1891
1965

1891
1965

# THE UNIVERSITY
# OF CHICAGO PRESS

## Catalogue of Books
## & Journals

THE UNIVERSITY OF CHICAGO PRESS
CHICAGO AND LONDON

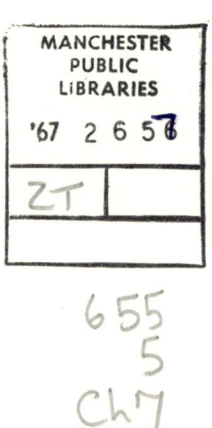
*Library of Congress Catalog Card Number: 66-13859*

THE UNIVERSITY OF CHICAGO PRESS, CHICAGO & LONDON
The University of Toronto Press, Toronto 5, Canada

# List of Abbreviations

ACLA — AMERICAN COUNTRY LIFE ASSOCIATION

ADA — AMERICAN DENTAL ASSOCIATION: PUBLICATIONS OF THE COMMITTEE ON THE STUDY OF DENTAL PRACTICE

AISL — AMERICAN INSTITUTE OF SACRED LITERATURE

AM — ASTROPHYSICAL MONOGRAPHS

AN — UNIVERSITY OF CHICAGO PUBLICATIONS IN ANTHROPOLOGY

ANB — UNIVERSITY OF CHICAGO DEPARTMENT OF ANTHROPOLOGY BULLETINS

AOPPS — CONFERENCE FOR ADMINISTRATIVE OFFICERS OF PUBLIC AND PRIVATE SCHOOLS. PROCEEDINGS

AP — AMERICAN PRIMERS

APA — AMERICAN POLICIES ABROAD

AR — ANCIENT RECORDS

AS — ASSYRIOLOGICAL STUDIES

BJP — MONOGRAPH SUPPLEMENTS TO THE BRITISH JOURNAL OF PSYCHOLOGY

BL — BARROWS LECTURES

BM — A PUBLICATION SPONSORED BY THE COMMITTEE ON PUBLICATIONS IN BIOLOGY AND MEDICINE

BR — BEHAVIOR RESEARCH FUND PUBLICATIONS

CA — CLASSICS IN ANTHROPOLOGY

CC — CITY CLUB OF CHICAGO PUBLICATIONS

CE — CHICAGO EDITIONS

CE — CONTRIBUTIONS TO EDUCATION

CEH — CAMBRIDGE ECONOMIC HANDBOOKS

CEM — CURRICULUM ENRICHMENT MATERIALS

CF — CHICAGO IN FICTION

CGT — COMPLETE GREEK TRAGEDIES

CHAC — CHICAGO HISTORY OF AMERICAN CIVILIZATION

CLBS — COLLEGE LIBRARY OF BIOLOGICAL SCIENCE

CLCP — CHICAGO LIBRARY OF COMPARATIVE POLITICS

CLM — CHICAGO LECTURES IN MATHEMATICS

CLP — CHICAGO LECTURES IN PHYSICS

CMC — COMMITTEE ON THE COSTS OF MEDICAL CARE

CMM — UNIVERSITY OF CHICAGO MONOGRAPHS IN MEDICINE

CP — STUDIES IN CLASSICAL PHILOLOGY

CR — HASKELL LECTURES IN COMPARATIVE RELIGION

CS — CONSTRUCTIVE STUDIES

CSAFP — CENTER FOR THE STUDY OF AMERICAN FOREIGN POLICY

CSC — UNIVERSITY OF CHICAGO SETTLEMENT. CHICAGO STOCK YARDS COMMUNITY STUDIES

CSCC — COMPARATIVE STUDIES OF CULTURES AND CIVILIZATIONS

CSS — CONTRASTIVE STRUCTURE SERIES

DBC — DEVELOPMENTAL BIOLOGICAL CONFERENCE SERIES

DM — PUBLICATIONS OF THE UNIVERSITY OF CHICAGO DEPARTMENT OF METEOROLOGY

DMMR — PUBLICATIONS OF THE UNIVERSITY OF CHICAGO DEPARTMENT OF METEOROLOGY. MISCELLANEOUS REPORTS

DP — DECENNIAL PUBLICATIONS OF THE UNIVERSITY OF CHICAGO

EC — ECONOMIC STUDIES OF THE UNIVERSITY OF CHICAGO

EHI — EVALUATION OF HIGHER INSTITUTIONS (North Central Association of Colleges and Secondary Schools: Monographs)

ENG — ENGLISH STUDIES OF THE UNIVERSITY OF CHICAGO

ERS — ECONOMICS RESEARCH SERIES

FW — FOLKTALES OF THE WORLD

| | | | | |
|---|---|---|---|---|
| GER | GERMANIC STUDIES | NPL | NEW PLAN TEXTS AT THE UNIVERSITY OF CHICAGO |
| GFL | GREEN FOUNDATION LECTURES | | |
| GN | STUDIES IN GREEK NOUN FORMATION | NS | UNIVERSITY OF CHICAGO NATURE STUDY SERIES |
| GSC | GEOGRAPHIC SOCIETY OF CHICAGO | | |
| HB | CONTRIBUTIONS FROM THE HULL BOTANICAL LABORATORY | NSSE | NATIONAL SOCIETY FOR THE STUDY OF EDUCATION |
| HCLS | HEATH-CHICAGO LANGUAGE SERIES | OIC | ORIENTAL INSTITUTE COMMUNICATIONS |
| HE | UNIVERSITY OF CHICAGO HOME ECONOMIC SERIES | | |
| HER | HANDBOOKS OF ETHICS AND RELIGION | OIE | ORIENTAL INSTITUTE ESSAYS |
| | | OIP | ORIENTAL INSTITUTE PUBLICATIONS |
| HFL | HARRIS MEMORIAL FOUNDATION LECTURES ON INTERNATIONAL RELATIONS | P | PHOENIX BOOKS |
| | | PA | STUDIES IN PUBLIC ADMINISTRATION |
| | | PHI | UNIVERSITY OF CHICAGO CONTRIBUTIONS TO PHILOSOPHY |
| HI | INSTITUTE FOR ADMINISTRATIVE OFFICERS OF HIGHER INSTITUTIONS. PROCEEDINGS | | |
| | | PLC | PATTERNS OF LITERARY CRITICISM |
| | | PLS | PUBLICATIONS OF THE LABORATORY SCHOOL |
| HLL | UNIVERSITY OF CHICAGO HISTORICAL AND LINGUISTIC STUDIES IN LITERATURE RELATED TO THE NEW TESTAMENT | | |
| | | PM | PRINCIPLES AND METHODS OF RELIGIOUS EDUCATION |
| | | PMS | PSYCHOMETRIC MONOGRAPHS |
| HS | HERITAGE OF SOCIOLOGY | POL | STUDIES IN POLITICAL SCIENCE |
| HSG | HANDBOOKS OF SOCIAL GERONTOLOGY | PP | PHOENIX POETS |
| | | PPP | PUBLIC POLICY PAMPHLETS |
| IEUS | INTERNATIONAL ENCYCLOPEDIA OF UNIFIED SCIENCE | PS | PHILOSOPHIC STUDIES |
| | | PS | A PUBLICATION SPONSORED BY THE COMMITTEE ON PUBLICATIONS IN THE PHYSICAL SCIENCES |
| IMP | INSTITUTE OF MEAT PACKING STUDIES | | |
| IPR | INSTITUTE OF PACIFIC RELATIONS | PSS | PHOENIX SCIENCE SERIES |
| LG | LINGUISTIC STUDIES IN GERMANIC | RSS | RICE UNIVERSITY SEMICENTENNIAL SERIES |
| LS | UNIVERSITY OF CHICAGO STUDIES IN LIBRARY SCIENCE | | |
| | | SAOC | STUDIES IN ANCIENT ORIENTAL CIVILIZATION |
| LT | STUDIES IN THE LECTIONARY TEXT OF THE GREEK NEW TESTAMENT | | |
| | | SB | UNIVERSITY OF CHICAGO STUDIES IN BALZAC |
| MA | STUDIES OF MEANING IN ART | | |
| MAD | MATERIALS FOR THE ASSYRIAN DICTIONARY | SBA | STUDIES IN BUSINESS ADMINISTRATION |
| | | SCI | UNIVERSITY OF CHICAGO SCIENCE SERIES |
| ME | MEDICAL ECONOMICS SERIES | | |
| MM | STUDIES IN MUNICIPAL MANAGEMENT | SE | UNIVERSITY OF CHICAGO STUDIES IN ECONOMICS |
| MPM | MODERN PHILOLOGY MONOGRAPHS OF THE UNIVERSITY OF CHICAGO | SEM | SUPPLEMENTARY EDUCATIONAL MONOGRAPHS |
| MRM | MONUMENTS OF RENAISSANCE MUSIC | SL | SCAMMON LECTURES AT THE ART INSTITUTE OF CHICAGO |
| MSB | MATERIALS FOR THE STUDY OF BUSINESS | | |
| | | SLBM | SCIENTIST'S LIBRARY. BIOLOGY AND MEDICINE |
| MSE | MATERIALS FOR THE STUDY OF ECONOMICS | | |
| | | SMC | STUDIES IN THE MAKING OF CITIZENS |
| NACRE | NATIONAL ADVISORY COUNCIL ON RADIO IN EDUCATION | SOC | UNIVERSITY OF CHICAGO SOCIOLOGICAL SERIES |
| NHS | NATURE OF HUMAN SOCIETY | SRM | STATISTICAL RESEARCH MONOGRAPHS |
| NPA | NATIONAL PLANNING ASSOCIATION | SSCI | SOCIAL SCIENCE STUDIES |

| | |
|---|---|
| SSM | University of Chicago Social Service Monographs |
| SSS | University of Chicago Social Service Series |
| TAS | Scales for the Measurement of Social Attitudes |
| UCMS | University of Chicago Mathematical Series |
| UCS | University of Chicago Survey |
| WFL | Walgreen Foundation Lectures |
| WIL | Weil Institute Lectures |
| WM | Contributions from the Walker Museum |
| WP | University of Chicago War Papers |
| YDS | Youth Development Series |
| YO | Yerkes Observatory Publications |
| YOB | Yerkes Observatory Bulletins |

## Code

ˢ Short discount

ᵗ Text discount

*o.p.* Out of print

| | |
|---|---|
| OBE | World Rights except in the British Commonwealth |
| COBE | World Rights except in the British Commonwealth but including Canada |
| USA | United States and its dependencies only |
| CUSA | United States and its dependencies plus Canada |
| SOUTH ASIA | Burma, Ceylon, India, Pakistan |

# Order Information

Books from The University of Chicago Press may be ordered from the following:

**UNITED STATES OF AMERICA AND ASIA, INCLUDING PAKISTAN, INDIA, CEYLON, AND BURMA:**

The University of Chicago Press, 11030 South Langley Avenue, Chicago, Illinois 60628

**LATIN AMERICA:**

Centro Interamericano de Libros Academicos, Sullivan 31 Bis, Mexico 4, D.F.

**BRITISH COMMONWEALTH (except Canada), EUROPEAN CONTINENT, AFRICA, THE NEAR EAST:**

The University of Chicago Press, 70 Great Russell Street, London, W.C. 1, England

**CANADA:**

The University of Toronto Press, Front Campus, University of Toronto, Toronto 5, Canada

**AUSTRALASIA:**

Thomas C. Lothian, 4-12 Tattersalls Lane, Melbourne, Victoria, Australia

**JAPAN:**

Donald Moore (Japan) Limited, 4-1 Kojimachi Chiyoda-ku, Tokyo, Japan

Xerographic reproductions of most out-of-print books can be obtained in paper covers for approximately $0.04 per page. Address requests to the Order Department, University of Chicago Press, 11030 South Langley Avenue, Chicago, Illinois 60628.

Journals from The University of Chicago Press may be ordered from The University of Chicago Press, 5750 Ellis Avenue, Chicago, Illinois 60637.

# The Organization of This Catalogue

The catalogue is divided into three principal sections: author and title listing of books, subject listing of books, and journals listing.

**Author and title listing.** This section, which includes main entries, series, and cross-references, begins on page 3.

*Main entries* are alphabetized under the author, editor, or primary contributor. Size, pagination, Library of Congress number, and price are given for titles in print only. Prices are subject to change without notice.

*Joint authors, editors, joint editors,* and *translators* are listed with cross-references to the main entries.

*Series* are included under the series name, each followed by a list of series titles in shortened form. The main entries for such titles appear under the authors' names and include the series abbreviation. A list of abbreviations appears on page v.

*Proceedings of annual meetings* of associations and other organizations are entered under the name of the association or organization. *Proceedings of occasional conferences* or *symposia* may have the main entry under the title of the conference.

**Subject listing.** An alphabetical listing of subject areas, each followed by titles in shortened form, begins on page 311.

**Journals.** Journals are listed under their present title, with reference in the descriptive copy to changes in title where this has occurred. Present editors' names are given. Subscription rates are current for the year 1966. The most recent available data are supplied for those journals transferred from The University of Chicago Press to another publisher. The journals listing begins on page 359.

**Other sections.** A historical introduction to The University of Chicago Press begins on page xi.

A Brief History of the University Press

# PUBLISHING AT CHICAGO

THE true character of a publishing house is to be read, not in its statements of purposes and intentions, but in the list of the authors and works it publishes. In the record of seventy-five years of publishing that follows in these pages, the character of the University of Chicago Press is made manifest, so that the reader may judge to what extent it has justified the vision that moved President William Rainey Harper to conceive the Press as one of the three main divisions of his new University.

Expecting his professors to be scholars as well as teachers, President Harper judged it essential that the University include a press to publish the products of their research. Wanting to extend the influence of the University far beyond its campus and classrooms, he insisted on having a press to give it the added power of the printed page, "not as an incident, an attachment, but . . . as an organic part of the institution." He firmly believed and said that through its publishing the University could expand its work to cover the globe. And today, each year, the Press sends throughout the world some two million books and another half million copies of its scholarly journals, each and all bearing the name of the University of Chicago.

*The Press in the old horse-and-buggy days*
*when the camera had room to take a long shot . . .*

But in the beginning President Harper must sometimes have doubted his own convictions. The Press was no more than a printer of announcements and bulletins in that first year of 1891. Its publishing did not begin until D. C. Heath and Company of Boston joined the University in organizing the Press as a private corporation in 1892. Even with Daniel C. Heath himself as director, serious financial deficits appeared at once, and in 1894 the private corporation was dissolved and the University resumed sole ownership of the Press.

By that time the fledgling publishing house had issued five books and initiated or taken over the publication of five scholarly journals. Three of those journals are still very much alive: the *Journal of Political Economy,* the *Journal of Geology,* and the *Journal of Near Eastern Studies* (then entitled *Hebraica*). None of the five books survives. The earliest Press book that remains in print appeared in 1899; it was that truly seminal work, John Dewey's *The School and Society.*

For six years a succession of short-term directors struggled to keep the Press going in spite of inadequate funds, recurring deficits, scattered quarters, and disruptive changes in organization. One hundred and twenty-seven books and pamphlets were published, largely on biblical and philosophical subjects, and six new journals were added to the list, among them the still flourishing *American Journal of Sociology, Astrophysical Journal, School Review,* and

*Today, in the VW age, the campus and people crowd us in,
but our books reach far horizons*

*Botanical Gazette.* By 1906 the number of journals had grown to fourteen, with *Modern Philology, Classical Philology,* and the *Elementary School Teacher* among the newcomers. By 1898 President Harper's insistence on publishing the research of the faculty had brought into being eight series of monographs, ranging from Studies in Classical Philology to Physiological Archives.

The appointment of Newman Miller as director in 1900 gave to the Press the advantages of a stable administration that lasted for nineteen years. But the chronic problems of scholarly publishing continued to plague Mr. Miller and President Harper, who until his death in 1906 gave the Press his personal attention and supervision. This, it must be admitted, was not always to its advantage; the surviving archives contain many a letter from Mr. Miller to the President pleading for long-delayed decisions on urgent matters of organization, housing, and budget.

By this time the structure of the Press had jelled into three fairly well defined divisions: publication, manufacturing (i.e., printing), and "purchase and retail." The third of these included not only the University Bookstore but also the purchasing and accounting services for a number of the University's departments, principally its laboratories. The responsibility for handling laboratory supplies so annoyed Newman Miller that he made it the scapegoat whenever he was pressed to reduce staff and expenditures. Eventually he was relieved of this irritant and the Press settled down to printing, publishing, and selling books and journals.

The problem of housing was solved in 1902 when the component parts of the Press were brought together in its own new building at 5750 Ellis Avenue. This red brick building, four stories high with Dutch gables, cost $105,852, which was paid from funds supplied by John D. Rockefeller.

With space always at a premium, the new building housed not only the Press, with its printing plant and bookstore, but also the Library, the Law School, and offices for the Auditor, Registrar, and Superintendent of Buildings and Grounds. Mr. Miller was soon spending much more time than he liked trying to dislodge these occupants so as to gain space for new staff, new printing equipment, and his growing stock of books and journals.

Chief among the books contributing to this growing stock were those in the series called the Decennial Publications, with which the University celebrated the end of its first ten years. Thinking "there could be no more appropriate way for the celebration of the anniversary of a University than the production and publication of books by its scholars," President Harper planned to issue three volumes: two containing departmental reports and a third devoted to articles and monographs by faculty members "prepared in honor of this occasion and published for the first time in this volume." He appropriated $2,000 for the project and called upon the faculty for material. Manuscripts poured in, the three volumes expanded into twenty-eight, and the publishing costs mounted to more than $50,000.

Undoubtedly the Decennial Publications helped immeasurably to draw the attention of the academic world to the young University of Chicago; their contents included substantial works by well-known, or soon to be well-known, scholars, among them Robert A. Millikan, Albert A. Michelson, Jacques Loeb, Shailer Mathews, Thorstein Veblen, George Herbert Mead. But the books were more impressive than salable, and the financial loss incurred in publishing them jeopardized the very existence of the Press.

Stanchly, however, President Harper declared the deficit to be a wise investment. "The value of this enterprise to the University and the University Press has been, and will continue to be, inestimable," he wrote in 1904; "it is safe to say that no series of scientific publications so comprehensive in its scope and of so great a magnitude has ever been issued at one time by any learned society or institution, or by private enterprise."

This certainty of achievement was in part responsible for a major change in policy. As stated in official bulletins, the function of the Press until then had been "the printing and publishing of books prepared or edited by University instructors." In 1905, at the President's urging, this self-defeating limitation was dropped; the Trustees' Committee on Press and Extension explicitly instructed the Press to "solicit suitable books . . . among scholars outside the University."

In carrying out this instruction, with increasing vigor and effectiveness over the years, the University of Chicago Press became what every mature university press must be and is proud to be, not a mere public relations agency of its university, but a "servant to the learned world" as a whole.

The Decennial Publications were the Press's first great venture in the field of book publishing, and in both content and typographical format they attained standards far beyond any of their predecessors. As part of this process an expertly efficient copyediting and proofreading section was organized in the printing division in 1904–5, and from this section came the first few typewritten sheets of rules for typographical accuracy, consistency, and style that developed into the well-known book, *A Manual of Style,* first published in 1906. Having become a standard working tool for authors, editors, printers, and proofreaders everywhere, it is soon to appear in a revised twelfth edition.

The constant problem of those early years was, of course, financial stringency. In 1903 the Trustees granted the Press a capital fund of $140,000, agreed to meet its operating deficits within reason, and established an annual appropriation to subsidize publication of the journals. Lavish as this support was for that day, it fell substantially short of the need. Book publication in

*The business office in the 1920's,*
*with the neat efficient ladies in their subdued office garb . . .*

particular was left to chance financing, title by title, when and as resources permitted.

Receipts from book sales and journal subscriptions were meager, and though profits earned by the printing division and the bookstore were applied to the publishing operation, for many years these were too small to make any appreciable difference. Manuscripts accepted for publication piled up in the vault and sometimes lay there for years before the money to publish them was found. In the editorial records of the Press one can trace the reluctant but relentless march toward a change of policy: toward acceptance for publication of what were called "property books"—books of wide enough appeal to sell more than a few hundred copies and so add to the income of the Press.

President Harper expressed this acceptance of necessity when he wrote Mr. Miller about a manuscript under consideration in 1905, "I am not enthusiastic. . . . I think we can get along just as well without this book, but of course if you think there is money in it, I have no objection."

A decade later the situation was easing a little. The monetary surplus produced by printing and the bookstore had grown large enough to reduce materially the deficits of the publishing division and even sometimes to provide the subsidies required for the journals. In 1915 the University at last undertook to subsidize book publication by assuming all composition and plate

*Today the furniture and the ladies look more colorful,*
*but the efficiency hasn't wavered*

costs, charging to the Press only its operating expenses and the costs of paper, presswork, and binding. Even so, two years later the Trustees were forced to increase the capital of the Press, "by appropriation from general funds," to $155,000 and simultaneously grant it a loan of $40,000, "bringing the total investment in the Press to $196,521." Publishing scholarship was expensive.

When Newman Miller died in 1919, the Trustees decided to try a major reorganization. First they separated the Bookstore from the Press, moved it to new quarters in Ellis Hall, and gave it the status of an independent service enterprise; then they abolished the position of director and made the two remaining divisions autonomous units, each with its own manager. Donald P. Bean was named manager of the Publication Department and A. C. McFarland manager of the Manufacturing Department. Together the two departments still constituted the Press; they remained in the same building and of necessity worked closely together. The surpluses earned by both the Bookstore and the Manufacturing Department were still allocated to the Publication Department.

At this same time the Press was given a new governing body. Since its inception it had been directly responsible to the Trustees, through a committee of the Board at first called the Committee on Press and Extension, then the Committee of University Publishing, and later simply the Press Committee. This relationship had been spelled out in a Constitution for the Press in

1903, which also defined its threefold structure and the duties of each of its divisions. Now the Trustees decided to transfer their responsibility in part to a Board of University Publications made up of faculty members appointed to determine the editorial policy of the Press and to pass on the manuscripts it proposed to publish.

Supervision of the business affairs of the Press remained with a committee of the Trustees until 1931, when the Business Manager of the University was made responsible for the management and operation of the Press. Thereafter both Mr. Bean and Mr. McFarland reported to him on all financial matters.

This divided authority—which in fact accurately reflected the essential duality of university publishing as half service to scholarship and half business enterprise—was duplicated within the Publication Department. Gordon J. Laing, dean of humanities, had been acting also as General Editor of the Press since 1909. Thoroughly conversant and sympathetic with the ways and aims of scholars and scholarship, he was responsible for the character and quality of the Press list, took care of manuscripts and authors, and worked closely with the Board of University Publications, while Donald Bean devoted his time primarily to sales and promotion, contracts, budgets, billing, accounting, warehousing, shipping, and the like.

Sometimes the dual arrangement caused trouble. The Board of University Publications might accept a manuscript and Dean Laing inform the author that it was to be published, only to have the Business Manager and Mr. Bean refuse publication on the grounds of financial impracticality.

But confusing though the chart of reorganization may have been, it was effective. Within three years sales income jumped from $83,000 to $198,000 and continued to rise. With equally growing surpluses from the Bookstore and printing plus subsidies and benefactions from outside sources, the Publication Department began to operate in the black and even to accumulate a small reserve. Through the 1920's and 1930's it was an exciting focus of big projects, proliferating series, and experimental ventures.

From the first the Press list had been especially strong in biblical studies, and, next perhaps to President Harper himself, who had found time to write thirteen books for the Press to publish, the most prolific author in this field was Dr. Edgar J. Goodspeed. When his impressive scholarship crystallized in the manuscript for *The New Testament: An American Translation*, its publication in 1923 created a sensation. Newspapers syndicated it and radio stations broadcast it in daily installments; reviewers, ministers, and men in the street praised and condemned it.

Recognizing that the original New Testament had been written, not in literary Greek, but in the plain speech of everyday life, Dr. Goodspeed had sought to translate it into English of the same kind for twentieth-century Americans. He had succeeded admirably, and when the initial furor subsided, his version of the Gospels and the Epistles came to be much loved for the simple directness of its style.

A decade later the Press combined Dr. Goodspeed's New Testament with a similar translation of the Old Testament edited by J. M. Powis Smith, in *The Complete Bible: An American Translation.* This Bible, in its multiple editions and bindings, has been the Press's all-time best seller if paperback reissues are excluded.

Interest in American English led to another outstanding item on the Press list. In 1925 the University appointed to its faculty in English Sir William Alexander Craigie, the distinguished co-editor of the *Oxford English Dictionary,* with the understanding that he was to organize and direct the compilation of a dictionary of American English by a resident staff of American scholars. Hailed as a great project in humanistic scholarship, Sir William's work was partly financed by the General Education Board and the American Council of Learned Societies. It was published in parts as the work progressed, and each five parts were assembled in a bound volume. When *A Dictionary of American English on Historical Principles* was completed and the last of its four volumes was published in 1943, it won for the Press the Carey-Thomas Award for Creative Publishing.

From American English Sir William turned his time and talents to Scottish. He did not live to complete his *Dictionary of the Older Scottish Tongue, from the Twelfth Century to the End of the Seventeenth,* but another British lexicographer, A. J. Aitken, is going on with the task, and the latest published part, the twenty-second, is appearing in 1966 and carries the work into the letter "M."

Under way concurrently with Craigie's compilation of American English was the "Chaucer project" of two incomparable Chicago scholars, John M. Manly and Edith Rickert. For fourteen years this pair devoted their lives to the prodigious task of collating all the eighty-three known texts of *The Canterbury Tales.* They finished it in time for publication, in eight volumes, in 1940, the six hundredth anniversary of Chaucer's birth. It was designated also as a Fiftieth Anniversary Publication of the University of Chicago Press. It is still considered a model of textual criticism and editing.

It is not likely that the Press could have financed the publication of these monumental and costly works of scholarship without the monetary stimulus it received in 1926–27 from a grant of $100,000 by the Laura Spelman Rockefeller Memorial Foundation. Now the manuscripts grown dusty in the vault could be pulled out and put into production and fewer good new ones need be declined for lack of funds. In one year the number of titles published an-

*That was the warehouse that was . . .*

*Today
it is a lot easier
to get the books rolling*

nually jumped from fifty-nine to eighty-nine, and throughout the 1930's, excepting only two years, it ranged from 100 to 140.

The stimulation extended from the Press into the ranks of University scholars. Old series took on new life and new ones multiplied. The University of Chicago Science Series, for example, begun in 1914 and graced in 1917 by the publication of Robert A. Millikan's *The Electron,* added two other Nobel Prize winners to its list with the publication in 1927 of Albert A. Michelson's *Studies in Optics* and in 1930 of a translation of Werner Heisenberg's *Physical Principles of the Quantum Theory.* This series also began to reflect the University's growing eminence in mathematics with monographs on the theory of numbers by Leonard E. Dickson and *Modern Higher Algebra* by A. Adrian Albert.

Typical of the new series were Studies in Public Administration, initiated in 1934, in which appeared the early works of Leonard D. White, Marshall E. Dimock, and Charles E. Merriam, and the University of Chicago Sociological Series, launched in 1926, which within ten years had produced E. Franklin Frazier's *The Negro Family in the United States,* Edwin H. Sutherland's *The Professional Thief,* Frederic M. Thrasher's *The Gang,* Louis Wirth's *The Ghetto,* and Harvey W. Zorbaugh's *The Gold Coast and the Slum.*

Not so typical was the Home Economics Series, begun in 1924 to improve the teaching of domestic science and carry new facts about food to the educated homemaker. It did result in a popular textbook, the *Hows and Whys of Cooking* by Evelyn G. Halliday and Isabel T. Noble, but the series was short-lived.

Most productive of series was the vigorous young Oriental Institute established in 1919 by James H. Breasted. This Institute and its work were a natural outgrowth of the interest in Near Eastern studies that had marked the early years of both the University and the Press. Unflagging in research and writing, Breasted and his colleagues inaugurated several series that still go merrily on: Oriental Institute Publications (now 93 volumes), Studies in Ancient Oriental Civilizations (32 volumes), Oriental Institute Communications (20 volumes), Assyriological Studies (15 volumes). Outside these series, the scholars of the Oriental Institute gave the Press some of its notable "property books"—Edward Chiera's charming *They Wrote on Clay,* for example, and the lavishly handsome three-volume *Ancient Egyptian Paintings* by Nina Cummings Davies and Alan H. Gardiner.

But the most profitable Press books in this period, next to the Goodspeed Bibles, proved to be the New Plan textbooks in the physical and biological sciences.

The writing and publishing of improved textbooks was a legitimate, indeed necessary, activity of a University in the opinion of President Harper, who was himself one of the editors of the Press's first venture in this area: the Constructive Bible Series for religious education. This textbook series began in 1900 and had grown to thirty-five titles by 1939, when it was transferred to commercial publication by Harper and Brothers.

Experimentation with teaching methods in the mathematics department of the University High School led to a series of high-school textbooks in mathematics which the Press published for thirty years before handing them over in 1937 to Laidlaw Brothers. And a series of foreign-language textbooks for high schools and colleges, in French, German, Spanish, Italian, and Latin, developed by experimental work in the classrooms of the University, was successfully established by the Press in the years 1925 to 1934. Then a joint publishing arrangement was made with D. C. Heath and Company by which they became the well-known Heath-Chicago Language Series.

The Press was therefore no newcomer to the textbook field when in 1931 introductory survey courses were organized to implement the University's New Plan for the undergraduate curriculum. Unable to find textbooks that fitted this new kind of course, the teachers wrote their own, nine in all, and the Press published these as a service, with no expectation of national markets or adoptions elsewhere. But the idea of general education spread and with it went the Chicago textbooks. Entirely novel in format and illustrations as well as in content and style of writing, they were widely adopted by instructors and gratefully read by students. Thousands of copies were sold also to the general public when nonacademic reviewers discovered them and recommended them as good leisure-time reading for those who were curious about science and the world we live in.

With few exceptions these books are still in print and in use, familiar names in the college world: Ralph M. Buchsbaum, *Animals without Backbones;* Anton J. Carlson and Victor Johnson, *The Machinery of the Body;* Carey G. Croneis, *Down to Earth;* Merle C. Coulter, *The Story of the Plant Kingdom;* Alfred S. Romer, *Man and the Vertebrates;* Harvey B. Lemon, *From Galileo to Cosmic Rays* (in a later revision *From Galileo to the Nuclear Age*).

Underlying this dynamic publishing program were Donald P. Bean's persistent efforts to improve the sales of Press books, not merely to increase income, but to discharge the task of getting each book into the hands of as many as possible of the readers for whom it had been written. This, he felt, was a special duty and challenge for a university publisher.

Newman Miller had done what he could to attract the attention of booksellers and librarians to Chicago books, by advertising in *Publisher's Weekly,* preparing catalogues to be included in the national *Publishers' Trade List Annual,* establishing sales agencies and book depositories on the East and

West coasts, and making contractual arrangements with universities or companies abroad to represent the Press in Great Britain, Germany, Japan, Central Europe, and China. He established the fruitful association with Cambridge University Press in England that endured for fifty years. But for lack of staff and funds his efforts were sporadic and relatively ineffective. Mr. Bean concentrated on improving and extending them.

Toward that end he strove to cultivate cooperation with commercial publishers, other university presses, and learned societies in studying and experimenting with methods for improving the distribution of books and reducing its costs. As an outstanding example, in 1934 he instituted a program of cooperative arrangements with commercial textbook and trade publishing houses. Books with a kind or size of market that the Press seemed unlikely to reach effectively were edited and produced by the Press but promoted and distributed by the commercial house. By 1937–38 ten commercial publishers were promoting and distributing 133 books originally published by the University of Chicago Press.

Most beneficial and enduring was the association developed during this period with other university presses. Mr. Bean had made the Chicago Press a member of the National Association of Book Publishers and he and Rollin D. Hemens, his assistant, attended its annual meetings faithfully. There they would gather together the other university press directors present to spend an evening discussing the peculiar problems and needs of university publishing. Purely informal, these discussions proved to be of such benefit that the number participating grew, the sessions lengthened, planned agenda came into being, and Donald Bean was elected chairman of the group, which presently became the Association of American University Presses. Today this Association has sixty-seven members and maintains a central office in New York City where a salaried staff carries on its extensive program of cooperative activities.

Two of these activities Mr. Bean launched at Chicago in the 1930's: the Educational Directory and the Exhibits Program.

The Educational Directory is a mailing list of college and university faculty members classified according to the subjects they teach. Established in 1931 with an underwriting grant of $12,000 from the Rockefeller Foundation, its mailing service proved so useful to the university presses, and eventually to commercial publishers as well, that it had become self-supporting by 1936. Chicago continued to operate the Directory until 1954, when ownership and management were transferred to the Association. Today the income derived from its 8,000,000 or so mailings a year goes far toward supporting the central office of the Association.

No single press could then afford to exhibit its books at the annual meet-

*The latest in office equipment is used to speed customer service . . .*

ings of learned and professional societies, but cooperatively they might do so. In 1935 some of them began to send joint displays of their books to a few selected conventions. The University of Chicago Press managed this Exhibits Program at first, then passed the chore on to other participating presses in succession. Today the central office of the Association handles the scheduling, supervision, and bookkeeping for all joint exhibits, and the larger presses, including Chicago, exhibit independently at the major conventions.

Chicago took the lead in these early phases of cooperation among university presses partly because of Mr. Bean's belief in the process and partly because Chicago was at that time the largest and most active among them. Thanks largely to the pump-priming gift from the Laura Spelman Rockefeller Memorial Foundation, Chicago had been able to expand its program and size just when other presses were having to curtail theirs in the wake of the Depression.

In 1940 the University drafted Donald Bean from the Press to run its Fiftieth Anniversary celebration, and this chore concluded, he requested a recuperative leave of absence at the end of which he resigned. A few years later he returned to university publishing as director of the presses at Stanford and Syracuse.

Mr. Bean's departure and the coincidental retirement of Dean Laing

*but manuscripts still need the human touch*

ushered in fourteen years of changing administrations and policies at the Press.

Rollin D. Hemens as Acting Manager and W. K. Jordan, professor of English history, as General Editor held the fort until President Hutchins in 1944 called Joseph A. Brandt from the presidency of the University of Oklahoma to take full charge of the Press, both printing and publication departments, with the reinstituted title of director. Mr. Hemens was named associate director.

Mr. Brandt was returning to, not entering, university publishing. He had been director of the presses at Oklahoma and Princeton before trying his hand at university administration. A journalist by training and publicist at heart, he was impatient with bad writing by scholars and their attempt to defend it by the plea that they were writing only for other scholars. He felt that with clearer thinking and a more lucid style they could just as well communicate their knowledge to a much wider audience. Though he stayed at Chicago only eighteen months, resigning in 1946 to become president of a major commercial publishing house in New York, he left an unmistakable mark on the Press's list. In his time it contained fewer esoteric monographs and incidental pamphlets and more "trade" books such as Donald Culross Peattie's *Immortal Village,* B. A. Botkin's *Lay My Burden Down,* Graham Hutton's *Midwest at Noon,* and Saul D. Alinsky's *Reveille for Radicals.*

As frequently happens, however, much to the consternation of editors and publishers, the Press's best trade book in that period was a piece of solid writing by a German economist. Everyone, even Mr. Brandt, was surprised when Friedrich A. Hayek's *The Road to Serfdom* made its own way onto the national best-seller lists.

Mr. Brandt's successor was William T. Couch, who had won great repute for the distinguished publishing he had fostered as director of the University of North Carolina Press. He was a person of strong moral and social conscience, and together with Fred D. Wieck, a man of like mind whom he named his editor, he did much to strengthen the Press list in philosophy and problems of public policy. His tenure saw the publication, for instance, of Rudolph Carnap's *Meaning and Necessity* and *Logical Foundations of Probability;* Chicago editions of Kant, Hegel, and Cicero in English (and initiation of the monumental translation of the *Complete Greek Tragedies*); Ernst Cassirer's *The Renaissance Philosophy of Man;* and Paul Tillich's *The Protestant Era* and the initial volume of his vastly influential *Systematic Theology.* On the lists of these years appeared also such sources of public controversy as Richard M. Weaver's *Ideas Have Consequences,* A. Frank Reel's *The Case of General Yamashita,* and Morton Grodzins' *Americans Betrayed: Politics and the Japanese Evacuation.*

Although Mr. Couch had been appointed with the rank of a full professor, his productive career at Chicago was cut short in 1950 by insurmountable disagreements with the University administration over editorial and fiscal policies. Mr. Wieck left the Press with him. Again Rollin D. Hemens took charge for a year as Acting Director.

Fittingly that year was marked by the publication of *A Dictionary of Americanisms on Historical Principles* in two volumes, edited by Mitford M. Mathews. Fittingly because Mr. Hemens had for some seven years made the nurture of this project one of his special concerns. Mr. Mathews had worked with Sir William Alexander Craigie for nineteen years as assistant editor of his *Dictionary of American English* and thereafter had headed a "Dictionary Department" set up within the Press to prepare this compilation of words and word meanings that have entered the English language from the United States. Along the way he had supervised the preparation by his staff of the *University of Chicago Spanish Dictionary* compiled by Carlos Castillo and Otto F. Bond, both University professors, which the Press had published in 1948.

Investment in these two projects had been substantial since neither had been subsidized in any way, but both proved to be good income producers as well as works of fine scholarship. Their indirect contribution in adding to the Press's eminence in lexicography was demonstrated in this same year by the arrangements made for publication of *A Greek-English Lexicon of the New Testament and Other Early Christian Literature,* a translation and revision of a famous German lexicon by W. F. Arndt and F. W. Gingrich under the sponsorship of the Missouri Synod of the Lutheran Church. When the book was published in 1957, its reception by critics and its astonishing sales amply demonstrated its quality and usefulness.

Mr. Hemens' primary editorial responsibility was in the sciences. At a time when publishing in scientific fields was less fashionable than today, Chicago was continuing the tradition established in the early years by flourishing series in science and medicine. The Monographs in Medicine had been replaced in 1941 by a broader program in the biological sciences guided by a faculty Committee on Biology and Medicine. The series designation was dropped but each title bore a note indicating its approval by the committee. In 1946 the distinguished old Science Series similarly gave way to publications sponsored by a faculty Committee on the Physical Sciences and Mathematics.

Although the Press never achieved a list in the physical sciences as extensive as its list in biology and medicine, this catalogue cites scores of titles in both divisions of the sciences. It is a truism, of course, that any university press tends to be strongest in publishing in the areas where its faculty is most active in research and writing, and as the University of Chicago became preeminent in the sciences during the chancellorship of a humanist, Robert Maynard Hutchins, Press publications reflected the fact. On its list appeared titles like Enrico Fermi's *Nuclear Physics,* Willard F. Libby's *Radiocarbon Dating,* Nicolas Rashevsky's *Mathematical Biology of Social Behavior,* Frieda Fromm-Reichmann's *Principles of Intensive Psychotherapy,* Franklin McLean's *Bone,* and Stephen Rothman's *Physiology and Biochemistry of the Skin.*

In 1951, after the departure of Mr. Couch, the University decided once again to separate the publishing and printing operations, and this time the divorce was made complete in all except domicile. Charles E. Trout, superintendent of the printing division, who had succeeded Amos W. Bishop, in turn the successor to A. C. McFarland, became Director of the Printing Department. The Press was made exclusively the publishing department, and Morton Grodzins, a professor of political science, took charge of it as General Editor with Rollin D. Hemens continuing as Manager. The Printing Department remained under the supervision of the business officers of the University, but responsibility for the Press was transferred to the academic officers. The faculty Board of University Publications continued to watch over editorial policy and the selection of manuscripts to be published. The surpluses earned by the Printing Department and the Bookstore were

The crossroads—downstairs, house editors negotiate publishing coups; upstairs, printing machines clatter and thud; right, manuscript editors quietly blue-pencil; left, production staff hopefully produces schedules, and sales, advertising, and publicity departments add the necessary dash of commerce.

henceforth to be absorbed into the general funds of the University, the consequent loss of income to the Press to be made up by annual subsidies to meet operating deficits.

For two and a half years Morton Grodzins proved what an imaginative and energetic professor could do in publishing. He expanded what Mr. Couch had started—procurement editing—by appointing staff members in all four of the traditional divisions of learning, the humanities and social sciences as well as the biological and physical sciences. He grappled with the problem of deficits on many of the University journals by trying to increase the number from outside organizations that would earn a profit. When the Oriental Institute was temporarily unable to pay the costs of its archaeological monographs, the Press shouldered these costs without delaying the publication even of books as expensive as the studies of Erich Schmidt on the excavations at Persepolis, though these volumes were inevitably limited to printings of 500 copies and necessarily priced at $75 and $100 a copy.

Among other notable books published by the Press at this time were *Atoms in the Family,* Laura Fermi's memoir of her husband Enrico, the pioneer atomic physicist, which became a best seller after serialization in *The New Yorker,* and many books on public affairs, including George F. Kennan's *American Diplomacy 1900–1950* and Senator Paul H. Douglas's *Economy in the National Government.* The Press returned to the traditional policy of recruiting its list from faculty-written books but ventured boldly into new fields as well. Professor Daniel J. Boorstin's series, the Chicago History of American Civilization, was launched, and publication of *The Correspondence of Edmund Burke* was undertaken in cooperation with Cambridge University Press.

This venturesome period in the history of the Press came to an end when Mr. Grodzins was appointed Dean of the Social Sciences. In 1954 Roger W. Shugg was named to succeed him, first as executive editor, then as director, of the Press. Mr. Shugg has been greatly aided in the subsequent twelve years by a succession of highly competent assistant directors: William B. Harvey, Carroll G. Bowen, William A. Wood, John B. Goetz, Anders Richter, and Marshall Townsend. Four of these men have moved on to become directors of other university presses, giving Chicago good reason to be proud of its publishing "alumni."

Since the University, after 1951 under the chancellorship of Lawrence A. Kimpton, was having to save itself by spending millions of dollars on urban renewal, the annual subsidies to the Press were terminated in 1955, and severe economies were required to make the Press self-sufficient. Staff size was reduced by limiting the Press's work to the publication of books and journals: the Educational Directory was transferred to the Association of

American University Presses and the local letter and mailing services were abolished. An accumulated overstock of books was cut down by drastic remaindering and special sales by direct mail. Some works of esoteric scholarship were of necessity denied publication; others were published by offset printing from typewritten copy.

By such measures the Press was soon made to pay its own way again, and it has been operating in the black ever since 1956, thanks in large part to the subsidy for printing costs which the Ford Foundation granted to most of the university presses, amounting in the case of Chicago to $265,000. The Press has even been able to reverse the money flow of earlier years and repay some of the University's investment in publishing by contributing to its general funds more than half a million dollars.

Although the multiplication and prosperity of university presses in the last decade or so must be explained by the general state of the American economy and the phenomenal growth in college and university enrollments, Chicago's Press grew strong again in its resources because of certain changes and innovations peculiar to its own situation. It developed a large and expert manuscript editing staff to take over and expand the copy work of the Printing Department's proofroom; organized an effective production department of its own and put renewed emphasis on fine typography and design; greatly improved royalties and terms for authors so as to keep old friends and win new ones; more than doubled salaries in order to secure people experienced in publishing for key positions; and sought at every turn to emulate the practices and match the expenditure percentages of the most efficient commercial houses. At no time, however, did the Press turn its back on its fundamental duty to publish the most significant scholarship it could find, inside or outside the University, and the number of books published, even at a loss, steadily increased every year.

Contributing to this increase have been other universities and organizations for which the Press is pleased to serve as publisher: Rice University in Houston, Washington University in St. Louis, and in Chicago the Newberry Library and the American Bar Foundation.

Fully aware of the importance of journal publication to scholars and scholarship, the Press has tried, especially since 1956, to make its journals a valued part of its program rather than merely a necessary nuisance. It has been receptive to proposals for new journals that had reasonable prospects of survival without undue deficits, and it has invited the transfer of good established journals to Chicago. It has been as generous as resources permitted in giving secretarial assistance to editors, allowing them more pages per issue, and absorbing unbudgeted deficits, and it is making intensive efforts to secure more advertising to increase revenue.

The result is a "journals division" of increasing size and expertness, which is now publishing 158 issues of 30 journals a year, plus a goodly number of annual or occasional supplements, some of which reach full book size. The subjects of Press journals cover the academic spectrum from astrophysics to zoology, and the number of subscribers ranges from 450 to 18,500.

In 1956, only a few months after Cornell University Press led the way, Chicago embarked on a large-scale program of publishing paperbacks, the now familiar Phoenix Books, reprinting them chiefly from its own backlist at the "democratic" prices that students could afford to pay. It quickly learned what every other paperback publisher knew or came to know: scholarly monographs that sold only two thousand copies in cloth bindings at the high prices required by the postwar inflation of printing costs could be expected to sell five, ten, and twenty thousand copies at lower paperback prices. Where the Press had published textbooks in the 1930's, it now supplied the same needs of students and teachers with paperbacks. Its list of Phoenix titles has grown to more than three hundred, of which it sells more than a million copies a year.

Only those who live at the University of Chicago know how much housekeeping the Press has had to do in recent years. Just as the University transformed its environs from slums into livable neighborhoods, so the Press has cleaned the charming face of its old building, refurbished and relighted all its offices, and moved its warehouse from cramped quarters in a garage to a new location in the old village of Pullman, where a railway car barn has been completely rebuilt and air-conditioned to provide business offices for some fifty men and women, a mechanized shipping room, and stacked shelves that now house a stock of two million books. Automated machines have taken over all billing and bookkeeping, so that the Press now runs with records of perpetual inventory and accounts receivable that are equal to those of any modern publishing house.

The Press is still concerned first and foremost, however, with what it publishes, and it has enjoyed its share of notable books in recent years. It is publishing *The Papers of James Madison*, now in their fifth volume, and has contracted to publish at its own expense, including even the cost of editorial preparation, *The Selected Papers of Adlai Stevenson*. It has launched some major new series, such as Folktales of the World, edited by Richard M. Dorson, Chicago in Fiction, edited by Saul Bellow, Patterns of Literary Criticism, published jointly with the University of Toronto Press, and Monuments of Renaissance Music, edited by Edward E. Lowinsky. Under its imprint have appeared significant works in history such as William H. McNeill's *The Rise of the West*, which won the National Book Award in History in 1964, and the first volume of Donald F. Lach's *Asia in the Making of Europe.* In the sciences there have been such works as those of George B. Schaller on the mountain gorilla, Gerard P. Kuiper's series on the sun and on the stars and stellar systems, John Paul Scott's studies of animal behavior as observed in dogs, and *The Collected Papers of Enrico Fermi.* The social sciences have contributed many works of uncommon merit, among them Hannah Arendt's *The Human Condition,* Milton Friedman's *Capitalism and Freedom,* Tang Tsou's *America's Failure in China,* Harold Leavitt's *Managerial Psychology,* and the annual volumes of *The Supreme Court Review* edited by Philip B. Kurland.

Without neglecting original works by contemporary scholars, the Press has sought of late to retrieve some of the heritage of the past by reprinting, in cloth and in paper, from the lists of many publishers important books in sociology, anthropology, and literature that have long been out of print. It has also made available in English translation many classics of scholarship or wisdom from a dozen different languages—among them *The Colloquies of Erasmus,* Marc Bloch's *Feudal Society,* Émile Bréhier's *History of Philosophy,* Moses Maimonides' *The Guide of the Perplexed,* Karl Jaspers' *The Future of Mankind* and his *General Psychopathology.*

Reaching out to the international world of scholarship in its distribution as in its editorial selection, the Press in 1961 organized its own chartered company in England and joined the presses of Yale and Columbia in establishing an office in London with a British staff to look after the promotion and sales of its books in Great Britain and on the European continent. Every book published in Chicago is now immediately stocked also in London. And in cooperation with several foreign publishers the Press is importing or co-publishing scholarly works that might otherwise suffer for want of international distribution, or even not be published at all.

To achieve maximum distribution of its books in the United States, the Press has in turn tried commission salesmen and sales agencies, its own New York office, and franchised sales representation by Harper and Row. Now in its seventy-fifth year it resumes maintaining a salaried sales staff of its own to carry Chicago books from coast to coast. The efforts of all its salesmen are buttressed by continuous and extensive advertising, both in newspapers and magazines and by direct mail. Most provocative of its advertising campaigns in recent years has been the series of institutional ads called "Great Moments at Chicago."

The Press has been privileged to share, at one stage or another, in many of those great moments, and its staff hopes its participation in the basic and ongoing work of the University will continue and increase. Looking ahead to the Centennial twenty-five years hence, they hope their successors at that time will be able to report some essential achievements: an endowment for the Press substantial enough to relieve pressure on the sensitive money nerve and permit untrammeled service to scholarship however esoteric; a doubled backlist with a larger proportion of it in print, since it is to the interest of authors and publisher alike that books remain in constant demand during a long life on the backlist; an extensive development of effective communication among scholars, especially in the sciences, through "publication" on magnetic tapes or by computer printouts; and a new or enlarged building to house a necessarily enlarged staff and increased stock of books.

Twenty-five years ago, in the Fiftieth Anniversary Catalogue of the Press, Dean Gordon J. Laing wrote: "Perhaps there is no better index of the real character of any university than the catalogue of its press. And if one wishes to get some idea of the chief objective of the institution, to know what its highest purpose is, to understand its essential nature, he should read the catalogue of its press." If that is still true, this 75th Anniversary Catalogue of the University of Chicago Press, added to those of all the other university presses laboring in the vineyard of scholarly publishing, may reveal to the thoughtful reader the true character of American scholarship.

ROGER W. SHUGG

March 15, 1966

## Best Sellers
(In-Print Titles)

| Year of Publication | Author | Title | Total Sales to 6/30/66 |
|---|---|---|---|
| 1955 | Turabian | *A Manual for the Writers of Term Papers, Theses, and Dissertations* | 883,000 |
| 1935 | Smith and Goodspeed | *The Bible. An American Translation* | 440,000 |
| 1951 | Lattimore (trans.) | *The Iliad* | 311,000 |
| 1924 | Kornhauser | *How To Study* | 286,000 |
| 1922 | Hyman | *Comparative Vertebrate Anatomy* | 273,000 |
| 1938 | Buchsbaum | *Animals without Backbones* | 222,000 |
| 1924 | Goodspeed | *New Testament. American Translation* | 210,000 |
| 1937 | Carlson and Johnson | *Machinery of the Body* | 205,000 |
| 1906 | Press Staff | *A Manual of Style* | 149,000 |
| 1963 | Turabian | *Student's Guide for Writing College Papers* | 145,000 |
| 1953 | Grene and Lattimore (eds.) | *Aeschylus I* | 141,000 |
| 1944 | Hayek | *The Road to Serfdom* | 136,000 |
| 1960 | Grene and Lattimore (eds.) | *Greek Tragedies*, Volume I | 134,000 |
| 1954 | Grene and Lattimore (eds.) | *Sophocles I* | 102,000 |
| 1957 | Clark | *History of the Primates* | 102,000 |
| 1956 | Morgan | *The Birth of the Republic, 1763–89* | 101,000 |
| 1899 | Dewey | *The School and Society* | 100,000 |
| 1916 | Goodspeed | *The Story of the New Testament* | 96,000 |
| 1958 | Leuchtenburg | *The Perils of Prosperity, 1914–32* | 94,000 |
| 1954 | Potter | *People of Plenty* | 90,000 |

# Annual Summary of Books Published and Book Sales

| Year | Number of Books Published | Total Net Book Sales* (in Dollars) | Year | Number of Books Published | Total Net Book Sales* (in Dollars) |
|---|---|---|---|---|---|
| 1892–93 | 1 | . . . . . . . . . | 1929–30 | 119 | $   360,528 |
| 1893–94 | 4 | . . . . . . . . . | 1930–31 | 100 | 388,469 |
| 1894–95 | 11 | . . . . . . . . . | 1931–32 | 132 | 342,616 |
| 1895–96 | 8 | . . . . . . . . . | 1932–33 | 139 | 248,013 |
| 1896–97 | 31 | . . . . . . . . . | 1933–34 | 129 | 223,030 |
| 1897–98 | 27 | . . . . . . . . . | 1934–35 | 88 | 205,041 |
| 1898–99 | 22 | . . . . . . . . . | 1935–36 | 97 | 221,219 |
| 1899–1900 | 28 | . . . . . . . . . | 1936–37 | 114 | 234,138 |
| 1900–01 | 28 | . . . . . . . . . | 1937–38 | 110 | 259,454 |
| 1901–02 | 40 | . . . . . . . . . | 1938–39 | 119 | 269,122 |
| 1902–03 | 118 | . . . . . . . . . | 1939–40 | 100 | 255,513 |
| 1903–04 | 53 | . . . . . . . . . | 1940–41 | 83 | 252,843 |
| 1904–05 | 36 | . . . . . . . . . | 1941–42 | (1941)  69† | 247,329 |
| 1905–06 | 23 | . . . . . . . . . | 1942–43 | (1942)  79 | 320,229 |
| 1906–07 | 33 | . . . . . . . . . | 1943–44 | (1943)  59 | 445,762 |
| 1907–08 | 37 | . . . . . . . . . | 1944–45 | (1944)  49 | 546,026 |
| 1908–09 | 43 | . . . . . . . . . | 1945–46 | (1945)  41 | 581,106 |
| 1909–10 | 41 | . . . . . . . . . | 1946–47 | (1946)  46 | 757,565 |
| 1910–11 | 37 | $    36,596 | 1947–48 | (1947)  53 | 765,591 |
| 1911–12 | 30 | 38,598 | 1948–49 | (1948)  65 | 836,033 |
| 1912–13 | 27 | 46,103 | 1949–50 | (1949)  45 | 820,838 |
| 1913–14 | 31 | 53,749 | 1950–51 | (1950)  50 | 842,924 |
| 1914–15 | 32 | 49,320 | 1951–52 | (1951)  58 | 769,256 |
| 1915–16 | 34 | 61,703 | 1952–53 | (1952)  62 | 718,819 |
| 1916–17 | 42 | 87,610 | 1953–54 | (1953)  68 | 719,159 |
| 1917–18 | 55 | 87,753 | 1954–55 | (1954)  52 | 821,337 |
| 1918–19 | 27 | 82,917 | 1955–56 | (1955)  58 | 878,183 |
| 1919–20 | 28 | 111,613 | 1956–57 | (1956)  51 | 1,041,254 |
| 1920–21 | 28 | 132,250 | 1957–58 | (1957)  70 | 1,393,719 |
| 1921–22 | 35 | 197,902 | 1958–59 | (1958)  64 | 1,421,567 |
| 1922–23 | 39 | 210,152 | 1959–60 | (1959)  74 | 1,668,334 |
| 1923–24 | 43 | 267,923 | 1960–61 | (1960)  92 | 1,803,576 |
| 1924–25 | 48 | 266,485 | 1961–62 | (1961) 131 | 2,240,610 |
| 1925–26 | 43 | 292,593 | 1962–63 | (1962) 135 | 2,199,747 |
| 1926–27 | 59 | 323,033 | 1963–64 | (1963) 136 | 2,769,521 |
| 1927–28 | 89 | 336,838 | 1964–65 | (1964) 137 | 3,092,043 |
| 1928–29 | 85 | 338,098 |  | (1965) 139 |  |

* The income from journals is not included. Totals for book sales are not available for the years preceding 1910–11.

† From 1941 on the count of number of books is by calendar year, total book sales as before by the fiscal year, ending June 30.

*Here our wares are housed, our orders shipped, and a busy business office sees that we don't get too carried away with the idea of being a non-profit organization.*

# THE CATALOGUE

# Author and Title Listing

**L'Abbé Constantin (Halévy):** POLLARD.

**Abbott, Edith.** Democracy and Social Progress in England. 1918. WP. *o.p.*

**Abbott, Edith.** Historical Aspects of the Immigration Problem. Select Documents. 1926. SSS. *o.p.*

**Abbott, Edith.** Immigration. Select Documents and Case Records. 1924. SSS. *o.p.*

**Abbott, Edith.** Public Assistance. 2 vols. *Vol. I:* American Principles and Politics. In Five Parts. With Select Documents. 1940. SSS. *o.p.*

**Abbott, Edith.** Social Welfare and Professional Education. 1931. Rev. ed. 1941. *o.p.*

**Abbott, Edith.** Some American Pioneers in Social Welfare. Select Documents with Editorial Notes. 1937. SSS. *o.p.*

**Abbott, Edith.** The Tenements of Chicago, 1908–1935. By Edith Abbott, assisted by Sophonisba P. Breckinridge and Other Associates in the School of Social Service Administration of the University of Chicago. 1936. SSM. *o.p.*

**Abbott, Edith.** Truancy and Non-attendance in the Chicago Schools. A Study of the Social Aspects of the Compulsory Education and Child Labor Legislation of Illinois, by Edith Abbott and Sophonisba P. Breckinridge. 1917. *o.p.*

**Abbott, Frank Frost.** The Toledo Manuscript of the *Germania* of Tacitus, with Notes on a Pliny Manuscript. 1903. *o.p.*

**Abbott, Frank Frost.** The Use of Repetition in Latin To Secure Emphasis, Intensity, and Distinctness of Impression. 1900. Preprint from Vol. III, STUDIES IN CLASSICAL PHILOLOGY. *o.p.*

**Abbott, Grace.** The Child and the State. Select Documents, with Introductory Notes. 1938. 2 vols. *Vol. I:* Legal Status in the Family. Apprenticeship and Child Labor. *Vol. II:* The Dependent and the Delinquent Child. The Child of Unmarried Parents. SSS. *o.p.*

**Abbott, Grace.** From Relief to Social Security. The Development of the New Public Welfare Services and Their Administration. 1941. *o.p.*

**Abbott, Nabia.** Aishah, the Beloved of Mohammed. 1942. *o.p.*

**Abbott, Nabia.** The Kurrah Papyri from Aphrodito in the Oriental Institute. xviii, 101 p. Illus. 25 cm. 40-458. 1938. SAOC 15. *o.p.*

**Abbott, Nabia.** The Monasteries of the Fayyūm. 1937. SAOC 16. *o.p.*

**Abbott, Nabia.** The Rise of the North Arabic Script and Its Ḳurʾānic Development. With a Full Description of the Ḳurʾān Manuscripts in the Oriental Institute. 1939. xxii, 103 p. Illus. 30 cm. 39-21170. OIP, L. $10.00.

**Abbott, Nabia.** Studies in Arabic Literary Papyri. I. Historical Texts. 1956. 136 p. Illus. 30 cm. 56-5027. OIP, LXXV. $30.00.

**Abbott, Nabia.** Two Queens of Baghdad. 1946. *o.p.*

**ABC of Acid-Base Chemistry:** DAVENPORT.

**Abenteuer der Neujahrsnacht:** HAGBOLDT.

**Ability To Pay for Medical Care:** REED.

**Above Pompeii:** WILKINS.

**Abraham, W. E.** The Mind of Africa. 1963. 208 p. 22 cm. 63-9733. NHS. $4.00ˢ. OBE.

**Abraham Lincoln:** SELBY.

**Abramson, David I.** Vascular Responses in the Extremities of Man in Health and Disease. 1944. BM. *o.p.*

**Abstracts of Theses:** *see* UNIVERSITY OF CHICAGO, Abstracts of Theses.

**Abundance of Chemical Elements:** CHERDYNTSEV.

**Academic Illusions:** SCHÜTZE.

**Academic and Professional Preparation:** GRAY.

**Accounting Method:** ROREM.

**Acculturation in the Americas:** TAX.

**Acheson, Eunice Mae.** The Effective Dean of Women. A Study of the Personal and Professional Characteristics of a Selected Group of Deans of Women. 1932. *o.p.*

**Achievement Tests To Be Used with** *Beginning Spanish:* CASTILLO.

**Achievement Tests To Be Used with** *Primeras lecturas españolas:* CASTILLO.

**Achromatic Spindle in the Spore Mother-Cells of** *Osmunda regalis:* SMITH.

**Ackerman, Edward A.** Japan's Natural Resources and Their Relation to Japan's Economic Future. 1953. xxv, 655 p. Illus. 26 cm. 53-12889. PS. $25.00ˢ.

**Ackerman, Edward A.** New England's Fishing Industry. 1941. *o.p.*

**Ackerman, Joseph,** *ed.* Family Farm Policy. Edited by Joseph Ackerman and Marshall Harris. 1947. *o.p.*

**Ackerson, Luton.** Children's Behavior Problems. A Statistical Study Based upon 5,000 Children Examined Consecutively at the Illinois Institute for Juvenile Research. *Vol. I:* Incidence, Genetic, and Intellectual Factors. 1931. BR. *o.p.*

**Ackoff, Russell L.** The Design of Social Research. 1953. xi, 420 p. 26 cm. 53-12546. $8.50ᵗ.

**Acquisition and Cataloging of Books:** RANDALL.

**Acrobatics for All:** BEYER.

**Activity Movement:** MOSSMAN.

**Adair, Fred Lyman,** *ed.* Maternal Care. The Principles of Antepartum, Intrapartum, and Postpartum Care for the Practitioner of Obstetrics. Prepared by Drs. W. C. Danforth, G. W. Kosmak, R. L. DeNormandie, and F. L. Adair. 1937. 2d ed. 1941. *o.p.*

**Adair, Fred Lyman,** *ed.* Maternal Care Complications. The Principles of Management of Some Serious Complications Arising during the Antepartum, Intrapartum, and Postpartum Periods. Prepared by Drs. R. D. Mussey, P. F. Williams, and F. H. Falls. 1938. 2d ed. 1941. *o.p.*

**Adair, Fred Lyman,** *ed.* Maternal Care and Some Complications. The Principles of Antepartum, Intrapartum, and Postpartum Care and the Management of Some Serious Complications. Prepared by Drs. W. C. Danforth, G. W. Kosmak, R. D. Mussey, R. L. DeNormandie, F. L. Adair, P. F. Williams, and F. H. Falls. 1939. *o.p.*

**Adair, Fred Lyman,** *joint author:* POTTER, Fetal and Neonatal Death.

**Adam Smith:** CLARK.

**Adam Smith and Modern Sociology:** SMALL.

**Adams, Elizabeth Kemper.** The Aesthetic Experience. Its Meaning in a Functional Psychology. 1907. *o.p.*

**Adams, James Luther,** *trans.:* TILLICH, Protestant Era.

**Adams, John A. S.,** *ed.* The Natural Radiation Environment. Edited by John A. S. Adams and Wayne M. Lowder. 1964. 1069 p. 24 cm. 64-12256. RSS. $15.00ˢ.

**Adams, John Clinton,** *trans.:* PAVLOV, Leningrad 1941.

**Adams, Nicholson B.,** *ed.:* NORTHUP, Introduction to Spanish Literature.

**Adams, Robert J.,** *trans.:* SEKI, *ed.,* Folktales of Japan.

**Adams, Robert McC.** Land behind Baghdad. A History of Settlement on the Diyala Plains. 1965. xvi, 187 p. Illus. 30 cm. 65-17279. $8.50.

**Adams, Robert McC.,** *joint ed.:* Kraeling, City Invincible.

**Adams, Thomas S.:** *see* Financial Mobilization for War.

**Adams, Walter Sydney,** *joint author:* Frost, Radial Velocities of Twenty Stars.

**Adapting Reading Programs:** Gray.

**Adapting the Schools to Individual Differences:** Washburne.

**Adapting the Secondary-School Program to the Needs of Youth:** Brink.

**Additon, Henrietta.** City Planning for Girls. A Study of the Social Machinery for Case Work with Girls in Philadelphia, with Comments on Present Methods, Brief Histories of Past Experiments, and Recommended Plans for the Future. 1928. SSM. *o.p.*

**Ade, George.** Artie *and* Pink Marsh, 1896–97. Reissue, 1 vol. 1963. Introduction by James T. Farrell. xi, 224 p. Illus. 21 cm. 63-22584. CF. $3.95.

**Adjusting Reading Programs to Individuals:** Gray.

**Adler, Mortimer J.** The Revolution in Education. By Mortimer J. Adler and Milton Mayer. 1958. viii, 224 p. 22 cm. 58-7348. $4.25†.

**Administering Unemployment Compensation:** White.

**Administration:** Russell.

**Administration of Criminal Law:** Puttkammer.

**Administration of Higher Institutions:** Burns.

**Administration of Justice from Homer to Aristotle:** Bonner.

**Administration of Mathematics in Secondary Schools:** Breslich.

**Administration of Private Social Service Agencies:** Burke.

**Administration of Schools for Better Living:** Cooper.

**Administration of Secondary-School Units:** Koos.

**Administration of Technical Assistance:** Glick.

**Administrative Adjustments Required by Socio-economic Change:** Reavis.

**Administrative Decentralization:** Truman.

**Administrative Planning for School Programs and Plants:** Cooper.

**Administrative Powers over Persons and Property:** Freund.

**Administrative Regulation:** Leiserson.

**Administrative State:** Morstein Marx.

**Administrative Theories of Hamilton and Jefferson:** Caldwell.

**Administrative Use of Intelligence Tests:** Holmes.

**Admiral:** Kennedy, *in his* Plays for Three Players. Vol. I.

**Admission and Retention of University Students:** Reeves.

**Adolescence:** Jones.

**Adult Education and Rural Life:** American Country Life Association, Proceedings, No. 15.

**Adult Reading:** Clift.

**Advanced Conversational Chinese:** Têng.

**Advances and Applications of Mathematical Biology:** Rashevsky.

**Advertising Agency Compensation:** Young.

**Aeschylus:** *see* Complete Greek Tragedies.

**Aesop's Fables:** Hull.

**Aesthetic Aspects of Art:** Scranton.

**Aesthetic Experience:** Adams.

**Aesthetics of the Novel:** Ames.

**Africa in the Modern World:** Stillman.

**Africanisms in the Gullah Dialect:** Turner.

**Against the Current. The Life of Karl Heinzen:** WITTKE.

**Agar, Herbert.** The Price of Power. America since 1945. 1957. xi, 199 p. 21 cm. 57-8575. CHAC. Cloth. $4.50ˢ. Paper. $1.75. COBE.

**Agar, Herbert:** *see* HUTCHINSON, Democracy and National Unity.

**Agard, Frederick B.** The Grammatical Structures of English and Italian. By Frederick B. Agard and Robert J. Di Pietro. 1965. vii, 91 p. 24 cm. 65-25119. CSS. Paper. $2.00ᵗ.

**Agard, Frederick B.** The Sounds of English and Italian. By Frederick B. Agard and Robert J. Di Pietro. 1965. vii, 76 p. 24 cm. 65-25118. CSS. Paper. $2.00ᵗ.

**Agassiz, Louis:** LURIE.

**Aggeler, Paul M.** Hemorrhagic Disorders. A Guide to Diagnosis and Treatment. By Paul M. Aggeler and S. P. Lucia. 1949. BM. *o.p.*

**Aggression:** SCOTT.

**Aging and Levels of Biological Organization:** BRUES.

**Aging in Western Societies:** BURGESS.

**Agrarian China:** INSTITUTE OF PACIFIC RELATIONS. *Research Staff of the Secretariat.*

**Agricultural Economics:** NOURSE.

**Agricultural Education:** DAVIS.

**Agricultural Education in Secondary Schools:** MONAHAN.

**Agriculture in the Chicago Region:** DUDDY.

**Aim of the Yerkes Observatory:** HALE.

**Aims, Scope, and Methods of a University Course in Public-School Administration:** SPAULDING.

**Air Transportation in the United States:** KNOWLTON.

**Aishah, the Beloved of Mohammed:** ABBOTT.

**Aitken, A. J.,** *ed.:* CRAIGIE, Dictionary of the Older Scottish Tongue. Part 17 *et seq.*

**Albert, A. Adrian.** College Algebra. 1946. Paper. PSS 517. 21 cm. $1.95.

**Albert, A. Adrian.** Fundamental Concepts of Higher Algebra. 1956. 176 p. 56-5129. Cloth. 24 cm. $6.50ˢ. Paper. PSS 507. 21 cm. $1.35.

**Albert, A. Adrian.** Introduction to Algebraic Theories. 1941. 138 p. 24 cm. 41-3957. $3.50ˢ.

**Albert, A. Adrian.** Modern Higher Algebra. 1937. xiv, 319 p. 26 cm. 38-2937. SCI. $6.50ˢ. ". . . the serious student of mathematics will find Professor Albert's book stimulating and packed with ideas. It is in a class quite apart from the mediocre and nearly identical 'college algebras' which American commercial publishers seem to prefer. . . . [A]n indispensable book which every specialist in algebra should own."—Garrett Birkhoff, in *Science.*

**Alden, William Clinton,** *joint author:* SALISBURY, Geography of Chicago.

**Alexander, Franz,** *ed.* Dynamic Psychiatry. Edited by Franz Alexander and Helen Ross. 1952. xii, 578 p. 24 cm. 52-9733. BM. $12.50ˢ.

**Alexander, Franz,** *ed.* The Impact of Freudian Psychiatry. Edited by Franz Alexander and Helen Ross. An abridgment of *Dynamic Psychiatry.* 1961. Paper. P62. $1.95.

**Alexander, William Picken.** Intelligence, Concrete and Abstract. A Study in Differential Traits. 1935. BJP. *o.p.*

**Alfred the Great:** DUCKETT.

**Alfred Weber's Theory of the Location of Industries:** FRIEDRICH.

**Algae of Illinois:** TIFFANY.

**Algebras and Their Arithmetics:** DICKSON.

**Algol Variable +17°4367. W. Delphini:** PICKERING.

**Alien Enemies and Alien Friends:** PUTTKAMMER.

**Alienation and Freedom:** BLAUNER.

**Alimentary Tract:** CARLSON.

**Alinsky, Saul D.** Reveille for Radicals. 1946. *o.p.*

**Alishar Hüyük, Season of 1927:** OSTEN.

**Alishar Hüyük, Seasons of 1928 and 1929:** SCHMIDT.

**Alishar Hüyük, Seasons of 1930–32:** OSTEN.

**All Coherence Gone:** HARRIS.

**All the King's Ladies:** WILSON.

**Allee, Warder Clyde.** Animal Aggregations. A Study in General Sociology. 1931. o.p.

**Allee, Warder Clyde.** Synoptic Key to the Phyla, Classes, and Orders of Animals. With Particular Reference to Fresh-Water and Terrestrial Forms of the Moist Temperate Region in North America. Based on a Compilation Originally Made by V. E. Shelford and Compiled by W. C. Allee. 1923. o.p.

**Allee, Warder Clyde,** joint author: PARK, Laboratory Introduction to Animal Ecology and Taxonomy.

**Allee, Warder Clyde:** see MOULTON, World and Man.

**Allee, Warder Clyde:** see NEWMAN, Nature of the World and of Man.

**Allen, Francis A.** The Borderland of Criminal Justice. Essays in Law and Criminology. 1964. ix, 139 p. 21 cm. 64-24972. $3.75ˢ.

**Allen, Hamilton Ford.** The Infinitive in Polybius Compared with the Infinitive in Biblical Greek. 1907. HLL. o.p.

**Allen, Henry Elisha.** The Turkish Transformation. A Study in Social and Religious Development. 1935. o.p.

**Allen, Henry Elisha:** see HAYDON, Modern Trends in World-Religions.

**Allen, J. Garrott.** The Physiology and Treatment of Peptic Ulcer. 1959. x, 236 p. Illus. 24 cm. 59-10421. BM. $7.50ˢ.

**Allen, Philip Schuyler.** Medieval Latin Lyrics. 1931. o.p.

**Allen, Philip Schuyler.** Studies in Popular Poetry. 1902. o.p.

**Allen, Philip Schuyler,** ed. Diary and Letters of Wilhelm Müller. With Explanatory Notes and a Biographical Index. Edited by Philip Schuyler Allen and James Taft Hatfield. 1903. o.p.

**Allen, Thomas George.** A Handbook of the Egyptian Collection, The Art Institute of Chicago. Published for the Art Institute of Chicago. 1923. o.p.

**Allen, Thomas George.** Occurrences of Pyramid Texts with Cross Indexes of These and Other Egyptian Mortuary Texts. 1950. vii, 149 p. 25 cm. 50-9024. Paper. SAOC 27. $10.00.

**Allen, Thomas George,** ed. The Egyptian Book of the Dead Documents in the Oriental Institute Museum at the University of Chicago. 1960. 282 p. Illus. 31 cm. 59-7290. Paper. OIP, LXXXII. $17.50.

**Aller, Lawrence H.** Stellar Structure. Edited by Lawrence H. Aller and Dean B. McLaughlin. 1965. ("Stars and Stellar Systems," Vol. VIII.) xx, 648 p. Illus. 25 cm. 63-16723. $17.50ˢ.

**Allerlei:** HAGBOLDT.

**Alphabet:** SPRENGLING.

**Alschuler, Rose H.** Painting and Personality. A Study of Young Children. By Rose H. Alshuler and L. W. Hattwick. 2 vols. 1947. o.p.

**Alternative Laboratory Exercises for Rorem's Accounting Method:** GRAHAM.

**Altick, Richard D.** The English Common Reader. A Social History of the Mass Reading Public, 1800–1900. 1957. x, 418 p. 24 cm. Cloth. 57-6975. $6.00ˢ. Paper. P140. $2.45.
"The confident assertion that free libraries, secondary schools, mechanics' institutes, the industrial revolution, and a general bias in favor of the moral life led to great advancements in reading and intelligence in Victorian England has not hitherto received the thorough documentation such an assertion warrants. . . . A much needed realistic evaluation of the reciprocity between social change and reading. . . ."—Journal of English and Germanic Philology.

**Altman, Charles B.,** joint author: LOUD, Khorsabad.

**Altrocchi, Rudolph.** Deceptive Cognates. Italian-English and English-Italian. 1935. o.p.

**Altrocchi, Rudolph,** ed. Tristi Amori. By Giuseppe Giacosa. Edited by Rudolph Altrocchi and Benjamin M. Woodbridge. HCLS. o.p.

**Alumni Directory:** UNIVERSITY OF CHICAGO. *Alumni Council.*

**Alumni of the Colleges:** REEVES.

**Alvord, Clarence Walworth.** The Old Kaskaskia Records. 1906. CHS. *o.p.*

**Amateur Democrat:** WILSON.

**Amateurs and Professionals in British Politics:** BUCK.

**Ambler, Charles Henry.** Sectionalism in Virginia from 1776 to 1861. 1910. *o.p.*

**America in Contemporary Fiction:** BOYNTON.

**America and the Strife of Europe:** RIPPY.

**American, Sadie.** The Vacation School Movement. 1898. *Bound with* MILLIKEN, Chicago Vacation Schools. *o.p.*

**American Adam:** LEWIS.

**American Automobile:** RAE.

**American Bar Association,** *Council on Legal Education and Admissions to the Bar, ed.* The Lawyer and the Public. 1933. *o.p.*

**American Catholicism:** ELLIS.

**American Country Life Association (ACLA).** (Formerly the National Country Life Association.)

In 1921, the University of Chicago Press became exclusive publishers for the Association, issuing all proceedings from the Third National Country Life Conference. All volumes are out of print.

Town and Country Relations. Fourth Conference. New Orleans, 1921. 1922.

Country Community Education. Fifth Conference. Columbia University, New York City, 1922. 1923.

The Rural Home. Sixth Conference. St. Louis, 1923. 1924.

Religion in Country Life. Seventh Conference. Columbus, Ohio, 1924. 1925.

Needed Readjustments in Rural Life. Eighth Conference. Richmond, 1925. 1926.

Farm Youth. Ninth Conference. Washington, D.C., 1926. 1927.

A Decade of Rural Progress. Tenth Conference. East Lansing, Mich., 1927. The Proceedings of the Eleventh Conference. Urbana, Ill., 1928. Edited by Benson Y. Landis and Nat T. Frame. 1928.

Rural Organization, 1929. Twelfth Conference. Ames, Iowa, 1929. 1930.

Standards of Living. Thirteenth Conference. Madison, Wis., 1930. 1931.

Rural Government. Fourteenth Conference. Ithaca, N.Y., 1931. 1932.

Adult Education and Rural Life. Fifteenth Conference. Wheeling, W.Va., 1932. 1933.

National Policies Affecting Rural Life. Sixteenth Conference. Blacksburg, Va., 1933. 1934.

National Planning and Rural Life. Seventeenth Conference. Washington, D.C., 1934. 1935.

Country Life Programs. Eighteenth Conference. Columbus, Ohio, 1935. 1936.

Education for Democracy. Nineteenth Conference. Kalamazoo, Mich., 1936. 1937.

The People and the Land. Twentieth Conference. Manhattan, Kan., 1937. 1938.

Disadvantaged People in Rural Life. Twenty-first Conference. Lexington, Ky., 1938. 1939.

What's Ahead for Rural America? Twenty-second Conference. State College, Pa., 1939. 1940.

Building Rural Communities. Twenty-third Conference. Purdue University, 1940. 1941.

**American Country Life Association.** Farm Income and Farm Life. A Symposium on the Relation of the Social and Economic Factors in Rural Progress. Edited by Dwight Sanderson, 1927. ACLA. *o.p.*

**American Daughter:** THOMPSON.

**American Democracy and Military Power:** SMITH.

**American Dental Association,** *Committee on the Study of Dental Practice* (ADA):

1. LEVEN, Practice of Dentistry.
2. BECK, Cost of Equipping a Dental Office.
3. LEUCK, Study of Dental Clinics in the United States.
4. LEUCK, Further Study of Dental Clinics in the United States.
5. (Never published.)
6. SIMONS, Way to Health Insurance.

**American Diplomacy, 1900–1951:** KENNAN.

**American Discount Market:** BALABANIS.

**American Drama and Its Critics:** DOWNER.

**American Education:** DEWEY.

**American Education in the Postwar Period. Curriculum Reconstruction:** TYLER.

**American Education in the Postwar Period. Structural Reorganization:** GOODYKOONTZ.

**American Empire:** HAAS.

**American Folklore:** DORSON.

**American Foreign Policy toward International Stability:** HARRIS FOUNDATION COMMITTEE.

**American Girl:** MONTGOMERY.

**American Governor:** LIPSON.

**American and His Food:** CUMMINGS.

**American Immigration:** JONES.

**American Indian and White Children:** HAVIGHURST.

**American Indians:** HAGAN.

**American Institute of Sacred Literature.** Outline Bible-Study Courses (AISL):
BEWER, Religion of the Bible.
BURTON, Founding of the Christian Church.
BURTON, Four Letters of the Apostle Paul.
BURTON, Jesus of Nazareth.
BURTON, Life of Christ. A Series of Direction Sheets.
BURTON, Origin and Teaching of the New Testament Books.
CASE, Book of Revelation.
CHAMBERLIN, Old Testament Books.
GOODSPEED, Gospel of John.
GOODSPEED, Paul.
GORDON, Truth about the Bible.
HARPER, Book of Job.
HARPER, Foreshadowings of the Christ.
HARPER, Work of the Old Testament Priests.
HARPER, Work of the Old Testament Sages.
MATHEWS, Message of Jesus.
MATHEWS, Social and Ethical Teaching of Jesus.
SMITH, Problem of Suffering.
SMITH, Realities of the Christian Religion.
SMITH, Universal Element in the Psalter.
SOARES, How To Enjoy the Bible.
WILLETT, Message of the Prophets.

**American Judaism:** GLAZER.

**American Labor:** MILLER.

**American Labor:** PELLING.

**American Labor from Defense to Reconversion:** SEIDMAN.

**American Lawyer:** BLAUSTEIN.

**American Library Association,** *joint publications* with The University of Chicago Press:
RANDALL, College Library.
RANDALL, Principles of College Library Administration.
WAPLES, What People Want To Read About.
WILSON, Geography of Reading.

**American Life:** WARNER.

**American Newspaper:** ROGERS.

**American Newspaperman:** WEISBERGER.

**American Participation in the China Consortiums:** FIELD.

**American Partnership:** ELAZAR.

**American Permian Vertebrates:** WILLISTON.

**American Philanthropy:** BREMNER.

**American Philosophy of Equality:** SMITH.

**American Poems:** BRONSON.

**American Policies Abroad** (APA). Published for the Chicago Council on Foreign Relations:
FISH, United States and Great Britain.
JONES, United States and the Caribbean.
RIPPY, Mexico.

**American Political Science Association:** *see* REED, Four Years of Network Broadcasting.

**American Primers** (AP):
CANTOR, Crime.
CRIGHTON, Business and Government.
DAVIS, Youth in the Depression.
DE NOOD, Jobs or the Dole?
HORNE, The Farm Business.
OGBURN, You and Machines.
PRATT, Friends or Enemies?
ROSE, Money.
SENTURIA, Strikes.
WIESE, Let's Talk It Over.

**American Prisons:** MCKELVEY.

**American Prose:** BRONSON.

**American Radio:** WHITE.

**American Railroads:** STOVER.

**American Schools:** MORRISON.

**American Short Story in the Twenties:** WRIGHT.

**American Society in Wartime:** OGBURN.

**American Sociological Society,** Annual Proceedings (AS).
The University of Chicago Press discontinued publication of the annual proceedings with Vol. XXIX (1935). All volumes are out of print.
Vol. I. (1906) Papers and Proceedings of the First Annual Meeting, Providence, R.I. 1907.

Vol. II. (1907) Social Conflicts. Madison, Wis. 1908.

Vol. III. (1908) The Family. Atlantic City. 1909.

Vol. IV. (1909) Papers and Proceedings. New York City. 1910.

Vol. V. (1910) Papers and Proceedings. St. Louis. 1911.

Vol. VI. (1911) Papers and Proceedings. Washington, D.C. 1912.

Vol. VII. (1912) The Conception of Human Interrelations as a Variant of Social Theory. Boston. 1913.

Vol. VIII. (1913) Problems of Social Assimilation. Minneapolis. 1914.

Vol. IX. (1914) Freedom of Communication. Princeton. 1915.

Vol. X. (1915) War and Militarism in Their Sociological Aspects. Washington, D.C. 1916.

Vol. XI. (1916) The Sociology of Rural Life. Columbus, Ohio. 1917.

Vol. XII. (1917) Social Control. Philadelphia. 1918.

Vol. XIII. (1918) Sociology and Education. Richmond. 1919.

Vol. XIV. (1919) The Problem of Democracy. Chicago. 1920.

Vol. XV. (1920) Some Newer Problems, National and Social. Washington, D.C. 1921.

Vol. XVI. (1921) Factors in Social Evolution. Pittsburgh. 1922.

Vol. XVII. (1922) Constructive Social Analysis. Chicago. 1923.

Vol. XVIII. (1923) The Trend of Population. Washington, D.C. 1924.

Vol. XIX. (1924) The Trend of Our Civilization. Chicago. 1925.

Vol. XX. (1925) The City. New York. 1926. Issued as Part 2, The American Journal of Sociology, July, 1926.

Vol. XXI. (1926) The Progress of Sociology. St. Louis. 1927.

Vol. XXII. (1927) The Relation of the Individual to the Group. Washington. 1928.

Vol. XXIII. (1928) The Rural Community. Chicago. 1929.

Vol. XXIV. No. 1. February, 1930. Proceedings. 1930.

No. 2. May, 1930. Studies in Quantitative and Cultural Sociology. Washington, D.C., 1929. 1930.

No. 3. August, 1930. List of Members. 1930.

No. 4. November, 1930. Yearbook of the Section on Rural Sociology. General Topic: Rural Social Conflict. 1930.

Vol. XXV. No. 1. February, 1931. Proceedings. 1931.

No. 2. May, 1931. Social Conflict. Twenty-fifth Annual Meeting. Cleveland, 1930. 1931.

No. 3. August, 1931. List of Members, 1931. 1931.

No. 4. November, 1931. Yearbook of the Section on Rural Sociology. 1930.

Vol. XXVI. No. 1. February, 1932. Proceedings. 1932.

No. 2. June, 1932. Organization for Research in the American Sociological Society. Report and Recommendations of the Special Committee on the Scope of the Research of the American Sociological Society. 1932.

No. 3. March, 1933. Social Process. Twenty-sixth Annual Meeting. Washington, D.C., 1931. 1933.

No. 4. December, 1932. Letter from the President. Program of the Twenty-seventh Annual Meeting. Supplemental List of Members of the American Sociological Society. 1932.

Vol. XXVII. No. 1. February, 1933. Proceedings. 1933.

No. 2. May, 1933. Sociological Problems and Methods. Twenty-seventh Annual Meeting. Cincinnati, 1932. 1933.

No. 3. August, 1933. Tentative Program of the Twenty-eighth Annual Meeting. Philadelphia, 1933. 1933.

No. 4. November, 1933. Proposed Constitution of the American Sociological Society, Submitted by the Committee on the Revision of the Constitution. Supplementary List of Members of the American Sociological Society. 1933.

Vol. XXVIII. No. 1. February, 1934. Proceedings. 1934.

No. 2. May, 1934. Racial Contacts and Social Research. Twenty-eighth Annual Meeting. Philadelphia, 1933. 1934.

No. 3. August, 1934. Twenty-ninth Annual Meeting. A Brief from the Report of the Committee To Consider a Plan for the Control of the Official Journal and Other Publications of the American Sociological Society. 1934.

No. 4. November, 1934. List of Members of the American Sociological Society. Letter from the President. Final Program of the Twenty-ninth Annual Meeting of the American Sociological Society. Chicago, 1934.

Vol. XXIX. No. 1. February, 1935. Proceedings. 1935.

No. 2. June, 1935. Plans for the Retirement of the Deficit of the American Sociological Society. Message from the President concerning the Status of the Program for the Annual Meeting. Note from the Managing Editor of the *Publication of the American Sociological Society*. 1935.

**American-Spanish Syntax:** KANY.

**American State Archives:** POSNER.

**American Suffrage Medley:** McGOVNEY.

American Supreme Court: McCloskey.

American Tariff and Oriental Trade: Wright.

Americanization of Carl Schurz: Easum.

Americans Betrayed: Grodzins.

Americans and the World-Crisis: Small.

America's Failure in China, 1941–50: Tsou.

Ames, Edward Scribner. The New Orthodoxy. 1918. 2d ed. 1925. *o.p.*

Ames, Edward Scribner: *see* Bower, Church at Work in the Modern World.

Ames, Edward Scribner: *see* Haydon, Modern Trends in World-Religions.

Ames, Van Meter. Aesthetics of the Novel. 1928. *o.p.*

Ames, Van Meter, *ed.* Beyond Theology. The Autobiography of Edward Scribner Ames. 1959. xii, 224 p. 22 cm. 59-10763. $5.00ˢ.

Amiable Humorist: Tave.

Amici di scuola: Cioffari.

Amusements and Sports: Weaver.

Analysis of the Electric Railway Problem: Wilcox.

Analysis of the Retail Trading Relationships of Elgin, Illinois: Read.

Analysis of the Social Structure of a Western Town: Dunn.

Analytical Bibliography of Modern Language Teaching, 1927–1932: Coleman.

Analytical Bibliography of Modern Language Teaching, 1932–1937: Coleman.

Analytical Didactic: Comenius.

Analytical Experimental Physics: Ference.

Anatolia through the Ages: Schmidt.

Anatomy of the Anecdote: Brownlow.

Anatomy of Woody Plants: Jeffrey.

Ancient Egypt: Kees.

Ancient Egyptian Paintings: Davies.

Ancient Italy: Pais.

Ancient Mesopotamia: Oppenheim.

Ancient Oriental Cylinder and Other Seals: Eisen.

Ancient Oriental Seals in the Collection of Mr. Edward T. Newell: Osten.

Ancient Records (AR).

A series proposed by William Rainey Harper, first President of the University of Chicago, to contain for the first time complete English versions of documentary sources for the history of Assyria and Babylonia (First Series); Egypt (Second Series); and Palestine, Phoenicia, and Syria (Third Series). "Ancient Records" were to appear in twenty-three volumes under the general editorship of President Harper: six volumes in the First Series, to be edited by Robert Francis Harper; twelve volumes of Egyptian sources, to be edited by James Henry Breasted; and five volumes of Palestinian, Phoenician, and Syrian records, to be edited by President Harper.

Upon the President's death, the general editorship passed to Professor Breasted, who published in five volumes the Egyptian sources concerned with political history. Daniel David Luckenbill, succeeding Robert Francis Harper as editor of the First Series, planned to expand it to seven volumes; published two before his death: *Vol. I,* Historical Records of Assyria from the Earliest Times to Sargon; *Vol. II, . . .* from Sargon to the End. *Vol. III,* Babylonian Historical Inscriptions; *Vol. IV,* Ancient Law and Business; *Vol. V,* Literary and Religious Texts; *Vol. VI,* Letters, Official and Private; *Vol. VII,* Index, to cover the entire First Series, were not completed. None of the Third Series was published.

Breasted, Ancient Records of Egypt.

Luckenbill, Ancient Records of Assyria and Babylonia.

Ancient Records of Assyria and Babylonia: Luckenbill.

Ancient Records of Egypt: Breasted.

And Call It Peace: Knappen.

And the War Came: Stampp.

Anders, Edward, *joint trans.:* Heide, Meteorites.

Anderson, Eugene Newton. The First Moroccan Crisis, 1904–1906. 1930. *o.p.*

Anderson, Eugene Newton, *joint ed.:* Cate, Medieval and Historiographical Essays.

Anderson, F. H. The Philosophy of Francis Bacon. 1948. *ȯ.p.*

**Anderson, Galusha.** The Elements of Chrysostom's Power as a Preacher. 1903. *o.p.*

**Anderson, G. Lester.** Educating for the Professions. Prepared by G. Lester Anderson, Chairman of the Yearbook Committee. 1962. NSSE, 61st Yrbk., Part II. xii, 312, cxii p. 24 cm. 62-2235. $4.50ᵗ.

**Anderson, G. Lester.** Learning and Instruction. Prepared by G. Lester Anderson, Chairman of the Yearbook Committee. 1950. NSSE, 49th Yrbk., Part I. xii, 352 p. 24 cm. 50-14227. Cloth. $4.50ᵗ. Paper. $3.75ᵗ.

**Anderson, Harold A.** Classroom Procedure Test in English Composition. For Rating Methods of Teaching in Junior and Senior High Schools. By Harold A. Anderson and Douglas Waples. 1928. *o.p.*

**Anderson, Harold A.** Instruction in English in the University High School. By Harold A. Anderson and others. 1941. PLS. *o.p.*

**Anderson, Harold A.,** *joint ed.:* CHASE, High School in a New Era.

**Anderson, Harold A.:** *see* UNIVERSITY OF CHICAGO, University High School, Department of English.

**Anderson, Nels.** Desert Saints. The Mormon Frontier in Utah. 1942. *o.p.*

**Anderson, Nels.** The Hobo. The Sociology of the Homeless Man. 1923. Paper. P71. $1.95.

**Anderson, Nels.** Men on the Move. 1940. SOC. *o.p.*

**Anderson, Odin W.,** *joint author:* LERNER, Health Progress in the United States.

**Anderson, Oscar E.** The Health of a Nation. Harvey W. Wiley and the Fight for Pure Food. 1958. 312 p. Illus. 25 cm. 58-11945. $6.00ˢ.

**Anderson, Sherwood.** Windy McPherson's Son. 1916. *Reissue,* 1965. Introduction by Wright Morris. xix, 330 p. 21 cm. 65-17280. CF. $5.95.

**Andrea dal Castagno:** RICHTER.

**Andrew Johnson and Reconstruction:** McKITRICK.

**Andrewartha, H. G.** The Distribution and Abundance of Animals. By H. G. Andrewartha and L. C. Birch. 1954. xv, 782 p. Illus. 26 cm. 54-13016. BM. $16.50ˢ.

**Andrewartha, H. G.** Introduction to the Study of Animal Populations. 1961. xvii, 282 p. 61-14538. Paper. PSS 519. 21 cm. $1.95. COBE.

**Andrews, Katharine.** Experiments in Plant Physiology: *see* ELEMENTARY SCHOOL RECORD, No. 4.

**Anekdoten und Erzählungen:** HAGBOLDT.

**Angell, James Rowland.** A Preliminary Study of the Significance of Partial Tones in the Localization of Sound. 1902. *o.p.*

**Angell, James Rowland.** The Relations of Structural and Functional Psychology to Philosophy. 1903. *o.p.*

**Angell, James Rowland:** *see* STUDIES FROM THE PSYCHOLOGICAL LABORATORY.

**Angell, Sir Norman:** *see* FISH, United States and Great Britain.

**Angell, Robert Cooley.** A Study in Undergraduate Adjustment. Sponsored by the Sociology Department and Financed by the Faculty Research Fund of the University of Michigan. Staff of the study: Director, Robert Cooley Angell; Interviewers, Helen Goodrich Campbell, L. Wallace Hoffman, W. Lloyd Berridge; In Charge of Tests, Emma McDonald Dawson; Advice on Analysis of Test Results, Edward B. Greene. 1930. *o.p.*

**L'Anglais tel qu'on le parle (Bernard):** BOND.

**Angle, Paul M.** Created Equal? The Complete Lincoln-Douglas Debates of 1858. Edited and with an Introduction by Paul M. Angle. 1958. xxxiii, 421 p. Frontispiece. 25 cm. 58-6885. $7.50ˢ.

**Anibal, Fred G.:** *see* DOWNING, Our Physical World.

**Animal Aggregations:** ALLEE.

**Animal Behavior:** SCOTT.

**Animal Communities in Temperate America:** SHELFORD.

**Animal Ecology of the Cold Spring Sand Spit:** DAVENPORT.

**Animal Education:** WATSON.

**Animal Micrology:** GUYER.

**Animal Remains from Tell Asmar:** HILZ-HEIMER.

**Animals without Backbones:** BUCHSBAUM.

**Annals of Sennacherib:** LUCKENBILL.

**Annotated Bibliography of Robert M. La Follette:** STIRN.

**Annual Tables of Constants and Numerical Data:** *see* TABLES ANNUELLES DE CONSTANTES ET DONNÉES NUMÉRIQUES.

**Annual Temperature Cycle of Lake Michigan:** CHURCH.

**Anonyms and Pseudonyms:** MORRIS.

**Anoxia:** VAN LIERE.

**Anthes, Rudolf:** *see* HÖLSCHER, Excavation of Medinet Habu. II.

**Anthropology Today:** KROEBER.

**Anthropology Today. Selections:** TAX.

**Anti-Chain-Store Tax Legislation:** LEE.

**Anticipations, Uncertainty, and Dynamic Planning:** HART.

**Anticipatory Subjunctive in Greek and Latin:** HALE.

**Antiquity of Disease:** MOODIE.

**Antología de la literatura mexicana:** CASTILLO.

**Apache Life-Way:** OPLER.

**Apes, Giants, and Man:** WEIDENREICH.

**Apocrypha. An American Translation:** GOODSPEED.

*Apologie and Treatise of Ambroise Paré:* KEYNES.

**Apostle, Hippocrates G.** Aristotle's Philosophy of Mathematics. 1952. x, 228 p. $6.00ˢ.

**Apostles of the Self-made Man:** CAWELTI.

**Appleton, Lilla Estelle.** A Comparative Study of the Play Activities of Adult Savages and Civilized Children. An Investigation of the Scientific Basis of Education. 1910. *o.p.*

**Appositionell bestimmte Pronomen:** POEBEL.

**Appraisal of American Business Forecasts:** COX.

**Appraisal of Anthropology:** TAX.

**Appraisal of Current Practices in Reading:** GRAY.

**Apter, David.** The Politics of Modernization. 1965. xvi, 481 p. 23 cm. 65-24421. $7.50ˢ.

**Aquinas, Thomas:** *see* GILBY, Political Thought of Thomas Aquinas.

**Arbaugh, George Bartholomew.** Revelation in Mormonism. Its Character and Changing Forms. 1932. *o.p.*

**Arc-Spectra:** ROWLAND.

**Archaeological Explorations:** BENNETT.

**Archeology of Eastern United States:** GRIFFIN.

**Archeology and the Sumerian Problem:** FRANKFORT.

**Architecture in Old Chicago:** TALLMADGE.

**Architecture of the Old Northwest Territory:** NEWCOMB.

**Arendt, Hannah.** The Human Condition. 1958. vi, 333 p. 25 cm. 58-5535. WFL. $6.50ˢ. "She offers no pat solutions which can be extracted from their context and used as slogans. Her politics are those of human dignity, not dogma. There is, in fact, only one 'solution' to the predicament she has so profoundly analysed: that is the example of her book itself, and the free, serenely mature and disinterested intelligence it exhibits at every turn. Her plan to do 'nothing more than to think what we are doing' has involved her in an intense, systematic critique of the whole tradition of political philosophy and the full sterility of our contemporary situation. The result is the first important revaluation of the human condition since Marx."—*New Statesman.*

**Ariel (Rodo):** RICE.

**Aristocracy and the Middle-Classes in Germany:** BRAMSTED.

**Aristotle's Philosophy of Mathematics:** APOSTLE.

**Aristotle's Poetics and English Literature:** OLSON.

**Arithmetic, 1947:** BUSWELL.

**Arithmetic, 1948:** BUSWELL.

**Arithmetic, 1949:** BUSWELL.

**Arithmetic Tests:** COUNTS.

**Arkell, William Joscelyn,** *joint author:* SANDFORD, Prehistoric Survey of Egypt and Western Asia.

**Armenian Awakening:** ARPEE.

**Armington, John Howard,** *joint author:* Cox, Weather and Climate of Chicago.

**Army Air Forces in World War II:** CRAVEN.

**Army with Banners:** KENNEDY, *in his* Plays for Seven Players.

**Army French:** WILKINS.

**Arndt, Christian O.,** *ed.* Community Education. 1959. NSSE, 58th Yrbk., Part I. 420 p. 24 cm. 59-751. Cloth. $4.50t. Paper. $3.75t.

**Arndt, W. F.,** *ed. and trans.* A Greek-English Lexicon of the New Testament and Other Early Christian Literature. Edited and translated by W. F. Arndt and F. W. Gingrich. Revision of W. Bauer, *Griechisch-deutsches Wörterbuch zu den Schriften des Neuen Testaments und der übrigen urchristlichen Literatur.* 1957. xxxvii, 909 p. 26 cm. 56-5028. $14.00ˢ. COBE. *See also* GINGRICH, Shorter Lexicon of the Greek New Testament.

"This handsome volume . . . is an outstanding contribution to New Testament Scholarship and an outstanding example of international co-operation . . . the English version faithfully represents the German original . . . the great masses of references both to biblical and other Greek texts and to the relevant literature are accurately reproduced."—*Times Literary Supplement.*

"Tous ceux qui ont contribué à cette splendide réalisation méritent d'être chaudement félicités. On ne manquera pas d'apprécier aussi la largeur de vue de W. Bauer et de son éditeur qui ont autorisé cette publication. Si l'on se réjouit sans réserve de voir le public de langue anglaise pourvu désormais d'un instrument de travail d'une haute tenue scientifique, on se prend à regretter que nous n'ayons rien, en langue française, qui puisse lui être comparé."—*Nouvelle revue théologique.*

**Arnett, Trevor.** Blank Accounting Blanks, Forms 1–12. 1911. *o.p.*

**Arnett, Trevor.** Sigma Chi Accounting System Booklets. 1911. *o.p.*

**Arnett, Trevor.** Sigma Chi Fraternity Blanks, Forms 1–12. 1911. *o.p.*

**Arnett, Trevor.** Sigma Chi Indices. 1911. *o.p.*

**Arnold, Julean Herbert:** *see* WOODHEAD, Occidental Interpretations of the Far Eastern Problem.

**Arnoldson, Torild Washington.** Parts of the Body in Older Germanic and Scandinavian. 1915. LG. *o.p.*

**Arpee, Leon.** The Armenian Awakening. A History of the Armenian Church, 1820–1860. 1909. *o.p.*

**Arrest and Movement:** FRANKFORT.

**Art in America from 1600 to 1865:** STARK.

**Art in American Life and Education:** MUNRO.

**Art in Arnhem Land:** ELKIN.

**Art of Chinese Poetry:** LIU.

**Art Education:** HASTIE.

**Art in Home Economics:** CLARK.

**Art of Jean Racine:** WEINBERG.

**Art and the Social Order:** GOTTSCHALK.

**Artaxerxes III:** HIRSCHY.

**Arte or Crafte of Rhethoryke:** Cox.

**Arthurian Romance and Modern Poetry and Music:** NITZE.

**Artie:** ADE.

**Artificial Parthenogenesis and Fertilization:** LOEB.

**Artificial Production of Spores in Monas:** GREELEY.

**Artz, Frederick B.** From the Renaissance to Romanticism. Trends in Style in Art, Literature, and Music, 1300–1830. 1962. x, 312 p. 62-20021. Cloth. 24 cm. $5.00t. Paper. P186. 21 cm. $2.25.

**Āryabhaṭa, b. 476.** The Āryabhaṭiya of Āryabhaṭa. An Ancient Indian Work on Mathematics and Astronomy. Translated with Notes by Walter Eugene Clark. 1930. *o.p.*

**As Others See Chicago:** PIERCE.

**Asada, Eiji.** The Hebrew Text of Zechariah, 1–8, Compared with the Different Ancient Versions. 1896. *o.p.*

**Ashbaugh, E. J.** The Measurement of Educational Products. By E. J. Ashbaugh and others. 1918. NSSE, 17th Yrbk., Part II. *o.p.*

**Asheim, Lester,** *ed.* New Directions in Public Library Development. Twenty-second Annual Conference, Graduate Library School. 1957. v, 104 p. 25 cm. 58-8610. LS. $3.75ˢ.

**Asheim, Lester,** *ed.* The Persistent Issues in American Librarianship. Twenty-fifth Anniversary Conference, Graduate Library School. 1961. v, 104 p. 25 cm. 61-15050. LS. $3.75ˢ.

**Ashton, E. B.,** *trans.:* JASPERS, Future of Mankind.

**Asia for the Asiatics?:** WARD.

**Asia in the Making of Europe:** LACH.

**Asoka, Edicts of:** NIKAM.

**Aspects of American Astronomy:** NEWCOMB.

**Aspects of the Depression:** MORLEY.

**Aspects of Mexican Civilization:** VASCONCELOS.

**Assembly of Gods:** LYDGATE.

**Assembly of the League of Nations:** BURTON.

**Association of American Universities.** Journal of Proceedings and Addresses.
Proceedings of 1st to 27th conferences published by the Association. The University of Chicago Press began publication with the 28th conference in 1926 and assumed the agency for all earlier volumes. The Press ceased publication and agency in 1941. All volumes are out of print.
Journal of Proceedings and Addresses, 1900–1940.
Index of Proceedings and Addresses, 1900–1918.
Special Report of the Executive Committee in Regard to the Intellectual Cooperation between the Institutions of Latin America and the Members of the Association. Reprinted from the Journal of Proceedings and Addresses of the Tenth Annual Conference of the Association, 1909.

**Association of Collegiate Schools of Business.** Social Studies in Secondary Schools. The Commission on Correlation of Secondary and Collegiate Education, with Particular Reference to Business Education. 1922. MSB. *o.p.*

**Association of Ideas:** TANNER.

**Assyrian and Babylonian Letters:** HARPER.

**Assyriological Studies:** *see* ORIENTAL INSTITUTE, PUBLICATIONS OF.

**Astonished Music:** DENNEY.

**Astrometric and Photometric Statistics of Certain of Hagen's Fields:** PARSONS.

**Astronomical Photographs:** YERKES OBSERVATORY.

**Astronomical Photography:** RITCHEY.

**Astronomical Techniques:** HILTNER.

**Astrophysical Monographs** (AM). Sponsored by *The Astrophysical Journal:*
BOK, Distribution of the Stars in Space.
CHANDRASEKHAR, Introduction to the Study of Stellar Structure.
CHANDRASEKHAR, Principles of Stellar Dynamics.
MERRILL, Spectra of Long-Period Variable Stars.
MORGAN, Atlas of Stellar Spectra.
RUSSELL, Masses of the Stars.

**Atactocrinus:** WELLER.

**Athearn, Walter Scott.** The City Institute for Religious Teachers. 1915. PM. *o.p.*

**Atheism in the English Renaissance:** BUCKLEY.

**Atkins, Elizabeth.** Edna St. Vincent Millay and Her Times. 1936. *o.p.*

**Atkins, Willard Earl,** *joint author:* DOUGLAS, Worker in Modern Economic Society.

**Atkinson, Louise Warren.** The Story of Paul of Tarsus. 1910. CS. *o.p.*

**Atlas of Cat Anatomy:** FIELD.

**Atlas of Economic Development:** GINSBURG.

**Atlas of the Northern Milky Way:** ROSS.

**Atlas of Stellar Spectra:** MORGAN.

**Atmospheres of Earth and Planets:** KUIPER.

**Atoms in the Family:** FERMI.

**Atoms and Men:** LEPRINCE-RINGUET.

**Atoms for the World:** FERMI.

**L'Attaque du moulin (Zola):** BOND.

**Attempt To Frame a Working Hypothesis of the Cause of Glacial Periods:** CHAMBERLIN.

**Attempt To Test the Nebular Hypothesis:** MOULTON.

**Attitude Scales:** *see* Scales for the Measurement of Social Attitudes.

**Aucassin et Nicolette (Bida):** BOND.

**Audio-Visual Materials of Instruction:** COREY.

**Auerbach, Erich.** Dante, Poet of the Secular World. Translated by Ralph Manheim. Edited by Theodore Silverstein. 1961. viii, 195 p. 21 cm. Index. 61-11893. $5.00ˢ.

**Auger, Pierre.** What Are Cosmic Rays? Translated from the French by Maurice Shapiro. 1945. *o.p.*

**Aurelianus, Caelius.** On Acute and Chronic Diseases. Translated by I. E. Drabkin. BM. 1950. *o.p.*

**Aus deutscher Vergangenheit:** HAGBOLDT.

**Aus Wald und Heide (Lons):** GUDDE.

**Autarchy:** TIPPETTS.

**Aventuras de Gil Blas:** CASTILLO.

**Avogadro, Amedo:** *see* DALTON, Foundations of the Molecular Theory.

**Awakening Valley:** COLLIER.

**Axtell, Harold Lucius.** The Deification of Abstract Ideas in Roman Literature and Inscriptions. 1907. *o.p.*

**Ayer, F. C.** Fourth Report of the Committee on Economy of Time in Education. By F. C. Ayer and Others. 1919. NSSE, 18th Yrbk., Part II. 123 p. 24 cm. Paper. $1.10ᵗ.

**Ayres, Clarence Edwin.** The Nature of the Relationship between Ethics and Economics. 1918. PS. *o.p.*

**Ayres, James Garrett,** *joint author:* GRAY, Growth in Private-School Children.

**Baber, Zonia.** Stony Island. A Plea for Its Conservation. 1917. GSC. *o.p.*

**Babkin, Boris P.** Pavlov. A Biography. 1949. xiii, 365 p. 22 cm. 49-11887. $6.00ˢ.

**Babylonian Chronology:** PARKER.

**Babylonian Genesis:** HEIDEL.

**Babylonian Texts:** *see* AKKADIAN TEXTS.

**Bach, G. Leland:** *see* LELAND, State-Local Fiscal Relations.

**Background of Swedish Immigration:** JANSON.

**Backlund, Helge G.:** *see* STUDIES IN PETROLOGY.

**Bacon, Georgia F.** History: *see* ELEMENTARY SCHOOL RECORD, No. 8.

**Baer, Klaus.** Rank and Title in the Old Kingdom. The Structure of the Egyptian Administration in the Fifth and Sixth Dynasties. 1960. x, 310 p. 24 cm. 60-7231. $7.50ˢ.

**Bagley, W. C.** Second Report of the Committee on Minimum Essentials in Elementary-School Subjects. By W. C. Bagley and others. 1917. NSSE, 16th Yrbk., Part I. *o.p.*

**Bagley, W. C.** Third Report of the Committee on Economy of Time in Education. By W. C. Bagley and others. 1918. NSSE, 17th Yrbk., Part I. *o.p.*

**Baharav, Gena,** *trans.:* NOY, *ed.,* Folktales of Israel.

**Bail System in Chicago:** BEELEY.

**Bailey, Dana Clark.** A New Approach to American History. Students' Guide Sheets. 1927. 3d ed., 1931, revised by E. T. Smith. *o.p.*

**Bailey, Percival.** Intracranial Tumors of Infancy and Childhood. By Percival Bailey, M.D.; Douglas N. Buchanan, M.D.; and Paul C. Bucy, M.D. 1939. xiii, 598 p. 24 cm. CMM. $12.50ˢ.

". . . a needed and desirable monograph. It is the result of a study of an unselected series of 100 consecutive cases from infancy to the sixteenth birthday . . . should be read by every neurologist, neurosurgeon and neuropathologist because it will prove to be an excellent reference. It contains so much valuable information, suggestions and points that studying it is the only way to appreciate it."—*Journal of the American Medical Association.*

**Bailiff, L. D.,** *ed.* Las Inquietudes de Shanti Andía. By Pio Baroja. Edited by L. D. Bailiff and Maro B. Jones. HCLS.

**Bain, Harry Foster.** Relations of the Wisconsin and Kansan Drift Sheets in Central Iowa, and Related Phenomena. 1897. *o.p.*

**Baker, Archibald Gillies.** A Short History of Christianity. Written in collaboration by Archibald G. Baker, *editor*, Massey H. Shepherd, Jr., John T. McNeill, Matthew Spinka, Winfred E. Garrison, and William W. Sweet. 1940. vii, 279 p. 40-34185. Cloth. 20 cm. $5.00ˢ. Paper. P95. 21 cm. $1.50.

**Baker, Archibald Gillies:** *see* BOWER, Church at Work in the Modern World.

**Baker, Archibald Gillies:** *see* SMITH, Religious Thought in the Last Quarter-Century.

**Baker, Florence M.** Las Cuevas de Artá: A Tale of Mallorca. HCLS.

**Baker, Gladys.** The County Agent. 1939. PA. *o.p.*

**Baker, Newman Freese.** Legal Aspects of Zoning. 1927. MSB. *o.p.*

**Baker, Oliver Edwin:** *see* GINI, Population.

**Baker, Oliver Edwin:** *see* HUTCHINSON, Democracy and National Unity.

**Baker, Richard Philip.** The Problem of the Angle-Bisectors. 1911. *o.p.*

**Baker-Crothers, Hayes.** Virginia and the French and Indian War. 1928. *o.p.*

**Baking Industry under N.R.A.:** STONE.

**Balabanis, Homer P.** The American Discount Market. 1935. MSB. *o.p.*

**Balancing the Budget:** UNIVERSITY OF CHICAGO ROUND TABLE.

**Balduf, E. W.,** *joint ed.:* KAUFMANN, Inductive Readings in German. Book III.

**Baldwin, Bird T.,** *joint author:* CUBBERLEY, Research within the Field of Education.

**Baldwin, James Fosdick.** Scutage and Knight Service in England. 1897. *o.p.*

**Baldwin, Ralph B.** The Face of the Moon. 1949. *o.p.*

**Baldwin, Ralph B.** The Measure of the Moon. 1963. xx, 488 p. Illus. 24 cm. 62-20025. $13.50ˢ.

**Baldwin, Raymond William.** Price Differentials in Wheat Futures between Kansas City and Chicago. 1934. SBA, IV. *o.p.*

**Ball, Frank H.** Manual Training: *see* ELEMENTARY SCHOOL RECORD, No. 7.

**Ballad of Manila Bay:** FISKE.

**Ballad Revival:** FRIEDMAN.

**Ballard, Philip Boswood.** Obliviscence and Reminiscence. 1913. BJP. *o.p.*

**Balzac Bibliography:** ROYCE.

**Banking and the New Deal:** WHITTLESEY.

**Bantu Bureaucracy:** FALLERS.

**Baptist Congress.** Annual Sessions. All volumes are out of print.
26th Annual Session, Chicago, 1908. 1909.
27th Annual Session, New York City, 1909. 1909.
28th Annual Session, Augusta, Georgia, 1910. 1911.
29th Annual Session, Atlantic City, 1911. 1912.
30th Annual Session, Ithaca, N.Y., 1912. 1913.
An Author, Title, and Subject Index to the Proceedings of the Baptist Congress, Vols. 1–30, 1882–1912. By Frank Grant Lewis and Edith Maddock West. 1913.

**Baptists, 1783–1830:** SWEET.

**Barhebraeus' Scholia on the Old Testament:** GREGORIUS.

**Barker, J. F.** Industrial Education. Typical Experiments Described and Interpreted. By J. F. Barker and others. 1912. NSSE, 11th Yrbk., Part I. *o.p.*

**Barker, James M.,** *joint author:* LYON, Your Business and Postwar Readjustment.

**Barker, Lewellys Franklin.** A Description of the Brains and Spinal Cords of Two Brothers Dead of Hereditary Ataxia. Cases XVIII and XX of the Series in the Family Described by Dr. Sanger Brown. With a Clinical Introduction by Dr. Sanger Brown. 1903. *o.p.*

**Barlow, Melvin L.,** *ed.* Vocational Education. 1965. NSSE, 64th Yrbk., Part I. x, 301 p. 24 cm. $5.00ᵗ.

**Barnard, Edward Emerson.** Celestial Photographs with a "Magic Lantern" Lens. 1895. *o.p.*

**Barnard, Edward Emerson.** Micrometric Measures of Star Clusters. Edited by Edwin B. Frost, George Van Biesbroeck, and Mary R. Calvert. 1931. YO, VI. *o.p.*

**Barnard, Edward Emerson.** Micrometrical Observations of Eros Made with the Forty-Inch Refractor of the Yerkes Observatory during the Opposition of 1900–1901. 1902. YO, II. *o.p.*

**Barnard, J. Darrel,** *ed.* Rethinking Science Education. 1960. NSSE, 59th Yrbk., Part I. xviii, 34, vi p. 22 cm. 60-1514. Cloth. $4.50[t].

**Barnes, Harry Elmer,** *ed.* An Introduction to the History of Sociology. 1948. xvi, 960 p. 25 cm. 47-12522. $10.00[t].

**Barnes, Helen Elcessor.** A Study of the Variations between the Original and the Standard Editions of Balzac's *Les Chouans.* 1923. *o.p.*

**Barnes, Nathaniel Waring.** Marketing the Stephens Brake Shoe. Prepared by Nathaniel W. Barnes and Leverett S. Lyon. 1922. MSB. *o.p.*

**Barnett, Albert E:** Paul Becomes a Literary Influence. 1941. *o.p.*

**Barnett, Paul.** Business-Cycle Theory in the United States, 1860–1900. 1941. SBA, XI. *o.p.*

**Baroja, Julio Caro.** The World of the Witches. Translated by O. N. V. Glendinning. 1965. xiv, 313 p. 22 cm. NHS. 64-15829. $6.50[s]. OBE.

**Barr, A. S.** The Social Studies in the Elementary and Secondary School. By A. S. Barr and others. 1923. NSSE, 22d Yrbk., Part II. *o.p.*

**Barr, Stringfellow.** Let's Join the Human Race. 1950. *o.p.*

**Barrett, Oliver Rogers,** *ed.:* LINCOLN, Lincoln's Last Speech.

**Barrett, Storrs Barrows.** The Geography of the Heavens. 24 Slides Selected for High-School Use. Accompanied by a forty-minute lecture by Storrs B. Barrett. 1935. *o.p.*

**Barrett, Storrs Barrows,** *joint author:* FROST, Radial Velocities of 500 Stars.

**Barrows, David Prescott.** The Ethno-Botany of the Coahuilla Indians of Southern California. 1900. *o.p.*

**Barrows, Harlan Harland:** *see* COLBY, Geographic Aspects of International Relations.

**Barrows Lectures** (BL). The Barrows Lectureship Foundation was established at the University of Chicago in 1894 by Caroline E. Haskell:

1902–3 HALL, Christian Belief Interpreted by Christian Experience.
1906–7 HALL, Christ and the Eastern Soul.
1912–13 HENDERSON, Social Programmes in the West.
1924–25 GILKEY, Jesus and Our Generation.
1930–31 McCONNELL, The Christian Ideal and Social Control.

*See also* HASKELL LECTURES IN COMPARATIVE RELIGION.

**Bartelme, Phyllis Frances,** *joint author:* HESS, Physical and Mental Growth of Prematurely Born Children.

**Bartelmez, George W.:** *see* NEWMAN, Nature of the World and of Man.

**Barth, G.,** *joint author:* WACHSMANN, Moving Field Radiation Therapy.

**Bartholdy, Albrecht Mendelssohn:** *see* WHITE, New Social Science.

**Bartky, Walter.** Highlights of Astronomy. PSS 509. 1935. x, 278 p. 24 cm. NPL. Paper. $1.95.

**Bartlett, Lester William.** The Y.M.C.A. Executive Secretary. An Analysis of the Activities of the Secretary Who Is Responsible for the Administration of a Local Y.M.C.A. By Lester W. Bartlett, Ralph M. Hogan, and Alden W. Boyd. 1929. *o.p.*

**Bartlett, Lester William.** The Y.M.C.A. Physical Director. An Analysis of the Activities of the Secretary Who Is Responsible for Physical Education in a Local Y.M.C.A. By Lester Bartlett and Alden W. Boyd. 1929. *o.p.*

**Barton, George Aaron.** The Religions of the World. 1917. 4th ed. 1937. *o.p.*

**Barton, R. F.** The Kalingas. Their Institutions and Custom Law. 1949. *o.p.*

**Barton, William Eleazar.** The Influence of Chicago upon Abraham Lincoln. 1923. *o.p.*
A publication of the Chicago Historical Society.

**Bascom, William R.,** *ed.* Continuity and Change in African Cultures. Edited by William R. Bascom and Melville J. Herskovits. 1958. x, 309 p. 58-13135. Cloth. 24 cm. $7.00ˢ. Paper. P85. 21 cm. $1.95.

**Basic Astronomical Data:** STRAND.

**Basic Concepts of Music Education:** MADISON.

**Basic French:** EDDY.

**Basic Instruction in Reading:** GRAY.

**Basic List of Spanish Words:** KENISTON.

**Basic Physiology:** D'AMOUR.

**Basic Postulates:** FRENCH.

**Basic Russian Publications:** HORECKY.

**Baskervill, Charles Read.** The Elizabethan Jig and Related Song Drama. 1929. *o.p.*

**Baskervill, Charles Read,** *ed.* Pierre Gringore's Pageants for the Entry of Mary Tudor into Paris. An Unpublished Manuscript. Edited by Charles Read Baskervill. 1934. *o.p.*

**Baskett, William D.** Parts of the Body in the Later Germanic Dialects. 1920. LG. *o.p.*

**Baskin, Wade,** *trans.:* BRÉHIER, Hellenistic and Roman Age.

**Baskin, Wade,** *trans.:* BRÉHIER, Middle Ages and the Renaissance.

**Bates, Marston,** *joint ed.:* THOMAS, Man's Role in Changing the Face of the Earth.

**Batt, Max.** The Treatment of Nature in German Literature from Günther to the Appearance of Goethe's *Werther.* 1902. *o.p.*

**Battan, Louis J.** Radar Meteorology. 1959. xii, 161 p. Illus. 24 cm. 59-10422. $6.00ˢ.

**Batten, J. Minton.** John Drury, Advocate of Christian Reunion. 1944. *o.p.*

**Battle against Isolation:** JOHNSON.

**Battle of Kadesh:** BREASTED.

**Bauer, Peter.** The Economics of Underdeveloped Countries. By Peter Bauer and Basil Yamey. 1957. xiii, 271 p. 19 cm. 57-11204. Paper. CEH 1. $1.75. USA.

**Bauer, W.:** *see* ARNDT: Greek-English Lexicon of the New Testament.

**Baumgart, Guenther,** *joint author:* LYON, Your Business and Postwar Readjustment.

**Bay, Emmet Blackburn.** Medical Administration of Teaching Hospitals. 1931. ME. *o.p.*

**Bay Psalm Book:** HARASZTI.

**Bayer, Leona.** Growth Diagnosis. Selected Methods for Interpreting and Predicting Physical Development from One Year to Maturity. By Leona Bayer and Nancy Bayley. 1959. xvi, 241 p. Illus. 28 cm. 59-11171. BM. $10.00ˢ.

**Bayley, Nancy,** *joint author:* BAYER, Growth Diagnosis.

**Beach, Joseph Warren.** Meek Americans and Other European Trifles. 1925. *o.p.*

**Beach, Joseph Warren.** The Outlook for American Prose. 1926. *o.p.*

**Beach, Joseph Warren.** The Technique of Thomas Hardy. 1922. *o.p.*

**Bean, Elizabeth Anita Smith:** *see* GUYER, Animal Micrology.

**Beardslee, John Walter, Jr.** The Use of $\Phi\acute{\nu}\sigma\iota\varsigma$ in Fifth-Century Greek Literature. 1918. *o.p.*

**Beardsley, Richard K.** Village Japan. By Richard K. Beardsley, John W. Hall, and Robert E. Ward. 1959. xiv, 498 p. Illus. 25 cm. 58-13802. $10.00ˢ.
"The best and most detailed study of a Japanese social microcosm that has ever been produced in a Western language."—Edwin O. Reischauer, United States Ambassador to Japan.

**Beatty, Edward Corbyn Obert.** Herbert Levi Osgood, *in* HUTCHINSON, Marcus W. Jernegan Essays.

**Bebel, Ferdinand August.** My Life. 1912. *o.p.*

**Bechtel, Edward Ambrose.** Sanctae Silviae peregrinatio. 1902. Preprint from Vol. IV, STUDIES IN CLASSICAL PHILOLOGY. *o.p.*

**Beck, Dorothy Fahs.** The Cost of Equipping a Dental Office. A Study of the Initial Expenditures of Dental Graduates when Equipping an Office for Practice. 1932. ADA. *o.p.*

**Beck, Dorothy Fahs:** *see* LEVEN, Practice of Dentistry.

**Beck, Lewis White.** A Commentary on Kant's Critique of Practical Reason. 1960. xvi, 308 p. 24 cm. 60-5461. Cloth. $6.00ˢ. Paper. P114. $1.95.

**Beck, Lewis White,** *ed. and trans.:* KANT, Critique of Practical Reason.

**Beck, Lewis White,** *ed. and trans.:* KANT, Foundations of the Metaphysics of Morals.

**Becker, Gary S.** The Economics of Discrimination. 1957. x, 137 p. 22 cm. 57-8578. ERS. $5.00ˢ.

**Becker, Howard S.** Boys in White. Student Culture in Medical School. By Howard S. Becker, Blanche Geer, Everett C. Hughes, and Anselm Strauss. 1961. xiv, 456 p. 24 cm. 61-16622. $10.00ˢ.

**Beckner, Earl Rucker.** A History of Labor Legislation in Illinois. 1929. SSCI. *o.p.*

**Beckwith, Martha.** The Kumulipo. A Hawaiian Creation Chant. 1951. *o.p.*

**Beeley, Arthur Lawton.** An Experimental Study in Left-Handedness, with Practical Suggestions for Schoolroom Tests. 1918. SEM 8. *o.p.*

**Beeley, Arthur Lawton.** The Bail System in Chicago. By Arthur Lawton Beeley. Introduction by Herman M. Adler. 1927. SSM. xii, 189 p. $4.50ˢ.

**Beggar's Gift:** KENNEDY, *in his* Plays for Three Players. Vol. III.

**Beginning French:** EDDY.

**Beginning Spanish:** SPARKMAN.

**Beginnings of American English:** MATHEWS.

**Beginnings of Graduate Education in America:** STORR.

**Behavior Mechanisms in Monkeys:** KLÜVER.

**Behavior and Neurosis:** MASSERMAN.

**Behavior Research Fund** (BR):
ACKERSON, Children's Behavior Problems.
GRAY, Growth in Private School Children.
HESS, Physical and Mental Growth of Prematurely Born Children.
KAWIN, Children of Preschool Age.
KAWIN, Comparative Study of a Nursery-School versus a Non-Nursery-School Group.
KAWIN, Problems of Preschool Age.
KLÜVER, Behavior Mechanisms in Monkeys.
LARSON, Lying and Its Detection.
LASHLEY, Brain Mechanisms and Intelligence.
LASHLEY, Studies in the Dynamics of Behavior.
MONROE, Children Who Cannot Read.
SHAW, Brothers in Crime.
SHAW, Delinquency Areas.
SHAW, Jack-Roller.
SHAW, Natural History of a Delinquent Career.
THURSTONE, Order of Birth, Parent-Age, and Intelligence.
TULCHIN, Intelligence and Crime.
VAN ALSTYNE, Play Behavior and Choice of Play Materials.

**Behavioral Science and Educational Administration:** GRIFFITHS.

**Behaviorism:** WATSON.

**Behaviorism and Phenomenology:** WANN.

**Beiträge zum assyrischen Wörterbuch:** MEISSNER.

**Belaunde, Victor Andres:** *see* WRIGHT, Interpretations of American Foreign Policy.

**Belden, Don A., Jr.,** *joint author:* D'AMOUR, Manual for Laboratory Work in Mammalian Physiology.

**Belitt, Ben.** The Enemy Joy. New and Selected Poems. 1964. 21 cm. 64-15805. Cloth. $3.95. Paper. P177. $1.95.

**Bellamy, John.** Horizontal Temperature and Pressure Gradient Scale. 1943. *o.p.*

**Bellamy, John.** Pressure-Height Slide Rule. 1943. *o.p.*

**Bellow, Saul,** *Advisory Editor,* CHICAGO IN FICTION SERIES.

**Bélopolsky, A.** New Investigations of the Spectrum of $\beta$ Lyræ. 1897. *o.p.*

**Bélopolsky, A.** Researches on the Spectrum of the Variable Star $\eta$ Aquilæ. 1897. *o.p.*

**Beneš, Eduard.** International Security. By Eduard Beneš, Arthur Feiler, Rushton Coulborn. Edited by Walter H. C. Laves. 1939. HFL. *o.p.*

**Benítez, Fernando.** The Century after Cortés. Translated by Joan MacLean. 1965. 296 p. Illus. 24 cm. 65-25121. $7.50.

**Benjamin, F. S. and L. T.,** *joint eds.:* THORNDIKE, The Herbal of Rufinus.

**Benjamin Franklin and American Foreign Policy:** STOURZH.

**Benjamin H. Hill:** PEARCE.

**Bennett, H. E.,** *joint author:* CUBBERLEY, Research within the Field of Education.

**Bennett, John W.** Archaeological Explorations in Jo Daviess County, Illinois. 1945. AN. *o.p.*

**Bennett, Josephine W.** The Evolution of the *Faerie Queene.* 1942. *o.p.*

**Bennett, Wendell Clark.** The Tarahumara, an Indian Tribe of Northern Mexico. By Wendell C. Bennett and Robert M. Zingg. 1935. AN. *o.p.*

**Bensley, Robert Russell.** Handbook of Histological and Cytological Technique. By R. R. Bensley and S. H. Bensley. 1938. *o.p.*

**Bensley, Robert Russell.** The Structure of the Glands of Brunner. 1903. *o.p.*

**Bensley, Sylvia Holton,** *joint author:* BENSLEY, Handbook of Histological and Cytological Technique.

**Benson, George Charles Sumner,** *joint author:* DIMOCK, Can Interstate Compacts Succeed?

**Bentley, Arthur Fisher.** The Process of Government. A Study of Social Pressures. 1908. *o.p.*

**Bentley, Gerald E.** Shakespeare and Jonson. Their Reputations in the Seventeenth Century Compared. Two vols. in one. 1945. lx, 307 p. 21 cm. A45-1235. $10.00ˢ.

**Berelson, Bernard R.** Voting. A Study of Opinion Formation in a Presidential Campaign. By Bernard R. Berelson, Paul F. Lazarsfeld, and William N. McPhee. 1954. xix, 395 p. Illus. 24 cm. 54-11205. $8.50ˢ.

**Berelson, Bernard R.,** *joint author:* WAPLES, What Reading Does to People.

**Bergin, Thomas G.,** *ed.* Modern Italian Short Stories. Selected and edited by Thomas G. Bergin. HCLS.

**Bergsträsser, Arnold,** *ed.* Deutsche Beiträge: Zur geistigen Überlieferung. 1947. *o.p.*

**Bernard, Luther Lee.** The Transition to an Objective Standard of Social Control. 1911. *o.p.*

**Bernard of Cluny.** The Source of "Jerusalem the Golden," Together with Other Pieces Attributed to Bernard of Cluny. In English translation by Henry Preble. Introduction, Notes, and Annotated Bibliography by Samuel Macauley Jackson. 1910. *o.p.*

**Berndt, Catherine H.** From Black to White in South Australia. By Catherine H. and Ronald M. Berndt. 1952. *o.p.*

**Berndt, Catherine H.,** *joint author:* BERNDT, World of the First Australians.

**Berndt, Catherine H. and Ronald M.,** *joint authors:* ELKIN, Art in Arnhem Land.

**Berndt, Ronald M.** Excess and Restraint. Social Control among a New Guinea Mountain People. 1962. xxii, 474 p. 24 cm. 62-10996. $8.95ˢ.

**Berndt, Ronald M.** The World of the First Australians. An Introduction to the Traditional Life of the Australian Aborigines. By Ronald M. Berndt and Catherine H. Berndt. 1965. xxii, 509 p. Illus. 24 cm. 64-15806. $10.95ˢ. CUSA.

**Bernert, Eleanor H.,** *joint author:* WIRTH, Local Community Fact Book.

**Bernstein, Enoch.** Quickness and Intelligence. An Enquiry concerning the Existence of a General Speed Factor. 1924. BJP. *o.p.*

**Berry, Brian J. L.:** *see* GINSBURG, Atlas of Economic Development.

**Berry, George Ricker.** The Letters of the Rᵐ 2 Collection. 1896. *o.p.*

**Berry, George Ricker.** Premillennialism and Old Testament Prediction. A Study in Interpretation. 1929. *o.p.*

**Berthollet, Count Claude Louis:** *see* SCHEELE, Early History of Chlorine.

**Better Homes Manual:** HALBERT.

**Beveridge,** Sir **William:** *see* WHITE, New Social Science.

**Bewer, Julius August.** Religion of the Bible. By Nine Great Teachers. By Julius Bewer, G. L. Chamberlin, Frederick C. Eiselen, Henry T. Fowler, Alexander R. Gordon, Shailer Mathews, Theophile J. Meek, H. Franklin Rall, Ernest F. Scott. 1925. *o.p.*

**Beyer, Erwin F.** Acrobatics for All. 1947. *o.p.*

**Beyle, Herman Carey.** Governmental Reporting in Chicago. 1928. SSCI. *o.p.*

**Beyle, Herman Carey.** Identification and Analysis of Attribute-Cluster-Blocs. A Technique for Use in the Investigation of Behavior in Governance, Including Report on Identification and Analysis of Blocs in a Large Non-Partisan Legislative Body, the 1927 Session of the Minnesota State Senate. 1931. *o.p.*

**Beyond Theology:** AMES.

**Bhagavad-gita:** RYDER.

**Bible: An American Translation:** SMITH.

**Biblical Ideas of Atonement:** BURTON.

**Biblical Religion and the Search for Ultimate Reality:** TILLICH.

**Bibliographical History of Anonyma and Pseudonyma:** TAYLOR.

**Bibliographic Organization:** SHERA.

**Bibliographical Guide to English Studies:** CROSS.

**Bibliographical Guide to the History of Christianity:** CASE.

**Bibliographical Society of America.**
The University of Chicago Press served as publisher for the Society from April 1, 1911, to June 30, 1939, and also handled all volumes published prior to 1911, including the four yearbooks and the one reprint issued by the Bibliographical Society of Chicago. In 1939 all books not out of print were transferred to the Society.

**BIBLIOGRAPHICAL SOCIETY OF CHICAGO:**

*Yearbooks. o.p.*
 1899–1900. 1900.
 1900–1901. 1901.
 1901–2. 1902.
 1902–3. 1903.

*Reprints:*
 DE MORGAN, On the Difficulty of the Correct Description of Books. *o.p.*

**BIBLIOGRAPHICAL SOCIETY OF AMERICA:**

*Bulletins.* Vols. I–IV. May, 1907–October, 1912. *o.p.*

*Proceedings and Papers.* 1904–8. Vols. I–III, 1906–9. *o.p.*

*Papers.* 1909–37. Vols. IV–XXXI, 1910–39. *o.p.*

*Reprints:*
 FEIPEL, Elements of Bibliography.
 JOSEPHSON, Bibliographies of Bibliographies.
 KERNER, Foundations of Slavic Bibliography.
 NORTHUP, Present Bibliographical Status of Modern Philology.

*Miscellaneous:*
 COLE, Index to Bibliographical Papers.
 Index to Vol. I of the *Bulletins. o.p.*
 Index to the Publications of the Bibliographical Society of America and of the Bibliographical Society of Chicago, 1899–1931. 1931. *o.p.*

**Bibliographies of Bibliographies:** JOSEPHSON.

**Bibliography of Congo Language:** STARR.

**Bibliography of Crystal Structure:** MORSE.

**Bibliography of Economics:** UNIVERSITY OF CHICAGO. *Department of Political Economy.*

**Bibliography on Educational Broadcasting:** COOPER.

**Bibliography of French Translations:** ROCHEDIEU.

**Bibliography of Human Morphology:** KROGMAN.

**Bibliography and Index:** NEURATH.

**Bibliography of Internal Medicine:** BLOOMFIELD.

**Bibliography on Meteorites:** BROWN.

**Bibliography of Secondary Education:** LOCKE.

**Bibliography of Sociology:** HASTINGS.

**Bibliography of the Works of Ambroise Paré:** DOE.

**Bice, E. G.** Correlations of Isallobaric Patterns in the High Atmosphere with Those at the Surface. Edited by E. G. Bice and G. T. Stephens. 1945. DMMR 12. *o.p.*

**Biddle, Francis.** The World's Best Hope. 1949. WFL. *o.p.*

**Biddle, Nicholas:** GOVAN.

**Bidwell, Percy Wells,** *ed.:* AMERICAN PRIMERS.

**Biel, Erwin R.** Climatology of the Mediterranean Area. 1944. DMMR 13. *o.p.*

**Bile:** HORRALL.

**Bill, V. Tschebotarioff.** The Russian People. A Reader on Their History and Culture. (Text in Russian.) 1959. 2d ed. 1965. ix, 163 p. Maps. 23 cm. 59-10301. $4.00ᵗ.

**Billings, Thomas Henry.** The Platonism of Philo Judaeus. 1919. *o.p.*

**Billingsley, Patrick.** Statistical Inference for Markov Processes. 1961. vii, 75 p. 25 cm. 61-8646. SRM, II. $4.00ˢ.

**Billy Budd, Sailor:** MELVILLE.

**Billy Sunday Was His Real Name:** McLOUGHLIN.

**Binger, Carl.** More about Psychiatry. 1949. *o.p.*

**Bingham, Walter V.,** *ed.* Psychology Today. Lectures and Study Manual. 1932. *o.p.*

**Biochemical Studies:** EVANS.

**Biochemistry of Intracellular Parasitism:** MOULDER.

**Biographical Sketch of Enoch Long:** REID.

**Biographical Sketch of Gurdon Saltonstall Hubbard:** HAMILTON.

**Biographical Sketch of the Hon. John Peter Altgeld:** BROWN.

**Biographical Sketch of Hon. Joseph Duncan:** BLATCHFORD.

**Biography and Bibliography of Edgar Johnson Goodspeed:** COBB.

**Biological Action of the Vitamins:** EVANS.

**Biology of Mind:** HESS.

**Biology of the Negro:** LEWIS.

**Biology of Twins:** NEWMAN.

**Birch, L. C.,** *joint author:* ANDREWARTHA, Distribution and Abundance of Animals.

**Birds of Mexico:** BLAKE.

**Birren, James E.,** *ed.* A Handbook of Aging and the Individual. Psychological and Biological Aspects. 1960. xii, 939 p. Illus. Index. 25 cm. 59-12106. HSG. $12.50ᵗ.

**Birth of the Republic:** MORGAN.

**Bixby Gospels:** GOODSPEED.

**Bjorklund, Einar.** A Study of the Prices of Chain and Independent Grocers in Chicago. By Einar Bjorklund and James L. Palmer. 1930. BA, I. *o.p.*

**Blaauw, Adriaan,** *ed.* Galactic Structure. Edited by Adriaan Blaauw and Maarten Schmidt. ("Stars and Stellar Systems," Vol. V.) 1965. xx, 606 p. Illus. 25 cm. 64-23428. $15.00ˢ.

**Blachly, Clarence Dan.** The Treatment of the Problem of Capital and Labor in Social-Study Courses in the Churches. 1920. *o.p.*

**Black, Joseph.** Experiments upon Magnesia Alba, Quicklime, and Some Other Alcaline Substances. (1755). 1902. AC. *o.p.*

**Black Nationalism:** ESSIEN-UDOM.

**Blackburn, Bonnie:** *see* DARGAN, Studies in Balzac's Realism.

**Blair, Emily Newell.** More for Your Money. Consumers Radio Series. 1935. *o.p.*

**Blair, Walter.** Horse Sense in American Humor. From Benjamin Franklin to Ogden Nash. 1942. *o.p.*

**Blair, Walter,** *ed.* Half Horse Half Alligator. The Growth of the Mike Fink Legend. Edited by Walter Blair and Franklin J. Meine. 1956. ix, 289 p. $1.50.

**Blake, Emmet Reid.** Birds of Mexico. A Guide for Field Identification. Illustrated by Douglas E. Tibbitts. 1953. xxx, 644 p. Frontispiece (in color). 21 cm. 53-8737. BM. $8.50ˢ.

**Blakeslee, George Hubbard:** *see* WRIGHT, Interpretations of American Foreign Policy.

**Blanchard, W. O.:** *see* HAAS, American Empire.

**Blank Accounting Blanks:** ARNETT.

**Blanksten, George I.** Perón's Argentina. 1953. *o.p.*

**Blass, F.:** *see* FUNK, Greek Grammar of the New Testament.

**Blatchford, Eliphalet Wickes.** Biographical Sketch of Hon. Joseph Duncan, Fifth Governor of Illinois. By E. W. Blatchford. (?)1905. *o.p.*
A publication of the Chicago Historical Society.

**Blau, Peter M.** The Dynamics of Bureaucracy. A Study of Interpersonal Relationships in Two Government Agencies. 2d ed., rev. 1963. xiv, 322 p. 22 cm. 63-22822. $7.50ˢ.

**Blauch, Lloyd E.,** *joint author:* REEVES, Liberal Arts College.

**Blauner, Robert.** Alienation and Freedom. The Factory Worker and His Industry. 1964. xvi, 222 p. 23 cm. 64-15820. $7.50ˢ.

**Blaustein, Albert P.** The American Lawyer. A Summary of the Survey of the Legal Profession. By Albert P. Blaustein and Charles O. Porter. With Charles T. Duncan. 1954. *o.p.*

**Blichfeldt, Hans Frederick.** Finite Collineation Groups. With an Introduction to the Theory of Groups of Operators and Substitution Groups. 1917. SCI. *o.p.*

**Blinde Geronimo und sein Bruder (Schnitzler):** PRICE.

**Blindness in Children:** NORRIS.

**Bliss, Gilbert Ames.** Lectures on the Calculus of Variations. 1946. ix, 296 p. 25 cm. A46-5369. 1961. Paper. PSS 504. $1.95.

**Bliss, Gilbert Ames,** *ed.* Contributions to the Calculus of Variations, 1930. Theses Submitted to the Department of Mathematics of the University of Chicago. Written under the direction of G. A. Bliss and L. M. Graves. 1931. *o.p.*

**Bliss, Gilbert Ames,** *ed.* Contributions to the Calculus of Variations, 1931–32. Theses Submitted to the Department of Mathematics of the University of Chicago. Written under the direction of G. A. Bliss and L. M. Graves. 1933. *o.p.*

**Bliss, Gilbert Ames,** *ed.* Contributions to the Calculus of Variations, 1933–37. Theses Submitted to the Department of Mathematics of the University of Chicago. Written under the direction of G. A. Bliss, L. M. Graves, or W. T. Reid. 1937. *o.p.*

**Bliss, Gilbert Ames,** *ed.* Contributions to the Calculus of Variations, 1938–41. 1942. *o.p.*

**Bloch, Henry S.** Economics of Military Occupation. By Henry S. Bloch and B. F. Hoselitz. 1944. *o.p.*

**Bloch, Marc.** Feudal Society. 1961. Translated by L. A. Manyon. xxi, 498 p. 61-4322. Cloth. 24 cm. $8.50ˢ. COBE. Paper. 2 vols. 21 cm. P156, P157. Each $1.95. COBE.
"Here is one of those rare books of impeccable scholarship which no intelligent person could possibly read without pleasure and interest and excitement. . . . Place-names, *chansons*, heraldry, technology, demography: every source is pillaged that can possibly cast light on how men thought and lived and acted. It is this and the wealth of concrete illustration that give Bloch's work its enduring value: what he shows us is not a bloodless system but the living and vitalising force which shaped society in western Europe for four creative centuries."—Geoffrey Barraclough, in *The Observer* (London).

**Blood, Frank R.,** *joint author:* D'AMOUR, Manual for Laboratory Work in Mammalian Physiology.

**Bloom, Benjamin S.** Problem-solving Processes of College Students: An Exploratory Investigation. By Benjamin S. Bloom and Lois J. Broder. 1950. SEM 73 *o.p.*

**Bloomfield, Arthur I.** Capital Imports and the American Balance of Payments, 1934–39. 1950. *o.p.*

**Bloomfield, Arthur L.,** *ed.* A Bibliography of Internal Medicine. *Vol. I:* Communicable Diseases. 1958. vii, 560 p. 24 cm. 58-11470. BM. $10.00ˢ. *Vol. II:* Selected Diseases. 1960. viii, 312 p. 24 cm. 60-6775. BM. $6.00ˢ.
"Dr. Bloomfield has compiled a fascinating history of some 30 communicable diseases, by selecting excerpts from the literature published over the past 150 years. These excerpts, as well as

being carefully selected, are commendably brief. . . . The research work carried out by Dr. Bloomfield in compiling his excerpts must have been tremendous, and one can have nothing but praise for the way in which he has carried out his task." —*The Medical Journal of Australia.*

**Bloomfield, Leonard.** Linguistic Aspects of Science. 1939. viii, 59 p. 25 cm. A41-3425. Paper. IEUS, I, 4. $1.50ˢ.

**Blount, Ralph Earl.** Excursion on the Rock River of Illinois between Rockford and Dixon. Prepared October, 1911, by R. E. Blount. GSC. *o.p.*

**Blount, Ralph Earl.** Excursion through the Rivers and Harbors of Chicago. Prepared October, 1905, by R. E. Blount and C. S. Jewell. Revised October, 1911, by H. T. Lukens, O. D. Whalin, F. Schapper, C. P. Dawley, and H. T. Mortenson, Chairman. GSC. *o.p.*

**Blue and the Gray on the Nile:** HESSELTINE.

**Blum, Walter J.** The Uneasy Case for Progressive Taxation. By Walter J. Blum and Harry Kalven, Jr. 1953. viii, 107 p. 21 cm. 53-3592. Cloth. $3.50ˢ. Paper. P130. $1.50.

**Blumenthal, Albert.** Small-Town Stuff. 1932. SOC. *o.p.*

**Blunt, Katharine.** Ultraviolet Light and Vitamin D in Nutrition. By Katharine Blunt and Ruth Cowan. 1930. HE. *o.p.*

**Boan, Fern.** A History of Poor Relief Administration in Missouri. 1941. SSM *o.p.*

**Boardman Robinson:** CHRIST-JANER.

**Boas, Franz:** *see* WHITE, New Social Science.

**Bobbitt, Franklin.** Curriculum Investigation. By Franklin Bobbitt and others. 1926. SEM 31. *o.p.*

**Bobbitt, Franklin.** Curriculum-making in Los Angeles. 1922. SEM 20. *o.p.*

**Bobbitt, Franklin.** The Supervision of City Schools. By Franklin Bobbitt, J. W. Hall, and J. D. Wolcott. 1913. NSSE, 12th Yrbk., Part I. *o.p.*

**Boccaccio and His Imitators:** JONES.

**Body Defenses against Disease:** CANNON.

**Boehner, Philotheus, O.F.M.** Medieval Logic. An Outline of Its Development from 1250 to *ca.* 1400. 1952. *o.p.*

**Bogardus, Emory S.,** *ed.* Social Problems and Social Processes. Selected Papers from The Proceedings of the American Sociological Society, 1932. 1933. SOC. *o.p.*

**Bogart, Ernest L.:** *see* Financial Mobilization for War.

**Bogert, Jean L.** Good Nutrition for Everybody. 1942. *o.p.*

**Boggess, Arthur Clinton.** The Settlement of Illinois, 1778–1830. 1908. *o.p.*
A publication of the Chicago Historical Society.

**Boggs, Ralph S.** Leyendas épicas de España. A prosificación moderna. By Ralph S. Boggs and Carlos Castillo. HCLS.

**Bogue, Allen G.** From Prairie to Corn Belt. Farming on the Illinois and Iowa Prairies in the Nineteenth Century. 1963. x, 310 p. Maps. Index. 22 cm. 63-20913. $6.95ˢ.

**Bogue, Donald J.,** *joint ed.:* BURGESS, Contributions to Urban Sociology.

**Bohannan, Paul,** *General Editor:* Classics in Anthropology.

**Bohannan, Paul,** *ed.:* TYLOR, Researches into the Early History of Mankind.

**Bohr, Niels:** *see* NEURATH, Encyclopedia and Unified Science.

**Bok, Bart Jan.** The Distribution of the Stars in Space. 1937. AM. *o.p.*

**Bolton, Frederick E.,** *joint author:* SUTTON, Organization of the Department of Education in Relation to Other Departments in Colleges.

**Bolza, Oskar.** Concerning the Geodesic Curvature and the Isoperimetric Problem on a Given Surface. 1902. *o.p.*

**Bolza, Oskar.** Lectures on the Calculus of Variations. 1904. *o.p.*

**Bolza, Oskar.** Proof of the Sufficiency of Jacobi's Condition for a Permanent Sign of the Second Variation in the So-called Isoperimetric Problems. 1902. *o.p.*

**Bomb:** HARRIS.

**Bond, Donald F.** A Reference Guide to English Studies. 1962. xii, 172 p. 21 cm. 62-9112. Index. Cloth. $5.00ˢ. Paper. P83. $1.95.

**Bond, Otto F.** En route. French Grammar for Reading. HCLS.

**Bond, Otto F.** Fifty Foreign Films. Reviewed by Otto F. Bond. 1939. *o.p.*

**Bond, Otto F.** Graded French Readers. HCLS.
L'Anglais tel qu'on le parle. By Tristan Bernard.
L'Attaque du moulin. By Émile Zola.
Aucassin et Nicolette. (After the Modern French Version of Alexandre Bida.)
Les Chandeliers de l'évêque. Épisodes des *Misérables* de Victor Hugo.
Contes. Par Mendès, Saint Juvis, Pouvillon, Coppée, Erckmann-Chatrain.
L'Évasion du duc de Beaufort. By Alexandre Dumas.
La Grammaire. By Eugène Labiche.
Les pauvres gens. Quatre contes par Maupassant, Daudet, Bazin, et Bordeau.
Première étape. Basic French Readings. Books 1–5, together with Vocabulary Drill Book.
Sept-d'un-coup. After the French of Alexandre Dumas.
Vocabulary Drill Book for Graded French Readers. (Books 1–5.)

**Bond, Otto F.** An Introduction to the Study of French. HCLS.

**Bond, Otto F.** The Reading Method. An Experiment in College French. 1953. *o.p.*

**Bond, Otto F.** The Sounds of French. An Elementary Phonetic Manual. HCLS.

**Bond, Otto F.** Terre de France. Premières lectures. HCLS.

**Bond, Otto F.,** *joint comp.:* CASTILLO, University of Chicago Spanish Dictionary.

**Bond, Otto F.,** *joint author:* WEST, Grouped-Frequency French Word List.

**Bond, Otto F.** HCLS.
Language Reading Report Blanks (Heath-Chicago French Series).
Language Reading Report Blanks (Heath-Chicago Italian Series).
Language Reading Report Blanks (Heath-Chicago Junior College Series: French).
Language Reading Report Blanks (Heath-Chicago Junior College Series: German).
Language Reading Report Blanks (Heath-Chicago Junior College Series: Spanish).

**Bondurant, Bernard Camillus.** Decimus Junius Brutus Albinus. A Historical Study. 1907. *o.p.*

**Bone:** McLEAN.

**Bonner, Robert Johnson.** The Administration of Justice from Homer to Aristotle. By Robert J. Bonner and Gertrude Smith. 2 vols. Vol. I, 1930. Vol. II, 1938. *o.p.*

**Bonner, Robert Johnson.** Evidence in Athenian Courts. 1905. *o.p.*

**Bonner, Robert Johnson.** Lawyers and Litigants in Ancient Athens. The Genesis of the Legal Profession. 1927. *o.p.*

**Book of Canadian Poetry:** SMITH.

**Book of Esther:** HAUPT.

**Book of God and Man:** GORDIS.

**Book of Illustrations:** MOULTON.

**Book of Job:** HARPER.

**Book and Job Printing in Chicago:** BROWN.

**Book of Lake Geneva:** JENKINS.

**Book of Lord Shang:** DUYVENDAK.

**Book of Micah:** HAUPT.

**Book of Revelation:** CASE.

**Book of Thekla:** GOODSPEED.

**Books of the Holy Bible:** CHAMBERLIN.

**Books and Libraries in Wartime:** BUTLER.

**Books and Library Reading for Pupils in the Intermediate Grades:** COLBURN.

**Books for Old Testament Study:** SMITH.

**Books Recommended for New Testament Study:** VOTAW.

**Boorstin, Daniel J.** The Genius of American Politics. 1953. ix, 202 p. 22 cm. 53-9434. Cloth. WFL. $4.00ˢ. Paper. P27. 21 cm. $1.50.

**Boorstin, Daniel J.,** *General Editor,* Chicago History of American Civilization Series.

**Booth, Wayne C.** The Rhetoric of Fiction. 1961. xx, 455 p. 24 cm. 61-14947. $6.95ˢ. Paper. $3.95ᵗ.

"This book makes good the claim on the dust jacket that it offers 'the most significant analysis of the novelist's art' since Percy Lubbock's *Craft of Fiction*. But it differs from that classic study, indeed from much of the criticism of fiction which it ably surveys, in that it is written with no overspecific commitment. . . . A good critical terminology, such as we are given in this fruitful study, helps us to solve problems by encouraging us to ask the right questions. . . . Booth's work is required reading for all serious students of prose fiction. . . ."—Alan D. McKillop, in *Modern Philology*.

**Borderland of Criminal Justice:** ALLEN.

**Bore-Hole Investigations:** FENNER.

**Borgese, Elisabeth Mann,** *trans.:* SCHENKER, Harmony.

**Borgese, G. A.** Foundations of the World Republic. 1953. *o.p.*

**Borgese, G. A.** Preliminary Draft of a World Constitution. By G. A. Borgese and Robert M. Hutchins. 1948. *o.p.*

**Borja, Luis J.:** *see* HAAS, American Empire.

**Borland, Belle McCullough.** Philippe de Lasalle. His Contribution to the Textile Industry of Lyons. 1936. *o.p.*

**Boss Platt:** GOSNELL.

**Botkin, B. A.,** *ed.* Lay My Burden Down. A Folk History of Slavery. 1945. xxi, 286 p. Illus. 21 cm. 45-5576. Paper. P24. $1.95.

**Boucher, Chauncey Samuel.** The Chicago College Plan. By Chauncey Samuel Boucher. 1935. Revised and Enlarged after Ten Years' Operation of the Plan, by A. J. Brumbaugh. 1940. *o.p.*

**Boucher, Chauncey Samuel.** The Nullification Controversy in South Carolina. 1916. *o.p.*

**Bouglé, Célestin:** *see* WHITE, New Social Science.

**Boundary Dispute:** RADEBAUGH.

**Bovie, Smith Palmer,** *trans.:* HORACE, Satires and Epistles.

**Bovie, Smith Palmer,** *trans.:* VIRGIL, Georgics.

**Bowen, Clayton Raymond.** Studies in the New Testament. Collected Papers of Clayton R. Bowen. Edited by Robert J. Hutcheon. Published for The Meadville Theological School by The University of Chicago Press. 1936. *o.p.*
". . . an indispensable volume for the New Testament student . . . an appropriate memorial to . . . one of the most productive New Testament scholars of our generation. He combined a devotion to exhaustive and meticulous research with unusual capacity for brilliant insight and creative organization. . . ."—John Knox, in *The Christian Century*.

**Bowen, J. Donald.** Patterns of Spanish Pronunciation. A Drill Book. By J. Donald Bowen and Robert P. Stockwell. 1960. x, 137 p. 25 cm. 60-16841. Paper. $2.75t.

**Bowen, J. Donald,** *joint author:* STOCKWELL, Grammatical Structures of English and Spanish.

**Bowen, J. Donald,** *joint author:* STOCKWELL, Sounds of English and Spanish.

**Bowen, Merlin.** The Long Encounter. Self and Experience in the Writings of Herman Melville. 1960. vii, 280 p. 60-7232. Cloth. 22 cm. $5.00s. Paper. P132. 21 cm. $1.95.

**Bowen, N. L.:** *see* STUDIES IN PETROLOGY.

**Bower, William C.** Character through Creative Experience. 1930. HER. *o.p.*

**Bower, William C.** Church and State in Education. 1944. *o.p.*

**Bower, William C.** A Survey of Religious Education in the Local Church. 1919. PM. *o.p.*

**Bower, William C.,** *ed.* The Church at Work in the Modern World. Written in Collaboration by William Clayton Bower, editor, Edward Scribner Ames, Archibald Gillies Baker, Shirley Jackson Case, Winfred Ernest Garrison, Charles Thomas Holman, Samuel C. Kincheloe, Shailer Mathews. 1935. *o.p.*

**Bowers, Alfred W.** Mandan Society and Ceremonial Organization. 1950. *o.p.*

**Bowers, Fredson,** *ed.* Whitman's Manuscripts. *Leaves of Grass,* 1860. A Parallel Text. 1955. lxxiv, 264 p. Illus. 25 cm. $12.50s.

**Bowman, Isaiah:** *see* COLBY, Geographic Aspects of International Relations.

**Bowman, Leona Florence.** Problems in Home Economics Teaching. 1925. *o.p.*

**Bowman, Paul H.** Mobilizing Community Resources for Maladjusted and Delinquent Youth. By Paul H. Bowman, Gordon Liddle, and Jack Kough. 1956. SEM 85. *o.p.*

**Bowman, Paul H.** Studying Children and Training Counselors in a Community Program. By Paul H. Bowman, William J. Dietrich, Robert F. DeHaan, Henry Hackamack, Robert J. Havighurst, LaVona A. Johnson, Robert D. King, and Lester O. Litler. 1953. SEM 78. *o.p.*

**Boyce, Arthur C.,** *ed.* Methods for Measuring Teachers' Efficiency. 1915. NSSE, 14th Yrbk., Part II. *o.p.*

**Boyd, Alden W.,** *joint author:* BARTLETT, Y.M.C.A. Executive Secretary.

**Boyd, Alden W.,** *joint author:* BARTLETT, Y.M.C.A. Physical Director.

**Boyd, Andrew.** Chinese Architecture and Town Planning, 1500 B.C.—A.D. 1911. 1962. vi, 166 p. Illus. 19 cm. 63-9735. $7.50ˢ. USA.

**Boyd, Clarence Eugene.** Public Libraries and Literary Culture in Ancient Rome. 1915. *o.p.*

**Boyden, Mildred W.,** *joint author:* ROSSBY, Weather Estimates from Local Aerological Data.

**Boyeff, Ivan V.:** *see* HARPER, Soviet Union and World-Problems.

**Boyer, Paul.** Russian Reader. Accented Texts, Grammatical and Explanatory Notes. Vocabulary. By Paul Boyer and N. Speranski. Adapted for English-speaking Students by Samuel Northrup Harper. 1906.

**Boyland, E.,** *et al.* On Cancer and Hormones. Essays in Experimental Biology. 1962. ix, 346 p. Illus. 24 cm. 63-13921. $8.50ˢ.

**Boynton, Percy Holmes.** America in Contemporary Fiction. 1940. *o.p.*

**Boynton, Percy Holmes.** Changing Ideas of American Patriotism. 1936. PPP 21. *o.p.*

**Boynton, Percy Holmes.** London in English Literature. 1913. *o.p.*

**Boynton, Percy Holmes.** More Contemporary Americans. 1927. *o.p.*

**Boynton, Percy Holmes.** The Rediscovery of the Frontier. 1931. *o.p.*

**Boynton, Percy Holmes.** Some Contemporary Americans. The Personal Equation in Literature. 1924. *o.p.*

**Boys in White:** BECKER.

**Bradbury, Samuel.** The Cost of Adequate Medical Care. 1937. ME. *o.p.*

**Bradley, Charles Frederick,** *joint author:* VOTAW, Books Recommended for New Testament Study.

**Bradley, John Hodgdon.** Fauna of the Kimmswick Limestone of Missouri and Illinois. 1930. WM. *o.p.*

**Bradner, Leicester.** Edmund Spenser and the *Faerie Queene.* 1948. xi, 194 p. 21 cm. 48-6359. $5.00ˢ.

**Bradner, Leicester.** The Latin Epigrams of Thomas More. By Leicester Bradner and Charles A. Lynch. 1953. *o.p.*

**Bradshaw, Franklyn Royer,** *joint author:* WAPLES, What Reading Does to People.

**Bradway, John Saeger.** Law and Social Work. An Introduction to the Study of the Legal-Social Field for Social Workers. 1929. SSM. *o.p.*

**Bragdon, Claude Fayette:** *see* CRAM, Six Lectures on Architecture.

**Braidwood, Linda S.,** *joint author:* BRAIDWOOD, Excavations in the Plain of Antioch. I. The Earlier Assemblages.

**Braidwood, Robert J.** Excavations in the Plain of Antioch. I. The Earlier Assemblages. Phases A–J. By Robert J. Braidwood and Linda S. Braidwood. Appendixes by Joan Crowfoot Payne and Hans Helbaek. Technical notes by Frederick R. Matson and others. 1960. xxvii, 601 p. Illus. (10 in color). 31 cm. 57-12749. OIP, LXI. $100.00.

"... will ... long be an essential frame of reference for this important area. ... The systematic way in which the material is set out and the abundant illustrations of notable integrity make it delightfully easy to consult what is by any standards a massive volume." Grahame Clark, in *The Proceedings of the Prehistoric Society*.

**Braidwood, Robert J.** Mounds in the Plain of Antioch. An Archeological Survey. 1937. OIP, XLVIII. *o.p.*

**Braidwood, Robert J.** Prehistoric Investigations in Iraqi Kurdistan. By Robert J. Braidwood and Bruce Howe. With contributions by Hans Helbaek, Frederick R. Matson, Charles A. Reed, and Herbert E. Wright, Jr. 1960. xxvii, 183 p. Illus. 25 cm. 60-8960. SAOC 31. $5.00.

**Braidwood, Robert J.** Time, Space, and Man. 1946. *o.p.*

**Brain and Intelligence:** HALSTEAD.

**Brain Mechanisms and Intelligence:** LASHLEY.

**Brain of the Tiger Salamander:** HERRICK.

**Brains of Rats and Men:** HERRICK.

**Brameld, Theodore Burghard Hurt.** A Philosophic Approach to Communism. By Theodore B. H. Brameld. With a Foreword by T. V. Smith. 1933. *o.p.*

**Bramhall, Frederick Dennison.** Democracy the Basis of a World-Order. 1918. WP. *o.p.*

**Bramsted, Ernest.** Aristocracy and the Middle-Classes in Germany. Social Types in German Literature, 1830–1900. 1937. Rev. ed. 1964. xxiv, 364 p. 21 cm. 64-15031. Cloth. $7.00ˢ. Paper. P163. $2.95.

**Branch, Mary Sydney.** Women and Wealth. A Study of the Economic Status of American Women. 1934. *o.p.*

**Brandt, Joseph August.** Toward the New Spain. 1933. *o.p.*

**Brandt, Richard B.** Hopi Ethics. A Theoretical Analysis. 1954. *o.p.*

**Branscombe, Martha.** The Courts and the Poor Laws in New York State, 1784–1929. 1943. *o.p.*

**Branson, E. B.** Notes on Some Carboniferous Cochliodonts, with Descriptions of Seven New Species. 1905. WM. *o.p.*

**Branton, James Rodney.** The Common Text of the Gospel Lectionary in the Lenten Lections. 1934. LT. *o.p.*

**Bratter, Herbert Max.** Should We Turn to Silver? 1933. PPP 6. *o.p.*

**Bray, William L.** The Weekly Lessons from Luke in the Greek Gospel Lectionary. 1959. xii, 72 p. 25 cm. 59-8733. LT. $2.00ˢ.

**Bray, William L.** The Ecological Relations of the Vegetation of Western Texas. 1901. HB. *o.p.*

**Breaking the Building Blockade:** LASCH.

**Breasted, James Henry.** The Battle of Kadesh. A Study in the Earliest Known Military Strategy. 1903. *o.p.*

**Breasted, James Henry.** The Edwin Smith Surgical Papyrus. Published in Facsimile and Hieroglyphic Transliteration with Translation and Commentary in Two Volumes. *Vol. I:* Hieroglyphic Transliteration, Translation, and Commentary. 1930. xxiv, 596 p. Illus. 30 cm. *Vol. II:* Facsimile Plates and Line for Line Hieroglyphic Transliteration. 1930. xiv p., 46 collotype plates, 30 cm. 31-7595. OIP, III–IV. The set, $35.00.

**Breasted, James Henry.** The Monuments of Sudanese Nubia. Oriental Exploration Fund of the University of Chicago. Second Preliminary Report of the Egyptian Expedition. Preprinted from *The American Journal of Semitic Languages and Literatures,* October, 1908. *o.p.*

**Breasted, James Henry.** Oriental Forerunners of Byzantine Painting. First-Century Wall Paintings from the Fortress of Dura on the Middle Euphrates. 1924. OIP, I. *o.p.*

**Breasted, James Henry.** The Oriental Institute. 1933. UCS. *o.p.*

**Breasted, James Henry.** The Oriental Institute of the University of Chicago. A Beginning and a Program. Preprinted from *The American Journal of Semitic Languages and Literatures,* July, 1922. OIC 1. *o.p.*

**Breasted, James Henry.** The Temples of Lower Nubia. Oriental Exploration Fund of the University of Chicago. First Preliminary Report of the Egyptian Expedition. 1906. *o.p.*

**Breasted, James Henry,** *ed. and trans.* Ancient Records of Egypt. Historical Documents from the Earliest Times to the Persian Conquest. Collected, edited, and translated with commentary by James Henry Breasted. 5 vols. *Vol. I:* The First to the Seventeenth Dynasties. 1906. *Vol. II:* The Eighteenth Dynasty. 1906. *Vol. III:* The Nineteenth Dynasty. 1906. *Vol. IV:* The Twentieth to the Twenty-sixth Dynasties. 1906. *Vol. V:* Indices. 1907. AR. *o.p.*
". . . a scope and a degree of accuracy never before attained in this field of research. . . . [A] standard translation at once scholarly, accurate, and idiomatic."—*Asiatic Quarterly Review.*

**Breckinridge, Sophonisba Preston.** The Family and the State. Select Documents. 1934. SSS. *o.p.*

**Breckinridge, Sophonisba Preston.** Family Welfare Work in a Metropolitan Community. Selected Case Records. 1924. SSS. *o.p.*

**Breckinridge, Sophonisba Preston.** The Illinois Poor Law and Its Administration. 1939. SSM. *o.p.*

**Breckinridge, Sophonisba Preston.** Legal Tender. A Study in English and American Monetary History. 1903. *o.p.*

**Breckinridge, Sophonisba Preston.** Madeline McDowell Breckinridge. A Leader in the New South. 1921. *o.p.*

**Breckinridge, Sophonisba Preston.** Marriage and the Civic Rights of Women. Separate Domicil and Independent Citizenship. 1931. SSM. *o.p.*

**Breckinridge, Sophonisba Preston.** Public Welfare Administration in the United States. Select Documents. 1927. 2d ed. 1938. SSS. *o.p.*

**Breckinridge, Sophonisba Preston.** Social Work and the Courts. Select Statutes and Judicial Decisions. 1934. SSS. *o.p.*

**Breckinridge, Sophonisba Preston,** *ed.:* BROWNING, Development of Poor Relief Legislation in Kansas.

**Breckinridge, Sophonisba Preston,** *ed.:* BRUCE, Michigan Poor Law.

**Breckinridge, Sophonisba Preston,** *ed.:* KENNEDY, Ohio Poor Law.

**Breckinridge, Sophonisba Preston,** *ed.:* PUTTEE, Illegitimate Child in Illinois.

**Breckinridge, Sophonisba Preston,** *ed.:* VEEDER, Development of the Montana Poor Law.

**Breckinridge, Sophonisba Preston,** *joint author:* ABBOTT, Truancy and Non-Attendance.

**Breckinridge, Sophonisba Preston,** *joint author:* SHAFFER, Indiana Poor Law.

**Breckinridge, Sophonisba Preston:** *see* ABBOTT, Tenements of Chicago.

**Breckinridge, Sophonisba Preston:** *see* MERIAM, Stepfather in the Family.

**Breckinridge, Sophonisba Preston:** *see* SMITH, Chicago.

**Breese, Gerald.** Daytime Population of the Central Business District of Downtown Chicago. 1949. *o.p.*

**Bréhier, Émile.** The Hellenic Age. Translated by Joseph Thomas. 1963. ("The History of Philosophy.") vii, 242 p. 21 cm. 63-20912. Cloth. $6.75s. Paper. P198. $1.95.

**Bréhier, Émile.** The Hellenistic and Roman Age. Translated by Wade Baskin. 1965. ("The History of Philosophy.") 261 p. 21 cm. 65-14433. Cloth. $6.75s. Paper. P199. $1.95.

**Bréhier, Émile.** The Middle Ages and the Renaissance. Translated by Wade Baskin. 1965. ("The History of Philosophy.") 272 p. 21 cm. 65-25122. $6.75s.

**Bréhier, Émile.** The Philosophy of Plotinus. Translated by Joseph Thomas. 1958. viii, 206 p. 22 cm. 58-11946. $5.00s.

**Bremner, Robert H.** American Philanthropy. 1960. x, 230 p. Illus. 21 cm. 60-7246. CHAC 2. $4.50s. Paper. $1.75.

**Brennecke, Ernest.** Shakespeare in Germany: 1590–1700. By Ernest Brennecke and Henry Brennecke. 1964. 308 p. 64-13949. $7.50s.

**Breslich, Ernst Rudolph.** The Administration of Mathematics in Secondary Schools. 1933. *o.p.*

Breslich, Ernst Rudolph. Classroom Procedure Test in Mathematics for Rating Methods of Teaching in Junior and Senior High Schools. By E. R. Breslich and Charles A. Stone. 1928. *o.p.*

Breslich, Ernst Rudolph. First-Year Mathematics for Junior Colleges. 1919. 2d ed. 1923. UCMS. *o.p.*

Breslich, Ernst Rudolph. First-Year Mathematics for Secondary Schools. 4th ed. 1915. UCMS. *o.p.*

First edition privately printed 1906.

Breslich, Ernst Rudolph. Logarithmic and Trigonometric Tables and Mathematical Formulas. 1917. *o.p.*

Breslich, Ernst Rudolph. Mathematical Achievement Tests, Senior Mathematics. Grade X. 1928. *o.p.*

Breslich, Ernst Rudolph. Problems in Teaching Secondary-School Mathematics. 1931. Rev. ed. 1940. *o.p.*

Breslich, Ernst Rudolph. Second-Year Mathematics for Secondary Schools. 1916. UCMS. *o.p.*

Breslich, Ernst Rudolph. Senior Mathematics. Book I. 1928. UCMS. *o.p.*

Breslich, Ernst Rudolph. Senior Mathematics. Book II. 1927. UCMS. *o.p.*

Breslich, Ernst Rudolph. Senior Mathematics. Book III. 1929. UCMS. *o.p.*

Breslich, Ernst Rudolph. The Slide Rule. By Ernst R. Breslich and Charles A. Stone. 1929. UCMS. *o.p.*

Breslich, Ernst Rudolph. Solid Geometry. 1929. UCMS. *o.p.*

Breslich, Ernst Rudolph. The Technique of Teaching Secondary-School Mathematics. 1930. *o.p.*

Breslich, Ernst Rudolph, Third-Year Mathematics for Secondary Schools. 1924. UCMS. *o.p.*

Breslich, Ernst Rudolph. Trigonometry with Tables, for Use in Senior High Schools and Junior Colleges. By Ernst R. Breslich and Charles A. Stone. 1928. UCMS. *o.p.*

Breslich, Ernst Rudolph, *joint author:* MYERS, First-Year Mathematics.

Breslich, Ernst Rudolph, *joint author:* MYERS, Geometric Exercises for Algebraic Solution.

Breslich, Ernst Rudolph, *joint author:* MYERS, Second-Year Mathematics.

Breslich, Ernst Rudolph, *joint author:* MYERS, Teacher's Manual for First-Year Mathematics.

Breslich, Ernst Rudolph, *joint author:* REAVIS, Diagnostic Tests in the Fundamental Operation of Arithmetic and in Problem Solving.

Brett, Agnes Baldwin: *see* OSTEN, Ancient Oriental Seals in the Collection of Mrs. Agnes Baldwin Brett.

Bretz, J Harlen: *see* NEWMAN, Nature of the World and of Man.

Brewington, Ann. The Social Concept of Money. A Bibliography. By Ann Brewington and Verona B. Knisely. 1935. MSB. *o.p.*

Brewington, Ann. The Women Graduates of a Collegiate School of Business. By Ann Brewington and Evelyn van Emden Berg. 1942. *o.p.*

Brewington, Ann, *ed.* Business as a Social Institution. Proceedings of the University of Chicago Conference on Business Education, 1938. 1938. *o.p.*

Brewster, John Monroe, *joint ed.:* MEAD, Philosophy of the Act.

Bridenbaugh, Carl. The Colonial Craftsman. 1950. 50-7479. P80. Paper. $1.95.

Brief Course in German: HAGBOLDT.

Briggs, Asa. Victorian People. A Reassessment of Persons and Themes, 1851–67. 1955. *o.p.*

Briggs, Katharine M. Folktales of England. Edited by Katharine M. Briggs and Ruth L. Tongue. 1965. xxxiv, 174 p. 22 cm. 65-18341. FW. $5.00. COBE.

Brim, Orville G. The Status of Rural Education. Prepared by Orville G. Brim, Chairman of the Society's Committee. 1931. NSSE, 30th Yrbk., Part I. *o.p.*

**Brink, William G.** Adapting the Secondary-School Program to the Needs of Youth. Prepared by William G. Brink, Chairman of the Yearbook Committee. 1953. NSSE, 52d Yrbk., Part I. xiii, 316 p. 24 cm. 53-6956. Cloth. $4.50t. Paper. $3.75t.

**Bristol, Margaret Isabelle Cochran.** Handbook for Field Work Students (Family Welfare). Edited by Margaret Cochran Bristol, assisted by Catherine M. Dunn. 1935. Third Edition edited by Margaret Cochran Bristol. 1937. SSM. *o.p.*

**Bristol, Margaret Isabelle Cochran.** Handbook on Social Case Recording. 1936. 2d ed. 1937. SSM. *o.p.*

**Britain—Uneasy Ally:** EPSTEIN.

**Britain and the Bulgarian Horrors of 1876:** HARRIS.

**Britain between the Wars:** MOWAT.

**British Institute of Adult Education.** Group Listening. A Report Prepared for the National Advisory Council on Radio in Education, Inc. By the British Institute of Adult Education. 1934. *o.p.*

**British Public Utilities and National Development:** DIMOCK.

**Britnell, G. E.** The Wheat Economy. Editor's Preface by H. A. Innis. 1939. *o.p.*

**Britton, M. E.,** *joint author:* TIFFANY, The Algae of Illinois.

**Broadcasting Abroad:** UNION INTERNATIONALE DE RADIO-DIFFUSION.

**Broder, Lois J.,** *joint author:* BLOOM, Problem-solving Processes of College Students.

**Brodie, Fern H.,** *joint author:* NORRIS, Blindness in Children.

**Brody, Maurice S.** Wage Rates and Living Costs in a War Economy. 1943. *o.p.*

**Brombert, Victor.** The Intellectual Hero. Studies in the French Novel, 1880–1955. *Reissue,* 1964. 255 p. 21 cm. 61-8673. Paper. P158. $1.95. COBE.

**Bronson, Walter Cochrane,** *ed.* American Poems (1625–1892). Selected and Edited, with Illustrative and Explanatory Notes and a Bibliography, by Walter C. Bronson. 1912. *o.p.*

**Bronson, Walter Cochrane,** *ed.* American Prose (1607–1685). Selected and Edited, with Illustrative and Explanatory Notes and a Bibliography, by Walter C. Bronson. 1916. *o.p.*

**Bronson, Walter Cochrane,** *ed.* English Poems. Selected and Edited with Illustrative and Explanatory Notes and Bibliographies, by Walter C. Bronson. 1907–10. 4 vols. *o.p.*

*Vol. I:* Old English and Middle English Periods (450–1550). 1910.
*Vol. II:* The Elizabethan Age and the Puritan Period (1550–1660). 1909.
*Vol. III:* The Restoration and the Eighteenth Century (1660–1800). 1908.
*Vol. IV:* The Nineteenth Century. 1907.

**Brooks, Eugene C.** Report of the Commission on Length of Elementary Education. By Eugene C. Brooks and others. 1927. SEM 34. *o.p.*

**Brooks, Robert Clarkson.** Civic Training in Switzerland. A Study of Democratic Life. 1930. SMC. *o.p.*

**Broome, Myrtle F.,** *joint author:* CALVERLEY, Temple of King Sethos I.

**Brothers in Crime:** SHAW.

**Brown, Bolton Coit.** Lithography for Artists. A Complete Account of How To Grind, Draw upon, Etch, and Print from the Stone, together with Instructions for Making Crayon, Transferring, etc. 1930. SL. *o.p.*

**Brown, Carleton:** *see* BRYAN, Sources and Analogues of Chaucer's *Canterbury Tales.*

**Brown, E. K.** Matthew Arnold. A Study in Conflict. 1948. *o.p.*

**Brown, Edward Osgood.** Biographical Sketch of Hon. John Peter Altgeld, Twentieth Governor of Illinois. By Edward Osgood Brown. 1905. *o.p.*
A publication of the Chicago Historical Society.

**Brown, Emily Clark.** Book and Job Printing in Chicago. A Study of Organizations of Employers and Their Relations with Labor. 1931. SSCI. *o.p.*

**Brown, Emily Clark,** *joint author:* MILLIS, From the Wagner Act to Taft-Hartley.

**Brown, Francis,** *joint ed.:* HARPER, Old Testament and Semitic Studies.

**Brown, Frank Clyde.** Elkanah Settle. His Life and Works. 1910. *o.p.*

**Brown, G. P.** On the Teaching of English in the Elementary and High Schools. By G. P. Brown and Emerson Davis. 1906. NSSE, 5th Yrbk., Part I. *o.p.*

**Brown George.** The New Economic Education. At the Secondary Level. 1941. *o.p.*

**Brown, Harrison,** *ed.* A Bibliography on Meteorites. An International Catalogue of Meteorites. Harrison Brown, *Editor;* Gunnar Kullerud and Walter Nichiporuk, *Associate Editors.* 1953. PS. *o.p.*

**Brown, J. S.** The Place of Vocational Subjects in the High School. By J. S. Brown and others. 1905. NSSE, 4th Yrbk., Part II. *o.p.*

**Brown, James.** The History of Public Assistance in Chicago, 1833–1893. 1941. *o.p.*

**Brown, Kenneth Irving.** A Campus Decade. The Hiram Study Plan of Intensive Courses, 1930–40. 1940. *o.p.*

**Brown, Sanger:** *see* BARKER, A Description of the Brains and Spinal Cords of Two Brothers.

**Brown, William Adams.** The Case for Theology in the University. 1938. *o.p.*

**Browne, Sir Thomas.** The Works of Sir Thomas Browne. Edited by Geoffrey Keynes. 4 vols. 2d ed. 1964. 1,970 p. 64-14539. $37.50ˢ. OBE.

**Brownell, William A.** The Development of Children's Number Ideas in the Primary Grades. 1928. SEM 35. *o.p.*

**Brownell, William A.** The Measurement of Understanding. Prepared by William A. Brownell, Chairman of the Society's Committee. 1946. NSSE, 45th Yrbk., Part I. *o.p.*

**Browning, Grace Alta.** The Development of Poor Relief Legislation in Kansas. By Grace A. Browning. Appendixes with Court Decisions edited by Sophonisba P. Breckinridge. 1935. SSM. *o.p.*

**Browning, Grace Alta.** Rural Public Welfare. Selected Records with Introductory Notes and Comments. 1941. SSS. *o.p.*

**Browning, Grace Alta,** *joint ed.:* DIXON, Social Case Records.

**Brownlow, Louis.** The Anatomy of the Anecdote. 1960. vi, 154 p. Illus. 22 cm. 60-7233. $3.75ˢ.

**Brownlow, Louis.** Autobiography. *Vol. I:* A Passion for Politics. The Autobiography of Louis Brownlow. The First Half. 1955. xii, 606 p. Illus. $7.50ˢ. *Vol. II:* A Passion for Anonymity. 1958. x, 499 p. Illus. 24 cm. 55-5111. $7.50ˢ.

**Brubacher, John S.** Modern Philosophies and Education. Prepared by John S. Brubacher, Chairman of the Society's Committee. 1955. NSSE, 54th Yrbk., Part I. x, 374 p. 24 cm. 54-14177. Cloth. $4.50ᵗ. Paper. $3.75ᵗ.

**Brubacher, John S.** Philosophies of Education. Prepared by John S. Brubacher, Chairman of the Society's Committee. 1942. NSSE, 41st Yrbk., Part I. xi, 331 p. 24 cm. E42-207. Cloth. $4.00ᵗ. Paper. $3.25ᵗ.

**Bruce, Isabel Campbell.** The Michigan Poor Law. Its Development and Administration with Special Reference to State Provision for Medical Care of the Indigent. By Isabel Campbell Bruce and Edith Eickhoff. Edited with an Introductory Note and Selected Court Decisions by Sophonisba P. Breckinridge. 1936. SSM. *o.p.*

**Brueckner, Leo J.** Educational Diagnosis. Prepared by Leo J. Brueckner, Chairman of the Society's Committee. 1935. NSSE, 34th Yrbk. x, 523 p. 24 cm. 35-177. Cloth. $4.25ᵗ. Paper. $3.00ᵗ.

**Bruère, Henry:** *see* WIRTH, Eleven Twenty-six.

**Brues, Austin M.** Aging and Levels of Biological Organization. Edited by Austin M. Brues and George A. Sacher. 1965. xi, 353 p. 22 cm. 65-17281. $5.00ˢ.

**Brumbaugh, Aaron John,** *joint author:* REEVES, Liberal Arts College.

**Brunschwig, Alexander.** Radical Surgery in Advanced Abdominal Cancer. 1947. *o.p.*

**Brunstetter, Max Russell.** How To Use the Educational Sound Film. 1937. *o.p.*

**Brunstetter, Max Russell.** Introduction to Spanish Pronunciation and Diction.

**Brunswik, Egon.** The Conceptual Framework of Psychology. 1952. iv, 102 p. Illus. 25 cm. 52-8500. Paper. IEUS, I, 10. $2.00ˢ.

**Brux, Adolf A.,** *trans.:* HILZHEIMER, Animal Remains from Tell Asmar.

**Bryan, William Frank,** *ed.* Sources and Analogues of Chaucer's *Canterbury Tales.* W. F. Bryan, *General Editor;* Germaine Dempster, *Associate General Editor.* 1941. *o.p.*

**Bryson, Frederick Robertson.** The Sixteenth-Century Italian Duel. A Study in Renaissance Social History. 1938. *o.p.*

**Bryson, Lyman Lloyd,** *joint author:* WIESE, Let's Talk It Over.

**Buber, Martin:** FRIEDMAN.

**Buchanan, Douglas Nisbet,** *joint author:* BAILEY, Intracranial Tumors.

**Buchsbaum, Ralph.** Animals without Backbones. An Introduction to the Invertebrates. 2d ed. 1948. xiii, 405 p. Illus. 25 cm. 48-9508. Text ed. NPL. $7.00ᵗ. Trade ed. $9.00.

"Should be hailed as a distinct educational asset by every zoölogy teacher and as an open sesame to the world of invertebrates for every would-be zoölogist."—George H. Childs, in *Natural History.*

"Not a popularization of science but a textbook of science; yet because of its simplicity, its beautiful and modern design and its interesting presentation, it is entirely suitable and will appeal to non-scientific readers. The illustrations consist of hundreds of superb photographs, line drawings and diagrams such as cannot be found in any other published work."—*Saturday Review.*

**Buchsbaum, Ralph.** Methods of Tissue Culture in Vitro. By Ralph Buchsbaum. *And* Outlines of Histological Methods, with Special Reference to Tissue Culture. By Clayton G. Loosli. 1936. *o.p.*

**Buchsbaum, Ralph.** Readings in Ecology. 1949. *o.p.*

**Buchsbaum, Ralph,** *ed.:* College Library of Biological Science.

**Buck, Adriaan de.** The Egyptian Coffin Texts. *Vol. I:* Texts of Spells 1–75. 1935.

xix, 405 p. Illus. 30 cm. OIP, XXXIV. $7.00. *Vol. II:* Texts of Spells 76–163. 1938. xiv, 405 p. Illus. OIP, XLIX. $8.00. *Vol. III:* Texts of Spells 164–267. 1947. xvi, 400 p. Illus. OIP, LXIV. $10.00. *Vol. IV:* Texts of Spells 268–354. 1951. xiv, 418 p. Illus. 30 cm. OIP, LXVII. $10.00. *Vol. V:* Texts of Spells 355–471. 1954. xv, 400 p. 30 cm. OIP, LXXIII. $10.00. *Vol. VI:* Texts of Spells 472–786. 1956. xiv, 415 p. Illus. OIP, LXXXI. $15.00. *Vol. VII:* Texts of Spells 787–1185. 1963. 546 p. Illus. 30 cm. OIP, LXXXVII. $15.00.

**Buck, Carl Darling.** A Comparative Grammar of Greek and Latin. 1933. xvi, 405 p. 23 cm. 33-11254. $8.00ᵗ.

**Buck, Carl Darling.** Dental Terminations I. 1918. GN. *o.p.*

**Buck, Carl Darling.** A Dictionary of Selected Synonyms in the Principal Indo-European Languages. A Contribution to the History of Ideas. With the co-operation of colleagues and assistants. 1949. xix, 1,515 p. 26 cm. 49-11769. $25.00ˢ.

"We have had, so far, no work of this sort, and this large and substantial volume, which is so much more than a bare compilation, will render excellent service . . . a remarkable achievement."—André Martinet, in *Word.*

**Buck, Carl Darling.** The Greek Dialects. Grammar. Selected Inscriptions. Glossary. 3d rev. ed. 1955. xiii, 373 p. 24 cm. 55-5115. $12.50ˢ.

**Buck, Carl Darling.** The Oscan-Umbrian Verb-System. 1895. *o.p.*

**Buck, Carl Darling.** A Sketch of the Linguistic Conditions of Chicago. 1903. *o.p.*

**Buck, Carl Darling,** *ed.* A Reverse Index of Greek Nouns and Adjectives. Edited by Carl D. Buck and Walter Peterson. 1948. *o.p.*

**Buck, Carl Darling:** *see* STUDIES IN GREEK NOUN-FORMATION.

**Buck, Harry M.** The Johannine Lessons in the Greek Gospel Lectionary. 1958. viii, 83 p. 24 cm. 58-5537. LT. $2.00ˢ.

**Buck, John Lossing.** Chinese Farm Economy. A Study of 2,866 Farms in Seventeen Localities and Seven Provinces in China. 1929. Published in China by the University of Nanking. American edition published by the University of Chicago Press. 1930. IPR. *o.p.*

**Buck, John Lossing.** Land Utilization in China. A Study of 16,786 Farms in 168 Localities, and 38,256 Farm Families in Twenty-two Provinces in China, 1929–1933. 3 vols. 1937. IPR. *o.p.*

**Buck, Peter H.** Vikings of the Pacific. First published as *Vikings of the Sunrise*. Reissue, 1959. xiii, 339 p. 21 cm. 59-16101. Paper. P31. $1.95. (Not for sale in Australia and New Zealand.)

**Buck, Philip W.** Amateurs and Professionals in British Politics, 1918–59. 1963. xii, 144 p. Illus. Index. 23 cm. 63-13073. $5.00ˢ.

**Buckley, Edmund.** Phallicism in Japan. 1895. *o.p.*

**Buckley, George Truett.** Atheism in the English Renaissance. 1932. *o.p.*

**Bucy, Paul Clancy,** *joint author:* BAILEY, Intracranial Tumors.

**Buddhism in India, Ceylon, China, and Japan:** HAMILTON.

**Buddhist Cave Paintings:** GRAY.

**Budy, Ann. M.,** *joint ed.:* GAILLARD, The Parathyroid Glands.

**Buechner, Frank Robert.** Municipal Self-Insurance of Workmen's Compensation. 1931. MM. *o.p.*

**Buell, Raymond Leslie.** Death by Tariff. Protectionism in State and Federal Legislation. 1939. PPP. *o.p.*

**Buenaventura y otros cuentos:** CASTILLO.

**Building Character:** CHICAGO ASSOCIATION FOR CHILD STUDY.

**Building the German Vocabulary:** HAGBOLDT.

**Building Industry and Business Cycles:** NEWMAN.

**Building Lenin's Russia:** LIBERMAN.

**Building Rural Communities:** AMERICAN COUNTRY LIFE ASSOCIATION, Proceedings, No. 23.

**Buitron, Anibal,** *joint author:* COLLIER, The Awakening Valley.

**Bullard, Dexter M.,** *ed.:* FROMM-REICHMANN, Psychoanalysis and Psychotherapy.

**Burden of Egypt:** WILSON.

**Bureau of Railway Economics.** Railway Economics. A Collective Catalogue of Books in Fourteen American Libraries. Prepared by The Bureau of Railway Economics. 1912. *o.p.*

**Bureaucratic Phenomenon:** CROZIER.

**Burgess, Ernest W.** Environment and Education. By Ernest W. Burgess and others. 1942. SEM 54. *o.p.*

**Burgess, Ernest W.** The Function of Socialization in Social Evolution. 1916. *o.p.*

**Burgess, Ernest W.,** *ed.* Aging in Western Societies. A Survey of Social Gerontology. 1960. xvi, 492 p. Illus. 25 cm. 60-5465. HSG. $7.50ᵗ.

**Burgess, Ernest W.,** *ed.* Census Data of the City of Chicago, 1920. Edited by Ernest W. Burgess and Charles Newcomb. 1931. *o.p.* Census Data of the City of Chicago, 1930. 1933. *o.p.*

**Burgess, Ernest W.,** *ed.* Contributions to Urban Sociology. Edited by Ernest W. Burgess and Donald J. Bogue. 1964. xi, 673 p. 25 cm. 63-21309. $12.00ᵗ.

**Burgess, Ernest W.,** *ed.* Personality and the Social Group. 1929. SOC. *o.p.*

**Burgess, Ernest W.,** *ed.* The Urban Community. Selected Papers from The Proceedings of the American Sociological Society, 1925. 1926. SOC. *o.p.*

**Burgess, Ernest W.,** *joint author:* PARK, Introduction to the Science of Sociology.

**Burgess, Ernest W.:** *see* PARK, The City.

**Burgess, Ernest W.:** *see* SHAW, Brothers in Crime.

**Burgess, Ernest W.:** *see* SMITH, Chicago.

**Burgess, Isaac Bronson.** The Life of Christ for Use of Students of High-School Age. 1908. CS. *o.p.*

**Burgess, M. A.** Report of the Society's Committee on Silent Reading. By M. A. Burgess and others. 1921. NSSE, 20th Yrbk., Part II. *o.p.*

**Burgess, Theodore Chalon.** Epideictic Literature. 1902. Preprint from Vol. III, STUDIES IN CLASSICAL PHILOLOGY. *o.p.*

**Burgevin, Leslie Gale:** *see* SAINTONGE, Horace.

**Burke, Edmund.** The Correspondence of Edmund Burke. Thomas W. Copeland, *General Editor.* 24 cm. 58-5615. *Vol. I.* Edited by Thomas W. Copeland. 1958. xxvi, 377 p. $8.00ˢ. COBE. *Vol. II.* Edited by Lucy S. Sutherland. 1960. xxiii, 567 p. $12.00ˢ. COBE. *Vol. III.* Edited by George H. Guttridge. 1961. xxvi, 479 p. $12.00ˢ. *Vol. IV.* Edited by J. A. Woods. 1963. xxiv, 476 p. Index. $12.00ˢ. COBE. *Vol. V.* Edited by Holden Furber. 1965. xxx, 496 p. 24 cm. 58-5616. $12.00ˢ. COBE.

"Professor Copeland has organized a team of dedicated Anglo-American editors, and the volumes of his correspondence are flowing from the press, beautifully and skillfully edited in the highest traditions of American scholarship."—J. H. Plumb, in *The New York Review of Books.*

**Burke, Kenneth.** Counter-Statement. 1957. *o.p.*

**Burke, William Willard.** Administration of Private Social Service Agencies. A Topical Bibliography with Supplement. 1927. *o.p.*

**Burnham, Sherburne Wesley.** A General Catalogue of 1290 Double Stars. Discovered from 1871 to 1899 by S. W. Burnham. Arranged in Order of Right Ascension with All the Micrometrical Measures of Each Pair. 1900. YO. *o.p.*

**Burnham, Sherburne Wesley.** Measures of Double Stars with the 40-Inch Refractor of the Yerkes Observatory in 1900 and 1901. 1902. YO, II. *o.p.*

**Burnham, William H.** The History of Education as a Professional Subject. By William H. Burnham and Henry Suzzallo. 1908. *o.p.*

**Burns, Norman,** *ed.* The Administration of Higher Institutions under Changing Conditions. 1947. *o.p.*

**Burns, Norman,** *ed.* The Community Responsibilities of Institutions of Higher Learning. Compiled and edited by Norman Burns and Cyril O. Houle. 1948. v, 88 p. 24 cm. 48-9710. Paper. $3.00ˢ.

**Burris, William Paxton,** *joint author:* SPAULDING, Aims, Scope, and Methods of a University Course in Public-School Administration.

**Burton, Ernest DeWitt.** Biblical Ideas of Atonement. Their History and Significance. By Ernest DeWitt Burton, John Merlin Powis Smith, and Gerald Birney Smith. 1909. *o.p.*

**Burton, Ernest DeWitt.** Christianity in the Modern World. Papers and Addresses by Ernest DeWitt Burton. Edited by Harold R. Willoughby. 1927. *o.p.*

**Burton, Ernest DeWitt.** Education in a Democratic World. By Ernest DeWitt Burton. Edited by Harold R. Willoughby. 1927. *o.p.*

**Burton, Ernest DeWitt.** Four Letters of the Christian Church. A Series of Direction Sheets for Individual or Class Study of the History of the Early Church as It Is Recorded in the Acts, the Epistles, and the Revelation. 1904. AISL. *o.p.*

**Burton, Ernest DeWitt.** Four Letters of the Apostle Paul. A Short Course. 1908. AISL. *o.p.*

**Burton, Ernest DeWitt.** A Handbook of the Life of the Apostle Paul. An Outline for Classroom and Private Study. 1899. 5th ed. 1906. AISL. *o.p.*
First three editions privately printed.

**Burton, Ernest DeWitt.** A Harmony of the Synoptic Gospels in Greek. By Ernest DeWitt Burton and Edgar Johnson Goodspeed. 1920. xxx, 316 p. 21 cm. 17-25996. $5.75ˢ.

**Burton, Ernest DeWitt.** Jesus of Nazareth, How He Thought, Lived, Worked, and Achieved. 1920. AISL. *o.p.*

**Burton, Ernest DeWitt.** The Life of Christ. By Ernest DeWitt Burton and Shailer Mathews. 1901. 3d ed. 1927. CS. *o.p.*

**Burton, Ernest DeWitt.** The Life of Christ. A Series of Direction Sheets for Individual or Class Study of the Life of The Christ as It Is Recorded in the Four Gospels. 1906. AISL. *o.p.*

**Burton, Ernest DeWitt.** New Testament Word Studies. By Ernest DeWitt Burton. Edited by Harold R. Willoughby. 1927. HLL. *o.p.*

**Burton, Ernest DeWitt.** Notes on New Testament Grammar. 1904. *o.p.*

**Burton, Ernest DeWitt.** The Origin and Teaching of the New Testament Books. By Ernest DeWitt Burton and Fred Merrifield. 1913. AISL. *o.p.*

**Burton, Ernest DeWitt.** Principles and Ideals for the Sunday School. An Essay in Religious Pedagogy. By Ernest DeWitt Burton and Shailer Mathews. 1903. *o.p.*

**Burton, Ernest DeWitt.** A Short Introduction to the Gospels. 1904. 2d ed. Revised by Harold R. Willoughby. 1926. CS. *o.p.*

**Burton, Ernest DeWitt.** Some Principles of Literary Criticism and Their Application to the Synoptic Problem. 1904. *o.p.*

**Burton, Ernest DeWitt.** A Source Book for the Study of the Teaching of Jesus in Its Historical Relationships. 1923. 2d ed. 1924. HER. *o.p.*

**Burton, Ernest DeWitt.** Spirit, Soul, and Flesh. The Usage of Πνεῦμα, Ψυχή, and Σάρξ in Greek Writings and Translated Works from the Earliest Period to 180 A.D.; and of Their Equivalents רוּחַ, נֶפֶשׁ, and בָּשָׂר in the Hebrew Old Testament. 1918. HLL. *o.p.*

**Burton, Ernest DeWitt.** Studies in the Gospel According to Mark. For the Use of Classes in Secondary Schools and in the Secondary Division of the Sunday School. 1904. CS. *o.p.*

**Burton, Ernest DeWitt.** Syntax of the Moods and Tenses in New Testament Greek. 1888. 3d ed. 1898. *o.p.*

**Burton, Ernest DeWitt,** *joint author:* STEVENS, Harmony of the Gospels.

**Burton, Ernest DeWitt:** *see* SMITH, Guide to the Study of the Christian Religion.

**Burton, Ian.** Readings in Resource Management and Conservation. Edited by Ian Burton and Robert W. Kates. 1965. xi, 609 p. 25 cm. 65-14427. $8.50ᵗ.

**Burton, Margaret Ernestine.** The Assembly of the League of Nations. 1941. *o.p.*

**Burwash, Edward Moore Jackson.** The Geology of Vancouver and Vicinity. 1918. *o.p.*

**Business Administration:** MARSHALL.

**Business Behavior:** PAYNE.

**Business Cases and Problems:** MARSHALL.

**Business Cycle:** MATTHEWS.

**Business-Cycle Theory in the United States:** BARNETT.

**Business Education for Everybody:** SHIELDS.

**Business Education and Money Management:** DUDDY.

**Business Education in School Situations:** DUDDY.

**Business Education for What?** KORNHAUSER.

**Business and Government:** CRIGHTON.

**Business Life of Ancient Athens:** CALHOUN.

**Business and Personal Failure and Readjustment in Chicago:** COVER.

**Business as a Social Institution:** BREWINGTON.

**Buswell, Guy T.** Diagnostic Studies in Arithmetic. By Guy T. Buswell and Lenore John. 1926. SEM 30. *o.p.*

**Buswell, Guy T.** An Experimental Study of the Eye-Voice Span in Reading. 1920. SEM 17. *o.p.*

**Buswell, Guy T.** Fundamental Reading Habits. A Study of Their Development. 1922. SEM 21. *o.p.*

**Buswell, Guy T.** How Adults Read. 1937. SEM 45. *o.p.*

**Buswell, Guy T.** How People Look at Pictures. A Study of the Psychology of Perception in Art. 1935. *o.p.*

**Buswell, Guy T.** Remedial Reading at the College and Adult Levels. An Experimental Study. 1939. SEM 50. *o.p.*

**Buswell, Guy T.** Summary of Educational Investigations Relating to Arithmetic. By Guy T. Buswell and Charles H. Judd. 1925. SEM 27. *o.p.*

**Buswell, Guy T.** The Teaching of Arithmetic. Prepared by Guy T. Buswell, Chairman of the Society's Committee. 1951. NSSE, 50th Yrbk., Part II. xii, 302 p. 24 cm. 51-9871. Cloth. $4.50ᵗ. Paper. $3.75ᵗ.

**Buswell, Guy T.** The Vocabulary of Arithmetic. By Guy T. Buswell and Lenore John. 1931. SEM 38. *o.p.*

**Buswell, Guy T.,** *ed.* Arithmetic, 1947. Papers Presented at the Second Annual Conference on Arithmetic Held at the University of Chicago, 1947. 1947. SEM 63. *o.p.*

**Buswell, Guy T.,** *ed.* Arithmetic, 1948. Papers Presented at the Third Annual Conference on Arithmetic Held at the University of Chicago, 1948. 1948. SEM 66. *o.p.*

**Buswell, Guy T.,** *ed.* Arithmetic, 1949. Papers Presented at the Fourth Annual Conference on Arithmetic Held at the University of Chicago, 1949. Edited by Guy T. Buswell and Maurice Hartung. 1949. SEM 70. *o.p.*

**Buswell, Guy T.,** *ed.* Non-oral Reading: A Study of Its Use in the Chicago Public Schools. 1945. SEM 60. *o.p.*

**Buswell, Guy T.,** *joint author:* JUDD: Silent Reading.

**Buswell, Guy T.:** *see* EDWARDS, Education in a Democracy.

**Butler, Frank A.** The Improvement of Teaching in Secondary Schools. 1939. 3d ed. 1954. xii, 433 p. 24 cm. 54-10718. $5.50ᵗ.

**Butler, Pierce.** An Introduction to Library Science. 1933. Reprint, 1961, with Introduction by Lester E. Asheim. xvi, 118 p. 21 cm. 33-16039. Paper. P59. LS. $1.25.

"Its ability still to provoke thought, raise questions, engender argument, and shake convictions deservedly wins for *An Introduction to Library Science* the name of 'classic.' "—Lester E. Asheim, from the new Introduction.

**Butler, Pierce.** The Origin of Printing in Europe. 1940. LS. *o.p.*

**Butler, Pierce,** *ed.* Books and Libraries in Wartime. 1945. *o.p.*

**Butler, Pierce,** *ed.* Librarians, Scholars, and Booksellers at Mid-Century. 1953. LS. *o.p.*

**Butler, Pierce,** *ed.* The Reference Function of the Library. 1943. LS. *o.p.*

**Butler, R. L.,** *joint ed.:* PARGELLIS, Nathaniel Moore's Diary.

**Buttenwieser, Moses.** The Psalms, Chronologically Treated with a New Translation. 1938. *o.p.*

**Butterbaugh, Grant.** Measurement of Business Activity in the Puget Sound Area. 1943. *o.p.*

**Butterfield, Kenyon Leech.** Chapters in Rural Progress. 1907. *o.p.*

**Butterfield, Kenyon Leech.** The Country Church and the Rural Problem. The Carew Lectures at Hartford Theological Seminary, 1909. 1911. *o.p.*

**Buying Happiness:** GOODSPEED.

**Buying the Wind:** DORSON.

**Buytendijk, F. I. J.** Pain. Its Modes and Functions. 1962. vi, 190 p. 21 cm. 62-9737. $3.95ˢ. OBE.

**By-Products in the Packing Industry:** CLEMEN.

**Byers, Horace R.** Elements of Cloud Physics. 1965. ix, 191 p. Illus. 24 cm. 65-17282. $7.50ˢ.

**Byers, Horace R.** Nonfrontal Thunderstorms. 1943. *o.p.*

**Byers, Horace R.,** *ed.* Thunderstorm Electricity. 1953. PS. *o.p.*

**Byrne, Lee,** *ed.* The Syntax of High-School Latin. A Co-operative Study by Fifty Collaborators. 1909. 2d ed. 1918. *o.p.*

**Byzantine Church at Khirbat-al-Karak:** DELOUGAZ.

**Byzantine and Romanesque Architecture:** JACKSON.

**Caballeros y escuderos:** HENDRIX.

**Cadbury, Edward.** Women's Work and Wages. A Phase of Life in an Industrial City. By Edward Cadbury, M. Cécile Matheson and George Shann. 1907. *o.p.*

**Cade, G. N.** The Professional Preparation of High-School Teachers. By G. N. Cade and others. 1919. NSSE, 18th Yrbk., Part I. *o.p.*

**Cady, Gilbert Haven,** *joint author:* SAUER, Starved Rock State Park.

**Caffee, Gabrielle L.,** *joint trans.:* GENNEP, Rites of Passage.

**Calciphylaxis:** SELYE.

**Calculation of Elliptic Elements:** DUNÉR.

**Calculus. A Genetic Approach:** TOEPLITZ.

**Calder, Ritchie.** Living with the Atom. 1962. ix, 275 p. Illus. 22 cm. 62-13562. $5.95ˢ.

**Caldwell, Ernest Leroy,** *joint author:* MYERS, Second-Year Mathematics.

**Caldwell, Ernest Leroy,** *joint author:* MYERS, Teacher's Manual for First-Year Mathematics.

**Caldwell, Lynton K.** The Administrative Theories of Hamilton and Jefferson. Their Contribution to Thought on Public Administration. 1944. PA. *o.p.*

**Caldwell, Otis W.** On Life-History of Lemna Minor. 1899. HB. *o.p.*

**Calef, Wesley.** Private Grazing and Public Lands. Comparative Studies of the Local Management of the Taylor Grazing Act. 1960. xviii, 292 p. Illus. 25 cm. 60-15936. $9.50ˢ.

**Calendars of Ancient Egypt:** PARKER.

**Calhoun, George Miller.** The Business Life of Ancient Athens. Introduction by Wigginton E. Creed. 1926. *o.p.*

**Calkins, Fay.** The CIO and the Democratic Party. 1952. *o.p.*

**Callahan, Raymond E.** Education and the Cult of Efficiency. 1962. xii, 276 p. 21 cm. 62-17961. $5.50ˢ. Paper. P149. $2.25.
"This is an excellent history of the influence of business ideology on American schools during this century. Professor Callahan dwells especially on the craze for 'scientific management' after Frederick Taylor. . . . is at his best . . . in showing how during these sixty years there has developed a strangling network of baneful mutually-causing influences. . . ."—Paul Goodman, in *The Harvard Educational Review*.

**Callender, Charles,** *joint ed.:* TAX, Issues in Evolution.

**Calverley, Amice M.** The Temple of King Sethos I at Abydos. With the assistance of Myrtle F. Broome. Edited by Alan H. Gardiner. Joint Publication of the Oriental Institute and Egypt Exploration Society. *Special Publication of the Oriental Institute of the University of Chicago.* 34-1455. COBE. *Vol. I.:* The Chapels of Osiris, Isis, and Horus. 1933. 11 p. Illus. (4 in color). 60×47 cm. Cloth. $20.00. *Vol. II.:* The Chapels of Amen-rē, ʿRē-Harakhti, Ptah and King Sethos. 1935. 9 p. Illus. (4 in color). 60×47 cm. Cloth. $20.00. *Vol. III.:* The Osiris Complex. 1938. Illus. (13 in color). 60×47 cm. Cloth. $25.00. *Vol. IV.:* The Great Hypostyle Hall. 1959. 18 p. Illus. (7 in color). 60×47 cm. Cloth. $32.50.

**Calvert, Mary Ross,** *joint author:* Ross, Atlas of the Northern Milky Way.

**Cambridge Economic Handbooks** (CEH). *Edited by* MILTON FRIEDMAN and C. W. GUILLEBAUD:

BAUER, Economics of Under-developed Countries (CEH 1).
HARROD, International Economics (CEH 2).
HENDERSON, Supply and Demand (CEH 3).
MATTHEWS, Business Cycle (CEH 4).
REES, Economics of Trade Unions (CEH 7).
ROBERTSON, Money (CEH 5).
ROBINSON, Structure of Competitive Industry (CEH 6).

**Camden, Carroll,** *ed.* Literary Views. Critical and Historical Essays. 1964. xiii, 193 p. 24 cm. 64-13715. RSS. $5.00ˢ.

**Camden, Carroll,** *ed.* Restoration and Eighteenth-Century Literature. Essays in Honor of Alan Dugald McKillop. 1963. xi, 435 p. 24 cm. RSS. $8.50ˢ.

**Cameralists:** SMALL.

**Cameron, George G.** History of Early Iran. 1936. *o.p.*

**Cameron, George G.** Persepolis Treasury Tablets. 1948. OIP, LXV. *o.p.*

**Cameron, George G.**, *ed.*: CHIERA, They Wrote on Clay.

**Camp, Katherine B.** Science in Elementary Education: *see* ELEMENTARY SCHOOL RECORD, No. 6.

**Campbell, Frank L.**, *ed.* Physiology of Insect Development. 1959. xi, 167 p. 24 cm. 59-9701. DBC. $4.00s.

**Campbell, William Wallace.** The Mills Spectrograph of the Lick Observatory; Some Stars with Great Velocities in the Line of Sight; The Variable Velocity of $\eta$ *Pegasi* in the Line of Sight. 1898. *o.p.*

**Campus Decade:** BROWN.

**Can Interstate Compacts Succeed?** DIMOCK.

**Canadian Marketing Problems:** KEMP.

**Canadian Penal Institutions:** TOPPING.

**Cannizzaro, Stanislao.** Sketch of a Course of Chemical Philosophy. (1858.) 1911. AC. *o.p.*

**Canterbury Tales:** MANLY.

**Cantharus from the Factory of Brygos:** TARBELL.

**Cantor, Nathaniel.** Crime. 1935. 2d ed. 1938. AP. *o.p.*

**Capital Imports and Balance of Payments:** BLOOMFIELD.

**Capital Investment in Hospitals:** ROREM.

**Capital, the Money Market, and Gold:** EDIE.

**Capital Punishment and British Politics:** CHRISTOPH.

**Capitalism and Freedom:** FRIEDMAN.

**Capitalism and the Historians:** HAYEK.

**Capitalistic Warmongers:** SULZBACH.

**Capps, Edward.** The Introduction of Comedy into the City Dionysia. A Chronological Study in Greek Literary History. 1903. *o.p.*

**Capps, Edward.** Vitruvius and the Greek Stage. 1893. *o.p.*

**Carbohydrate Metabolism:** SOSKIN.

**Carbon in the Chromosphere:** HALE.

**Care of the Aged:** RUBINOW.

**Careers for Students of Chinese Language:** HODOUS.

**Carlson, Anton J.** The Control of Hunger in Health and Disease. 1916. *o.p.*

**Carlson, Anton J.** The Machinery of the Body. By Anton J. Carlson, Victor Johnson, and H. Mead Cavert. 5th ed. rev. and enlarged. 1961. xix, 752 p. Illus. 24 cm. 61-14536. $6.50t.

". . . interestingly and concisely written, simplified, yet accurate . . . the authors have succeeded more completely than any others with whom the reviewer is acquainted in bringing together in close integration all the physiologic relationships of the human race."—*Journal of the American Medical Association*.

**Carlson, Anton J.** Studies on the Possible Intoxicating Action of 3.2 Per Cent Beer. By A. J. Carlson, N. Kleitman, C. W. Muehlberger, F. C. McLean, H. Gulliksen, and R. B. Carlson. 1934. *o.p.*

**Carlson, Anton J.:** *see* MOULTON, World and Man.

**Carlson, Anton J.:** *see* NEWMAN, Nature of the World and of Man.

**Carlson, Robert Bernard:** *joint author:* CARLSON, Studies on the Possible Intoxicating Action of 3.2 Per Cent Beer.

**Carmina Latina:** FLICKINGER.

**Carmody, Sister Winifred Mary.** The Subjunctive in Tacitus. 1926. *o.p.*

**Carnap, Rudolf.** The Continuum of Inductive Methods. 1952. *o.p.*

**Carnap, Rudolf.** Foundations of Logic and Mathematics. 1939. viii, 71 p. 25 cm. A40-3146. Paper. IEUS, I, 3. $1.50s.

**Carnap, Rudolf.** Logical Foundations of Probability. 2d ed. 1962. xxviii, 614 p. 24 cm. 62-52505. $10.00s. CBBE.

". . . Carnap's book is of fundamental importance. His distinction between the two concepts of probability clears up a great deal of confusion. Most of his postulates and theorems are certainly correct. He makes a strong case for using this approach to find a logical foundation for statistics and for the inductive method . . . [W]hether fully right or not [he] lays down the foundations for many years of future research."—John G. Kemeny, in *The Journal of Symbolic Logic*.

**Carnap, Rudolf.** Meaning and Necessity. A Study in Semantics and Modal Logic. 2d ed., 1956. viii, 260 p. 21 cm. 56-9132. Paper. $1.95.

**Carnap, Rudolf.** The Nature and Application of Inductive Logic. 1951. *o.p.*

**Carnap, Rudolf,** *joint ed.:* Neurath, International Encyclopedia of Unified Science.

**Carnovsky, Leon,** *ed.* International Aspects of Librarianship. Eighteenth Annual Conference, Graduate Library School. 1954. vii, 124 p. 24 cm. 54-11303. LS. $4.00ˢ.

**Carnovsky, Leon,** *ed.* The Library in the Community. Edited by Leon Carnovsky and Lowell Martin. 1944. LS. *o.p.*

**Carnovsky, Leon,** *ed.* The Medium-sized Public Library. Its Status and Future. Edited by Leon Carnovsky and Howard W. Winger, Twenty-seventh Annual Conference, Graduate Library School. 1963. ii, 142 p. 24 cm. 63-5298. LS. $3.75ˢ.

**Carnovsky, Leon,** *joint author:* Joeckel, Metropolitan Library in Action.

**Carnovsky, Leon,** *joint author:* Waples, Libraries and Readers.

**Carnovsky, Leon:** *see* Waples, Library.

**Carolus et Maria:** Fay.

**Carpender, J. W. J.,** *joint ed.:* Wachsmann, Moving Field Radiation Therapy.

**Carpenter, Frederic Ives.** Metaphor and Simile in the Minor Elizabethan Drama. 1895. ENG. *o.p.*

**Carpenter, Frederic Ives.** A Reference Guide to Edmund Spenser. 1923. *o.p.*

**Carpenter, Frederic Ives,** *ed.:* Cox, Arte or Crafte of Rhethoryke.

**Carpenter, Frederic Ives,** *ed.:* Jonson, Case Is Altered.

**Carpenter, Frederic Ives,** *ed.:* Wager, Life and Repentaunce of Marie Magdalene.

**Carpenter, Niles.** Hospital Service for Patients of Moderate Means. A Study of Certain American Hospitals. 1930. CMC 4. *o.p.*

**Carpenter, Niles.** Medical Care for 15,000 Workers and Their Families. A Survey of the Endicott Johnson Workers Medical Service. 1928. By Niles Carpenter, with reports on certain phases of the organization by Nellis B. Foster, Ransom S. Hooker, and Michael M. Davis. 1930. CMC 5. *o.p.*

**Carpenter, Rhys.** Greek Sculpture. A Critical Review. 1960. 304 p. Illus. 24 cm. 60-14233. $6.95.

**Carpi, Jacopo Berengario da.** A Short Introduction to Anatomy (*Isagogae breves*). Translated by L. R. Lind. With Anatomical Notes by Paul G. Roofe. 1959. *o.p.*

**Carrington, Fitz Roy.** Engravers and Etchers. Six Lectures Delivered on the Scammon Foundation at the Art Institute of Chicago, March, 1916. 1917. SL. *o.p.* Publication by The University of Chicago Press assumed in 1921.

**Carrothers, William A.:** *see* Young, The Japanese Canadians.

**Carson, William Glasgow Bruce.** The Theatre on the Frontier. The Early Years of the St. Louis Stage. 1932. *o.p.*

**Carter, Edward Clark,** *ed.* China and Japan in Our University Curricula. With a Special Section on the University of Hawaii. 1930. IPR. *o.p.*

**Carter, William Giles Harding.** The Life of Lieutenant General Chaffee. 1917. *o.p.*

**Carter Henry Harrison I:** Johnson.

**Carver, Arthur Henry.** Personnel and Labor Problems in the Packing Industry. 1928. IMP. *o.p.*

**Case, Carl Delos.** The Incarnation and Modern Thought. 1908. *o.p.*

**Case, Ermine C.** New or Little-known Vertebrates from the Permian of Texas. 1903. WM. *o.p.*

**Case, Ermine C.** The Osteology of the Skull of the Pelycosaurian Genus, Dimetrodon. *And* On the Structure of the Fore Foot of Dimetrodon. 1904. WM. *o.p.*

**Case, Ermine C.** Palæontological Notes. 1902. WM. *o.p.*

**Case, Ermine C.** The Vertebrates from the Permian Bone Bed of Vermilion County, Illinois. 1901. WM. *o.p.*

**Case, Shirley Jackson.** The Book of Revelation. 1918. AISL. *o.p.*

**Case, Shirley Jackson.** The Christian Philosophy of History. 1943. *o.p.*

**Case, Shirley Jackson.** The Evolution of Early Christianity. A Genetic Study of First-Century Christianity in Relation to Its Religious Environment. 1914. ix, 385 p. 21 cm. 14-17216. $6.00ˢ.

**Case, Shirley Jackson.** The Historicity of Jesus. Criticism of the Contention that Jesus Never Lived, a Statement of the Evidence for His Existence, an Estimate of His Relation to Christianity. 1912. 2d ed. 1928. *o.p.*

**Case, Shirley Jackson.** Jesus. A New Biography. 1927. *o.p.*

". . . masterpiece of scholarship . . . a work of surpassing literary . . . qualities. . . . The Jesus of history, not the Christ of dogma, in his [Professor Case's] theme, and this Jesus he depicts as a man, inspired by genius, but saturated with the thoughts, habits, and superstitions of his age . . . [the] book is delightful to read."—John Haynes Holmes, in the *New York Herald Tribune.*

**Case, Shirley Jackson.** Jesus through the Centuries. 1932. *o.p.*

**Case, Shirley Jackson.** The Millennial Hope. 1918. *o.p.*

**Case, Shirley Jackson.** The Origins of Christian Supernaturalism. 1946. *o.p.*

**Case, Shirley Jackson.** The Revelation of John. A Historical Interpretation. 1919. *o.p.*

**Case, Shirley Jackson.** The Social Origins of Christianity. 1923. *o.p.*

**Case, Shirley Jackson,** *ed.* A Bibliographical Guide to the History of Christianity. Compiled by S. J. Case, J. T. McNeill, W. W. Sweet, W. Pauch, and M. Spinka. 1931. HER. *o.p.*

**Case, Shirley Jackson:** *see* BOWER, Church at Work in the Modern World.

**Case, Shirley Jackson:** *see* SMITH, Guide to the Study of the Christian Religion.

**Case, Shirley Jackson:** *see* SMITH, Religious Thought in the Last Quarter-Century.

**Case of Frank L. Smith:** WOODDY.

**Case of General Yamashita:** REEL.

**Case Is Altered:** JONSON.

**Case for Theology in the University:** BROWN.

**Casebook of Law and Business:** SPENCER.

**Cases and Problems:** MARSHALL.

**Casey, Robert J.,** *joint author:* HILLMAN, Tomorrow's Chicago.

**Caspari, Fritz.** Humanism and the Social Order in Tudor England. 1954. *o.p.*

**Cassel, Carl Gustav.** Foreign Investments. By Gustav Cassel, Theodore E. Gregory, Robert E. Kuczynski, and Henry Kittredge Norton. 1928. HFL. *o.p.*

**Cassels, Edwin Henry.** The Short Ballot in Illinois. Report of the Short Ballot Committee of the City Club of Chicago [Edwin H. Cassels, Chairman]. 1912. CC. *o.p.*

**Cassirer, Ernst,** *ed.* The Renaissance Philosophy of Man. Petrarca, Valla, Ficino, Pico, Pomponazzi, Vives. Edited by Ernst Cassirer, Paul Oskar Kristeller, and John Herman Randall, Jr. 1948. viii, 405 p. 22 cm. 48-9358. Cloth. CE. $5.00ˢ. Paper. P1. 21 cm. $1.95.

**Castillo, Carlos,** *ed.* Antología de la literatura mexicana. Introducción, selecciones y crítica con un apéndice bibliográfico. Edited by Carlos Castillo and Luis Leal. 1944. *o.p.*

**Castillo, Carlos,** *ed.* Graded Spanish Readers. Edited by Carlos Castillo and Colley F. Sparkman. HCLS.
Aventuras de Gil Blas.
La Buenaventura y otros cuentos.
La Gitanilla (Cervantes).
En Guatemala. Lecturas.
De México a Guatemala. Lecturas.
Sigamos leyendo.
De todo un poco.
Un Vuelo a México. Lecturas.

**Castillo, Carlos,** *ed.* HCLS.

Achievement Tests To Be Used with *Beginning Spanish.*

Achievement Test To Be Used with *Primeras lecturas españolas.*

Cuaderno To Accompany *España en América.*

Cuaderno To Accompany *La Nela.*

España en América. Segundas lecturas.

La Nela. An Adaptation of Galdos' *Marianela.* With Cuaderno.

Lecturas introductorias.

Primeras lecturas españolas.

Spanish Wall Charts, for Use with *Repasemos.*

Spanish Workbook To Accompany *Beginning Spanish.*

**Castillo, Carlos,** *comp.* The University of Chicago Spanish Dictionary. A New Concise Spanish-English and English-Spanish Dictionary of Words and Phrases Basic to the Written and Spoken Languages of Today. Compiled by Carlos Castillo and Otto F. Bond, with the assistance of Barbara M. Garcia. 1948. xxxvi, 226 p., xvii, 252 p. 24 cm. 48-9151. $5.50.

**Castillo, Carlos,** *joint author:* BOGGS, Leyendas épicas de España. A prosificación moderna.

**Castle, William Ernest.** Heredity and Eugenics. A Course of Lectures Summarizing Recent Advances in Knowledge in Variation, Heredity, and Evolution and Its Relation to Plant, Animal, and Human Improvement and Welfare. By William Ernest Castle, John Merle Coulter, Charles Benedict Davenport, Edward Murray East, and William Lawrence Tower. 1912. *o.p.*

**Castor, George Dewitt.** Matthew's Sayings of Jesus. The Non-Markan Common Source of Matthew and Luke. 1918. *o.p.*

**Castro, Mathilde.** The Respective Standpoints of Psychology and Logic. 1913. PS. *o.p.*

**Cat Musculature:** GREENBLATT.

**Catalogues and Counters:** EMMET.

**Catalysis:** LEMON.

**Cate, James Lea,** *ed.* Medieval and Historiographical Essays in Honor of James Westfall Thompson. Edited by James Lea Cate and Eugene N. Anderson. 1938. *o.p.*

**Cate, James Lea,** *joint ed.:* CRAVEN, Army Air Forces in World War II.

**Categorical Imperative:** PATON.

**Catlin, George Edward Gordon,** *ed.:* DURKHEIM, Rules of Sociological Method.

**Cattell, Raymond Bernard.** The Subjective Character of Cognition and the Presensational Development of Perception. 1930. BJP. *o.p.*

**Catterall, Ralph C. H.** The Second Bank of the United States. 1903. iv, 538 p. Illus. 21 cm. 3-19. $6.50s.

**Caughey, John W.** In Clear and Present Danger. The Crucial State of Our Freedoms. 1958. (O.I.)

**Caughey, John W.** Their Majesties the Mob. 1960. xi, 214 p. 22 cm. 60-6473. $5.00s.

**Cavan, Ruth Shonle.** The Family and the Depression. A Study of One Hundred Chicago Families. By Ruth Shonle Cavan and Katherine Howland Ranck. 1938. SSCI. *o.p.*

**Cavan, Ruth Shonle.** Suicide. 1928. SOC. *o.p.*

**Cavendish, Henry.** Experiments on Air. Papers Published in the Philosophical Transactions. By The Hon. Henry Cavendish, F.R.S. (1784–85). 1902. AC. *o.p.*

**Cavert, H. Mead,** *joint author:* CARLSON, Machinery of the Body.

**Cavins, Lorimer Victor.** Standardization of American Poetry for School Purposes. 1928. *o.p.*

**Cawelti, John G.** Apostles of the Self made Man. 1965. xiv, 279 p. 22 cm. 65-25123. $6.95.

**Cecil, David.** Victorian Novelists. 1958. xi, 331 p. 21 cm. Cloth. $5.00s. Paper. P26. $2.25. USA.

**Celestial Photographs:** BARNARD.

**Cell:** GERARD.

**Census Data of the City of Chicago, 1920:** BURGESS.

**Census Data of the City of Chicago, 1930:** BURGESS.

**Census Data of the City of Chicago, 1934:** NEWCOMB.

**Center for the Study of American Foreign and Military Policy (CSAFP):**
EPSTEIN, Britain—Uneasy Ally.
LISKA, New Statecraft.
OSGOOD, Limited War.

**Century after Cortés:** BENÍTEZ.

**Certification of Teachers:** CUBBERLY.

**Certification of Teachers:** WOELLNER.

**Chafee, Zechariah.** Government and Mass Communication. 2 vols. 1947. *o.p.*

**Challenge of Israel's Faith:** WRIGHT.

**Challenges of Space:** ODISHAW.

**Chamberlain, Basil Hall.** A Simplified Grammar of the Japanese Language (Modern Written Style). Revised Edition by Colonel James Garfield McIlroy. 1924. *o.p.*

**Chamberlain, Charles Joseph.** Contribution to the Life-History of Salix. 1897. HB. *o.p.*

**Chamberlain, Charles Joseph.** The Embryo-Sac of Aster Novae-Angliae. 1895. HB. *o.p.*

**Chamberlain, Charles Joseph.** Gymnosperms. Structure and Evolution. 1935. *o.p.*

**Chamberlain, Charles Joseph.** The Living Cycads. 1919. SCI. *o.p.*

**Chamberlain, Charles Joseph.** Methods in Plant Histology. 1901. 5th rev. ed. 1932. *o.p.*

**Chamberlain, Charles Joseph.** Mitosis in Pellia. 1903. *o.p.*

**Chamberlain, Charles Joseph.** Oögenesis in Pinus laricio. 1899. HB. *o.p.*

**Chamberlain, Charles Joseph.** Winter Characters of Certain Sporangia. 1898. HB. *o.p.*

**Chamberlain, Charles Joseph,** *joint author:* COULTER, Contributions to the Life-History of Lilium Philadelphicum.

**Chamberlain, Charles Joseph,** *joint author:* COULTER, Morphology of Gymnosperms.

**Chamberlin, Georgia Louise.** The Books of the Holy Bible. A Notebook for Homework. 1907. 3d ed. 1925. CS. *o.p.*

**Chamberlin, Georgia Louise.** Child Religion in Song and Story. For Teachers of Children from Six to Eight Years of Age. By Georgia Louise Chamberlin and Mary Root Kern. 2 vols. and looseleaf notebooks. 1907–9. *o.p.*

**Chamberlin, Georgia Louise.** The Hebrew Prophets or Patriots and Leaders of Israel. A Textbook for Students of High-School Age and Above. 1911. 2d ed. 1911. CS. *o.p.*

**Chamberlin, Georgia Louise.** An Introduction to the Bible for Teachers of Children. A Manual for Use in the Sunday School, the Week-Day School or in the Home. 1904. 2d ed. 1926. CS. *o.p.*

**Chamberlin, Georgia Louise.** Making the Bible Live. 1939. *o.p.*

**Chamberlin, Georgia Louise.** The Old Testament Books. Their Origin and Religious Values for Today. 1908. 2d ed. 1923. AISL. *o.p.* (First edition entitled *The Origin and Religious Teaching of the Old Testament Books.*)

**Chamberlin, Georgia Louise,** *joint author:* SMITH, Universal Element in the Psalter.

**Chamberlin, Georgia Louise:** *see* BEWER, Religion of the Bible.

**Chamberlin, Rollin T.:** *see* MOULTON, World and Man.

**Chamberlin, Rollin T.:** *see* NEWMAN, Nature of the World and of Man.

**Chamberlin, Thomas Chrowder.** An Attempt To Frame a Working Hypothesis of the Cause of Glacial Periods on an Atmospheric Basis. 1900. *o.p.*

**Chamberlin, Thomas Chrowder.** Classification of American Glacial Deposits. 1895. *o.p.*

**Chamberlin, Thomas Chrowder.** A Contribution to the Theory of Glacial Motion. 1904. *o.p.*

**Chamberlin, Thomas Chrowder.** The Origin of the Earth. 1916. SCI. *o.p.*

**Chamberlin, Thomas Chrowder.** Proposed Genetic Classification of Pleistocene Glacial Formations. 1894. *o.p.*

**Chamberlin, Thomas Chrowder.** The Two Solar Families. The Sun's Children. 1928. SCI. *o.p.*

**Chambers, Robert:** *see* COWDRY, General Cytology.

**Chan Kom:** REDFIELD.

**Chance and Symbol:** HERTZ.

**Chandeliers de l'évêque:** BOND.

**Chandrasekhar, S.** An Introduction to the Study of Stellar Structure. 1939. AM. *o.p.*

**Chandrasekhar, S.** Plasma Physics. Notes compiled by S. K. Trehan. 1960. x, 217 p. 21 cm. 60-7234. Paper. PSS 513. $1.75.

**Chandrasekhar, S.** Principles of Stellar Dynamics. 1942. *o.p.*

**Chaney, Ralph Works.** The Flora of the Eagle Creek Formation. 1920. WM. *o.p.*

**Chang, Chih-I,** *joint author:* FEI, Earthbound China.

**Chang, Tsung-ch'ien,** *joint ed.:* CREEL, Literary Chinese by the Inductive Method.

**Chang Hsi and the Treaty of Nanking, 1842:** TÊNG.

**Changes and Experiments in Liberal-Arts Education:** MCHALE.

**Changes in the Spectrum of Nova Persei:** HALE.

**Changes in the Wave-Frequencies of the Lines of Emission Spectra of Elements:** HUMPHREYS.

**Changing College:** WILKINS.

**Changing Conceptions in Educational Administration:** GRACE.

**Changing Ideas of American Patriotism:** BOYNTON.

**Changing Relative Importance of the Central Livestock Market:** DUDDY.

**Chapin, Elsa.** A New Approach to Poetry. By Elsa Chapin and Russell Thomas. 1929. *o.p.*

**Chaplin, Ralph.** Wobbly. The Rough-and-Tumble Story of an American Radical. 1948. *o.p.*

**Chapman, B. B.** Climate Reprints: *see* BUCK, Land Utilization in China.

**Chapters in the History of Actors and Acting:** O'CONNER.

**Chapters in the History of Greek Noun-Formation:** STRATTON.

**Chapters in Rural Progress:** BUTTERFIELD.

**Character Building through Recreation:** HEATON.

**Character and Citizenship Training:** JONES.

**Character through Creative Experience:** BOWER.

**Character Emphasis in Education:** HEATON.

**Character and Intelligence:** WEBB.

**Charters, Werrett Wallace.** Check-List of Teachers' Activities. By W. W. Charters and Douglas Waples. 1929. *o.p.*

**Charters, Werrett Wallace.** The Commonwealth Teacher-Training Study. Directed by W. W. Charters and Douglas Waples. Introduction by Samuel P. Capen. 1929. *o.p.*

**Charters, Werrett Wallace,** *joint author:* CUBBERLEY, Research within the Field of Education.

**Charters of the City of Chicago:** JAMES.

**Chase, Francis S.,** *ed.* The High School in a New Era. Edited by Francis S. Chase and Harold A. Anderson. 1958. xiv, 465 p. 24 cm. 58-11947. $6.00$^t$.

**Chastening:** KENNEDY, *in his* Plays for Three Players. Vol. I.

**Chaucer Gazetteer:** MAGOUN.

**Chave, Ernest J.** Attitude toward the Bible. 1933. TAS 29. *o.p.*

**Chave, Ernest J.** Attitude toward God. Forms A and B: The Reality of God. Forms C and D: Influence on Conduct. Prepared by E. J. Chave and L. L. Thurstone. Form E: Definitions of God. Prepared by E. J. Chave. 1931. TAS 22. *o.p.*

**Chave, Ernest J.** A Functional Approach to Religious Education. 1947. *o.p.*

**Chave, Ernest J.** The Junior. Life-Situations of Children Nine to Eleven Years of Age. 1905. 2d ed. 1932. PM. *o.p.*

**Chave, Ernest J.** Personality Development in Children. A Multiple Approach to a Complex Problem. 1937. HER. *o.p.*

**Chave, Ernest J.** Supervision of Religious Education. 1931. HER. *o.p.*

**Chave, Ernest J.**, *joint author:* THURSTONE, The Measurement of Attitude.

**Chave, Ernest J.**, *joint author:* THURSTONE. A Scale for Measuring Attitude toward the Church.

**Checagou:** QUAIFE.

**Check-List of Teachers' Activities:** CHARTERS.

**Chemical Anthropology:** MACY.

**Chemical Dynamics of Bone Mineral:** NEUMAN.

**Chemical Sign of Life:** TASHIRO.

**Cherdyntsev, V. V.** Abundance of Chemical Elements. (Moscow, 1956.) Translated by Walter Nichiporuk. English rev. ed., 1961. x, 304 p. Index. 24 cm. 61-11892. $10.00ˢ.

**Chesky, Jane**, *joint author:* JOSEPH, The Desert People.

**Chicago, An Experiment in Social Science Research:** SMITH.

**Chicago Art Institute:** *see* SCAMMON LECTURES AT THE ART INSTITUTE OF CHICAGO.

**Chicago Association for Child Study and Parent Education.** Building Character. Proceedings of the Mid-West Conference on Character Development, February, 1928. 1928. *o.p.*

**Chicago Association for Child Study and Parent Education.** The Child's Emotions. Proceedings of the Mid-West Conference on Character Development, February, 1930. 1930. *o.p.*

**Chicago Association for Child Study and Parent Education.** Developing Attitudes in Children. Proceedings of the Mid-West Conference of the Chicago Association for Child Study and Parent Education, March, 1932. 1933. *o.p.*

**Chicago Association for Child Study and Parent Education.** Intelligent Parenthood. Proceedings of the Mid-West Conference on Parent Education, March, 1926. 1926. *o.p.*

**Chicago and the Baptists:** STACKHOUSE.

**Chicago Civic Agencies.** A Directory of Associations of Citizens of Chicago Interested in Civic Welfare, 1927. Published for the Public Affairs Committee of the Union League Club of Chicago and the Committee on Local Community Research of the University of Chicago. 1927. SSCI. *o.p.*

**Chicago College Plan:** BOUCHER.

**Chicago Commission on Race Relations.** The Negro in Chicago. A Study of Race Relations and a Race Riot. 1922. *o.p.*

**Chicago Common Council:** MANN.

**Chicago Council on Foreign Relations:** *see* AMERICAN POLICIES ABROAD.

**Chicago Credit Market:** PALYI.

**Chicago Editions** (CE):
CASSIRER, Renaissance Philosophy of Man.
SIMON, *Material Logic* of John of St. Thomas.

**Chicago Families:** MONROE.

**Chicago in Fiction** (CF). SAUL BELLOW, *Advisory Editor:*
ADE, Artie *and* Pink Marsh.
ANDERSON, Windy McPherson's Son.
FULLER, With the Procession.
HARRIS, Bomb.
HECHT, Erik Dorn.
LARDNER, Gullible's Travels, Etc.

**Chicago Foundry Company:** DUDDY.

**Chicago Historical Society.** In Memoriam. John Nelson Jewett, LL.D., President of the Chicago Historical Society, 1899–1904. 1904(?). *o.p.*
A publication of the Chicago Historical Society.

**Chicago Historical Society:** McCAGG.

**Chicago Historical Society Publications.** The Chicago Historical Society was founded in 1856. From February, 1914, through June, 1935, The University of Chicago Press served as agent for the publications of the Society, handling the volumes dating from 1881, which are listed below. These publications consist of the *Collections,* which include historical and biographical material; *Pamphlets,* which publish lectures given at the Society's meetings; the *Fort Dearborn Series;* and miscellaneous volumes.

INGRAHAM, Elmer E. Ellsworth.
JENKINS, Book of Lake Geneva.
*Collections:*
    Vol. I. FLOWER, History of the English Settlement.
      II. REID, Biographical Sketch of Enoch Long.
      III. WASHBURNE, Edwards Papers.
      IV. MASON, Early Chicago.
      V. BOGGESS, Settlement of Illinois.
    VI–IX. Never published.
      X. PUTNAM, Illinois and Michigan Canal.
*Fort Dearborn Series:*
REED, Masters of the Wilderness.
*Pamphlets:*
ALVORD, Old Kaskaskia Records.
BARTON, Influence of Chicago.
BLATCHFORD, Biographical Sketch of Hon. Joseph Duncan.
BROWN, Biographical Sketch of Hon. John Peter Altgeld.
CHICAGO HISTORICAL SOCIETY, In Memoriam.
COLE, Lincoln's "House-divided" Speech.
COX, Indian as a Diplomatic Factor.
GROVER, Some Indian Landmarks.
HAMILTON, Biographical Sketch of Gurdon Saltonstall Hubbard.
JAMES, Preamble and Boundary Clauses of the Illinois Constitution.
McCAGG, Chicago Historical Society.
McCULLOUGH, Early Days of Peoria.
MacNAUL, Jefferson-Lemen Compact.
MANN, Chicago Common Council.
PATTERSON, Early Society in Southern Illinois.
PEASE, Diary of Orville H. Browning.
PROCTOR, Lincoln and the Convention of 1860.
RADEBAUGH, Boundary Dispute.
RAY, Convention That Nominated Lincoln.
REED, Masters of the Wilderness. A Study of the Hudson's Bay Company.
SELBY, Abraham Lincoln.
WHITE, Lincoln and Douglas Debates.
WIGHT, Eleazer Williams.

**Chicago History of American Civilization** (CHAC). *Edited by* DANIEL J. BOORSTIN:
AGAR, Price of Power.
BREMNER, American Philanthropy.
COLES, War of 1812.
CUNLIFFE, Nation Takes Shape.
DORSON, American Folklore.
ELLIS, American Catholicism.
FRANKLIN, Reconstruction after the Civil War.
GLAZER, American Judaism.
HAGAN, American Indians.
HAYS, Response to Industrialism.
HUDSON, American Protestantism.
JONES, American Immigration.

LEUCHTENBURG, Perils of Prosperity.
McCLOSKEY, American Supreme Court.
MORGAN, Birth of the Republic.
PECKHAM, Colonial Wars.
PECKHAM, War for Independence.
PELLING, American Labor.
PERKINS, New Age of Franklin Roosevelt.
RAE, American Automobile.
ROLAND, Confederacy.
SINGLETARY, Mexican War.
STOVER, American Railroads.
WEISBERGER, American Newspaperman.

**Chicago Home Rule Commission,** LEVERETT S. LYON, *Chairman.* Modernizing a City Government. 1954. *o.p.*

**Chicago Lectures in Physics** (CLP):
LEVI SETTI, Elementary Particles.

**Chicago Lectures in Mathematics** (CLM):
SWAN, Theory of Sheaves.

**Chicago Library of Comparative Politics** (CLCP). *Edited by* ROY C. MACRIDIS:
DUVERGER, French Political System.
HAZARD, Soviet System of Government.
MORSTEIN MARX, Administrative State.

**Chicago Literary Papyri:** GOODSPEED.

**Chicago Mental Growth Battery:** FREEMAN.

**Chicago and the Old Northwest:** QUAIFE.

**Chicago Police Problems:** CITIZENS' POLICE COMMITTEE.

**Chicago Press-Feeders' Wage Arbitration Case:** MEINE.

**Chicago Primary of 1926:** WOODDY.

**Chicago Public Library:** SPENCER.

**Chicago Regional Planning Association:** *see* JETER, Trends of Population in the Region of Chicago.

**Chicago Regional Planning Association,** *The Committee on General Surveys: see* FRYXELL, Physiography of the Region of Chicago.

**Chicago Review Anthology:** RAY.

**Chicago School of Architecture:** CONDIT.

**Chicago Syllabary and the Louvre Syllabary AO 7661:** HALLOCK.

**Chicago Vacation Schools for 1898:** MILLIKEN.

**Chicago's Famous Buildings:** SIEGEL.

**Chiera, Edward.** Sumerian Epics and Myths. 1934. xi, 9 pages. 112 plates with 117 texts in facsimile. 29 cm. OIP, XV. $5.00.

**Chiera, Edward.** Sumerian Lexical Texts from the Temple School of Nippur. 1929. xi, 19 p. 126 plates with 256 texts in facsimile. 30 cm. 29-28966. OIP, XI. $5.00.

**Chiera, Edward.** Sumerian Texts of Varied Contents. 1934. ix, 8 p. 109 plates with 135 texts in facsimile. 30 cm. 34-22547. OIP, XVI. $5.00.

**Chiera, Edward.** They Wrote on Clay. The Babylonian Tablets Speak Today. By Edward Chiera. Edited by George G. Cameron. 1938. xvi, 235 p. Illus. 38-27631. Cloth. 19 cm. $5.00ˢ. Paper. P2. 21 cm. $1.50.
". . . no mystery story can be as exciting as this revelation of the discovery of ancient life."—*Harper's Magazine*.

**Chiera, Edward:** *see* SMITH, Origin and History of Hebrew Law.

**Child, Charles Manning.** Individuality in Organisms. 1915. SCI. *o.p.*

**Child, Charles Manning.** The Origin and Development of the Nervous System, from a Physiological Viewpoint. 1921. SCI. *o.p.*

**Child, Charles Manning.** Patterns and Problems of Development. 1941. *o.p.*

**Child, Charles Manning.** Senescence and Rejuvenescence. 1915. *o.p.*

**Child and the Curriculum:** DEWEY.

**Child Development and the Curriculum:** WASHBURNE.

**Child and His Religion:** DAWSON.

**Child Psychology:** STEVENSON.

**Child Religion in Song and Story:** CHAMBERLIN.

**Child and the State:** ABBOTT.

**Child Study Association of America:** *see* GRUENBERG, Use of Radio in Parent Education.

**Child Welfare Case Records:** WALKER.

**Child Welfare in Germany:** FRIEDLANDER.

**Childbirth:** LEE.

**Childhood in Contemporary Cultures:** MEAD.

**Children and Movies:** MITCHELL.

**Children of Preschool Age:** KAWIN.

**Children Who Cannot Read:** MONROE.

**Children's Behavior Problems:** ACKERSON.

**Children's Drawings of the Human Figure:** ZESBAUGH.

**Children's Preferences for Colors:** GALE.

**Children's Preferences for Pictures:** MORRISON.

**Childress, J. R.,** *joint ed.:* MCSWAIN, Opportunities for Education.

**Child's Emotions:** CHICAGO ASSOCIATION FOR CHILD STUDY.

**China and Japan in Our Museums:** MARCH.

**China and Japan in Our University Curricula:** CARTER.

**China in Revolution:** MACNAIR.

**China's Gentry:** FEI.

**Chinese Architecture and Town Planning:** BOYD.

**Chinese Calligraphy:** DRISCOLL.

**Chinese Farm Economy:** BUCK.

**Chinese Painting:** FERGUSON.

**Chinese Poems in English Rhyme:** TS'AI T'INGKAN.

**Chinese Renaissance:** HU.

**Chinese Social Origins:** RUDD.

**Chinese Thought from Confucius to Mao Tsê-tung:** CREEL.

**Chinese Thought and Institutions:** FAIRBANK.

**Chiricahua and Mescalero Apache Texts:** HOIJER.

**Chirol, Sir Valentine.** The Occident and the Orient. 1924. HFL. *o.p.*

**Choldin, Mariana,** *joint trans.:* JENSEN, Myth and Cult.

**Cholera Years:** ROSENBERG.

**Chorti Indians of Guatemala:** WISDOM.

**Choulant, Johann Ludwig.** History and Bibliography of Anatomic Illustration in Its Relation to Anatomic Science and the Graphic Arts. Translated and Edited with Notes and a Biography by Mortimer Frank. With a Biographical Sketch of the Translator and Two Additional Sections by Fielding H. Garrison and Edward C. Streeter. 1920. *o.p.*

**Christ, Jay Finley,** *joint author:* MARSHALL, Outlines of the Economic Order.

**Christ and the Eastern Soul:** HALL.

**Christenson, Carroll Lawrence.** Collective Bargaining in Chicago, 1929–30. A Study of the Economic Significance of the Industrial Location of Trade-Unionism. 1933. SSCI. *o.p.*

**Christian Belief:** HALL.

**Christian Faith for Men of Today:** COOK.

**Christian Ideal:** McCONNELL.

**Christian Philosophy of History:** CASE.

**Christian Salvation:** CROSS.

**Christian Way:** LEBERMAN.

**Christianity:** BURTON.

**Christianity and Its Bible:** WARING.

**Christiansen, Reidar Th.,** *ed.* Folktales of Norway. Translated by Pat Shaw Iversen. 1964. 328 p. 64-15830. FW. $5.50. COBE.

**Christie, Francis Albert:** *see* SMITH, Guide to the Study of the Christian Religion.

**Christ-Janer, Albert.** Boardman Robinson. 1946. *o.p.*

**Christ-Janer, Albert.** Eliel Saarinen. 1948. *o.p.*

**Christology:** STARK.

**Christology of the Epistle to the Hebrews:** MacNEILL.

**Christoph, James B.** Capital Punishment and British Politics. 1962. iv, 202 p. 22 cm. 62-12639. $4.00ˢ. USA.

**Chronicle of Jeopardy:** TUGWELL.

**Chronicle of John Malalas:** SPINKA.

**Chronologies in Old World Archaeology:** EHRICH.

**Chudoba, Bohdan.** Spain and the Empire. 1952. *o.p.*

**Church, Phil E.** The Annual Temperature Cycle of Lake Michigan. *Part I:* Cooling from Late Autumn to the Terminal Point, 1941–42. *Part II:* Spring Warming and Summer Stationary Period, 1942. 1943. DMMR 4 and 18. *o.p.*

**Church School:** HOBEN.

**Church School Projects:** SHAVER.

**Church and State in Education:** BOWER.

**Church at Work in the Modern World:** BOWER.

**Cicero, Marcus Tullius.** Brutus, *On the Nature of the Gods, On Divination, On Duties.* Translated by Hubert M. Poteat. 1950. C.E. *o.p.*

**CIO and the Democratic Party:** CALKINS.

**Cioffari, Vincenzo,** *joint author:* HCLS.
Amici di scuola (with John Van Horne).
Giulietta e Romeo, e altre novelle (with John Van Horne).
Raccontini (with John Van Horne).

**Citizen Co-operation for Better Public Schools:** MORPHET.

**Citizens' Police Committee.** Chicago Police Problems. By the Citizens' Police Committee, Bruce Smith, director. 1931. *o.p.*

**City, The:** AMERICAN SOCIOLOGICAL SOCIETY, Annual Proceedings, Vol. XX.

**City, The:** PARK.

**City Club of Chicago.** The Railway Terminal Problem of Chicago. A Series of Addresses before the City Club, June Third to Tenth, 1913, Dealing with the Proposed Reorganization of the Railway Terminals of Chicago, Including All Terminal Proposals Now before the City Council Committee on Railway Terminals. 1913. CC. *o.p.*

**City Club of Chicago:** *see* Financial Mobilization for War.

**City Club of Chicago Publications** (CC). From May, 1916, to March, 1938, The University of Chicago Press was publisher for the Club.

CASSELS, Short Ballot.
CITY CLUB OF CHICAGO, Railway Terminal Problem of Chicago.
HOOKER, Through Routes for Chicago's Steam Railroads.
MEAD, Report on Vocational Training.
MERRIAM, Municipal Revenues.
YEOMANS, City Residential Land Development.

**City Institute for Religious Teachers:** ATHEARN.

**City Invincible:** KRAELING.

**City Manager:** WHITE.

**City-Manager Profession:** RIDLEY.

**City Planning for Girls:** ADDITON.

**City Planning in Soviet Russia:** PARKINS.

**City Residential Land Development:** YEOMANS.

**City School as a Community Center:** LEIPZIGER.

**Cityward Migration. Swedish Data:** MOORE.

**Civic Attitudes in American School Textbooks:** PIERCE.

**Civic Training in Soviet Russia:** HARPER.

**Civic Training in Switzerland:** BROOKS.

**Civil Liberties and the Vinson Court:** PRITCHETT.

**Civil-Military Relationships:** KERWIN.

**Civil Service in the Modern State:** WHITE.

**Civil Service in Wartime:** WHITE.

**Civil War:** HENDERSON.

**Civilization and Disease:** SIGERIST.

**Civilization of the Renaissance:** THOMPSON.

**Civilizations of Ancient America:** TAX.

**Clancy, Joseph P.,** *trans.:* HORACE, Odes and Epodes.

**Clapp, Gordon R.** The TVA. An Approach to the Development of a Region. 1955. WFL. *o.p.*

**Clark, Frank Lowry.** A Study of the Iliad in Translation. 1927. *o.p.*

**Clark, Hannah Belle.** The Public Schools of Chicago. A Sociological Study. 1897. *o.p.*

**Clark, John Maurice.** Adam Smith, 1776–1926. Lectures To Commemorate the Sesquicentennial of the Publication of *The Wealth of Nations.* By John Maurice Clark, Paul H. Douglas, Jacob H. Hollander, Glenn R. Morrow, Melchior Palyi, and Jacob Viner. 1928. SE. *o.p.*

**Clark, John Maurice.** Studies in the Economics of Overhead Costs. 1923. xiv, 502 p. Illus. 21 cm. 24-2488. SE. $9.50ˢ.

**Clark, John Maurice,** *ed.* Readings in the Economics of War. Edited by J. Maurice Clark, Walton H. Hamilton, and Harold G. Moulton. 1918. MSE. *o.p.*

**Clark, John Roscoe,** *joint author:* RUGG, Scientific Method in the Reconstruction of Ninth-Grade Mathematics.

**Clark, Kenneth Willis.** A Descriptive Catalogue of Greek New Testament Manuscripts in America. Introduction by Edgar J. Goodspeed. 1937. *o.p.*

**Clark, Kenneth Willis.** Eight American Praxapostoloi. 1941. *o.p.*

**Clark, Marion Elizabeth.** Art in Home Economics. A Bibliography of Costume Design, History of Costume, Interior Decoration, History of Furniture, Architecture, Art Principles, and Art Appreciation. Compiled by Marion E. Clark and others. 1925. HE. *o.p.*

**Clark, W. E. LeGros.** The Fossil Evidence for Human Evolution. An Introduction to the Study of Paleoanthropology. 2d ed. 1964. xii, 200 p. 22 cm. 64-22250. SLBM. $6.00.

"In a short survey for nonspecialists, the reader expects to find sharp corners rounded off, controversies glibly evaded or ignored. Professor LeGros Clark has no such intention. On the contrary, he has written a highly stimulating book which not only summarizes the cogent material, but also expresses some unorthodox theories. . . . Anyone who wishes to explore the subject further will appreciate the detailed bibliography."—*Journal of the American Medical Association.*

**Clark, W. E. LeGros.** History of the Primates. 4th ed. 1963. 188 p. 21 cm. 57-14053. Paper. P21. $1.25. COBE.

**Clark, Walter Eugene,** *trans.:* ĀRYABHAṬA, Āryabhaṭiya.

**Clarke, E. R.** Predictable Accuracy in Examinations. 1940. BJP. *o.p.*

**Class Size and University Costs:** REEVES.

**Classics in Anthropology** (CA). *Edited by* PAUL BOHANNAN:
MOONEY, Ghost-Dance Religion and the Sioux Outbreak of 1890.
TYLOR, Researches into the Early History of Mankind.

**Classification of American Glacial Deposits:** CHAMBERLIN.

**Classification of European Glacial Deposits:** GEIKIE.

**Classroom Problems in the Education of Gifted Children:** HENRY.

**Classroom Procedure Test in English Composition:** ANDERSON.

**Classroom Procedure Test in English Literature:** POLEY.

**Classroom Procedure Test in History:** WILSON.

**Classroom Procedure Test in Mathematics:** BRESLICH.

**Classroom Procedure Test in Natural Science:** CUNNINGHAM.

**Classroom Procedure Test for Rating Methods of Teaching in Junior and Senior High Schools.** WAPLES.

**Classroom Techniques in Improving Reading:** GRAY.

**Clemen, Rudolf Alexander.** By-Products in the Packing Industry. 1927. *o.p.*

**Clement, Ernest Wilson.** A Short History of Japan. 1915. *o.p.*

**Clement, John Addison.** Standardization of the Schools of Kansas. 1912. *o.p.*

**Cleveland, Catharine Caroline.** The Great Revival in the West, 1797–1805. 1916. *o.p.*

**Clifford, Esther Rowland.** A Knight of Great Renown. 1961. xvii, 313 p. Illus. 22 cm. 60-14361. $6.50ˢ.

**Clift, David H.** Adult Reading. Prepared by David H. Clift, Chairman of the Society's Committee. 1956. NSSE, 55th Yrbk., Part II. 24 cm. 56-1104. Cloth. $4.50ᵗ. Paper. $3.75ᵗ.

**Climate Reprints:** CHAPMAN.

**Climatic Study of Cloudiness over Japan:** LANSBERG.

**Climatology of the Mediterranean Area:** BIEL.

**Cline, Dorothy I.** Training for Recreation under the W.P.A. An Account of the In-Service Training Program Division of Recreation, October, 1935–October, 1937. 1940. *o.p.*

**Clinical Epidemiology:** PAUL.

**Clinical Studies in Reading. I:** STAFF OF THE READING CLINICS.

**Clinical Studies in Reading. II:** ROBINSON.

**Clough, Shepard Bancroft,** *joint author:* SCHNEIDER, Making Fascists.

**Cobb, James Harrel.** A Biography and Bibliography of Edgar Johnson Goodspeed. By James Harrel Cobb and Louis B. Jennings. 1948. *o.p.*

**Cobban, Alfred.** National Self-determination. 1948. *o.p.*

**Cochran, Grace.** Si nous lisions. By Grace Cochran and Helen M. Eddy. HCLS. *o.p.*

**Cochran, Grace,** *ed.* Pierrille. By Jules Clarétie. Adapted and edited by Grace Cochran and Helen M. Eddy. HCLS. *o.p.*

**Cochran, Grace,** *joint author:* EDDY, Basic French.

**Cochrane, Eric W.** Tradition and Enlightenment in the Tuscan Academies, 1690–1800. 1962. xxii, 268 p. 25 cm. 60-14232. $6.00ᵒ.

**Coe, George Albert.** Law and Freedom in the School. "Can and Cannot," "Must and Must Not," "Ought and Ought Not" in Pupils' Projects. 1924. *o.p.*

**Coe, George Albert.** The Psychology of Religion. 1916. HER. *o.p.*

**Coffinberry, A. S.,** *ed.* The Metal Plutonium. Edited by A. S. Coffinberry and W. N. Miner. 1961. xi, 446 p. Illus. 24 cm. 61-17072. $9.50ˢ.

**Cohen, Arthur A.** The Communism of Mao Tse-tung. 1964. 210 p. 22 cm. 64-23420.

**Cohen, Hymen Ezra.** Recent Theories of Sovereignty. 1937. *o.p.*

**Cohn, Alfred Einstein.** Medicine, Science, and Art. Studies in Interrelations. 1931. *o.p.*

**Cohn, Gustav.** The Science of Finance. By Gustav Cohn. Translated by T. V. Veblen. 1895. EC. *o.p.*

**Colburn, Evangeline.** Books and Library Reading for Pupils in the Intermediate Grades. 1942. PLS 10. *o.p.*

**Colby, Charles Carlyle.** Source Book for the Economic Geography of North America. 1921. 3d ed. 1926. *o.p.*

**Colby, Charles Carlyle,** *ed.* Geographic Aspects of International Relations. By Isaiah Bowman, Pierre Dennis, Harlan H. Barrows, Derwent Whittlesey, Richard Hartshorne, Preston E. James, Robert S. Platt. 1938. HFL. *o.p.*

**Colby, Charles Carlyle,** *ed.:* FINCH, Geographic Surveys.

**Colby, Charles Carlyle:** *see* LAVES, Foundations of a More Stable World Order.

**Colby, Mary Ruth,** *joint author:* PUTTEE, Illegitimate Child in Illinois.

**Cold-Storage Industry in the United States:** DUDDY.

**Cole, Arthur Charles.** Lincoln's "Housedivided" Speech. Did It Reflect a Doctrine of Class Struggle? 1923. *o.p.*

**Cole, Fay-Cooper.** Kincaid. A Prehistoric Illinois Metropolis. 1951. AN. *o.p.*

**Cole, Fay-Cooper.** Rediscovering Illinois. Archaeological Explorations in and around Fulton County. By Fay-Cooper Cole and Thorne Deuel. 1937. AN. *o.p.*

**Cole, Fay-Cooper:** *see* MOULTON, World and Man.

**Cole, Fay-Cooper:** *see* NEWMAN, Nature of the World and of Man.

**Cole, George Watson.** An Index to Bibliographical Papers. Published by the Bibliographical Society and the Library Association, London, 1877–1932. 1933. *o.p.*

**Coleman, Algernon.** An Analytical Bibliography of Modern Language Teaching, Vol. I, 1927–32. Compiled for the Committee on Modern Language Teaching by Algernon Coleman with the assistance of Agnes Jacques. 1933. *o.p.*

**Coleman, Algernon.** An Analytical Bibliography of Modern Language Teaching, Vol. II, 1927–37. Compiled and edited for the Committee on Modern Languages by Algernon Coleman with the assistance of Clara Breslove King. 1938. *o.p.*

**Coleman, Algernon.** Experiments and Studies in Modern Language Teaching. Compiled for the Committee on Modern Language Teaching by Algernon Coleman. 1934. *o.p.*

**Coleman, Algernon.** Le Soldat américain en France. By Algernon Coleman and A. Marin La Meslée. Cover design by Walter Sargent. 1917. *o.p.*

**Coleman, Algernon,** *joint author:* WILKINS, Army French.

**Coleman, Algernon,** *joint author:* WILKINS, First Lessons in Spoken French for Doctors and Nurses.

**Coleman, Algernon,** *joint author:* WILKINS, First Lessons in Spoken French for Men in Military Service.

**Coleridge, Opium, and Kubla Khan:** SCHNEIDER.

**Coles, Harry L.** The War of 1812. 1965. ix, 298 p. Illus. 21 cm. 65-17283. CHAC. $5.95.

**Collected Papers of Enrico Fermi:** FERMI.

**Collected Poems:** OLSON.

**Collective Bargaining in Chicago:** CHRISTENSON.

**Collective Bargaining under Section 7(a) of the National Industrial Recovery Act:** SPENCER.

**Collective Security:** POTTER.

**College Algebra:** ALBERT.

**College Course of Laboratory Experiments:** STRATTON.

**College Course in the Principles of Education:** MacVANNEL.

**College Courses in Education:** NATIONAL SOCIETY OF COLLEGE TEACHERS OF EDUCATION, *Proceedings*, No. 8.

**College Curriculum Based on Functional Needs of Students:** HEATON.

**College Library:** RANDALL.

**College Library of Biological Science** (CLBS). *Edited by* RALPH BUCHSBAUM:

LI, Population Genetics.
NEEL, Human Heredity.
SCOTT, Animal Behavior.

**College Professor of the Renaissance:** LYNN.

**Collegiate School of Business:** MARSHALL.

**Collier, Donald,** *joint author:* MARTIN, Indians before Columbus.

**Collier, John, Jr.** The Awakening Valley. By John Collier, Jr., and Anibal Buitron. 1949. *o.p.*

**Colligan, F. J.,** *joint author:* JOHNSON, Fulbright Program.

**Collins, Leo C.** Hercules Seghers. 1953. xi, 149 p. Illus. 31 cm. 53-12895. $20.00ˢ.

**Collins, Tom** [Joseph Furphy]. Such Is Life. 1948. *o.p.*

**Colloids:** LEMON.

**Colloquies of Erasmus:** ERASMUS.

**Colonial Craftsman:** BRIDENBAUGH.

**Colonial Policy:** KAT ANGELINO.

**Colonial Wars:** PECKHAM.

**Colwell, Ernest Cadman.** The Greek of the Fourth Gospel. A Study of Its Aramaisms in the Light of Hellenistic Greek. 1931. *o.p.*

**Colwell, Ernest Cadman.** A Hellenistic Greek Reader. Selections from the Koine of the New Testament Period. With Vocabulary and Notes. By Ernest Cadman Colwell and Julius R. Mantey. 1939. *o.p.*

**Colwell, Ernest Cadman.** The Study of the Bible. Rev. ed. 1964. xv, 202 p. 21 cm. 64-23411. Cloth. $5.00ˢ. Paper. P164. $1.75.

**Colwell, Ernest Cadman.** What Is the Best New Testament? 1952. *o.p.*

**Colwell, Ernest Cadman,** *ed.* The Four Gospels of Karahissar. Edited by Ernest Cadman Colwell and Harold Rideout Willoughby. 2 vols. 1936. *o.p.*

**Colwell, Ernest Cadman,** *ed.* Prolegomena to the Study of the Lectionary Text of the Gospels. Edited by Ernest Cadman Colwell and Donald W. Riddle. 1933. LT. *o.p.*

**Colwell, Ernest Cadman,** *joint author:* GOODSPEED, Greek Papyrus Reader.

**Colwell, Ernest Cadman,** *joint ed.* STUDIES IN THE LECTIONARY TEXT OF THE GREEK NEW TESTAMENT.

**Colwell, Ernest Cadman,** *joint ed.* WILLOUGHBY, Elizabeth Day McCormick Apocalypse.

**Comenius, Johann Amos.** The Analytical Didactic of Comenius [Jan Amos Komensky]. Translated from the Latin by Vladimir Jelinek. 1953. *o.p.*

**Comic and the Realistic in English Drama:** MOORE.

**Coming of the Age of Steel:** WERTIME.

**Coming of the Civil War:** CRAVEN.

**Commager, Henry Steele.** Henry Adams: *see* HUTCHINSON, Marcus W. Jernegan Essays.

**Commentariolum petitionis:** HENDRICKSON.

**Commentary on Kant's Critique of Practical Reason:** BECK.

**Commerce and Administration:** *see* JOURNAL OF BUSINESS OF THE UNIVERSITY OF CHICAGO.

**Committee on the Costs of Medical Care** (CMC):

1. Five-Year Program of the Committee on the Costs of Medical Care.
2. MILLS, Extent of Illness.
3. PEEBLES, Survey of Statistical Data on Medical Facilities.
4. CARPENTER, Hospital Service.
5. CARPENTER, Medical Care for 15,000 Workers.
6. PEEBLES, Survey of the Medical Facilities of Shelby County, Indiana.
7. ROREM, Capital Investment in Hospitals.
8. ROREM, Private Group Clinics.
9. SINAI, Survey of the Medical Facilities of the City of Philadelphia.
10. SINAI, Study of Physicians and Dentists.

11. ROREM, "Municipal Doctor" System in Rural Saskatchewan.
12. SINAI, Survey of the Medical Facilities of San Joaquin County, California.
13. PEEBLES, Survey of the Medical Facilities of the State of Vermont.
14. ROREM, Costs of Medicines.
15. REED, Midwives, Chiropodists, and Optometrists.
16. REED, Healing Cults.
17. PEEBLES, Nursing Services and Insurance for Medical Care in Brattleboro, Vermont.
18. REED, Medical Service of the Homestake Mining Company.
19. GRISWOLD, University Student Health Services.
20. FALK, Community Medical Service Organized under Industrial Auspices in Roanoke Rapids, North Carolina.
21. FALK, Organized Medical Service at Fort Benning, Georgia.
22. LEE, Fundamentals of Good Medical Care.
23. GUILD, Surveys of the Medical Facilities in Three Representative Southern Counties.
24. LEVEN, Incomes of Physicians.
25. REED, Ability To Pay for Medical Care.
26. FALK, Incidence of Illness and the Receipt and Costs of Medical Care.
27. FALK, Costs of Medical Care.
28. Medical Care for the American People.

**Committee on the Costs of Medical Care.** Five-Year Program of the Committee on the Costs of Medical Care. 1928. CMC 1. *o.p.*

**Committee on the Costs of Medical Care.** Medical Care for the American People. The Final Report of the Committee on the Costs of Medical Care. 1932. CMC 28. *o.p.*

**Committee on Materials.** New Materials of Instruction. Prepared by the Society's Committee on Materials of Instruction. 1920. NSSE, 19th Yrbk., Part I. *o.p.*

**Committee on Materials.** New Materials of Instruction. Prepared by the Society's Committee on Materials of Instruction, Second Report. 1921. NSSE, 20th Yrbk., Part I. *o.p.*

**Commodity Dollar:** GIDEONSE.

**Common Stocks and Bonds as Long-Term Investments:** SPURRIER.

**Common Text of the Gospel Lectionary:** BRANTON.

**Commonwealth Teacher-Training Study:** CHARTERS.

**Communication in Management:** REDFIELD.

**Communism of Mao Tse-tung:** COHEN.

**Communitas:** GOODMAN.

**Community Church:** ZUMBRUNNEN.

**Community Education:** ARNDT.

**Community Life and Social Policy:** WIRTH.

**Community Medical Service Organized under Industrial Auspices in Roanoke Rapids, N.C.:** FALK.

**Community Organization for Social Welfare:** McMILLEN.

**Community Responsibilities of Institutions of Higher Learning:** BURNS.

**Community School:** SEAY.

**Community Youth Development Program:** HAVIGHURST.

**Comparative Archeology of Early Mesopotamia:** PERKINS.

**Comparative Grammar of Greek and Latin:** BUCK.

**Comparative Stratigraphy of Early Iran:** McCOWN.

**Comparative Studies of Cultures and Civilizations (CSCC):**

FAIRBANK, Chinese Thought and Institutions.
GRUNEBAUM, Unity and Variety in Muslim Civilization.
HOIJER, Language in Culture.
MARRIOTT, Village India.
REDFIELD, Little Community.
WRIGHT, Studies in Chinese Thought.

**Comparative Study of Cataloging Rules Based on the Anglo-American Code of 1908:** HANSON.

**Comparative Study of Hesiod and Pindar:** SCOTT.

**Comparative Study of the Lower Cretaceous Formations:** STANTON.

**Comparative Study of a Nursery-School versus a Non-Nursery-School Group:** KAWIN.

**Comparative Study of the Play Activities of Adult Savages and Civilized Children:** APPLETON.

**Comparative Vertebrate Anatomy:** HYMAN.

**Comparison of the Photometric Fields of the 6-Inch Doublet, 24-Inch Reflector, and 40-Inch Refractor of the Yerkes Observatory:** FARNSWORTH.

**Comparison of Stellar Spectra:** HALE.

**Complete Bible:** SMITH.

**Complete Greek Tragedies** (CGT). *Edited by* DAVID GRENE *and* RICHMOND LATTIMORE:

**Aeschylus I.** Oresteia. Agamemnon, The Libation Bearers, The Eumenides. Translated and with an Introduction by Richmond Lattimore. 1953. vii, 171 p. 22 cm. 53-9655. Paper. $1.50t.

**Aeschylus II.** Four Tragedies. Prometheus Bound, Seven against Thebes. Translated by David Grene. The Persians, The Suppliant Maidens. Translated by Seth G. Benardete. 1956. vii, 179 p. 22 cm. 56-11262. Paper. $1.75t.

**Euripides I.** Four Tragedies. Alcestis. Translated by Richmond Lattimore. The Medea. Translated by Rex Warner. The Heracleidae. Translated by Ralph Gladstone. Hippolytus. Translated by David Grene. With an Introduction by Richmond Lattimore. 1955. ix, 221 p. 22 cm. 55-5787. Paper. $1.65t.

**Euripides II.** Four Tragedies. The Cyclops. Translated by William Arrowsmith. Heracles. Translated by William Arrowsmith. Iphigenia in Tauris. Translated by Witter Bynner. Helen. Translated by Richmond Lattimore. 1956. vi, 264 p. 22 cm. 55-5787. Paper. $1.50t.

**Euripides III.** Four Tragedies. Hecuba. Translated by William Arrowsmith. Andromache. Translated by John Frederick Nims. The Trojan Women. Translated by Richmond Lattimore. Ion. Translated by Ronald Frederick Willets. 1958. v, 255 p. 22 cm. 55-5787. Paper. $1.95t.

**Euripides IV.** Four Tragedies. Rhesus. Translated by Richmond Lattimore. The Suppliant Women. Translated by Frank William Jones. Orestes. Translated by William Arrowsmith. Iphigenia in Aulis. Translated by Charles R. Walker. 1958. v, 308 p. 22 cm. 55-5787. Paper. $1.95t.

**Euripides V.** Three Tragedies. Electra. Translated by Emily Townsend Vermeule. The Phoenician Women. Translated by Elizabeth Wyckoff. The Bacchae. Translated by William Arrowsmith. 1959. v, 228 p. 22 cm. 55-5787. Paper. $1.95t.

**Sophocles I.** Oedipus the King. Translated by David Grene. Oedipus at Colonus. Translated by Robert Fitzgerald. Antigone. Translated by Elizabeth Wyckoff. With an Introduction by David Grene. 1954. vii, 206 p. 22 cm. 54-10731. Paper. $1.25t.

**Sophocles II.** Ajax. Translated by John Moore. The Women of Trachis. Translated by Michael Jameson. Electra. Translated by David Grene. Philoctetes. Translated by David Grene. 1957. v, 254 p. 22 cm. 54-10731. Paper. $1.95t.

**The above complete in a four-volume boxed set. $25.00. (Clothbound.)**

*See:* GREEK TRAGEDIES: PHOENIX.

"For the Greekless reader, there is no other translation to be considered."—Douglas Parker, in *The Hudson Review*.

"Offers better value than any other existing verse translation."—*Times Literary Supplement*.

**Complete Works of the Gawain-Poet:** GARDNER.

**Completion of the Yerkes Telescope:** HALE.

**Composing for the Jazz Orchestra:** RUSSO.

**Compound Oosphere of Albugo Bliti:** STEVENS.

**Comte de Monte-Cristo (Dumas):** MILLER.

**Concept of Time:** HEATH.

**Conception of Human Interrelations as a Variant of Social Theory:** AMERICAN SOCIOLOGICAL SOCIETY, Annual Proceedings. Vol. VII.

**Conception of a Kingdom of Ends:** STOKES.

**Conceptual Framework of Psychology:** BRUNSWIK.

**Conceptual Structure of Educational Research:** McCONNELL.

**Concerning Geodesic Curvature:** BOLZA.

**Concerning the Modern German Relatives, "Das" and "Was":** CUTTING.

**Concordance to the Complete Poetical Works of Sir Thomas Wyatt:** HANGEN.

**Condensations with Benzoin:** GARNER.

**Condit, Carl W.** The Chicago School of Architecture. A History of Commercial and Public Building in the Chicago Area. 1875–1925. 1964. xviii, 238 p. 196 plates. 25 cm. 64-13287. $8.50.

**Condit, Carl W.** The Rise of the Skyscraper. 1952. *o.p.*

**Condit, Lester.** A Pamphlet about Pamphlets. 1939. LS. *o.p.*

**Condit, Lester.** A Provisional Index to Roman Printing Types of the Fifteenth Century. 1935. *o.p.*

**Condliffe, John Bell.** New Zealand in the Making. A Survey of Economic and Social Development. 1930. *o.p.*

**Condliffe, John Bell,** *ed.* Problems of the Pacific. Proceedings of the Second Conference of the Institute of Pacific Relations, Honolulu, July, 1927. 1928. IPR. *o.p.*

**Condliffe, John Bell,** *ed.* Problems of the Pacific, 1929. Proceedings of the Third Conference of the Institute of Pacific Relations, Nara and Kyoto, Japan, Oct.–Nov., 1929. 1930. IPR. *o.p.*

**Condliffe, John Bell:** *see* HURST, Great Britain and the Dominions.

**Confederacy:** ROLAND.

**Confederate Ironclad "Virginia" ("Merrimac"):** TREXLER.

**Conference for Administrative Officers of Public and Private Schools. Proceedings (AOPPS):**
  I. REAVIS, Critical Issues in Educational Administration.
  II. REAVIS, Democratic Practices in School Administration.
  III. REAVIS, Evaluating the Work of the School.
  IV. REAVIS, Administrative Adjustments Required by Economic Change.
  V. REAVIS, The School and the Urban Community.
  VI. REAVIS, War and Postwar Responsibilities of American Schools.
  VII. REAVIS, Significant Aspects of American Life.
  VIII. REAVIS, Forthcoming Developments in American Education.
  IX. REAVIS, Educational Administration.
  X. COOPER, Administrative Planning for School Programs and Plants.
  XI. COOPER, Administration of Schools for Better Living.
  XII. LAWLER, Educational Administration in an Era of Transition.
  XIII. GRACE, Leadership in American Education.
  XIV. McSWAIN, Opportunities for Education in the Next Decade.

**Conference on Consumer Financing:** *see* COVER, Financing the Consumer.

**Conference on Economic Policy:** DUDDY.

**Conflicting Penal Theories in Statutory Criminal Law:** ELLIOTT.

**Congregationalists, 1783–1850:** SWEET.

**Congress and the Court:** MURPHY.

**Conjunktiv bei Hartmann von Aue:** CUTTING.

**Conklin, Edwin G.:** *see* COWDRY, General Cytology.

**Connecticut Wits:** HOWARD.

**Conquest of the Material World:** NEF.

**Conrad, Abram H.** A Contribution to the Life-History of Quercus. 1900. HB. *o.p.*

**Conrad, Joseph:** *see* HAY, Political Novels of Joseph Conrad.

**Constitution of the Argentine Republic and . . . Brazil:** WALLACE.

**Constitutional Right of Association:** FELLMAN.

**Constitutions of the Americas:** FITZGIBBONS.

**Constructive Social Analysis:** AMERICAN SOCIOLOGICAL SOCIETY, Annual Proceedings, Vol. XVII.

**Constructive Studies (CS):** Formerly *Constructive Bible Studies:*
ATKINSON, Story of Paul of Tarsus.
BURGESS, Life of Christ.
BURTON, Life of Christ.
BURTON, Studies in the Gospel According to Mark.
CHAMBERLIN, Books of the Holy Bible.
CHAMBERLIN, Child Religion in Song and Story.
CHAMBERLIN, Introduction to the Bible.
COOK, Christian Faith for Men of Today.
COPE, Religious Education in the Family.
CORBETT, Old Testament Story.

COWLES, Problems in Living.
DOWNING, Third and Fourth Generation.
FERRIS, Sunday Kindergarten.
GATES, Life of Jesus.
GILBERT, Short History of Christianity.
HARPER, Priestly Element in the Old Testament.
HARPER, Prophetic Element in the Old Testament.
HENDERSON, Social Duties from the Christian Point of View.
HENRY, Paul, Son of Kish.
JOHNSON, Problems of Boyhood.
LEBERMAN, Christian Way.
LOBINGIER, Hebrew Home Life.
LOBINGIER, Our Church.
LOBINGIER, Stories of Shepherd Life.
NEUBERG, Right Living.
PEABODY, Lives Worth Living.
RHODES, Religion in Kindergarten.
SHAVER, Young People's Projects.
SLATEN, What Jesus Taught.
SOARES, Heroes of Israel.
SOARES, Story of Paul.
STEREOGRAPH ILLUSTRATIONS.
WALKER, Great Men of the Christian Church.
WARING, Christianity and Its Bible.
WILLETT, Studies in First Book of Samuel.

**Constructive Studies in the Life of Christ:** *see* BURTON, Life of Christ.

**Consumers' Co-operative Movement in Illinois:** WARNE.

**Consumption of Meat and Meat Products:** COVER.

**Contemporary Social Problems:** WIRTH.

**Content and Style of an Oral Literature:** JACOBS.

**Contes** (Mendès, Saint Juvis, Pouvillon, Coppée, Erckmann-Chatrain): BOND.

**Contes de Maupassant:** ROWLAND.

**Contest for Liberty of Conscience:** ST. JOHN.

**Continued Fractions:** KHINCHIN.

**Continuity and Change in African Cultures:** BASCOM.

**Continuum of Inductive Methods:** CARNAP.

**Contrastive Structure Series (CSS).** CHARLES A. FERGUSON, *General Editor:*

AGARD, Grammatical Structures of English and Italian.

AGARD, Sounds of English and Italian.
KUFNER, Grammatical Structures of English and German.
MOULTON, Sounds of English and German.
STOCKWELL, Grammatical Structures of English and Spanish.
STOCKWELL, Sounds of English and Spanish.

**Contribution to the Comparative Physiology of Compensatory Motions:** LYON.

**Contribution to the Life-History of Euphorbia corollata:** LYON.

**Contribution to the Life-History of Lilium Philadelphicum:** COULTER.

**Contribution to the Life-History of the Pontederiaceae:** SMITH.

**Contribution to the Life-History of Quercus:** CONRAD.

**Contribution to the Life-History of Ranunculus:** COULTER.

**Contribution to the Life-History of Sagittaria variabilis:** SCHAFFNER.

**Contribution to the Life-History of Salix:** CHAMBERLAIN.

**Contribution to the Life-History of Silphium:** MERRELL.

**Contribution to the Physical Analysis of the Phenomena of Absorption:** WEBSTER.

**Contribution to the Theory of Glacial Motion:** CHAMBERLAIN.

**Contributions to the Calculus of Variations, 1930:** BLISS.

**Contributions to the Calculus of Variations, 1931–32:** BLISS.

**Contributions to the Calculus of Variations, 1933–37:** BLISS.

**Contributions to the Calculus of Variations, 1938–41:** BLISS.

**Contributions to Education (CE):**
1. YOUNG, Isolation in the School.
2. DEWEY, Psychology and Social Practice.
3. DEWEY, Educational Situation.
4. YOUNG, Ethics in the School.
5. DEWEY, Child and the Curriculum.
6. YOUNG, Some Types of Modern Educational Theory.

**Contributions from the Hull Botanical Laboratory (HB):**

I. CHAMBERLAIN, Embryo-Sac of Aster Novae-Angliae.

II. COULTER, Notes on the Fertilization and Embryogeny of Conifers.

III. CHAMBERLAIN, Contribution to the Life-History of Salix.

IV. SCHAFFNER, Contribution to the Life-History of Sagittaria variabilis.

V. COULTER, Contribution to the Life-History of Lilium Philadelphicum.

VI. SCHAFFNER, Development of the Stamens and Carpels of Typha latifolia.

VII. COULTER, Contribution to the Life-History of Ranunculus.

VIII. CHAMBERLAIN, Winter Characters of Certain Sporangia.

IX. SMITH, Contribution to the Life-History of the Pontederiaceæ.

X. LYON, Contribution to the Life-History of Euphorbia corollata.

XI. STEVENS, Effect of Aqueous Solutions upon the Germination of Fungus Spores.

XII. CALDWELL, On the Life-History of Lemna minor.

XIII. COWLES, Ecological Relations of the Vegetation on the Sand Dunes of Lake Michigan.

XIV. CHAMBERLAIN, Oögenesis in Pinus laricio.

XV. DAVIS, Spore Mother-Cell of Anthoceros.

XVI. STEVENS, Compound Oosphere of Albugo bliti.

XVII. MERRELL, Contribution to the Life-History of Silphium.

XVIII. SMITH, Structure and Development of the Sporophylls and Sporangia of Isoetes.

XIX. DAVIS, Fertilization of Albugo candida.

XX. CONRAD, Contribution to the Life-History of Quercus.

XXI. LAND, Double Fertilization in Compositae.

XXII. LIVINGSTON, On the Nature of the Stimulus Which Causes the Change in Form in Polymorphic Green Algæ.

XXIII. SMITH, Achromatic Spindle in the Spore Mother-Cells of Osmunda regalis.

XXIV. COWLES, Physiographic Ecology of Chicago and Vicinity.

XXV. DAVIS, Nuclear Studies on Pellia.

XXVI. LIFE, Tuber-like Rootlets of Cycas revoluta.

XXVII. WHITFORD, Genetic Development of the Forests of Northern Michigan.

XXVIII. HOLFERTY, Ovule and Embryo of Potamogeton natans.

XXIX. STEVENS, Gametogenesis and Fertilization in Albugo.

XXX. BRAY, Ecological Relations of the Vegetation of Western Texas.

XXXI. LYON, Study of the Sporangia and Gametophytes of Selaginella apus and Selaginella rupestris.

XXXII. FRYE, Development of the Pollen in Some Asclepiadaceae.

XXXIII. Not published.

XXXIV. Not published.

XXXV. OVERTON, Parthenogenesis in Thalictrum purpurascens.

XXXVI. WEBB, Morphological Study of the Flower and Embryo of Spiraea.

XXXVII. McCALLUM, On the Nature of the Stimulus Causing the Change of Form and Structure in Proserpinaca palustris.

XXXVIII. COPELAND, Rise of the Transpiration Stream.

XXXIX. LAND, Morphological Study of Thuja.

XL. SNOW, Some Notes on the Ecology of the Delaware Coast.

XLI. FRYE, Morphological Study of Certain Asclepiadaceae.

**Contributions to Medical Science:** RICKETTS.

**Contributions to Urban Sociology:** BURGESS.

**Contributions from Walker Museum of the University of Chicago (WM):**

Vol. I. 1917:

No. 1. CASE, Vertebrates from the Permian Bone Bed of Vermilion County, Illinois.

2. SMITH, Prodromites.

3. CASE, Palæontological Notes.

4. CASE, New or Little-known Vertebrates.

5. WELLER, Stokes Collection of Antarctic Fossils.

6. CASE, Osteology of the Skull of . . . Dimetrodon.

Vol. II. Not published as a single volume.

No. 1. DOUTHITT, Structure and Relationship of Diplocaulus.

2. WILLISTON, Labidosaurus Cope.

3. WILLISTON, Phylogeny and Classification of Reptiles.

4. WILLISTON, Evolution of Vertebrae.

5. CHANEY, Flora of the Eagle Creek Formation.
6. BRADLEY, Fauna of the Kimmswick Limestone.
7. BRANSON, Notes on Some Carboniferous Cochliodonts.
8. WILLISTON, Osteology of Some American Permian Vertebrates. I.
9. WILLISTON, Osteology of Some American Permian Vertebrates. II.
10. WELLER, Atactocrinus.

**Control of Body Temperature:** CARLSON.

**Control of Hunger:** CARLSON.

**Control of Radio:** KERWIN.

**Controlled Reading:** TAYLOR.

**Controversial Issues in Reading and Promising Solutions:** ROBINSON.

**Convalescent Care in Great Britain:** GARDINER.

**Convention That Nominated Lincoln:** RAY.

**Conversational Chinese:** TÊNG.

**Cook, Ezra Albert.** Christian Faith for Men of Today. 1913. 2d ed. 1920. CS. *o.p.*

**Cook, Mercer,** *ed.* Portraits américains. Collection "Arts et sciences" Series. HCLS. *o.p.*

**Cooper, Dan H.,** *ed.* The Administration of Schools for Better Living. 1948. AOPPS, XI. *o.p.*

**Cooper, Dan H.,** *ed.* Administrative Planning for School Programs and Plants. 1947. AOPPS, X. *o.p.*

**Cooper, Dan H.,** *joint author:* LAWLER, Educational Administration.

**Cooper, Dan H.,** *joint author:* REAVIS, Evaluation of Teacher Merit.

**Cooper, Grosvenor.** Learning To Listen. A Handbook for Music. 1957. xiii, 188 p. 23 cm. 57-8579. Paper. P79. $1.50.

**Cooper, Grosvenor.** The Rhythmic Structure of Music. By Grosvenor Cooper and Leonard B. Meyer. 1960. ix, 212 p. Index. 60-14068. Cloth. 25 cm. $6.00ˢ. Paper. P118. 23 cm. $1.95.

**Cooper, Isabella.** Bibliography on Educational Broadcasting. 1942. *o.p.*

**Co-operative Efforts in Schools To Improve Reading:** GRAY.

**Co-operative Society of America:** WARNE.

**Cooperman, Norman Roy:** *see* KLEITMAN, Sleep Characteristics.

**Co-ordination of the Kindergarten and the Elementary School:** GREGORY.

**Cope, Henry Frederick.** Religious Education in the Family. 1915. CS. *o.p.*

**Copeland, Edwin B.** The Rise of the Transpiration Stream. 1902. HB 38. *o.p.*

**Copeland, Thomas,** *General Editor:* BURKE, Correspondence of Edmund Burke.

**Copperheads in the Middle West:** KLEMENT.

**Coptic Ostraca from Medinet Habu:** STEFANSKI.

**Cora. Vier Lausbubengeschichten (Thoma):** DIAMOND.

**Corbett, Charles H.** Old Testament Story. 1912. CS. *o.p.*

**Corbett, Percy Ellwood:** *see* WRIGHT, Interpretations of American Foreign Policy.

**Coregency of Ramses II with Seti I:** SEELE.

**Corey, Stephen M.** Audio-Visual Materials of Instruction. Prepared by Stephen M. Corey, Chairman of the Society's Committee. 1949. NSSE, 48th Yrbk., Part I. x, 320 p. 24 cm. 49-8494. Cloth. $4.50ᵗ.

**Corey, Stephen M.,** *ed.* In-Service Education for Teachers, Supervisors, and Administrators. 1956. NSSE, 56th Yrbk., Part I. xlv, 376 p. 24 cm. 57-631. Cloth. $4.50ᵗ. Paper. $3.75ᵗ.

**Cornelia:** MAXEY.

**Corrective Reading in Classroom and Clinic:** ROBINSON.

**Correlated Mathematics for Junior Colleges:** BRESLICH.

**Correlations of Isallobaric Patterns:** BICE.

**Correspondence of Edmund Burke:** BURKE.

**Cosenza, Mario Emilio.** Francesco Petrarca and the Revolution of Cola di Rienzo. 1913. *o.p.*

**Cosenza, Mario Emilio,** *trans.* Petrarch's Letters to Classical Authors. Translated from the Latin with a Commentary by Mario Emilio Cosenza. 1910. *o.p.*

**Cosmology:** FINLAY-FREUNDLICH.

**Cost of Adequate Medical Care:** BRADBURY.

**Cost of Equipping a Dental Office:** BECK.

**Cost under the Unfair Practices Acts:** TANNENBAUM.

**Costs of Medical Care:** FALK.

**Costs of Medicines:** ROREM.

**Cotton Kingdom:** TRYON.

**Cottrell, Leonard S., Jr.,** *joint author:* FOOTE, Identity and Interpersonal Competence.

**Cottrell, Leonard S., Jr.:** *see* SHAW, Delinquency Areas.

**Coulborn, Rushton.** A Farewell to Leadership. Britain and the World, 1919–39: *see* BENES, International Security.

**Coulter, John Merle.** Contribution to the Life-History of Lilium Philadelphicum. By John M. Coulter, Charles J. Chamberlain, and John H. Schaffner. 1897. HB. *o.p.*

**Coulter, John Merle.** Contribution to the Life-History of Ranunculus. 1898. HB. *o.p.*

**Coulter, John Merle.** The Evolution of Sex in Plants. 1914. SCI. *o.p.*

**Coulter, John Merle.** Morphology of Gymnosperms. By John M. Coulter and Charles J. Chamberlain. 1910. Rev. ed. 1917. *o.p.*

**Coulter, John Merle.** Notes on the Fertilization and Embryogeny of Conifers. 1897. HB. *o.p.*

**Coulter, John Merle.** The Phylogeny of Angiosperms. 1903. *o.p.*

**Coulter, John Merle.** Plant Genetics. By John M. Coulter and Merle C. Coulter. 1918. *o.p.*

**Coulter, John Merle:** *see* CASTLE, Heredity and Eugenics.

**Coulter, John Merle:** *see* GORDON, Truth about the Bible.

**Coulter, John Wesley.** Fiji. The Little India of the Pacific. 1942. *o.p.*

**Coulter, John Wesley:** *see* HAAS, American Empire.

**Coulter, Merle C.** Outline of Genetics. With Special Reference to Plant Material. 1923. *o.p.*

**Coulter, Merle C.** The Story of the Plant Kingdom. Revised by Howard J. Dittmer. 3d ed. 1964. ix, 467 p. Illus. 23 cm. 64-10093. $5.75ᵗ.

**Coulter, Merle C.,** *ed.* Introductory General Course in the Biological Sciences Syllabus. Edited by Merle C. Coulter with the co-operation of Warder C. Allee, Ralph Buchsbaum, Anton J. Carlson, Fay-Cooper Cole, Lester R. Dragstedt, Alfred Emerson, Ralph W. Gerard, Victor Johnson, Carl R. Moore, F. Joseph Mullin, Horatio H. Newman, Alfred S. Romer, Joseph Schwab, Herluf H. Strandskow, William Taliaferro, Louis L. Thurstone, H. Gideon Wells, and Dael Wolfle. 1931. 11th ed. 1941. *o.p.*

**Coulter, Merle C.,** *joint author:* COULTER, Plant Genetics.

**Coulter, Merle C.:** *see* MOULTON, World and Man.

**Coulter, Merle C.:** *see* NEWMAN, Nature of the World and of Man.

**Counter-Statement:** BURKE.

**Country Church:** BUTTERFIELD.

**Country Community Education:** AMERICAN COUNTRY LIFE ASSOCIATION, Proceedings, No. 5.

**Country Life Programs:** AMERICAN COUNTRY LIFE ASSOCIATION, Proceedings, No. 18.

**Country School:** SCHATZMANN.

**Countryman, Vern,** *ed.* Discrimination and the Law. Foreword by Erwin Griswold. 1965 xiv, 170 p. 21 cm. 65-24422. $5.00.

**Counts, George S.** Arithmetic Tests and Studies in the Psychology of Arithmetic. 1917. SEM 4. *o.p.*

**Counts, George S.** The Selective Character of American Secondary Education. 1922. SEM 19. *o.p.*

**Counts, George S.** The Senior High School Curriculum. 1926. SEM 29. *o.p.*

**Counts, George S.** The Social Composition of Boards of Education. A Study in the Social Control of Public Education. 1927. SEM 33. *o.p.*

**County Agent:** BAKER.

**County Library Service in the South:** WILSON.

**Cours complet de langue française:** INGRES.

**Course of Study in History in the Common School:** LAWRENCE.

**Courts, the Constitution, and Parties:** McLAUGHLIN.

**Courts and the Poor Laws in New York State:** BRANSCOMBE.

**Courts and Public-School Property:** PUNKE.

**Courts and the Public Schools:** EDWARDS.

**Cover, John Higson.** Business and Personal Failure and Readjustment in Chicago. 1933. SBA, III. *o.p.*

**Cover, John Higson.** Consumption of Meat and Meat Products with Particular Reference to Price. 1936. *o.p.*

**Cover, John Higson.** Neighborhood Distribution and Consumption of Meat in Pittsburgh, as Related to Other Social and Economic Factors. 1932. *o.p.*

**Cover, John Higson.** Retail Price Behavior. 1935. SBA, V. *o.p.*

**Cover, John Higson,** *ed.* Financing the Consumer. Report of a Conference on Consumer Financing Held at the University of Chicago, May, 1937. 1937. SBA, VII. *o.p.*

**Cowan, Donald Ross Gront.** Sales Analysis from the Management Standpoint. 1938. MSB. *o.p.*

**Cowan, Ruth,** *joint author:* BLUNT, Ultraviolet Light and Vitamin D in Nutrition.

**Cowdry, Edmund Vincent,** *ed.* General Cytology. A Textbook of Cellular Structure and Function for Students of Biology and Medicine. By Robert Chambers, Edwin G. Conklin, Edmund V. Cowdry, Merkel H. Jacobs, Ernest E. Just, Margaret R. Lewis, Warren H. Lewis, Frank R. Lillie, Ralph S. Lillie, Clarence E. McClung, Albert P. Mathews, Thomas H. Morgan, Edmund B. Wilson. 1924. *o.p.*

**Cowles, Henry Chandler.** The Ecological Relations of the Vegetation on the Sand Dunes of Lake Michigan. 1899. HB. *o.p.*

**Cowles, Henry Chandler.** The Physiographic Ecology of Chicago and Vicinity. A Study of the Origin, Development, and Classification of Plant Societies. 1901. HB. *o.p.*

**Cowles, Henry Chandler.** The Plant Societies of Chicago and Vicinity. 1901. GSC. *o.p.*

**Cowles, Henry Chandler,** *joint author:* SAUER, Starved Rock State Park.

**Cowles, Henry Chandler:** *see* NEWMAN, Nature of the World and of Man.

**Cowles, May K.** Problems in Living. A Course for Week-Day Religious Instruction. 1927. CS. *o.p.*

**Cowper, F. A. G.** Italian Folk Tales and Folk Songs. HCLS.

**Cox, Garfield Vestal.** An Appraisal of American Business Forecasts. 1929. 2d ed. 1930. SBA, I. *o.p.*

**Cox, Henry Joseph.** The Weather and Climate of Chicago. By Henry J. Cox and John E. Armington. 1914. GSC. *o.p.*

**Cox, Isaac Joslin.** The Indian as a Diplomatic Factor in the History of the Old Northwest. 1910. *o.p.*
A publication of the Chicago Historical Society.

**Cox, Isaac Joslin:** *see* HAAS, American Empire.

**Cox, Leonard** (*fl.* 1572). The Arte or Crafte of Rhethoryke. A Reprint. Edited with an Introduction, Notes, and Glossarial Index, by Frederic Ives Carpenter. 1899. ENG. *o.p.*

**Coxe, Louis O.** The Middle Passage. A Narrative Poem. Illustrations and script by Gobin Stair. 1960. iv, 156 p. 24 cm. 60-7235. $3.75<sup>s</sup>.

**Coxe, W. W.** The Grouping of Pupils. Prepared by W. W. Coxe, Chairman of the Society's Committee. 1936. NSSE, 35th Yrbk., Part I. *o.p.*

**Cozens, Frederick W.** Sports in American Life. By Frederick W. Cozens and Florence Scovil Stumpf. 1953. *o.p.*

**Crabb, Wilson Drane.** Culture History in the Chanson de geste—Aymeri de Narbonne. 1898. *o.p.*

**Craigie, Sir William A.** A Dictionary of American English on Historical Principles. 4 vols. 1938. 31 cm. 36-21500. $100.00ˢ. COBE.

"... a scholarly event of the highest importance. ... It is conceived on a large and comprehensive scale, it shows skillful and judicious editing on every page, and it will be of solid value for all time."—H. L. Mencken, in the *New York Herald Tribune.*

"... an enormous repository of information ... a great work, an indispensable and trustworthy tool for all students of the history of civilization in these United States."—Kemp Malone, in *The American Historical Review.*

"Avec cet ouvrage l'Amérique nous donne un merveilleux exemple d'activité intelligente et de bonne organisation, exemple digne de rendre un peu confus les Français qui, jadis fiers de leur Littré, ne possèdent pas encore aujourd'hui de dictionnaire historique au courant de l'état des connaissances et n'aperçoivent même pas le moment où ils le posséderont. Mais ceci est une autre histoire.'—F. Mossé in *Études Anglaises.*

**Craigie, Sir William A.** A Dictionary of the Older Scottish Tongue. From the Twelfth Century to the End of the Seventeenth. 31 cm. Twenty parts published to date. Seventeenth and following parts edited by A. J. Aitken. Each part, $7.50ˢ. COBE.

"... will long, if not ever, remain *the* and not merely *a* 'Dictionary of the Older Scottish Tongue.' It will remain so not primarily because the interest and value of its subject have not been hitherto fully realized, but because of the high order of workmanship amply supplying the needs of twentieth-century scholarship."—Percy W. Long, in *The Journal of English and Germanic Philology.*

**Craigie, Sir William A.** The Northern Element in English Literature. 1931. *o.p.*

**Crain, William Leeper:** *see* DARGAN, Studies in Balzac's Realism.

**Cram, Ralph Adams.** Six Lectures on Architecture. By Ralph Adams Cram, Thomas Hastings, and Claude Bragdon. The Scammon Lectures for 1915. 1917. SL. *o.p.*

**Crandall, Lee S.** The Management of Wild Mammals in Captivity. 1964. xv, 761 p. 8 plates. 23 cm. 64-10498. $13.50ˢ.

"... an exhaustive treatise, and there can be little of importance relating to the subject that has been overlooked. ... It goes systematically through the orders of living mammals, omitting only the Cetacea, dealing with all the species that have ever been kept in zoos and mentioning some others that have not ... well documented and well indexed, and the typography and format are excellent. It is embellished with some splendid photographic illustrations. ... Crandall's book will be the zoo-keeper's bible for many a year."—L. Harrison Matthews, in *Nature.*

**Crane, Esther.** The Place of the Hypothesis in Logic. 1923. PS. *o.p.*

**Crane, Milton.** Shakespeare's Prose. 1951. iv, 220 p. 21 cm. 51-10894. Paper. P127. $1.50.

**Crane, Ronald S.,** *ed.* Critics and Criticism, Ancient and Modern. By Ronald S. Crane, W. R. Keast, Richard McKeon, Norman Maclean, Elder Olson, and Bernard Weinberg. 1952. v, 647 p. Cloth. 26 cm. 52-7330. $10.00ˢ. Abridged. Paper. P15. 21 cm. $1.95.

"Even a casual reading of *Critics and Criticism* would reveal one salient fact: these men are starting from 'professional' knowledge not only of philosophical problems but of the whole history of thought and philosophical discussion. Together, if in no one man, they show a mastery of a variety of languages, a phenomenal amount of specific historical knowledge, and considerable analytic prowess, all integrated within a coherent and unified system of principles and methods."—Robert Marsh, in *The Hopkins Review.*

**Crane, Ronald S.,** *ed.:* GOLDSMITH, New Essays.

**Craven, Avery.** The Coming of the Civil War. 2d ed. 1957. xi, 491 p. 24 cm. 57-8572. $6.50ˢ.

**Craven, Avery.** Democracy in American Life. A Historical View. 1941. WFL. *o.p.*

**Craven, Avery.** An Historian and the Civil War. 1964. v, 233 p. 24 cm. 64-15802. $6.95ˢ.

**Craven, Avery,** *ed.* Essays in Honor of William E. Dodd. By His Former Students at the University of Chicago. 1935. ix, 362 p. 24 cm. 36-7460. $6.00ˢ.

**Craven, Avery:** *see* HUTCHINSON, Marcus W. Jernegan Essays.

Craven, Wesley Frank, *ed.* The Army Air Forces in World War II. Prepared under the editorship of Wesley Frank Craven and James Lea Cate. 7 vols. *Vol. I:* Plans and Early Operations, January 1939 to August 1942. 1948. xxxi, 788 p. Illus. 26 cm. $10.00ˢ. *Vol. II:* Europe. Torch to Pointblank, August 1942 to December 1943. 1949. xxi, 897 p. Illus. 26 cm. $10.00ˢ. *Vol. III:* Europe. Argument to V-E Day, January 1944 to May 1945. 1951. xxxix, 948 p. Illus. 26 cm. $10.00ˢ. *Vol. IV:* The Pacific. Guadalcanal to Saipan, August 1942 to July 1944. 1950. xxxii, 825 p. Illus. 26 cm. $10.00ˢ. *Vol. V:* The Pacific. Matterhorn to Nagasaki, June 1944 to August 1945. 1953. xxxvii, 878 p. Illus. 26 cm. $10.00ˢ. *Vol. VI:* Men and Planes. 1955. lii, 807 p. Illus. 26 cm. $10.00ˢ. *Vol. VII:* Services around the World. 1958. lii, 667 p. Illus. 26 cm. $10.00ˢ. Set of seven volumes. 48-3657. $60.00ˢ.

"This official and scholarly work . . . will take an important place in the military history of this great war. . . . From the historical view, the success of these volumes rests principally on the completeness and accuracy of the account . . . this is military history at its best."—Capt. Ralph Weymouth, USN, in *United States Naval Institute Proceedings.*

Crawford, John Forsyth. The Relation of Inference to Fact in Mill's Logic. 1916. PS. *o.p.*

Created Equal?: ANGLE.

Creative Critic: GRABO.

Creative Organization: STEINER.

Credit: LAUGHLIN.

Creech, Margaret. Three Centuries of Poor Law Administration. A Study of Legislation in Rhode Island. With an Introductory Note by Edith Abbott. 1936. SSM. *o.p.*

Creel, Herrlee Glessner. Chinese Thought from Confucius to Mao Tsê-tung. 1953. ix, 293 p. 24 cm. 53-10054. $6.00ˢ. CUSA.

Creel, Herrlee Glessner, *ed.* Literary Chinese by the Inductive Method. Prepared by Herrlee Glessner Creel, *editor,* Chang Tsung-ch'ien, and Richard C. Rudolph. 3 vols. *Vol. I:* The *Hsiao Ching.* Rev. ed. 1948. iv, 188 p. 26 cm. 48-8466. Planographed.

$4.00ᵗ. *Vol. II:* Selections from the *Lun Yü.* 1939. x, 252 p. 26 cm. 38-1458. Planographed. $4.50ᵗ. *Vol. III:* The *Mencius,* Books I–III. 1952. viii, 332 p. 26 cm. 38-1458. $6.00ᵗ.

Creel, Herrlee Glessner, *ed.* Newspaper Chinese by the Inductive Method. Edited by Herrlee Glessner Creel and Têng Ssŭ-yü. 1943. viii, 265 p. 26 cm. 43-2570. $5.50ᵗ.

Creel, Herrlee Glessner, *ed.* Translations of Text Selections and Exercises in Newspaper Chinese. Edited by Herrlee Glessner Creel and Têng Ssŭ-yü. 1943. *o.p.*

Cressey, George Babcock. The Indiana Sand Dunes and Shore Lines of the Lake Michigan Basin. 1928. GSC. *o.p.*

Cressey, Paul Goalby. The Taxi-Dance Hall. A Sociological Study in Commercialized Recreation and City Life. 1932. SOC. *o.p.*

Cressman, George P., *joint author:* RIEHL, Studies of Upper Air Conditions.

Cresswell, Major H. T. A Dictionary of Military Terms, Japanese-English, English-Japanese. By Major H. T. Cresswell, Major J. Hiraoki, and Major R. Namba. 1942. *o.p.*

Crick, Bernard. In Defence of Politics. 1962. xi, 156 p. 22 cm. 62-17138. NHS. $3.75ˢ. OBE.

Crighton, John Clarke. Business and Government. By John C. Crighton and Joseph J. Senturia. 1935. 2d ed. 1938. AP. *o.p.*

Crime: CANTOR.

Crime of Galileo: SANTILLANA.

Criminal Law in Colonial Virginia: SCOTT.

Crisis of Democracy: RAPPARD.

Crisis in Hospital Finance: DAVIS.

Critical Guide to *Leaves of Grass:* MILLER.

Critical Issues in Educational Administration: REAVIS.

Critical Study of Current Theories of Moral Education: HART.

Critics and Criticism: CRANE.

Critique of Logical Positivism: JOAD.

Critique of Practical Reason: KANT.

**Crocheron, B. H.** The Rural School as a Community Center. By B. H. Crocheron and others. 1911. NSSE, 10th Yrbk., Part II. *o.p.*

**Crocker, Lionel George.** Henry Ward Beecher's Art of Preaching. 1934. *o.p.*

**Cronbach, Abraham:** *see* HAYDON, Modern Trends in World-Religions.

**Croneis, Carey Gardiner.** Down to Earth. An Introduction to Geology. By Carey Croneis and William C. Krumbein. 1936. xviii, 501 p. Illus. 24 cm. 36-10420. Cloth. NPL. $8.50ˢ. Paper. PSS 501. $2.95.

". . . remarkable in content and emphasis . . . this book proceeds to picture the earth for what it is—the theater of human enterprise. . . . The world will never look the same to you after you have read it, and read it you will, if you look between its covers."—Paul B. Sears, in the *New York Herald Tribune*.

**Croquis d'un flâneur:** STANLEY.

**Cross, Barbara M.** Horace Bushnell. Minister to a Changing America. 1958. *o.p.*

**Cross, Cecil Merne Putnam.** The Development of Self-Government in India, 1858–1914. 1922. *o.p.*

**Cross, Earle Bennett.** The Hebrew Family. A Study in Historical Sociology. 1927. *o.p.*

**Cross, George.** Christian Salvation. A Modern Interpretation. 1925. *o.p.*

**Cross, George.** The Theology of Schleiermacher. A Condensed Presentation of His Chief Work, *The Christian Faith*. 1911. *o.p.*

**Cross, George.** What Is Christianity? A Study of Rival Interpretations. 1918. *o.p.*

**Cross, George:** *see* SMITH, Guide to the Study of the Christian Religion.

**Cross, Tom Peete.** Bibliographical Guide to English Studies. 1919. 10th ed. 1951. *o.p.* (*See* BOND, A Reference Guide to English Studies.)

**Cross, Tom Peete.** Lancelot and Guenevere. A Study on the Origins of Courtly Love. By Tom Peete Cross and William Albert Nitze. 1930. MPM. *o.p.*

**Cross, Tom Peete,** *joint author:* PLOMER, Life and Correspondence of Lodowick Bryskett.

**Cross, Whitman.** Quantitative Classification of Igneous Rocks. Based on Chemical and Mineral Characters, with a Systematic Nomenclature. By Whitman Cross, Joseph P. Iddings, Louis V. Pirsson, Henry S. Washington. With an Introductory Review of the Development of Systematic Petrography in the Nineteenth Century. 1903. *o.p.*

**Crosskey, William W.** Politics and the Constitution in the History of the United States. 2 vols. 1953. xi, viii, 1,410 p. 26 cm. 53-7433. $20.00ˢ.

"Like [Darwin's *Origin of Species*] Crosskey's [book] is the product of extraordinary powers of analysis and synthesis applied to myriad, newly uncovered, brilliantly researched facts which seem at first to be separated by more dimensions than one . . . [Exposes] vast flaws in the pre-existing general understanding, requires as a condition of its acceptance the abandonment of views institutionalized by a great deal of academic work, upsets patterns of thought and allegiances which have acquired deep emotional significance, and tenders perceptions so new and large as to be staggering."—Sylvester Petro, in *The Michigan Law Review*.

"The approximately 1,400 tightly packed pages of this work constitute an impressive and indeed an amazing performance in the way of a reinterpretation of the original meaning of the Constitution."—Carl Brent Swisher, in *The American Historical Review*.

**Crozier, Michel.** The Bureaucratic Phenomenon. 1964. x, 320 p. 23 cm. 63-20916. $7.50ˢ.

**Crumbs:** KENNEDY, *in his* Plays for Three Players. Vol. II.

**Cruz, Cornelio C.:** *see* HAAS, American Empire.

**Cuaderno To Accompany *España en América*. Segundas lecturas:** CASTILLO.

**Cuaderno To Accompany *La Nela*:** CASTILLO.

**Cubberley, Ellwood P.** The Certification of Teachers. 1906. NSSE, 5th Yrbk., Part II. *o.p.*

**Cubberley, Ellwood P.** Research within the Field of Education. By Ellwood P. Cubberley, Walter F. Dearborn, Paul Monroe, Edward L. Thorndike, Bird T. Baldwin, H. E. Bennett, W. W. Charters, Edward C. Elliott, H. H. Foster, John W. Hall, Paul H. Hanus, Charles M. McConn, M. V. O'Shea, W. S. Sutton, Guy M. Whipple. 1911. CTE. *o.p.*

Cuento de Tristan de Leonis: NORTHUP.

Cuevas de Artá: BAKER.

Cult of Antiquity and the French Revolutionaries: PARKER.

Cultural Reality: ZNANIECKI.

Cultural Relations on the Kansu-Tibetan Border: EKVALL.

Culture Agencies of a Typical Manufacturing Group: GILLETTE.

Culture of Ancient Egypt: WILSON.

Culture and Conscience: GRAHAM.

Culture and Faith: KRONER.

Culture History: CRABB.

Cummings, Richard Osborn. The American and His Food. A History of Food Habits in the United States. 1940. Rev. ed. 1941. o.p.

Cunha, Euclides da. Rebellion in the Backlands. Translated from Os Sertões, with an Introduction and Notes, by Samuel Putnam. 1944. xxx, 532 p. 21 cm. A44-346. Paper. P22. $2.95.
"Os Sertões is one of the books that has most profoundly affected Brazilian intellectual history. . . . In outline it is very simple, for it describes the human geography of the interior of northeast Brazil, the origin and growth there of a fanatic religious sect that came into conflict with the authority of the newly founded Brazilian republic, and the desperate and losing struggle of the back-country men against the republican army."—Alexander Marchant, in The American Historical Review.

"If I had to choose just one book in Brazilian literature to be translated into other languages . . . I would certainly pick up 'Os Sertões.' . . . Mr. Putnam's translation . . . is accurate, beautiful and packed with illuminating footnotes."—Erico Verissimo, in The New York Times Book Review.

Cunliffe, Marcus. The Nation Takes Shape. 1789–1837. 1959. vii, 223 p. 21 cm. 59-5770. Cloth. CHAC. $4.50s. Paper. $1.75.

Cunningham, Harry A. Classroom Procedure Test in Natural Science. For Rating Methods of Teaching in Junior and Senior High Schools. By Harry A. Cunningham and Douglas Waples. 1928. o.p.

Curare: MCINTYRE.

Cure of Souls: HOLMAN.

Curran, Barbara A. Trends in Consumer Credit Legislation. 1965. xi, 394 p. 29 cm. 65-17284. $8.50s.

Current Anthropology: THOMAS.

Current Christian Thinking: SMITH.

Current Economic Problems: HAMILTON.

Current Educational Readjustments in Higher Institutions: NATIONAL SOCIETY OF COLLEGE TEACHERS OF EDUCATION, Proceedings, No. 17.

Current Issues in Higher Education: GRAY.

Current Issues in Library Administration: JOECKEL.

Curriculum of the Common School: MORRISON.

Curriculum Development in City-School Systems: LAWSON.

Curriculum Enrichment Materials (CEM):
WEAVER, Amusement and Sports.
WEAVER, Men and Oil.
WEAVER, Struggle over Slavery.
WITTICK, Development of Power.

Curriculum Investigation: BOBBITT.

Curriculum-making in Los Angeles: BOBBITT.

Curriculum-making: RUGG.

Curriculum Practices in the Junior High School: GLASS.

Currie, David P. ed. Federalism in the New Nations. 1964. 440 p. 24 cm. 64-23421. $8.50s.

Curtis, Charles Densmore, trans.: PAIS, Ancient Italy.

Cushman, Lillian. Principles of Education Applied to Art. See ELEMENTARY SCHOOL RECORD, No. 1.

Customer Turnover Experience: GREER.

Cutting, Starr Willard. Der Conjunktiv bei Hartmann von Aue. 1894. GER. o.p.

Cutting, Starr Willard. Concerning the Modern German Relatives, "Das" and "Was," in Clauses Dependent upon Substantivized Adjectives. 1902. o.p.

Cutting the Cost of Bank Loans: KEENER.

Cytodifferentiation: RUDNICK.

**Dack, G. M.** Food Poisoning. Rev. and enl. ed. 1956. xi, 251 p. 24 cm. 55-12510. BM. $6.75ˢ.

**Dafoe, John Wesley:** *see* HURST, Great Britain and the Dominions.

**Dafoe, John Wesley:** *see* WRIGHT, Public Opinion and World-Politics.

**Dahl, Clothilde,** *joint ed.:* DAHL, Le Roi des montagnes.

**Dahl, Lief Christopher,** *ed.* Le Roi des montagnes. By Edmond About. Edited by Lief Christopher Dahl, Henri Pochard, and Clothilde Dahl. HCLS. *o.p.*

**Dahl, Robert A.** A Preface to Democratic Theory. 1956. xi, 155 p. 21 cm. 56-6642. Cloth. WFL. $3.50ˢ. Paper. P115. $1.50.

**Daiches, David.** The King James Version of the English Bible. An Account of the Development and Sources of the English Bible of 1611 with Special Reference to the Hebrew Tradition. 1941. *o.p.*

**Daiches, David.** The Novel and the Modern World. 1939. Rev. ed. 1960. xi, 220 p. 21 cm. 60-11134. Cloth. $5.00ˢ. Paper. P180. $1.75.

**Daiches, David.** Poetry and the Modern World. A Study of Poetry in England between 1900 and 1939. 1940. *o.p.*

**Dale, Edgar.** Mass Media and Education. Prepared by Edgar Dale, Chairman of the Yearbook Committee. 1954. x, 290, lxxvi p. NSSE, 53d Yrbk., Part II. 24 cm. 54-8086. Cloth. $4.50ᵗ. Paper. $3.75ᵗ.

**Dalton, John.** Foundations of the Atomic Theory. Comprising Papers and Extracts by John Dalton, Wm. Hyde Wollaston, M.D., and Thomas Thomson, M.D. (1802–1808). 1902. AC. *o.p.*

**Dalton, John.** Foundations of the Molecular Theory. Comprising Papers and Extracts by John Dalton, Joseph-Louis Gay-Lussac, and Amedo Avogadro (1808–1811). 1902. AC. *o.p.*

**D'Amour, Fred E.** Basic Physiology. 1961. xxii, 642 p. Illus. 24 cm. 61-5603. $7.95ᵗ.

**D'Amour, Fred E.** Manual for Laboratory Work in Mammalian Physiology. By Fred E. D'Amour, Frank R. Blood, and Don A. Belden. 1948. 3d ed. 1965. 200 p. Illustrated with photographs, graphs, and drawings. 28 × 22 cm. 65-17285. Paper. BM. $6.00ᵗ.

**Danforth, W. C.:** *see* ADAIR, Maternal Care.

**Daniel, Samuel.** Poems and A Defence of Ryme. Edited with an Introduction by Arthur Colby Sprague. *Reissue,* 1965. xxxvii, 215 p. 21 cm. Paper. P200. $2.25.

**Danner-Kraft Dry Goods Company:** MOULTON.

**Dante: Poet and Apostle:** WILKINS.

**Dante, Poet of the Secular World:** AUERBACH.

**Dargan, Edwin Preston.** Honoré de Balzac. A Force of Nature. 1932. *o.p.*

**Dargan, Edwin Preston.** Studies in Balzac's Realism. By E. Preston Dargan, W. L. Crain, and others. 1932. S.B. *o.p.*

**Dargan, Edwin Preston,** *ed.* The Evolution of Balzac's *Comédie humaine.* Edited by E. Preston Dargan and B. Weinberg. 1942. S.B. *o.p.*

**Dargan, Edwin Preston,** *ed.:* UNIVERSITY OF CHICAGO STUDIES IN BALZAC.

**Dargan, Marion, Jr.:** *see* Clarence Walworth Alvord, *in* HUTCHINSON, Marcus W. Jernegan Essays.

**Darrow, Chester W.:** *see* LASHLEY, Studies in the Dynamics of Behavior.

**Darwin, Charles.** The Expression of the Emotions in Man and Animals. *Reissue,* 1965. Preface by Konrad Lorenz. xiii, 372 p. Illus. 21 cm. 65-17286. Cloth. $5.00ˢ. Paper. PSS 526. $1.95.

**Darwin among the Poets:** STEVENSON.

**Davenport, Charles Benedict.** The Animal Ecology of the Cold Spring Sand Spit, with Remarks on the Theory of Adaptation. 1903. *o.p.*

**Davenport, Charles Benedict:** *see* CASTLE, Heredity and Eugenics.

**Davenport, Herbert Joseph.** Exercises in Value Theory. To accompany *Value and Distribution.* 1908. *o.p.*

**Davenport, Herbert Joseph.** Value and Distribution. A Critical and Constructive Study. 1908. *o.p.*

**Davenport, Horace W.** The ABC of Acid-Base Chemistry. The Elements of Physiological Blood-Gas Chemistry for Medical Students and Physicians. 4th rev. ed. 1958. vii, 87 p. 25 cm. 58-6974. Paper. BM. $2.00ᵗ.

**Davidson, Philip G.:** *see* Claude Halstead Van Tyne, *in* HUTCHINSON, Marcus W. Jernegan Essays.

**Davie, Donald.** Russian Literature and Modern English Fiction. A Collection of Critical Essays. Edited with an Introduction by Donald Davie. 1965. vi, 224 p. 21 cm. 65-18337. PLC 3. Cloth. $5.50ˢ. Paper. $1.95.

**Davies, James William Frederick.** Out of Doors with Youth. For Leaders of Boys' and Girls' Camps. 1927. PM. *o.p.*

**Davies, Nina M. Cummings.** Ancient Egyptian Paintings. Selected, Copied, and Described by Nina M. Davies, with the editorial assistance of Alan H. Gardiner. 3 vols. 1936. *o.p.*

"For a full appreciation of Egyptian painting as art there can be no substitute for a visit to the tombs themselves. The best alternative is a study of the volumes *Ancient Egyptian Paintings.* . . . The excellent coloured reproductions of her careful tempera copies have never been excelled for fidelity of colour."—*Times Literary Supplement.*

**Davis, Allison.** Deep South. A Social Anthropological Study of Caste and Class. By Allison Davis, Burleigh B. Gardner, and Mary Gardner. Directed by W. Lloyd Warner. 1941. xvi, 558 p. Illus. 20 cm. 41-23645. $8.50ˢ. Paper. Abridged. Foreword by James W. Silver. P204. $2.95.

**Davis, Allison,** *joint author:* EELLS, Intelligence and Cultural Differences.

**Davis, Benjamin Marshall.** Agricultural Education in the Public Schools. A Study of Its Development with Particular Reference to the Agencies Concerned. Introduction by Charles Hubbard Judd. 1912. *o.p.*

**Davis, Bradley Moore.** The Fertilization of Albugo candida. 1900. HB. *o.p.*

**Davis, Bradley Moore.** Nuclear Studies on Pellia. 1901. HB. *o.p.*

**Davis, Bradley Moore.** Oögenesis in Saprolegnia. 1903. *o.p.*

**Davis, Bradley Moore.** The Spore Mother-Cell of Anthoceros. 1900. HB. *o.p.*

**Davis, Emerson,** *joint author:* BROWN, On the Teaching of English.

**Davis, James A.** Stipends and Spouses. The Finances of American Arts and Sciences Graduate Students. With David Gottlieb, Jan Hajda, Carolyn Huson, and Joe L. Spaeth. 1962. viii, 294 p. 25 cm. 62-12630. $5.00ˢ.

**Davis, Kingsley.** Youth in the Depression. 1935. AP. *o.p.*

**Davis, Michael Marks.** The Crisis in Hospital Finance, and Other Studies in Hospital Economics. By Michael M. Davis and Clarence Rufus Rorem. 1932. ME. *o.p.*

**Davis, Michael Marks.** Paying Your Sickness Bills. 1931. ME. *o.p.*

**Davis, Michael Marks.** Public Medical Services. A Survey of Tax-supported Medical Care in the United States. 1937. ME. *o.p.*

**Davis, Ozora Stearns.** The Gospel in the Light of the Great War. 1919. *o.p.*

**Davis, Ozora Stearns.** Preaching on Church and Community Occasions. 1928. HER. *o.p.*

**Davis, Ozora Stearns.** Principles of Preaching. A Textbook, Based on the Inductive Method, for Class Use and Private Study. 1924. HER. *o.p.*

**Davis, Ozora Stearns:** *see* SMITH, Religious Thought in the Last Quarter-Century.

**Davis, William Morris.** Physical Geography in the University. 1894. *o.p.*

**Davis, William Morris.** The Progress of Geography in the Schools. By W. M. Davis and H. M. Wilson. 1902. NSSE, 1st Yrbk., Part II. *o.p.*

**Davy, Sir Humphry.** The Decomposition of the Fixed Alkalies and Alkaline Earths (1807–1808). 1902. AC. *o.p.*

**Davy, Sir Humphry.** The Elementary Nature of Chlorine. Papers by Humphry Davy (1809–1818). 1902. AC. *o.p.*

**Dawn of a New Age:** RABINOWITCH.

**Dawson, George Ellsworth.** The Child and His Religion. 1909. *o.p.*

**Day, Kenneth,** *joint author:* MORISON, Typographic Book.

**Day of the Cattleman:** OSGOOD.

**Day of Yahweh:** SMITH.

**Daytime Population:** BREESE.

**De México a Guatemala. Lecturas:** CASTILLO.

**De morbis artificum:** RAMAZZINI.

**De todo un poco:** CASTILLO.

**Dead Sea Scrolls and the Early Church:** MOWRY.

**Dean, James Elmer,** *ed.:* EPIPHANIUS, Epiphanius' Treatise on Weights and Measures.

**Dean, Joel.** The Long-Run Behavior of Costs in a Chain of Shoe Stores. By Joel Dean and Warren James. 1942. *o.p.*

**Dean, Joel.** Statistical Cost Functions of a Hosiery Mill. 1941. SBA, XI. *o.p.*

**Dean, Joel.** Statistical Determination of Costs. With Special Reference to Marginal Costs. 1936. SBA, VII. *o.p.*

**Dean, John P.** A Manual of Intergroup Relations. By John P. Dean and Alex Rosen. Foreword by Charles S. Johnson. 1955. xiv, 194 p. 21 cm. 56-5141. Cloth. $4.50ˢ. Paper. P129. $1.65.

**Dean, Mabel:** *see* MANLY, Text of *The Canterbury Tales.*

**Dearborn, Walter F.,** *joint author:* CUBBERLEY, Research within the Field of Education.

**Death by Tariff:** BUELL.

**Debate. Resolved: That the United States Should Adopt the Essential Features of the British System of Radio:** TYSON.

**Debevoise, Neilson Carel.** A Political History of Parthia. 1938. *o.p.*

**Debrunner, A.:** *see* FUNK, Greek Grammar of the New Testament.

**DeBruyn, Peter P. H.,** *General Editor,* SCIENTISTS' LIBRARY.

**Decade of Civic Development:** ZUEBLIN.

**Decade of Corporate Incomes:** NERLOVE.

**Decade of Radio Advertising:** HETTINGER.

**Decade of Rural Progress:** AMERICAN COUNTRY LIFE ASSOCIATION, Proceedings, Nos. 10 and 11.

**Decennial Papers on Astronomy and Astrophysics (1903).** 1904. YO, II *o.p.*

Also issued as Volume VIII, *Astronomy and Astrophysics,* of the *First Series* of the DECENNIAL PUBLICATIONS and as seven separate reprints:

BARNARD, Micrometrical Observations of Eros.
BURNHAM, Measures of Double Stars.
FROST, Radial Velocities of Twenty Stars.
HALE, Spectra of Stars of Secchi's Fourth Type.
LAVES, Orbit of the Minor Planet (334).
MOULTON, On Certain Rigorous Methods of Treating Problems in Celestial Mechanics.
RITCHEY, Astronomical Photography.

**Decennial Publications of the University of Chicago.** (DP). Issued in Commemoration of the Completion of the First Ten Years of the University of Chicago's Existence. Authorized by the Board of Trustees of the University of Chicago on the recommendation of the President and the Senate. Edited by a committee appointed by the Senate: James Rowland Angell, Oskar Bolza, Carl Darling Buck, Edward Capps, Frederic Ives Carpenter, Starr Willard Cutting, Jacques Loeb, Shailer Mathews, William I. Thomas. *First Series,* 10 volumes. *Second Series,* 17 volumes.

William Rainey Harper, first President of the University of Chicago, considered the production and publication of books by the University's scholars to be the most appropriate way of celebrating the University of Chicago Decennium. Two series of DECENNIAL PUBLICATIONS were published.

The *First Series* consists of two volumes of reports and eight volumes of investigations which were also issued as reprints, in heavy paper covers, but all these separates are now out of print.

The *Second Series* consisted of seventeen volumes of systematic treatises, unpublished documents, collections of articles on allied subjects, etc., by seventeen individual authors. The volumes are numbered from I through XVIII, however, because Volume XIII, in preparation for many years, was never completed for publication.

*First Series:*

Vol.

I. THE PRESIDENT'S REPORT. ADMINISTRATION. 1903.

II. THE REPORT OF THE PRESIDENT. PUBLICATIONS OF THE MEMBERS OF THE UNIVERSITY. 1904.

III. INVESTIGATONS REPRESENTING THE DEPARTMENTS. *Part I:* Systematic Theology, Church History, Practical Theology. *Part II:* Philosophy, Education. 1903.

*Part I:*

1. JOHNSON, Have We the Likeness of Christ?
2. HENDERSON, Practical Sociology.
3. ANDERSON, Elements of Chrysostom's Power.
4. SMITH, Practical Theology.

*Part II:*

1. TUFTS, On the Genesis of the Aesthetic Categories.
2. ANGELL, Preliminary Study of the Significance of Partial Tones.
3. MOORE, Existence, Meaning, and Reality.
4. ANGELL, Relations of Structural and Functional Psychology to Philosophy.
5. MEAD, Definition of the Psychical.
6. DEWEY, Logical Conditions of a Scientific Treatment of Morality.
7. YOUNG, Scientific Method in Education.

IV. INVESTIGATIONS REPRESENTING THE DEPARTMENTS. Political Economy, Political Science, History, Sociology, Anthropology. 1903.

1. LAUGHLIN, Credit.
2. VEBLEN, Use of Loan Credit.
3. STARR, Physical Characters of the Indians.
4. SMALL, Significance of Sociology for Ethics.
5. THATCHER, Studies Concerning Adrian IV.
6. THOMAS, Relation of the Medicine-Man to the Origin of the Professional Occupations.
7. FREUND, Empire and Sovereignty.
8. THOMPSON, Decline of the Missi Dominici.
9. JUDSON, Essentials of a Written Constitution.

V. INVESTIGATIONS REPRESENTING THE DEPARTMENTS. Semitic Languages and Literatures, Biblical and Patristic Greek. 1904.

1. GOODSPEED, Greek Papyri from the Cairo Museum.
2. BREASTED, Battle of Kadesh.

3. HARPER, Structure of the Text of the Book of Amos.
4. PRICE, Some Literary Remains of Rim-Sin.
5. BURTON, Some Principles of Literary Criticism.

VI. INVESTIGATIONS REPRESENTNG THE DEPARTMENTS. Greek, Latin, Comparative Philology, Classical Archeology. 1904.

1. TARBELL, Greek Hand-Mirror.
2. TARBELL, Cantharus from the Factory
3. FLICKINGER, Meaning of $\epsilon\pi\iota$ $\tau\hat{\eta}s$ $\sigma\kappa\eta\nu\hat{\eta}s$. of Brygos.
4. HENDRICKSON, Proconsulate of Julius Agricola.
5. FRANK, Stichometric Scholium to the Medea of Euripides.
6. HENDRICKSON, Commentariolum petitionis.
7. BUCK, Sketch of the Linguistic Conditions of Chicago.
8. MEYER, Two Twice-told Tales.
9. SHOREY, Unity of Plato's Thought.
10. ABBOTT, Toledo Manuscript of the Germania of Tacitus.
11. CAPPS, Introduction of Comedy into the City Dionysia.

VII. INVESTIGATIONS REPRESENTING THE DEPARTMENTS. Romance Languages and Literatures, Germanic Languages and Literatures, English. 1903.

1. HAMMOND, On the Text of Chaucer's Parlement of Foules.
2. KLENZE, Treatment of Nature in the Works of Nikolaus Lenau.
3. CUTTING, Concerning the Modern German Relatives "Das" and "Was."
4. ALLEN, Studies in Popular Poetry.
5. TOLMAN, What Has Become of Shakespeare's Play, "Love's Labour's Won"?
6. PIETSCH, Preliminary Notes on Two Old Spanish Versions of the Disticha Catonis.
7. JENKINS, Espurgatoire Saint Patriz.
8. MACCLINTOCK, Some Paradoxes of the English Romantic Movement.

VIII. INVESTIGATION REPRESENTING THE DEPARTMENTS. Astronomy and Astrophysics. 1903.

1. BURNHAM, Measures of Double Stars.
2. BARNARD, Micrometrical Observations of Eros.
3. MOULTON, On Certain Rigorous Methods of Treating Problems in Celestial Mechanics.
4. FROST, Radial Velocities of Twenty Stars.
5. HALE, Spectra of Stars of Secchi's Fourth Type.
6. RITCHEY, Astronomical Photography.
7. LAVES, Orbit of the Minor Planet (334).

IX. INVESTIGATIONS REPRESENTING THE DEPART-

MENTS. Physics, Chemistry, Geology, Mathematics. 1904.
1. MICHELSON, Velocity of Light.
2. BOLZA, Concerning Geodesic Curvature.
3. BOLZA, Proof of the Sufficiency of Jacobi's Condition.
4. DICKSON, Ternary Orthogonal Group.
5. DICKSON, Groups Defined for a General Field.
6. SMITH, On Amorphous Sulphur.
7. MILLIKAN, New Instruments of Precision.
8. STIEGLITZ, On the "Beckmann Rearrangement."
9. KINSLEY, Systematic Method of Calculating the Dimensions of Direct Current Dynamo-electric Machines.
10. McCOY, Equilibrium.
11. MASCHKE, Invariants and Covariants of Quadratic Differential Quantics of $n$ Variables.
12. MOORE, Subgroups of the Generalized Finite Modular Group.
13. CHAMBERLIN, Contribution to the Theory of Glacial Motion.

X. INVESTIGATIONS REPRESENTING THE DEPARTMENTS. Zoölogy, Anatomy, Physiology, Neurology, Botany, Pathology, Bacteriology. 1903.
1. LOEB, On the Production and Suppression of Muscular Twitchings.
2. DONALDSON, On a Formula for Determining the Weight of the Central Nervous System of the Frog.
3. TOWER, Development of the Colors and Color Patterns of Coleoptera.
4. GREELEY, Artificial Production of Spores in Monas.
5. JORDAN, Self-purification of Streams.
6. KOCH, Lecithans.
7. WEBSTER, Contribution to the Physical Analysis of the Phenomena of Absorption.
8. SHAMBAUGH, Distribution of Blood-vessels.
9. DAVENPORT, Animal Ecology of the Cold Spring Sand Spit.
10. HATAI, Finer Structure of Neurones.
11. COULTER, Phylogeny of Angiosperms.
12. WELLS, Studies in Fat Necrosis.
13. DAVIS, Oögenesis in Saprolegnia.
14. EYCLESHYMER, Early Development of Lepidosteus osseus.
15. BENSLEY, Structure of the Glands of Brunner.
16. CHAMBERLAIN, Mitosis in Pellia.
17. BARKER, Description of the Brains and Spinal Cords of Two Brothers.

*Second Series:*
VOL.
I. WAGER, Life and Repentaunce of Marie Magdalene.
II. CATTERALL, Second Bank of the United States.
III. MICHELSON, Light Waves.
IV. HARPER, Assyrian and Babylonian Letters, Part VIII.
V. REYNOLDS, Poems of Anne.
VI. LEÓN, La perfecta casada.
VII. BRECKINRIDGE, Legal Tender.
VIII. LIVINGSTON, Role of Diffusion.
IX. MITCHELL, History of the Greenbacks.
X. HALE, Study of Stellar Evolution.
XI. DEWEY, Studies in Logical Theory.
XII. MATHEWS, Messianic Hope.
XIII. CHAMBERLIN, Glacial Studies in Greenland. (Never published.)
XIV. BOLZA, Lectures on the Calculus of Variations.
XV. LOEB, Studies in General Physiology.
XVI. FOSTER, Finality of the Christian Religion.
XVII. KLENZE, Interpretation of Italy.
XVIII. HOFF, Physical Chemistry.

**Deceptive Cognates: Italian-English and English-Italian:** ALTROCCHI.

**Decimus Junius Brutus Albinus:** BONDURANT.

**Decker, Charles Elijah.** Studies in Minor Folds. 1920. *o.p.*

**Decline of Hell:** WALKER.

**Decline of the Missi Dominici in Frankish Gaul:** THOMPSON.

**Decomposition of the Fixed Alkalies:** DAVY.

**Dedication of the Yerkes Observatory:** HALE.

**Deep South:** DAVIS.

**Defense, Controls, and Inflation:** DIRECTOR.

**Definition of the Psychical:** MEAD.

**Definitive Orbit of Comet Delavan:** VAN BIESBROECK.

**Definitive Orbit of Comet Geddes:** VAN BIESBROECK.

**Definitive Orbit of Comet Morehouse:** VAN BIESBROECK.

**Definitive Orbits of Comets Van Biesbroeck, 1935 d, and of Barnard-Brooks, 1889 I:** VAN BIESBROECK.

**Defoe, Daniel:** MOORE.

**Degan, J. W.** Dimensions of Functional Psychoses. 1952. PMS. *o.p.*

**Dégh, Linda,** *ed.* Folktales of Hungary. Translated by Judit Halasz. 1964. 424 p. 64-19846. FW. $6.00. COBE.

**DeHaan, Robert F.** Educating Gifted Children. By Robert F. DeHaan and Robert J. Havighurst. 1957. Rev. ed. 1961. x, 362 p. 24 cm. 61-8648. $5.00ᵗ.

**DeHaan, Robert F.,** *joint author:* BOWMAN, Mobilizing Community Resources for Delinquent and Maladjusted Youth.

**DeHaan, Robert F.,** *joint author:* BOWMAN, Studying Children.

**DeHaan, Robert F.,** *joint author:* HAVIGHURST, Community Youth Development Program.

**DeHaan, Robert F.,** *joint author:* HAVIGHURST, Survey of the Education of Gifted Children.

**De Haven, James C.,** *joint author:* HIRSHLEIFER, Water Supply.

**Deification of Abstract Ideas:** AXTELL.

**De Jong, Louis.** The German Fifth Column in the Second World War. Translated from the Dutch by C. M. Geyl. 1956. *o.p.*

**Delay, Jean.** The Youth of André Gide. Translated and abridged by June Guicharnaud. 1963. x, 498 p. 22 cm. Illus. 63-13063. $7.95ˢ.

**Delayed Implantation:** ENDERS.

**Deléry, Simone de la Souchère.** France d'Amérique. By Simone de la Souchère Deléry and Gladys Anne Renshaw. HCLS. *o.p.*

**Delinquency Areas:** SHAW.

**Delougaz, Pinhas.** A Byzantine Church at Khirbat-al-Karak. By Pinhas Delougaz and Richard C. Haines. 1960. 72 p. Illus. 31 cm. 59-13607. Paper. OIP, LXXXV. $6.50.

**Delougaz, Pinhas.** I. Plano-convex Bricks and the Methods of Their Employment. II. The Treatment of Clay Tablets in the Field. 1933. xi, 57 p. Illus. 25 cm. Paper. SAOC 7. $1.00.

**Delougaz, Pinhas.** Pottery from the Diyala Region. 1952. xxii, 182 p. Illus. 31 cm. 52-6876. OIP, LXIII. $30.00.

**Delougaz, Pinhas.** Pre-Sargonid Temples in the Diyala Region. By Pinhas Delougaz and Seton Lloyd. With chapters by Henri Frankfort and Thorkild Jacobsen. 1942. xviii, 320 p. Illus. 31 cm. 42-25390. OIP, LVIII. $15.00.

**Delougaz, Pinhas.** The Temple Oval at Khafājah. 1940. xix, 175 p. Illus. 27 cm. 40-14640. OIP, LIII. $10.00.

**Delphic Maxims in Literature:** WILKINS.

**Demand for Durable Goods:** HARBERGER.

**Democracy:** BRAMHALL.

**Democracy in American Life:** CRAVEN.

**Democracy and American Schools:** JUDD.

**Democracy and National Unity:** HUTCHINSON.

**Democracy and Proportional Representation:** HERMENS.

**Democracy and Social Progress:** ABBOTT.

**Democracy in a World of Tensions:** McKEON.

**Democratic Practices in School Administration:** REAVIS.

**Democratic Way of Life:** SMITH.

**Demonstration Laboratory of Physics:** LEMON.

**De Morgan, Augustus.** On the Difficulty of Correct Description of Books. Originally printed in *Companion to the Almanac;* or, *Year-book of General Information for 1853, London.* Edited by Aksel G. S. Josephson. 1902. *o.p.*

**Demotic Ostraca from Medinet Habu:** LICHTHEIM.

**Dempster, Germaine Collette,** *joint ed.:* BRYAN, Sources and Analogues of Chaucer's *Canterbury Tales.*

**Denis, Pierre:** *see* COLBY, Geographic Aspects of International Relations.

**Denney, Reuel.** The Astonished Muse. 1957. viii, 264 p. 22 cm. 57-6985. $4.50ˢ.

**Denney, Reuel.** In Praise of Adam. 1961. 70 p. 21 cm. 61-18887. Paper. P89. $1.50.

**Dennis, Charles Henry.** Victor Lawson. His Time and His Work. 1935. *o.p.*

**DeNood, Neal Breaule.** Jobs or the Dole? 1935. 2d ed. 1938. AP. *o.p.*

**DeNormandie, R. L.:** *see* ADAIR, Maternal Care.

**DeNormandie, R. L.:** *see* ADAIR, Maternal Care. and Some Complications.

**Dental Education Today:** HORNER.

**Dental Terminations:** BUCK.

**Department of Meteorology.** Tephigram Chart. *No. 1:* Low Level 1100mb to 200mb. *No. 2:* High Level 1100 mb to 20mb. *No. 3:* Pressure Altitude Tephigram with Altimeter Correction Data. Each $0.03.

**Desai, Mahesh M.** Surprise. A Historical and Experimental Study. 1939. BJP. *o.p.*

**Description of Aptitude and Achievement Tests:** FRENCH.

**Description of the Brains and Spinal Cords of Two Brothers:** BARKER.

**Descriptive Catalogue of Greek New Testament Manuscripts in America:** CLARK.

**Descriptive Catalogue of Manuscripts in the Libraries of the University of Chicago:** GOODSPEED.

**Descriptive Petrography of the Igneous Rocks:** JOHANNSEN.

**Descriptive Study of the Spectra of the A-Type Stars:** MORGAN.

**Desert People:** JOSEPH.

**Desert People:** MEGGITT.

**Desert Saints:** ANDERSON.

**Design of Social Research:** ACKOFF.

**Detweiler, Frederick German.** The Negro Press in the United States. 1922. *o.p.*

**Deuel, Thorne,** *joint author:* COLE, Rediscovering Illinois.

**Deutsch, J. A.** The Structural Basis of Behavior. 1960. ix, 186 p. Index. 22 cm. 60-12466. $4.00ˢ. COBE.

**Deutsch für Anfänger:** HAGBOLDT.

**Deutsche Beiträge:** BERGSTRÄSSER.

**Devaluation of the Dollar:** HARDY.

**Developing America's Waterways. Administration of the Inland Waterways Corporation:** DIMOCK.

**Developing Attitudes in Children:** CHICAGO ASSOCIATION FOR CHILD STUDY.

**Developing Permanent Interest in Reading:** ROBINSON.

**Development of Children's Number Ideas in the Primary Grades:** BROWNELL.

**Development of the Colors and Color Patterns of Coleoptera:** TOWER.

**Development of the French Monarchy:** THOMPSON.

**Development of High-School Curricula in the North Central States:** STOUT.

**Development of the Historic Drama:** KUEFFNER.

**Development of Logical Empiricism:** JOERGENSEN.

**Development of the Montana Poor Law:** VEEDER.

**Development of the Pollen in Some Asclepiadaceae:** FRYE.

**Development of Poor Relief Legislation in Kansas:** BROWNING.

**Development of Power:** WITTICK.

**Development of Rationalism and Empiricism:** SANTILLANA.

**Development in and through Reading:** WITTY.

**Development of Self-government in India:** CROSS.

**Development of the Stamens and Carpels of Typha latifolia:** SCHAFFNER.

**Development of Virgil's Art:** PRESCOTT.

**Development of Western Civilization:** FORREST.

**Development of the Young People's Movement:** ERB.

**Developmental Biology Conference** (1956) **Series** (DBC):
CAMPBELL, Physiology of Insect Development.
DUCOFF, Mitogenesis.
EDDS, Immunology and Development.
MINTZ, Environmental Influences on Prenatal Development.
PATTERSON, Wound Healing and Tissue Repair.
PRICE, Dynamics of Proliferating Tissues.
RUDNICK, Cytodifferentiation.
RUDNICK, Embryonic Nutrition.
THORNTON, Regeneration in Vertebrates.
WATTERSON, Endocrines in Development.

**Devereux, Frederick Leonard.** The Educational Talking Picture. By Frederick L. Devereux. In Collaboration with Nickolaus L. Engelhardt, Paul R. Mort, Alexander J. Stoddard, V. C. Arnspiger, Howard G. Stokes, M. R. Brunstetter, and Laura Krieger Eads. 1933. 2d ed. 1935. *o.p.*

**De Visscher, Charles.** The Stabilization of Europe. 1924. HFL. *o.p.*

**Dewey, Ethel Lillian,** *ed.:* DEWEY, Recollections of Richard Dewey.

**Dewey, John.** The Aim of History in Elementary Education: *see* ELEMENTARY SCHOOL RECORD, No. 8.

**Dewey, John.** American Education, Past and Future. 1931. *o.p.*

**Dewey, John.** The Child and the Curriculum. 1902. 40 p. 20 cm. 2-20883. Cloth. CE. $1.50ˢ.

**Dewey, John.** The Child and the Curriculum *and* The School and Society. With an Introduction by Leonard Carmichael. 1956. 21 cm. 56-13578. Paper. P3. $1.25.

**Dewey, John.** The Educational Situation. 1902. CE. *o.p.*

**Dewey, John.** Essays in Experimental Logic. 1916. *o.p.*

**Dewey, John.** Ethical Principles Underlying Education. 1908. *o.p.*

**Dewey, John.** Froebel's Educational Principles: *see* ELEMENTARY SCHOOL RECORD, No. 5.

**Dewey, John.** The General Principles of Work, Educationally Considered: *see* ELEMENTARY SCHOOL RECORD, No. 1.

**Dewey, John.** Logical Conditions of a Scientific Treatment of Morality. 1903. *o.p.*

**Dewey, John.** Psychology and Social Practice. 1901. CE. *o.p.*

**Dewey, John.** The Psychology of an Elementary Curriculum: *see* ELEMENTARY SCHOOL RECORD, No. 9.

**Dewey, John.** The Psychology of Occupation: *see* ELEMENTARY SCHOOL RECORD, No. 3.

**Dewey, John.** Reflective Attention: *see* ELEMENTARY SCHOOL RECORD, No. 4.

**Dewey, John.** The Relation of Theory to Practice in the Education of Teachers. By John Dewey and others. 1904. NSSE, 3d Yrbk., Part I. *o.p.*

**Dewey, John.** The School and Society. 1899. 2d ed. 1915. xvi, 164 p. Illus. 20 cm. 15-18118. $4.00ˢ.
"No other American work on education has had greater influence . . ."—Frank A. Manny, in *The Survey.*

**Dewey, John.** The Significance of the Problem of Knowledge. 1897. PHI. *o.p.*

**Dewey, John.** Studies in Logical Theory. By John Dewey with the Co-operation of Members and Fellows of the Department of Philosophy. 1903. *o.p.*

**Dewey, John.** Theory of Valuation. 1939. vii, 67 p. 25 cm. A42-5466. Paper. IEUS, II, 4. $1.50ˢ.

**Dewey, John:** *joint author:* NEURATH, Encyclopedia and Unified Science.

**Dewey, John:** *see* THOMAS, John Dewey.

**Dewey, Richard Smith.** Recollections of Richard Dewey, Pioneer in American Psychiatry. An Unfinished Autobiography with an Introduction by Clarence B. Farrar, M.D. Edited by Ethel L. Dewey. 1936. *o.p.*

**Dewhurst, Frederic Eli.** The Investment of Truth and Other Sermons. By Frederic E. Dewhurst with an Introduction by Albion W. Small. 1907. *o.p.*

**Dewsnup, Ernest Ritson,** *ed.* Railway Organization and Working. A Series of Lectures Delivered before the Railway Classes of the University of Chicago. 1906. *o.p.*

**Diagnostic Studies in Arithmetic:** BUSWELL.

**Diagnostic Tests in the Fundamental Operation in Arithmetic:** REAVIS.

**Dialogue on the Great World Systems:** GALILEI.

**Diamond, William,** *ed.* Cora. Vier Lausbubengeschichten. By Ludwig Thoma. Edited by William Diamond and Selma Rosenfeld. HCLS.

**Diary and Letters of Wilhelm Müller:** ALLEN.

**Diary of Orville H. Browning:** PEASE.

**Diatessaron of Tatian:** HOBSON.

**Dickerman, Philip J.,** *ed.* Optical Spectrometric Measurements of High Temperatures. 1961. viii, 268 p. Illus. Index. 25 m. 61-5607. $12.50ˢ.

**Dickinson, Edwin DeWitt:** *see* WRIGHT, Neutrality and Collective Security.

**Dickman, Adolphe-Jacques,** *joint ed.:* MOUSSIEGT, Histoires de bêtes.

**Dickson, Leonard Eugene.** Algebras and Their Arithmetics. 1923. SCI. *o.p.*

**Dickson, Leonard Eugene.** The Groups Defined for a General Field by the Rotation Groups. 1902. *o.p.*

**Dickson, Leonard Eugene.** Introduction to the Theory of Numbers. 1929. *o.p.*

**Dickson, Leonard Eugene.** Modern Elementary Theory of Numbers. 1939. viii, 309 p. 20 cm. 39-31899. $6.00ˢ.

**Dickson, Leonard Eugene.** Studies in the Theory of Numbers. 1930. SCI. *o.p.*

**Dickson, Leonard Eugene.** Ternary Orthogonal Group in a General Field. 1902. *o.p.*

**Dictionary of American English:** CRAIGIE.

**Dictionary of Americanisms:** MATHEWS.

**Dictionary of Military Terms:** CRESSWELL.

**Dictionary of the Older Scottish Tongue:** CRAIGIE.

**Dictionary of Selected Synonyms in the Principal Indo-European Languages:** BUCK.

**Diet and Dental Health:** HANKE.

**Diet and Efficiency:** HOLCK.

**Dietrich, William J.,** *joint author:* BOWMAN, Studying Children.

**Dietrich, William J.,** *joint author:* HAVIGHURST, Community Youth Development Program.

**Diffraction of Light, X-Rays, and Material Particles:** MEYER.

**Digestion of Foods:** CARLSON.

**Dignan, Frank Winans.** The Idle Actor in Æschylus. 1905. *o.p.*

**Dilemmas of Politics:** MORGENTHAU.

**Diller, Robert.** Farm Ownership, Tenancy, and Land Use in a Nebraska Community. 1941. *o.p.*

**Dillon, George,** *trans.:* RACINE, Three Plays.

**Dillon, Myles.** Early Irish Literature. 1948. xix, 192 p. 25 cm. $5.00ˢ.

**Dimensions of Functional Psychoses:** DEGAN.

**Dimock, Edward C.,** *ed. and trans.* The Thief of Love. Bengali Tales from Court and Village. 1963. xiv, 306 p. 22 cm. 63-11396. $5.95ˢ.

**Dimock, Marshall Edward.** British Public Utilities and National Development. 1933. PA. *o.p.*

**Dimock, Marshall Edward.** Can Interstate Compacts Succeed? The Uses and Limitations of Interstate Agreements. By Marshall E. Dimock and George C. S. Benson. 1937. PPP 22. *o.p.*

**Dimock, Marshall Edward.** Developing America's Waterways. Administration of the Inland Waterways Corporation. 1935. PA. *o.p.*

**Dimock, Marshall Edward.** Government-operated Enterprises in the Panama Canal Zone. With an Introduction by Louis Brownlow. 1934. PA. *o.p.*

**Dimock, Marshall Edward,** *joint author:* GAUS, Frontiers of Public Administration.

**Di Pietro, Robert J.:** *joint author:* AGARD, Grammatical Structures of English and Italian.

**Di Pietro, Robert J.:** *joint author:* AGARD, Sound of English and Italian.

**Diplomat under Stress:** HALPERIN.

**Direct Contribution of Educational Psychology to Teacher Training:** NATIONAL SOCIETY OF COLLEGE TEACHERS OF EDUCATION, Proceedings, No. 20.

**Direction of Writing on Attic Vases:** TARBELL.

**Director, Aaron.** The Economics of Technocracy. 1933. PPP 2. *o.p.*

**Director, Aaron,** *ed.* Defense, Controls, and Inflation. A Conference Sponsored by the University of Chicago Law School. 1952. *o.p.*

**Disadvantaged People in Rural Life:** AMERICAN COUNTRY LIFE ASSOCIATION, Proceedings, No. 21.

**Discoveries in Anatolia:** OSTEN.

**Discovery of Oxygen.** Part I: PRIESTLEY.

**Discovery of Oxygen.** Part II: SCHEELE.

**Discrimination and the Law:** COUNTRYMAN.

**Diseases of Workers:** RAMAZZINI, De morbis artificum.

**Dissolution of the Habsburg Monarchy:** JÁSZI.

**Distinct Glacial Epochs:** SALISBURY.

**Distribution and Abundance of Animals:** ANDREWARTHA.

**Distribution of Attention:** McQUEEN.

**Distribution of Blood-Vessels:** SHAMBAUGH.

**Distribution of Livestock from the Chicago Market:** DUDDY.

**Distribution of the Stars in Space:** BOK.

**Dittmer, Howard J.,** *ed.:* COULTER, Story of the Plant Kingdom.

**Divine, Robert A.** The Illusion of Neutrality. 1962. x, 370 p. Index. 22 cm. 62-10993. $6.50ˢ.

**Dixon, Elizabeth S.** *ed.* Social Case Records. Family Welfare. Edited by Elizabeth S. Dixon and Grace A. Browning. 1938. SSS. *o.p.*

**Dobbin, Leonard,** *trans.:* LADENBURG, Lectures on the History of the Development of Chemistry.

**Doberck, William.** On the Magnitudes of 919 Fixed Stars Determined from Sequences Observed by Sir John Herschel during the Years 1835 to 1838. 1900. *o.p.*

**Doctors, Dollars, and Disease:** FOSTER.

**Dr. Johnson's** *Dictionary:* SLEDD.

**Documentary History of American Higher Education:** HOFSTADTER.

**Dodd, Sue Hutchison,** *joint author:* DODD, Government in Illinois.

**Dodd, Walter Fairleigh.** Government in Illinois. By Walter F. Dodd and Sue Hutchison Dodd. 1923. *o.p.*

**Dodd, Walter Fairleigh.** Modern Constitutions. A Collection of the Fundamental Laws of Twenty-two of the Most Important Countries of the World, with Historical and Bibliographical Notes. 2 vols. 1909. *o.p.*

**Dodd, William Edward:** *see* RANEY, If Lincoln Had Lived.

**Dodd, William Edward:** *see* WRIGHT, Neutrality and Collective Security.

**Doe, Janet.** A Bibliography of the Works of Ambroise Paré: Premier chirurgien & conseiller du roy. 1937. *o.p.*

**Dolejší, Robert.** Modern Viola Technique. 1939. *o.p.*

**Domestic Discord:** MOWRER.

**Donahue, Wilma,** *General Editor,* HANDBOOKS OF SOCIAL GERONTOLOGY.

**Donaldson, Henry Herbert.** On a Formula for Determining the Weight of the Central Nervous System of the Frog from the Weight and Length of Its Entire Body. 1902. *o.p.*

**Donnelly, Thomas W.,** *ed.* The Earth Sciences. Problems and Progress in Current Research. With Contributions by Sydney P. Clark, Jr., Fred A. Donath, W. S. Frye, Heinz A. Lowenstein, John O'Keefe, and S. S. Wilks. 1963. vii, 195 p. 24 cm. 63-20901. RSS. $6.00ˢ.

**Donovan, Frances R.** The Saleslady. 1929. *o.p.*

**Donovan, William Joseph,** *joint author:* TY-SON, Retrospect and Forecast in Radio Education.

**Dopp, Katharine Elizabeth.** The Place of Industries in Elementary Education. 1902. 2d ed. 1905. *o.p.*

**Dornbusch, Sanford M.,** *joint author:* SCHNEIDER, Popular Religion.

**Dorson, Richard M.** American Folklore. 1959. ix, 313 p. 21 cm. 59-12283. Cloth. CHAC. $4.50ˢ. Paper. $1.95.

". . . fills a gap in the historical literature of our subject by bringing together from many sources a rich store of material in a critical and scholarly manner."—Beatrice Blackwood, in *Folklore.*

"I know of nobody who would have done a better job in furnishing a historical background and perspective from which American folklore can be profitably studied . . ."—Mody C. Boatright, in *American Literature.*

**Dorson, Richard M.** Buying the Wind. Regional Folklore in the United States. 1964. 573 p. 23 cm. 64-13010. $7.95.

**Dorson, Richard M.,** *General Editor,* FOLK-TALES OF THE WORLD.

**Doty, George Lewis,** *ed.* Novelle (Panzini). HCLS. *o.p.*

**Double Fertilization in Compositae:** LAND.

**Douglas, Paul Howard.** Economy in the National Government. 1952. WFL. *o.p.*

**Douglas, Paul Howard.** The Movement of Money and Real Earnings in the United States, 1926–28. By Paul H. Douglas and Florence Tye Jennison. 1930. SBA, I, 3. *o.p.*

**Douglas, Paul Howard.** Standards of Unemployment Insurance. 1933. SSM. *o.p.*

**Douglas, Paul Howard.** Wages and the Family. 1925. 2d ed. 1927. MSB. *o.p.*

**Douglas, Paul Howard.** The Worker in Modern Economic Society. By Paul H. Douglas, Curtice N. Hitchcock, and Willard E. Atkins. 1923. 2d ed. 1925. MSB. *o.p.*

**Douglas, Paul Howard,** *joint author:* CLARK, Adam Smith, 1776–1926.

**Douglas, R. Langton.** Leonardo da Vinci. His Life and Pictures. 1944. *o.p.*

**Douglas, R. Langton.** Piero di Cosimo. 1946. *o.p.*

**Douglass, Aubrey A.** The Junior High School. 1916. NSSE, 15th Yrbk., Part III. *o.p.*

**Douthitt, Herman.** The Structure and Relationships of Diplocaulus. 1917. WM. *o.p.*

**Doutt, Howard MacKenzie:** *see* ZOOK, Principles of Accrediting Higher Institutions.

**Dowd, Quincy Lamartine.** Funeral Management and Costs. A World-Survey of Burial and Cremation. 1921. *o.p.*

**Down to Earth:** CRONEIS.

**Downer, Alan.** American Drama and Its Critics. A Collection of Critical Essays. Edited with an Introduction by Alan Downer. 1965. xxi, 258 p. 21 cm. 65-24424. PLC 4. Cloth. $6.50ˢ. Paper. $2.45.

**Downey, Glanville,** *joint ed.:* SPINKA, Chronicle of John Malalas.

**Downing, Elliot Rowland.** Elementary Eugenics. A Revision of *The Third and Fourth Generation.* 1928. *o.p.*

**Downing, Elliot Rowland.** A Field and Laboratory Guide in Biological Nature-Study. 1918. NS. *o.p.*

**Downing, Elliot Rowland.** A Field and Laboratory Guide in Physical Nature-Study. 1920. NS. *o.p.*

**Downing, Elliot Rowland.** An Introduction to the Teaching of Science. A Revision of *Teaching Science in the Schools.* 1934. *o.p.*

**Downing, Elliot Rowland.** A Naturalist in the Great Lakes Region. 1922. NS. *o.p.*

**Downing, Elliot Rowland.** Our Living World. A Source Book of Biological Nature-Study. 1919. 2d ed. 1924. NS. *o.p.*

The first edition was entitled *A Source Book of Biological Nature-Study.*

**Downing, Elliot Rowland.** Our Physical World. A Source Book of Physical Nature-Study. With a chapter on Radio Communication by Fred G. Anibal. 1924. NS. *o.p.*

**Downing, Elliot Rowland.** Teaching Science in the Schools. 1929. *o.p.*

**Downing, Elliot Rowland.** The Third and Fourth Generation. An Introduction to Heredity. 1918. CS. *o.p.*

**Downing, Elliot Rowland:** *see* NEWMAN, Nature of the World and of Man.

**Downing, George E.:** *see* DARGAN, Studies in Balzac's Realism.

**Downs, Norton,** *ed.* Essays in Honor of Conyers Read. 1953. xxii, 304 p. 25 cm. 53-5817. $6.00ˢ.

**Doyle, Bertram Wilbur.** The Etiquette of Race Relations in the South. A Study in Social Control. 1937. *o.p.*

**Dozen Doctors:** INGLE.

**Drabkin, I. E.,** *trans.:* AURELIANUS, On Acute and Chronic Diseases.

**Dramatic Traditions:** TUNISON.

**Dramatization of Bible Stories:** MILLER.

**Dramatization in the Church School:** MILLER.

**Drawings of the Florentine Painters:** BERENSON.

**Dreadful Freedom:** *see* GRENE, Introduction to Existentialism.

**Dresden, Arnold,** *joint author:* MYERS, Second-Year Mathematics.

**Dressel, Paul L.,** *ed.* The Integration of Educational Experiences. 1958. NSSE, 57th Yrbk., Part III. xi, 273, cix p. 24 cm. 58-1376. Cloth. $4.50ᵗ. Paper. $3.75ᵗ.

**Drew, Katherine Fisher,** *ed.* Perspectives in Medieval History. Edited by Katherine Fisher Drew and Floyd Seyward Lear. 1963. xi, 93 p. 24 cm. 63-20902. RSS. $4.00ˢ.

**Drinnon, Richard.** Rebel in Paradise. A Biography of Emma Goldman. 1961. xv, 349 p. Illus. 24 cm. 61-17074. $5.95ˢ.

**Driscoll, Lucy Catherine.** Chinese Calligraphy. By Lucy Driscoll and Kenji Toda. 1935. *o.p.*

**Driver, Harold E.** Indians of North America. 1961. xviii, 668 p. Illus. Index. 25 cm. 61-5604. Cloth. $10.95ˢ. Paper. $5.00ᵗ.

". . . a worthy successor to Wissler's classic, insofar as the Indians of North America are concerned. It is a systematic, sound description of the ways in which the Indians lived before their traditional customs were altered greatly through contacts with European civilization."—John C. Ewers, in *Natural History*.

". . . the best comprehensive book on the North American Indians of any so far published . . . in a form much more usable for the beginning student and for the general reader."—Charles H. Fairbanks, in *Science*.

**Droba, Daniel D.** Attitude toward War. Forms A and B. 1930. TAS 2. *o.p.*

**Drôles aventures de renard:** PASSARELLI.

**Drury, John.** Old Chicago Houses. 1941. *o.p.*

**Duab of Turkestan:** RICKMERS.

**Dualism of Fact and Idea:** TALBERT.

**Dubberstein, W. H.,** *joint author:* PARKER, Babylonian Chronology.

**Dubs, Homer H.** Rational Induction. An Analysis of the Method of Science and Philosophy. 1930. *o.p.*

**Duckett, Eleanor Shipley.** Alfred the Great. The King and His England. 1956. viii, 220 p. 22 cm. 56-13050. Cloth. $3.75ˢ. Paper. P29. $1.95. USA.

**Ducoff, Howard S.** Mitogenesis. Edited by H. S. Ducoff and C. F. Ehret. 1959. xiii, 114 p. 24 cm. 59-8806. DBC. $3.25ˢ.

**Duddy, Edward Augustin.** Agriculture in the Chicago Region. 1929. SSCI. *o.p.*

**Duddy, Edward Augustin.** The Changing Relative Importance of the Central Livestock Market. By Edward A. Duddy and David A. Revzan. 1938. SBA, VIII. *o.p.*

**Duddy, Edward Augustin.** The Chicago Foundry Company. 1924. MSB. *o.p.*

**Duddy, Edward Augustin.** The Cold-Storage Industry in the United States. 1929. MSB. *o.p.*

**Duddy, Edward Augustin.** Distribution of Livestock from the Chicago Market, 1924–29. By Edward A. Duddy and David A. Revzan. 1932. SBA, III. *o.p.*

**Duddy, Edward Augustin.** The Grain Supply Area of the Chicago Market. By Edward A. Duddy and David A. Revzan. 1934. SBA, IV. *o.p.*

**Duddy, Edward Augustin.** The Physical Distribution of Fresh Fruits and Vegetables. By Edward A. Duddy and David A. Revzan. 1937. SBA, VII. *o.p.*

**Duddy, Edward Augustin.** The Supply Area of the Chicago Livestock Market. By Edward A. Duddy and David A. Revzan. 1931. SBA, II. *o.p.*

**Duddy, Edward Augustin.** The Use of Transportation Facilities in the Chicago Fruit and Vegetable Market. By Edward A. Duddy and David A. Revzan. 1940. SBA, X. *o.p.*

**Duddy, Edward Augustin,** *ed.* Business Education in School Situations. Proceedings of the University of Chicago Conference on Business Education, 1939. 1939. *o.p.*

**Duddy, Edward Augustin,** *ed.* Conference on Economic Policy for American Agriculture. The University of Chicago, September, 1931. 1932. *o.p.*

**Duell, Prentice:** *see* SAKKARAH EXPEDITION, Mastaba of Mereruka.

**DuFresne, Eugene,** *joint trans.:* HEIDE, Meteorites.

**Duk-Duks. Primitive and Historic Types of Citizenship:** WEBER.

**DuMond, Jesse W. M.,** *ed.:* MILLIKAN, Electron.

**Dumping:** VINER.

**Dunbar, Olivia Howard.** A House in Chicago. 1947. *o.p.*

**Duncan, Beverly,** *joint author:* DUNCAN, Negro Population of Chicago.

**Duncan, Charles T.:** *see* BLAUSTEIN, American Lawyer.

**Duncan, Hugh D.** Language and Literature in Society. 1953. *o.p.*

**Duncan, Kunigunde.** Mentor Graham. The Man Who Taught Lincoln. By Kunigunde Duncan and D. F. Nickols. 1944. *o.p.*

**Duncan, Otis Dudley.** The Negro Population of Chicago. A Study of Residential Succession. By Otis Dudley Duncan and Beverly Duncan. 1957. xxiv, 367 p. 24 cm. 57-5271. $7.50ˢ.

**Duncan, Otis Dudley,** *ed.:* OGBURN, William F. Ogburn on Culture and Social Change.

**Duncan, Otis Dudley,** *joint author:* HAUSER, Study of Population.

**Dunér, Nils Christofer.** Calculation of Elliptic Elements of the System of Y Cygni. 1900. *o.p.*

**Dunér, Nils Christofer.** On the Spectra of Stars of Class IIIb. 1899. *o.p.*

**Dunham, Albert Millard,** *joint ed.:* MEAD, The Philosophy of the Act.

**Dunham, Allison,** *ed.* Mr. Justice. Edited by Allison Dunham and Philip B. Kurland. 2d ed., 1964. xi, 344 p. Illus. 21 cm. 64-15821. Cloth. $7.50ˢ. Paper. P152. $2.95.

**Dunham, Henry Warren,** *joint author:* FARIS, Mental Disorders in Urban Areas.

**Dunkel, Harold B.** French in the Elementary School. Five Years' Experience. By Harold B. Dunkel and Roger A. Pillet. 1962. 150 p. 22 cm. 62-12636. $3.75ᵗ.

**Dunkel, Wilbur Dwight.** Sir Arthur Pinero. A Critical Biography with Letters. 1941. *o.p.*

**Dunn, Arthur William.** An Analysis of the Social Structure of a Western Town. A Specimen Study According to Small and Vincent's Method. 1896. *o.p.*

**Dunn, Catherine Merriam,** *joint ed.:* BRISTOL, Handbook for Field Work Students.

**Durand, Edward Dana:** *see* Financial Mobilization for War.

**Durkheim, Émile.** Primitive Classification. By Émile Durkheim and Marcel Mauss. Translated by Rodney Needham. 1963. xlviii, 96 p. 22 cm. 63-9737. $3.00ˢ. OBE.

**Durkheim, Émile.** The Rules of Sociological Method. By Émile Durkheim. Eighth edition, translated by Sarah A. Solovay and John H. Mueller and edited by George E. G. Catlin. 1938. SOC. *o.p.*

**DuShane, Graham P.** Supplemental Drawings for Embryology. 1955. iv, 44 p. Illus. Planographed. 28 cm. 55-5121. Paper. BM. $1.50ᵗ.

**Dushkin, David.** Fun with Flutes. Book design and illustrations by Alfred D. Sterges. 1934. *o.p.*

**Duverger, Maurice.** The French Political System. 1958. CLCP. *o.p.*

**Duyvendak, J. J. L.,** *trans.* The Book of Lord Shang. A Classic of the Chinese School of Law. Translated and with an Introduction by J. J. L. Duyvendak. *Reissue,* 1963. xiv, 346 p. 19 cm. 63-22585. $6.50. CUSA.

**Dvorin, Eugene P.** Racial Separation in South Africa. 1952. *o.p.*

**Dykeman, Wilma.** Seeds of Southern Change. The Life of Will Alexander. By Wilma Dykeman and James Stokely. Foreword by Alexander Heard. 1962. xvi, 344 p. Illus. 23 cm. 62-13923. $5.95s.

**Dymond, Rosalind F.,** *joint ed.:* ROGERS, Psychotherapy and Personality Change.

**Dynamic Psychiatry:** ALEXANDER.

**Dynamics of Bureaucracy:** BLAU.

**Dynamics of Business Cycles:** TINBERGEN.

**Dynamics of Groups at Work:** THELEN.

**Dynamics of Instructional Groups:** JENSEN.

**Dynamics of Proliferating Tissues:** PRICE.

**Eakin, Mary K.,** *comp.* Good Books for Children. A Selection of Outstanding Children's Books Published 1948–61. 2d ed. 1962. 21 cm. 62-17962. Cloth. $6.50s. Paper. P98. $1.95.

**Earhart, Mary.** Frances Willard. From Prayers to Politics. 1944. *o.p.*

**Earle, Homer Price,** *joint ed.:* ROSENBERG, Horas vividas.

**Earlier and Later Forms of Petrarch's Canzoniere:** PHELPS.

**Early Chicago:** MASON.

**Early Childhood Education:** LIGHT.

**Early Days of Peoria:** McCULLOUGH.

**Early Development of Lepidosteus osseus:** EYCLESHYMER.

**Early History of Chlorine:** SCHEELE.

**Early Irish Literature:** DILLON.

**Early Society in Southern Illinois:** PATTERSON.

**Early Theater in Eastern Iowa:** SCHICK.

**Earth as a Planet:** *see* KUIPER, Solar System.

**Earth Sciences:** DONNELLY.

**Earthbound China:** FEI.

**East, Edward Murray:** *see* CASTLE, Heredity and Eugenics.

**Easterbrook, W. T.** Farm Credit in Canada. Foreword by H. A. Innis. 1938. *o.p.*

**Easterby, J. H.,** *ed.* The South Carolina Rice Plantation as Revealed in the Papers of Robert F. W. Allston. 1945. *o.p.*

**Easum, Chester Verne.** The Americanization of Carl Schurz. 1929. *o.p.*

**Eaton, Helen Slocomb.** Semantic Frequency List for English, French, German, and Spanish. A Correlation of the First Six Thousand Words in Four Single-Language Frequency Lists. Issued by the Committee on Modern Languages of the American Council of Education. 1940. *o.p.*

**Eaton, Leonard K.** Landscape Artist in America. The Life and Work of Jens Jensen. 1964. x, 240 p. 28 cm. 64-23422. Illus. $10.00.

**Eberhard, Wolfram.** Folktales of China. Edited and translated by Wolfram Eberhard. 1965. xlii, 267 p. 22 cm. 65-25440. FW. $5.50. COBE.

**Eby, Kermit.** The God in You. With a Foreword by Reinhold Niebuhr. 1954. xi, 162 p. 20 cm. 55-8454. $3.50s.

**Echelon Spectroscope:** MICHELSON.

**Eckhardt, Carl Conrad.** The Papacy and World-Affairs as Reflected in the Secularization of Politics. 1937. *o.p.*

**Eckhart, Carl Henry,** *trans.:* HEISENBERG, Physical Principles of the Quantum Theory.

**Ecological Relations of the Vegetation on the Sand Dunes of Lake Michigan:** COWLES.

**Ecological Relations of the Vegetation of Western Texas:** BRAY.

**Economic Geography Maps:** JONES.

**Economic History of the United States:** WRIGHT.

**Economic Meaning of the Townsend Plan:** UNIVERSITY OF CHICAGO ROUND TABLE.

**Economic Policy and Democracy:** HEILPERIN.

**Economic Policy for a Free Society:** SIMONS.

**Economic Policy for Rearmament:** HART.

**Economic Position of the Chinese in the Netherlands Indies:** CATOR.

**Economic Problems of War:** WRIGHT.

**Economic Role of the State:** ORTON.

**Economic Studies of the University of Chicago (EC):**
1. COHN, Science of Finance.
2. WHITE, History of the Union Pacific.
3. ELLSTAETTER, Indian Silver Currency.
4. MILLION, State Aid to Railways.
5. WILLIS, History of the Latin Monetary Union.

**Economic World Today:** MORLEY.

**Economics of Competitive Bidding:** WESTON.

**Economics of Discrimination:** BECKER.

**Economics of Labor:** MILLIS.

**Economics of Military Occupation:** BLOCH.

**Economics of Overhead Costs:** CLARK.

**Economics Research Studies (ERS):**
BECKER, Economics of Discrimination.
FRIEDMAN, Studies in the Quantity Theory of Money.
HAAVELMO, Study in the Theory of Investment.
HARBERGER, Demand for Durable Goods.
LEWIS, Unionism and Relative Wages in the United States.
MEIGS, Free Reserves and the Money Supply.
PESEK, Gross National Product of Czechoslovakia.

**Economics of Technocracy:** DIRECTOR.

**Economics of Trade Unions:** REES.

**Economics of Underdeveloped Countries:** BAUER.

**Economies in Food. Quantity Recipes Using Evaporated Milk:** McAULEY.

**Economy in the National Government:** DOUGLAS.

**Economy of Time in Education:** BAGLEY.

**Écrivons:** EDDY.

**Edds, Mac V., Jr.,** ed. Immunology and Development. 1958. xi, 59 p. 24 cm. 58-13251. DBC. $2.50s.

**Eddy, Helen M.** Basic French. Vol. I (*Avant de lire, Si nous lisions, Pierrille*), by Helen M. Eddy, Grace Cochran, and Isabel C. Redfield. Vol. II (*Madame Thérèse, Les trois mousquetaires, Écrivons, Grammaire*), by Helen M. Eddy, Marguirette M. Struble, Grace Cochran, and Florence B. Williams. HCLS. *o.p.*

**Eddy, Helen M.** HCLS. *o.p.*
Beginning French.
Écrivons (with Marguirette Struble).
French Workbook.
Progress Tests in French.

**Eddy, Helen M.,** *joint ed.:* COCHRAN, Pierrille.

**Edel, Abraham.** Science and the Structure of Ethics. 1961. iv, 101 p. 24 cm. 61-8082. Paper. IEUS, II, 3. $2.25s.

**Edfelt, Ake W.** Silent Speech and Silent Reading. 1960. vii, 165 p. Illus. 24 cm. 60-8125. $3.50t. COBE.

**Edgerton, A. H.** Vocational Guidance and Vocational Education for Industries. By A. H. Edgerton and others. 1924. NSSE, 23d Yrbk., Part II. *o.p.*

**Edgerton, William Franklin.** Notes on Egyptian Marriage, Chiefly in the Ptolemaic Period. 1931. SAOC 1. *o.p.*

**Edgerton, William Franklin.** The Thutmosid Succession. 1933. SAOC 8. *o.p.*

**Edgerton, William Franklin,** ed. Medinet Habu Graffiti. Facsimiles. 1937. xi, 6 p. 103 plates (3 in color), 11 plans. 41 cm. 42-23005. OIP, XXXVI. $15.00.

**Edgerton, William Franklin,** *trans.* Historical Records of Ramses III. The Texts in *Medinet Habu*, Volumes I–II. Translated, with Explanatory Notes, by William F. Edgerton and John A. Wilson. 1936. xv, 159 p. 30 cm. 36-477. Paper. SAOC 12. $5.00.

**Edicts of Asoka:** NIKAM.

**Edie, Lionel Danforth.** Capital, the Money Market, and Gold. 1929. SBA, I. *o.p.*

**Edie, Lionel Danforth:** *see* WRIGHT, Gold and Monetary Stabilization.

**Edmonson, J. B.** The Textbook in American Education. Prepared by J. B. Edmonson, Chairman of the Society's Committee. 1931. NSSE, 30th Yrbk., Part II. viii, 364 p. 24 cm. E31-416. Cloth. $2.50$^t$. Paper. $1.75$^t$.

**Edmund Spenser and the *Faerie Queene*:** BRADNER.

**Edna St. Vincent Millay and Her Times:** ATKINS.

**Educating Gifted Children:** DeHAAN.

**Educating for the Professions:** ANDERSON.

**Education:** BURTON.

**Education on the Air . . . and Radio and Education, 1935.** Proceedings of the Sixth Annual Institute for Education by Radio Combined with the Fifth Annual Assembly of the National Advisory Council on Radio in Education. Edited by Levering Tyson and Josephine MacLatchy. 1935. *o.p.*

**Education of an Army:** LUVAAS.

**Education for Business:** LYON.

**Education of Business Men:** JAMES.

**Education and the Cult of Efficiency:** CALLAHAN.

**Education for Democracy:** AMERICAN COUNTRY LIFE ASSOCIATION, Proceedings, No. 19.

**Education in a Democracy:** EDWARDS.

**Education of Exceptional Children:** KIRK.

**Education of Gifted Children:** WHIPPLE.

**Education for the Gifted in School and College:** HAVIGHURST.

**Education versus Indoctrination in the Schools:** KALLEN.

**Education of a Navy:** SCHURMAN.

**Education with Reference to Sex. Agencies and Methods:** HENDERSON.

**Education with Reference to Sex. Pathological, Economic, and Social Aspects:** HENDERSON.

**Education for Rural America:** REEVES.

**Education in Rural Communities:** STRANG.

**Education and Social Change in Ghana:** FOSTER.

**Education for Social Work:** STEINER.

**Education of Teachers:** NATIONAL SOCIETY OF COLLEGE TEACHERS OF EDUCATION, Proceedings, No. 23.

**Education and Training of Secondary Teachers:** ELLIOTT.

**Education of Women:** TALBOT.

**Educational Administration:** REAVIS.

**Educational Administration in an Era of Transition:** LAWLER.

**Educational Broadcasting. A Bibliography:** LINGEL.

**Educational Broadcasting, 1936.** Proceedings of the First National Conference on Educational Broadcasting, Held in Washington, D.C., December, 1936. Edited by C. S. Marsh. 1937. *o.p.*

**Educational Broadcasting, 1937.** Proceedings of the Second National Conference on Educational Broadcasting, Held in Chicago, Nov.–Dec., 1937. Edited by C. S. Marsh. 1938. *o.p.*

**Educational Conference of the Academies and High Schools Affiliating or Co-operating with the University of Chicago.** Proceedings of the 16th Educational Conference. 1903. *o.p.*

**Educational Diagnosis:** BRUECKNER.

**Educational Frontier:** NATIONAL SOCIETY OF COLLEGE TEACHERS OF EDUCATION, Proceedings, No. 21.

**Educational Legislation and Administration:** HOBSON.

**Educational Objectives for Colleges and Schools of Education:** NATIONAL SOCIETY OF COLLEGE TEACHERS OF EDUCATION, Proceedings, No. 13.

**Educational Program:** HAGGERTY.

**Educational Situation:** DEWEY.

**Educational Surveys:** NATIONAL SOCIETY OF COLLEGE TEACHERS OF EDUCATION, Proceedings, No. 5.

**Educational Talking Picture:** DEVEREUX.

**Education's Own Stations. The History of Broadcast Licenses Issued to Educational Institutions:** FROST.

**"Edward" and "Sven i Rosengård":** TAYLOR.

**Edwards, Edgar O.,** ed. The Nation's Economic Objectives. With Contributions by Edward S. Mason, Lester V. Chandler, Arthur F. Burns, Fritz Machlup, Kenneth R. Boulding, Seymour E. Harris, and Jacob Viner. 1964. viii, 167 p. 64-15816. RSS. $4.95.

**Edwards, Lyford Paterson.** The Natural History of Revolution. 1927. SOC. o.p.

**Edwards, Newton.** The Courts and the Public Schools. The Legal Basis of School Organization and Administration. 1933. Rev. ed. 1955. xvii, 622 p. 24 cm. SSCI. $11.50ᵗ.

**Edwards, Newton,** ed. Education in a Democracy. By Newton Edwards, Robert J. Havighurst, Guy T. Buswell, Mandel Sherman, Ralph W. Tyler, William C. Reavis, John Dale Russell, George A. Works. 1941. WFL. o.p.

**Edwards, Owen Morgan.** A Short History of Wales. 1907. o.p.

**Edwards Papers:** WASHBURNE.

**Edwin Smith Surgical Papyrus:** BREASTED.

**Eells, Kenneth.** Intelligence and Cultural Differences. A Study of Cultural Learning and Problem-solving. By Kenneth Eells, Allison Davis, Robert J. Havighurst, Virgil E. Herrick, and Ralph Tyler. 1951. o.p.

**Effect of Aqueous Solutions upon the Germination of Fungus Spores:** STEVENS.

**Effective Dean of Women:** ACHESON.

**Effective English:** HULBERT.

**Efficiency of College Students:** PITTENGER.

**Efficiency and Scarcity Profits:** FOREMAN.

**Efficiency and Uplift:** HABER.

**Egan, Margaret E.,** joint ed.: SHERA, Bibliographic Organization.

**Eggan, Fred.** Social Organization of the Western Pueblos. 1950. xviii, 373 p. Illus. 22 cm. 50-9388. AN. $6.00ˢ.

**Eggan, Fred,** ed. Social Anthropology of North American Tribes. By Fred Eggan, editor, William H. Gilbert, Jr., J. Gilbert McAllister, Philleo Nash, Morris Edward Opler, John H. Province, and Sol Tax. 1950. Rev. enl. ed. 1955. xv, 574 p. Illus. 22 cm. 55-5123. $8.00ˢ.

**Egoism:** WALLIS.

**Egypt Exploration Society:** see CALVERLEY, The Temple of King Sethos I at Abydos.

**Egyptian Antiquities:** PIER.

**Egyptian Book of the Dead Documents:** ALLEN.

**Egyptian Coffin Texts:** BUCK.

**Ehrensvärd, Gösta.** Life. Origin and Development. 1962. x, 164 p. Illus. 21 cm. 62-19620. Cloth. $4.50ˢ. Paper. PSS 515. $1.50.

**Ehrensvärd, Gösta.** Man on Another World. Translated by Lennart and Kajsa Rodén. 1965. vii, 182 p. 21 cm. 65-17287. $5.95.

**Ehret, Charles F.,** joint ed.: DUCOFF, Mitogenesis.

**Ehrich, Robert W.,** ed. Chronologies in Old World Archaeology. Edited by Robert W. Ehrich. 1965. Illus. 24 cm. 65-17296. Cloth. $7.50. Paper. $5.00.

**Ehrich, Robert W.,** ed. Relative Chronologies in Old World Archeology. Edited by Robert W. Ehrich. o.p.

**Eickhoff, Edith,** joint author: BRUCE, Michigan Poor Law.

**Eight American Praxapostoloi:** CLARK.

**Eikenberry, W. L.** The Teaching of General Science. 1922. o.p.

**Einstein, Albert.** Symposium on America and the World Situation. By Albert Einstein, Henry M. Robinson, and William B. Munro. A Radio Presentation Delivered January 23, 1933. Introduction by Robert A. Millikan. Program Sponsored by the

Southern California College Student Body Presidents' Association and Presented under the Auspices of the National Advisory Council on Radio in Education. 1933. *o.p.*

**Eiselen, Frederick Carl:** *see* BEWER, Religion of the Bible.

**Eiseley, Loren C.,** *joint ed.:* TAX, Appraisal of Anthropology.

**Eisen, Gustavus Augustus.** Ancient Oriental Cylinder and Other Seals, with a Description of the Collection of Mrs. William H. Moore. 1940. xiii, 94 p. Illus. 30 cm. 40-13161. OIP, XLVII. $5.00.

**Eisinger, Chester E.** Fiction of the Forties. 1963. xii, 392 p. 21 cm. 63-2090. Cloth. $7.95. Paper. P188. $2.25.

**Eitel, Wilhelm.** The Physical Chemistry of the Silicates. 1954. xvii, 1,592 p. Illus. 25 cm. 54-8733. PS. $45.00s.

**Eitner, Lorenz.** Géricault. An Album of Drawings in the Art Institute of Chicago. 1960. 48 p. of text. 101 plates. 28 cm. 60-14231. $10.00s.

**Ekvall, Robert B.** Cultural Relations on the Kansu-Tibetan Border. 1939. AN. *o.p.*

**Ekvall, Robert B.** Religious Observances in Tibet. Patterns and Function. 1964. xiii, 313 p. 24 cm. 64-23423. $8.50s.

**Elasticity and Anelasticity of Metals:** ZENER.

**Elazar, Daniel.** The American Partnership. Intergovernmental Co-operation in Nineteenth Century United States. 1962. xvi, 358 p. 24 cm. 62-17132. $6.50s.

**Eleazer Williams:** WIGHT.

**Electrochemistry:** LEMON.

**Electrodynamics:** LEMON.

**Electrolysis of Organic Compounds:** KOLBE.

**Electromagnetic Field:** MASON.

**Electron:** MILLIKAN.

**Electrons:** LEMON.

**Electrons (+ and —), Protons, Photons, Neutrons, and Cosmic Rays:** MILLIKAN.

**Electrostatics:** LEMON.

**Elementary Course in English:** HOSIC.

**Elementary Eugenics:** DOWNING.

**Elementary Nature of Chlorine:** DAVY.

**Elementary Particles:** LEVI SETTI.

**Elementary Russian Grammar:** PROKOSCH.

**Elementary School:** REAVIS.

**Elementary School Record.** A Series of Nine Monographs on the Elementary School of the University of Chicago. Edited by John Dewey and Laura L. Runyon. 1900. *o.p.*

1. *Art:* Principles of Education Applied to Art. By Lillian Cushman. School Reports of Groups III and IV. The General Principles of Work, Educationally Considered. By John Dewey.
2. *Music:* Song Composition. By Mrs. May Root Kern. School Reports of Groups V and VI. With Introduction by John Dewey.
3. *Textiles:* Textile Industries. By Althea Harmer. The Psychology of Occupation. By John Dewey. School Reports of Groups VII and VIII.
4. *Botany:* Experiments in Plant Physiology. By Katharine Andrews. Reflective Attention. By John Dewey. School Reports of Groups IX and X.
5. *Kindergarten:* The Subprimary (Kindergarten) Department. By Georgia P. Scates. Froebel's Educational Principles. By John Dewey.
6. *Science:* Science in Elementary Education. By Katherine B. Camp. School Reports of Groups III and IV.
7. *Manual Training:* Manual Training. By Frank H. Ball. School Reports of Groups V and VI.
8. *History:* The Aim of History in Elementary Education. By John Dewey. History. By Georgia F. Bacon. School Reports of Groups VII and VIII.
9. *Curriculum:* The Psychology of an Elementary Curriculum. By John Dewey. School Reports of Groups IX and X.

**Elements of Acoustic Phonetics:** LADEFOGED.

**Elements of the Acoustics of Speech:** LADEFOGED.

**Elements of Bibliography:** FEIPEL.

**Elements of Chrysostom's Power:** ANDERSON.

**Elements of Cloud Physics:** BOWERS.

**Elements of Debating:** LYON.

**Elements of Electrocardiographic Interpretation:** KATZ.

**Elements of General Linguistics:** MARTINET.

**Elements of the Geological Time-Scale:** WILLIAMS.

**Elements of Hebrew by an Inductive Method:** HARPER.

**Elements of Judicial Strategy:** MURPHY.

**Eleven Twenty-six:** WIRTH.

**Elford, C. R.,** *joint author:* RIEHL, Ocean Analysis from Coastal Reports.

**Eliade, Mircea,** *ed.* The History of Religions. Essays in Methodology. Edited by Mircea Eliade and Joseph M. Kitagawa. 1959. xi, 164 p. 22 cm. 59-11621. $5.00ˢ.

**Eliel Saarinen:** CHRIST-JANER.

**Eliot, T. S.:** *see* SMITH, The Poetry and Plays of T. S. Eliot.

**Elizabeth Day McCormick Apocalypse:** WILLOUGHBY.

**Elizabethan Jig and Related Song Drama:** BASKERVILL.

**Elizabethan and Metaphysical Imagery:** TUVE.

**Elizur Wright. The Father of Life Insurance:** WRIGHT.

**Elkanah Settle:** BROWN.

**Elkin, A. P.** Art in Arnhem Land. By A. P. Elkin and Catherine and Ronald Berndt. 1951. *o.p.*

**Elkins, Stanley M.** Slavery. A Problem in American Institutional and Intellectual Life. 1959. viii, 248 p. 22 cm. 59-12284. $4.50ˢ.

**Ellerman, Ferdinand,** *joint author:* HALE, Rumford Spectroheliograph.

**Ellerman, Ferdinand,** *joint author:* HALE, Spectra of Stars of Secchi's Fourth Type.

**Ellingson, Mark,** *joint author:* JARVIE, Handbook on the Anecdotal Behavior Journal.

**Elliott, Edward Charles.** The Education and Training of Secondary Teachers. By E. C. Elliot and others. 1905. NSSE, 4th Yrbk., Part I. *o.p.*

**Elliott, Edward Charles,** *joint author:* SPAULDING, Aims, Scope, and Methods of a University Course in Public-School Administration.

**Elliott, Edward Charles:** *see* CUBBERLEY, Research in the Field of Education.

**Elliott, Mabel Agnes.** Conflicting Penal Theories in Statutory Criminal Law. 1931. *o.p.*

**Ellis, John Tracy.** American Catholicism. 1956. xiii, 208 p. 21 cm. 56-11002. Cloth. CHAC. $3.50ˢ. Paper. $1.75.

**Ellis, Lewis Ethan.** James Schouler, *in* HUTCHINSON, Marcus W. Jernegan Essays.

**Ellstaetter, Karl.** The Indian Silver Currency. An Historical and Economic Study. Translated by J. Laurence Laughlin. 1895. EC. *o.p.*

**Elmer E. Ellsworth:** INGRAHAM.

**Elvey, Christian Thomas,** *joint author:* FROST, Study of the Spectrum of 7ε Aurigae.

**Embree, Edwin Rogers.** Island India Goes to School. By Edwin R. Embree, Margaret Sargent Simon, and W. Bryant Mumford. 1934. *o.p.*

**Embree, John Fee.** Suye Mura. A Japanese Village. 1939. xxviii, 354 p. Illus. 21 cm. AN. Cloth. $6.00ˢ. Paper. P173. $2.95.

"Professor Embree's research embraces village organization, the family and household, classes and associations, religion, economics, and the life history of the individual. His is not another book for those who would linger over the tea ceremony, the kabuki, or ukiyoye prints; it is designed not only for those genuinely interested in the Far East, but for all who in their regard for the interests of the human race as a whole seek to find realities, and as such it is to be recommended." —*Time.*

**Embryo-Sac of Aster Novae-Angliae:** CHAMBERLAIN.

**Embryonic Nutrition:** RUDNICK.

**Emergence of the American University:** VEYSEY.

**Emergent Responsibilities in Higher Education:** RUSSELL.

**Emmet, Boris.** Catalogues and Counters. A History of Sears, Roebuck and Company. By Boris Emmet and John E. Jeuck. 1950. xix, 788 p. 50-7387. 25 cm. $8.95ˢ.

**Emotion and Meaning in Music:** MEYER.

**Empire and Sovereignty:** FREUND.

**En Guatemala. Lecturas:** CASTILLO.

**En route:** BOND.

**Encyclopedia and Unified Science:** NEURATH.

**Enders, Allen C.,** *ed.* Delayed Implantation. 1963. viii, 318 p. Illus. 24 cm. 63-18851. RSS. $8.50ˢ.

**Endocrine Glands:** CARLSON.

**Endocrines in Development:** WATTERSON.

**Enemy Joy:** BELITT.

**Energy and Its Transformations:** LEMON.

**Engberg, Robert Martin.** The Hyksos Reconsidered. 1939. SAOC 18. *o.p.*

**Engberg, Robert Martin.** Notes on the Chalcolithic and Early Bronze Age Pottery of Megiddo. By Robert M. Engberg and Geoffrey M. Shipton. 1934. SAOC 10. *o.p.*

**Engberg, Robert Martin:** *see* GUY, Megiddo Tombs.

**Engberg, Robert Martin:** *see* MAY, Material Remains of the Megiddo Cult.

**England and America:** READ.

**Englehardt, N. L.** The Planning and Construction of School Buildings. Prepared by N. L. Englehardt, Chairman of the Society's Committee. 1934. NSSE, 33d Yrbk., Part I. xi, 337 p. 24 cm. E34-429. $2.50ᵗ.

**English Common Reader:** ALTICK.

**English Composition:** HUDELSON.

**English Poems:** BRONSON.

**English Radicalism, 1832–1852:** MACCOBY.

**English Radicalism, 1853–1886:** MACCOBY.

**English Reformation:** HULBERT.

**English Studies of the University of Chicago** (ENG):
    I. LYDGATE, Assembly of Gods.
    II. LEWIS, History of the English Paragraph.
    III. REYNOLDS, Treatment of Nature in English Poetry.
    IV. CARPENTER, Metaphor and Simile.
    V. COX, Arte or Crafte of Rhethoryke.

**English Words with Native Roots:** NICHOLSON.

**Engravers and Etchers:** CARRINGTON.

**Enjoyment and Use of Art in the Elementary School:** TODD.

**Ennis, Philip,** *ed.* Seven Questions about the Profession of Librarianship. Edited by Philip Ennis and Howard W. Winger. Twenty-sixth Annual Conference, Graduate Library School. 1962. v, 104 p. 25 cm. 62-994. LS. $3.75ˢ.

**Ennis, Thomas E.** French Policy and Developments in Indochina. 1936. *o.p.*

**Enquiry into Goodness:** SPARSHOTT.

**Enrichment of the English Curriculum:** LYMAN.

**Environment and Education:** BURGESS.

**Environment and Nation:** TAYLOR.

**Environment, Race, and Migration:** TAYLOR.

**Environmental Factors in Christian History:** McNEILL.

**Environmental Influences on Prenatal Development:** MINTZ.

**Epideictic Literature:** BURGESS.

**Epidemiology and Control of Malaria in Palestine:** KLIGLER.

**Epigraphic Survey:**

*Medinet Habu.* 5 vols. *Vol. I:* Earlier Historical Records of Ramses III. 1930. Harold H. Nelson, Field Director. xviii, 12 p. Illus. 48 cm. OIP, VIII. $25.00. *Vol. II:* Later Historical Records of Ramses III. 1932. Harold H. Nelson, Field Director. x, 2 p. Illus. 48 cm. OIP, IX. $25.00. *Vol. III:* The Calendar, the "Slaughterhouse," and Minor Records of Ramses III. 1934. Harold H. Nelson, Field Director. xvi, 2 p. Illus. 48 cm. OIP, XXIII. $15.00. *Vol. IV:* Festival Scenes of Ramses III. 1940. Harold H. Nelson, Field Director. xii p. Illus. 48 cm. OIP, LI. $30.00. *Vol. V:* The Temple Proper, Part I. 1957. George R. Hughes, Field Director. OIP, LXXXIII. $25.00. *The set.* $100.00. *Vol. VI:* The Temple

Proper, Part II. George R. Hughes, Field Director. 1963. 48 cm. 120 plates. OIP, LXXXIV. $30.00. *Vol. VII:* The Temple Proper, Part III. The Third Hypostyle Hall and All Rooms Accessible from It. OIP, XCIII. $35.00.

*Reliefs and Inscriptions at Karnak.* 3 vols. *Vol. I:* Ramses III's Temple within the Great Inclosure of Amon, Part I. 1936. Harold H. Nelson, Field Director. xiv, 2 p. Illus. 48 cm. OIP, XXV. $30.00. *Vol. II:* Ramses III's Temple within the Great Inclosure of Amon (Part II) and Ramses III's Temple in the Precinct of Mut. xi, 2 p. Illus. 48 cm. OIP, XXXV. $20.00. *Vol. III:* The Bubastite Portal. 1954. George R. Hughes, Field Director. 20 p. Illus. 48 cm. OIP, LXXIV. $10.00.

**Epiphanius.** Epiphanius' Treatise on Weights and Measures. The Syriac Version. Edited by James Elmer Dean. With a Foreword by Martin Sprengling. 1935. xv, 145 p. 25 cm. 35-1907. Paper. SAOC 11. $2.50.

**Epiphyseal Chart:** HODGES.

**Epistle of Pelagia:** GOODSPEED.

**Epochs in Buddhist History:** SAUNDERS.

**Epstein, Leon D.** Britain—Uneasy Ally. 1954. viii, 279 p. 24 cm. 54-12795. CSAFP. $4.00ˢ.

**Equilibrium in the System Composed of Sodium Carbonate, Sodium Bicarbonate, Carbon Dioxide, and Water:** McCOY.

**Erasmus.** The Colloquies of Erasmus. Translated with an Introduction by Craig R. Thompson. 1965. xxxiv, 662 p. 25 cm. 64-22246. $15.00.

The "Colloquies" are extremely varied in theme and manner. Typically each takes its rise from an idea, a note or observation on life, a proposition to be proved, disproved or at least examined. The interlocutors represent human types or attitudes or convictions. Thus each colloquy is a clash of opinion or a conflict of behavior.

This new, handsome, valuable edition of the "Colloquies" is the first Englishing of the complete text since the 18th century. Mr. Thompson has been working on Erasmus for a good many years; his book is a tribute of love. His delightful translation is in racy modern colloquial English when Erasmus was racy; it is sober and profound when the master was sober.—Willie Lee Rose, in *The New York Times Book Review.*

**Erb, Frank Otis.** The Development of the Young People's Movement. 1917. *o.p.*

**Ercker, Lazarus.** Treatise on Ores and Assaying. Translated by Anneliese G. Sisco and Cyril S. Smith. 1951. PS. *o.p.*

**Ericksen, Ephraim Edward.** The Psychological and Ethical Aspects of Mormon Group Life. 1922. *o.p.*

**Erik Dorn:** HECHT.

**Ernest De Witt Burton:** GOODSPEED.

**Erosion, Transportation, and Sedimentation:** UDDEN.

**España en América. Segundas lecturas:** CASTILLO.

**España y la cultura española:** KRAUSE.

**Espurgatoire St. Patriz:** JENKINS.

**Essays concerning Jesus and His Times.** Reprinted from the *The Biblical World,* Vols. IV, V, VI, and VIII, 1894–1896. 1897. *o.p.*

**Essays in Criticism:** JORDAN.

**Essays in Experimental Logic:** DEWEY.

**Essays in the History of Economics:** STIGLER.

**Essays in Honor of Conyers Read:** DOWNS.

**Essays in Honor of William E. Dodd:** CRAVEN.

**Essays of Jean Rey.**

**Essays in Linguistics:** GREENBERG.

**Essays in Political Economy:** INNIS.

**Essays on Population:** FIELD.

**Essays in Positive Economics:** FRIEDMAN.

**Essen, Leon van der.** A Short History of Belgium. 1916. 2d rev. ed. 1920. *o.p.*

**Essentials of German Reviewed:** HAGBOLDT.

**Essentials for the Microscopical Determination of Rock-forming Minerals:** JOHANNSEN.

**Essentials of a Written Constitution:** JUDSON.

**Essien-Udom, E. U.** Black Nationalism. The Search for an Identity. 1962. xiii, 367 p. Illus. 24 cm. 62-12632. $6.95ˢ.

**Estimates of Moral Values Expressed in Cicero's Letters:** GORDIS.

**Ethical Principles:** DEWEY.

**Ethical Significance of Feeling:** WRIGHT.

**Ethical World-Conception of the Norse People:** FORS.

**Ethics of the Old Testament:** MITCHELL.

**Ethics in the School:** YOUNG.

**Ethiopic Martyrdoms:** GOODSPEED.

**Ethnic Survey of Woonsocket, Rhode Island:** WESSEL.

**Ethno-Botany of the Coahuilla Indians:** BARROWS.

**Etiquette of Race Relations:** DOYLE.

**Etkin, William,** *ed.* Social Behavior and Organization among Vertebrates. With Contributions by Frank A. Beach, David E. Davis, William Etkin, Daniel S. Lehrman, J. P. Scott, and Niko Tinbergen. 1964. xii, 307 p. 64-13947. Illus. $7.50<sup>t</sup>.

**Etruscans:** RICHARDSON.

**Études critiques sur *Manon Lescaut*:** HAZARD.

**Eucken, Walter.** Foundations of Economics. History and Theory in the Analysis of Economic Reality. Translated from the German by T. W. Hutchinson. 1951. *o.p.*

**Eulenspiegel und Münchhausen:** HAGBOLDT.

**Eurich, Alvin C.** General Education in the American College. Prepared by Alvin C. Eurich, Chairman of the Society's Committee. 1939. NSSE, 38th Yrbk., Part II. xii, 382, xxxiv p. 24 cm. E39-669. Cloth $2.75<sup>t</sup>. Paper $2.00<sup>L</sup>.

**Euripides:** *see* COMPLETE GREEK TRAGEDIES.

**Europa: Argument to V-E Day, January 1944 to May 1945:** CRAVEN.

**Europe: Torch to Pointblank, August 1942 to December 1943:** CRAVEN.

**Europe's Steppe Frontier, 1500–1800:** McNEILL.

**Evaluating the Work of the School:** REAVIS.

**Evaluation of Higher Institutions. (EHI):**

VOL.
1. ZOOK, Principles of Accrediting Higher Institutions.

2. HAGGERTY, Faculty.
3. HAGGERTY, Educational Program.
4. WAPLES, Library.
5. GARDNER, Student Personnel Service.
6. RUSSELL, Administration.
7. RUSSELL, Finance.

**Evaluation of Reading:** ROBINSON.

**Evaluation of Teacher Merit:** REAVIS.

**Evans, E. A., Jr.** Biochemical Studies of Bacterial Viruses. 1952. BM. *o.p.*

**Evans, E. A., Jr.,** *ed.* The Biological Action of the Vitamins. A Symposium. 1942. BM. *o.p.*

**Evans, Eldon Cobb.** A History of the Australian Ballot System in the United States. 1917. *o.p.*

**Evans, Herbert Francis.** The Sunday-School Building and Its Equipment. 1914. PM. *o.p.*

**L'Évasion du duc de Beaufort (Dumas):** BOND.

**Everyday Greek:** HOFFMAN.

**Evidence in Athenian Courts:** BONNER.

**Evolution of the Atherosclerotic Plaque:** JONES.

**Evolution of Balzac's *Comédie humaine*:** DARGAN.

**Evolution, the Bible, and Religion:** GURNEY.

**Evolution after Darwin:** TAX.

**Evolution of Early Christianity:** CHASE.

**Evolution of *The Faerie Queene*:** BENNETT.

**Evolution, Genetics, and Eugenics:** NEWMAN.

**Evolution of the Human Brain:** VON BONIN.

**Evolution of Life:** TAX.

**Evolution of Man:** TAX.

**Evolution and Modification of Behavior:** LORENZ.

**Evolution of Sex in Plants:** COULTER.

**Evolution et structure de la langue française:** WARTBURG.

**Evolution of Vertebrae:** WILLISTON.

**Evolutionist and Missionary: John Thomas Gulick:** GULICK.

**Ewing, A. C.** A Short Commentary on Kant's *Critique of Pure Reason*. 1938. viii, 278 p. 19 cm. $4.50s. OBE.

**Excavation of Armageddon:** FISHER.

**Excavation of Medinet Habu:** HÖLSCHER.

**Excavations at Ancient Thebes:** HÖLSCHER.

**Excavations in the Plain of Antioch. I:** BRAIDWOOD.

**Excess and Restraint:** BERNDT.

**Excursion through the Rivers and Harbors of Chicago:** BLOUNT.

**Excursion on the Rock River of Illinois:** BLOUNT.

**Exercises in Current Economics:** HAMILTON.

**Exercises and Questions for Use with *Principles of Money*:** MOULTON.

**Exercises in Value Theory:** DAVENPORT.

**Existence and Inquiry:** LEE.

**Existence, Meaning, and Reality:** MOORE.

**Expanding Horizons in Medical Social Work:** GOLDSTINE.

**Experience and the Analytic:** PASCH.

**Experience and Prediction:** REICHENBACH.

**Experiment in Alien Labor:** PAYNE.

**Experimental Design and Its Statistical Basis:** FINNEY.

**Experimental Study of Eye-Voice Span:** BUSWELL.

**Experimental Study of Frustration:** PHILP.

**Experimental Study in Left-Handedness:** BEELEY.

**Experimental Study of the Mental Processes:** STEVANOVIC.

**Experimental Study in the Psychology of Reading:** SCHMIDT.

**Experimental Study of the Porosity and Permeability of Clastic Sediments:** FRASER.

**Experiments on Air:** CAVENDISH.

**Experiments in General Psychology:** SCHEIDEMANN.

**Experiments upon Magnesia Alba:** BLACK.

**Experiments in Plant Physiology:** ANDREWS.

**Experiments and Studies in Modern Language Teaching:** COLEMAN.

**Explication de textes:** VIGNERON.

**Exploration of the Colorado River:** POWELL.

**Exploration in Reading Patterns:** STRANG.

**Explorations in Central Anatolia:** OSTEN.

**Explorations in Hittite Asia Minor. A Preliminary Report:** OSTEN.

**Explorations in Hittite Asia Minor, 1927–28:** OSTEN.

**Explorations in Hittite Asia Minor, 1929:** OSTEN.

**Exploring in Physics:** STEPHENSON.

**Expression of the Emotions in Man and Animals:** DARWIN.

**Extension Program of the University of Chicago:** THOMPSON.

**Extent of Enterprise Monopoly:** NUTTER.

**Extent of Illness:** MILLS.

**Extracts from Micrographia:** HOOKE.

**Extra-Curricular Activities:** KOOS.

**Eycleshymer, Albert Chauncey.** The Early Development of Lepidosteus osseus. 1903. *o.p.*

**Ezra Studies:** TORREY.

**Fabeln:** HAGBOLDT.

**Fabulous Voyager:** KAIN.

**Face of God:** KENNEDY, *in his* Plays for Three Players. Vol. III.

**Face of the Moon:** BALDWIN.

**Factor Analysis. A Synthesis of Factorial Methods:** HOLZINGER.

**Factor Analysis to 1940:** WOLFLE.

**Factorial Studies of Intelligence:** THURSTONE.

**Factorial Study of Perception:** THURSTONE.

**Factors in Social Evolution:** AMERICAN SOCI-
OLOGICAL SOCIETY, Vol. XVI.

**Faculty:** HAGGERTY.

**"Faculty" of Imagination:** HARGREAVES.

**Fahrney, Ralph Ray.** Edward Channing, *in*
HUTCHINSON, Marcus W. Jernegan Essays.

**Failing Student:** HEATON.

**Fairbank, John K.,** *ed.* Chinese Thought
and Institutions. 1957. xvi, 422 p. 25 cm.
57-5272. CSCC. $8.50ˢ.

**Fairweather, George Owen.** Wanted: Intelligent Local Self-Government. Restoring the
Parties to the People. 1934. *o.p.*

**Fakhry, Ahmed.** The Pyramids. 1961. 266 p.
Illus. 24 cm. 61-8645. $5.95.

**Falk, Isidore Sydney.** A Community Medical
Service Organized under Industrial Aus-
pices in Roanoke Rapids, North Carolina.
By I. S. Falk, Don M. Griswold, M.D., and
Hazel I. Spicer. With Reports on Certain
Phases of the Organization by David Ries-
man, M.D., and George P. Muller, M.D.
1932. CMC 20. *o.p.*

**Falk, Isidore Sydney.** The Costs of Medical
Care. A Summary of Investigations on the
Economic Aspects of the Prevention and
Care of Illness. By I. S. Falk, C. Rufus
Rorem, and Martha D. Ring. With a Fore-
word by Ray Lyman Wilbur, M.D. 1933.
*o.p.*

**Falk, Isidore Sydney.** The Incidence of Illness and the Receipt and Costs of Medical
Care among Representative Families. Experiences in Twelve Consecutive Months
during 1928–1931. By I. S. Falk, Margaret
C. Klem, and Nathan Sinai. 1933. CMC 26.
*o.p.*

**Falk, Isidore Sydney.** Organized Medical
Service at Fort Benning, Georgia. By I. S.
Falk. With Reports on Certain Phases of
the Organization by David Riesman, M.D.,
and George P. Muller, M.D. 1932. CMC 21.
*o.p.*

**Falk, Isidore Sydney,** *joint author:* NORTON,
Laboratory Outlines in Bacteriology and
Immunology.

**Falk, Isidore Sydney,** *joint ed.:* JORDAN,
Newer Knowledge of Bacteriology and Immunology.

**Falk, Isidore Sydney:** *see* GUILD, Surveys of
the Medical Facilities in Three Representative Southern Counties.

**Fallers, Lloyd A.** Bantu Bureaucracy. A
Century of Political Evolution among the
Basoga of Uganda. *Reissue,* 1965. xix, 283 p.
21 cm. 65-25124. Cloth. $5.00ˢ. Paper. P197.
$1.95.

**Falls, Frederick Howard:** *see* ADAIR, Maternal
Care Complications.

**Family:** AMERICAN SOCIOLOGICAL SOCIETY, Vol.
III.

**Family:** MOWRER.

**Family in the American Economy:** KYRK.

**Family and the Depression:** CAVAN.

**Family Disorganization:** MOWRER.

**Family Farm Policy:** ACKERMAN.

**Family and the State:** BRECKINRIDGE.

**Family Welfare Work in a Metropolitan Com-
munity:** BRECKINRIDGE.

**Family Worlds:** HESS.

**Far Peoples:** PHILLIPS.

**Faraday, Michael.** The Liquefaction of Gases.
Papers by Michael Faraday (1823–1845).
With an Appendix Consisting of Papers
by Thomas Northmore on the Compression
of Gases (1805–1806). 1902. AC. *o.p.*

**Faris, Ellsworth,** *ed.* Intelligent Philanthropy.
Edited by Ellsworth Faris, Ferris Laune,
and Arthur J. Todd. 1930. *o.p.*

**Faris, Robert E. L.** Mental Disorders in
Urban Areas. An Ecological Study of
Schizophrenia and Other Psychoses. By
Robert E. L. Faris and H. Warren Dunham.
1939. xxxviii, 270 p. 21 cm. Paper. P183.
SOC. $1.95.

**Farm Business:** HORNE.

**Farm Credit in Canada:** EASTERBROOK.

**Farm Income and Farm Life:** AMERICAN
COUNTRY LIFE ASSOCIATION.

**Farm Ownership, Tenancy, and Land Use in a Nebraska Community:** DILLER.

**Farm Youth:** AMERICAN COUNTRY LIFE ASSOCIATION, Proceedings No. 9.

**Farmers' Mutual Fire Insurance:** VALGREN.

**Farnsworth, Alice Hall.** A Comparison of the Photometric Fields of the 6-Inch Doublet, 24-Inch Reflector, and 40-Inch Refractor of the Yerkes Observatory, with Some Investigation of the Astrometric Field of the Reflector. 1926. YO, IV. *o.p.*

**Farnsworth, Alice Hall:** *ed.* PARKHURST, Zone +45° of Kapteyn's Selected Areas.

**Farrington, Frederick Ernest.** Observation and Practice Teaching in College and University Departments of Education. By F. E. Farrington, G. D. Strayer, and W. B. Jacobs. 1909. *o.p.*

**Fashoda:** GIFFEN.

**Father Pierre François Pinet:** GROVER.

**Fauna of the Kimmswick Limestone:** BRADLEY.

**Faunce, William Herbert Perry:** *see* SMITH, Guide to the Study of the Christian Religion.

**Favill, John.** Outline of the Cranial Nerves. 1933. *o.p.*

**Fay, Marjorie J.** Carolus et Maria. Second Extensive Reader. HCLC.

**Federal Aid and Public Assistance in Illinois:** MILES.

**Federal Grants for Vocational Rehabilitation:** MACDONALD.

**Federal Reserve Bank Policy in Iowa:** PICKETT.

**Federal Tax Reform:** SIMONS.

**Federalism and the New Nations of Africa:** CURRIE.

**Fei, Hsiao-tung.** China's Gentry. Essays in Rural-Urban Relations. Revised and edited by Margaret Park Redfield. 1953. *o.p.*

**Fei, Hsiao-tung.** Earthbound China. A Study of Rural Economy in Yunnan. By Hsiao-tung Fei and Chih-I Chang. 1945. *o.p.*

**Feidelson, Charles N., Jr.** Symbolism and American Literature. 1953. x, 356 p. 21 cm. 53-6890. 1959. Paper. P37. $1.95.

". . . belongs in that small company of critical writings which have sought . . . to reappraise the entire American literary tradition within the vocabulary most influential today."—R. W. B. Lewis, in *The Hudson Review.*

**Feiler, Arthur.** Farewell to Security. Germany and the World, 1919–39: *in* BENEŠ, International Security.

**Feipel, Louis Nicholas.** Elements of Bibliography. 1916. *o.p.*

**Fellman, David.** The Constitutional Right of Association. 1963. x, 110 p. Index. 22 cm. 63-9728. $3.95ˢ.

**Fenner, Clarence Norman.** Bore-Hole Investigations in Yellowstone Park. 1936. *o.p.*

**Fenton, Frances.** The Influence of Newspaper Presentations upon the Growth of Crime and Other Anti-social Activity. 1911. *o.p.*

**Fenwick, Sara Innis,** *ed.* New Definitions of School-Library Service. Twenty-fourth Annual Conference, Graduate Library School. 1960. v, 90 p. 25 cm. 60-2341. LS. $3.75ˢ.

**Ference, Michael, Jr.** Analytical Experimental Physics. By Michael Ference, Jr., Harvey Brace Lemon, and Reginald J. Stephenson. 3d ed., 2d rev. 1956. xv, 623 p. Illus. 26 cm. 55-5124. PS. $8.00ᵗ.

"Its form makes its perusal a pleasure, its matter is simply but fully expounded, and it achieves a happy combination of mathematical theory and experimental atmosphere."—*American Journal of Science.*

**Ference, Michael, Jr.** A Mobile Weather Unit with an Example of a Field Forecast. By Michael Ference, Jr., and M. Snodgrass. 1943. *o.p.*

**Ferguson, Charles A.,** *General Editor,* CONTRASTIVE STRUCTURE SERIES.

**Ferguson, John Calvin.** Chinese Painting. 1927. *o.p.*

**Ferguson, John Calvin.** Outlines of Chinese Art. The Scammon Lectures for 1918. Published for the Art Institute of Chicago. 1919. SL. *o.p.*

**Ferguson, William Duncan.** The Legal Terms Common to the Macedonian Inscriptions and the New Testament. 1913. HLL. *o.p.*

**Fermi, Enrico.** The Collected Papers of Enrico Fermi. 27 cm. 60-12465. *Vol. I:* 1921–38. 1962. xlii, 1,044 p. $15.00ˢ. *Vol. II:* 1939–54. 1965. xvi, 1083 p. $22.50ˢ. (Excluding Continent of Europe.)

**Fermi, Enrico.** Notes on Quantum Mechanics. 1961. vii. 171 p. 21 cm. 61-9447. Paper. PSS 512. $1.75.

**Fermi, Enrico.** Nuclear Physics. A Course Given by Enrico Fermi at the University of Chicago. Notes compiled by Jay Orear, A. H. Rosenfeld, and R. A. Schluter. Rev. ed. 1950. ix, 248 p. Planographed. 26 cm. 50-6826. Paper. PS. $3.50ᵗ. (Not for sale in South Asia.)

**Fermi, Laura.** Atoms in the Family. My Life with Enrico Fermi. 1954, ix, 267 p. Illus. 54-12114. Cloth. 24 cm. $4.75ˢ. Paper. P58. 21 cm. $1.95. COBE.

". . . a charmingly written and informative story of the career of one of the world's foremost physicists."—John Pfeiffer in *Saturday Review.*

**Fermi, Laura.** Atoms for the World. 1957. xii, 227 p. Illus. 22 cm. 57-6977. $4.50ˢ.

**Fermi, Laura.** Mussolini. 1961. vii, 477 p. Illus. 22 cm. 61-17075. $5.95.

**Fernsemer, Oscar F. W.** *ed.* Der Meister. By Josef Ponten. HCLS. *o.p.*

**Ferris, Carrie Sivyer.** The Sunday Kindergarten. Game, Gift, and Story. 1909. CS. *o.p.*

**Fertig, James Walter.** The Secession and Reconstruction of Tennessee. 1898. *o.p.*

**Fertilization of Albugo candida:** DAVIS.

**Fetal and Neonatal Death:** POTTER.

**Fetter, Frank Whitson.** The New Deal and Tariff Policy. 1933. 2d ed. 1937. PPP, 7. *o.p.*

**Feudal Germany:** THOMPSON.

**Feudal Relations between the Kings of England and Scotland:** WYCKOFF.

**Feudal Society:** BLOCH.

**Fichter, Joseph H., S.J.** Social Relations in the Urban Parish. 1954. vii, 263 p. 24 cm. 54-11207. $5.50ˢ.

**Fichter, Joseph H., S.J.** Sociology. 1957. xii, 432 p. 24 cm. 57-6272. $5.00ᵗ.

**Fichter, Joseph H., S.J.** Southern Parish. The Dynamics of a City Church. 1951. *o.p.*

**Fiction of the Forties:** EISINGER.

**Field, Frederick Vanderbilt.** American Participation in the China Consortiums. 1931. IPR *o.p.*

**Field, Hazel E.** An Atlas of Cat Anatomy. By Hazel E. Field and Mary E. Taylor. 1950. 134 p. Illus. 31 × 26 cm. 50-6520. Wire-X binding. Stain-resistant cover. BM. $5.75ᵗ.

**Field, James Alfred.** Essays on Population and Other Papers. By James Alfred Field. Together with Material from his Notes and Lectures. Compiled and edited by Helen Fisher Hohman. With a Foreword by James Bonar. 1931. SE *o.p.*

**Field, James Alfred,** *joint editor:* MARSHALL, Materials for the Study of Elementary Economics.

**Field, Marshall.** Freedom Is More than a Word. 1945. *o.p.*

**Field and Laboratory Guide in Biological Nature-Study:** DOWNING.

**Field and Laboratory Guide in Physical Nature:** DOWNING.

**Field Studies in Sociology:** PALMER.

**Field Work:** JUNKER.

**Fifty Foreign Films:** BOND.

**Fiji:** COULTER.

**Fijian Village:** QUAIN.

**Filipino Immigration:** LASKER.

**Finality of the Christian Religion:** FOSTER.

**Finance:** RUSSELL.

**Finance of Higher Education:** RUSSELL.

**Financial Mobilization for War.** Papers Presented at a Joint Conference of the Western Economic Society, and the City Club of Chicago, June 21 and 22, 1917. By Edwin R. A. Seligman, E. Dana Durand, Harold G. Moulton, Ernest L. Bogart, Carl C. Plehn, Lucius Teter, Thomas S. Adams, William A. Scott and A. C. Miller. 1917. *o.p.*

**Financial Organization of Society:** MOULTON.

**Financial Reports for Colleges and Universities:** NATIONAL COMMITTEE ON STANDARD REPORTS.

**Financing the Consumer:** COVER.

**Finch, Vernor Clifford.** Geographic Surveys. Geographic Surveying, by Vernor C. Finch. Montfort—A Study in Landscape Types in Southwestern Wisconsin, by Vernor C. Finch. Magdalena Atlipac. A Study in Terrene Occupancy in Mexico, by Robert S. Platt. Edited by Charles C. Colby. 1933. GSC. *o.p.*

**Findley, Warren G.,** *ed.* The Impact and Improvement of School Testing Programs. Prepared by Warren G. Findley, Chairman of the Society's Committee. 1963. NSSE, 62d Yrbk., Part II. 22 cm. 63-5289. $4.50ᵗ.

**Finer, Herman.** The Presidency: Crisis and Regeneration. An Essay in Possibilities. 1960. xi, 374 p. 22 cm. 60-14230. $5.00ˢ.

**Finer Structure of Neurones:** HATAI.

**Finite Collineation Groups:** BLICHFELDT.

**Finlay-Freundlich, E.** Cosmology. 1951. iv, 59 p. 25 cm. 51-4594. Paper. IEUS, I, 8. $1.50ˢ.

**Finney, D. J.** Experimental Design and Its Statistical Basis. 1955. xi. 169 p. Illus. 22 cm. 55-10245. SLBM. $4.50ᵗ.

**Finney, D. J.** An Introduction to the Theory of Experimental Design. 1960. xii, 223 p. 22 cm. 60-8126. Paper. $3.50ᵗ.

**First Annual Report of the Director of the Yerkes Observatory:** HALE.

**First Authorized English Bible:** WILLOUGHBY.

**First Five Lives of Annie Besant:** NETHERCOT.

**First Italian Book:** WILKINS.

**First Lessons in Spoken French for Doctors and Nurses:** WILKINS.

**First Lessons in Spoken French for Men in Military Service:** WILKINS.

**First Moroccan Crisis:** ANDERSON.

**First Report of the Prehistoric Survey Expedition:** SANFORD.

**First-Year Mathematics for Secondary Schools:** BRESLICH.

**First-Year Mathematics for Secondary Schools:** MYERS.

**Fischelis, Robert Philipp,** *joint author:* ROREM, Costs of Medicines.

**Fish, Carl Russell.** The United States and Great Britain. By Carl Russell Fish, Sir Norman Angell, and Rear Admiral Charles L. Hussey, U.S.N. Retired. 1932. APA. *o.p.*

**Fisher, Clarence Stanley.** The Excavation of Armageddon. 1929. OIC 4 *o.p.*

**Fisher, I. Z.** Statistical Theory of Liquids. Translated by Theodore Switz. With a Supplement by Stuart Rice and Peter Gray. 1964. xii, 335 p. 22 cm. 64-22249. $12.50ˢ.

**Fishman, Mildred:** *see* LELAND, State-Local Fiscal Relations.

**Fiske, Horace Spencer.** The Ballad of Manila Bay and Other Verses. 1900. *o.p.*

**Fitzgibbons, Russell H.,** *ed.* The Constitutions of the Americas. 1948. *o.p.*

**Fitz-Hugh, Thomas.** The Philosophy of the Humanities. 1897. *o.p.*

**5 Sight-Reading and Vocabulary Tests for Inductive Readings in German. Book I:** HAGBOLDT.

**Five-Year Program of the Committee on the Costs of Medical Care:** COMMITTEE ON THE COSTS OF MEDICAL CARE.

**Fixed Investment Trust:** KETCHUM.

**Flaming Ministers:** KENNEDY, *in his* Plays for Three Players. Vol. II.

**Fletcher, Angus S.:** *see* HURST, *Great Britain and the Dominions.*

**Fletcher, Harris Francis.** Milton's Semitic Studies and Some Manifestations of Them in His Poetry. 1926. *o.p.*

**Flexible Exchange Rates:** SOHMEN.

**Flickinger, Roy Caston.** The Greek Theatre and Its Drama. 4th ed. 1936. xxi, 384 p. 23 cm. 36-11686. $7.50ˢ.

". . . Professor Flickinger's life work is still an indispensable book which has the additional advantage over its rivals in that it comprises a fairly comprehensive treatment of a vast subject within the compass of a single volume."—Alfred Gudeman, in *The Classical Weekly.*

**Flickinger, Roy Caston.** The Meaning of ἐπὶ τῆς σκηνῆς in Writers of the Fourth Century. 1902. *o.p.*

**Flickinger, Roy Caston.** Plutarch as a Source of Information on the Greek Theatre. 1904. *o.p.*

**Flickinger, Roy Caston,** *ed.* Carmina Latina. Selected and Edited by Roy C. Flickinger. 1923. *o.p.*

**Flickinger, Roy Caston,** *ed.* Songs for the Latin Club. Selected and Edited by Roy C. Flickinger. 1924. *o.p.*

**Flights over Ancient Cities of Iran:** SCHMIDT.

**Flights over the United States (Meteorological Conditions in the Upper Reaches):** WULF.

**Flint, Nott William.** The University of Chicago. A Sketch. 1905. *o.p.*

**Flor de las ystorias de Orient:** HAYTON.

**Flora of the Eagle Creek Formation:** CHANEY.

**Flory, Charles David.** Osseous Development in the Hand as an Index of Skeletal Development. 1936. CD. *o.p.*

**Flower, George.** History of the English Settlement in Edwards County, Illinois, Founded in 1817 and 1818, by Morris Birkbeck and George Flower. With Preface and Footnotes by E. B. Washburne. 1882. *o.p.*

A publication of the Chicago Historical Society.

**Fluctuations in Human Output:** PHILPOTT.

**Flügel, John Carl.** Practice, Fatigue, and Oscillation. A Study of Work at High Pressure. 1928. BJP. *o.p.*

**Fobes, Francis H.** Philosophical Greek. An Introduction. 1957. xii, 322 p. 25 cm. 57-8580. $5.00ᵗ.

**Folk Culture of Yucatan:** REDFIELD.

**Folklore in the English and Scottish Ballads:** WIMBERLY.

**Folktales of China:** EBERHARD.

**Folktales of England:** BRIGGS.

**Folktales of Hungary:** DÉGH.

**Folktales of Israel:** NOY.

**Folktales of Japan:** SEKI.

**Folktales of Norway:** CHRISTIANSEN.

**Folktales of the World (FW).** RICHARD M. DORSON, *General Editor:*

BRIGGS, Folktales of England.
CHRISTIANSEN, Folktales of Norway.
DÉGH, Folktales of Hungary.
EBERHARD, Folktales of China.
NOY, Folktales of Israel.
SEKI, Folktales of Japan.

**Food Chemistry and Cookery:** HALLIDAY.

**Food as a Factor in Student Life:** RICHARDS.

**Food for Life:** GERARD.

**Food Poisoning:** DACK.

**Food Poisoning and Food-borne Infection:** JORDAN.

**Food Supply and Raw Materials in Japan:** PENROSE.

**Food for the World:** SCHULTZ.

**Foods and Nutrition:** CARLSON.

**Food from the Hills:** KENNEDY, in his Plays for Seven Players.

**Foote, Nelson N.** Identity and Interpersonal Competence. A New Direction in Family Research. By Nelson N. Foote and Leonard S. Cottrell, Jr. 1955. ix, 305 p. 24 cm. 56-11957. $6.00ˢ.

**For Future Doctors:** GREGG.

**Forced To Be Free:** MONTGOMERY.

**Foreign Economic Policy:** RANDALL.

**Foreign Investment and War:** STALEY.

**Foreign Investments:** CASSEL.

**Foreign Policy for the United States:** WRIGHT.

**Foreman, Clarence James.** Efficiency and Scarcity Profits. An Economic and Legal Analysis of the Residual Surplus. 1930. MSB. *o.p.*

**Foreman, Grant.** The Last Trek of the Indians. 1946. *o.p.*

**Foreshadowings of the Christ:** HARPER.

**Formation of the New Testament:** GOODSPEED.

**Forms and Motions of the Solar Prominences:** PETTIT.

**Forms, Records, and Reports in Personnel Administration:** HITCHCOCK.

**Forrer, Emil O.** Die hethitische Bilderschrift. 1932. ix, 62 p. Illus. 26 cm. A33-1105. Paper. SAOC 3. $2.50.

**Forrest, Jacob Dorsey.** The Development of Western Civilization. A Study in Ethical Economic and Political Evolution. 1907. *o.p.*

**Fors, Andrew Peter.** The Ethical World-Conception of the Norse People. 1904. *o.p.*

**Forthcoming Developments in American Education:** REAVIS.

**Fortunatus:** PURIN.

**Forward Prices for Agriculture:** JOHNSON.

**Fossil Evidence for Human Evolution:** CLARK.

**Foster, Frank Hugh.** A Genetic History of the New England Theology. 1907. *o.p.*

**Foster, George Burman.** The Finality of the Christian Religion. 1906. 2d ed. 1909. *o.p.*

**Foster, George Burman.** The Function of Death in Human Experience. 1919. *o.p.*

**Foster, George Burman.** The Function of Religion of Man's Struggle for Existence. 1909. *o.p.*

**Foster, George Burman:** *see* SMITH, Guide to the Study of the Christian Religion.

**Foster, H. H.,** *joint author:* CUBBERLEY, Research within the Field of Education.

**Foster, Philip.** Education and Social Change in Ghana. 1965. 448 p. 65-12040. $7.50ˢ. COBE.

**Foster, William Trufant,** *chairman.* Doctors, Dollars, and Disease. Public Health Series. 19 pamphlets. 1934–35. *o.p.*

**Foundations of the Atomic Theory:** DALTON.

**Foundations of Biology:** MAINX.

**Foundations of Curriculum-making:** RUGG.

**Foundations of Economics:** EUCKEN.

**Foundations of English for Foreign Students:** WALPOLE.

**Foundations of Logic and Mathematics:** CARNAP.

**Foundations of the Metaphysics of Morals:** KANT.

**Foundations of the Molecular Theory:** DALTON.

**Foundations of a More Stable World Order:** LAVES.

**Foundations of Physics:** FRANK.

**Foundations of the Public Library:** SHERA.

**Foundations of Slavic Bibliography:** KERNER.

**Foundations of the Social Sciences:** NEURATH.

**Foundations of Systematization within Empiricism:** HEMPEL.

**Foundations of the Theory of Signs:** MORRIS.

**Foundations of the World Republic:** BORGESE.

**Founding of the Christian Church:** BURTON.

**Founding of the Federal Republic of Germany:** GOLAY.

**Four Dialectical Theories of Poetry:** MARSH.

**Four Gospels of Karahissar:** COLWELL.

**Four Letters of the Apostle Paul:** BURTON.

**4 Vocabulary Tests for *Inductive Readings in German*. Book II:** HAGBOLDT.

**Four Years of Network Broadcasting:** REED.

**14 Tests on *A Modern German Grammar*:** HAGBOLDT.

**Fourth Report of the Committee on Economy of Time in Education:** AYER.

**Fowler, Frank Hamilton.** The Negatives of the Indo-European Languages. 1896. *o.p.*

**Fowler, Henry Thatcher.** The Origin and Growth of the Hebrew Religion. 1916. HER. *o.p.*

**Fowler, Henry Thatcher:** *see* BEWER, Religion of the Bible.

**Fowler, William A.** Nucleosynthesis in Massive Stars and Supernovae. By William A. Fowler and Fred Hoyle. 1965. vi, 148 p. 25 cm. 65-14516. $4.50ˢ.

**Fowlie, Wallace.** Mallarmé. With Ten Line Drawings by Henri Matisse. 1953. 299 p. Illus. 21 cm. 53-9931. Paper. P93. $1.75.

**Fox, Annette Baker.** The Power of Small States. Diplomacy in World War II. 1959. ix, 212 p. 22 cm. 59-12285. $5.50ᵗ.

**Fox, Philip.** The Rotation Period of the Sun as Determined from Measures of Plates Taken with the Rumford Spectrohelio-graph. 1921. YO III. *o.p.*

**Fra le corde d'un contrabasso** (Farino): SCHOBINGER.

**Fragments from Graeco-Jewish Writers:** STEARNS.

**France d'Amérique:** DELÉRY.

**Francesco di Giorgio:** WELLER.

**Francesco Petrarca:** COSENZA.

**Francis Willard:** EARHART.

**Fränger, Wilhelm.** The Millennium of Hieronymus Bosch. Outlines of a New Interpretation. Translated by Eithne Wilkins and Ernst Kaiser. 1951. *o.p.*

**Frank, Philip.** Foundations of Physics. 1946. vi, 78 p. 25 cm. 46-4908. Paper. IEUS, I, 7. $1.50ᵗ.

**Frank, Tenny.** A Stichometric Scholium to the *Medea* of Euripides, with Remarks on the Text of Didymus. 1903. *o.p.*

**Frank, Mortimer,** *ed.* and *trans.: see* CHOULANT, History and Bibliography of Anatomic Illustration.

**Frankfort, H. A.** Arrest and Movement. An Essay on Space and Time in the Representational Art of the Near East. 1951. *o.p.*

**Frankfort, H. A.,** *joint author:* FRANKFORT, Intellectual Adventure of Ancient Man.

**Frankfort, Henri.** Archeology and the Sumerian Problem. 1932. SAOC 4. *o.p.*

**Frankfort, Henri.** The Gimilsin Temple and the Palace of the Rulers at Tell Asmar. By Henri Frankfort, Seton Lloyd, and Thorkild Jacobsen. With a Chapter by Günter Martiny. 1940. xviii, 271 p. Illus. 30 cm. 40-14630. OIP, XLIII. $12.00.

**Frankfort, Henri.** The Intellectual Adventure of Ancient Man. An Essay on Speculative Thought in the Ancient Near East. By Henri and H. A. Frankfort, John A. Wilson, Thorkild Jacobsen, and William A. Irwin. 1946. viii, 401 p. 23 cm. 47-1318. OIE. $7.50ᵗ.

**Frankfort, Henri.** Iraq Excavations of the Oriental Institute, 1932/33. Third Preliminary Report of the Iraq Expedition. 1934. ix, 92 p. Illus. 26 cm. 33-6601. Paper. OIC 17. $2.00.

**Frankfort, Henri.** Kingship and the Gods. A Study of Ancient Near Eastern Religion as the Integration of Society and Nature. 1948. xxvi, 444 p. Illus. 26 cm. 48-5158. OIE. $9.00ˢ.

". . . the student should be grateful for such an excellent guide to the understanding of difficult material much of which is buried in scattered studies of a highly technical nature, frequently in a foreign language. The skillful treatment of such a complex subject is all the more to be admired for its simple clarity of expression."—William Stevenson Smith, in *The American Journal of Archaeology.*

**Frankfort, Henri.** More Sculpture from the Diyala Region. 1943. xiii, 48 p. 95 plates, 1 map. 31 cm. 43-3190. OIP, LX. $10.00.

**Frankfort, Henri.** Oriental Institute Discoveries in Iraq, 1933/34. Fourth Preliminary Report of the Iraq Expedition. By Henri Frankfort. With a Chapter by Thorkild Jacobsen. 1935. xi, 103 p. Illus. 25 cm. 33-6601. Paper. OIC 19. $2.00.

**Frankfort, Henri.** Progress of the Work of the Oriental Institute in Iraq, 1934/35. Fifth Preliminary Report of the Iraq Expedition. 1936. xi, 108 p. Illus. 25 cm. Paper. OIC 20. $2.75.

**Frankfort, Henri.** Sculpture of the Third Millennium B.C. from Tell Asmar and Khafajah. 1939. xviii, 271 p. Illus. 30 cm. 39-31400. OIP, XLIV. $9.00.

**Frankfort, Henri.** Stratified Cylinder Seals from the Diyala Region. 1955. xi, 78 p. 96 plates of photographs and maps. 31 cm. 54-11976. OIP, LXXII. O.S.

**Frankfort, Henri.** Tell Asmar and Khafaje. The First Season's Work in Eshnunna, 1930/31. By Henri Frankfort, Thorkild Jacobsen, and Conrad Preusser. 1932. ix, 112 p. Illus. 26 cm. 33-6601. Paper. OIC 13. $1.50.

**Frankfort, Henri.** Tell Asmar, Khafaje, and Khorsabad. Second Preliminary Report of the Iraq Expedition. 1933. ix, 102 p. Illus. 26 cm. 33-6601. Paper. OIC 16. $1.50.

**Frankfort, Henri:** *see* DELOUGAZ, Pre Sargonid Temples in the Diyala Region.

**Frankfort, Henri:** *see* LOUD, Khorsabad. I.

**Franklin, Frank George.** The Legislative History of Naturalization in the United States from the Revolutionary War to 1861. 1906. *o.p.*

**Franklin, John Hope.** Reconstruction after the Civil War. 1961. x, 258 p. 21 cm. 61-15931. Cloth. CHAC. $5.00s. Paper. $1.95.

**Fraser, Gladys Genevra.** The Licensing of Boarding Homes, Maternity Homes, and Child Welfare Agencies. 1937. SSM. *o.p.*

**Fraser, Horace J.** Experimental Study of the Porosity and Permeability of Clastic Sediments *in* GRATON, Systematic Packing of Spheres.

**Frazier, E. Franklin.** The Negro Family in Chicago. 1932. SOC. *o.p.*

**Frazier, E. Franklin.** The Negro Family in the United States. 1939. Rev. and abr. ed., 1966. xxii, 372 p. 21 cm. 66-15868. Cloth. $6.00. Paper. P205. $2.45.

"Few studies have done as much to illuminate the obscure processes of social change as this thorough-going treatment."—T. Lynn Smith, in *The Annals of the American Academy of Political and Social Science.*

**Frazier, E. Franklin.** Racial Variations in Immunity to Syphilis. A Study of the Disease in the Chinese, White, and Negro Races. By E. Franklin Frazier and Li Hung-Chiung. 1948. BM. *o.p.*

**Fred Newton Scott Anniversary Papers.** Contributed by Former Students and Colleagues of Professor Scott and Presented to Him in Celebration of His Thirty-eighth Year of Distinguished Service in the University of Michigan. 1888–1926. *Editors:* Clarence DeWitt Thorpe and Charles E. Whitmore. 1929. *o.p.*

**Free Reserves and the Money Supply:** MEIGS.

**Free and Responsible Press:** LEIGH.

**Freedman, Ronald.** Recent Migration to Chicago. 1950. *o.p.*

**Freedom in Agricultural Education:** HARDIN.

**Freedom of Communication:** AMERICAN SOCIOLOGICAL ASSOCIATION, Vol. IX.

**Freedom and the Economic System:** HAYEK.

**Freedom is More than a Word:** FIELD.

**Freedom of the Movies:** INGLIS.

**Freedom of the Press:** HOCKING.

**Freeman, Frank N.** The Chicago Mental Growth Battery. Ten Tests of Graded Difficulty for the Study of Intellectual Development. By Frank N. Freeman and M. A. Wenger. 1943. *o.p.*

**Freeman, Frank N.** The Handwriting Movement; a Study of the Motor Factors of Excellence in Penmanship. By Frank N. Freeman with the Assistance of H. W. Nutt, Mary L. Dougherty, C. F. Dunn and P. V. West. 1918. SEM 9. *o.p.*

**Freeman, Frank N.** Individual Pupil Graph Assembled from Teacher's Rating Scales for Pupil Adjustment. By Frank N. Freeman and Ethel Kawin. 1937. *o.p.*

**Freeman, Frank N.** The Scientific Movement in Education. Prepared by Frank N. Freeman, Chairman of the Society's Committee. 1938. NSSE, 37th Yrbk., Part II. xii, 529, ix p. 22 cm. E38-148. Paper. $3.00t.

**Freeman, Frank N.** Teacher's Rating Scales for Pupil Adjustment. By Frank N. Freeman and Ethel Kawin. 1937. *o.p.*

**Freeman, Frank N.,** *ed.* Visual Education. A Comparative Study of Motion Pictures and Other Methods of Instruction. The Report of an Investigation Made with the Aid of a Grant from the Commonwealth Fund. By Frank N. Freeman, F. D. McClusky, H. W. James, E. H. Reeder, A. P. Hollis, Caroline Hoefer, Edna Keith, H. Y. McClusky, E. C. Rolfe, Lena A. Shaw, D. E. Walker, Nina J. Beglinger, Jean A. Thomas. 1924. *o.p.*

**Freeman, Frank N.,** *joint author:* NEWMAN, Twins.

**Freeman, Otis W.:** *see* HAAS, American Empire.

**Freer Gospels:** GOODSPEED.

**French, John W.** The Description of Aptitude and Achievement Tests in Terms of Rotated Factors. 1951. *o.p.*

**French, Thomas M.** The Integration of Behavior. *Vol. I:* Basic Postulates. 1952. xi, 272 p. $6.00ˢ. *Vol. II:* The Integrative Process in Dreams. 1954. xi, 367 p. $7.50ˢ. *Vol. III:* The Reintegrative Process in Psychoanalytic Treatment. 1958. xi, 512 p. 22 cm. 52-7329. BM. $11.50ˢ.

**French Canada in Transition:** HUGHES.

**French in the Elementary School:** DUNKEL.

**French Policy and Developments in Indochina:** ENNIS.

**French Political System:** DUVERGER.

**French Verb:** NITZE.

**French Verb Blanks:** WILKINS.

**French Workbook:** EDDY.

**Freund, Ernst.** Administrative Powers over Persons and Property. A Comparative Survey. 1928. *o.p.*

**Freund, Ernst.** Empire and Sovereignty. 1903. *o.p.*

**Freund, Ernst.** The Legal Nature of Corporations. 1897. POL. *o.p.*

**Freund, Ernst.** The Police Power. Public Policy and Constitutional Rights. 1904. *o.p.*

**Freund, Ernst.** Standards of American Legislation. 1917. *Reissue,* 1965. Preface by Francis A. Allen. li, 327 p. 21 cm. 65-17289. Cloth. $5.50ˢ. Paper. P182. $2.45.

**Friedenberg, Edgar Z.** Self-perception in the University. A Study of Successful and Unsuccessful Graduate Students. By Edgar Z. Friedenberg and Julius A. Roth. 1954. x, 102 p. 25 cm. 53-13548. Paper. SEM 80. $2.00ᵗ.

**Friedlander, Walter.** Child Welfare in Germany before and after Naziism. By Walter Friedlander and Earl Dewey Myers. 1940. SSM. *o.p.*

**Friedman, Albert B.** The Ballad Revival. 1961. vii, 376 p. 22 cm. 61-11894. $6.00ˢ.

**Friedman, Maurice S.** Martin Buber. The Life of Dialogue. 1955. *O.I.*

**Friedman, Milton.** Capitalism and Freedom. 1962. vi, 202 p. 21 cm. 62-19619. Cloth. $3.95ˢ. Paper. P111. $1.50.

**Friedman, Milton.** Essays in Positive Economics. 1953. vi, 328 p. 25 cm. 53-3533. $6.25ˢ.

"In its subjects . . . this volume falls roughly into two halves, one devoted to methodology . . . the other to monetary policy and theory. . . . There is, of course, much to disagree with. . . . But there is so much that is acute, independent and stimulating, that this collection of essays should be widely and warmly welcomed."—T. W. Hutchinson, in *The Economic Journal*.

**Friedman, Milton,** *ed.* Studies in the Quantity Theory of Money. 1956. v, 265 p. 24 cm. 56-10999. ERS. $6.00ˢ.

**Friedman, Milton,** *joint ed.:* CAMBRIDGE ECONOMIC HANDBOOKS.

**Friedmann, Eugene A.** The Meaning of Work and Retirement. By Eugene A. Friedmann and Robert J. Havighurst. 1954. *o.p.*

**Friedrich, Carl Joachim.** Alfred Weber's Theory of the Location of Industries. English edition with Introduction and Notes by Carl J. Friedrich. 1929. xxxiv, 256 p. Illus. 21 cm. 29-18915. $5.00ˢ.

**Friedrich, Carl Joachim.** The Philosophy of Law in Historical Perspective. 2d ed. 1963. xii, 298 p. 57-9546. 21 cm. Cloth. $6.50ˢ. Paper. P135. $1.95.

**Friends or Enemies?** PRATT.

**From Art to Theatre: Form and Convention in the Renaissance:** KERNODLE.

**From Black to White in South Australia:** BERNDT.

**From Descartes to Kant:** SMITH.

**From Economic Theory to Policy:** WALKER.

**From Galileo to the Nuclear Age:** LEMON.

**From Prairie to Corn Belt:** BOGUE.

**From Rationalism a Priori to Empiricism:** ROUGIER.

**From Relief to Social Security:** ABBOTT.

**From the Renaissance to Romanticism:** ARTZ.

**From Versailles to Munich:** SCHMITT.

**From the Wagner Act to Taft-Hartley:** MILLIS.

**Fromm-Reichmann, Frieda.** Principles of Intensive Psychotherapy. 1950. xviii, 246 p. 22 cm. 50-9782. BM. $4.50ˢ. 1960. Paper. P49. $1.75.

**Fromm-Reichmann, Frieda.** Psychoanalysis and Psychotherapy. Selected Papers. Edited by Dexter M. Bullard. 1959. xiv, 350 p. 24 cm. 59-10746. $7.50ˢ.

"Frieda Fromm-Reichmann was outstanding on the contemporary scene as a psychoanalyst in the humanitarian tradition; her concern with the totality of man's existence, coupled with an exceptional sensitivity to the most delicate nuances of human behavior, allowed her to transcend the narrow confines of any particular school of thought. . . . These are qualities that make Fromm-Reichmann's papers classics in the field of psychotherapy, and evoke . . . gratitude for the opportunity to have the best of them collected into one volume."—Eugene B. Brody, in *The Journal of Nervous and Mental Diseases.*

**Frontier Moves West:** TRYON.

**Frontiers of Public Administration:** GAUS.

**Frost, Edwin Brant.** Radial Velocities of 500 Stars of Spectral Class A. By Edwin B. Frost, Storrs B. Barrett, and Otto Struve. 1929. YO VII. *o.p.*

**Frost, Edwin Brant.** Radial Velocities of Twenty Stars Having Spectra of the Orion Type. By Edwin B. Frost and Walter S. Adams. 1903. *o.p.*

**Frost, Edwin Brant.** A Study of the Spectrum of $7_\epsilon$ Aurigae. By Edwin B. Frost, Otto Struve, and C. T. Elvey. 1932. YO, VII. *o.p.*

**Frost, Edwin Brant,** *joint ed.:* BARNARD, Micrometric Measures of Star Clusters.

**Frost, Edwin C.** Frost's Culture Chart (Modified). 1911. *o.p.*

Originally for use with HEINEMANN, Laboratory Guide in Bacteriology.

**Frost, S. E., Jr.** Education's Own Stations. The History of Broadcast Licenses Issued to Educational Institutions. 1937. *o.p.*

**Frost, S. E., Jr.** Is American Radio Democratic? 1937. *o.p.*

**Frost's Culture Charts:** FROST.

**Frye, Theodore C.** Development of the Pollen in Some Asclepiadaceae. 1901. HB. *o.p.*

**Frye, Theodore C.** A Morphological Study of Certain Asclepiadaceae. 1902. HB. *o.p.*

**Fryxell, Fritiof Melvin.** The Physiography of the Region of Chicago. By F. M. Fryxell. Prepared by the University of Chicago Local Community Research Committee, and the Chicago Commonwealth Club, for the Committee on General Surveys of the Chicago Regional Planning Association. 1927. SSCI. *o.p.*

**Fucilla, Joseph G.** *ed.* Il Vecchio della montagna. By Grazia Deledda. HCLS.

**Fulbright Program:** JOHNSON.

**Fuller, George Damon.** The Vegetation of the Chicago Region. An Outline of Some of the Principal Plant Associations Together with Lists of Their Principal Species. 1925. *o.p.*

**Fuller, Henry B.** With the Procession. 1894. *Reissue,* 1965. Introduction by Mark Harris. xiv, 274 p. 21 cm. 65-17288. CF. $4.95.

**Fuller, John L.,** *joint author:* SCOTT, Genetics and the Social Behavior of the Dog.

**Fullerton, Kemper:** *see* GORDON, Truth about the Bible.

**Fultz, Dave.** Upper-Air Trajectories and Weather Forecasting. 1945. DMMR 19. *o.p.*

**Fun with Flutes:** DUSHKIN.

Function of Death: FOSTER.

Function of Religion: FOSTER.

Function of Socialization: BURGESS.

Functional Approach to Religious Education: CHAVE.

Functional versus the Representational Theories of Knowledge: MOORE.

Fund Theory of Accounting and Its Implications for Financial Reports: VATTER.

Fundamental Astrometry: PODOBED.

Fundamental Concepts of Higher Algebra: ALBERT.

Fundamental Reading Habits. A Study of Their Development: BUSWELL.

Fundamentals of Acoustics: LEMON.

Fundamentals of Concept Formation in Empirical Science: HEMPEL.

Fundamentals of Good Medical Care: LEE.

Funeral Management: DOWD.

Fünf berühmte Märchen: HAGBOLDT.

Funk, Robert W., *ed. and trans.* Greek Grammar of the New Testament and Other Early Christian Literature. A revision of F. Blass and A. Debrunner, "Grammatik der neutestamentlichen Griechisch," incorporating supplementary notes by A. Debrunner. 1961. xxxviii, 325 p. Index. 26 cm. 61-8077. $10.00t. COBE.

"The American student now has available in his own language one of the finest tools for the interpretation of the New Testament."—*The Journal of Religion.*

Furber, Holden, *ed.:* BURKE, Correspondence of Edmund Burke, *Vol. V.*

Furst, Henry, *ed.* Novelle e poesie. By Renato Fucini. HCLS.

Further Contributions to the Prestige Value of Public Employment: WHITE.

Further Study of Dental Clinics in the United States: LEUCK.

Fussler, Herman. Photographic Reproduction for Libraries. 1942. *o.p.*

Future of Cities and Urban Redevelopment: WOODBURY.

Future of Government in the United States: WHITE.

Future of Mankind: JASPERS.

Future of Peace: KALLEN.

Future of Public Education: LIEBERMAN.

Future of Radio: TYSON.

Gaenssle, Carl. The Hebrew Particle אֲשֶׁר. 1915. *o.p.*

Gaillard, Pieter J. The Parathyroid Glands. Ultrastructure, Secretion, and Function. Edited by Pieter J. Gaillard, Roy V. Talmage, and Ann M. Budy. Foreword by Franklin C. McLean. 1965. xii, 353 p. 24 cm. 65-17290. $15.00s.

Galactic Structure: BLAAUW.

Galdston, Iago. Medicine in Transition. 1965. Foreword by Lord Cohen of Birkenhead. xii, 220 p. 22 cm. 65-24425. $5.95.

Gale, Ann Van Nice. Children's Preferences for Colors, Color Combinations and Color Arrangements. 1933. *o.p.*

Gale, Ann Van Nice, *joint author:* TODD, Enjoyment and Use of Art in the Elementary School.

Gale, Esson McDowell: *see* HODOUS, Careers for Students of Chinese Language and Civilization.

Galilei, Galileo. Dialogue on the Great World Systems. In the Translation of T. Salusbury. Revised, annotated, and with an Introduction by Giorgio de Santillana. 1953. lviii, 506 p. Illus. 26 cm. 53-11771. $15.00s.

Galton, D. A. G., *ed.* Haematology and Blood Groups. Edited by D. A. G. Galton and K. L. A. Goldsmith. 1961. 169 p. 29 cm. 61-7252. $4.00s. CUSA.

Game, Josiah Bethea. Teaching High-School Latin. A Handbook. 1916. 2d ed. 1925. *o.p.*

Gametogenesis and Fertilization in Albugo: STEVENS.

**Gamio, Manuel.** The Indian Basis of Mexican Civilization, *in* VASCONCELOS, Aspects of Mexican Civilization.

**Gamio, Manuel.** Mexican Immigration to the United States. A Study of Human Migration and Adjustment. 1930. *o.p.*

**Gamio, Manuel,** *ed.* The Mexican Immigrant, His Life-Story. Autobiographic Documents Collected by Manuel Gamio. 1931. *o.p.*

**Gang:** THRASHER.

**Garden and the Wilderness:** HOWE.

**Gardiner, Alan Henderson,** *ed.:* CALVERLEY, Temple of King Sethos I.

**Gardiner, Alan Henderson,** *ed.:* DAVIES, Ancient Egyptian Paintings.

**Gardiner, Elizabeth Greene.** Convalescent Care in Great Britain. 1935. SSM. *o.p.*

**Gardner, Burleigh,** *joint author:* DAVIS, Deep South.

**Gardner, Donfred Huber.** Student Personnel Service. 1936. EHI. *o.p.*

**Gardner, Isabella.** The Looking Glass. New Poems. 1961. 45 p. 21 cm. 61-15932. Paper. PP. $1.50.

**Gardner, John.** The Complete Works of the Gawain-Poet. Modern English Version with a Critical Introduction by John Gardner. 1965. xiii, 347 p. 25 cm. 65-17291. $10.00.

**Gardner, Mary,** *joint author:* DAVIS, Deep South.

**Garner, James Bert.** Condensations with Benzoin by Means of Sodium Ethylate. 1897. *o.p.*

**Garner, Ross.** Henry Vaughan. Experience and the Tradition. 1959. viii, 176 p. 22 cm. 59-11357. $5.00ˢ.

**Garrison, Fielding Hudson:** *see* CHOULANT, History and Bibliography of Anatomic Illustration.

**Garrison, Winfred E.,** *joint author:* BAKER, Short History of Christianity.

**Garrison, Winfred E.:** *see* BOWER, Church at Work in the Modern World.

**Gartland, Ruth Marie.** Psychiatric Social Service in a Children's Hospital. Two Years of Service in Bobs Roberts Memorial Hospital for Children, University of Chicago Clinics. 1937. SSM. *o.p.*

**Gastroscopy:** SCHINDLER.

**Gates, Arthur I.** Reading in the Elementary School. Prepared by Arthur I. Gates, Chairman of the Yearbook Committee. 1949. NSSE, 48th Yrbk., Part II. x, 350 p. 22 cm. 49-8506. Cloth. $4.50ᵗ. Paper. $3.75ᵗ.

**Gates, Errett:** *see* SMITH, Guide to the Study of the Christian Religion.

**Gates, Herbert Wright.** The Life of Jesus. Published in three parts: A Manual for Teachers. 1907; Pupil's Notebook. 1907; Helps for Home Study. 1921. CS. *o.p.*

**Gates, Herbert Wright.** Recreation and the Church. 1917. PM. *o.p.*

**Gaus, John Merriman.** The Frontiers of Public Administration. By John M. Gaus, Leonard D. White, and Marshall E. Dimock. 1936. PA. *o.p.*

**Gaus, John Merriman.** Great Britain. A Study of Civic Loyalty. 1929. SMC. *o.p.*

**Gawain-Poet:** *see* GARDNER, Complete Works of the Gawain-Poet.

**Gay-Lussac, Joseph-Louis,** *joint author:* DALTON, Foundations of the Molecular Theory.

**Gay-Lussac, Joseph-Louis:** *see* SCHEELE. Early History of Chlorine.

**Geer, Blanche,** *joint author:* BECKER, Boys in White.

**Geertz, Clifford.** Peddlers and Princes, Social Development and Economic Change in Two Indonesian Towns. 1963. x, 162 p. Illus. 22 cm. 63-18844. $5.00ˢ.

**Geheimnisvolle Dorf:** HINZ.

**Geiger, Joseph Roy.** Some Religious Implications of Pragmatism. 1919. PS. *o.p.*

**Geikie, James.** Classification of European Glacial Deposits. 1895. *o.p.*

**Gelb, Ignace J.** Glossary of Old Akkadian. 1957. xxiv, 318 p. 25 cm. MAD, III. $5.00.

**Gelb, Ignace J.** Hurrians and Subarians. 1944. SAOC 22. *o.p.*

**Gelb, Ignace J.** Hittite Hieroglyphs. *Vol. I.* 1931. *o.p. Vol. III.* 1942 SAOC 2;21. *o.p.*

**Gelb, Ignace J.** Hittite Hieroglyphs. 1935. *Vol. II.* xx, 37 p. Illus. 25 cm. 32-11984. Paper. SAOC 14. $1.25.

**Gelb, Ignace J.** Nuzi Personal Names. By Ignace J. Gelb, Pierre M. Purves, and Allan MacRae. 1943. xvii, 324 p. 31 cm. A43-1880. OIP, LVII. $10.00.

**Gelb, Ignace J.** Researches in Anatolia. VI. Inscriptions from Alishar and Vicinity. 1935. xv, 84 p. Illus. 30 cm. 35-5136. OIP, XXVII. $6.00.

**Gelb, Ignace J.** Sargonic Texts from the Diyala Region. 1952. xv, 251 p. 25 cm. 53–69. MAD, I. $3.00.

**Gelb, Ignace J.** Old Akkadian Writing and Grammar. 1952. Rev. ed. 1962. x, 235 p. 25 cm. 61-6577. MAD, II. $3.00.

**Gelb, Ignace J.** Study of Writing. 1952. xvi, 295 p. Illus. Index. 22 cm. 52-10599. Cloth. $6.50s. Paper. P109. $2.95.

**Gelb, Ignace J.,** *ed.* Hittite Hieroglyphic Monuments. 1939. xviii, 40 p. Illus. 23 cm. 40-4831. OIP, XLV. $10.00.

**Gellner, Ernest,** *Joint Editor,* Nature of Human Society Series.

**Gellner, Ernest.** Thought and Change. 1965. 224 p. 22 cm. NHS. $5.00s. OBE.

**General Biology and the Philosophy of Organism:** LILLIE.

**General Catalogue of 1290 Double Stars:** BURNHAM.

**General, Civil and Military Administration of Noricum and Raetia:** PEAKS.

**General Cytology:** COWDRY.

**General Diagnosis and Treatment of Skin Diseases:** SIEMENS.

**General Education:** GRAY.

**General Education:** McCONNELL.

**General Education in the American College:** EURICH.

**General Psychopathology:** JASPERS.

**General Sociology:** SMALL.

**Generalization in Writing of History:** GOTTSCHALK.

**Generalized Foreign Politics:** RICHARDSON.

**Genesis of Hand Preference:** GIESECKE.

**Genetic Development of the Forests of Northern Michigan:** WHITFORD.

**Genetic History of the New England Theology:** FOSTER.

**Genetic Neurology:** WEISS.

**Genetics and the Social Behavior of Dogs:** SCOTT.

**Genitive of Value in Latin and Other Constructions with Verbs of Rating:** LAING.

**Genius of American Politics:** BOORSTIN.

**Gennep, Arnold van.** The Rites of Passage. Translated by Monika B. Vizedom and Gabrielle L. Caffee. With an Introduction by Solon T. Kimball. 1960. xxvi, 198 p. 60-1087. Cloth. 23 cm. $4.50s. Paper. P64. 21 cm. $1.50. COBE.

**Geochemistry:** RANKAMA.

**Geographic Aspects of International Relations:** COLBY.

**Geographic Background of Chicago:** GOODE.

**Geographic Society of Chicago (GSC).**
*Bulletins:*
  1. SALISBURY, Geography of Chicago.
  2. COWLES, Plant Societies.
  3. Cox, Lantern Slide Illustrations.
  4. Cox, Weather and Climate of Chicago.
  5. SHELFORD, Animal Communities.
  6. SAUER, Starved Rock State Park.
  7. SAUER, Geography of the Ozark Highland.
  8. CRESSEY, Indiana Sand Dunes.
  9. FINCH, Geographic Surveys.

*Excursion Bulletins:*
  1. BLOUNT, Excursion through the Rivers and Harbors of Chicago.
  2. BLOUNT, Excursion on the Rock River of Illinois.
  3. BABER, Stony Island.

**Geographic Surveys:** FINCH.

**Geography of Chicago:** SALISBURY.

**Geography of the Heavens:** BARRETT.

**Geography of Illinois:** RIDGLEY.

**Geography of the Ozark Highland:** SAUER.

**Geography of Reading:** WILSON.

**Geological Work of Ice:** CRONEIS.

**Geology of Coal:** STUTZER.

**Geology of Vancouver:** BURWASH.

**Geometric Exercises for Algebraic Solution:** MYERS.

**Georg Friedrich Hegel:** KNOX.

**George Ellett Coghill:** HERRICK.

**George Herbert Mead on Social Psychology:** MEAD.

**Georgics:** VIRGIL.

**Gerard, Ralph W.,** *ed.* Food for Life. With Contributions by Richard J. Block, Ralph W. Gerard, Norman Jolliffe, Clive M. McCay, Sedgwick E. Smith, and Samuel Soskin. 1952. xiv, 306 p. Illus. 22 cm. 52-14880. BM. Paper. PSS527. $2.45.

**Géricault:** EITNER.

**German Fifth Column:** DE JONG.

**German Histories of American Literature:** LOCHER.

**German Review and Composition:** HAGBOLDT.

**Germanic Studies** (GER):

    I. CUTTING, Der Conjunktiv bei Hartmann von Aue.
    II. WOOD, Verner's Law in Gothic.
    III. SCHMIDT-WARTENBERG, Inedita des Heinrich Kaufringer.

**Germany and the Future of Europe.** MORGENTHAU.

**Germany in Transition:** KRAUS.

**Gerould, Gordon Hall:** *see* BRYAN, Sources and Analogues of Chaucer's *Canterbury Tales.*

**Getting Out the Vote:** GOSNELL.

**Gettys, Cora Luella.** The Law of Citizenship in the United States. By Luella Gettys. With a Foreword by Quincy Wright. 1934. *o.p.*

**Gevirtz, Stanley.** Patterns in the Early Poetry of Israel. 1963. 136 p. SAOC 32. $3.00.

**Geyl, C. M.,** *trans.:* DE JONG, The German Fifth Column.

**Ghetto:** WIRTH.

**Ghost-Dance Religion:** MOONEY.

**Ghosts of the Heart:** LOGAN.

**Giannella, Donald A.,** *ed.* Religion and the Public Order, 1963. 1964. x, 338 p. 24 cm. 64-17164. $6.00$^s$.

**Giannella, Donald A.,** *ed.* Religion and the Public Order, 1964. 1965. viii, 280 p. 24 cm. 64-17164. $6.00$^s$.

**Giant African Snail:** MEAD.

**Gibb, H. A. R.** Modern Trends in Islam. 1947. CR. *o.p.*

**Gide, André.** Self-Portraits. The Gide-Valéry Letters. Edited by Robert Mallet. Abridged and translated by June Guicharnaud. 1965. 384 p. $10.00.

**Gide, André:** *see* DELAY, The Youth of André Gide.

**Gideonse, Harry David.** The Commodity Dollar. 1938. PPP 26. *o.p.*

**Gideonse, Harry David.** Organized Scarcity and Public Policy. 1940. PPP 30 *o.p.*

**Gideonse, Harry David.** War Debts. 1933. PPP 4. *o.p.*

**Giesecke, Minnie.** The Genesis of Hand Preference. 1936. CD. *o.p.*

**Giffen, Morrison Beall.** Fashoda. The Incident and Its Diplomatic Setting. 1930 *o.p.*

**Giffen, Naomi Musmaker.** The Rôles of Men and Women in Eskimo Culture. 1930. AN. *o.p.*

**Gilbert, George Holley.** A Short History of Christianity in the Apostolic Age. 1906. CS. *o.p.*

**Gilbert, William H., Jr.,** *joint author:* EGGAN, Social Anthropology of North American Tribes.

**Gilby, Thomas.** The Political Thought of Thomas Aquinas. 1958. xxvi, 357 p. 22 cm. 58-5534. $6.00$^s$. COBE.

**Gilgamesh and the *Ḫuluppu-Tree*:** KRAMER.

**Gilgamesh Epic and Old Testament Parallels:** HEIDEL.

**Gilkey, Charles Whitney.** Jesus and Our Generation. 1925. BL. *o.p.*

**Gilland, Thomas McDowell.** The Origin and Development of the Power and Duties of the City-School Superintendent. 1935. *o.p.*

**Gillespie, Frances E.,** *joint ed.:* WALLACE, The Journal of Benjamin Moran.

**Gillette, John Morris.** Culture Agencies of a Typical Manufacturing Group: South Chicago. 1901. *o.p.*

**Gilson, Mary Barnett.** Unemployment Insurance. 1933. PPP, 3. *o.p.*

**Gimilsin Temple and the Palace of the Rulers at Tell Asmar:** FRANKFORT.

**Gingrich, F. W.,** *ed.* Shorter Lexicon of the Greek New Testament. 1965. 241 p. 21 cm. 65-24434. $4.50.

**Gingrich, F. W.,** *joint ed. and trans.:* ARNDT, Greek-English Lexicon of the New Testament and Other Early Christian Literature.

**Gini, Corrado.** Population. By Corrado Gini, Shiroshi Nasu, Robert R. Kuczynski, Oliver E. Baker. 1930. HFL. *o.p.*

**Ginsburg, Norton.** Atlas of Economic Development. Foreword by Bert F. Hoselitz. Statistical Analysis by Brian J. L. Berry. 1961. vii, 119 p. 48 two-color maps. 25 × 36 cm. 61-6. Cloth. $7.50ˢ. Paper. $5.00ᵗ.

**Giordano Bruno and the Hermetic Tradition:** YATES.

**Giorgio da Castelfranco:** RICHTER.

**Gitanilla (Cervantes):** CASTILLO.

**Giulietta e Romeo, e altre novelle:** CIOFFARI.

**Glanville, John J.,** *joint trans.:* SIMON, *Material Logic* of John of St. Thomas.

**Glass, James M.** Curriculum Practices in the Junior High School and Grades V and VI. 1924. SEM 25. *o.p.*

**Glazer, Nathan.** American Judaism. 1957. x, 178 p. 21 cm. 57-8574. Cloth. CHAC. $3.50ˢ. Paper. $1.75.

**Gleason, Eliza V. Atkins.** The Southern Negro and the Public Library: The Government and Administration of Public Library Service to Negroes in the South. 1941. LS. *o.p.*

**Glendinning, O. N. V.,** *trans.:* BAROJA, World of the Witches.

**Glick, Frank Ziegler.** The Illinois Emergency Relief Commission. A Study of Administrative and Financial Aspects of Emergency Relief. 1940. SSM. *o.p.*

**Glick, Philip M.** The Administration of Technical Assistance. Growth in the Americas. 1957. NPA. *o.p.*

**Glossary of Old Akkadian:** GELB.

**God and the Social Process:** WALLIS.

**God in You:** EBY.

**Goddard, Harold C.** The Meaning of Shakespeare. 1951. xii, 691 p. 26 cm. 51-2288. Cloth. $10.00ˢ. 2 vols. Paper. 21 cm. A63-194. P50. $1.95. P51. $1.95.

"... has a range and depth unusual in this day of specialization. ... written by one who has *enjoyed* the plays and who sees in them both aesthetic values and a genuine moral relevance to our own time. It is literary criticism which is sensitive and stimulating but definitely *ad hominem*, for it is what Shakespeare means to Professor Goddard that stands most clearly—and delightfully—revealed."—*College English.*

**Goethe as Revealed in His Poetry:** FAIRLEY.

**Goins, Jean Turner.** Visual Perceptual Abilities and Reading Progress. 1957. x, 109 p. 21 cm. 57-11930. SEM 87. $2.75ᵗ.

**Golay, John Ford.** The Founding of the Federal Republic of Germany. 1958. xii, 299 p. $6.00ˢ.

**Gold Coast and the Slum:** ZORBAUGH.

**Gold and Monetary Stabilization:** WRIGHT.

**Gold and Prices:** LAUGHLIN.

**Gold's Gloom:** RYDER.

**Goldin, Judah,** *trans. and ed.* The Living Talmud. 1957. *o.p.*

**Goldman, Solomon.** The Ten Commandments. Edited by Maurice Samuel. 1956. xxv, 225 p. 21 cm. 56-10081. Paper. P141. $1.75.

**Goldman, Solomon:** *see* HAYDON, Modern Trends in World-Religions.

**Goldsmith, K. L. A.,** *joint ed.:* GALTON, Haematology and Blood Groups.

**Goldsmith, Oliver.** New Essays by Oliver Goldsmith. Now First Collected and Edited with an Introduction and Notes by Ronald S. Crane. 1927. *o.p.*

**Goldstine, Dora,** *ed.* Expanding Horizons in Medical Social Work. 1955. viii, 275 p. 24 cm. 54-11423. $5.00ˢ.

**Goldstine, Dora,** *ed.* Readings in the Theory and Practice of Medical Social Work. 1954. vi, 342 p. 24 cm. 54-8906. $5.00ˢ.

**Golembiewski, Robert T.** The Small Group. An Analysis of Research Concepts and Operations. 1962. xii, 303 p. 22 cm. 62-12633. $6.00.ˢ

**Gomer, Robert,** *ed.* Structure and Properties of Solid Surfaces. Edited by Robert Gomer and Cyril S. Smith. 1953. PS. *o.p.*

**Gomori, George.** Microscopic Histochemistry. Principles and Practice. 1952. vi, 273 p. 22 cm. 52-12501. BM. $6.75ˢ.

**Good Books for Children:** EAKIN.

**Good Life:** JORDAN.

**Good Nutrition for Everybody:** BOGERT.

**Good Will and Ill Will:** SHARP.

**Goode, John Paul.** The Geographic Background of Chicago. 1926. SSCI. *o.p.*

**Goode, John Paul,** *joint ed.:* Cox, Lantern Slide Illustrations for the Teaching of Meteorology.

**Goodheart, Eugene.** The Utopian Vision of D. H. Lawrence. 1963. x, 190 p. 22 cm. 63-22817. $5.00ˢ.

**Goodman, Paul.** Communitas. Means of Livelihood and Ways of Life. By Paul and Percival Goodman. 1947. *o.p.*

**Goodman, Paul.** The Structure of Literature. 1954. vii, 280 p. 21 cm. 54-9577. Paper. P91. $1.75.

**Goodman, Percival,** *joint author:* GOODMAN, Communitas.

**Goodrich, Francis Lee Dewey,** *joint author:* RANDALL, Principles of College Library Administration.

**Goodrich, H. B.,** *joint author:* KNAPP, Origins of American Scientists.

**Goodspeed, Charles Ten Broeke.** Thomas Wakefield Goodspeed. 1932. *o.p.*

**Goodspeed, Charles Ten Broeke,** *ed.:* GOODSPEED, William Rainey Harper.

**Goodspeed, Edgar Johnson.** The Bixby Gospels. 1915. HLL. *o.p.*

**Goodspeed, Edgar Johnson.** Buying Happiness. 1932. *o.p.*

**Goodspeed, Edgar Johnson.** Chicago Literary Papyri. 1908. *o.p.*

**Goodspeed, Edgar Johnson.** A Descriptive Catalogue of Manuscripts in the Libraries of the University of Chicago. Prepared by Edgar Johnson Goodspeed with the Assistance of Martin Sprengling. 1912. *o.p.*

**Goodspeed, Edgar Johnson.** The Formation of the New Testament. 1926. *o.p.*

**Goodspeed, Edgar Johnson.** The Freer Gospels. 1914. HLL. *o.p.*

**Goodspeed, Edgar Johnson.** The Gospel of John. 1917. AISL. *o.p.*

**Goodspeed, Edgar Johnson.** Greek Gospel Texts in America. 1902–1918. HLL. *o.p.*

**Goodspeed, Edgar Johnson.** Greek Papyri from the Cairo Museum. Together with Papyri of Roman Egypt from American Collections. 1902. *o.p.*

**Goodspeed, Edgar Johnson.** The Harvard Gospels. 1918. HLL *o.p.*

**Goodspeed, Edgar Johnson.** The Haskell Gospels. 1918. HLL *o.p.*

**Goodspeed, Edgar Johnson.** A History of Early Christian Literature. 1942. *o.p.*

**Goodspeed, Edgar Johnson.** An Introduction to the New Testament. 1937. xviii, 362 p. Illus. 20 cm. 37-28550. $5.00ˢ.

**Goodspeed, Edgar Johnson.** The Key to Ephesians. 1956. xvi, 75 p. 25 cm. 56-6550. $2.50ˢ.

Goodspeed, Edgar Johnson. The Making of the English New Testament. 1925. *o.p.*

Goodspeed, Edgar Johnson. The Meaning of Ephesians. 1933. *o.p.*

Goodspeed, Edgar Johnson. New Solutions of New Testament Problems. 1927. *o.p.*

Goodspeed, Edgar Johnson. The Newberry Gospels. 1902. HLL *o.p.*

Goodspeed, Edgar Johnson. Papyri from Karanis. 1900. Reprint from Vol. III, STUDIES IN CLASSICAL PHILOLOGY *o.p.*

Goodspeed, Edgar Johnson. Paul. 1922. AISL. *o.p.*

Goodspeed, Edgar Johnson. Problems of New Testament Translation. 1945. *o.p.*

Goodspeed, Edgar Johnson. The Story of the Apocrypha. 1939. x, 150 p. 20 cm. 39-31175. $2.75ˢ.

Goodspeed, Edgar Johnson. The Story of the Bible. 1936. xx, 336 p. 20 cm. 36-21666. $3.75.

Goodspeed, Edgar Johnson. The Story of the New Testament. 2d ed. 1929. xiv, 150 p. 17 cm. 35-4089. HER. $2.75.

Goodspeed, Edgar Johnson. The Story of the Old Testament. 1934. xii, 187 p. 17 cm. 34-35866. $2.75.

Goodspeed, Edgar Johnson. Strange New Gospels. 1931. *o.p.*

Goodspeed, Edgar Johnson. The Synoptic Gospels, Matthew, Mark, Luke. From *The New Testament. An American Translation.* 1930. *o.p.*

Goodspeed, Edgar Johnson. Things Seen and Heard. 1925. *o.p.*

Goodspeed, Edgar Johnson. The Toronto Gospels. 1911. HLL. *o.p.*

Goodspeed, Edgar Johnson. The University Chapel. 1933. *o.p.*

Goodspeed, Edgar Johnson. The University of Chicago Chapel. A Guide. 1928. *o.p.*

Goodspeed, Edgar Johnson, *trans.* The Apocrypha. An American Translation. 1938. x, 493 p. Illus. 20 cm. $6.00ˢ.

Goodspeed, Edgar Johnson, *ed. and trans.* The Book of Thekla. 1901. *o.p.*

Goodspeed, Edgar Johnson, *ed. and trans.* Epistle of Pelagia. 1931. *o.p.*

Goodspeed, Edgar Johnson, *ed. and trans.* Ethiopic Martyrdoms. 1931. *o.p.*

Goodspeed, Edgar Johnson, *trans.* Goodspeed Parallel New Testament. The American Translation and the King James Version in Parallel Columns. With Introductions and Explanatory Notes by Edgar J. Goodspeed. 1943. viii, 600 p. 21 cm. 43-2501. $4.00ˢ.

Goodspeed, Edgar Johnson, *ed.* A Greek Papyrus Reader. With Vocabulary. Edited by Edgar J. Goodspeed and Ernest Cadman Colwell. 1935. *o.p.*

Goodspeed, Edgar Johnson, *ed. and trans.* The Martyrdom of Cyprian and Justa. 1903. *o.p.*

Goodspeed, Edgar Johnson, *trans.* The New Testament. An American Translation. Popular ed. 1923. x, 481 p. 17 cm. 23-15842. Single column. Black cloth. $2.50.

Goodspeed, Edgar Johnson, *ed.* The Rockefeller McCormick New Testament. Edited by Edgar J. Goodspeed, Donald W. Riddle, and Harold R. Willoughby. 3 volumes. 1932. *o.p.*

Goodspeed, Edgar Johnson, *ed.* The Short Bible. An American Translation. Edited by Edgar J. Goodspeed and J. M. Powis Smith. 1933. x, 549 p. 20 cm. 33-32388. $5.00ˢ.

Goodspeed, Edgar Johnson, *ed. and trans.* The Story of Eugenia and Philip. 1931. *o.p.*

Goodspeed, Edgar Johnson, *ed. and trans.* The Student's New Testament. (Parallel Greek and English.) 1954. x, 1,055 p. 22 cm. 54-8092. $7.50ˢ.

Goodspeed, Edgar Johnson, *ed.* The Translators to the Reader. Preface to the King James Version 1611. 1935. *o.p.*

Goodspeed, Edgar Johnson, *joint author:* OWEN, Homeric Vocabularies.

**Goodspeed, Edgar Johnson,** *joint author:* BURTON, Harmony of the Synoptic Gospels in Greek.

**Goodspeed, Edgar Johnson,** *joint author:* GOODSPEED, William Rainey Harper.

**Goodspeed, Edgar Johnson,** *joint ed. and trans.:* SMITH, Bible.

**Goodspeed, Edgar Johnson:** *see* SMITH, Guide to the Study of the Christian Religion.

**Goodspeed, Thomas Wakefield.** Ernest De Witt Burton. A Biographical Sketch. 1926. *o.p.*

**Goodspeed, Thomas Wakefield.** A History of the University of Chicago, Founded by John D. Rockefeller. The First Quarter-Century [1891–1916]. 1916. *o.p.*

**Goodspeed, Thomas Wakefield.** The Story of the University of Chicago, 1890–1925. 1925. *o.p.*

**Goodspeed, Thomas Wakefield.** The University of Chicago Biographical Sketches. *Vol. I.* 1922. 2d ed. 1924. *o.p. Vol. II.* 1925. *o.p.*

**Goodspeed, Thomas Wakefield.** William Rainey Harper, First President of the University of Chicago. Completed and Revised after the Author's Death by his Sons, Charles T. B. Goodspeed and Edgar J. Goodspeed. 1928. *o.p.*

**Goodwin, Grenville.** The Social Organization of the Western Apache. 1942. *o.p.*

**Goodykoontz, Bess.** American Education in the Postwar Period. Structural Reorganization. Prepared by Bess Goodykoontz, Chairman of the Society's Committee. 1945. NSSE, 44th Yrbk., Part II. x, 324 p. 24 cm. E46-51. Paper. $2.25t.

**Gordis, Robert.** The Root and the Branch. Judaism and the Free Society. 1962. xvi, 254 p. 22 cm. 62-17133. $3.95.

**Gordis, Warren Stone.** The Estimates of Moral Values Expressed in Cicero's Letters. A Study of the Motives Professed or Approved. 1905. *o.p.*

**Gordon, Alexander Reid.** The Truth about the Bible. By Alexander R. Gordon, Ernest F. Scott, Edward I. Bosworth, Kemper Fuller- ton, John M. Coulter, Daniel D. Luckenbill, J. M. Powis Smith, Theodore G. Soares, Chester C. McCown, Shailer Mathews. 1923. AISL. *o.p.*

**Gordon, Alexander Reid:** *see* BEWER, Religion of the Bible.

**Gordon, Alexander Reid:** *see* SMITH, Bible; Complete Bible; Old Testament.

**Gordon, Bernard K.** New Zealand Becomes a Pacific Power. 1960. xi, 283 p. Index. 22 cm. 60-15106. $6.50s.

**Gordon, William Clark.** The Social Ideals of Alfred Tennyson as Related to His Time. 1906. *o.p.*

**Gore, Willard Clark.** The Imagination in Spinoza and Hume. A Comparative Study in the Light of Some Recent Contributions to Psychology. 1902. PHI. *o.p.*

**Gosnell, Harold Foote.** Boss Platt and His New York Machine. A Study of the Political Leadership of Thomas C. Platt, Theodore Roosevelt, and Others. With an Introduction by Charles R. Merriam. 1924. *o.p.*

**Gosnell, Harold Foote.** Getting Out the Vote. An Experiment in the Stimulation of Voting. 1927. SSCI. *o.p.*

**Gosnell, Harold Foote.** Machine Politics. Chicago Model. Foreword by William F. Ogburn. 1937. SSCI. *o.p.*

**Gosnell, Harold Foote.** Negro Politicians. The Rise of Negro Politics in Chicago. With an Introduction by Robert E. Park. 1935. SSCI. *o.p.*

**Gosnell, Harold Foote.** Why Europe Votes. 1930. SSCI. *o.p.*

**Gosnell, Harold Foote,** *joint author:* MERRIAM, Non-voting.

**Gosnell, Harold Foote:** *see* SMITH, Chicago.

**Gospel of John:** GOODSPEED.

**Gospel in the Light of the Great War:** DAVIS.

**Gospel before Mark:** PARKER.

**Gospels, Their Origin and Growth:** RIDDLE.

**Gossard, Arthur Paul.** Superior and Backward Children in Public Schools. 1940. *o.p.*

**Gothic Architecture:** JACKSON.

**Gotshalk, D. W.** Art and the Social Order. 1947. *o.p.*

**Gotshalk, D. W.** Metaphysics in Modern Times. A Present-Day Perspective. 1940. *o.p.*

**Gottschalk, Louis.** Lafayette between the American and the French Revolution (1783–1789). 1950. xii, 461 p. 24 cm. 50-5286. $7.50s.

**Gottschalk, Louis.** Lafayette and the Close of the American Revolution. 1942. xiv, 458 p. 24 cm. 42-12337. $7.50s.

**Gottschalk, Louis.** Lafayette Comes to America. 1935. xiv, 184 p. 24 cm. $4.50s.

**Gottschalk, Louis.** Lafayette Joins the American Army. 1937. xvi, 364 p. 24 cm. $6.50s.

"The way in which he has managed to gather this mass of material and sift it by the most enlightened process is a model for all research historians. . . . His book is really more than a history of Lafayette—it is Lafayette himself."—B. Fay, reviewing *Lafayette Joins the American Army*, in *The American Historical Review*.

"With precise and full documentation, and with every effort of accuracy Mr. Gottschalk follows his hero almost day by day, with much of the absorbing story told in Lafayette's own words. . . . Countless manuscripts have been ransacked, countless monographs consulted and checked for original materials. . . ."—Carl Van Doren reviewing *Lafayette and the Close of the American Revolution*, in the *New York Herald Tribune*.

**Gottschalk, Louis,** *ed.* Generalization in the Writing of History. 1963. xiv, 256 p. 22 cm. 63-13064. $5.00s.

**Govan, Thomas Payne.** Nicholas Biddle. Nationalist and Public Banker, 1786–1844. 1959. xii, 429 p. Illus. 25 cm. 59-12286. $7.50s.

**Government of the American Public Library:** JOECKEL.

**Government Career Service:** WHITE.

**Government Corporations and Federal Funds:** McDIARMID.

**Government in a Depression:** REED.

**Government of Education in Metropolitan Chicago:** VIEG.

**Government and Mass Communication:** CHAFEE.

**Government of the Metropolitan Region of Chicago:** MERRIAM.

**Government in Illinois:** DODD.

**Government Publicity:** McCAMY.

**Government-operated Enterprises in the Panama Canal Zone:** DIMOCK.

**Governmental Problems in the Chicago Metropolitan Area:** LYON.

**Governmental Reporting in Chicago:** BEYLE.

**Grabar, Oleg,** *joint author:* HILL: Islamic Architecture.

**Grabo, Carl.** The Creative Critic. 1948. *o.p.*

**Grace, Alonzo G.** Changing Conceptions in Educational Administration. Prepared by Alonzo G. Grace, Chairman of the Society's Committee. 1946. NSSE, 45th Yrbk., Part II. vii, 186, xlvii p. 24 cm. A46-5124. Cloth. $2.50t.

**Grace, Alonzo G.,** *ed.* Leadership in American Education. 1950. AOPPS, XIII. *o.p.*

**Graded French Word and Idiom Book:** LANDRY.

**Graded French Readers,** *see* HEATH-CHICAGO LANGUAGE SERIES.

**Graded German Readers,** *see* HEATH-CHICAGO LANGUAGE SERIES.

**Graded Italian Readers,** *see* HEATH-CHICAGO LANGUAGE SERIES.

**Graded Social Service for the Sunday School:** HUTCHINS.

**Graded Spanish Readers,** *see* HEATH-CHICAGO LANGUAGE SERIES.

**Graduate and Undergraduate Courses and Degrees in Education:** NATIONAL SOCIETY OF COLLEGE TEACHERS OF EDUCATION, Proceedings, No. 2.

**Graduate Study in Education:** TYLER.

**Graham, Malbone Watson:** *see* HARPER, Soviet Union and World-Problems.

**Graham Taylor:** WADE.

**Graham, Thomas.** Researches on the Arseniates, Phosphates, and Modifications of Phosphoric Acid. (1833). 1902. AC. *o.p.*

**Graham, Willard J.** Alternative Laboratory Exercises for Rorem's *Accounting Method*. 1930. MSB. *o.p.*

**Graham, Willard J.** Public Utility Valuation. Reproduction Cost as a Basis for Depreciation and Rate-Base Determination. 1934. SBA, IV. *o.p.*

**Graham, Willard J.** Solutions to Alternative Laboratory Exercises for Rorem's *Accounting Method*. 1930. MSB. *o.p.*

**Graham, Willard J.** Teacher's Manual for *Accounting Method*. By W. J. Graham and C. Rufus Rorem. 1928. MSB. *o.p.*

**Graham, William Creighton.** Culture and Conscience. An Archeological Study of the New Religious Past in Ancient Palestine. By William Creighton Graham and Herbert Gordon May. 1936. HER. *o.p.*

**Graham, William Creighton.** The Prophets and Israel's Culture. 1934. HER. *o.p.*

**Graham, William Creighton,** *joint ed.:* GREGORIUS, Barhebraeus' Scholia on the Old Testament.

**Grain Yields and the American Food Supply:** JOHNSON.

**Grammaire (Labiche):** BOND.

**Grammatical Structures of English and German:** KUFNER.

**Grammatical Structures of English and Italian:** AGARD.

**Grammatical Structures of English and Spanish:** STOCKWELL.

**Granbery, John Cowper.** Outline of New Testament Christology. A Study of Genetic Relationships within the Christology of the New Testament Period. 1909. HLL. *o.p.*

**Graphic Arts:** PENNELL.

**Graphic Method of Obtaining Partial-Correlation Coefficients:** WOOD.

**Graton, Louis Cary.** Systematic Packing of Spheres—with Particular Relation to Porosity and Permeability, by L. C. Graton. *And* Experimental Study of the Porosity and Permeability of Clastic Sediments, by H. J. Fraser. 1935. *o.p.*

**Graves, Lawrence Murray,** *joint ed.:* BLISS, Contributions to the Calculus of Variations.

**Gravitational Collapse:** ROBINSON.

**Gravitation Theory and Gravitational Collapse:** HARRISON.

**Gray, Basil.** Buddhist Cave Paintings at Tun-huang. With a Preface by Arthur Waley. Photographs by John B. Vincent. 1959. *o.p.*

**Gray, Charles Henry.** Lodowick Carliell. His Life, a Discussion of His Plays, and *The Deserving Favourite*, a Tragi-Comedy Reprinted from the Original Edition of 1629, with Introduction and Notes. 1905. *o.p.*

**Gray, Clarence Truman.** Types of Reading Ability as Exhibited through Tests and Laboratory Experiments. 1917. SEM, 5. *o.p.*

**Gray, Clifton Daggett.** The Šamaš Religious Texts. Classified in the British Museum Catalogue as Hymns, Prayers, and Incantations. With Twenty Plates of Texts Hitherto Unpublished, and a Transliteration and Translation of K. 3182. Collated and Copied by Clifton Daggett Gray. 1901. *o.p.*

**Gray, Horace.** Growth in Private School Children. With Averages and Variabilities Based on 3,110 Measurings on Boys, and 1,473 on Girls, from the Ages of One to Nineteen Years. By Horace Gray and J. G. Ayres. 1931. BR. *o.p.*

**Gray, Lewis Cecil.** Land Planning. 1936. PPP 19. *o.p.*

**Gray, William Scott.** Maturity in Reading. By William Scott Gray and Bernice Rogers. 1956. xi, 273 p. Tables and charts. 24 cm. 56-13942. $5.75t.

**Gray, William Scott.** Report of the National Committee on Reading. Prepared by William S. Gray, Chairman of the Society's Committee. 1925. NSSE, 24th Yrbk., Part I. *o.p.*

**Gray, William Scott.** Studies of Elementary-School Reading through Standardized Tests. 1917. SEM, 1. *o.p.*

**Gray, William Scott.** Reading in the High School and College. Prepared by William S. Gray, Chairman of the Yearbook Committee. 1948. NSSE, 47th Yrbk., Part II. x, 318, xlix p. 24 cm. 48-6851. Cloth. $4.50^t. Paper. $3.75^t.

**Gray, William Scott.** The Teaching of Reading. Prepared by William S. Gray, Chairman of the Society's Committee. 1937. NSSE, 36th Yrbk., Part I. *o.p.*

**Gray, William Scott.** What Makes a Book Readable. With Special Reference to Adults of Limited Reading Ability. An Initial Study. By William S. Gray and Bernice E. Leary. 1935. LS. *o.p.*

**Gray, William Scott,** *ed.* The Academic and Professional Preparation of Secondary-School Teachers. 1935. HI. *o.p.*

**Gray, William Scott,** *ed.* Adapting Reading Programs to Wartime Conditions. Proceedings of the Sixth Annual Conference on Reading Held at The University of Chicago, 1943. 1943. SEM 57. *o.p.*

**Gray, William Scott,** *ed.* The Appraisal of Current Practices in Reading. Proceedings of the Eighth Annual Conference on Reading Held at the University of Chicago, 1945. 1946. SEM 61. *o.p.*

**Gray, William Scott,** *ed.* Adjusting Reading Programs to Individuals. Proceedings of the Fourth Annual Conference on Reading Held at the University of Chicago, 1941. 1941. SEM 52. *o.p.*

**Gray, William Scott,** *ed.* Basic Instruction in Reading in Elementary and High Schools. Proceedings of the Eleventh Annual Conference on Reading Held at the University of Chicago. 1948. SEM 65. *o.p.*

**Gray, William Scott,** *ed.* Classroom Techniques in Improving Reading. Proceedings of the Twelfth Annual Conference on Reading Held at the University of Chicago, 1949. 1949. SEM 69. *o.p.*

**Gray, William Scott,** *ed.* Co-operative Efforts in Schools To Improve Reading. Proceedings of the Fifth Annual Conference on Reading Held at the University of Chicago, 1942. 1942. SEM 56. *o.p.*

**Gray, William Scott,** *ed.* Current Issues in Higher Education. Edited by William S. Gray. 1937. HI. *o.p.*

**Gray, William Scott,** *ed.* General Education. Its Nature, Scope, and Essential Elements. 1934. HI. *o.p.*

**Gray, William Scott.** Improving Instruction in Reading. An Experimental Study. By William S. Gray and Gertrude Whipple. 1933. SEM 40 *o.p.*

**Gray, William Scott,** *ed.* Improving Reading in All Curriculum Areas. Proceedings of the Fifteenth Annual Conference on Reading Held at the University of Chicago, 1952. 1952. SEM 76. *o.p.*

**Gray, William Scott.** Improving Reading in Content Fields. Proceedings of the Ninth Annual Conference on Reading Held at the University of Chicago, 1947. 1947. SEM 62. *o.p.*

**Gray, William Scott,** *ed.* The Junior-College Curriculum. 1929. HI. *o.p.*

**Gray, William Scott,** *ed.* Keeping Reading Programs Abreast of the Times. Proceedings of the Thirteenth Annual Conference on Reading Held at the University of Chicago, 1950. 1950. SEM 72. *o.p.*

**Gray, William Scott,** *ed.* Needed Readjustments in Higher Education. 1933. HI. *o.p.*

**Gray, William Scott,** *ed.* The Preparation and In-Service Training of College Teachers. 1938. HI. *o.p.*

**Gray, William Scott,** *ed.* Promoting Growth toward Maturity in Interpreting What Is Read. Proceedings of the Fourteenth Annual Conference on Reading Held at the University of Chicago, 1951. 1951. vii, 264 p. 24 cm. 51-8579. Paper. SEM 74. $3.85^t.

**Gray, William Scott.** Promoting Personal and Social Development through Reading. Proceedings of the Tenth Annual Conference on Reading Held at the University of Chicago, 1947. 1947. SEM 64. *o.p.*

**Gray, William Scott,** *ed.* Provision for the Individual in College Education. 1932. HI. *o.p.*

Gray, William Scott, *ed.* Reading and Pupil Development. Proceedings of the Third Annual Conference on Reading Held at the University of Chicago, 1940. 1940. SEM 51. *o.p.*

Gray, William Scott, *ed.* Reading in Relation to Experience. Proceedings of the Seventh Annual Conference on Reading Held at the University of Chicago, 1944. 1944. SEM 58. *o.p.*

Gray, William Scott, *ed.* Recent Trends in American College Education. 1931. HI. *o.p.*

Gray, William Scott, *ed.* Recent Trends in Reading. Proceedings of the Second Annual Conference on Reading Held at the University of Chicago, 1939. 1939. SEM 49. *o.p.*

Gray, William Scott. Remedial Cases in Reading. Their Diagnosis and Treatment. By William S. Gray and others. 1922. SEM 22. *o.p.*

Gray, William Scott. Summary of Investigations Relating to Reading. 1925. SEM 28. *o.p.*

Gray, William Scott, *ed.* Tests and Measurements in Higher Education. 1936. HI. *o.p.*

Gray, William Scott, *ed.* The Training of College Teachers Including Their Preliminary Preparation and In-Service Improvement. 1930. HI. *o.p.*

Gray, Wood: Ulrich Bonnell Phillips, *in* HUTCHINSON, Marcus W. Jernegan Essays.

Grayson, Cecil, *trans.*: RIDOLFI, Life of Niccolò Machiavelli.

Grazia, Sebastian de. The Political Community. A Study of Anomie. 1948. xx, 258 p. 48-9544. Cloth. 25 cm. $5.00. Paper. P116. 21 cm. $2.45.

Great Awakening in the Middle Colonies: MAXSON.

Great Britain. A Study of Civic Loyalty: GAUS.

Great Britain and the Dominions: HURST.

Great EB: KOGAN.

Great Elector: SCHEVILL.

Great Men of the Christian Church: WALKER.

Great Revival in the West: CLEVELAND.

Great University Memorials: UNIVERSITY OF CHICAGO, *Committee on Development.*

Greece in the Bronze Age: VERMEULE.

Greek Dialects: BUCK.

Greek-English Lexicon of the New Testament and Other Early Christian Literature: ARNDT.

Greek of the Fourth Gospel: COLWELL.

Greek Grammar of the New Testament: FUNK.

Greek Gospel Texts in America: GOODSPEED.

Greek Hand-Mirror: TARBELL.

Greek Lyrics: LATTIMORE.

Greek Papyri from the Cairo Museum: GOODSPEED.

Greek Papyrus Reader: GOODSPEED.

Greek Political Theory: GRENE.

Greek Sculpture: CARPENTER.

Greek Theater and Its Drama: FLICKINGER.

Greek Tragedies: Phoenix. *Edited by* DAVID GRENE and RICHMOND LATTIMORE:

*Vol. I:* Aeschylus: Agamemnon. Translated by Richmond Lattimore. Prometheus Bound. Translated by David Grene. Sophocles: Oedipus the King. Translated by David Grene. Antigone. Translated by Elizabeth Wyckoff. Euripides: Hippolytus. Translated by David Grene. 1960. vii, 304 p. 21 cm. 60-950. P41. $1.50.

*Vol. II:* Aeschylus: The Libation Bearers. Translated by Richmond Lattimore. Sophocles: Electra. Translated by David Grene. Euripides: Iphigenia in Tauris. Translated by Witter Bynner. Electra. Translated by Emily T. Vermeule. The Trojan Women. Translated by Richmond Lattimore. 1960. vii, 312 p. 21 cm. 60-950. P42. $1.50.

*Vol. III:* Aeschylus: The Eumenides. Translated by Richmond Lattimore. Sophocles: Philoctetes. Translated by David Grene. Oedipus at Colonus. Translated by Robert Fitzgerald. Euripides: The Bacchae. Translated by William Arrowsmith. Alcestis. Translated by Richmond Lattimore. 1960. vii, 320 p. 21 cm. 60-950. P43. $1.50.

**Greeley, Arthur White.** The Artificial Production of Spores in Monas by a Reduction of the Temperature. 1902. *o.p.*

**Green Foundation Lectures** (GFL):
SAYRE, Protection of American Export Trade.
SFORZA, The Totalitarian War and After.
SKELTON, Our Generation.
SMITH, Legislative Way of Life.

**Greenberg, Joseph H.** Essays in Linguistics. 1957. vii, 108 p. 57–6273. Cloth. 26 cm. $3.00ˢ. Paper. P119. 21 cm. $1.25.

**Greenberg, Moshe,** *trans.*: KAUFMANN, Religion of Israel.

**Greenblatt, Gordon M.** Cat Musculature. 1954. 32 p. Illus. 22 cm. 54-2082. Paper. $1.25ᵗ.

**Greenhood, David.** Mapping. Rev. ed. 1964. 289 p. Illus. xiii, 289 p. 24 cm. 63-20905. Cloth. $6.00ˢ. Paper. PSS521. $2.95.

**Greenstein, Jesse L.,** *ed.* Stellar Atmospheres. ("Stars and Stellar Systems," Vol. VI.) 1961. xv, 725 p. Index. 25 cm. 61-9138. $17.50ˢ.

**Greer, Howard Clark.** Customer Turnover Experience of Meat Packing Companies. 1933. SBA, III. *o.p.*

**Greer, Howard Clark.** Packinghouse Accounting. Prepared by the Committee on Accounting of the Institute of American Meat Packers. 1929. IMP. *o.p.*

**Gregg, Alan.** For Future Doctors. 1957. xii, 164 p. 22 cm. 57–11207. Cloth. BM. $3.50ˢ. Paper. P126. $1.50.

**Gregg, H. C.,** *joint author:* REEVES, Liberal Arts College.

**Gregorius, Abū al-Faraj, called Bar-Hebraeus, 1226–1286.** Barhebraeus' Scholia on the Old Testament. *Part I: Genesis–II Samuel.* Edited by Martin Sprengling and William Creighton Graham. 1931. xvi, 393 p. 30 cm. 32-461. OIP, XIII. $15.00.

**Gregory, B. J.** The Co-ordination of the Kindergarten and the Elementary School. By B. J. Gregory and others. 1908. NSSE, 7th Yrbk., Part II. *o.p.*

**Gregory, Charles Oscar.** Legislative Loss Distribution in Negligence Actions. A Study in Administrative Aspects of Comparative Negligence and Contribution in Tort Litigation. 1936. *o.p.*

**Gregory, Charles Oscar,** *joint author:* SHARP, Social Change and Labor Law.

**Gregory, Theodor Emanuel Gugenheim:** *see* CASSEL, Foreign Investments.

**Grene, David.** Complete Greek Tragedies. Edited by David Grene and Richmond Lattimore. 4 vols. boxed. *See* COMPLETE GREEK TRAGEDIES.

**Grene, David.** Greek Political Theory. The Image of Man in Thucydides and Plato. (First published as *Man in His Pride,* 1950.) *Reissue,* 1965. x, 299 p. 21 cm. Paper. P201. $1.95.

**Grene, David.** Greek Tragedies. Edited by David Grene and Richmond Lattimore. 3 vols. (*Phoenix.*) *See* GREEK TRAGEDIES: PHOENIX.

**Grene, David.** Man in His Pride. A Study in the Political Philosophy of Thucydides and Plato. *See* GRENE, Greek Political Theory.

**Grene, David.** Three Greek Tragedies in Translation. Translated by David Grene. 1942. *o.p.*

**Grene, Marjorie.** Introduction to Existentialism. (First published as *Dreadful Freedom. A Critique of Existentialism.*) 1959. x, 150 p. 59-1934. Cloth. 23 cm. $5.00ˢ. Paper. P34. 21 cm. $1.50.

**Grene, Marjorie.** A Portrait of Aristotle. 1963. 272 p. 23 cm. $6.00ˢ. OBE.

**Grene, Marjorie,** *joint ed.:* SMITH, Philosophers Speak for Themselves: Berkeley, Hume, and Kant.

**Grene, Marjorie,** *joint ed.:* SMITH, Philosophers Speak for Themselves: From Descartes to Locke.

**Grene, Marjorie,** *trans.:* WEIZSÄCKER, The World View of Physics.

**Griffith, Helen:** *see* SAINTONGE, Horace.

**Griffin, James B.,** *ed.* Archeology of Eastern United States. 1952. x, 598 p. Illus. 31 cm. 52-14698. $13.50ˢ.

**Griffith, Reginald Harvey.** Sir Perceval of Galles. A Study of the Sources of the Legend. 1911. *o.p.*

**Griffiths, Daniel E.,** *ed.* Behavioral Science and Educational Administration. 1964. NSSE, 63d Yrbk., Part II. xi, 360 p. 24 cm. $4.50ᵗ.

**Grillparzer's Attitude toward Romanticism:** WILLIAMSON.

**Griswold, Don Morse.** University Student Health Services. A Study of Organization, Services Rendered, and Costs in Cornell University, Yale University, the University of Michigan, the University of Minnesota, the University of California, and Oregon State Agricultural College. By Don M. Griswold, M.D., and Hazel I. Spicer. 1932. CMC 19. *o.p.*

**Griswold, Don Morse,** *joint author:* FALK, Community Medical Service.

**Grodinsky, Julius.** The Iowa Pool. A Study in Railroad Competition, 1870–84. 1950. xii, 184 p. Illus. 25 cm. 50-8974. $4.00ˢ.

**Grodzins, Morton.** Americans Betrayed. Politics and the Japanese Evacuation. 1949. *o.p.*

**Grodzins, Morton.** The Loyal and the Disloyal. 1956. x, 319 p. 22 cm. 56-7201. $4.00ˢ.

**Grose, Clyde Leclare.** A Select Bibliography of British History, 1660–1760. 1939. *o.p.*

**Gross National Product of Czechoslovakia:** PESEK.

**Ground Water:** CRONEIS.

**Group Listening:** BRITISH INSTITUTE OF ADULT EDUCATION.

**Group Process and Gang Delinquency:** SHORT.

**Grouped-Frequency French Word List:** WEST.

**Grouping of Pupils:** COXE.

**Groups Defined for a General Field:** DICKSON.

**Grover, Frank Reed.** Father Pierre François Pinet, S.J., and His Mission of the Guardian Angel of Chicago (L'Ange gardien), A.D. 1696–1699. 1907. *o.p.*

A publication of the Chicago Historical Society.

**Grover, Frank Reed.** Some Indian Landmarks of the North Shore. 1905. *o.p.*

A publication of the Chicago Historical Society.

**Groves, Ernest Rutherford.** The Rural Mind and Social Welfare. With Foreword by Kenyon L. Butterfield. 1922. *o.p.*

**Growth of Constitutional Power in the United States:** SWISHER.

**Growth Diagnosis:** BAYER.

**Growth of Medical Thought:** KING.

**Growth in Private-School Children:** GRAY.

**Growth Regulators:** MITCHELL.

**Growth and Variability of Intelligence:** RICHARDSON.

**Growth of Visual Perception in Children:** LINE.

**Gruenberg, Sidonie Matsner.** The Use of the Radio in Parent Education. Report of a Study Conducted by the Child Study Association of America in Co-operation with the National Council of Parent Education and the National Advisory Council on Radio in Education. 1939. *o.p.*

**Grunebaum, Gustave E. von.** Medieval Islam. A Study in Cultural Orientation. 1946. 2d ed. 1953. viii, 378 p. Index. 46-5260. Cloth. 23 cm. OIE. $6.75ˢ. Paper. P69. 21 cm. $1.95.

**Grunebaum, Gustave E. von.** A Tenth-Century Document of Arabic Literary Theory and Criticism. The Sections on Poetry of al-Bâgillâni's Icjâz al-Qur'ân. 1951. *o.p.*

**Grunebaum, Gustave E. von.,** *ed.* Unity and Variety in Muslim Civilization. 1955. xii, 385 p. 25 cm. 55-11191. CSCC. $8.50ˢ.

**Gudde, Erwin G.,** *ed.* Aus Wald und Heide. Sagen, Erzählungen, Tiergeschichten, Gedichte. By Hermann Löns. HCLS.

**Guicharnaud, June,** *trans.:* DELAY, Youth of André Gide.

**Guicharnaud, June,** *trans.:* GIDE, Self-Portraits.

**Guicharnaud, June,** *trans.:* TOUSSAINT, History of the Indian Ocean.

**Guidance in Educational Institutions:** KE-FAUVER.

**Guide of the Perplexed:** MAIMONIDES.

**Guide to the Solar Phenomena Film:** MARSHALL.

**Guide to the Study of the Christian Religion:** SMITH.

**Guild, Cameron St. Clair.** Surveys of the Medical Facilities in Three Representative Southern Counties. With a Statistical Appendix on the Method of Selecting Representative Counties, by I. S. Falk. 1932. CMC 23. *o.p.*

**Gulick, Addison.** Evolutionist and Missionary: John Thomas Gulick. Portrayed through Documents and Discussions. 1932. *o.p.*

**Guillebaud, C. W.,** *joint ed.:* CAMBRIDGE ECONOMIC HANDBOOKS.

**Gullible's Travels:** LARDNER.

**Gulliksen, Harold,** *joint author:* CARLSON, Studies on the Possible Intoxicating Action of 3.2 Per Cent Beer.

**Gunn, Thom.** My Sad Captains and Other Poems. 1961. 48 p. 21 cm. 61-15933. Cloth. $2.50ˢ. Paper. PP. $1.50. USA.

**Gunn, Thom.** The Sense of Movement. 1959. 62 p. 23 cm. 59-8734. $2.75ˢ. USA.

**Gunnerson, William Cyrus.** History of U-Stems in Greek. 1905. *o.p.*

**Gunsaulus, Frank Wakeley.** Martin Luther and the Morning Hour in Europe. Two Lectures Delivered at the University of Chicago, October 16 and 17, 1917. 1917. *o.p.*

**Gurney, Frederick J.** Evolution, the Bible and Religion. 1922. *o.p.*

**Gustafson, Robert L.,** *joint author:* JOHNSON, Grain Yields and the American Food Supply.

**Guttridge, George H.,** *ed.:* BURKE, The Correspondence of Edmund Burke, *Vol. III.*

**Guy, Philip Langstaffe Ord.** Megiddo Tombs, 1938. With Contributions by Robert M. Engberg. xxiv, 224 p. Illus. 30 cm. 39-2230. OIP, XXXIII. $15.00.

**Guy, Philip Langstaffe Ord.** New Light from Armageddon. Second Provisional Report (1927–29) on the Excavations at Megiddo in Palestine. By P. L. O. Guy. With a Chapter on "An Inscribed Scaraboid" by W. E. Staples. 1931. ix, 68 p. Illus. 26 cm. 31-16113. Paper. OIC 9. $1.00.

**Guyer, Michael F.** Animal Micrology. Practical Exercises in Zoölogical Micro-Technique. With a Chapter on Drawing by Elizabeth A. (Smith) Bean. 1906. 5th ed. 1953. xviii, 327 p. Illus. 24 cm. 53-8741. $6.00ᵗ.

"This useful manual of microscopical technique, which has guided both the beginner and the more experienced worker in almost every biological laboratory . . . for some thirty years, has now reached its fourth revised edition. Such formulas and methods as have been found superior to the older procedures have been added, including the dioxan technique. This revision is essential to every laboratory where microscopical preparations are made . . ."—*American Journal of Science.*

**Gymnosperms: Structure and Evolution:** CHAMBERLAIN.

**Haas, William Herman.** Outposts of Defense. PPP *special.* 1942. *o.p.*

**Haas, William Herman,** *ed.* The American Empire. A Study of the Outlying Territories of the United States. Contributors: W. O. Blanchard, Luis J. Borja, John Wesley Coulter, Isaac J. Cox, Cornelio C. Cruz, Otis W. Freeman, William H. Haas, Rafael Picó, Earl B. Shaw. 1940. *o.p.*

**Haavelmo, Trygve.** A Study in the Theory of Investment. 1960. viii, 221 p. 24 cm. 60-13057. ERS. $5.00ˢ.

**Haber, Samuel.** Efficiency and Uplift. Scientific Management in the Progressive Era, 1890–1920. xiii, 181 p. 22 cm. 64 15828. 1964. $5.00ˢ.

**Haberler, Gottfried:** *see* WRIGHT, Gold and Monetary Stabilization.

**Hackamack, Henry,** *joint author:* BOWMAN, Studying Children.

**Hackamack, Henry,** *joint author:* HAVIGHURST, Community Youth Development Program.

**Haden, Ernest F.,** *ed.* Science française. Readings in General Science. Edited by Ernest F. Haden and R. C. Trotter. HCLS.

**Haematology and Blood Groups:** GALTON.

**Hagan, William T.** American Indians. 1961. viii, 190 p. Illus. Index. 21 cm. 61-1555. Cloth. CHAC. $4.50ˢ. Paper. $1.95.

**Hagboldt, Peter Herman.** How To Study Modern Languages in College. 1925. *o.p.*

**Hagboldt, Peter Herman.** How To Study Modern Languages in High School. 1925. *o.p.*

**Hagboldt, Peter Herman.** Language Learning. Some Reflections from Teaching Experience. 1935. *o.p.*

**Hagboldt, Peter Herman.** HCLS.

Das Abenteuer der Neujahrsnacht.
Allerlei.
Anekdoten und Erzählungen.
Aus deutscher Vergangenheit.
Brief Course in German (*with* KAUFMANN).
Building the German Vocabulary.
Deutsch für Anfänger (*with* KAUFMANN).
Essentials of German Reviewed.
Eulenspiegel und Münchhausen.
Fabeln.
5 Sight-reading and Vocabulary Tests for Inductive Readings in German. Book I.
4 Vocabulary Tests for Inductive Readings in German. Book II.
14 Tests on A Modern German Grammar.
Fünf berühmte Märchen.
German Review and Composition (*with* KAUFMANN).
Inductive Readings in German. Book I (*with* KAUFMANN).
Inductive Readings in German. Book II. An Introduction to the Spirit of German Life and Literature.
Land und Leute.
Lesebuch für Anfänger.
Modern German Grammar.
Pechvogel und Glückskind (Volkmann-Leander).
Teaching of German, The.
Tests To Accompany *A Brief Course in German.*
Von deutscher Sprache und Dichtung.
Word Book for *Graded German Readers,* Books 1–10.

**Haggerty, Melvin Everett.** The Educational Program. 1937. EHI. *o.p.*

**Haggerty, Melvin Everett.** The Faculty. 1937. EHI. *o.p.*

**Haggerty, Melvin Everett,** *joint author:* ZOOK, Principles of Accrediting Higher Institutions.

**Hagstrum, Jean H.** The Sister Arts. The Tradition of Literary Pictorialism in English Poetry from Dryden to Gray. 1958. xxii, 337 p. Illus. 25 cm. 59-11948. $8.50ˢ.

**Hagstrum, Jean H.** William Blake, Poet and Painter. An Introduction to the Illuminated Verse. 1964. xi, 156 p. 80 p. plates. 25 cm. 64-13950. $7.50ˢ.

**Haile, Father Bernard.** Navaho Sacrificial Figurines. 1947. *o.p.*

**Haile, Father Bernard.** Prayer Stick Cutting in a Five Night Navaho Ceremonial of the Male Branch of Shootingway. 1948. *o.p.*

**Haile, Father Bernard,** *ed. and trans.* Origin Legend of the Navaho Flintway. Text and Translation. 1943. AN *o.p.*

**Haines, Richard C.,** *joint author:* DELOUGAZ, Byzantine Church at Khirbat-al-Karak.

**Halbert, Blanche,** *ed.* The Better Homes Manual. (Published in Co-operation with Better Homes in America.) 1931. HE. *o.p.*

**Hale, George Ellery.** The Aim of the Yerkes Observatory. Address Delivered at the Conferences Held in Connection with the Dedication of the Yerkes Observatory, October 19, 1897. 1897. *o.p.*

**Hale, George Ellery.** Carbon in the Chromosphere. Some New Forms of Spectroheliographs. 1899. YOB. *o.p.*

**Hale, George Ellery.** Changes in the Spectrum of Nova Persei. 1901. YOB. *o.p.*

**Hale, George Ellery.** Comparison of Stellar Spectra of the Third and Fourth Types. 1899. YOB. *o.p.*

**Hale, George Ellery.** Completion of the Yerkes Telescope. 1897. YOB. *o.p.*

**Hale, George Ellery.** Dedication of the Yerkes Observatory. 1897. YOB. *o.p.*

**Hale, George Ellery.** First Annual Report of the Director of the Yerkes Observatory of the University of Chicago, for the Year Ending September 30, 1898. 1899. *o.p.*

**Hale, George Ellery.** Heat Radiation of the Stars. 1899. YOB. *o.p.*

**Hale, George Ellery.** Latitude and Longitude of the Yerkes Observatory. 1901. YOB. *o.p.*

**Hale, George Ellery.** The New Star in Gemini. 1903. YOB. *o.p.*

**Hale, George Ellery.** The New Star in Perseus. 1901. YOB. *o.p.*

**Hale, George Ellery.** Observations of the Total Solar Eclipse of May 28, 1900, at Wadesboro, N.C. 1900. YOB. *o.p.*

**Hale, George Ellery.** Opportunities for Students at the Yerkes Observatory. 1899. YOB. *o.p.*

**Hale, George Ellery.** Organization of the Yerkes Observatory. 1896. YOB. *o.p.*

**Hale, George Ellery.** Parallax of the Andromeda Nebula. The Spectrum of Saturn's Rings. 1899. YOB *o.p.*

**Hale, George Ellery.** Period and Elongation Distance of the Fifth Satellite of Jupiter. 1899. YOB. *o.p.*

**Hale, George Ellery.** Photographs of Star Clusters Made with the Forty-Inch Visual Telescope. 1900. YOB. *o.p.*

**Hale, George Ellery.** The Rumford Spectroheliograph of the Yerkes Observatory. By George E. Hale and Ferdinand Ellerman. 1903. YO, III. *o.p.*

**Hale, George Ellery.** Second Annual Report of the Director of the Yerkes Observatory of the University of Chicago, for the Year Ending June 30, 1899. 1899. *o.p.*

**Hale, George Ellery.** Solar Eclipse Problems. 1900. *o.p.*

**Hale, George Ellery.** Spectra of Stars of Secchi's Fourth Type. 1899. YOB. *o.p.*

**Hale, George Ellery.** The Spectra of Stars of Secchi's Fourth Type. By George E. Hale, Ferdinand Ellerman, and J. A. Parkhurst. 1903. *o.p.*

**Hale, George Ellery.** The Spectrum of the High Potential Discharge between Metallic Electrodes in Liquids and in Gases at High Pressures. By George E. Hale and Norton A. Kent. 1907. YO, III. *o.p.*

**Hale, George Ellery.** The Study of Stellar Evolution. An Account of Some Recent Methods of Astrophysical Research. 1909. *o.p.*

**Hale, George Ellery.** Variable Star Observations with the 12-Inch and 40-Inch Refractors. 1900. YOB. *o.p.*

**Hale, William Gardner.** The Anticipatory Subjunctive in Greek and Latin. 1894. Preprint from Vol. I, STUDIES IN CLASSICAL PHILOLOGY. *o.p.*

**Hale, William Gardner.** Synopsis of the Modal Uses of the Finite Verb in Latin. 1901. *o.p.*

**Half Horse Half Alligator:** BLAIR.

**Halich, Wasyl.** Ukrainians in the United States. 1937. *o.p.*

**Hall, Arthur Jackson.** Religious Education in the Public Schools of the State and City of New York. A Historical Study. 1914. *o.p.*

**Hall, Charles Cuthbert.** Christ and the Eastern Soul. The Witness of the Oriental Consciousness to Jesus Christ. 1909. BL *o.p.*

**Hall, Charles Cuthbert.** Christian Belief Interpreted by Christian Experience. Lectures delivered in India, Ceylon, and Japan on the Barrows Foundation. With an Introductory Note by the Vice-Chancellor of the University of Bombay. 1905. BL. *o.p.*

**Hall, Everett W.** Philosophical Systems. A Categorical Analysis. 1960. x, 172 p. 22 cm. 60-11824. $4.00⁸.

**Hall, John W.,** *joint author:* BEARDSLEY, Village Japan.

**Hall, John W.,** *joint author:* BOBBITT, Supervision of City Schools.

**Hall, John W.,** *joint author:* CUBBERLEY, Research within the Field of Education.

**Hall, Leonard.** Stars Upstream. Life along an Ozark River. 1959. ix, 252 p. Illus. 23 cm. 59-5772. $4.50.

**Hallenbeck, Wilbur Chapman,** *joint author:* WIESE, Let's Talk It Over.

**Halliday, Evelyn G.** Food Chemistry and Cookery. By Evelyn G. Halliday and Isabel T. Noble. 1943. *o.p.*

**Halliday, Evelyn G.** How To Buy Beef. By Evelyn G. Halliday and Isabel T. Noble. 1933. HE. *o.p.*

**Halliday, Evelyn G.** Hows and Whys of Cooking. By Evelyn G. Halliday and Isabel T. Noble. 1928. 3d ed. 1946. xii, 328 p. Illus. 22 cm. 46-2063. $4.75ᵗ.

**Hallock, Richard Treadwell.** The Chicago Syllabary and the Louvre Syllabary AO 7661. 1940. xiv, 79 p. Illus. 30 cm. 41-15403. Paper. AS, 7. $4.00.

**Hallowell, John H.** The Moral Foundation of Democracy. 1954. ix, 134 p. 21 cm. 54-11938. WFL. $3.50ˢ.

**Halperin, S. William.** Diplomat under Stress. Visconti-Venosta and the Crisis of July, 1870. 1963. xii, 196 p. Index. 22 cm. 63-13065. $5.00ˢ.

**Halperin, S. William.** Italy and the Vatican at War. A Study of Their Relations from the Outbreak of the Franco-Prussian War to the Death of Pius IX. 1937. *o.p.*

**Halperin, S. William.** The Separation of Church and State in Italian Thought from Cavour to Mussolini. 1937. *o.p.*

**Halperin, S. William,** *ed.* Some 20th Century Historians. Essays on Eminent Europeans. 1961. xxi, 298 p. 22 cm. 61-568. $5.95ˢ.

**Halpern, Bruce P.,** *joint author:* KARE, Physiological and Behavioral Aspects of Taste.

**Halstead, Ward C.** Brain and Intelligence. A Quantitative Study of the Frontal Lobes. 1947. xiv, 206 p. Illus. 24 cm. 47-2506. BM. $7.50ˢ.

**Hamburger, Viktor.** A Manual of Experimental Embryology. 1942. Illus. 26 cm. 42-22518. Rev. ed. 1960. xvii, 221 p. BM. $4.00ᵗ.

**Hamilton, Clarence Herbert.** Buddhism in India, Ceylon, China, and Japan. A Reading Guide. 1931. *o.p.*

**Hamilton, Earl J.,** *ed.* Landmarks in Political Economy. Edited by Earl J. Hamilton, Harry G. Johnson, and Albert Rees. 1962. xii, 622 p. 24 cm. 62-17134. Cloth. $10.00ˢ. Paper, 2 vols. 21 cm. P100. $1.95. P101. $1.95.

**Hamilton, Henry E.** Biographical Sketch of Gurdon Saltonstall Hubbard. 1908. *o.p.*

A publication of the Chicago Historical Society.

**Hamilton, Marian W.,** *trans.:* JASPERS, General Psychopathology.

**Hamilton, Walton Hale,** *ed.* Current Economic Problems. A Series of Readings in the Control of Industrial Development. 1915. 3d ed. 1925. MSE. *o.p.*

**Hamilton, Walton Hale.** Exercises in Current Economics. 1916. 2d ed. 1920. MSE. *o.p.*

**Hamilton, Walton Hale,** *joint ed.:* CLARK, Readings in the Economics of War.

**Hamlet Bibliography and Reference Guide, 1877–1935:** RAVEN.

**Hamlet and the Philosophy of Literary Criticism:** WEITZ.

**Hammond, Eleanor Prescott.** On the Text of Chaucer's *Parlement of Foules*. 1902. *o.p.*

**Hammurabi, King of Babylon.** The Code of Ḥammurabi, King of Babylon about 2250 B.C. Autographed Text, Transliteration, Translation, Glossary, Index of Subjects, Lists of Proper Names, Signs, Numerals, Corrections and Erasures, with Map, Frontispiece, and Photograph of Text. By Robert Francis Harper. 1904. *o.p.*

**Hancock, John Leonard.** Studies in Stichomythia. 1917. *o.p.*

**Handbook of Aging and the Individual:** BIRREN.

**Handbook on the Anecdotal Behavior Journal:** JARVIE.

**Handbook of Biological Illustration:** ZWEIFEL.

**Handbook of Diet Therapy:** TURNER.

**Handbook of the Egyptian Collection:** ALLEN.

**Handbook for Field Work Students:** BRISTOL.

**Handbook of Histological and Cytological Technique:** BENSLEY.

**Handbook of the Life of the Apostle Paul:** BURTON.

**Handbook of Rural Social Resources, 1926:** ISRAEL.

**Handbook of Rural Social Resources, 1928:** LANDIS.

**Handbook on Social Case Recording:** BRISTOL.

**Handbook of Social Gerontology:** TIBBITTS.

**Handbooks of Ethics and Religion** (HER): Edited by Shailer Mathews, W. C. Bower, and Edwin E. Aubrey.

BARTON, Religions of the World.
BOWER, Character through Creative Experience.
BURTON, Source Book for the Study of the Teaching of Jesus.
CASE, Bibliographical Guide to the History of Christianity.
CHAVE, Personality Development in Children.
CHAVE, Supervision of Religious Education.
COE, Psychology of Religion.
DAVIS, Preaching.
DAVIS, Principles of Preaching.
FOWLER, Origin and Growth of the Hebrew Religion.
GOODSPEED, Story of the New Testament.
GRAHAM, Culture and Conscience.
GRAHAM, Prophets and Israel's Culture.
HOLMAN, Cure of Souls.
LEWIS, How the Bible Grew.
MITCHELL, Ethics of the Old Testament.
MOORE, Spread of Christianity.
NORTON, Rise of Christianity.
ROBINSON, Life of Paul.
SMITH, Current Christian Thinking.
SMITH, Moral Life of the Hebrews.
SMITH, Origin and History of Hebrew Law.
SMITH, Principles of Christian Living.
SMITH, Prophets and Their Times.
SOARES, Religious Education.

**Handel, Gerald,** *joint author:* HESS, Family Worlds.

**Handwork in Religious Education:** WARDLE.

**Handwriting Movement:** FREEMAN.

**Haney, George Walker:** *see* LARSON, Lying and Its Detection.

**Hangen, Eva Catherine,** *comp.* A Concordance to the Complete Poetical Works of Sir Thomas Wyatt. 1941. *o.p.*

**Hanke, Milton Theodore.** Diet and Dental Health. 1933. *o.p.*

**Hanson, Harold B.:** *see* SHAW, Brothers in Crime.

**Hanson, James Christian Meinich.** A Comparative Study of Cataloging Rules Based on the Anglo-American Code of 1908, with Comments on the Rules and on the Prospects for a Further Extension of International Agreement and Co-operation. 1939. LS. *o.p.*

**Hanus, Paul H.,** *joint author:* CUBBERLEY, Research within the Field of Education.

**Haraszti, Zoltán.** The Bay Psalm Book. A Facsimile Edition. With an Introduction by Zoltán Haraszti. 1956. xiii, 448 p. 19 cm. 56-5128. 2 vols. boxed. $11.00ˢ.

"Dr. Haraszti demonstrates his wide knowledge of the *Scriptures* and his ability to work in the difficult field of Biblical criticism. . . . The two volumes, beautifully bound with matching case, form an interesting addition to the literature on the history of Massachusetts Bay Colony: *The Bay Psalm Book* as an example of scholarly zeal and curious rendition of the *Psalms* now no longer a rarity, and *The Enigma of the Bay Psalm Book* a work of historical investigation and criticism worthy of emulation."—Harry A. Poole, in *The William and Mary Quarterly.*

**Harberger, Arnold,** *ed.* The Demand for Durable Goods. Studies by Richard F. Muth, Meyer L. Burstein, Gregory C. Chow, Zvi Griliches, and Yehuda Grunfeld. 1960. vi, 274 p. 24 cm. 60-7236. ERS. $6.00ˢ.

**Harbison, F. H.,** *joint ed.:* McCARTHY, Labor Looks at Unemployment Insurance.

**Hard Winter Wheat Pools:** KNAPP.

**Hardee, Melvene D.,** *ed.* Personnel Services in Education. 1959. NSSE, 58th Yrbk., Part II. 398 p. 24 cm. 59-3793. Cloth. $4.50ᵗ. Paper. $3.75ᵗ.

**Hardesty, Irving.** Neurological Technique. Some Special Histological Methods Employed for the Study of the Nervous System, together with a Laboratory Outline for the Dissections of the Central Nervous System and the Neurological Nomenclature. 1902. *o.p.*

**Hardesty, Irving.** The Number and Arrangement of the Fibers Forming the Spinal Nerves of the Frog (Rana virescens). 1899. *o.p.*

**Hardin, Charles M.** Freedom in Agricultural Education. 1955. xviii, 275 p. Planographed. 24 cm. 55-5127. $4.50ˢ.

**Hardy, Charles Oscar.** Devaluation of the Dollar. 1933. PPP, 8. *o.p.*

**Hardy, Charles Oscar,** *ed.* Readings in Risk and Risk-bearing. 1924. MSB. *o.p.*

**Hardy, Charles Oscar.** Risk and Risk-bearing. 1923. 2d ed. 1931. MSB. *o.p.*

**Hardy, Martha Crumpton.** Healthy Growth. A Study of the Influence of Health Education on Growth and Development of School Children. By Martha Crumpton Hardy and Carolyn H. Hoefer. 1936. xii, 360 p. Illus. 24 cm. 37-27069. $6.00ˢ.

**Hargreaves, Herbert Lyde.** The "Faculty" of Imagination. An Enquiry Concerning the Existence of a General "Faculty," or Group Factor of Imagination. 1927. BJP. *o.p.*

**Harman, Harry H.** Modern Factor Analysis. 1960. xvi, 470 p. Index. 25 cm. 60-11591. $10.00ᵗ.

**Harman, Harry H.,** *joint author:* HOLZINGER, Factor Analysis.

**Harmer, Althea.** Textile Industries. *See* ELEMENTARY SCHOOL RECORD, No. 3.

**Harmony:** SCHENKER.

**Harmony of the Synoptic Gospels in Greek:** BURTON.

**Harper, Paul V.,** *ed.:* HARPER, The Russia I Believe In.

**Harper, Robert Francis.** Assyrian and Babylonian Letters Belonging to the Kouyunjik Collections of the British Museum. 14 Parts. 1892–1914. *o.p.*

Part I, issued in 1892, was the first book published by The University of Chicago Press.

**Harper, Robert Francis,** *ed.* Old Testament and Semitic Studies in Memory of William Rainey Harper. Edited by Robert Francis Harper, Francis Brown, George Foot Moore. 2 vols. 1908. *o.p.*

**Harper, Robert Francis,** *ed. and trans.:* ḤAMMURABI, Code.

**Harper, Samuel Northrup.** The Russia I Believe In. The Memoirs of Samuel N. Harper. Edited by Paul V. Harper. 1945. *o.p.*

**Harper, Samuel Northrup.** Civic Training in Soviet Russia. 1929. SMC. *o.p.*

**Harper, Samuel Northrup.** Making Bolsheviks. 1931. *o.p.*

**Harper, Samuel Northrup.** The New Electoral Law for the Russian Duma. 1908. POL. *o.p.*

**Harper, Samuel Northrup,** *ed.* The Soviet Union and World-Problems. By Alexander A. Troyanovsky, Ivan V. Boyeff, Vladimir Romm, Hans Kohn, Malbone W. Graham. 1935. HFL. *o.p.*

**Harper, Samuel Northrup:** *see* BOYER, Russian Reader.

**Harper, William Rainey.** The Book of Job. A Study of the Problem of Suffering as Treated in the Old Testament. 1908. AISL. *o.p.*

**Harper, William Rainey.** Elements of Hebrew by an Inductive Method. Revised by J. M. Powis Smith. 1959. xvii, 204 p. 22 cm. 59-7625. Paper. $2.25ᵗ.

**Harper, William Rainey.** The Foreshadowings of the Christ. A Series of Direction Sheets for Individual or Class Study of the Messianic Idea in Relation to the Old Testament History through Which It Was Developed—Genesis to Malachi. 1904. AISL. *o.p.*

**Harper, William Rainey.** Introductory Hebrew. Method and Manual. Revised by J. M. Powis Smith. 1959. xiv, 269 p. 22 cm. 59-7624. Paper. $2.50ᵗ.

**Harper, William Rainey.** The Priestly Element in the Old Testament. An Aid to Historical Study. 1902. 2d ed. 1905. CS. *o.p.*

Formerly *Constructive Studies in the Priestly Element in the Old Testament.*

**Harper, William Rainey.** The Prophetic Element in the Old Testament. An Aid to Historical Study. 1905. CS. *o.p.*

**Harper, William Rainey.** Prospects of the Small College. 1900. *o.p.*

**Harper, William Rainey.** Religion and the Higher Life. Talks to Students. 1904. *o.p.*

**Harper, William Rainey.** The Structure of the Text of the Book of Amos. 1904. 38 *o.p.*

**Harper, William Rainey.** The Structure of the Text of the Book of Hosea. 1905. 5 *o.p.*

**Harper, William Rainey.** The Trend in Higher Education. 1905. *o.p.*

**Harper, William Rainey.** The Utterances of Amos Arranged Strophically. 1900. *o.p.*

**Harper, William Rainey.** The Work of the Old Testament Priests. A Study of the Development of Ideas Concerning Worship. 1908. AISL. *o.p.*

**Harper, William Rainey.** The Work of the Old Testament Sages. A Series of Direction Sheets for Individual or Class Study of the Wisdom Element in the Old Testament, Especially in the Books of Proverbs, Job, The Song of Songs, and Ecclesiastes. 1904. AISL *o.p.*

**Harper, William Rainey,** *ed.* Report of the Educational Commission of the City of Chicago. The Commission was appointed by Hon. Carter H. Harrison, January 19, 1898. 1901. *o.p.*

**Harrington, K. P.** Medieval Latin. *Reissue,* 1962. xxx, 698 p. 21 cm. 62-18114. Paper. $5.50t.

**Harris, Ada Van Stone.** The Kindergarten and Its Relation to Elementary Education. 1907. NSSE, 6th Yrbk., Part II. *o.p.*

**Harris, David.** Britain and the Bulgarian Horrors of 1876. 1939. *o.p.*

**Harris Foundation Committee.** An American Foreign Policy toward International Stability. A Memorandum Prepared under the Auspices of the Norman Wait Harris Memorial Foundation. With a Preface by Quincy Wright. 1934. HFL. PPP 14. *o.p.*

**Harris, Frank.** The Bomb. *Reissue,* 1963. Introduction by John Dos Passos. xxiii, 332 p. 21 cm. 63-22587. CF. $4.95.

**Harris, Marshall,** *joint ed.:* ACKERMAN, Family Farm Policy.

**Harris Memorial Foundation Lectures on International Relations (HFL):**

BENEŠ, International Security.
CASSEL, Foreign Investments.
CHIROL, Occident and the Orient.
COLBY, Geographic Aspects of International Relations.
DE VISSCHER, Stabilization of Europe.
GINI, Population.

HARPER, Soviet Union and World-Problems.
HARRIS FOUNDATION COMMITTEE, American Foreign Policy toward International Stability.
HOSELITZ, Progress of Underdeveloped Areas.
HURST, Great Britain and the Dominions.
IRELAND, The Near East.
KRAUS, Germany in Transition.
LAVES, Foundations of a More Stable World Order.
LAVES, Inter American Solidarity.
MACNAIR, Voices from Unoccupied China.
MORGENTHAU, Germany and the Future of Europe.
MORGENTHAU, Peace, Security, and the United Nations.
OGBURN, Technology and International Relations.
RAPPARD, Crisis of Democracy.
SAENZ, Some Mexican Problems.
SCHULTZ, Food for the World.
STILLMAN, Africa in the Modern World.
SOYESHIMA, Oriental Interpretations of the Far Eastern Problem.
TALBOT, South Asia in the World Today.
VASCONCELOS, Aspects of Mexican Civilization.
WOODHEAD, Occidental Interpretations of the Far Eastern Problem.
WRIGHT, A Foreign Policy for the United States.
WRIGHT, Gold and Monetary Stabilization.
WRIGHT, Interpretations of American Foreign Policy.
WRIGHT, Neutrality and Collective Security.
WRIGHT, Public Opinion and World-Politics.
WRIGHT, Unemployment as a World-Problem.
WRIGHT, The World Community.

**Harris, Victor.** All Coherence Gone. 1949. *o.p.*

**Harris, Zellig S.** Structural Linguistics. (First published in 1951 as *Methods in Structural Linguistics.*) 1960. xvi, 384 p. 21 cm. 51-4864. Paper. P52. $2.25.

"Harris' contribution [is] epoch marking in a double sense: first in that it marks the culmination of a development of linguistic methodology *away* from a stage of intuitionism, frequently culture-bound; and second in that it marks the beginning of a new period, in which the new methods will be applied ever more rigorously to ever widening areas in human culture."—NORMAN A. MCQUOWN, in *Language.*

**Harrison, B. Kent.** Gravitation Theory and Gravitational Collapse. By B. Kent Harrison, Kip S. Thorne, Masami Wakano, and John Archibald Wheeler. 1965. xvii, 177 p. 25 cm. 65-17293. $6.50s.

**Harrison, Caleb N.,** *joint author:* ROWLAND, Arc-Spectra.

**Harrod, Roy F.** International Economics. 1958. xiv, 186 p. 21 cm. 58-5161. Paper. CEH 2. $1.50. USA.

**Harsh, Philip Whaley.** Studies in Dramatic "Preparation" in Roman Comedy. 1935. *o.p.*

**Hart, Albert Gailord.** Anticipations, Uncertainty, and Dynamic Planning. 1940. SBA, XI. *o.p.*

**Hart, Albert Gailord.** Economic Policy for Rearmament. 1940. PPP 33. *o.p.*

**Hart, Albert Gailord.** How the National Income Is Divided. 1937. PPP 23. *o.p.*

**Hart, Joseph Kinmont.** A Critical Study of Current Theories of Moral Education. 1910. *o.p.*

**Hart, Walter Morris:** *see* BRYAN, Sources and Analogues of Chaucer's *Canterbury Tales.*

**Harth, Phillip.** Swift and Anglican Rationalism. The Religious Background of *A Tale of a Tub.* 1961. vii, 171 p. 22 cm. 61-15934. $5.00ˢ.

**Hartshorne, Charles.** Philosophers Speak of God. By Charles Hartshorne and William L. Reese. 1953. xiv, 535 p. 24 cm. 53-10041. Cloth. $9.50ˢ. Paper. P142. $3.45.

**Hartshorne, Charles.** The Philosophy and Psychology of Sensation. 1934. *o.p.*

**Hartshorne, Richard:** *see* COLBY, Geographic Aspects of International Relations.

**Hartstall, Paul K.** Si nous écrivions. By Paul K. Hartstall and James C. Babcock. HCLS.

**Hartung, Maurice,** *joint ed.:* BUSWELL, Arithmetic, 1949.

**Harvard Gospels:** GOODSPEED.

**Haskell Gospels:** GOODSPEED.

**Haskell Lectures in Comparative Religion** (CR):

GIBB, Modern Trends in Islam.
HAYDON, Modern Trends in World-Religions.
HOLTON, Modern Japan and Shinto Nationalism.
HU, Chinese Renaissance.
LANDON, Southeast Asia.
MACDONALD, Religious Attitude.
MEEK, Hebrew Origins.
SAUNDERS, Epochs in Buddhist History.
*See also* Barrows Lectures.

**Hastie, W. Reid,** *ed.* Art Education. 1965. NSSE, 64th Yrbk., Part II. x, 310 p. 24 cm. $5.00ᵗ.

**Hastings, Charles Harris.** Bibliography of Sociology, 1897–98. 1898. *o.p.*

**Hastings, George Everett.** The Life and Works of Francis Hopkinson. 1926. *o.p.*

**Hastings, Thomas,** *joint author:* CRAM, Six Lectures on Architecture.

**Hastings, William Thomson.** Syllabus of American Literature. 1923. 3d ed. 1941. *o.p.*

**Hatai, Shinkishi.** The Finer Structure of the Neurones in the Nervous System of the White Rat. 1903. *o.p.*

**Hatch, William Henry Paine.** The Principal Uncial Manuscripts of the New Testament. 1939. *o.p.*

**Hatfield, Henry Rand,** *ed.* Lectures on Commerce. Delivered before the College of Commerce and Administration of the University of Chicago. 1907. *o.p.*

**Hatfield, James Taft,** *joint ed.:* ALLEN, Diary and Letters of Wilhelm Müller.

**Hathway, Marion.** The Migratory Worker and Family Life. The Mode of Living and Public Provision for the Needs of the Family of the Migratory Worker in Selected Industries of the State of Washington. 1934. SSM. *o.p.*

**Hathway, Marion.** The Young Cripple and His Job. 1928. SSM. *o.p.*

**Hattwick, L. W.,** *joint author:* ALSHULER, Painting and Personality.

**Haupt, Paul.** The Book of Esther. Critical Edition of the Hebrew Text with Notes. 1908. *o.p.*

**Haupt, Paul.** The Book of Micah. A New Metrical Translation with Restoration of the Hebrew Text and Explanatory and Critical Notes. 1910. *o.p.*

**Hauser, Elizabeth B.,** *trans.:* HÖLSCHER, Excavation of Medinet Habu, *Vol. IV, Vol. V.*

**Hauser, Elizabeth B.,** *trans.:* SCHOTT, Wall Scenes from the Mortuary Chapel of the Mayor Paser at Medinet Habu.

**Hauser, Philip M.,** *ed.* The Study of Population. An Inventory and Appraisal. Edited by Philip M. Hauser and Otis Dudley Duncan. 1959. xiv, 864 p. Illus. 25 cm. 58-11949. $15.00ˢ. (Not for sale in South Asia.)

**Haut livre du Graal. Perlesvaus:** Nitze.

**Have We the Likeness of Christ?** Johnson.

**Havighurst, Robert J.** American Indian and White Children. A Sociopsychological Investigation. By Robert J. Havighurst and Bernice L. Neugarten. 1955. *o.p.*

**Havighurst, Robert J.** A Community Youth Development Program. By Robert J. Havighurst, Robert F. DeHaan, William J. Dietrich, Henry Hackamack, LaVona Johnson, and Robert J. King. 1952. ("Youth Development Series," No. 1.) viii, 59 p. 25 cm. 52-11216. SEM 75. $1.50ᵗ.

**Havighurst, Robert J.** A Survey of the Education of Gifted Children. By Robert J. Havighurst, Eugene Stivers, and Robert F. DeHaan. 1955. SEM 83. $3.00ᵗ.

**Havighurst, Robert J.,** *ed.* Education for the Gifted in School and College. 1958. NSSE, 57th Yrbk., Part II. xi, 420, vii p. 24 cm. 56-5616. Cloth. $4.50ᵗ. Paper. $3.75ᵗ.

**Havighurst, Robert J.,** *joint author:* Bowman, Studying Children.

**Havighurst, Robert J.,** *joint author:* DeHaan, Educating Gifted Children.

**Havighurst, Robert,** *joint author:* Eells, Intelligence and Cultural Differences.

**Havighurst, Robert J.,** *joint author:* Friedmann, Meaning of Work and Retirement.

**Havighurst, Robert J.:** *see* Edwards, Education in a Democracy.

**Hawley, Florence.** Tree-Ring Analysis and Dating in the Mississippi Drainage. By Florence Hawley. With Appended Papers: Reflection of Precipitation and Temperature in Tree Growth. By Mildred Mott Wedel and Florence Hawley. A New Dendrochronograph. By E. J. Workman and Florence Hawley. 1941. AN. *o.p.*

**Hawthorne, John G.,** *joint trans.:* Theophilus, On Divers Arts.

**Hay, Eloise Knapp.** The Political Novels of Joseph Conrad. 1963. xiv, 350 p. 24 cm. 63-13066. $6.00ˢ.

**Haydon, Albert Eustace,** *ed.* Modern Trends in World-Religions. 1934. CR. *o.p.*

**Haydon, Albert Eustace:** *see* Smith, Religious Thought in the Last Quarter-Century.

**Hayek, Friedrich A.** The Constitution of Liberty. 1960. x, 570 p. 24 cm. 59-11618. $7.50. cusa.

**Hayek, Friedrich A.** Freedom and the Economic System. 1939. PPP 29. *o.p.*

**Hayek, Friedrich A.** Individualism and Economic Order. 1948. viii, 272 p. 21 cm. 48-4149. $6.00ˢ. cusa.

**Hayek, Friedrich A.** John Stuart Mill and Harriet Taylor. Their Friendship and Subsequent Marriage. 1951. *o.p.*

**Hayek, Friedrich A.** The Road to Serfdom. With a Foreword by John Chamberlain. 1944. viii, 248 p. 19 cm. A44-4381. $5.75ˢ. Paper. P4. 21 cm. $1.75. cusa.

**Hayek, Friedrich A.** The Sensory Order. An Inquiry into the Foundations of Theoretical Psychology. With an Introduction by Heinrich Klüver. 1952. xxii, 209 p. 24 cm. 52-14469. $5.00ˢ. Paper. PSS524. $1.95. cusa.

**Hayek, Friedrich A.,** *ed.* Capitalism and the Historians. Edited with an Introduction by F. A. Hayek. Essays by T. S. Ashton, L. M. Hacker, W. H. Hutt, and B. de Jouvenel. 1954. viii, 188 p. 54-64. Cloth. 19 cm. $3.75ˢ. Paper. P120. 21 cm. $1.75. cobe.

**Hayek, Friedrich A.** The Pure Theory of Capital. 1951. xxxi, 454 p. 24 cm. 41-2440. $8.00ˢ. cusa.

**Hayes, Augustus Washington.** Rural Community Organization. 1921. *o.p.*

**Hayes, William C.** Most Ancient Egypt. Edited with an Introduction by Keith C. Seele. 1965. xx, 160 p. 25 cm. 65-17294. $5.00ˢ.

**Hayford, Harrison,** *joint ed.:* Melville, Billy Budd, Sailor.

**Haygood, J. Douglas,** *ed.* Les Oberlé. By René Bazin. HCLS.

**Haygood, William Converse.** Who Uses the Public Library. A Survey of the Patrons of the Circulation and Reference Departments of the New York Public Library. 1938. LS. *o.p.*

**Hays, Samuel P.** The Response to Industrialism. 1957. x, 211 p. 21 cm. 57-6981. Cloth. CHAC. $4.50ˢ. Paper. $1.75.

**Hayton, Prince of Gorigos** (*ca.* 1235–*ca.* 1314). La Flor de las ystorias de Orient. Edited from the Unique MS, Escorial Z–I–2 with Introduction, Bibliography and Notes by Wesley Robertson Long. 1934. *o.p.*

**Hazard, John W.** The Soviet System of Government. 3d ed. 1964. x, 282 p. 24 cm. 64-15826. Cloth, $5.50. Paper. $2.50ᵗ.

**Hazard, Paul,** *ed.* Études critiques sur *Manon Lescaut*. Par Paul Hazard et ses étudiants américains. 1929. MPM. *o.p.*

**Head, Franklin Harvey,** *joint author:* Mc-Cagg, Chicago Historical Society.

**Heal the Hurt Child:** Riese.

**Healing Cults:** Reed.

**Health Dentistry for the Community:** New York Tuberculosis and Health Association, *Committee on Community Dental Service.*

**Health and Education:** Wood.

**Health of a Nation:** Anderson.

**Health Progress in the United States:** Lerner.

**Health Growth:** Hardy.

**Heart and Circulation:** Carlson.

**Heat Radiation of the Stars:** Hale.

**Heath-Chicago Language Series** (HCLS). Comprises the following series of language texts, published by the University of Chicago Press for many years, and transferred to D. C. Heath & Company August 1, 1934.

Heath-Chicago French Series:
Bond, En route.
Bond, Language Reading Report Blanks.
Cochran, Basic French, Vol. I.
Cochran, Pierrille (Clarétie).
Cochran, Si nous lisions.
Cook, Portraits américains. Collection "Arts et sciences" Series.
Dahl, Le Roi des montagnes (About).
Eddy, Basic French, Vol. II.
Eddy, Beginning French.
Eddy, French Workbook.
Eddy, Progress Tests in French.
Haygood, Les Oberlé (Bazin).
Johnson, Le Livre d'or (Yonge).
Limper, Le petit chose (Daudet).
Meade, Sans famille (Malot).
Miller, Le Comte de Monte-Cristo (Dumas).
Pollard, L'Abbé Constantin (Halévy).
Seibert, Perrine (Malot).
Struble, Les trois mousquetaires (Dumas).
West, Le petit roi d'Ys (G-Toudouze).
Williams, Madame Thérèse (Erckmann-Chatrian).

Heath-Chicago German Series:
Hagboldt, Building the German Vocabulary.
Hagboldt, A Brief Course in German.
Hagboldt, Deutsch für Anfänger.
Hagboldt, Lesebuch für Anfänger.
Hagboldt, The Teaching of German.
Leopold, Reise durch Deutschland.
Purin, A Standard German Vocabulary of 2,932 Words and 1,500 Idioms.

Heath-Chicago Italian Series:
Altrocchi, Tristi amori (Giacosa).
Bergin, Modern Italian Short Stories.
Bond, Language Reading Report Blanks.
Cowper, Italian Folk Tales and Folk Songs.
Fucilla, Il Vecchio della montagna (Deledda).
Furst, Novelle e poesie (Fucini).
McKenzie, Le Mie prigioni and Francesca da Rimini (Pellico).
Phelps, Una Partita a scacchi (Giacosa).
Schobinger, Fra le corde d'un contrabasso (Farina.)
Schobinger, Scampolo (Niccodemi).
Van Horne, Il Risorgimento.
Wilkins, First Italian Book.
Wilkins, L'Italia.

Heath-Chicago Latin Series:
Fay, Carolus et Maria.
Maxey, Cornelia.
Maxey, A New Latin Primer.

Heath-Chicago Spanish Series:
Baker, Las Cuevas de Artá, A Tale of Mallorca.
Boggs, Leyendas épicas de España, prosificación moderna.
Castillo, España en América.
Castillo, Primeras lecturas españolas.
Giesbert, Spanish Wall Charts, for Use with *Repasemos.*
Sparkman, Paso a paso.

SPARKMAN, Repasemos, A Spanish Review Grammar and Elementary Composition Book.

Spanish Workbook To Accompany *Beginning Spanish*.

Achievement Tests To Be Used with *Beginning Spanish*.

Achievement Tests To Be Used with *Primeras lecturas españolas*.

Cuaderno To Accompany *La Nela*.

Heath-Chicago Junior College Series: French:
BOND, An Introduction to the Study of French.
BOND, Language Reading Report Blanks.
BOND, The Sounds of French. An Elementary Phonetic Manual.
BOND, Terre de France: premières lectures.
DELERY, France d'Amérique.
French Phonograph Records. (5 records.)
HARSTALL, Si nous écrivions.
LANDRY, Graded French Word and Idiom Book.
MOUSSIEGT, Histoires de bêtes (Pergaud).
PALMBALD, Impressions de voyage (Dumas).
ROWLAND, Contes de Maupassant.
STANLEY, Croquis d'un flaneur.
WOODBRIDGE, Las Semeuse.

Heath-Chicago Junior College Series: German:
BOND, Language Reading Report Blanks.
DIAMOND, Cora: Vier Lausbubengeschichten (Thoma).
FERNSEMER, Der Meister (Ponten).
GUDDE, Aus Wald und Heide (Lons).
HAGBOLDT, Essentials of German Reviewed.
HAGBOLDT, German Review and Composition.
HAGBOLDT, Inductive Readings in German. Book I.
HAGBOLDT, Inductive Readings in German. Book II. An Introduction to the Spirit of German Life and Literature.
HAGBOLDT, A Modern German Grammar.
KAUFMANN, Inductive Readings in German. Book III. Introduction to German Political and Cultural History.
PRICE, Der blinde Geronimo und sein Bruder (Schnitzler).
5 Sight-Reading and Vocabulary Tests for *Inductive Readings in German*. Book I.
4 Vocabulary Tests for *Inductive Readings in German*. Book II.
14 Tests on *A Modern German Grammar*.

Heath-Chicago Junior College Series: Spanish:
BAILIFF, Las Inquietudes de Shanti Andía (Baroja).
BOND, Language Reading Report Blanks.
CASTILLO, Lecturas introductorias.
HENDRIX, Caballeros y escuderos.
KENISTON, Standard List of Spanish Words and Idioms.
KRAUSE, España y la cultura española.
RANSMEIER, Sentence Drill Blanks.

RANSMEIER, Spanish Recognition Grammar.
RICE, Ariel.
ROSENBERG, Horas vividas. Selections from the Verse and Prose of Antonio Heras.

Graded French Readers:
BOND, L'Anglais tel qu'on le parle (Bernard).
BOND, L'Attaque du Moulin (Zola).
BOND, Aucassin et Nicolette (Bida).
BOND, Les Chandeliers de l'évêque (Hugo).
BOND, Contes (Mendés, *et al.*).
BOND, L'Évasion du Duc de Beaufort (Dumas).
BOND, La Grammaire (Labiche).
BOND, Les pauvres gens (Maupassant, *et al.*).
BOND, Première étape.
BOND, Sept-d'un-Coup (Dumas).
BOND, Vocabulary Drill Book for Graded French Readers.

Graded German Readers:
HAGBOLDT, Das Abenteuer der Neujahrsnacht.
HAGBOLDT, Allerlei.
HAGBOLDT, Anekdoten und Erzählungen.
HAGBOLDT, Aus deutscher Vergangenheit.
HAGBOLDT, Eulenspiegel und Münchhausen.
HAGBOLDT, Fabeln.
HAGBOLDT, Fünf berühmte Märchen.
HAGBOLDT, Land und Leute.
HAGBOLDT, Pechvogel und Glückskind.
HAGBOLDT, Von deutscher Sprache und Dichtung.
HAGBOLDT, Word Book for Graded German Readers, Books 1–10.
HINZ, Das geheimnisvolle Dorf.
LEOPOLD, Ein Sommer in Deutschland.
MORGAN, Das Peterle von Nürnberg.
PURIN, Fortunatus.

Graded Italian Readers:
CIOFFARI, Amici di scuola.
CIOFFARI, Guilietta e Romeo, e altre novelle.
CIOFFARI, Raccontini.

Graded Spanish Readers:
CASTILLO, Aventuras de Gil Blas.
CASTILLO, De México a Guatemala.
CASTILLO, De todo un poco.
CASTILLO, En Guatemala.
CASTILLO, La Buenaventura y otros cuentos.
CASTILLO, La Gitanilla (Cervantes).
CASTILLO, Sigamos leyendo.
CASTILLO, Un Vuelo a México.

**Heath, Lena L.:** *see* LASHLEY, Studies in the Dynamics of Behavior.

**Heath, Louise Robinson.** The Concept of Time. 1936. *o.p.*

**Heaton, Kenneth Lewis.** Character Building through Recreation. A Training Course in Recreational Leadership. 1929. PM. *o.p.*

**Heaton, Kenneth Lewis.** The Character Emphasis in Education. A Collection of Materials and Methods. 1933. *o.p.*

**Heaton, Kenneth Lewis.** A College Curriculum Based on Functional Needs of Students. An Experiment with the General Curriculum at Central State Teachers College, Mount Pleasant, Michigan. By Kenneth L. Heaton and G. Robert Koopman. 1936. *o.p.*

**Heaton, Kenneth Lewis.** The Failing Student. A Study of Academic Failure and the Implications for Education. By Kenneth L. Heaton and Vivian Weedon. 1939. *o.p.*

**Heber, Rick,** *joint ed.:* STEVENS, Mental Retardation.

**Hebrew Family:** CROSS.

**Hebrew Home Life:** LOBINGIER.

**Hebrew Life:** HOUGHTON.

**Hebrew Particle אֲשֶׁר :** GAENSSLE.

**Hebrew Prophets:** CHAMBERLIN.

**Hebrew Text of Zechariah:** ASADA.

**Hecht, Ben.** Erik Dorn. *Reissue,* 1963. Introduction by Nelson Algren. xix, 432 p. Illus. 21 cm. CF. $5.95.

**Hefelbower, Samuel Gring.** The Relation of John Locke to English Deism. 1918. *o.p.*

**Hegel, Georg Wilhelm Friedrich.** Early Theological Writings. Translated by T. M. Knox. With an Introduction and Fragments Translated by Richard Kroner. 1948. *o.p.*

**Heide, Fritz.** Meteorites. Translated by Edward Anders and Eugene DuFresne. 1964. 144 p. Illus. 21 cm. 63-20906. Cloth. $6.50ˢ. Paper. PSS522. $1.95.

**Heidel, Alexander.** The Babylonian Genesis. The Story of the Creation. 2d ed. 1951. xii, 153 p. 21 cm. 51-822. Paper. P133. $1.50.

**Heidel, Alexander.** The Gilgamesh Epic and Old Testament Parallels. 2d ed. 1949. x, 269 p. 49-5734. Cloth. 26 cm. $5.00ˢ. Paper. P136. 21 cm. $1.95.

**Heidel, Alexander.** The System of the Quadriliteral Verb in Akkadian. 1940. AS 13. *o.p.*

**Heidel, William Arthur.** The Necessary and the Contingent in the Aristotelian System. 1896. PHI. *o.p.*

**Heilperin, Michael A.** Economic Policy and Democracy. 1943. PPP 37. *o.p.*

**Heine, Ralph W.,** *ed.* The Student Physician as Psychotherapist. 1962. xiv, 242 p. 47 tables. Index. 22 cm. 62-19624. $5.00ˢ.

**Heinemann, Paul Gustav.** A Laboratory Guide in Bacteriology for the Use of Students, Teachers, and Practitioners. 1905 3d ed. 1915. *o.p.*

**Heisenberg, Werner.** The Physical Principles of the Quantum Theory. By Werner Heisenberg. Translated into English by Carl Eckart and Frank C. Hoyt. 1930. SCI. *o.p.*

**Heiserman, A. R.** Skelton and Satire. 1961. 328 p. 22 cm. 61-5606. $6.50ˢ.

**Heliographic Positions:** VERY.

**Hellenic Age:** BRÉHIER.

**Hellenistic Greek Reader:** COLWELL.

**Hellenistic Greek Texts:** WIKGREN.

**Hellenistic and Roman Age:** BRÉHIER.

**Hemleben, Sylvester.** Plans for World Peace through Six Centuries. 1943. *o.p.*

**Hemorrhagic Disorders:** AGGELER.

**Hempel, Carl G.** Fundamentals of Concept Formation in Empirical Science. 1952. iii, 93 p. 25 cm. 52-13426. Paper. IEUS, II, 7. $2.25ˢ.

**Hempel, Carl G.,** *joint author:* NEURATH, Bibliography and Index.

**Henderson, C. R.** Education with Reference to Sex. Agencies and Methods. By C. R. Henderson and Helen C. Putnam. 1909. NSSE, 8th Yrbk., Part II. *o.p.*

**Henderson, C. R.** Education with Reference to Sex. Pathological, Economic, and Social Aspects. 1909. NSSE, 8th Yrbk., Part I. *o.p.*

**Henderson, C. R.** Industrial Insurance in the United States. 1909. 2d ed. 1911. *o.p.*

**Henderson, C. R.** Outdoor Labor for Convicts. A Report to the Governor of Illinois. 1907. *o.p.*

**Henderson, C. R.** Practical Sociology in the Service of Social Ethics. 1902. *o.p.*

**Henderson, C. R.** Social Duties from the Christian Point of View. A Textbook for the Study of Social Problems. 1909. CS. *o.p.*

**Henderson, C. R.** Social Programmes in the West. Lectures Delivered in the Far East. 1913. BL. *o.p.*

**Henderson, C. R.:** *see* SMITH, Guide to the Study of the Christian Religion.

**Henderson, G. F. R.** The Civil War. A Soldier's View. Edited by Jay Luvaas. 1957. xi, 323 p. Illus. 24 cm. 57-11209. $6.75ˢ.

**Henderson, Hubert.** Supply and Demand. 1958. xi, 142 p. 21 cm. 58-14749. Paper. CEH 3. $1.35. USA.

**Henderson, Stella Van Petten.** Introduction to Philosophy of Education. 1947. xiii, 401 p. 25 cm. 47-12128. $5.75ᵗ.

**Hendrickson, George Lincoln.** The Commentariolum petitionis attributed to Quintus Cicero. 1903. 25. *o.p.*

**Hendrickson, George Lincoln.** The Proconsulate of Julius Agricola in Relation to History and to Encomium. 1902. *o.p.*

**Hendrix, William S.** Caballeros y escuderos. By William S. Hendrix and D. F. Porter. HCLS.

**Henke, Frederick Goodrich.** A Study in the Psychology of Ritualism. 1910. *o.p.*

**Henry, Lyman I.** Paul, Son of Kish. 1923. CS. *o.p.*

**Henry L. Stimson and Japan:** RAPPAPORT.

**Henry, Nelson B.** Schools and City Government. A Study of School and Municipal Relationships in Cities of 50,000 or More Population. By Nelson B. Henry and Jerome G. Kerwin. 1938. PA. *o.p.*

**Henry, Nelson B.,** *joint author:* REEVES, Class Size and University Costs.

**Henry, Nelson B.,** *joint author:* REEVES, University Faculty.

**Henry, Nelson B.,** *General Editor,* YEARBOOKS OF THE NATIONAL SOCIETY FOR THE STUDY OF EDUCATION.

**Henry, T. S.** Classroom Problems in the Education of Gifted Children. 1920. NSSE, 19th Yrbk., Part II. *o.p.*

**Henry Vaughan:** GARNER.

**Henry Ward Beecher's Art of Preaching:** CROCKER.

**Heralds of American Literature:** MARBLE.

**Herbal of Rufinus:** THORNDIKE.

**Herbert, George,** *see:* TUVE, Reading of George Herbert

**Heredity:** STRANDSKOV.

**Heredity and Eugenics:** CASTLE.

**Heritage of Sociology** (HS). *Edited by* MORRIS JANOWITZ:

MEAD, George Herbert Mead on Social Psychology.

OGBURN, William F. Ogburn on Culture and Social Change.

WIRTH, Louis Wirth on Cities and Social Life.

**Hermens, F. A.** Democracy and Proportional Representation. 1940. PPP 31. *o.p.*

**Hermens, F. A.** The Tyrant's War and The People's Peace. 1944. *o.p.*

**Heroes of Israel:** SOARES.

**Herrick, C. A.** Vocational Studies for College Entrance. By C. A. Herrick and others. 1907. NSSE, 6th Yrbk., Part I. *o.p.*

**Herrick, Charles Judson.** Brains of Rats and Men. A Survey of the Origin and Biological Significance of the Cerebral Cortex. 1926. *o.p.*

**Herrick, Charles Judson.** The Brain of the Tiger Salamander. Ambystoma tigrinum. 1948. x, 407 p. Illus. 25 cm. BM. $10.00ˢ.

**Herrick, Charles Judson.** George Ellett Coghill. Naturalist and Philosopher. 1949. BM. *o.p.*

**Herrick, Charles Judson.** The Thinking Machine. 2d ed. 1932. xii, 372 p. 21 cm. 32-28144. $6.00ˢ.

". . . easy as well as enjoyable to read, and moreover profitable since it has been written by one whose knowledge of the psychical apparatus, particularly of its anatomical patterns, is second to none here or elsewhere . . . an exceptionally fine work."—*Journal of Nervous and Mental Diseases.*

**Herrick, Charles Judson:** *see* WHITE, New Social Science.

**Herrick, Henry Martyn.** The Kingdom of God in the Writings of the Fathers. 1903. HLL. *o.p.*

**Herrick, James B.** Memories of Eighty Years. 1949. *o.p.*

**Herrick, Virgil E.** Toward Improved Curriculum Theory. Papers Presented at the Conference on Curriculum Theory Held at the University of Chicago, October, 1947. Edited by Virgil E. Herrick and Ralph W. Tyler. 1950. SEM 71. *o.p.*

**Herrick, Virgil E.,** *joint author:* EELLS, Intelligence and Cultural Differences.

**Herskovits, Melville J.,** *joint ed.:* BASCOM, Continuity and Change in African Cultures.

**Hertz, Richard.** Chance and Symbol. A Study in Aesthetic and Ethical Consistency. 1948. *o.p.*

**Herz, John H.** Political Realism and Political Idealism. A Study in Theories and Realities. 1951. xii, 275 p. 24 cm. 51-10397. $5.00ˢ.

**Herzfeld, Ernst Emil.** A New Inscription of Xerxes from Persepolis. 1932. viii, 14 p. Illus. 25 cm. A33-1107. Paper. SAOC 5. $0.50.

**Hess, Julius Hayes.** The Physical and Mental Growth of Prematurely Born Children. By Julius H. Hess, M.D., George H. Mohr, M.D., and Phyllis F. Bartelme, Ph.D. 1934. BR. *o.p.*

**Hess, Robert D.** Family Worlds. A Psychosocial Approach to Family Life. By Robert D. Hess and Gerald Handel. 1959. xiii, 306 p. 23 cm. 54-5773. $5.00ˢ.

**Hess, Walter Rudolf.** The Biology of Mind. Translated by Gerhardt von Bonin. 1964. 192 p. 64-15807. $6.00ˢ.

**Hesseltine, William B.** The Blue and the Gray on the Nile. By William B. Hesseltine and Hazel C. Wolf. 1961. xi, 290 p. Illus. Index. 22 cm. 61-8644. $5.00ˢ.

**Hethitische Bilderschrift:** FORRER.

**Hettinger, Herman Strecker.** A Decade of Radio Advertising. 1933. *o.p.*

**Hexaemeral Literature:** ROBBINS.

**Heywood, Robert B.,** *ed.* The Works of the Mind. Edited for the Committee on Social Thought. Contributions by Mortimer J. Adler, Heinrich Brüning, Marc Chagall, S. Chandrasekhar, Alfeo Faggi, J. W. Fulbright, Robert M. Hutchins, C. H. McIlwain, John von Neumann, Arnold Schoenberg, Yves R. Simon, and Frank Lloyd Wright. 1947. xi, 246 p. 24 cm. 47-11992. $4.50ˢ.

**Higgy, Robert Charles,** *joint author:* JANSKY, Problem of the Institutionally Owned Station.

**High-School Extracurricular Activities:** TRUMP.

**High School in a New Era:** CHASE.

**Higher Education and the Human Spirit:** MELAND.

**Higher Education in the Postwar Period:** RUSSELL.

**Higher Education as a Training for Business:** JUDSON.

**Higher Education Under War Conditions:** RUSSELL.

**Higher Life of Chicago:** RILEY.

**Highlights of Astronomy:** BARTKY.

**Hildebrandslied:** WOOD.

**Hilgard, Ernest R.,** *ed.* Theories of Learning. 1964. NSSE, 63d Yrbk., Part I. xi, 430 p. 24 cm. 64-3323. $5.50ᵗ.

**Hill, Derek.** Islamic Architecture and Its Decoration. A.D. 800–1500. A Photographic Survey. By Derek Hill and Oleg Grabar. 1965. 88 p. 527 photographs, 4 colorplates. 26 cm. 64-19844. $17.50. USA.

**Hill, Howard Copeland.** Roosevelt and the Caribbean. 1927. *o.p.*

**Hill, Jim Dan.** The Texas Navy in Forgotten Battles and Shirtsleeve Diplomacy. 1937. *o.p.*

**Hill, Lewis B.** Psychotherapeutic Intervention in Schizophrenia. 1955. vii, 216 p. 22 cm. 55-5128. BM. $5.75ˢ.

**Hiller, Ernest Theodore.** The Strike. A Study in Collective Action. 1928. SOC. *o.p.*

**Hillman, Arthur.** Tomorrow's Chicago. By Arthur Hillman and Robert J. Casey. 1953. x, 182 p. Illus. 25 cm. 53-6507. $0.75.

**Hiltner, William A.,** *ed.* Astronomical Techniques. ("Stars and Stellar Systems," *Vol. II.*) 1962. xxii, 636 p. Illus. 25 cm. 62-9113. $16.50ˢ.

**Hilzheimer, Max.** Animal Remains from Tell Asmar. Translated by Adolph A. Brux. 1941. xiii, 52 p. Illus. 25 cm. 41-3497. SAOC 20. $2.00.

**Himmelfarb, Gertrude.** Lord Acton. A Study in Conscience and Politics. 1952. x, 258 p. 52-14608. 21 cm. Paper. P97. $1.50. COBE.

**Hinckley, Elmer Dumond.** Attitude toward the Negro. Forms A and B. 1930. TAS 3. *o.p.*

**Hinz, Stella M.** Das geheimnisvolle Dorf. HCLS.

**Hiraoki, Maj. J.,** *joint author:* CRESSWELL, A Dictionary of Military Terms.

**Hirschy, Noah Calvin.** Artaxerxes III Ochus and His Reign. With Special Consideration of the Old Testament Sources Bearing upon the Period. 1909. *o.p.*

**Hirshleifer, Jack.** Water Supply. Economics, Technique, and Policy. By Jack Hirshleifer, James C. DeHaven, and Jerry Milliman. 1960. xii, 378 p. 25 cm. 60-14355. $7.50ˢ.

**Histoires de bêtes (Pergaud):** MOUSSIEGT.

**Historian and the Civil War:** CRAVEN.

**Historic Rôle of France:** LANGLOIS.

**Historical Aspects of the Immigration Problem:** ABBOTT.

**Historical Examination of Some Non-Markan Elements in Luke:** PARSONS.

**Historical and Linguistic Studies in Literature Related to the New Testament (HLL):**

*First Series: Texts.*
Vol. I. GOODSPEED, Ethiopic Martyrdoms.
  Part 1. The Book of Thekla.
  Part 2. The Martyrdom of Cyprian and Justa.

Part 3. The Story of Eugenia and Philip.
Part 4. The Epistle of Pelagia.

Vol. II. GOODSPEED, Greek Texts.
  Part 1. The Newberry Gospels.
  Part 2. The Toronto Gospels.
  Part 3. The Freer Gospels.
  Part 4. The Bixby Gospels.
  Part 5. The Haskell Gospels.
  Part 6. The Harvard Gospels.

*Second Series: Linguistic and Exegetical Studies.*
Vol. I. Linguistic and Exegetical Studies.
  Part 1. HOBEN, The Virgin Birth.
  Part 2. HERRICK, The Kingdom of God.
  Part 3. HOBSON, Diatessaron of Tatian.
  Part 4. ALLEN, Infinitive in Polybius.
  Part 5. THOMPSON, Μετανοέω and Μεταμέλει in Greek Literature.
  Part 6. NORTON, A Lexicographical and Historical Study of ΔΙΑΘΗΚΗ from the Earliest Times to the End of the Classical Period.
  Part 7. LEWIS, The Irenaeus Testimony to the Fourth Gospel.
  Part 8. STAUDT, The Idea of the Resurrection in the Ante-Nicene Period.

Vol. II. Linguistic and Exegetical Studies.
  Part 1. GRANBERY, Outline of New Testament Christology.
  Part 2. WICKES, The Sources of Luke's Perean Section.
  Part 3. FERGUSON, The Legal Terms Common to the Macedonian Greek Inscriptions and the New Testament.
  Part 4. MACNEILL, The Christology of the Epistle to the Hebrews.
  Part 5. ROBINSON, Syntax of the Particle in the Apostolic Fathers.
  Part 6. PARSONS, A Historical Examination of Some Non-Markan Elements in Luke.

Vol. III. BURTON, Spirit, Soul, and Flesh.

Vol. IV. Linguistic and Exegetical Studies.
  Part 1. SLATEN, Qualitative Nouns in the Pauline Epistles.
  Part 2. PERRY, The Sources of Luke's Passion-Narrative.

Vol. V. BURTON, New Testament World Studies.

**Historical Prism Inscriptions:** PIEPKORN.

**Historical Records of Ramses III:** EDGERTON.

**Historicity of Jesus:** CASE.

**History of Assyria:** OLMSTEAD.

**History of the Australian Ballot System:** EVANS.

History of Banking Theory in Great Britain and the United States: MINTS.

History and Bibliography of Anatomic Illustration: COULANT.

History of Chicago: PIERCE.

History of Contagious Disease Care: WEBB.

History of Early Christian Literature: GOODSPEED.

History of Early Iran: CAMERON.

History of Education: BURNHAM.

History of Educational Legislation in Mississippi: WEATHERSBY.

History of Educational Legislation in Ohio: MILLER.

History of the English Paragraph: LEWIS.

History of the English Settlement in Edwards County, Illinois: FLOWER.

History of Greek Economic Thought: TREVER.

History of Greek Noun-Formation: STRATTON.

History of the Greenbacks: MITCHELL.

History Handbook of Western Civilization: MCNEILL.

History of the Illinois State Federation of Labor: STALEY.

History of the Indian Ocean: TOUSSAINT.

History of Labor Legislation in Illinois: BECKNER.

History of Latin Monetary Union: WILLIS.

History of Literary Criticism in the Italian Renaissance: WEINBERG.

History of Matrimonial Institutions: HOWARD.

History of Metallography: SMITH.

History of Nature: WEIZSÄCKER.

History of the Persian Empire: OLMSTEAD.

History of Philosophy: see BRÉHIER, Hellenic Age.

History of Poor Relief Administration: BOAN.

History of the Primates: CLARK.

History of Public Assistance in Chicago: BROWN.

History of Public Welfare in New York State: SCHNEIDER.

History of the Quaker Oats Company: THORNTON.

History of Religions: ELIADE.

History of Stone & Kimball: KRAMER.

History of Suffrage: PORTER.

History of the Title *Imperator*: MCFAYDEN.

History of Trade-Union Organization in Canada: LOGAN.

History of U-Stems in Greek: GUNNERSON.

History of the Union Pacific: WHITE.

History of the United Typothetae: POWELL.

History of the University of Chicago: GOODSPEED.

History of the Working Classes in France: WERGELAND.

Hitchcock, Curtice Nelson, ed. Forms, Records, and Reports in Personnel Administration. 1922. 2d ed. 1923. MSB. *o.p.*

Hitchcock, Curtice Nelson, *joint author:* DOUGLAS, Worker in Modern Economic Society.

Hittite Hieroglyphic Monuments: GELB.

Hittite Hieroglyphs: GELB.

Hoben, Allan. The Church School of Citizenship. 1918. PM. *o.p.*

Hoben, Allan. The Minister and the Boy. A Handbook for Churchmen Engaged in Boys' Work. 1912. *o.p.*

Hoben, Allan. The Virgin Birth. 1903. HLL. *o.p.*

Hobo: ANDERSON.

Hobson, Alphonzo Augustus. The Diatessaron of Tatian and the Synoptic Problem. Being an Investigation of the Diatessaron for the Light Which It Throws upon the Solution of the Problem of the Origin of the Synoptic Gospels. 1904. 81 HLL. *o.p.*

**Hobson, Elsie Garland.** Educational Legislation and Administration in the State of New York from 1777 to 1850. 1918. SEM 11. *o.p.*

**Hobson, John Atkinson.** Some Aspects of Recent British Economics. By John A. Hobson, D. H. Macgregor, Reginald Lennard. 1923. MSB. *o.p.*

**Hocking, William Ernest.** Freedom of the Press. A Framework of Principle. 1947. *o.p.*

**Hocking, William Ernest:** *see* HAYDON, Modern Trends in World-Religions.

**Hodge, Albert Claire.** Laboratory Material To Accompany *Principles of Accounting.* 1922. MSB. *o.p.*

**Hodge, Albert Claire.** Principles of Accounting. By Albert Claire Hodge and James Oscar McKinsey. 1920. MSB *o.p.*

**Hodge, Albert Claire.** Retail Accounting and Control. 1925. MSB. *o.p.*

**Hodges, Paul C.** An Epiphyseal Chart. 1937. *o.p.*

**Hodges, Paul C.** The Life and Times of Emil H. Grubbe. 1964. xi, 135 p. 16 plates. 64-24977. $3.95.

**Hodous, Lewis:** *see* HAYDON, Modern Trends in World-Religions.

**Hoefer, Carolyn Harrison,** *joint author:* HARDY, Healthy Growth.

**Hoefer, Carolyn Harrison,** *joint author:* KAWIN, Comparative Study of a Nursery-School versus a Non Nursery-School Group.

**Hölscher, Uvo.** The Excavation of Medinet Habu. 34-38539. *Vol. I:* General Plans and Views. 1934. xiv, 6 p. Illus. Large Folio. OIP, XXI. $20.00. *Vol. II:* The Temples of the Eighteenth Dynasty. 1939. xvii, 123 p. Illus. Folio (30×40 cm.). OIP, XLI, $20.00. *Vols. III–IV:* The Mortuary Temple of Ramses III. *Part I.* By Uvo Hölscher. Translated by Mrs. Keith C. Seele. 1941. xiii, 87 p. Illus. 41 cm. OIP, LIV. $16.00. *Part II:* By Uvo Hölscher. With Contributions by Rudolf Anthes. Translated by Elizabeth B. Hauser. 1951. xiii, 54 p. Illus. 42 cm. OIP, LV. $18.00. *Vol. V:* Post-Ramessid Remains. Edited and translated by Elizabeth B. Hauser. 1954. xiii, 81 p. Illus. 42 cm. OIP, LXVI. $20.00. *The set.* $80.00.

**Hölscher, Uvo.** Excavations at Ancient Thebes, 1930/31. 1932. vii, 65 p. Illus. 25 cm. 33-6599. Paper. OIC 15. $2.00.

**Hölscher, Uvo.** Medinet Habu Studies, 1928/29. I. The Architectural Survey. By Uvo Hölscher. II. The Language of the Historical Texts Commemorating Ramses III. By John A. Wilson. 1930. ix, 33 p. Illus. 25 cm. 29-13423. Paper. OIC 7. $0.75.

**Hölscher, Uvo,** *joint author:* EPIGRAPHIC SURVEY, Medinet Habu, 1924–28.

**Hölscher, Uvo,** *joint author:* NELSON, Medinet Habu Reports.

**Hölscher, Uvo,** *joint author:* NELSON, Work in Western Thebes.

**Hoenig, J.,** *trans.:* JASPERS, General Psychopathology.

**Hoenigswald, Henry M.** Language Change and Linguistic Reconstruction. 1960. viii, 168 p. 21 cm. 59-12287. $5.00ˢ. Paper, P178. $1.50.

**Hoff, Jacobus Henry.** Physical Chemistry in the Service of the Sciences. Translated by Alexander Smith. 1903. *o.p.*

**Hoffman, Horace Addison.** Everyday Greek. Greek Words in English, Including Scientific Terms. 1919. *o.p.*

**Hofstadter, Richard.** A Documentary History of American Higher Education. By Richard Hofstadter and Wilson Smith. 1961. xv, viii, 1,016 p. 24 cm. 61-15935. 2 vols. $15.00ˢ.

".... without question the best available collection of documents on the history of American higher education."—Louis L. Tucker, in *The William and Mary Quarterly.*

**Hogan, Ralph Montague,** *joint author:* BARTLETT, Y.M.C.A. Executive Secretary.

**Hohman, Helen Fisher,** *ed.:* FIELD, Essays on Population.

**Hoijer, Harry.** Chiricahua and Mescalero Apache Texts. With Ethnological Notes by Morris Edward Opler. 1938. AN. *o.p.*

**Hoijer, Harry,** *ed.* Language in Culture. Conference on the Interrelations of Language and other Aspects of Culture. 1954. xi, 286 p. 25 cm. 54-4977. CSCC. $5.00ˢ.

**Holck, Harald Groth Oxholm.** Diet and Efficiency. A Five-Year Controlled Experiment on Man. 1929. CMM. *o.p.*

**Holferty, George M.** Ovule and Embryo of Potamogeton natans. 1901. HB. *o.p.*

**Holland, William L.,** *ed.* Problems of the Pacific, 1936. Aims and Results of Social and Economic Policies in Pacific Countries. Proceedings of the Sixth Conference of the Institute of Pacific Relations, Yosemite National Park, California, August, 1936. Edited by W. L. Holland and Kate L. Mitchell, assisted by Harriet Moore and Richard Pyke. 1938. IPR. *o.p.*

**Holland, William L.,** *joint ed.:* Lasker, Problems of the Pacific, 1931.

**Holland, William L.,** *joint ed.:* Lasker, Problems of the Pacific, 1933.

**Hollander, Jacob H.,** *joint author:* Clark, Adam Smith.

**Hollenhorst, G. Donald,** *joint trans.:* Simon, *Material Logic* of John of St. Thomas.

**Holley, Charles E.** The Relationship between Persistence in School and Home Conditions. 1916. NSSE, 15th Yrbk. Part II. *o.p.*

**Hollingsworth, J. Rogers.** The Whirligig of Politics. The Democracy of Cleveland and Bryan. 1963. xii, 263 p. Illus. 22 cm. 63-18846. $5.00ˢ.

**Holman, Charles Thomas.** The Cure of Souls. A Socio-psychological Approach. 1932. HER. *o.p.*

**Holman, Charles Thomas:** *see* Bower, Church at Work in the Modern World.

**Holmes, Ernest Shurtleff,** *joint author:* Sills, Values.

**Holmes, H. W.** The Administrative Use of Intelligence Tests. By H. W. Holmes and others. 1922. NSSE, 21st Yrbk., Part II. Bound with Part I, Intelligence Tests and Their Use. *o.p.*

**Holmes, M. J.** The Relation of Theory to Practice in Education. By M. J. Holmes and others. 1903. NSSE, 2d Yrbk., Part II. *o.p.*

**Holmes, Willis Boit,** *joint author:* Smith, On Amorphous Sulphur.

**Holt, Robert F.** Strategic Psychological Operations and American Foreign Policy. By Robert T. Holt and Robert M. van de Velde. 1960. x, 244 p. 22 cm. 60-14238. $5.00ˢ.

**Holton, D. C.** Modern Japan and Shinto Nationalism. A Study of Present-Day Trends in Japanese Religions. 1943. 2d ed. 1947. CP. *o.p.*

**Holzinger, Karl John.** Factor Analysis. A Synthesis of Factorial Methods. By Karl J. Holzinger and Harry H. Harman. 1941. *o.p.*

**Holzinger, Karl John.** Statistical Résumé of the Spearman Two-Factor Theory. 1930. *o.p.*

**Holzinger, Karl John.** Statistical Tables for Students in Education and Psychology. 1925. 3d ed., 1931. *o.p.*

**Holzinger, Karl John.** A Study in Factor Analysis. The Stability of a Bi-factor Solution. By Karl J. Holzinger and Frances Swineford. 1939. SEM 48. *o.p.*

**Holzinger, Karl John,** *joint author:* Newman, Twins.

**Holzinger, Karl John,** *joint author:* Swineford, A Study in Factor Analysis. The Reliability of Bi-Factors.

**Home Economics in American Schools:** Trilling.

**Home Rule for Metropolitan Chicago:** Lepawsky.

**Homer.** The Iliad. Translated and with an Introduction by Richmond Lattimore. New ed. 1962. Illustrated by Leonard Baskin. 582 p. 29 cm. 62-19604. Cloth. $13.50.

**Homer.** The Iliad. Translated and with an Introduction by Richmond Lattimore. 1951. 527 p. 21 cm. Paper. P63. $1.95.

"The finest translation of Homer ever made into the English language."—William Arrowsmith in *The Hudson Review.*

"The feat is so decisive that it is reasonable to foresee a century or so in which nobody will try again to put the *Iliad* in English verse."—Robert Fitzgerald in *The Kenyon Review*.

**Homeric Vocabularies:** OWEN.

**Honoré de Balzac:** DARGAN.

**Hooke, Robert.** Extracts from Micrographia. Or Some Physiological Descriptions of Minute Bodies Made by Magnifying Glasses with Observations and Inquiries Thereupon. (1665.) 1902. AC. *o.p.*

**Hooker, George Ellsworth.** Through Routes for Chicago's Steam Railroads. The Best Means for Attaining Popular and Comfortable Travel for Chicago and Suburbs. 1914. CC. *o.p.*

**Hooker, Richard.** Of the Laws of Ecclesiastical Polity. 1950. *o.p.*

**Hopi Ethics:** BRANDT.

**Hopi Way:** THOMPSON.

**Horace Bushnell:** CROSS.

**Horace.** Odes and Epodes. Translated by Joseph P. Clancy. 1960. x, 257 p. 21 cm. 60-10659. Paper. P47. $1.95.

**Horace.** Satires and Epistles. Translated by Smith Palmer Bovie. 1959. vii, 318 p. 21 cm. 59-16413. Cloth. $5.00ˢ. Paper. P39. $1.95.

**Horace. Three Phases of His Influence:** SAINTONGE.

**Horas vividas:** ROSENBERG.

**Horecky, Paul L.,** *ed.* Basic Russian Publications. A Selected and Annotated Bibliography on Russia and the Soviet Union. 1962. xxvi, 314 p. 24 cm. 62-20022. $6.50ˢ.

**Horecky, Paul L.** *ed.* Russia and the Soviet Union. A Bibliographic Guide to Western-Language Publications. 1965. xxii, 473 p. 24 cm. 65-12041. $8.95ˢ.

**Horizontal Temperature and Pressure Gradient Scale:** BELLAMY.

**Horne, Roman L.** The Farm Business. 1935. 3d ed. 1938. AP. *o.p.*

**Horne, Roman L.,** *joint author:* ROSE, Money.

**Horner, Harlan H.** Dental Education Today. 1947. BM. *o.p.*

**Horrall, Onis Harrison.** Bile. Its Toxicity and Relation to Disease. 1938. CMM *o.p.*

**Horse Sense in American Humor:** BLAIR.

**Hoselitz, Bert F.,** *ed.* The Progress of Underdeveloped Areas. 1952. x, 297 p. 25 cm. 52-14480. HFL. $5.50ˢ.

**Hoselitz, Bert F.,** *joint author:* BLOCH, Economics of Military Occupation.

**Hosic, James Fleming.** The Elementary Course in English. A Syllabus with Graded Lists and References. 1908. *o.p.*

**Hospital Service for Patients of Moderate Means:** CARPENTER.

**Houghteling, Leila.** The Income and Standard of Living of Unskilled Laborers in Chicago. 1927. SSCI. *o.p.*

**Houghton, Louise Seymour.** Hebrew Life and Thought. Being Interpretative Studies in the Literature of Israel. 1906. *o.p.*

**Houle, Cyril O.,** *joint ed.:* BURNS, Community Responsibilities of Institutions of Higher Learning.

**Hounds and Hunting in Ancient Greece:** HULL.

**House in Chicago:** DUNBAR.

**House, Julius Temple.** Purpose the Variant of Theory. 1925. *o.p.*

**Household Manufactures:** TRYON.

**Housing and Income:** REID.

**How Adults Read:** BUSWELL.

**How the National Income Is Divided:** HART.

**How the Bible Grew:** LEWIS.

**How Numerals Are Read:** TERRY.

**How People Look at Pictures:** BUSWELL.

**How To Buy Beef:** HALLIDAY.

**How To Enjoy the Bible:** SOARES.

**How To Study:** KORNHAUSER.

**How To Study Modern Languages in College:** HAGBOLDT.

**How To Study Modern Languages in High School:** HAGBOLDT.

**How To Use the Educational Sound Film:** BRUNSTETTER.

**How To Write Business Letters:** POWELL.

**How We Judge Intelligence:** MAGSON.

**Howard, George Elliott.** A History of Matrimonial Institutions Chiefly in England and the United States. With an Introductory Analysis of the Literature and the Theories of Primitive Marriage and the Family. 3 vols. 1904. *o.p.*

**Howard, Leon.** The Connecticut Wits. 1943. *o.p.*

**Howe, Bruce,** *joint author:* BRAIDWOOD, Prehistoric Investigations in Iraqi Kurdistan.

**Howe, Laurence.** The Pretorian Prefect from Commodus to Diocletian. 1942. *o.p.*

**Howe, Mark De Wolfe.** The Garden and the Wilderness. Religion and Government in American Constitutional History. 1965. x, 180 p. 21 cm. 65-24977. WIL. $4.50.

**Howell, A. Brazier.** Speed in Animals. Their Specialization for Running and Leaping. 1944. *o.p.*

**Hows and Whys of Cooking:** HALLIDAY.

**Hoyle, Fred,** *joint author:* FOWLER, Nucleosynthesis in Massive Stars and Supernovae.

**Hoyt, Frank Clark,** *joint trans.:* HEISENBERG, Physical Principles of the Quantum Theory.

**Hoyt, Homer.** One Hundred Years of Land Values in Chicago. The Relationship of the Growth of Chicago to the Rise in Its Land Values, 1830–1933. 1933. *o.p.*

**Hsiao Ching:** CREEL, Literary Chinese. Vol. I.

**Hu, Kuen-Sen:** *see* BLISS, Contributions to the Calculus of Variations, 1931–32.

**Hu Shih.** The Chinese Renaissance. 1934. CR. *o.p.*

**Hu Shih:** *see* HAYDON, Modern Trends in World-Religions.

**Hubbert, Marion King.** The Theory of Ground-Water Motion. 1940. *o.p.*

**Hubble, Edwin Powell.** Photographic Investigations of Faint Nebulae. 1920. YO, IV. *o.p.*

**Hubert, Henri.** Sacrifice. Its Nature and Function. By Henri Hubert and Marcel Mauss. Translated by W. D. Halls. With a Foreword by E. E. Evans-Pritchard. 1964. ix, 165 p. 23 cm. 64-12260. $3.25s. OBE.

**Hudelson, Earl.** English Composition. Its Aims, Methods, and Measurements. 1923. NSSE, 22d Yrbk., Part I. *o.p.*

**Hudson, Winthrop S.** American Protestantism. 1961. vii, 198 p. 21 cm. 61-15936. Cloth. CHAC. $4.50s. Paper. $1.75.

**Hudson, Winthrop S.** John Panet. Advocate of Limited Monarchy. 1942. *o.p.*

**Huff, Clay G.** A Manual of Medical Parasitology. 1943. BM. *o.p.*

**Huggins, Lady Margaret Lindsay Murray,** *joint author:* HUGGINS, Spectroscopic Notes.

**Huggins, Sir William.** Spectroscopic Notes. By Sir William and Lady Huggins. *o.p.*

**Hughes, Elizabeth Ann.** The Social Service Exchange in Chicago. By Elizabeth A. Hughes and Francelia Stuenkel. 1929. SSM. *o.p.*

**Hughes, Everett C.** French Canada in Transition. 1943. *Reprint,* with new Forewords by author and Nathan Keyfitz. 1963. xix, 227 p. 21 cm. A43-2759. Paper. P139. $1.75.

**Hughes, Everett C.,** *joint author:* BECKER, Boys in White.

**Hughes, George Robert.** Saite Demotic Land Leases. 1952. x, 111 p. Illus. 26 cm. A52-6588. Paper. SAOC 28. $6.00.

**Hughes, George Robert,** *Field Director.* Medinet Habu, VI, V. *See* EPIGRAPHIC SURVEY.

**Hughes, George Robert,** *Field Director.* Reliefs and Inscription at Karnak, III. *See* EPIGRAPHIC SURVEY.

**Hughes, Helen MacGill.** News and the Human Interest Story. 1940. SOC. *o.p.*

**Hugill, William Meredith.** Panhellenism in Aristophanes. 1936. *o.p.*

**Hulbert, Eri Baker.** The English Reformation and Puritanism. With other Lectures and Addresses by Eri B. Hulbert. A Memorial. Edited by A. R. E. Wyant. 1908. *o.p.*

**Hulbert, James Root.** Effective English. By J. R. and V. B. Hulbert. 1929. *o.p.*

**Hulbert, James Root,** *joint ed.:* CRAIGIE, Dictionary of American English.

**Hulbert, James Root:** *see* BRYAN, Sources and Analogues of Chaucer's *Canterbury Tales.*

**Hulbert, Viola Blackburn,** *joint author:* HULBERT, Effective English.

**Hull, Denison B.** Aesop's Fables. Told by Valerius Babrius. 1960. 112 p. 24 cm. 60-14237. $5.00.

**Hull, Denison B.** Hounds and Hunting in Ancient Greece. 1964. xx, 240 p. 64-23424. Illus. $15.00.

**Human Animal:** LA BARRE.

**Human Behavior:** HUNTER.

**Human Condition:** ARENDT.

**Human Heredity:** NEEL.

**Human Nature and the Study of Society: Papers of Robert Redfield.** *Vol. I.* Edited by Margaret Park Redfield.

**Humanism and the Social Order:** CASPARI.

**Humphreys, William Jackson.** Changes in the Wave-Frequencies of the Lines of Emission Spectra of Elements, Their Dependence upon the Elements Themselves and upon the Physical Conditions under Which They Are Produced. *o.p.*

**Hunter, Walter Samuel.** Human Behavior. 1919. 3d ed. 1928. *o.p.*

The first and second editions of this book were published under the title, *General Psychology.*

**Huntington, J. F.,** *trans.:* JOUVENEL, Sovereignty.

**Hurst, Sir Cecil James Barrington.** Great Britain and the Dominions. By Cecil J. B. Hurst, Timothy A. Smiddy, John W. Dafoe, William Harrison Moore, J. B. Condliffe, Eric H. Louw, Angus S. Fletcher. 1928. HFL. *o.p.*

**Huse, Howard Russell,** *joint author:* WILKINS, First Lessons in Spoken French for Men in Military Service.

**Hussey, Charles Lincoln:** *see* FISH, United States and Great Britain.

**Huszar, George B. de,** *ed.* New Perspectives on Peace. 1944. WFL. *o.p.*

**Hutcheon, Robert James,** *ed.:* BOWEN, Studies in the New Testament.

**Hutchins, Robert M.** No Friendly Voice. 1936. *o.p.*

**Hutchins, Robert M.** The University of Utopia. 1953. xiii, 103 p. 21 cm. Paper. P151. $1.50.

**Hutchins, Robert M.,** *joint author:* BORGESE, Preliminary Draft of a World Constitution.

**Hutchins, Robert M.:** *see* WHITE, New Social Science.

**Hutchins, Robert M.:** *see* WIRTH, Eleven Twenty-six.

**Hutchins, William Norman.** Graded Social Service for the Sunday School. 1913. PM. *o.p.*

**Hutchinson, William T.** Lowden of Illinois. The Life of Frank O. Lowden. *Vol. I:* City and State. *Vol. II:* Nation and Countryside. 2 vols. 1957. xii, 760 p. 25 cm. 57-6274. $15.00ˢ.

**Hutchinson, William T.** John Bach McMaster, *in his* Marcus W. Jernegan Essays.

**Hutchinson, William.,** *ed.* Democracy and National Unity. 1941. WFL. *o.p.*

**Hutchinson, William T.,** *ed.* The Marcus W. Jernegan Essays in American Historiography. By His Former Students at the University of Chicago. 1937. *o.p.*

**Hutchinson, William T.,** *joint ed.:* MADISON, Papers of James Madison.

**Hutchinson, T. W.,** *trans.:* EUCKEN, Foundations of Economics.

**Hutson, Harold H.,** *joint author:* RIDDLE, New Testament Life and Literature.

**Hutton, Graham.** Midwest at Noon. 1946. *o.p.*

**Hutton, Graham.** The War as a Factor in Human Progress. 1942. PPP 36. *o.p.*

**Huygens, Christiaan.** Treatise on Light, Translated from the French by Silvanus Thompson. 1945. *o.p.*

**Hurrians and Subarians:** GELB.

**Hydrogen in Metals:** SMITH.

**Hyers, Faith Holmes.** The Library and the Radio. 1938. NACRE. *o.p.*

**Hyksos Reconsidered:** ENGBERG.

**Hyman, Herbert H.** Interviewing in Social Research. With William J. Cobb, Jacob J. Feldman, Clyde W. Hart, and Charles Herbert Stember. 1954. xvi, 415 p. 24 cm. 54-11209. $8.00ˢ. *A Research Project of the National Opinion Research Center, Clyde W. Hart, Director.*

**Hyman, Herbert H.,** *ed.* Noble-Gas Compounds. 1963. xiii, 404 p. Illus. 25 cm. 63-20907. $12.50ˢ.

**Hyman, Libbie Henrietta.** Comparative Vertebrate Anatomy. 2d ed. 1942. xx, 544 p. Illus. 26 cm. 42-21814. $5.00ᵗ.

"What Miss Hyman has attempted is a comprehensive study of *research treatises* in order that she can dispense with dogmatic assertions and present the subject as a living, moving science, to give the student a picture of a vast field full of controversial issues and unsolved problems, depending for their solution on future painstaking embryological and anatomical researches. We are wholeheartedly in sympathy with her aims, and congratulate her on the success that has crowned her efforts."—*Nature* (England).

**Hyman, Libbie Henrietta.** A Laboratory Manual for Comparative Vertebrate Anatomy. 1922. *o.p.*

**Hyman, Libbie Henrietta.** A Laboratory Manual for Elementary Zoölogy. 2d ed. 1926. xviii, 182 p. 25 cm. $4.00ᵗ.

**Hyman, Ray,** *joint author:* VOGT, Water Witching U.S.A.

**Hypoxia:** VAN LIERE.

**Hyslop, James Hervey.** The Science of Sociology. Supplementary Number to *The American Journal of Sociology.* May, 1897, 1897. *o.p.*

**Hysteria:** VEITH.

**Ibn Khaldûn's Philosophy of History:** MAHDI.

**Idea of God:** READ.

**Idea of Good in Plato's Republic:** SHOREY.

**Idea and Practice of General Education:** WARD.

**Idea of the Resurrection:** STAUDT.

**Idea of the South:** VANDIVER.

**Ideals and Self-interest in America's Foreign Relations:** OSGOOD.

**Ideas Have Consequences:** WEAVER.

**Identification and Analysis of Attribute-Cluster-Blocs:** BEYLE.

**Identity and Interpersonal Competence:** FOOTE.

**Idle Actor in Æschylus:** DIGNAN.

**Idol-Breaker:** KENNEDY, *in his* Plays for Seven Players.

**If Lincoln Had Lived:** RANEY.

**Ignatius Donnelly:** RIDGE.

**Ihrig, Roscoe Myrl.** The Semantic Development of Words for "Walk, Run" in the Germanic Languages. 1916. *o.p.*

**Ilchman, Warren F.** Professional Diplomacy in the United States, 1779–1939. 1961. vii, 254 p. 25 cm. 61-11991. $6.00ˢ.

**Iliad:** HOMER.

**Illegitimate Child in Illinois:** PUTTEE.

**Illinois Adoption Law:** NIMS.

**Illinois Emergency Relief Commission:** GLICK.

**Illinois and Michigan Canal:** PUTNAM.

**Illinois Poor Law:** BRECKINRIDGE.

**Illinois Society of Child Study:** *see* TRANSACTIONS OF THE ILLINOIS SOCIETY OF CHILD STUDY.

**Illusion of Neutrality:** DIVINE.

**Imagination in Spinoza and Hume:** GORE.

**Immigration:** ABBOTT.

**Immunology and Development:** EDDS.

**Impact of Freudian Psychiatry:** ALEXANDER.

**Impact and Improvement of School Testing Programs:** FINDLEY.

**Impasse of American Foreign Policy:** MORGENTHAU.

**Impersonal Judgment:** MACLENNAN.

**Importance of Astrophysical Research:** KEELER.

**Impressions de voyage (Dumas):** PALMBLAD.

**Improvement of Teaching in the Secondary School:** BUTLER.

**Improving Instruction in Reading:** GRAY.

**Improving Reading in All Curriculum Areas:** GRAY.

**Improving Reading in Content Fields:** GRAY.

**In Clear and Present Danger:** CAUGHEY.

**In Defence of Politics:** CRICK.

**In Memoriam. John Nelson Jewett:** CHICAGO HISTORICAL SOCIETY.

**In Pennsylvania-German Land:** ROSENBERGER.

**In Praise of Adam:** DENNEY.

**In-Service Education for Teachers:** COREY.

**Incarnation:** CASE.

**Incidence of Illness:** FALK.

**Income and Standard of Living of Unskilled Laborers in Chicago:** HOUGHTELING.

**Incomes of Physicians:** LEVEN.

**Increase in Weight of Tin and Lead:** REY.

**Index to Bibliographical Papers:** COLE.

**Indexes to _A Balzac Bibliography_:** ROYCE.

**Indian as a Diplomatic Factor:** COX.

**Indian Life in the Upper Great Lakes:** QUIMBY.

**Indian Silver Currency:** ELLSTAETTER.

**Indian Tribes:** TAX.

**Indiana Poor Law:** SHAEFFER.

**Indiana Sand Dunes:** CRESSEY.

**Indians before Columbus:** MARTIN.

**Indians of North America:** DRIVER.

**Indians of South Mexico:** STARR.

**Individual and His Relation to Society:** TUFTS.

**Individual Pupil Graphs:** FREEMAN.

**Individualism and Economic Order:** HAYEK.

**Individuality in Organisms:** CHILD.

**Individualizing Instruction:** TYLER.

**Inductive Readings in German. Book I:** HAGBOLDT.

**Inductive Readings in German. Book II:** HAGBOLDT.

**Inductive Readings in German. Book III:** KAUFMANN.

**Industrial Education:** BARKER.

**Industrial Insurance:** HENDERSON.

**Industrial Relations in the Chicago Building Trades:** MONTGOMERY.

**Industrial Society:** MARSHALL.

**Inedita des Heinrich Kaufringer:** SCHMIDT-WARTENBERG.

**Infinitive in Polybius:** ALLEN.

**Influence of Chicago upon Abraham Lincoln:** BARTON.

**Influence of Newspaper Presentations:** FENTON.

**Inge, W. R.** Mysticism in Religion. 1948. _o.p._

**Ingle, Dwight J.,** _ed._ A Dozen Doctors. Autobiographic Sketches. 1963. vii, 287 p. Illus. 24 cm. 63-20908. $5.50ˢ.

**Inglis, Ruth A.** Freedom of the Movies. 1947. _o.p._

**Ingraham, Charles Anson.** Elmer E. Ellsworth and the Zouaves of '61. 1925. _o.p._

A publication of the Chicago Historical Society.

**Ingres, Maxime.** Cours complet de langue française. 1901. _o.p._

**Innis, Harold Adams,** _ed._ Essays in Political Economy in Honour of E. J. Urwick. With an Introduction by The Hon. and Rev. H. J. Cody. 1938. _o.p._

**Innis, Harold Adams,** *ed.:* YOUNG, The Japanese Canadians.

**Inquietudes de Shanti Andia (Baroja):** BAILIFF.

**Inscriptions from Adab:** LUCKENBILL.

**Inscriptions from Alishar:** GELB.

**Insects and Their World:** OLDROYD.

**Institute for Administrative Officers of Higher Institutions** (HI):

Vol.   I. Seventh Annual Institute, 1929. GRAY, Junior College Curriculum.
    II. GRAY, Training of College Teachers. 1930.
    III. GRAY, Recent Trends in American College Education. 1931.
    IV. GRAY, Provision for the Individual in College Education. 1932.
    V. GRAY, Needed Readjustments in Higher Education. 1933.
    VI. GRAY, General Education. 1934.
    VII. GRAY, Academic and Professional Preparation. 1935.
    VIII. GRAY, Tests and Measurements in Higher Education. 1936.
    IX. GRAY, Current Issues in Higher Education. 1937.
    X. GRAY, Preparation and In-Service Training of College Teachers. 1938.
    XI. RUSSELL, Outlook for Higher Education. 1939.
    XII. RUSSELL, Student Personnel Services. 1940.
    XIII. RUSSELL, New Frontiers in Collegiate Instruction. 1941.
    XIV. RUSSELL, Terminal Education in Higher Institutions. 1942.
    XV. RUSSELL, Higher Education under War Conditions. 1943.
    XVI. RUSSELL, Higher Education in Postwar Period. 1944.
    XVII. RUSSELL, Emergent Responsibilities in Higher Education. 1945.
    XVIII. RUSSELL, Problems of Faculty Personnel. 1946.
    XIX. BURNS, The Administration of Higher Institutions under Changing Conditions. 1947.
    XX. BURNS, The Community Responsibilities of Institutions of Higher Learning. 1948.

**Institute of American Meat Packers, Chicago.** The Packing Industry. A series of lectures given under the joint auspices of the School of Commerce and Administration of the University of Chicago and the Institute of American Meat Packers. 1924. MSB. *o.p.*

**Institute for Juvenile Research:** *see* Behavior Research Fund.

**Institute of Meat Packing Studies** (IMP):

CARVER, Personnel and Labor Problems.
GREER, Packinghouse Accounting.
MOULTON, Meat through the Microscope.
RHOADES, Merchandising Packinghouse Products.

**Institute of Pacific Relations** (IPR):

BUCK, Chinese Farm Economy.
BUCK, Land Utilization in China.
BUCK, 1931 Flood in China.
CARTER, China and Japan in Our University Curricula.
CATOR, Economic Position of the Chinese in the Netherlands Indies.
CONDLIFFE, Problems of the Pacific, 1927.
CONDLIFFE, Problems of the Pacific, 1929.
FIELD, American Participation in the China Consortiums.
HODOUS, Careers for Students of Chinese Language and Civilization.
HOLLAND, Problems of the Pacific, 1936.
KAT ANGELINO, Colonial Policy.
LASKER, Filipino Immigration.
LASKER, Problems of the Pacific, 1931.
LASKER, Problems of the Pacific, 1933.

**Institute of Pacific Relations,** *American Council: see* UNION INTERNATIONAL DE RADIO-DIFFUSION, Broadcasting Abroad.

**Institute of Pacific Relations.** *Research Staff of the Secretariat.* Agrarian China. Selected Source Materials from Chinese Authors. Compiled and translated by the Research Staff of the Secretariat, Institute of Pacific Relations. With an Introduction by R. H. Tawney. A Report in the International Research Series of the Institute of Pacific Relations. 1940. IPR. *o.p.*

**Instruction in English in the University High School:** ANDERSON.

**Instructional Problems in the University:** REEVES.

**Insull:** McDONALD.

**Integration of Behavior:** FRENCH.

**Integration of Educational Experiences:** DRESSEL.

**Integrative Process in Dreams:** FRENCH.

**Intellectual Adventure of Ancient Man:** FRANKFORT.

**Intellectual Foundations of Library Education:** SWANSON.

**Intellectual Hero:** BROMBERT.

**Intelligence, Concrete and Abstract:** ALEXANDER.

**Intelligence and Crime:** TULCHIN.

**Intelligence and Cultural Differences:** EELLS.

**Intelligence: Its Nature and Nurture. Original Studies and Experiments:** STODDARD.

**Intelligence Tests and Their Use:** THORNDIKE.

**Intelligent Parenthood:** CHICAGO ASSOCIATION FOR CHILD STUDY.

**Intelligent Philanthropy:** FARIS.

**Inter-American Solidarity:** LAVES.

**Interdependence of the Arts of Design:** STURGIS.

**International Aspects of Librarianship:** CARNOVSKY.

**International City Managers' Association:** *see* STUDIES IN MUNICIPAL MANAGEMENT.

**International Congress of Educational and Instructional Cinematography:** *see* KOON, Motion Pictures in Education.

**International Economic System:** POLAK.

**International Economics.** HARROD.

LEE, Land Utilization and Rural Economy in Korea.
LIN, New Monetary System of China.
LIN YUTANG, History of the Press and Public Opinion in China.
MCKENZIE, Oriental Exclusion.
MARCH, China and Japan in Our Museums.
MEARS, Resident Orientals.
NITOBÉ, Lectures on Japan.
NITOBÉ, Western Influences in Modern Japan.
PENROSE, Food Supply and Raw Materials in Japan.
QUIGLEY, Introductory Syllabus on Far Eastern Diplomacy.
RESEARCH STAFF OF THE SECRETARIAT, Agrarian China.
TS'AI T'ING-KAN, Chinese Poems in English Rhyme.
WRIGHT, American Tariff and Oriental Trade.
YOUNG, International Relations of Manchuria.
YOUNG, Japanese Canadians.

**International Encyclopedia of Unified Science (IEUS):**

I, 1. NEURATH, Encyclopedia and Unified Science.
I, 2. MORRIS, Foundations of the Theory of Signs.
I, 3. CARNAP, Foundations of Logic and Mathematics.
I, 4. BLOOMFIELD, Linguistic Aspects of Science.
I, 5. LENZEN, Procedures of Empirical Science.
I, 6. NAGEL, Principles of the Theory of Probability.
I, 7. FRANK, Foundations of Physics.
I, 8. FINLAY-FREUNDLICH, Cosmology.
I, 9. MAINX, Foundations of Biology.
I, 10. BRUNSWIK, Conceptual Framework of Psychology.
II, 1. NEURATH, Foundations of the Social Sciences.
II, 2. KUHN, Structure of Scientific Revolutions.
II, 3. EDEL, Science and the Structure of Ethics.
II, 4. DEWEY, Theory of Valuation.
II, 5. WOODGER, Technique of Theory Construction.
II, 7. HEMPEL, Fundamentals of Concept Formation in Empirical Science.
II, 8. SANTILLANA, Development of Rationalism and Empiricism.
II, 9. JOERGENSEN, Development of Logical Empiricism.

**International Journal of Ethics:** *see* ETHICS.

**International Relations of Manchuria:** YOUNG.

**International Security:** BENEŠ.

**International Servitudes in Law:** REID.

**International Understanding through the Public-School Curriculum:** KANDEL.

**Interpretation of the Electrocardiogram:** KATZ.

**Interpretation of Italy:** KLENZE.

**Interpretations of American Foreign Policy:** WRIGHT.

**Interviewing in Social Research:** HYMAN.

**Intracranial Tumors:** BAILEY.

**Introduction to Algebraic Theories:** ALBERT.

**Introduction to the Bible:** CHAMBERLIN.

**Introduction of Comedy into the City Dionysia:** CAPPS.

Introduction and Development of the Works Committee: MEINE.

Introduction to Economic Geography: JONES.

Introduction to Existentialism: GRENE.

Introduction to the History of Sociology: BARNES.

Introduction to the Interpretation of the Electrocardiogram: KATZ.

Introduction to Legal Reasoning: LEVI.

Introduction to Library Science: BUTLER.

Introduction to the New Testament: GOOD-SPEED.

Introduction to the Pathogenic Anaerobes: SMITH.

Introduction to the Peace Treaties: SCOTT.

Introduction to Philosophy of Education: HENDERSON.

Introduction to Protestant Dogmatics: LOBSTEIN.

Introduction to the Science of Sociology: PARK.

Introduction to Spanish Literature: NORTHUP.

Introduction to Study of Animal Populations: ANDREWARTHA.

Introduction to the Study of French: BOND.

Introduction to the Study of Obadiah: PECKHAM.

Introduction to the Study of Ore Deposits: HATCH.

Introduction to the Study of Stellar Structure: CHANDRASEKHAR.

Introduction to the Teaching of Science: DOWNING.

Introduction to the Theory of Experimental Design: FINNEY.

Introduction to the Theory of Numbers: DICKSON.

Introductory General Course in the Biological Sciences Syllabus: COULTER.

Introductory General Course in the Humanities Syllabus: KENISTON.

Introductory General Course in the Physical Sciences Syllabus: STEPHENSON.

Introductory Hebrew Method and Manual: HARPER.

Introductory Syllabus on Far Eastern Diplomacy: QUIGLEY.

Invariants and Covariants of Quadratic Differential Quantics of *n* Variables: MASCHKE.

Investigating Library Problems: WAPLES.

Investigation into the Factors in Tests Involving the Visual Perception of Space: KOUSSY.

Investigation into the Relation between Intelligence and Inheritance: LAWRENCE.

Investigation of the Zeeman Effect: REESE.

Investment of Truth: DEWHURST.

Iowa Pool: GRODINSKY.

Iraq Excavations of the Oriental Institute, 1932/33: FRANKFORT.

Ireland, Phillip, *ed.* The Near East: Problems and Prospects. 1942. WFL. *o.p.*

Irenaeus Testimony to the Fourth Gospel: LEWIS.

Iron Curtains and Scholarship: WINGER.

Irradiation of Mice and Men: LOUTIT.

Irwin, William A. The Problem of Ezekiel. An Inductive Study. 1943. *o.p.*

Irwin, William A., *joint author:* FRANKFORT, Intellectual Adventure of Ancient Man.

Irwin, William A.: *see* SMITH, The Prophets and Their Times.

Is American Radio Democratic? FROST.

al-Iṣfahānī: *see* MUḤAMMAD B. DĀWŪD.

Islamic Architecture and Its Decoration: HILL.

Island Community. Ecological Succession in Hawaii: LIND.

Island India Goes to School: EMBREE.

Isles of the Blest: KENNEDY, *in his* Plays for Three Players. Vol. III.

Isolation in the School: YOUNG.

Isotopes in Experimental Pharmacology: ROTH.

Israel, Henry. *ed.* Handbook of Rural Social Resources. Edited by Henry Israel and Benson Y. Landis. 1926. ACLA *o.p.*

Issues in Evolution: TAX.

L'Italia: WILKINS.

Italian Folk Tales and Folk Songs: COWPER.

Italy and the Vatican at War: HALPERIN.


Jack-Roller: SHAW.

Jackman, W. S. Nature Study. 1904. NSSE, 3d Yrbk., Part II. *o.p.*

Jackson, Samuel Macauley, *ed.*: BERNARD OF CLUNY, Source of "Jerusalem the Golden."

Jacobs, Melville. The Content and Style of an Oral Literature. Clackamas Chinook Myths and Tales. 1959. viii, 285 p. 25 cm. 59-8489. $5.00s.

Jacobs, Merkel H.: COWDRY, General Cytology.

Jacobs, Walter Ballou, *joint author:* FARRINGTON, Observation and Practice Teaching.

Jacobsen, Thorkild Peter Rudolph. Philological Notes on Eshnunna and Its Inscriptions. 1934. xiv, 35 p. Illus. 25 cm. 34-23074. Paper. AS 6. $1.00.

Jacobsen, Thorkild Peter Rudolph. Sennacherib's Aqueduct at Jerwan. By Thorkild Jacobsen and Seton Lloyd. 1935. xii, 52 p. Illus. 30 cm. 35-9202. OIP, XXIV. $5.00.

Jacobsen, Thorkild Peter Rudolph. The Sumerian King List. 1939. xvi, 216 p. AS 11. $5.00.

Jacobsen, Thorkild Peter Rudolph, *joint author:* FRANKFORT, Gimilsin Temple and the Palace of the Rulers of Tell Asmar.

Jacobsen, Thorkild Peter Rudolph, *joint author:* FRANKFORT, Intellectual Adventure of Ancient Man.

Jacobsen, Thorkild Peter Rudolph, *joint author:* FRANKFORT, Tell Asmar and Khafaje.

Jacobsen, Thorkild Peter Rudolph: *see* DELOUGAZ, Pre-Sargonid Temples.

Jacobsen, Thorkild Peter Rudolph: *see* FRANKFORT, Oriental Institute Discoveries in Iraq, 1933/34.

Jacobsen, Thorkild Peter Rudolph: *see* LOUD, Khorsabad. I.

Jacobson, Edmund. Progressive Relaxation. A Physiological and Clinical Investigation of Muscular States and Their Significance in Psychology and Medical Practice. 2d ed., 1938. xviii, 494 p. Illus. 24 cm. 38-13310. CMM. $13.50s.

Jacoby, Neil H.: *see* LELAND, State-Local Fiscal Relations.

Jacques, Agnes, *joint ed.*: COLEMAN, Analytical Bibliography of Modern Language Teaching, 1927–1932.

Jaffa, Harry V. Thomism and Aristotelianism. A Study of the Commentary by Thomas Aquinas on the *Nicomachean Ethics*. 1952. *o.p.*

Jaffary, Stuart K. The Mentally Ill and Public Provision for their Care in Illinois. 1943. *o.p.*

James, Edmund Janes. The Charters of the City of Chicago. 1898–1899. *Part I:* The Early Charters, 1833–1837. 1898. *Part II:* The City Charters, 1838–1851. 1899. POL. *o.p.*

James, Edmund Janes. The Education of Business Men. A View of the Organization and Courses of Study in the Commercial High Schools of Europe. A Report to the American Bankers' Association. 1898. *o.p.*

James, Edmund Janes. Municipal Administration in Germany. As Seen in the Government of a Typical Prussian City, Halle a.S. 1901. *o.p.*

James, Herman Gerlach. The Preamble and Boundary Clauses of the Illinois Constitution. 1910. *o.p.*

A publication of the Chicago Historical Society.

**James, James Alton.** The Life of George Rogers Clark. 1928. *o.p.*

**James, Preston Everett:** *see* COLBY, Geographic Aspects of International Relations.

**James, T. G. H.,** *ed. and trans.:* KEES, Ancient Egypt.

**James, Warren,** *joint author:* DEAN, The Long-Run Behavior of Costs.

**Janowitz, Morris.** The Military in the Political Development of New Nations. An Essay in Comparative Analysis. 1964. ix, 134 p. 64-13952. Cloth. 23 cm. $4.50ˢ. Paper. P174. 21 cm. $1.50.

**Janowitz, Morris,** *General Editor:* Heritage of Sociology.

**Jansky, Cyril Moreau.** The Problem of the Institutionally Owned Station. By C. M. Jansky, Jr., R. C. Higgy, Morse Salisbury. 1934. NACRE. *o.p.*

**Janson, Florence Edith.** The Background of Swedish Immigration, 1840–1930. 1931. SSM. *o.p.*

**Japanese Canadians:** YOUNG.

**Japanese Scroll Painting:** TODA.

**Japan's American Interlude:** KAWAI.

**Japan's Natural Resources and Their Relation to Japan's Economic Resources:** ACKERMAN.

**Jarvie, Lawrence Lee.** A Handbook on the Anecdotal Behavior Journal. By L. L. Jarvie and Mark Ellingson. 1940. *o.p.*

**Jashemski, Wilhelmine F.** The Origins and History of the Proconsular and Propraetorian Imperium to 27 B.C. 1950. *o.p.*

**Jasny, Naum.** Soviet Industrialization, 1928–1952. 1961. xvii, 467 p. Illus. 25 cm. 57-11551. $10.00ˢ.

**Jaspers, Karl.** The Future of Mankind. Translated by E. B. Ashton. 1961. xii, 342 p. 60-7237. Cloth. 25 cm. $5.95ˢ. Paper. P143. 21 cm. $1.95.

"This book deals with the crucial issue of the age with unparalleled seriousness, profundity and sense. . . . Its reception will put our intellectual and political maturity to the test." —Hans Morgenthau, in *Saturday Review.*

**Jaspers, Karl.** General Psychopathology. 1913. Translated from the German (7th ed.) by J. Hoenig and Marian W. Hamilton. 1963. xxii, 922 p. 25 cm. 63-9736. $12.50ˢ. COBE.

**Jaspers, Karl.** The Nature of Psychotherapy. (Excerpted from *General Psychopathology*). Translated by J. Hoenig and Marian W. Hamilton. 1965. xi, 52 p. Paper. P187. 21 cm. $1.50. COBE.

**Jászi, Oscar.** The Dissolution of the Habsburg Monarchy. 1929. xiv, 482 p. 21 cm. 29-22812. Paper. P70. $2.45.

"There have been many books written on the breakup of the Austro-Hungarian Empire, but there is none which goes so deeply into the causes . . . in this pitiless yet pitiful analysis, rigorously buttressed with statistics, the tragedy is described without bitterness but with deep feeling."—*The Manchester Guardian.*

**Jazz and the White Americans:** LEONARD.

**Jefferson-Lemen Compact:** MacNAUL.

**Jeffrey, Edward Charles.** The Anatomy of Woody Plants. 1917. *o.p.*

**Jelinek, Vladimir,** *ed. and trans.:* COMENIUS, Analytical Didactic of Comenius.

**Jenkins, Hilger Perry.** A Terminology of Operations of the University of Chicago Clinics. 1935. *o.p.*

**Jenkins, Paul Burrill.** The Book of Lake Geneva. 1922. *o.p.*

A publication of the Chicago Historical Society.

**Jenkins, Richard Leos,** *joint author:* THURSTONE, Order of Birth, Parent-Age, and Intelligence.

**Jenkins, Thomas Atkinson.** The Espurgatoire Saint Patriz of Marie de France, with a Text of the Latin Original. Preprint, 1903. *o.p.*

**Jenkins, Thomas Atkinson,** *joint ed.:* NITZE, Le haute livre du Graal. Perlesvaus. Vol. I.

**Jenkins, Thomas Atkinson,** *trans.:* LANGLOIS, Historic Rôle of France.

**Jenness, Diamond.** The People of the Twilight. 1959. viii, 251 p. Illus. 21 cm. 59-16100. Paper. P32. $1.75.

**Jennings, Jesse D.,** *ed.* Prehistoric Man in the New World. Edited by Jesse D. Jennings and Edward Norbeck. 1964. x, 633 p. 24 cm. 63-18852. RSS. $10.00ˢ.

**Jennings, Louis B.,** *joint author:* COBB, A Biography and Bibliography of Edgar Johnson Goodspeed.

**Jennison, Florence Tye,** *joint author:* DOUGLAS, Movement of Money.

**Jensen, Adolf E.** Myth and Cult among Primitive Peoples. Translated by Marianna Tax Choldin and Wolfgang Weissleder. 1963. x, 349 p. 23 cm. 63-20909. $8.75ˢ.

**Jensen, Christen.** The Pardoning Power in the American States. 1922. *o.p.*

**Jensen, Gale E.,** *ed.* Dynamics of Instructional Groups. 1960. NSSE, 59th Yrbk., Part II. xi, 286, ci p. 22 cm. 60-1494. Cloth. $4.50ᵗ. Paper. $3.75ᵗ.

**Jensen, Jens:** *see* EATON, Landscape Artist in America.

**Jensen, Jens Peter.** Property Taxation in the United States. 1931. SE. *o.p.*

**Jernegan, Marcus Wilson.** Laboring and Dependent Classes in Colonial America, 1607–1783. Studies of the Economic, Educational, and Social Significance of Slaves, Servants, Apprentices, and Poor Folk. 1931. SSM. *o.p.*

**Jerusalem:** PATON.

**Jesus through the Centuries:** CASE.

**Jesus of Nazareth:** BURTON.

**Jesus and Our Generation:** GILKEY.

**Jesus and the Pharisees:** RIDDLE.

**Jet-Stream Meteorology:** REITER.

**Jeter, Helen Rankin.** Trends of Population in the Region of Chicago. Prepared by the Local Community Research Committee of the University of Chicago and the Commonwealth Club of Chicago for the Chicago Regional Planning Association. 1927. SSCI. *o.p.*

**Jeter, Helen Rankin:** *see* SMITH, Chicago.

**Jeuck, John E.,** *joint author:* EMMET, Catalogues and Counters.

**Jewell, C. S.,** *joint author:* BLOUNT, Excursion through the Rivers and Harbors of Chicago.

**Jewett, James Richard:** *see* YŪSUF IBN ḲISUGHLI *called* SIBṬ IBN AL-JAUZĪ, Mir'ât za-Zamân.

**Jews in Medieval Germany:** KISCH.

**Joad, C. E. M.** A Critique of Logical Positivism. 1950. *o.p.*

**Job Analysis and the Training of Teachers:** NATIONAL SOCIETY OF COLLEGE TEACHERS OF EDUCATION, Proceedings, No. 13.

**Jobs or the Dole?** DENOOD.

**Joeckel, Carleton B.** The Government of the American Public Library. 1935. LS. *o.p.*

**Joeckel, Carleton B.** A Metropolitan Library in Action. A Survey of the Chicago Public Library. By Carleton Bruns Joeckel and Leon Carnovsky. 1940. LS. *o.p.*

**Joeckel, Carleton B.,** *ed.* Current Issues in Library Administration. Papers Presented before the [Third] Library Institute at the University of Chicago, 1938. Edited with an Introduction by Carleton B. Joeckel, 1939. LS. *o.p.*

**Joeckel, Carleton B.,** *ed.* Library Extension. Problems and Solutions. 1946. *o.p.*

**Joergensen, Joergen.** The Development of Logical Empiricism. 1951. iv, 100 p. 26 cm. A51-3740. Paper. IEUS, II, 9. $2.25ˢ.

**Joergensen, Joergen,** *joint author:* NEURATH, Bibliography and Index.

**Johannine Lessons in the Greek Gospel Lectionary:** BUCK.

**Johannsen, Albert.** A Descriptive Petrography of the Igneous Rocks. 4 vols. 26 cm. 40-4476. *Vol. I:* Introduction, Textures, Classifications, and Glossary. 1931 (2d ed., 1939). xxiv, 318 p. Illus. $7.50ˢ. *Vol. II:* The Quartz-bearing Rocks. 1932. xxxii, 428 p. Illus. $10.00ˢ. *Vol. III:* The Intermediate Rocks. 1937. xiv, 360 p. Illus. $8.00ˢ. *Vol. IV:* Two parts. 1938. xviii, 523 p. Illus. $11.50ˢ. *Part I,* The Feldspathoid Rocks, includes the plutonic, extrusive, and hypabyssal rocks which contain nepheline, leucite, sodalite, analcite, etc., or which are quartz-free and possess alkaline affinities. *Part II,* The Peridotites and Perknites, describes the melanocratic rocks from dunite to pyroxenite. Complete indexes of the authors, localities, and rock names in Vols. II, III, and IV. (Not for sale in South Asia.)

". . . the most compendious handbook of petrography ever issued. . . . The value of the work is independent of the classification or the nomenclature. An enormous amount of data, gathered from world-wide and often relatively inaccessible sources, is made available in one work. To petrographers it will be a mine of information and a great time-saver. It is the fruition of the life-work of a great petrographer and scholar." —*Nature* (England).

**Johannsen, Albert.** Essentials for the Microscopical Determination of Rock-forming Minerals and Rocks in Thin Sections. 1922. 2d ed. 1928. *o.p.*

**Johannsen, Albert.** "Phiz." Illustrations from the Novels of Charles Dickens. 1956. xi, 443 p. Illus. 28×22 cm. 56-10998. $8.95s.

**John, Lenore,** *joint author:* BUSWELL, Diagnostic Studies in Arithmetic.

**John, Lenore,** *joint author:* BUSWELL, The Vocabulary of Arithmetic.

**John Amos Comenius:** SPINKA.

**John Drury:** BATTEN.

**John Hus and Czech Reform:** SPINKA.

**John Panet:** HUDSON.

**John Stuart Mill:** HAYEK.

**Johnson, Arlien.** Public Policy and Private Charities. A Study of Legislation in the United States and of Administration in Illinois. 1931. SSM. *o.p.*

**Johnson, B. Lamar.** The Public Junior College. Prepared by B. Lamar Johnson, Chairman of the Society's Committee. 1956. NSSE, 55th Yrbk., Part I. xi, 352 p. 24 cm. 56-13752. Cloth. $4.50t. Paper. $3.75t.

**Johnson, Charles Spurgeon,** Shadow of the Plantation. 1934. *o.p.*

**Johnson, Claudius Osborne.** Carter Henry Harrison I. Political Leader. 1928. SSCI. *o.p.*

**Johnson, D. Gale.** Forward Prices for Agriculture. 1947. *o.p.*

**Johnson, D. Gale.** Grain Yields and the American Food Supply. By D. Gale Johnson and Robert L. Gustafson. 1962. xii, 148 p. 22 cm. 62-18115. $3.50s.

**Johnson, Franklin.** Have We the Likeness of Christ? The Testimony of Early Christian Art. 1902. *o.p.*

**Johnson, Franklin Winslow.** The Problems of Boyhood. A Course of Ethics for Boys of High-School Age. 1914. 2d ed. 1924. CS. *o.p.*

**Johnson, Glenn Howard.** Relief and Health Problems of a Selected Group of Non-Family Men. 1937. SSM. *o.p.*

**Johnson, Harry G.,** *joint ed.:* HAMILTON, Landmarks in Political Economy.

**Johnson, Laura B.,** *ed.* Le Livre d'or. By Charlotte M. Yonge. Adapted and edited by Laura B. Johnson. HCLS.

**Johnson, LaVona,** *joint author:* BOWMAN, Studying Children.

**Johnson, LaVona,** *joint author:* HAVIGHURST, Community Youth Development Program.

**Johnson, Pamela Hansford.** Proust Recaptured. Six Radio Sketches Based on the Author's Characters. 1959. *o.p.*

**Johnson, Victor E.,** *joint author:* CARLSON, Machinery of the Body.

**Johnson, Victor E.,** *joint author:* KATZ, Elements of Electrocardiographic Interpretation.

**Johnson, Walter.** The Battle against Isolation. 1944. *o.p.*

**Johnson, Walter.** The Fulbright Program. A History. By Walter Johnson and F. J. Colligan. With a Foreword by J. W. Fulbright. 1965. xv, 380 p. 24 cm. 65-24978. $8.50.

**Jonas, Oswald,** *ed.:* SCHENKER, Harmony.

**Jones, Barbara:** *see* LEE, Fundamentals of Good Medical Care.

**Jones, Chester Lloyd.** The United States and the Caribbean. By Chester Lloyd Jones, Henry Kittredge Norton, and Parker Thomas Moon. 1929. APA. *o.p.*

**Jones, Donald Forsha.** Selective Fertilization. 1928. SCI. *o.p.*

**Jones, Florence Nightingale.** Boccaccio and His Imitators in German, English, French, Spanish, and Italian Literature. "The Decameron." 1910. *o.p.*

**Jones, H. S. V.:** *see* BRYAN, Sources and Analogues of Chaucer's *Canterbury Tales.*

**Jones, Harold E.** Adolescence. Prepared by Harold E. Jones, Chairman of the Society's Committee. 1944. NSSE, 43d Yrbk., Part I. x, 358 p. 24 cm. E44-78. Cloth. $3.00ᵗ. Paper. $2.25ᵗ.

**Jones, Jenkin Lloyd.** Love and Loyalty. 1907. *o.p.*

**Jones, Lester Bartlett,** *joint author:* SHEPARDSON, Scripture and Song in Worship.

**Jones, Lewis Webster,** *joint author:* LEE, Fundamentals of Good Medical Care.

**Jones, Maldwyn Allen.** American Immigration. 1960. vi, 360 p. Illus. 21 cm. 60-8301. Cloth. CHAC. $6.00ˢ. Paper. $1.95.

**Jones, Maro B.,** *joint ed.:* BAILIFF, Las Inquietudes de Shanti Andía.

**Jones, Richard J.,** *ed.* Evolution of the Atherosclerotic Plaque. 1964. xiii, 360 p. Illus. 25 cm. 63-20918. $6.75ˢ.

**Jones, Vernon Augustus.** Character and Citizenship Training in the Public School. An Experimental Study of Three Specific Methods. 1936. *o.p.*

**Jones, Victor.** Metropolitan Government. 1942. *o.p.*

**Jones, Wellington Downing.** An Introduction to Economic Geography. Volume I. Natural Environment as Related to Economic Life. By Wellington D. Jones and Derwent S. Whittlesey. 1925. MSB. *o.p.*

**Jones, Wellington Downing.** Jones and Whittlesey Economic Geography Maps.

World-Maps for use with *An Introduction to Economic Geography.* By Wellington D. Jones and Derwent S. Whittlesey. *o.p.*

**Jones, William W.** Weather-Map Construction and Forecasting in the Westerlies from Single-Station Aerological Data. 1943. DMMR 7. *o.p.*

**Jonson, Ben.** The Case Is Altered. A Comedy. By Ben Jonson. Presented by Students in the University of Chicago at the Auditorium Theater, May Seventeenth, Nineteen Hundred and Two. Revised after the Original Edition of 1609. 1902. *o.p.*

**Jordan, E.** Essays in Criticism. 1952. *o.p.*

**Jordan, E.** The Good Life. 1949. *o.p.*

**Jordan, E.** Theory of Legislation. An Essay on the Dynamics of Public Mind. 1952. *o.p.*

**Jordan, Edwin Oakes.** Food Poisoning and Food-borne Infection. 1917. 2d ed. 1931. SCI. *o.p.*

First edition published under title *Food Poisoning.*

**Jordan, Edwin Oakes.** The Self-purification of Streams. Preprint, 1903. *o.p.*

**Jordan, Edwin Oakes,** *ed.* The Newer Knowledge of Bacteriology and Immunology. By Eighty-two Contributors. Edited by Edwin O. Jordan and I. S. Falk. 1928. *o.p.*

**Jordan, Edwin Oakes:** *see* NEWMAN, Nature of the World and of Man.

**Jordan, Rudolf.** The New Perspective. 1951. *o.p.*

**Jordan, W. K.** Men of Substance. A Study of the Thought of Two English Revolutionaries, Henry Parker and Henry Robinson. 1942. *o.p.*

**Joseph, Alice.** The Desert People. By Alice Joseph, Jane Chesky, and Rosamond Spicer. 1949. *o.p.*

**Joseph, Alice,** *joint author:* THOMPSON, The Hopi Way.

**Joseph Spence:** WRIGHT.

**Josephson, Aksel G. S.** Bibliographies of Bibliographies. Chronologically Arranged with Occasional Notes and an Index by Aksel G. S. Josephson. 1901. 2d ed. 1913. *o.p.*

**Joshi, S. L.:** *see* HAYDON, Modern Trends in World-Religions.

**Journal of Benjamin Moran:** WALLACE.

**Jouvenel, Bertrand de.** Sovereignty. An Inquiry into the Political Good. Translated by J. F. Huntington. 1957. 57-9548. Paper. P121. 21 cm. $1.95. COBE.

**Joy, Alfred Harrison:** *see* SLOCUM, Stellar Parallaxes.

**Judaism and Christianity:** PARKES.

**Judd, Charles Hubbard.** Democracy and American Schools. 1918. WP. *o.p.*

**Judd, Charles Hubbard.** Plans for Organizing School Surveys, with a Summary of Typical School Surveys. By Charles H. Judd and Henry L. Smith. 1914. NSSE, 13th Yrbk., Part II. *o.p.*

**Judd, Charles Hubbard.** Psychological Analysis of the Fundamentals of Arithmetic. 1927. SEM 32. *o.p.*

**Judd, Charles Hubbard.** Reading. Its Nature and Development. With the co-operation of William Scott Gray, Clarence Truman Gray, Katherine McLaughlin, Clara Schmitt, and Adam Raymond Gilliland. 1918. SEM 10. *o.p.*

**Judd, Charles Hubbard.** Silent Reading. A Study of the Various Types. By Charles H. Judd and Guy T. Buswell. 1922. SEM 23. *o.p.*

**Judd, Charles Hubbard,** *joint author:* BUSWELL, Summary of Educational Investigations.

**Judd, Charles Hubbard:** *see* NEWMAN, Nature of the World and of Man.

**Judicial System of Metropolitan Chicago:** LEPAWSKY.

**Judson, Alexander Corbin,** *ed.* Seventeenth-Century Lyrics. Edited with Short Biographies, Bibliographies, and Notes. 1927. *o.p.*

**Judson, Harry Pratt.** The Essentials of a Written Constitution. 1903. *o.p.*

**Judson, Harry Pratt.** The Higher Education as a Training for Business. 1896. 2d ed. 1911. *o.p.*

First edition published by Henry Altemus, Philadelphia.

**Judson, Harry Pratt.** The Threat of German World-Politics. 1918. WP. *o.p.*

**Junior College Business Education:** SHIELDS.

**Junior College Curriculum:** GRAY.

**Junior High School:** DOUGLASS.

**Junior:** CHAVE.

**Junker, Buford H.** Field Work. An Introduction to the Social Sciences. With an Introduction by Everett C. Hughes. 1960. xvii, 210 p. 25 cm. 60-7238. Paper. $3.50t.

**Jupiter:** MCMATH-HULBERT OBSERVATORY.

**Jurisprudence:** LLEWELLYN.

**Just, Ernest E.:** *see* COWDRY, General Cytology.

**Justices Black and Frankfurter:** MENDELSON.

**Juvenile Delinquency and the Schools:** STRANG.

**Juvenile Delinquency and Urban Areas:** SHAW.

**Juvenile Detention in the United States:** WARNER.

**Kahrl, George M.** Tobias Smollett, Traveler-Novelist. 1945. *o.p.*

**Kain, Richard M.** Fabulous Voyager. James Joyce's *Ulysses.* 1947. *o.p.*

**Kaiser, Ernst,** *joint trans.:* FRÄNGER, Millennium of Hieronymus Bosch.

**Kales, Albert Martin.** Unpopular Government in the United States. 1914. *o.p.*

**Kalingas:** BARTON.

**Kallen, Horace M.** Education versus Indoctrination in the Schools. 1934. PPP 13. *o.p.*

**Kallen, Horace M.** The Future of Peace. 1941. PPP, 34. *o.p.*

**Kallen, Horace M.** William James and Henri Bergson. A Study in Contrasting Theories of Life. 1914. *o.p.*

**Kalven, Harry, Jr.,** *joint author:* BLUM, Uneasy Case for Progressive Taxation.

**Kandel, I. L.** International Understanding through the Public-School Curriculum. Prepared by I. L. Kandel, Chairman, of the Society's Committee on International Understanding. 1937. NSSE, 36th Yrbk., Part II. xii, 406 p. 24 cm. 37-172. Cloth. $2.50ᵗ. Paper. $1.75ᵗ.

**Kansas City Power and Light Company:** MEECH.

**Kant, Immanuel.** Critique of Practical Reason and Other Writings in Moral Philosophy. Edited and translated by Lewis White Beck. 1949. *o.p.*

**Kant, Immanuel.** Foundations of the Metaphysics of Morals. What Is Enlightenment? and a Passage from *The Metaphysics of Morals*. Edited and translated by Lewis White Beck. 1950. *o.p.*

**Kant's Weltanschauung:** KRONER.

**Kany, Charles E.** American-Spanish Syntax. 1945. 2d ed. 1951. ix, 467 p. 24 cm. 51-3150. $7.00ᵗ.

**Kaplan, Mordecai M.:** *see* HAYDON, Modern Trends in World-Religions.

**Kare, Morley R.,** *ed.* Physiological and Behavioral Aspects of Taste. Edited by Morley R. Kare and Bruce P. Halpern. 1961. xvi, 149 p. Illus. 24 cm. 61-15937. $6.00ˢ.

**Karl Bitter:** SCHEVILL.

**Karsh, Bernard,** *joint author:* SEIDMAN, Worker Views His Union.

**Kates, Robert W.,** *joint ed.:* BURTON, Readings in Resource Management and Conservation.

**Katz, Daniel:** Attitude toward the Law. Forms A and B. 1931. TAS 27. *o.p.*

**Katz, Jerrold J.** The Problem of Induction and Its Solution. 1962. xiv, 128 p. 22 cm. 62-18116. $3.75ˢ.

**Katz, Louis N.** Elements of Electrocardiographic Interpretation. With Thirty-eight Plates Illustrating the More Important Deviations from the Normal. Selected from the Files of the Michael Reese Hospital.

By Louis N. Katz, M.D., and Victor Johnson, M.D. 1932. 2d ed. 1936. *o.p.*

**Katz, Louis N.** Interpretation of the Electrocardiogram. By Louis N. Katz, Richard Langendorf, and Alfred Pick. 1952. BM. *o.p.*

**Katz, Louis N.** Introduction to the Interpretation of the Electrocardiogram. With Sixty-one Plates Illustrating the More Important Deviations from the Normal. Selected from the Files of the Michael Reese Hospital. By Louis N. Katz, Richard Langendorf, and Alfred Pick. 1952. x, 78 p. Illus. 24 cm. 52-14734. Paper. BM. $2.50ˢ.

**Kaufman, Gordon D.** Relativism, Knowledge, and Faith. 1960. xiii, 141 p. 23 cm. 59-11620. $3.75ˢ.

**Kaufmann, F. W.** Inductive Readings in German. Book III. Introduction to German Political and Cultural History. By F. W. Kaufmann and E. W. Balduf. HCLS.

*See also:*
HAGBOLDT, Brief Course in German.
HAGBOLDT, Deutsch für Anfänger.
HAGBOLDT, German Review and Composition.
HAGBOLDT, Inductive Readings in German. Book I.
HAGBOLDT, Lesebuch für Anfänger.
HAGBOLDT, Modern German Grammar.

**Kaufmann, Yehezkel.** The Religion of Israel (*Tōledōth Hā'emūnā Hay-yisre'ēlith*). From Its Beginnings to the Babylonian Exile. Translated and abridged by Moshe Greenberg. 1960. x, 486 p. 24 cm. 60-5466. $8.50. COBE.

"Kaufmann's work is monumental—not only in the sense that it is very extensive but also that it offers a fundamental criticism of the prevailing view, which is based on the work of Julius Wellhauser, and presents an alternative to that view which is in no way fundamental or obscurantist, but makes use of critical methods."—J. Philip Hyatt, in *The Journal of Bible and Religion.*

**Kawabé, Kisaburō.** The Press and Politics in Japan. A Study of the Relation between the Newspaper and the Political Development of Modern Japan. 1921. SOC. *o.p.*

**Kawai, Kazuo.** Japan's American Interlude. 1960. vii, 257 p. Illus. 22 cm. 59-14111. $5.00ˢ.

**Kawin, Ethel.** Children of Preschool Age. Studies in Socio-economic Status. Social Adjustment and Mental Ability, with Illustrative Cases. 1934. BR. *o.p.*

**Kawin, Ethel.** A Comparative Study of a Nursery-School versus a Non-Nursery-School Group. By Ethel Kawin and Carolyn Hoefer assisted by Edna Mohr, Maria G. Linder, and Marian W. Taylor. Based upon Studies Made by the Elizabeth McCormick Memorial Fund and the Institute for Juvenile Research, Assisted by the Behavior Research Fund. 1931. BR. *o.p.*

**Kawin, Ethel.** Problems of Preschool Age. Nine Case Studies. A Preprint of Part I from "Children of Preschool Age." 1933. BR. *o.p.*

**Kawin, Ethel.** The Wise Choice of Toys. With an Introduction by Frank N. Freeman. 1934. 2d ed. 1938. x, 154 p. Illus. 24 cm. $4.00s.

**Kawin, Ethel,** *joint author:* FREEMAN, Individual Pupil Graph.

**Kawin, Ethel,** *joint author:* FREEMAN, Teacher's Rating Scales for Pupil Adjustment.

**Kayser, Heinrich Gustave Johannes.** On the Spectra of Argon. 1896. *o.p.*

**Keast, W. R.,** *joint author:* CRANE, Critics and Criticism.

**Kecskemeti, Paul.** Meaning, Communication, and Value. 1952. *o.p.*

**Keefer, Mary Wysor,** *joint author:* SHAFFER, Indiana Poor Law.

**Keeler, James Edward.** The Importance of Astrophysical Research and the Relation of Astrophysics to Other Physical Sciences. Address Delivered at the Dedication of the Yerkes Observatory, October 21, 1897. 1897. *o.p.*

**Keeler, James Edward.** On Some Photographs of the Great Nebula in Orion, Taken by Means of the Less Refrangible Rays of Its Spectrum. 1899. *o.p.*

**Keeler, James Edward.** The Ring Nebula in Lyra. 1899. *o.p.*

**Keeler, James Edward.** A Spectroscopic Proof of the Meteoric Constitution of Saturn's Rings. 1895. *o.p.*

**Keeler, Leonarde:** *see* LARSON, Lying and Its Detection.

**Keenan, P. C.,** *joint author:* MORGAN, An Atlas of Stellar Spectra.

**Keener, Jefferson Ward.** Cutting the Cost of Bank Loans. 1931. SBA, II. *o.p.*

**Keeping Reading Programs Abreast of the Times:** GRAY.

**Kees, Herman.** Ancient Egypt. A Cultural Topography. Translated and edited by T. G. H. James. 1961. 392 p. Illus. Index. 22 cm. 61-8078. $5.95s. USA.

**Kefauver, Grayson N.** Guidance in Educational Institutions. Prepared by Grayson N. Kefauver, Chairman of the Society's Committee. 1938. NSSE, 37th Yrbk., Part I. *op.*

**Keller, Franklin J.** Vocational Education. Prepared by Franklin J. Keller, Chairman of the Society's Committee. 1943. NSSE. 42d Yrbk., Part I. xvi, 494 p. 24 cm. E43-38. Cloth. $3.25t. Paper. $2.50t.

**Kellman, E.,** *joint author:* MORGAN, An Atlas of Stellar Spectra.

**Kellogg, Ruth Mary.** The United States Employment Service. 1933. SSCI. *o.p.*

**Kellogg, Winthrop N.** Porpoises and Sonar. 1961. xiv, 177 p. Illus. 21 cm. 61-11294. Paper. PSS518. $1.50.

**Kelly, Alfred H.** Richard Hildreth, *in* HUTCHINSON, Marcus W. Jernegan Essays.

**Kelly, Frederick James,** *joint author:* REEVES, Organization and Administration of the University.

**Kelly, Frederick James,** *joint author:* REEVES, University Faculty.

**Kelly, Frederick James,** *joint author:* REEVES, University Plant Facilities.

**Kelly, Harriet J.,** *joint author:* MACY, Chemical Anthropology.

**Kelsen, Hans.** Society and Nature. A Social Inquiry. 1943. *o.p.*

**Kelsey, Francis Willey.** Should Papers Dealing with Matters of Scholarship, or Papers on Method, Be the Chief Feature of Teachers' Meetings? 1896. *o.p.*

**Kemp, H. R.,** *ed.* Canadian Marketing Problems. Ten Essays. 1939. *o.p.*

**Kemperman, J. H. B.** The Passage Problem for a Stationary Markov Chain. 1961. vii, 136 p. 25 cm. 61-8080. SRM, I. $5.00ˢ.

**Keniston, Hayward.** A Basic List of Spanish Words and Idioms. 1933. HCLS. *o.p.*

**Keniston, Hayward.** The Syntax of Castilian Prose. The Sixteenth Century. 1937. xxx, 750. p. 24 cm. $9.00ˢ.

**Keniston, Hayward,** *ed.* Introductory General Course in the Humanities Syllabus. Edited by Hayward Keniston, Ferdinand Schevill, Arthur P. Scott. Third Preliminary Edition, September, 1933. *o.p.*

**Kennan, George F.** American Diplomacy. 1900–1950. 1951. ix, 154 p. 22 cm. 51–12883. WFL. $3.50ˢ. COBE.

**Kennan, George Frost.** Siberia and the Exile System. Abridged from the first edition, published by the Century Company, 1891. With an introduction by George Kennan. 1958. *o.p.*

**Kennedy, Aileen Elizabeth.** The Ohio Poor Law and Its Administration. Appendixes with Selected Decisions of the Ohio Supreme Court, Edited by Sophonisba P. Breckinridge. 1934. SSM. *o.p.*

**Kennedy, Charles Rann.** Plays for Seven Players. A Repertory of Plays for a Company of Seven Players and Two Short Plays for Smaller Casts. By Charles Rann Kennedy. 1930. *o.p.*

**Kennedy, Charles Rann.** Plays for Three Players. A Repertory of Plays for a Company of Three Players. 3 vols. 1927–1940. *o.p.*

**Kennedy, John Curtis.** Wages and Family Budgets in the Chicago Stockyards District. With Wage Statistics from Other Industries Employing Unskilled Labor. By J. C. Kennedy and Others. 1914. CSC. *o.p.*

**Kent, Norton Adams,** *joint author:* HALE, Spectrum of the High Potential Discharge between Metallic Electrodes.

**Kent, Rockwell:** *see* PORTINARI.

**Kentucky Poor Law:** SUNLEY.

**Kern, Mary Root.** Song Composition: *see* ELEMENTARY SCHOOL RECORD, No. 2.

**Kern, Mary Root,** *joint author:* CHAMBERLIN, Child Religion in Song and Story.

**Kerner, Robert Joseph.** The Foundations of Slavic Bibliography. 1916. *o.p.*

**Kernodle, George R.** From Art to Theatre. Form and Convention in the Renaissance. 1944. x, 255 p. Illus. 29 cm. A44-3462. $10.00ˢ.

**Kerwin, Jerome G.** The Control of Radio. 1934. PPP 10. *o.p.*

**Kerwin, Jerome G.,** *ed.* Civil-Military Relationships in American Life. 1948. WFL. *o.p.*

**Kerwin, Jerome G.,** *joint author:* HENRY, Schools and City Government.

**Ketchum, Marshall Dana.** The Fixed Investment Trust. 1937. SBA, VII. *o.p.*

**Key to Ephesians:** GOODSPEED.

**Key Plans Showing Locations of Theban Temple Decorations:** NELSON.

**Keynes, Geoffrey,** *ed.:* BROWNE, Works of Sir Thomas Browne.

**Keynes, Geoffrey,** *ed.:* PARÉ, Apologie and Treatise.

**Keynes, John Maynard:** *see* WRIGHT, Unemployment as a World-Problem.

**Khinchin, A. Ya.** Continued Fractions. 3d ed. 1964. xi, 95 p. 21 cm. 64-15819. Cloth. $5.00ˢ. Paper. PSS525. $1.95.

**Khorsabad, I.** Excavations in the Palace and at a City Gate: LOUD.

**Khorsabad, II.** The Citadel and Town: LOUD.

**Killingsworth, Charles C.** State Labor Relations Acts. A Study of Public Policy. 1948. *o.p.*

**Kimble, Grace Eleanor.** Social Work with Travelers and Transients. A Study of Travelers Aid Work in the United States. 1935. SSM. *o.p.*

**Kincaid:** COLE.

**Kincheloe, Samuel Clarence:** *see* BOWER, Church at Work in the Modern World.

**Kindergarten and Its Relation to Elementary Education:** HARRIS.

**Kinematic and Hydrostatic Properties of Long Waves:** ROSSBY.

**Kinetic Theory of Liquids:** FISHER.

**King, Clara Breslove,** *joint author:* COLEMAN, Analytical Bibliography of Modern Language Teaching, 1932–1937.

**King, Irving.** The Psychology of Child Development. With an Introduction by John Dewey. 1903. 2d ed. 1904. *o.p.*

**King, Lester S.** The Growth of Medical Thought. 1963. xii, 254 p. Index. 22 cm. 63-9729. $5.50ˢ.

**King, Lester S.** The Medical World of the Eighteenth Century. 1958. xvii, 346 p. Illus. 22 cm. 58-7332. $5.75ˢ.

**King, Robert J.,** *joint author:* BOWMAN, Studying Children.

**King, Robert J.,** *joint author:* HAVIGHURST, Community Youth Development Program.

**King, W. O. Redman,** *trans.:* LOEB, Artificial Parthenogenesis and Fertilization.

**King Cotton Diplomacy:** OWSLEY.

**King James Version of the English Bible:** DAICHES.

**Kingdom of God:** HERRICK.

**Kingsbury, Forrest Alva,** *joint author:* KORNHAUSER, Psychological Tests in Business.

**Kingship and the Gods:** FRANKFORT.

**Kinsley, Carl.** A Systematic Method of Calculating the Dimensions of Direct-Current Dynamo-Electric Machines. 1903. *o.p.*

**Kirk, Russell.** Randolph of Roanoke. A Study in Conservative Thought. 1951. *o.p.*

**Kirk, Samuel A.** The Education of Exceptional Children. Prepared by Samuel A. Kirk, Chairman of the Society's Committee. 1950. NSSE, 49th Yrbk., Part II. xiii, 356 p. 24 cm. 50-13996. Cloth. $4.50ᵗ. Paper. $3.75ᵗ.

**Kirk, William,** *ed.* A Modern City. Providence, Rhode Island, and Its Activities. 1909. *o.p.*

**Kisch, Guido.** The Jews in Medieval Germany. A Study of Their Legal and Social Status. 1949. *o.p.*

**Kishimoto, Hideo:** *see* HAYDON, Modern Trends in World-Religions.

**Kitāb al-Zahrah:** MUḤAMMAD B. DĀWŪD AL-IṢFAHĀNĪ.

**Kitagawa, Joseph M.,** *joint ed.:* ELIADE, History of Religion and Its Methodology.

**Kitch, Ethel May.** The Origin of Subjectivity in Hindu Thought. 1917. PS *o.p.*

**Klein, Arthur Jay,** *joint author:* REEVES, University Extension Services.

**Klein, Arthur Jay,** *joint author:* REEVES, University Faculty.

**Klein, Earl Edwin.** Work Accidents to Minors in Illinois. Editorial Note by Grace Abbott. 1938. SSM. *o.p.*

**Kleines Lehrbuch des Positivismus:** MISES.

**Kleitman, Nathaniel.** Sleep Characteristics. How They Vary and React to Changing Conditions in the Group and the Individual. By N. Kleitman, F. J. Mullin, N. R. Cooperman, S. Titelbaum. 1937. *o.p.*

**Kleitman, Nathaniel.** Sleep and Wakefulness. 1939. Rev. ed. 1963. x, 552 p. Illus. 25 cm. 63-17845. CMM. $12.50ˢ.

**Kleitman, Nathaniel,** *joint author:* CARLSON, Studies on the Possible Intoxicating Action of 3.2 Per Cent Beer.

**Klem, Margaret C.,** *joint author:* FALK, Incidence of Illness.

**Klement, Frank L.** Copperheads in the Middle West. 1960. xiii, 341 p. Illus. 22 cm. 59-11623. $7.50ˢ.

**Klenze, Camillo von.** The Interpretation of Italy during the Last Two Centuries. A Contribution to the Study of Goethe's "Italienische Reise." 1907. *o.p.*

**Klenze, Camillo von.** The Treatment of Nature in the Works of Nikolaus Lenau. An Essay in Interpretation. 1902. *o.p.*

**Kligler, Israel Jacob.** The Epidemiology and Control of Malaria in Palestine. 1930. *o.p.*

**Klüver, Heinrich.** Behavior Mechanisms in Monkeys. 1933. Reprint, with new Preface, 1957. xviii, 387 p. Illus. 24 cm. 33-12360. BR. Paper. PSS503. $1.95.

**Klüver, Heinrich,** *ed.*: POLYAK, Vertebrate Visual System.

**Knapp, Joseph Grant.** The Hard Winter Wheat Pools. An Experiment in Agricultural Marketing Integration. 1933. *o.p.*

**Knapp, Robert H.** Origins of American Scientists. By R. H. Knapp and H. B. Goodrich. 1952. *o.p.*

**Knapp, Robert H.** The Younger American Scholar. His Collegiate Origins. By Robert H. Knapp and Joseph J. Greenbaum. 1953. xiii, 122 p. 26 cm. 53-8206. $3.00ˢ. (*With Wesleyan University Press.*)

**Knappen, Marshall M.** And Call It Peace. 1947. *o.p.*

**Knappen, Marshall M.** Tudor Puritanism. A Chapter in the History of Idealism. 1939. xvi, 555 p. 21 cm. 39-10082. Paper. P194. 21 cm. $3.45.

**Knight, F. B.** Report of the Society's Committee on Arithmetic. 1930. NSSE, 29th Yrbk., Parts I and II. *Part I:* Some Aspects of Modern Thought on Arithmetic. *Part II:* Research in Arithmetic. x, 709 p. 24 cm. $5.00ᵗ.

**Knight, Frank H.** On the History and Method of Economics. Selected Essays. 1956. vii, 309 p. 21 cm. 56-6632. Paper. P122. $1.95.

". . . he brings to the wider problems of ethics and philosophy the same penetration and power as to the cruxes of economic theory."—*Times Literary Supplement.*

"This book of essays will give to a resolute and patient reader an insight into the mind of one of the greatest social philosophers of our time." —G.L.S. Shackle, in *Economica.*

**Knight of Great Renown:** CLIFFORD.

**Knisely, Verona Butzer,** *joint author:* BREWINGTON, Social Concept of Money.

**Knoepfle, John.** Rivers into Islands. A Book of Poems. 1965. viii, 55 p. 21 cm. 65-18338. $3.50.

**Knowlton, Hugh.** Air Transportation in the United States. 1941. *o.p.*

**Knox, John.** Marcion and the New Testament. 1942. *o.p.*

**Knox, John.** Philemon among the Letters of Paul. A New View of Its Place and Importance. 1935. *o.p.*

**Knox, John.** Religion and the Present Crisis. 1942. WFL. *o.p.*

**Knox, T. M.,** *trans.:* HEGEL, Early Theological Writings.

**Kobrak, Heinrich G.,** *ed.* The Middle Ear. 1959. xvi, 254 p. Illus. 26 cm. 58-5619. $15.00ˢ.

**Koch, Waldemar.** The Lecithans. Their Function in the Life of the Cell. 1902. *o.p.*

**Koch, Waldemar,** *joint author:* WEBSTER, Laboratory Manual of Physiological Chemistry.

**Koenker, Ernest.** The Liturgical Renaissance in the Roman Catholic Church. 1954. xi, 272 p. 24 cm. 54-12370. $5.00ˢ.

**Köthe, Gottfried,** *ed.:* TOEPLITZ, The Calculus.

**Kogan, Herman.** The Great EB. The Story of the *Encyclopaedia Britannica.* 1958. vii, 338 p. Illus. 25 cm. 58-8379. $4.95ˢ.

**Kohn, Clyde F.,** *joint ed.:* MAYER, Readings in Urban Geography.

**Kohn, Hans:** *see* HARPER, Soviet Union and World-Problems.

**Kolb, Gwin J.,** *joint author:* SLEDD, Dr. Johnson's *Dictionary.*

**Kolbe, Hermann.** The Electrolysis of Organic Compounds. Papers by Hermann Kolbe (1845–1868). 1902. AC. *o.p.*

**Koon, Cline Morgan.** Motion Pictures in Education in the United States. A Report Compiled for the International Congress of Educational and Instructional Cinematography. By Cline M. Koon, in Collaboration with C. F. Hoban, V. C. Arnspiger, Mrs. Robbins Gilman, William Reid, and Others. 1934. *o.p.*

**Koon, Cline Morgan.** Some Public Service Broadcasting. Being a Report on the Survey Made by the National Advisory Council on Radio in Education and the Federal Office of Education. 1934. *o.p.*

**Koop, Theodore F.** The Weapon of Silence. 1946. *o.p.*

**Koopman, George Robert,** *joint author:* HEATON, College Curriculum Based on Functional Needs of Students.

**Koos, Leonard Vincent.** The Administration of Secondary-School Units. 1917. SEM, 3. *o.p.*

**Koos, Leonard Vincent.** Extra-Curricular Activities. Prepared by Leonard V. Koos, Chairman of the Society's Committee. 1926. NSSE, 25th Yrbk., Part II. *o.p.*

**Koos, Leonard Vincent.** Private and Public Secondary Education. A Comparative Study. 1931. *o.p.*

**Kornhauser, Arthur William.** How To Study. Suggestions for High-School and College Students. 1924. 2d ed. 1937. viii, 55 p. 17 cm. 37-2272. Paper. MSB. $0.50t.

**Kornhauser, Arthur William.** Psychological Tests in Business. By Arthur W. Kornhauser and Forrest A. Kingsbury. 1924. MSB. *o.p.*

**Kornhauser, Arthur William,** *ed.* Business Education for What? Proceedings of the University of Chicago Conference on Business Education, 1940. 1941. *o.p.*

**Kornhauser, Arthur William:** *see* MARSHALL, Outlines of the Economic Order.

**Kosmak, G. W.:** *see* ADAIR, Maternal Care.

**Kosok, Paul.** Modern Germany. A Study of Conflicting Loyalties. 1933. SMC. *o.p.*

**Kough, Jack,** *joint author:* BOWMAN, Mobilizing Community Resources for Maladjusted and Delinquent Youth.

**Koussy, Abdel Aziz Hamid el.** An Investigation into the Factors in Tests Involving the Visual Perception of Space. 1935. BJP. *o.p.*

**Kovalevsky, Maxime.** Russian Political Institutions. The Growth and Development of These Institutions from the Beginnings of Russian History to the Present Time. 1902. *o.p.*

**Kraeling, Carl H.,** *ed.* City Invincible. A Symposium on Urbanization and Cultural Development in the Ancient Near East. Edited for Planning Committee by Carl H. Kraeling and Robert McC. Adams. 1960. *Special Publication of the Oriental Institute of the University of Chicago. o.p.*

**Kraeling, Carl H.** Ptolemais. City of the Libyan Pentapolis. 1962. xvii, 288 p. Illus. 30 cm. 62-9742. OIP, XC. $15.00.

**Kraft, Charles Franklin.** The Strophic Structure of Hebrew Poetry as Illustrated in the First Book of the Psalter. 1938. *o.p.*

**Kramer, Samuel Noah.** Gilgamesh and the Ḫuluppu-Tree. A Reconstructed Sumerian Text. 1938. AS 10. *o.p.*

**Kramer, Samuel Noah.** Lamentation over the Destruction of Ur. 1940. AS 12, *o.p.*

**Kramer, Samuel Noah.** The Sumerian Prefix Forms be- and bi- in the Time of the Earlier Princes of Lagaš. 1936. AS 8. *o.p.*

**Kramer, Samuel Noah.** The Sumerians. Their History, Culture, and Character. 1963. xiv, 354 p. Illus. 24 cm. 63-11398. $7.95. OBE.

**Kramer, Sidney David.** A History of Stone & Kimball and Herbert S. Stone & Co., with a Bibliography of Their Publications, 1893–1905. Preface by Frederic G. Melcher. 1940. *o.p.*

**Kraus, Arthur James Israel.** Sick Society. 1929. *o.p.*

**Kraus, Herbert.** Germany in Transition. 1924. HFL. *o.p.*

**Krause, Anna.** España y la cultura española. HCLS.

**Krieger, Crypa Cecilia,** *trans.:* SIERPÍNSKI, Introduction to General Topology.

**Krieger, Leonard.** The Politics of Discretion. Pufendorf and the Acceptance of Natural Law. 1965. xii, 311 p. 22 cm. 65-14428. $6.50.

**Kristeller, Paul Oskar,** *joint ed.:* CASSIRER, Renaissance Philosophy of Man.

**Kroeber, A. L.** The Nature of Culture. 1952. x, 438 p. Illus. 26 cm. 52-12545. $10.00ˢ.

**Kroeber, A. L.** ed. Anthropology Today. An Encyclopedic Inventory. Prepared under the chairmanship of A. L. Kroeber. 1953. xv, 966 p. 25 cm. 53-6171. $10.00. *See also* TAX, Anthropology Today. Selections.

**Krogman, Wilton Marion.** A Bibliography of Human Morphology, 1914–1939. 1941. AN. *o.p.*

**Krogman, Wilton Marion:** *see* OSTEN, The Alishar Hüyük, Seasons of 1930–32. Part III.

**Krogman, Wilton Marion:** *see* SCHMIDT, The Alishar Hüyük, Seasons of 1928 and 1929. Part II.

**Kroner, Richard.** Culture and Faith. 1951. xvi, 278 p. 25 cm. 51-7837. $6.00ˢ.

**Kroner, Richard.** Kant's Weltanschauung. Translated by John E. Smith. 1956. xi, 119 p. 20 cm. $3.50ˢ. *O.I.*

**Kroner, Richard,** *ed. and trans.:* HEGEL, Early Theological Writings.

**Krughoff, Merrill Franzlau.** Salaries and Professional Qualifications of Social Workers in Chicago, 1935. 1937. SSM. *o.p.*

**Krumbein, William Christian,** *joint author:* CRONEIS, Down to Earth.

**Krumbine, Miles Henry.** A Summer Program for the Church School. 1926. PM. *o.p.*

**Kuczynski, Robert René,** *joint author:* GINI, Population.

**Kuczynski, Robert René:** *see* CASSEL, Foreign Investments.

**Kueffner, Louise Mallinckrodt.** The Development of the Historic Drama. 1911. *o.p.*

**Kufner, Herbert,** The Grammatical Structures of English and German. 1962. xii, 100 p. 25 cm. 62-19625. Paper. $2.00ᵗ.

**Kuhn, Thomas S.** The Structure of Scientific Revolutions. 1962. xvi, 172 p. 62-19621. Cloth. 25 cm. $4.00ˢ. Paper. P159. 21 cm. $1.50. IEUS, II, 2. $3.00ˢ.

**Kuiper, Gerard P.** The Atmospheres of the Earth and Planets. 1949. Rev. ed. 1952. *o.p.*

**Kuiper, Gerard P.** Photographic Lunar Atlas. 1960. *O.I.*

**Kuiper, Gerard P.,** Telescopes. Edited by Gerard P. Kuiper and Barbara M. Middlehurst. ("Stars and Stellar Systems," Vol. I.) 1960. xv, 225 p. Illus. Index. 25 cm. 60-14356. $8.50ˢ.

**Kuiper, Gerard P.** The Solar System. Gerard P. Kuiper and Barbara M. Middlehurst, *general eds. Vol. I:* The Sun. Edited by Gerard P. Kuiper. 1953. xx, 745 p. Illus. 26 cm. 54-7183. PS. $12.50ˢ. *Vol. II:* The Earth as a Planet. Edited by Gerard P. Kuiper. 1954. xvii, 751 p. Illus. 26 cm. 54-7183. PS. $12.50ˢ. *Vol. III:* Planets and Satellites. Edited by Gerard P. Kuiper and Barbara M. Middlehurst. 1961. xx, 601 p. Illus. 26 cm. 54-7183. $12.50ˢ. *Vol. IV:* The Moon, Meteorites, and Comets. Edited by Barbara M. Middlehurst and Gerard P. Kuiper. 1963. xxii, 810 p. Illus. Index. 26 cm. 62-18117. $15.00ˢ.

**Kuiper, Gerard P.,** *general ed.:* Stars and Stellar Systems. Compendium of Astronomy and Astrophysics. With Barbara M. Middlehurst, *associate general ed.:*

*Vol. I:* Telescopes. Edited by Gerard P. Kuiper and Barbara M. Middlehurst. 1960. Published. $8.50ˢ.
*Vol. II:* Astronomical Techniques. Edited by W. A. Hiltner. 1962. Published. $16.50ˢ.
*Vol. III:* Basic Astronomical Data. Edited by K. Aa. Strand and Daniel Harris. 1963. Published. $12.50ˢ.
*Vol. IV:* Clusters and Binaries. Edited by Harold Weaver.
*Vol. V:* Galactic Structure. Edited by Adriaan Blaauw and Maarten Schmidt. 1965. Published. $15.00ˢ.
*Vol. VI:* Stellar Atmospheres. Edited by

Jesse L. Greenstein. 1961. Published. $17.50ˢ.

*Vol. VII:* Nebulae and Interstellar Matter. Edited by Barbara M. Middlehurst and Lawrence H. Aller.

*Vol. VIII:* Stellar Structure. Edited by Lawrence H. Aller and Dean McLaughlin. 1965. Published. $17.50ˢ.

*Vol. IX:* Galaxies and the Universe. Edited by Dr. Allan Sandage and Mrs. Allan Sandage.

**Kullerud, Gunnar,** *joint ed.:* BROWN, Bibliography on Meteorites.

**Kummer, Anna P.** Weed Seedlings. 1951. *o.p.*

**Kumulipo:** BECKWITH.

**Kuo, Ping Wen:** *see* SOYESHIMA, Oriental Interpretations of the Far Eastern Problem.

**Kurland, Philip B.,** *ed.* The Supreme Court and the Constitution. Essays in Constitutional Law from *The Supreme Court Review.* 1965. viii, 324 p. 21 cm. Paper. P203. $2.45.

**Kurland, Philip B.,** *ed.* The Supreme Court Review 1961. 1961. vii, 332 p. 24 cm. 60-14353. $6.50ˢ.

**Kurland, Philip B.,** *ed.* The Supreme Court Review 1962. 1962. vii, 327 p. 24 cm. 60-14353. $6.50ˢ.

**Kurland, Philip B.,** *ed.* The Supreme Court Review 1963. 1963. vii, 356 p. 24 cm. 60-14353. $6.50ˢ.

**Kurland, Philip B.,** *ed.* The Supreme Court Review 1964. 1964. vii, 316 p. 24 cm. 60-14353. $6.50ˢ.

**Kurland, Philip B.,** *ed.* The Supreme Court Review 1965. 1965. vii, 288 p. 24 cm. 60-14353. $6.95ˢ.

**Kurland, Philip B.,** *joint ed.:* DUNHAM, Mr. Justice.

**Kurrah Papyri from Aphrodito in the Oriental Institute:** ABBOTT.

**Kyrk, Hazel.** The Family in the American Economy. 1953. xiii, 407 p. 25 cm. 53-12266. $6.75ᵗ.

**La Barre, Weston.** The Human Animal. 1954. xv, 372 p. 54-12371. Cloth. 24 cm. $6.75ˢ. Paper. P45. 21 cm. $1.95.

"The biggest piece of business left unfinished by the first wave of Darwinians was to account for human social activity. . . . In 'The Human Animal,' Weston La Barre has written the first general book, and one entirely suited to the non-professional reader, addressed directly to this point. . . . Anyone can get a sound, lively, unhackneyed account of man's nature and evolution from the book."—William Howells, in *The Saturday Review.*

**Labial Terminations:** STURTEVANT.

**Labidosaurus Cope:** WILLISTON.

**Labor Looks at Unemployment Insurance:** MC-CARTHY.

**Labor Productivity Functions:** NICHOLLS.

**Laboratory Guide in Bacteriology:** HEINE-MANN.

**Laboratory Introduction to Animal Ecology and Taxonomy:** PARK.

**Laboratory Manual for Comparative Vertebrate Anatomy:** HYMAN.

**Laboratory Manual for Elementary Zoölogy:** HYMAN.

**Laboratory Manual for Physiological Chemistry:** WEBSTER.

**Laboratory Material To Accompany** *Principles of Accounting:* HODGE.

**Laboratory Outline of Embryology:** LILLIE.

**Laboratory Outlines in Bacteriology and Immunology:** NORTON.

**Laboring and Dependent Classes in Colonial America:** JERNEGAN.

**Labovitz, I. M.:** *see* LELAND, State-Local Fiscal Relations.

**Lach, Donald F.** Asia in the Making of Europe. 1965. *Vol. I, Books* 1 and 2. The Century of Discovery. xl, 965 p. 24 cm. 64-19848. Illus. The set, $20.00.

**Ladefoged, Peter.** Elements of Acoustic Phonetics. 1962. viii, 120 p. Index. 23 cm. 62-8349. $3.50ᵗ. CUSA.

**Ladenburg, Albert.** Lectures on the History of the Development of Chemistry since the Time of Lavoisier. By Dr. A. Ladenburg, Professor of Chemistry in the University of Breslau. Translated for the Second German Edition by Leonard Dobbin. (With additions and corrections by the author.) 1900. AC. *o.p.*

**Ladewick, Esther.** Scholarships for Children of Working Age. A Study Made for the Scholarship Association for Jewish Children in Chicago. With a Prefatory Note by Edith Abbott. 1929. SSM. *o.p.*

**La Farge, Oliver.** Santa Eulalia. The Religion of a Cuchumatán Indian Town. 1947. AN. *o.p.*

**Lafayette between the American and the French Revolution:** GOTTSCHALK.

**Lafayette and the Close of the American Revolution:** GOTTSCHALK.

**Lafayette Comes to America:** GOTTSCHALK.

**Lafayette Joins the American Army:** GOTTSCHALK.

**Lagendorf, Richard,** *joint author:* KATZ, Introduction to the Interpretation of the Electrocardiogram.

**Laing, Gordon Jennings.** The Genitive of Value in Latin and Other Constructions with Verbs of Rating. 1920. *o.p.*

**Laing, Gordon Jennings,** *ed.* Publications of the Members of the University [of Chicago], 1902–1916. Compiled on the Twenty-fifth Anniversary of the Foundation of the University by a Committee of the Faculty. Gordon J. Laing, Editor. 1917. *o.p.*

**Lamentation over the Destruction of Ur:** KRAMER.

**La Meslee, A. Marin,** *joint author:* COLEMAN, Soldat américain en France.

**Lamon, Robert Scott.** Megiddo. I. Seasons of 1925–34. Strata I–V. By Robert S. Lamon and Geoffrey M. Shipton. 1939. xxvii, 235 p. Illus. 30 cm. 40-1002. OIP, XLII. $20.00.

**Lamon, Robert Scott.** The Megiddo Water System. 1935. xii, 41 p. Illus. 30 cm. 35-22353. OIP, XXXII. $3.00.

**Lancelot and Guenevere:** CROSS.

**Land, W. J. G.** Double Fertilization in Compositae. 1900. HB. *o.p.*

**Land, W. J. G.** A Morphological Study of Thuja. 1902. HB. *o.p.*

**Land behind Baghdad:** ADAMS.

**Land und Leute:** HAGBOLDT.

**Land Planning:** GRAY.

**Land Utilization in China:** BUCK.

**Land Utilization and Rural Economy in Korea:** LEE.

**Landis, Benson Young.** Social Aspects of Farmers' Co-operative Marketing. Bulletin No. 4 of the Department of Research and Education, Federal Council of the Churches of Christ in America. 1925. *o.p.*

**Landis, Benson Young,** *ed.* Handbook of Rural Social Resources, 1928. 1928. ACLA. *o.p.*

**Landis, Benson Young,** *joint ed.:* ISRAEL, Handbook of Rural Social Resources.

**Landis, Carney:** *see* LASHLEY, Studies in the Dynamics of Behavior.

**Landmarks in Political Economy:** HAMILTON.

**Landon, Kenneth P.** Southeast Asia. Crossroad of Religions. 1949. CR. *o.p.*

**Landry, Joseph A.** Graded French Word and Idiom Book. HCLS.

**Landtman, Gunnar.** The Origin of the Inequality of the Social Classes. 1938. *o.p.*

**Lane, Ernest Preston.** Metric Differential Geometry of Curves and Surfaces. 1940. viii, 216 p. Illus. 24 cm. 40-12579. $6.00ˢ.

**Lane, Ernest Preston.** Projective Differential Geometry of Curves and Surfaces. 1932. SCI. *o.p.*

**Lane, Ernest Preston.** A Treatise on Projective Differential Geometry. 1942. *o.p.*

**Lang, Richard Otto,** *joint ed.:* NEWCOMB, Census Data of the City of Cihcago, 1934.

**Lange, Luise,** *trans.:* TOEPLITZ, The Calculus.

**Lange, Oscar,** *ed.* Studies in Mathematical Economics and Econometrics. In Memory of Henry Schultz. Edited by Oscar Lange, Francis McIntyre, and Theodore O. Yntema. 1942. *o.p.*

**Langendorf, Richard,** *joint author:* KATZ, Interpretation of Electrocardiogram.

**Langlois, Charles Victor.** The Historic Rôle of France among the Nations. An Address Delivered at the University of Chicago, October 18, 1904. [Translated by Thomas Atkinson Jenkins.] 1905. *o.p.*

**Langsdorff, Alexander.** Tall-i-Bakun A. Season of 1932. By Alexander Langsdorff and Donald E. McCown. 1942. xi, 81 p. Illus. 24 cm. 42-16461. OIP, LIX. $10.00.

**Language Change and Linguistic Reconstruction:** HOENIGSWALD.

**Language in Culture:** HOIJER.

**Language Learning:** HAGBOLDT.

**Language and Literature:** DUNCAN.

**Language Reading Report Blanks:** BOND.

**Lansberg, H.** A Climatic Study of Cloudiness over Japan. 1944. DMMR 15. *o.p.*

**Lanzl, Elisabeth P.,** *trans.:* LENZ, Medical Genetics.

**Lanzl, Elisabeth P.,** *trans.:* WACHSMANN, Moving Field Radiation Therapy.

**Lanzl, L. H.,** *joint ed.:* WACHSMANN, Moving Field Radiation Therapy.

**Lardner, Ring.** Gullible's Travels. 1925. *Reissue,* 1965. Introduction by Josephine Herbst. xvii, 140 p. 21 cm. 65-24435. CF. 160 p. $3.95.

**Larson, John Augustus.** Lying and Its Detection. A Study of Deception and Deception Tests. By John A. Larson in Collaboration with George W. Haney and Leonarde Keeler. With an Introduction by August Vollmer. 1922. *o.p.*

"The author is probably the best qualified person in the country to discuss the topic, having been a pioneer in the field and having devoted most of his interest to it in recent years. His treatment is scientific and conservative."— *New York University Law Quarterly Review.*

**Larson, Martin Alfred.** The Modernity of Milton. A Theological and Philosophical Interpretation. 1927. *o.p.*

**Lasch, Robert.** Breaking the Building Blockade. 1946. *o.p.*

**Lashley, Karl Spencer.** Brain Mechanisms and Intelligence. A Quantitative Study of Injuries to the Brain. 1929. BR. *o.p.*

**Lashley, Karl Spencer,** *ed.* Studies in the Dynamics of Behavior. By Calvin P. Stone, Chester W. Darrow, Lena L. Heath, and Carney Landis, 1932. BR. *o.p.*

**Lasker, Bruno.** Filipino Immigration to Continental United States and to Hawaii. 1931. IPR. *o.p.*

**Lasker, Bruno,** *ed.* Problems of the Pacific, 1931. Proceedings of the Fourth Conference of the Institute of Pacific Relations, Hangchow and Shanghai, China, October 21 to November 2, 1931. Edited by Bruno Lasker, Assisted by W. L. Holland. 1932. IPR. *o.p.*

**Lasker, Bruno,** *ed.* Problems of the Pacific, 1933. Economic Conflict and Control. Proceedings of the Fifth Conference of the Institute of Pacific Relations, Banff, Canada, August 14–26, 1933. Edited by Bruno Lasker and W. L. Holland. 1934. IPR. *o.p.*

**Lasswell, Harold Dwight.** Psychopathology and Politics. 1930. *o.p.*

**Lasswell, Harold Dwight,** *joint author:* WAPLES, National Libraries and Foreign Scholarship.

**Lasswell, Harold Dwight:** *see* SMITH, Chicago, An Experiment in Social Science Research.

**Lasswell, Harold Dwight:** *see* WRIGHT, Public Opinion and World-Politics.

**Last Four Lives of Annie Besant:** NETHERCOT.

**Last Trek of the Indians:** FOREMAN.

**Later Realism:** MYERS.

**Latham, Earl,** *ed.* The Philosophy and Policies of Woodrow Wilson. 1958. *O.I.*

**Latin Epigrams of Thomas More:** BRADNER.

**Latin Reader for Colleges:** LEVY.

**Latin Third Declension:** LINSCOTT.

**Latin Treatises on Comets:** THORNDIKE.

**Latitude and Longitude of the Yerkes Observatory:** HALE.

**Latourette, Kenneth Scott:** *see* HODOUS, Careers for Students of Chinese Language and Civilization.

**Lattimore, Richmond,** *trans.* Greek Lyrics. xvii, 82 p. 21 cm. 60-51619. Rev. ed. 1960. Cloth. $4.00ˢ. Paper. P48. $1.35.

**Lattimore, Richmond,** *trans.:* HOMER, Iliad.

**Lattimore, Richmond,** *trans.:* PINDAR, Odes.

**Lattimore, Richmond,** *joint ed.:* COMPLETE GREEK TRAGEDIES.

**Lattimore, Richmond,** *joint ed.:* GREEK TRAGEDIES.

**Laughlin, James Laurence.** Credit. 1902. *o.p.*

**Laughlin, James Laurence.** Gold and Prices since 1873. 1895. *o.p.*

**Laughlin, James Laurence.** A New Exposition of Money, Credit, and Prices. 2 vols. 1931. *o.p.*

**Laughlin, James Laurence,** *trans.:* ELLSTAETTER, Indian Silver Currency.

**Laune, Ferris Finley,** *joint ed.:* FARIS, Intelligent Philanthropy.

**Laves, Kurt.** The Orbit of the Minor Planet (334). 1904. *o.p.*

**Laves, Walter Herman Carl.** Inter-American Solidarity. 1941. HFL. *o.p.*

**Laves, Walter Herman Carl.** The Middle West Looks at War. By Walter H. C. Laves and Francis O. Wilcox. 1940. PPP 32. *o.p.*

**Laves, Walter Herman Carl,** *ed.* The Foundations of a More Stable World Order. By Ferdinand Schevill, Jacob Viner, Charles C. Colby, Quincy Wright, J. Fred Rippy, Walter H. C. Laves. 1941. HFL. *o.p.*

**Laves, Walter Herman Carl,** *ed.:* BENEŠ, International Security.

**Law and Business:** SPENCER.

**Law and Citizenship:** GETTYS.

**Law and Freedom:** COE.

**Law of Gravitation in Relativity:** LEVINSON.

**Law of Guardian and Ward:** TAYLOR.

**Law and Liability in Pupil Transportation:** PUNKE.

**Law and Social Work:** BRADWAY.

**Lawler, Eugene S.** Educational Administration in an Era of Transition. By Eugene S. Lawler and Dan H. Cooper. 1949. AOPPS, XII. *o.p.*

**Laws of Ecclesiastical Polity:** HOOKER.

**Laws of Social Psychology:** ZNANIECKI.

**Lawrence, D. H.:** *see* GOODHEART, The Utopian Vision of D. H. Lawrence.

**Lawrence, Evelyn Mary.** An Investigation into the Relation between Intelligence and Inheritance. 1931. BJP. *o.p.*

**Lawrence, Isabel.** The Course of Study in History in the Common School. By Isabel Lawrence and others. 1903. NSSE, 2d Yrbk., Part I. *o.p.*

**Lawson, Douglas E.** Curriculum Development in City School Systems. 1940. *o.p.*

**Lawyer and the Public:** AMERICAN BAR ASSOCIATION, *Council on Legal Education and Admissions to the Bar.*

**Lawyers and Litigants in Ancient Athens:** BONNER.

**Lay My Burden Down:** BOTKIN.

**Lazarsfeld, Paul F.,** *joint author:* BERELSON, Voting.

**Leadership in American Education:** GRACE.

**League of Nations Map:** MARTIN.

**Leal, Luis,** *joint ed.:* CASTILLO, Antología de la literatura mexicana.

**Lear, Floyd Seyward,** *joint ed.:* DREW, Perspectives in Medieval History.

**Learner in Education for the Professions:** TOWLE.

**Learning and Instruction:** ANDERSON.

**Learning To Draw:** TODD.

**Learning To Listen:** COOPER.

**Learning To Look:** TAYLOR.

**Leary, Bernice Elizabeth,** *joint author:* GRAY, What Makes a Book Readable.

**Leaves of Grass:** *see* BOWERS, Whitman's Manuscripts. *See also* MILLER, Critical Guide to *Leaves of Grass.*

**Leavitt, Harold J.** Managerial Psychology. 2d ed. 1964. 22 cm. 64-16950. Cloth. $6.00. Paper. $2.75ᵗ.

"L'ultimo capitolo sul comportamento degli imprenditori in talune situazioni correnti . . . reca spunti di vivo interesse."—*Rivista di economia politica L'Industria.*

". . . it is a remarkable example of the best in behavioral science knowledge distilled by an empathetic pro who wants his managerial audience to get the message painlessly. . . . The overall effect is a tremendously meaty volume of on-the-frontier knowledge for the manager, whether in a line or staff activity."—Julius E. Eitington in *Personnel Administration.*

**Leavitt, Harold J.** *ed.* Readings in Managerial Psychology. Edited by Harold J. Leavitt and Louis R. Pondy. 1964. 22 cm. 64-15811. Cloth. $8.50ˢ. Paper. $4.75ᵗ.

**Leberman, Josephine Marie.** The Christian Way. Stories by E. May Munsell, and Songs by Blanche D. Springer. 1929. CS. *o.p.*

**Lecithans:** KOCH.

**Lecturas introductorias:** CASTILLO.

**Lecture Demonstrations for General Psychology:** SCHEIDEMANN.

**Lectures on the Calculus of Variations:** BLISS.

**Lectures on Commerce:** HATFIELD.

**Lectures on Geology:** WALKER.

**Lectures on the History of the Development of Chemistry:** LADENBURG.

**Lectures on Japan:** NITOBÉ.

**Lee, John C.,** *joint author:* SNIDER, Stereotaxic Atlas of the Monkey Brain.

**Lee, Maurice Wentworth.** Anti-Chain-Store Tax Legislation. 1939. SBA, IX. *o.p.*

**Lee, Oliver Justin.** Parallaxes of Eighty Stars. 1936. YO, VIII. *o.p.*

**Lee, Oliver Justin.** Zone +45° of Kapteyn's Selected Areas. Parallaxes and Proper Motions of 1041 Stars. 1926. YO, IV. *o.p.*

**Lee, Oliver Justin:** *see* SLOCUM, Stellar Parallaxes.

**Lee, Otis.** Existence and Inquiry. A Study of Thought in the Modern World. 1949. *o.p.*

**Lee, Roger Irving.** The Fundamentals of Good Medical Care. An Outline of the Fundamentals of Good Medical Care and an Estimate of the Service Required To Supply the Medical Needs of the United States. By Roger I. Lee, M.D., and Lewis Webster Jones, assisted by Barbara Jones. 1933. CMC 22. *o.p.*

**Lee, William George.** Childbirth. An Outline of Its Essential Features and the Art of Its Management. 1928. CMM. *o.p.*

**Leech, Clifford.** Shakespeare. The Tragedies. A Collection of Critical Essays. Edited with an Introduction by Clifford Leech. 1965. xvii, 140 p. 21 cm. 65-17295. Cloth. $6.50ˢ. PLC 2. Paper. $2.45.

**LeFevre, Perry D.,** *ed.* The Prayers of Kierkegaard. 1956. ix, 245 p. 21 cm. 56-11000. Cloth. $4.50ˢ. Paper. P131. $1.75.

**Legacy of Asia and Western Man:** WATTS.

**Legal Aspects of Zoning:** BAKER.

**Legal Nature of Corporations:** FREUND.

**Legal Protection of Woman:** RULLKOETTER.

**Legal Tender:** BRECKINRIDGE.

**Legal Terms Common to the Macedonian Inscriptions:** FERGUSON.

**Legislative Background of the Fair Labor Standards Act:** PHELPS.

**Legislative History of Naturalization:** FRANKLIN.

**Legislative Loss Distribution in Negligence Actions:** GREGORY.

**Legislative Way of Life:** SMITH.

**Legislatures:** REED.

**Lehman, Paul,** *trans.:* RICHTER, Re-educating Germany.

**Lehmann, Karl.** Thomas Jefferson. American Humanist. Foreword by Dumas Malone. *Reissue,* 1965. xx, 273 p. 21 cm. 64-66318. Paper. P181. $2.45.

**Lehrbuch der koptischen Grammatik:** STEINDORFF.

**Leibniz:** LOEMKER.

**Leigh, Robert D.,** *ed.* A Free and Responsible Press. A General Report on Mass Communication: Newspapers, Radio, Motion Pictures, Magazines, and Books. By the Commission on Freedom of the Press. 1947. xii, 139 p. 21 cm. A46-13. $3.50s.

**Leigh, Robert D.,** *joint author:* WHITE, Peoples Speaking to Peoples.

**Leipziger, H. C.** The City School as a Community Center. By H. C. Leipziger and others. 1911. NSSE, 10th Yrbk., Part I. *o.p.*

**Leiserson, Avery.** Administrative Regulation. A Study in Representation of Interests. 1942. PA. *o.p.*

**Leisler's Rebellion:** REICH.

**Leland, Simeon Elbridge,** *ed.* State-Local Fiscal Relations in Illinois. By Neil H. Jacoby, Rex J. Morthland, I. M. Labovitz, Mildred Fishman, Daniel Scheinman, Clarence Philbrook, W. F. Lougheed, George W. Mitchell, G. Leland Bach. Some Observations on Intergovernmental Fiscal Relationships, by Simeon E. Leland. 1941. SSCI. *o.p.*

**Lemon, Harvey Brace.** The Demonstration Laboratory of Physics at the University of Chicago. By Harvey B. Lemon and Fitz-Hugh Marshall. 1939. *o.p.*

**Lemon, Harvey Brace.** From Galileo to the Nuclear Age. 1946. (Rev. ed. of *From Galileo to Cosmic Rays.*) xviii, 451 p. Illus. Index. A46-6075. Cloth. 26 cm. NPL. $7.50s. Paper. 24 cm. PSS506. $2.95.

"This is an extraordinary and notable volume: a 'text book' on one of the most abstruse of the sciences [physics] that can actually be read, enjoyed and depended upon by student and layman alike."—*The New Republic* reviewing the first edition.

"At last a delightful textbook! In all the years that I have been reviewing scientific texts I have been often fascinated but I have seldom used

exclamation points. But this book deserves a fanfare."—Gerald Wendt, in the *New York Herald Tribune.*

**Lemon, Harvey Brace,** *joint author:* FERENCE, Analytical Experimental Physics.

**Lemon, Harvey Brace:** *see* MOULTON, World and Man.

**Lemon, Harvey Brace:** *see* NEWMAN, Nature of the World and of Man.

**Leningrad, 1941:** PAVLOV.

**Lennard, Reginald Vivian,** *joint author:* HOBSON, Some Aspects of Recent British Economics.

**Lenz, Widukind.** Medical Genetics. Translated by Elisabeth P. Lanzl. 1963. xiv, 218 p. Illus. 26 cm. 63-11399. $6.50s.

**Lenzen, Victor F.** Procedures of Empirical Science. 1938. vii, 59 p. 26 cm. A42-5468. Paper. IEUS, I, 5. $1.50s.

**León, Luis Ponce de.** La perfecta casada. Texto del Siglo XVI. Reimpresión de la Tercera Edición, con Variantes de la Primera, y un Prólogo. Por Elizabeth Wallace. 1903. *o.p.*

**Leonard, Neil.** Jazz and the White Americans. The Acceptance of a New Art Form. 1962. iv, 216 p. 23 cm. 62-19626. $4.50s.

**Leonardo da Vinci:** DOUGLAS.

**Leonhardt, Hans L.** Nazi Conquest of Danzig. 1942. *o.p.*

**Leopard's Spots:** STANTON.

**Leopold, Werner F.** Reise durch Deutschland. A Cultural First Reader. HCLS.

**Leopold, Werner F.** Ein Sommer in Deutschland. HCLS.

**Lepawsky, Albert.** Home Rule for Metropolitan Chicago. 1935. SSCI. *o.p.*

**Lepawsky, Albert.** The Judicial System of Metropolitan Chicago. 1932. SSCI. *o.p.*

**Lepawsky, Albert,** *joint author:* MERRIAM, The Government of the Metropolitan Region of Chicago.

**Leppard, Henry Milton:** *see* COLBY, Geographic Aspects of International Relations.

**Leppard, Henry Milton:** *see* GOODE, Base Maps.

**Leprince-Ringuet, Louis.** Atoms and Men. 1961. ix, 118 p. 23 cm. 61-11292. $3.00ˢ.

**Lerner, Monroe.** Health Progress in the United States, 1900–1960. By Monroe Lerner and Odin W. Anderson. 1963. xvi, 354 p. Illus. 24 cm. 63-18854. $6.50ˢ.

**Lesebuch für Anfänger:** HAGBOLDT.

**Lesser, Simon,** *joint author:* WORKS, Rural America Today.

**Let's Join the Human Race:** BARR.

**Let's Talk It Over:** WIESE.

**Letters of the Rᵐ 2 Collection:** BERRY.

**Leuchtenburg, William E.** The Perils of Prosperity: 1914–32. 1958. ix, 313 p. 21 cm. 58-5680. Cloth. CHAC. $4.50ˢ. Paper. $1.95.
". . . this little survey of politics, diplomacy and social and economic changes retains considerable freshness because of its independent evaluations, its apt illustrations, its use of the latest scholarly studies and its skillfully organized narrative."—Harvey Wish, in *The New York Times Book Review.*

**Leuck, Miriam Eleanor Simons.** A Further Study of Dental Clinics in the United States. By Miriam Simons Leuck. Statistical Adviser: Charles A. R. Wardwell. 1932. ADA. *o.p.*

**Leuck, Miriam Eleanor Simons.** A Study of Dental Clinics in the United States: 1930. By Miriam Simons Leuck. Statistical Adviser: Charles A. R. Wardwell. 1932. ADA. *o.p.*

**Levarie, Siegmund.** Mozart's *Le Nozze di Figaro:* A Critical Analysis. 1952. *o.p.*

**Leven, Maurice.** The Incomes of Physicians. An Economic and Statistical Analysis. 1932. CMC 24. *o.p.*

**Leven, Maurice.** The Practice of Dentistry and the Incomes of Dentists in Twenty States, 1929. Based upon data collected under the direction of Dorothy Fahs Beck. 1932. ADA. *o.p.*

**Levi, Edward H.** An Introduction to Legal Reasoning. 1949. Rev. ed. 1962. viii, 104 p. 21 cm. 49-11213. $3.00ˢ. 1962. Paper. P84. $1.50.
". . . Law, even when it is devoutly capitalized as The Law, is not an independent entity, creating, acting, reasoning. . . . [It] certainly arises from these activities, but they are activities carried on by human beings. To know what the law is we must endeavor to follow . . . the mental processes. 'Legal Reasoning,' then, means the mental processes of judges, which, at our legal peril, we must understand. I cannot imagine a better introduction and guide . . . than this first rate book of Professor Levi of Chicago."—Max Radin, in *The Journal of Legal Education.*

**Levi, Julian H.** Municipal and Institutional Relations within Boston. The Benefits of the Federal Housing Act of 1961. 1964. 157 p. 28 cm. 64-10497. Paper. $4.00ˢ.

**Levin, M. G.,** *ed.* The Peoples of Siberia. Edited by M. G. Levin and L. P. Potapov. 1964. viii, 948 p. 24 cm. 62-18118. $20.00ˢ.

**Levine, Donald N.** Wax and Gold. Tradition and Innovation in Ethiopian Culture. 1965. Illus. xvi, 315 p. 24 cm. 65-18340. $10.00ˢ.

**Levine, Rachmiel,** *joint author:* SOSKIN, Carbohydrate Metabolism.

**Levinson, Horace Clifford.** The Law of Gravitation in Relativity. By Horace C. Levinson and Ernest Bloomfield Zeisler. 1929. 2d ed. 1931. *o.p.*

**Levi Setti, Riccardo.** Elementary Particles. Lecture Notes from a Course in Elementary Particles Given at the University of Chicago in 1963. 1963. 172 p. 22 cm. 63-22713. CLP. Paper. $2.00ᵗ.

**Levy, H. L.** A Latin Reader for Colleges. Reprint. 1962. x, 264 p. 21 cm. 62-18119. Paper. $2.50ᵗ.

**Lewis, Ben William.** Price and Production Control in British Industry. 1927. PPP 25. *o.p.*

**Lewis, Edwin Herbert.** The History of the English Paragraph. 1894. ENG. *o.p.*

**Lewis, Edwin Herbert.** University of Chicago Poems. 1923. *o.p.*

**Lewis, Exum Percival.** The Measurement of Some Standard Wave-Lengths in the Infra-Red Spectra of the Elements. 1895. *o.p.*

**Lewis, Frank Grant.** How the Bible Grew. The Story as Told by the Book and Its Keepers. 1919. HER. *o.p.*

**Lewis, Frank Grant.** The Irenaeus Testimony to the Fourth Gospel. Its Extent, Meaning, and Value. 1908. HLL. *o.p.*

**Lewis, Frank Grant:** *see* BAPTIST CONGRESS, Author, Title, and Subject Index.

**Lewis, H. Gregg.** Unionism and Relative Wages in the United States. An Empirical Inquiry. 1963. xvii, 308 p. 24 cm. 63-20915. ERS. $7.50ˢ.

**Lewis Henry Morgan:** STERN.

**Lewis, James C., Jr.** Teaching in the Army. 1920. *o.p.*

**Lewis, Julian H.** The Biology of the Negro. 1942. *o.p.*

**Lewis, Lloyd:** *see* RANEY, If Lincoln Had Lived.

**Lewis, Margaret R.:** *see* COWDRY, General Cytology.

**Lewis, R. W. B.** The American Adam. 1955. vi, 201 p. 21 cm. 55-5133. Cloth, $6.00ˢ. Paper. P38. $1.50.

**Lewis, Warren H.:** *see* COWDRY, General Cytology.

**Lexicographical and Historical Study of** Διαθήκη: NORTON.

**Lexicographical Study of the Greek Inscriptions:** SEARLES.

**Leyendas épicas de España, prosificación moderna:** BOGGS.

**Li, Ching Chun.** Population Genetics. 1955. xi, 366 p. Illus. 24 cm. 55-5134. BM. CLBS. $12.00ᵗ.

**Li, Fang-Kuei.** Mattole. An Athabaskan Language. 1930. viii, 152 p. AN. $3.00.

**Li, Hung-Chiung,** *joint author:* FRAZIER, Racial Variations in Immunity to Syphilis.

**Libby, Willard F.** Radiocarbon Dating. 1952. 2d rev. ed. 1955. xi, 175 p. Illus. 21 cm. 55-10246. PS. $5.00ˢ.

"Important book. . . . The radiocarbon method has by no means reached a final stage of devel-

opment. . . . It may be anticipated that the method will become more accurate and usable over a longer time span . . . and that greater insight will be gained into the biological and chemical problems of sample reliability. For an understanding of these future developments Libby's book is basic."—Donald Collier, in *The American Anthropologist.*

**Liberal Arts College:** REEVES.

**Liberman, Simon.** Building Lenin's Russia. Translated by Albert Parry. 1945. *o.p.*

**Librarians, Scholars, and Booksellers:** BUTLER.

**Libraries and Readers in the State of New York:** WAPLES.

**Library:** WAPLES.

**Library Catalogs:** STROUT.

**Library in the Community:** CARNOVSKY.

**Library Extension:** JOECKEL.

**Library Extension under the WPA:** STANFORD.

**Library in General Education:** WILSON.

**Library Institute at the University of Chicago:** *see* UNIVERSITY OF CHICAGO STUDIES IN LIBRARY SCIENCE.

**Library and the Radio:** HYERS.

**Library Science:** *see* UNIVERSITY OF CHICAGO STUDIES IN LIBRARY SCIENCE.

**Library Trends:** WILSON.

**Licensing of Boarding Homes, Maternity Homes, and Child Welfare Agencies:** FRASER.

**Lichtheim, Miriam.** Demotic Ostraca from Medinet Habu. 1957. 96 p. Illus. 31 cm. 57-9105. OIP, LXXX. $12.50.

**Lichtheim, Miriam,** *joint author:* STEFANSKI, Coptic Ostraca from Medinet Habu.

**Liddle, Gordon,** *joint author:* BOWMAN, Mobilizing Community Resources for Maladjusted and Delinquent Youth.

**Lieberman, Myron.** The Future of Public Education. 1960. ix, 294 p. 59-15108. Cloth. 23 cm. $5.00ˢ. Paper. P94. 21 cm. $1.75.

**Life, Andrew C.** The Tuber-like Rootlets of Cycas revoluta. 1901. HB. *o.p.*

**Life of Christ:** BURGESS.

**Life of Christ:** BURTON.

**Life of Christ. A Series of Direction Sheets:** BURTON.

**Life and Correspondence of Lodowick Bryskett:** PLOMER.

**Life of George Rogers Clark:** JAMES.

**Life-History of Polysiphonia Violacea:** YAMA-NOUCHI.

**Life of Jesus:** GATES.

**Life of Karl Follen:** SPINDLER.

**Life of Lieutenant General Chaffee:** CARTER.

**Life of Niccolò Machiavelli:** RIDOLFI.

**Life. Origin and Development:** EHRENSVÄRD.

**Life of Paul:** ROBINSON.

**Life of Petrarch:** WILKINS.

**Life and Repentaunce of Marie Magdalene:** WAGER.

**Life and Times of Emil H. Grubbe:** HODGES.

**Life and Works of Francis Hopkinson:** HASTINGS.

**Light, N. Searle.** Early Childhood Education. Prepared by N. Searle Light, Chairman of the Society's Committee. 1947. NSSE, 46th Yrbk., Part II. xii, 390, xlix p. 24 cm. 48-293. Cloth. $4.50$^t$. Paper. $3.75$^t$.

**Light Waves:** MICHELSON.

**Lillie, Frank Rattray.** A Laboratory Outline of Embryology with Special Reference to the Chick and the Pig. By Frank R. Lillie and Carl R. Moore. 1919. 3d ed. 1934. x, 67 p. 19 cm. Paper. $1.50$^t$.

**Lillie, Frank Rattray.** Problems of Fertilization. 1919. SCI *o.p.*

**Lillie, Frank Rattray.** The Woods Hole Marine Biological Laboratory. 1944. *o.p.*

**Lillie, Frank Rattray:** *see* COWDRY, General Cytology.

**Lillie, Ralph S.** General Biology and the Philosophy of Organism. 1945. BM. *o.p.*

**Lillie, Ralph S.** Protoplasmic Action and Nervous Action. 1923. 2d ed. 1932. SCI. *o.p.*

**Lillie, Ralph S.:** *see* COWDRY, General Cytology.

**Limited War:** OSGOOD.

**Limper, Louis H.,** *ed.* Le petit chose. By Alphonse Daudet. HCLS.

**Lincoln, Abraham.** Lincoln's Last Speech in Springfield in the Campaign of 1858. Edited and with an introduction by Oliver R. Barrett. 1925. *o.p.*

**Lincoln and the Convention of 1860:** PROCTOR.

**Lincoln and Douglas Debates:** WHITE.

**Lincoln, Living Legend:** SMITH.

**Lincoln's "House Divided" Speech:** COLE.

**Lincoln's Last Speech:** LINCOLN.

**Lind, Andrew William.** An Island Community. Ecological Succession in Hawaii. 1938. *o.p.*

**Lind, L. R.,** *trans.:* CARPI, Short Introduction to Anatomy.

**Lindman, Frank T.,** *ed.* The Mentally Disabled and the Law. Edited by Frank T. Lindman and Donald M. McIntyre, Jr. 1961. xiii, 445 p. 28 cm. 61-14537. $7.50$^s$.

**Lindsey, Almont.** The Pullman Strike. The Story of a Unique Experiment and of a Great Labor Upheaval. 1943. xi, 385 p. 21 cm. 64-23413. Paper. P165. $2.95.

**Line, William.** The Growth of Visual Perception in Children. 1931. BJP. *o.p.*

**Linear Polars of the $k$-Hedron in $n$-Space:** MACNEISH.

**Linford, Alton A.** Old Age Assistance in Massachusetts. 1949. SSM. *o.p.*

**Lingel, Robert.** Educational Broadcasting. A Bibliography. 1932. *o.p.*

**Linguistic Aspects of Science:** BLOOMFIELD.

**Linguistic Change:** STURTEVANT.

**Linguistic and Exegetical Studies:** *see* UNIVERSITY OF CHICAGO HISTORICAL AND LINGUISTIC STUDIES.

**Linguistic Studies in Germanic** (LG):

1. SCHWABE, Semantic Development of Words for Eating and Drinking.
2. ARNOLDSON, Parts of the Body in Older Germanic.
3. NICHOLSON, English Works with Native Roots.
4. IHRIG, Semantic Development of Words for "Walk, Run."
5. BASKETT, Parts of Body in the Later Germanic.

**Linscott, Henry Farrar.** The Latin Third Declension. A Study in Metaplasm and Syncretism. 1896. *o.p.*

**Lipson, Leslie.** The American Governor from Figurehead to Leader. Introduction by Marshall Edward Dimock. 1939. P.A. *o.p.*

**Lipson, Leslie.** The Politics of Equality. New Zealand's Adventures in Democracy. 1948. *o.p.*

**Liquefaction of Gases:** FARADAY.

**Liska, George.** The New Statecraft. Foreign Aid in American Foreign Policy. 1960. xv, 247 p. 22 cm. 60-6823. CSAFP. $5.00ˢ.

**List of Approved Colleges and Universities in the North Central Association of Colleges and Secondary Schools for 1913:** JUDD.

**Literary Chinese by the Inductive Method:** CREEL.

**Literary Views:** CAMDEN.

**Literature of Ancient Greece:** MURRAY.

**Literature in the Elementary School:** MAC-CLINTOCK.

**Lithography for Artists:** BROWN.

**Litler, Lester O.,** *joint author:* BOWMAN, Studying Children.

**Little Community:** REDFIELD.

**Little Pottery Objects:** STARR.

**Liturgical Renaissance in the Roman Catholic Church:** KOENKER.

**Litwack, Leon F.** North of Slavery. 1961. xi, 318 p. 23 cm. 61-10869. $6.00ˢ.

**Liu, James J. Y.** The Art of Chinese Poetry. 1962. xvi, 166 p. 22 cm. 62-7475. $4.50ˢ. OBE.

**Lives Worth Living:** PEABODY.

**Living with the Atom:** CALDER.

**Living Cycads:** CHAMBERLAIN.

**Living Talmud:** GOLDEN.

**Livingston, Burton Edward.** On the Nature of the Stimulus Which Causes the Change of Form in Polymorphic Green Algæ. 1900. HB. *o.p.*

**Livingston, Burton Edward.** The Role of Diffusion and Osmotic Pressure in Plants. 1903. *o.p.*

**Le Livre d'or (Yonge):** JOHNSON.

**Llewellyn, Karl N.** Jurisprudence. Realism in Theory and Practice. 1962. vii, 534 p. Index. 24 cm. 62-12634. $8.95ˢ.

Here, . . . no longer scattered through library stacks, is an unparalleled opportunity to view law and government up close and overall through the keenest eyes of our time. . . . The hub of Llewellyn's jurisprudence is not the rules of the law, nor even the conduct of public officials. He is concerned with the interrelationship between the behavior of public officials and the behavior of the public."—Charles D. Kelso in *The Michigan Law Review.*

**Lloyd, Seton,** *joint author:* DELOUGAZ, Pre-Sargonid Temples.

**Lloyd, Seton,** *joint author:* FRANKFORT, Gimilsin Temple and the Palace of the Rulers at Tell Asmar.

**Lloyd, Seton,** *joint author:* JACOBSEN, Sennacherib's Aqueduct.

**Lobingier, Elizabeth Erwin Miller.** Hebrew Home Life. A Third-Grade Course of Study Suitable for Primary Departments of Church Schools, Week-Day Schools of Religion, and Church Vacation Schools. 1926. CS. *o.p.*

**Lobingier, Elizabeth Erwin Miller.** Stories of Shepherd Life. A Second-Grade Course of Study Suitable for Primary Departments of Church Schools, Week-Day Schools of Religion, and Church Vacation Schools. 1924. CS. *o.p.*

**Lobingier, John Leslie.** Our Church. A Course of Study for Young People of the High-School Age. 1927. CS. *o.p.*

**Lobingier, John Leslie.** Projects in World-Friendship. 1925. PM. *o.p.*

**Lobingier, John Leslie.** World-Friendship through the Church School. A Training Course for Church Workers. 1923. PM. *o.p.*

**Lobstein, Paul.** An Introduction to Protestant Dogmatics. Authorized Translation from the Original French Edition by Arthur Maxson Smith. 1902. *o.p.*

Translated from Lobstein's *Essai d'une Introduction à la Dogmatique Protestante*, published in 1896 at Strassburg. The first impression of the English translation was privately printed by the translator. A second impression in 1911 was published by the University of Chicago Press.

**Local Broadcasts to Schools:** STEWART.

**Local Community Fact Book:** WIRTH.

**Locher, Kaspar T.** German Histories of American Literature, 1800–1950. 1955. *o.p.*

**Locke, George Herbert.** A Bibliography of Secondary Education. Being a Classified Index of the *School Review*, Vols. I–X. 1903. *o.p.*

**Lockwood, D. P.** A Survey of Classical Roman Literature. *Vol. I*, xvi, 334 p. *Vol. II*, x, 383 p. *Reissue*, 1962. 21 cm. 34-40316. Paper. Each volume, $3.00ᵗ.

**Lockwood, D. P.** Ugo Benzi. Medieval Philosopher and Physician, 1376–1439. 1951. BM. *o.p.*

**Lodge, Rupert C.** Philosophy of Business. 1945. *o.p.*

**Lodowick Carliell:** GRAY.

**Loeb, Jacques.** Artificial Parthenogenesis and Fertilization. Originally Translated from the German by W. O. Redman King. Supplemented and Revised by the Author. 1913. *o.p.*

**Loeb, Jacques.** The Mechanistic Conception of Life. Biological Essays. 1912. *o.p.*

"The work of the distinguished Jacques Loeb . . . has had a profound influence on the progress of biological science during the past twenty-five years. . . . The investigations regarding the influence of the chemical elements singly and in various combinations on the vital processes of living tissue have had far-reaching consequences for scientific medicine and experimental physiology, not only on account of the novelty and value of the results obtained, but also because they have furnished a new way of attacking problems. The salient results of all this research . . . make an imposing record of achievement. . . . While this book . . . ranges well over the whole field of biology in its subject matter, it attains a degree of unity not to be found in many works of much more limited scope."—Raymond Pearl, in *The Dial*.

**Loeb, Jacques.** On the Production and Suppression of Muscular Twitchings and Hypersensitiveness of the Skin by Electrolytes. 1902. *o.p.*

**Loeb, Jacques.** Studies in General Physiology. 2 vols. 1905. *o.p.*

**Loemker, LeRoy E.,** *trans.* Leibniz. Philosophical Papers and Letters. 2 vols. 1956. CE. *o.p.*

**Loewenstein, Karl.** Political Power and the Governmental Process. 1957. 2d ed. 1965. viii, 434 p. 21 cm. 57-9549. Cloth. $7.50ˢ. Paper. P190. $2.95.

**Löwith, Karl.** Meaning in History. The Theological Implications of the Philosophy of History. 1949. vii, 257 p. 21 cm. 57-7900. Paper. P16. $1.50.

**Logan, Harold Amos.** The History of Trade-Union Organization in Canada. 1928. SE. *o.p.*

**Logan, John.** Ghosts of the Heart. 1960. viii, 79 p. 22 cm. 60-7239. $2.75ˢ.

**Logan, William Newton.** A North American Epicontinental Sea of Jurassic Age. 1900. *o.p.*

**Logarithmic and Trigonometric Tables and Mathematical Formulas:** BRESLICH.

**Logic of Liberty:** POLANYI.

**Logical Basis of Educational Theory:** TEAR.

**Logical Conditions of a Scientific Treatment of Morality:** DEWEY.

**Logical Empiricism:** JOERGENSEN.

**Logical Foundations of Probability:** CARNAP.

**Logsdon, Mayme Irwin.** A Mathematician Explains. 2d ed. 1936. xii, 189 p. Illus. 24 cm. 36-8177. NPL. $4.00ˢ.

**London, Jack,** *joint author:* SEIDMAN, Worker Views His Union.

**London in English Literature:** BOYNTON.

**Long Encounter:** BOWEN.

**Long, Ralph B.** The Sentence and Its Parts. A Grammar of Contemporary English. 1961. v, 528 p. 21 cm. 61-11895. $6.00ᵗ.

**Long, Ralph B.** Structure Worksheets for Contemporary English To Accompany *The Sentence and Its Parts.* 1963. 256 p. 28 cm. Paper. $3.25ᵗ.

**Long, Wesley Robertson,** *ed.:* HAYTON, Flor de las ystorias de Orient.

**Long-Run Behavior of Costs:** DEAN.

**Looking Glass:** GARDNER.

**Loomis, Laura H.:** *see* BRYAN, Sources and Analogues of Chaucer's *Canterbury Tales.*

**Loosli, Clayton Garr.** Outlines of Histological Methods, *in* BUCHSBAUM, Methods of Tissue Culture in vitro.

**Lord Acton:** HIMMELFARB.

**Lorenz, Konrad.** Evolution and Modification of Behavior. 1965. 121 p. 22 cm. 65-24436. $3.50ˢ. COBE.

**Lost Panoramas of the Mississippi:** McDERMOTT.

**Lost Tribes and Sunken Continents:** WAUCHOPE.

**Loud, Gordon.** Khorsabad, I. Excavations in the Palace and at a City Gate. By Gordon Loud. With chapters by Henri Frankfort and Thorkild Jacobsen. 1936. xv, 139 p. Illus. 30 cm. 41-13760. OIP, XXXVIII. $10.00.

**Loud, Gordon.** Khorsabad, II. The Citadel and the Town. By Gordon Loud and Charles B. Altman. 1938. xxi, 115 p. Illus. 40 cm. 41-13760. OIP, XL. $30.00.

**Loud, Gordon.** Megiddo II. Seasons of 1935–39. 2 vols. 1948. OIP, LXII. *o.p.*

**Loud, Gordon.** The Megiddo Ivories. 1939. xi, 25 p. Illus. 30 × 40 cm. 40-4417. OIP, LII. $15.00.

**Lougheed, W. F.:** *see* LELAND, State-Local Fiscal Relations.

**Loutit, John F.** Irradiation of Mice and Men. 1962. xii, 154 p. Illus. Index. 23 cm. 62-12635. $5.00ˢ.

**Louw, Eric H.:** *see* HURST, Great Britain and the Dominions.

**Love, Knowledge, and Discourse in Plato:** SINAIKO.

**Love and Loyalty:** JONES.

**Lowden of Illinois:** HUTCHINSON.

**Lower Triassic Cephalopod Fauna:** MATHEWS.

**Lowie, Robert.** Toward Understanding Germany. 1954. *o.p.*

**Lowinsky, Edward E.,** *general ed.:* Monuments of Renaissance Music.

**Lowry, Charles D.** The Relation of Superintendents and Principals to the Training and Professional Improvement of Their Teachers. 1908. NSSE, 7th Yrbk., Part I. *o.p.*

**Loyal and the Disloyal:** GRODZINS.

**Lucia, S. P.,** *joint author:* AGGELER, Hemorrhagic Disorders.

**Luckenbill, Daniel David.** Ancient Records of Assyria and Babylonia. 2 vols. 1926–27. AR. *Vol. 1:* Historical Records of Assyria. From the Earliest Times to Sargon. 1926. *o.p. Vol. 2:* Historical Records of Assyria. From Sargon to the End. 1927. *o.p.*

". . . a definitely complete work . . . extremely useful . . . trustworthy . . . has resulted in clearing up and rectifying many difficult passages. This is a very important contribution to Assyriology."—S. Langdon, in *The Journal of the Royal Asiatic Society* (London).

**Luckenbill, Daniel David.** Inscriptions from Adab. Cuneiform Series, II. 1930. ix, 8 p. 87 plates with 198 texts in facsimile. 24 × 30 cm. 30-33015. OIP, XIV. $5.00.

**Luckenbill, Daniel David.** *ed.* The Annals of Sennacherib. 1924. xi, 196 p. Illus. 24 × 30 cm. 24-25205. OIP, II. $4.00.

**Luckenbill, Daniel David:** *see* GORDON, Truth about the Bible.

**Luckenbill, Daniel David:** *see* SMITH, Origin and History of Hebrew Law.

**Lurie, Edward.** Louis Agassiz. A Life in Science. 1960. xiv, 449 p. Illus. 24 cm. 59-11623. $7.50ˢ.

**Lush, Adaline Lincoln:** *see* DARGAN, Studies in Balzac's Realism.

**Lutz, Ralph Haswell:** *see* WRIGHT, Public Opinion and World-Politics.

**Luvaas, Jay.** The Education of an Army. British Military Thought, 1815–1940. 1964. xi, 454 p. 22 cm. 64-25717. $9.50. COBE.

**Luvaas, Jay.** The Military Legacy of the Civil War. The European Inheritance. 1959. xi, 253 p. Illus. 24 cm. 59-12288. $5.95s.

**Luvaas, Jay,** *ed.:* HENDERSON, Civil War.

**Luyten, Willem Jacob.** Reobservation of the Orbits of Ten Spectroscopic Binaries with a Discussion of Apsidal Motions. By W. J. Luyten, O. Struve, and W. W. Morgan. 1939. YO, VII. *o.p.*

**Lydgate, John.** The Assembly of Gods: or, The Accord of Reason and Sensuality in the Fear of Death. Edited from the MSS. with Introduction, Notes, Index of Persons and Places, and Glossary, by Oscar Lovell Triggs. 1895. ENG. *o.p.*

**Lying and Its Detection:** LARSON.

**Lyman, R. L.** The Enrichment of the English Curriculum. 1932. SEM 39. *o.p.*

**Lyman, R. L.** Summary of Investigations Relating to Grammar, Language, and Composition. 1929. SEM 36. *o.p.*

**Lyman, R. L.:** *see* UNIVERSITY OF CHICAGO, University High School, Department of English.

**Lynch, Charles A.,** *joint author:* BRADNER, Latin Epigrams of Thomas More.

**Lynn, Caro.** A College Professor of the Renaissance. Lucio Marineo Sículo among the Spanish Humanists. 1937. *o.p.*

**Lyon, Earl DeWitt:** *see* BRYAN, Sources and Analogues of Chaucer's *Canterbury Tales.*

**Lyon, Elias Potter.** A Contribution to the Comparative Physiology of Compensatory Motions. 1899. *o.p.*

**Lyon, Florence May.** A Contribution to the Life-History of Euphorbia corollata. 1898. HB. *o.p.*

**Lyon, Florence May.** A Study of the Sporangia and Gametophytes of Selaginella apus and Selaginella rupestris. 1901. HB. *o.p.*

**Lyon, Leverett S.** Education for Business. 1922. 3d ed. 1931. MSB. *o.p.*

**Lyon, Leverett S.** Elements of Debating. A Manual for Use in High Schools and Academies. 1913. 2d ed. 1932. *o.p.*

**Lyon, Leverett S.** A Survey of Commercial Education in the Public High Schools of the United States. 1919. SEM 12. *o.p.*

**Lyon, Leverett S.** Your Business and Postwar Readjustment. By Leverett S. Lyon, James M. Barker, and Guenther Baumgart. 1944. *o.p.*

**Lyon, Leverett S.,** *ed.* Governmental Problems in the Chicago Metropolitan Area. 1957. xii, 282 p. 28 cm. 57-8576. $8.00s.

**Lyon, Leverett Samuel,** *joint author:* BARNES, Marketing the Stephens Brake Shoe.

**Lyon, Leverett S.:** *see* CHICAGO HOME RULE COMMISSION, Modernizing a City Government.

**Lyons, William Nelson,** *ed.* New Testament Literature. An Annotated Bibliography. Edited by William Nelson Lyons and Merrill M. Parvis. 1948. *o.p.*

**Ma, Gioh-fang Dju.** One Hundred Years of Public Services for Children in Minnesota. 1949. SSM. *o.p.*

**McAllister, J. Gilbert,** *joint author:* EGGAN, Social Anthropology of North American Tribes.

**McAuley, Mary Faith.** Economies in Food. Quantity Recipes Using Evaporated Milk. By M. Faith McAuley and Mary Adele Wood. 1934. *o.p.*

**McCagg, Ezra Butler.** Chicago Historical Society, 1857–1907. Celebration of the Fiftieth Anniversary of Its Incorporation, February 7, 1907. Addresses by Ezra B. McCagg and Franklin H. Head. Roll of Officers and Members. 1907. *o.p.*

A publication of the Chicago Historical Society.

**McCallum, William Burnet.** On the Nature of the Stimulus Causing the Change of Form and Structure in Proserpinaca palustris. 1902. HB. *o.p.*

**McCamy, James Lucian.** Government Publicity. Its Practice in Federal Administration. 1939. PA. *o.p.*

**McCarthy, Henry L.,** *ed.* Labor Looks at Unemployment Insurance. Edited by Henry L. McCarthy and F. H. Harbison. 1946. *o.p.*

**MacClintock, Porter Lander.** Sainte-Beuve's Critical Theory and Practice after 1849. 1920. *o.p.*

**MacClintock, Porter Lander.** Literature in the Elementary School. 1907. 2d ed. 1928. *o.p.*

**MacClintock, William Darnall.** Some Paradoxes of the English Romantic Movement. 1903. *o.p.*

**McCloskey, Robert G.** The American Supreme Court. 1960. x, 260 p. 21 cm. 60-14235. Cloth. CHAC. $5.00ˢ. Paper. $1.75.
"Professor McCloskey's perceptive and penetrating study of the Court's role in exercising its power of judicial review sheds light and tenders good counsel in an area too often obscured by the heat and passion of controversy. This excellent book deserves wide reading."— Paul G. Kauper, in *The Michigan Law Review.*

**McClung, Clarence E.:** *see* COWDRY, General Cytology.

**McConn, Charles M.,** *joint author:* CUBBERLEY, Research within the Field of Education.

**McConnell, Francis John,** Bishop. The Christian Ideal and Social Control. 1932. BL. *o.p.*

**McConnell, Francis John,** Bishop: *see* HAYDON, Modern Trends in World-Religions.

**McConnell, T. R.** The Conceptual Structure of Educational Research. By T. R. McConnell and others. 1942. SEM 55. *o.p.*

**McConnell, T. R.** General Education. Prepared by T. R. McConnell, Chairman of the Society's Committee. 1952. NSSE, 51st Yrbk., Part I. xiii, 377 p. 24 cm. 52-7760. Cloth. $4.50ᵗ. Paper. $3.75ᵗ.

**McConnell, T. R.** The Psychology of Learning. Prepared by T. R. McConnell, Chairman of the Society's Committee. 1942. NSSE, 41st Yrbk., Part II. xiv, 463 p. 24 cm. E42-208. Cloth. $4.00ᵗ. Paper. 3.25ᵗ.

**McCown, Chester C.:** *see* GORDON, Truth about the Bible.

**McCown, Donald E.** The Comparative Stratigraphy of Early Iran. 1942. SAOC 23. *o.p.*

**McCown, Donald E.,** *joint author:* LANGSDORFF, Tall-i-Bakun A.

**McCoy, Herbert Newby.** Equilibrium in the System Composed of Sodium Carbonate, Sodium Bicarbonate, Carbon Dioxide, and Water. 1903. *o.p.*

**McCulloch, David.** Early Days of Peoria and Chicago. 1904(?). *o.p.*
A publication of the Chicago Historical Society.

**McDermott, John Francis.** The Lost Panoramas of the Mississippi. 1958. *o.p.*

**McDermott, Valeria Dunne,** *joint author:* PEEBLES, Nursing Services and Insurance for Medical Care in Brattleboro, Vermont.

**McDiarmid, Errett Weir, Jr.,** *joint author:* WAPLES, Library.

**McDiarmid, John.** Government Corporations and Federal Funds. 1938. PA. *o.p.*

**Macdonald, Duncan Black.** The Religious Attitude and Life in Islam. 1909. CR. *o.p.*

**McDonald, Forrest.** Insull. 1962. xvi, 252 p. Illus. 25 cm. 62-18110. $5.95.

**McDonald, Forrest.** We the People. The Economic Origins of the Constitution. 1958. 448 p. 58-14905. Cloth. 24 cm. $7.00ˢ. Paper. P144. 21 cm. $2.95.
"In *We the People* Forrest McDonald has written what may prove to be one of the most important books on American history in recent years. His formidable study . . . subjects Charles A. Beard's economic interpretation of the Constitution to one of the most smashing analyses ever mounted in the literature of historical criticism. . . . McDonald has done a staggering amount of research. . . ."—David M. Potter, in *The Saturday Review.*

**Macdonald, Mary E.** Federal Grants for Vocational Rehabilitation. 1944. xiii, 404 p. 25 cm. A44-2270. Paper. SSM. $2.50ˢ.

**McDonald, James F.,** *joint author:* SHAW, Brothers in Crime.

**Macdonald, John.** Mind, School, and Civilization. 1952. *o.p.*

**McEwan, Calvin Wells.** The Oriental Origin of Hellenistic Kingship. 1934. SAOC 13. *o.p.*

**McEwan, Calvin Wells.** Soundings at Tell Fakhariyah (Including Roman Resaina). By Calvin W. McEwan and others. 1957. 132 p. 87 plates. 30 cm. 57-11216. OIP, LXXIX. $35.00.

**McFarlane, Margaret Mary.** A Study of Practical Ability. 1925. BJP. *o.p.*

**McFayden, Donald.** The History of the Title *Imperator* under the Roman Empire. 1920. *o.p.*

**McGovney, Dudley O.** The American Suffrage Medley. The Need for a National Uniform Suffrage. 1949. *o.p.*

**McGrane, Reginald C.** The Panic of 1837. Some Financial Problems of the Jacksonian Era. 1924. viii, 260 p. 21 cm. Paper. P202. $1.95.

**Macgregor, David Hutchison,** *joint author:* HOBSON, Some Aspects of Recent British Economics.

**Macgregor, Gordon.** Warriors without Weapons. A Study of the Society and Personality Development of the Pine Ridge Sioux. 1946. *o.p.*

**McHale, Kathryn.** Changes and Experiments in Liberal-Arts Education. Prepared by Kathryn McHale. 1932. NSSE, 31st Yrbk., Part II. ix, 310 p. 24 cm. E33-66. Cloth. $2.50ᵗ. Paper. $1.75ᵗ.

**Machiavelli, Niccolò:** *see* RIDOLFI, Life of Niccolò Machiavelli.

**Machine Politics. Chicago Model:** GOSNELL.

**Machinery of the Body:** CARLSON.

**McIlroy, Colonel James Garfield,** *ed.:* CHAMBERLAIN, Simplified Grammar of the Japanese Language.

**McIntosh, Helen:** *see* MANLY, Text of *The Canterbury Tales.*

**McIntosh, John Strayer.** A Study of Augustine's Versions of Genesis. 1912. *o.p.*

**McIntyre, A. R.** Curare. Its History, Nature, and Clinical Use. 1947. BM. *o.p.*

**McIntyre, Donald M., Jr.,** *joint ed.:* LINDMAN, Mentally Disabled and the Law.

**McIntyre, Francis,** *joint ed.:* LANGE, Studies in Mathematical Economics.

**McKay, Henry Donald,** *joint author:* SHAW, Brothers in Crime.

**McKay, Henry Donald,** *joint author:* SHAW, Juvenile Deliquency and Urban Areas.

**McKay, Henry Donald:** *see* SHAW, Delinquency Areas.

**McKelvey, Blake Faus.** American Prisons. A Study in American Social History Prior to 1915. 1936. SSM. *o.p.*

**Mackenzie, Donald,** *joint ed.:* RUSSELL, Emergent Responsibilities in Higher Education.

**Mackenzie, Helen Frances:** *see* PICASSO, Understanding Picasso.

**McKenzie, Kenneth,** *ed.* Le Mie prigioni and Francesca da Rimini. By Silvio Pellico. HCLS.

**Mackenzie King Record:** PICKERSGILL.

**McKenzie, Roderick Duncan.** The Neighborhood. A Study of Local Life in the City of Columbus, Ohio. 1923. *o.p.*

**McKenzie, Roderick Duncan.** Oriental Exclusion. The Effect of American Immigration Laws, Regulations, and Judicial Decisions upon the Chinese and Japanese on the American Pacific Coast. 1928. IPR. *o.p.*

**McKenzie, Roderick Duncan:** *see* PARK, The City.

**McKeon, Richard.** Democracy in a World of Tensions. A Symposium prepared by UNESCO. 1951. *o.p.*

**McKeon, Richard.** Thought, Action, and Passion. 1954. ix, 305 p. 22 cm. $6.00ˢ.

**McKeon, Richard,** *joint author:* CRANE, Critics and Criticism.

**McKeon, Richard,** *joint ed. and trans.:* NIKAM, Edicts of Asoka.

**McKinsey, James Oscar.** Managerial Accounting. [Vol. I.] 1924. MSB. *o.p.*

**McKinsey, James Oscar.** Organization and Methods of the Walworth Manufacturing Company. 1922. MSB. *o.p.*

**McKinsey, James Oscar,** *joint author:* HODGE, Principles of Accounting.

**McKitrick, Eric L.** Andrew Johnson and Reconstruction. 1960. ix, 544 p. 60-5467. Cloth. 24 cm. $9.50ˢ. Paper. P153. 21 cm. $2.95.
"A contribution of prime importance to the reviving study of the Reconstruction period. Among ts merits are its originality in reshaping old problems, its imaginative use of analogy and comparative history, and its disciplined respect for the chronological order of events, ideas, hopes and despairs."—*New York Times Book Review.*

**MacLatchy, Josephine,** *joint ed.:* EDUCATION ON THE AIR . . . AND RADIO AND EDUCATION, 1935.

**McLaughlin, Andrew Cunningham.** The Courts, the Constitution, and Parties. Studies in Constitutional History and Politics. 1912. *o.p.*

**McLaughlin, Andrew Cunningham.** Sixteen Causes of War. 1918. WP. *o.p.*

**McLaughlin, Dean B.,** *joint ed.:* ALLER, Stellar Structure.

**McLean, Franklin C.** Bone. An Introduction to the Physiology of Skeletal Tissue. By Franklin C. McLean and Marshall R. Urist. Rev. ed. 1961. xvi, 261 p. Illus. 23 cm. 61-3979. SL. BM. $6.00ˢ.

**McLean, Franklin C.:** *see* CARLSON, Studies on the Possible Intoxicating Action of 3.2 Per Cent Beer.

**MacLean, Joan,** *trans.:* BENÍTEZ, Century after Cortés.

**Maclean, Norman,** *joint author:* CRANE, Critics and Criticism.

**MacLennan, Simon Fraser.** The Impersonal Judgment. Its Nature, Origin, and Significance. 1897. PHI. *o.p.*

**McLoughlin, William G., Jr.** Billy Sunday Was His Real Name. 1955. *o.p.*

**McLuhan, Marshall,** *joint general ed.:* Patterns of Literary Criticism.

**McMahon, A. Philip.** Preface to an American Philosophy of Art. 1945. *o.p.*

**McMillen, Wayne.** Community Organization for Social Welfare. 1945. *o.p.*

**McMillen, Wayne.** Measurement in Social Work. A Statistical Problem in Family and Child Welfare and Allied Fields. 1930. SSM. *o.p.*

**McMillen, Wayne.** Statistical Methods for Social Workers. 1952. xi, 564 p. Illus. 25 cm. 52-9736. $8.50ᵗ.

**MacNair, Harley Farnsworth.** China in Revolution. An Analysis of Politics and Militarism under the Republic. 1931. *o.p.*

**MacNair, Harley Farnsworth.** The Real Conflict between China and Japan. An Analysis of Opposing Ideologies. 1938. *o.p.*

**MacNair, Harley Farnsworth,** *ed.* Voices from Unoccupied China. 1944. *o.p.*

**McNair, James Birtley.** Rhus Dermatitis from Rhus Toxicodendron, Radicans and Diversiloba. (Poison Ivy.) Its Pathology and Chemotherapy. 1923. *o.p.*

**MacNaul, Willard C.** The Jefferson-Lemen Compact. The Relations of Thomas Jefferson and James Lemen in the Exclusion of Slavery from Illinois and the Northwest Territory with Related Documents, 1781–1818. 1915. *o.p.*
A publication of the Chicago Historical Society.

**MacNeill, Harris Lachlan.** The Christology of the Epistle to the Hebrews Including Its Relation to the Developing Christology of the Primitive Church. 1914. HLL. *o.p.*

**McNeill, John T.,** *ed.* Environmental Factors in Christian History. Edited by John McNeill, Matthew Spinka, and Harold R. Willoughby. 1939. *o.p.*

**McNeill, John T.,** *joint author:* BAKER, Short History of Christianity.

**McNeill, John T.:** *see* CASE, Bibliographical Guide to the History of Christianity.

**McNeill, John T.:** *see* SMITH, Religious Thought in the Last Quarter-Century.

**McNeill, William H.** Europe's Steppe Frontier, 1500–1800. 256 p. Illus. 64-22248. $5.50.

**McNeill, William H.** History Handbook of Western Civilization. Rev. ed. 1958. xiii, 739 p. Illus. 24 cm. 53-12590. Paper. $5.00ᵗ.

**McNeill, William H.** Past and Future. 1954. v, 217 p. 21 cm. 54-9578. Paper. P166. $1.75.

**McNeill, William H.** The Rise of the West. A History of the Human Community. 1963. xviii, 829 p. Illus. 25 cm. 63-13067. $12.50. ". . . this is not only the most learned and the most intelligent, it is also the most stimulating and fascinating book that has ever set out to recount and explain the whole history of mankind. . . . To read it is a great experience. It leaves echoes to reverberate, and seeds to germinate in the mind. . . .

"It covers 5,000 years of humanity. It is not merely a history of 'The West': it is a history of the world, written to show how and where civilization arose, how it developed and was transfered from place to place, what laws, if any, regulated its progress, why certain civilization throve at the expense of others, and finally, why, since 1500 A.D., European civilization imposed itself on the whole world."—H. R. Trevor-Roper, in *The New York Times Book Review*.

**MacNeish, Harris Franklin.** Linear Polars of the *k*-Hedron in *n*-Space. *o.p.*

**MacNeish, Harris Franklin,** *joint author:* MYERS, First Year Mathematics.

**McPhee, William N.,** *joint author:* BERELSON, Voting.

**McQueen, Ewen Neil.** The Distribution of Attention. 1917. BJP. *o.p.*

**MacRae, Allan,** *joint author:* GELB, Nuzi Personal Names.

**Macridis, Roy C.,** *Editor,* CHICAGO LIBRARY OF COMPARATIVE POLITICS.

**McSwain, E. T.,** *ed.* Opportunities for Education in the Next Decade. Edited by E. T. McSwain and J. R. Childress. 1951. AOPPS, XIV. *o.p.*

**MacVannel, John Angus.** College Course in the Principles of Education. 1906. *o.p.*

**Macy, Icie G.** Chemical Anthropology. A New Approach to the Growth of Children. By Icie G. Macy and Harriet J. Kelly. 1957. xviii, 149 p. Illus. 24 cm. 57-11931. BM. $3.75ˢ.

**Madame Thérèse (Erckmann-Chatrian):** WILLIAMS.

**Maddox, James G.** Technical Assistance by Religious Agencies in Latin America. 1956. NPA. *o.p.*

**Madeline McDowell Breckinridge:** BRECKINRIDGE.

**Madison, James.** The Papers of James Madison. Edited by William T. Hutchinson and William M. E. Rachal. With Ralph L. Ketcham, Robert R. Scribner, Donald O. Dewey, and Jean Schneider, assistant editors. 24 cm. 62-9114. *Vol. I:* 16 March 1751 —16 December 1779. 1962. xlii, 344 p. 8 plates. $10.00ˢ. *Vol. II:* 20 March 1780–23 February 1781. 1962. xix, 346 p. $10.00ˢ. *Vol. III:* March–December 1781. 1963. xxv, 381 p. Illus. $10.00ˢ. *Vol. IV:* 1 January— 31 July, 1782. 1965. xxvii, 486 p. Illus. $12.50ˢ.

"These papers in published form are especially welcome to anyone seriously interested in Madison and his period because in the past they have been so hard to come by. . . . These two volumes, like the first thirty years of the man whose career they document, are a highly promising beginning."—Raymond Walters, Jr., in *The William and Mary Quarterly*.

**Madison, Thurber H.,** *ed.* Basic Concepts of Music Education. 1958. NSSE, 57th Yrbk., Part I. xi, 362, vi p. 24 cm. 58-5681. Cloth. $4.50ᵗ. Paper. $3.75ᵗ.

**Magee, Mabel Agnes.** Trends in Location of the Women's Clothing Industry. 1930. MSB. *o.p.*

**Magson, Egbert Hockey.** How We Judge Intelligence. An Investigation into the Value of an Interview as a Means of Estimating General Intelligence. 1926. BJP. *o.p.*

**Mahaffy, Sir John Pentland.** The Progress of Hellenism in Alexander's Empire. 1905. *o.p.*

**Mahaffy, Sir John Pentland.** The Silver Age of the Greek World. 1906. *o.p.* This book was a second edition of the author's *Greek World under Roman Sway*, published in 1890.

**Mahdi, Muhsin.** Ibn Khaldûn's Philosophy of History. A Study in the Philosophic

Foundation of the Science of Culture. *Reissue*, 1964. 325 p. 21 cm. Paper. P167. $2.45. CUSA.

**Mahr, Alexander.** Monetary Stability and How To Achieve It. 1933. PPP 9. *o.p.*

**Maimonides.** The Guide of the Perplexed. Translated and with an Introduction and Notes by Shlomo Pines and with an Introductory Essay by Leo Strauss. 1963. cxxxiv, 658 p. Index. 26 cm. 62-18113. $15.00.
"The purpose of Maimonides was not primarily to write a philosophical treatise but to show that those elements of the Bible which acquaintance with the writings of the philosophers might make difficult of acceptance were not contrary to reason. Leo Strauss's penetrating essay alone would give high value to this volume, and it should certainly help the reader to break the seals. . . . an important volume, which is unlikely to be surpassed for a long time."— *Times Literary Supplement.*

**Mainx, Felix.** Foundations of Biology. 1955. ii, 86 p. 25 cm. 55-5135. Paper. IEUS, I, 9. $2.00ˢ.

**Mair, Lucy.** New Nations. 1963. 235 p. 22 cm. NHS. $5.00ˢ. OBE.

**Major Forms of Inhibition in Man:** SKAGGS.

**Making the Bible Live:** CHAMBERLIN.

**Making Bolsheviks:** HARPER.

**Making of Citizens:** MERRIAM.

**Making of *The Cloister and the Hearth*:** TURNER.

**Making of the English New Testament:** GOODSPEED.

**Making Fascists:** SCHNEIDER.

**Making of *Walden*:** SHANLEY.

**Mallarmé:** FOWLIE.

**Mallet, Robert,** *ed.:* GIDE, Self-Portraits.

**Man on Another World:** EHRENSVÄRD.

**Man in His Pride:** GRENE.

**Man Must Eat:** SLATER.

**Man and the State:** MARITAIN.

**Man the Tool-maker:** OAKLEY.

**Management of the School Money:** MORRISON.

**Management of Wild Mammals in Captivity:** CRANDALL.

**Management's Adjustment to the Changing National Economy:** MITCHELL.

**Managerial Accounting:** McKINSEY.

**Managerial Psychology:** LEAVITT.

**Mandan Society:** BOWERS.

**Mandates under the League of Nations:** WRIGHT.

**Manheim, Ralph,** *trans.:* AUERBACH, Dante, Poet of the Secular World.

**Manly, John Matthews.** A Manual for Writers. Covering the Needs of Authors for Information on Rules of Writing and Practices in Printing. By John Matthews Manly and John Arthur Powell. 1913. 2d ed. 1915. *o.p.*

**Manly, John Matthews.** The Text of *The Canterbury Tales.* Studied on the Basis of All Known Manuscripts. By John M. Manly and Edith Rickert. With the aid of Mabel Dean, Helen McIntosh, and Others. With a chapter on Illuminations, by Margaret Rickert. 8 vols. 1940. 24 cm. 40-4358. *Vol. I:* Descriptions of the Manuscripts. xxiv, 690 p. Illus. *Vol. II:* Classification of the Manuscripts. viii, 518 p. Illus. *Vol. III:* Text and Critical Notes, Part I. x, 537 p. *Vol. IV:* Text and Critical Notes, Part II. viii, 536 p. Illus. *Vol. V:* Corpus of Variants, Part I. x, 554 p. *Vol. VI:* Corpus of Variants, Part II. viii, 673 p. *Vol. VII:* Corpus of Variants, Part III. viii, 617 p. *Vol. VIII:* Corpus of Variants, Part IV. viii, 551 p. Illus. Planographed. Set, boxed, $75.00ˢ. O.S.
"The great merit of this vast accomplishment does not consist merely in the fact that it makes possible a better text of the 'Canterbury Tales' than any which has hitherto been published. It marks an epoch in the development of the art of editing a classical text from a large number of manuscripts. . . . The section in the introduction to Volume II, entitled 'Critics of the Genealogical Method,' should be read by everybody concerned with the formation of critical texts from numerous manuscripts."—*Times Literary Supplement.*

**Manly Anniversary Studies:** UNIVERSITY OF CHICAGO, *Department of English.*

**Mann, Charles Wesley.** The Chicago Common Council and the Fugitive Slave Law of 1850. 1903. *o.p.*

A publication of the Chicago Historical Society.

**Man's Role in Changing the Face of the Earth:** THOMAS.

**Mansfield, Harvey C., Jr.** Statesmanship and Party Government. A Study of Burke and Bolingbroke. 1965. 288 p. $7.50ˢ.

**Mantey, Julius Robert,** *joint author:* COLWELL, Hellenistic Greek Reader.

**Manual of Criminal Law:** PUTTKAMMER.

**Manual of Experimental Embryology:** HAMBURGER.

**Manual of Harmony:** OTTERSTRÖM.

**Manual of Intergroup Relations:** DEAN.

**Manual for Laboratory Work in Mammalian Physiology:** D'AMOUR.

**Manual of Medical Parasitology:** HUFF.

**Manual of Style:** UNIVERSITY OF CHICAGO PRESS.

**Manual for Writers:** MANLY.

**Manual for the Writers of Term Papers, Theses, and Dissertations:** TURABIAN.

**Manwaring, David R.** Render unto Caesar. The Flag-Salute Controversy. 1962. x, 322 p. Index. 22 cm. 62-13563. $5.50ˢ.

**Manyon, L. A.,** *trans.:* BLOCH, Feudal Society.

**Map of Chicago's Gangland:** THRASHER.

**Mapa de Cuauhtlantzinco:** STARR.

**Mapping:** GREENHOOD.

**Marble, Annie Russell.** Heralds of American Literature. A Group of Patriot Writers of the Revolutionary and National Periods. 1907. *o.p.*

**March, Benjamin Franklin.** China and Japan in Our Museums. Introduction by Frederick P. Keppel. 1929. IPR. *o.p.*

**Marcion and the New Testament:** KNOX.

**Marcus W. Jernegan Essays in American Historiography:** HUTCHINSON.

**Margold, Charles William.** Sex Freedom and Social Control. Introduction by Edward T. Devine. 1926. SOC. *o.p.*

**Marhofer, Esther:** *see* DARGAN, Studies in Balzac's Realism.

**Marie de France:** *see* JENKINS, Espurgatoire Saint Patriz.

**Marion, J. B.,** *joint ed.:* PHILLIPS, Progress in Fast Neutron Physics.

**Maritain, Jacques.** Man and the State. 1951. x, 219 p. 21 cm. 51-555. Cloth. WFL. $4.00ˢ. Paper. P5. $1.75.

**Maritain, Jacques.** Some Reflections on Culture and Liberty. 1933. *o.p.*

**Mark, Thiselton.** The Unfolding of Personality as the Chief Aim in Education. Some Chapters in Educational Psychology. 1911. *o.p.*

**Marketing the Stephens Brake Shoe:** BARNES.

**Markov, A. V.,** *ed.* The Moon. A Russian View. 1961. ix, 394 p. Illus. 25 cm. 62-9115. $8.00ˢ.

**Marriage and the Civic Rights of Women:** BRECKINRIDGE.

**Marriott, McKim,** *ed.* Village India. Studies in the Little Community. 1955. xix, 269 p. Illus. 25 cm. 55-9326. CSCC. $6.50ˢ. (Not for sale in South Asia.)

**Marsh, Clarence Stephen,** *ed.:* EDUCATIONAL BROADCASTING.

**Marsh, Robert.** Four Dialectical Theories of Poetry. An Aspect of English Neoclassical Criticism. 1965. xii, 223 p. 22 cm. 65-24432. $6.00ˢ.

**Marshall, Fitz-Hugh,** *joint author:* LEMON, Demonstration Laboratory of Physics.

**Marshall, Leon Carroll.** Business Administration. 1921. MSB. *o.p.*

**Marshall, Leon Carroll.** Business Cases and Problems. By Leon Carroll Marshall and Others. 1925. MSB. *o.p.*

**Marshall, Leon Carroll.** Cases and Problems. 10 preprints from MARSHALL, Business Cases and Problems. MSB.

1. MARSHALL, Noel Slate and Manufacturing Company.
2. MEECH, Kansas City Power and Light Company.
3. McKINSEY, Organization and Methods of the Walworth Manufacturing Company.
4. MOULTON, Danner-Kraft Dry Goods Company.
5. BARNES, Marketing the Stephens Brake Shoe.
6. MEINE, Chicago Press-Feeders' Wage Arbitration Case.
7. MEINE, Introduction and Development of the Works Committee.
8. DUDDY, Chicago Foundry Company.
9. WARNE, Co-operative Society of America.
10. PALMER, Organization and Methods of the Thayer Manufacturing Company.

**Marshall, Leon Carroll.** Industrial Society. 1918. 2d ed. 1929–30, 3 vols. MSB. *Part I.* The Emergence of the Modern Order. 1929. *o.p. Part II:* Production in the Modern Order. 1929. *o.p. Part III.* The Co-Ordination of Specialists through the Market. 1930. *o.p.*
The first edition was published under the title, *Readings in Industrial Society.*

**Marshall, Leon Carroll.** The Noel Slate and Manufacturing Company. 1922. MSB. *o.p.*

**Marshall, Leon Carroll.** Outlines of the Economic Order Developed in a Series of Problems. By L. C. Marshall, J. F. Christ, A. W. Kornhauser, L. W. Mints, S. H. Nerlove. 1930. MSB. *o.p.*

**Marshall, Leon Carroll,** *ed.* The Collegiate School of Business. Its Status at the Close of the First Quarter of the Twentieth Century. Edited by L. C. Marshall in collaboration with A. W. Fehling, K. Ficek, R. E. Heilman, W. H. Kiekhofer, E. C. Longobardi, C. O. Ruggles, Frances Ruml, I. L. Sharfman, J. G. Smith, and J. Wiesner. 1928. MSB. *o.p.*

**Marshall, Leon Carroll,** *ed.* Materials for the Study of Elementary Economics. Edited by Leon Carroll Marshall, Chester Whitney Wright, James Alfred Field. 1915. MSE. *o.p.*

**Marshall, Leon Carroll,** *ed.* Outlines of Economics Developed in a Series of Problems. Prepared by Members of the Department of Political Economy of the University of Chicago. 1910. MSE. *o.p.*

**Marshall, Leon Carroll,** *ed.* Quartermaster and Ordnance Supply. A Guide to the Principles of the Supply Service of the United States Army. By Instructors of the Army Supply Service Course, The University of Chicago. 1917. *o.p.*

**Marth, Paul C.,** *joint author:* MITCHELL, Growth Regulators.

**Martin Buber:** FRIEDMAN.

**Martin, Edgar W.** The Standard of Living in 1860. American Consumption Levels on the Eve of the Civil War. 1942. *o.p.*

**Martin, Edward Moss.** The Rôle of the Bar in Electing the Bench in Chicago. 1936. *o.p.*

**Martin, Ethel A.** Roberts' Nutrition Work with Children. 1936. Rev. ed. 1954. xvi, 527 p. Illus. 25 cm. 54-11210. $8.50ᵗ.
". . . analyzes at great length the causes of malnutrition and all its contributory factors, be they dietary, anatomical or sociological; bad habits, heredity and body build are considered properly. Physical and mental effects of undernutrition are broadly described; prevention and treatment practically presented . . . an excellent book."—*Modern Medicine.*

**Martin, John W.,** *joint author:* STOCKWELL, Grammatical Structures of English and Spanish.

**Martin, Laura H.** League of Nations Map. 1925. *o.p.*

**Martin, Lawrence:** *see* Washington's Map of Mount Vernon.

**Martin, Lowell A.,** *ed.* Personnel Administration in Libraries. 1946. *o.p.*

**Martin, Lowell A.,** *joint author:* MILES, Public Administration and the Library.

**Martin, Lowell A.,** *joint ed.:* CARNOVSKY, The Library in the Community.

**Martin, Paul S.** Indians before Columbus. Twenty Thousand Years of North American History Revealed by Archeology. By Paul S. Martin, George Irving Quimby, and Donald Collier. 1947. xxiv, 582 p. Illus. 25 cm. 47-1434. $8.50ᵗ.

**Martin, Richard Arthur,** *joint author:* OSTEN, Discoveries in Anatolia.

**Martin, Richard M.** Truth and Denotation. A Study in Semantical Theory. 1957. xii, 304 p. 22 cm. 57-12813. $7.50s. COBE.

**Martin Luther:** GUNSAULUS.

**Martinet, André.** Elements of General Linguistics. 1964. Translated from the French by Elisabeth Palmer. 205 p. 22 cm. $6.50s. OBE.

**Martiny, Günter:** *see* FRANKFORT, Gimilsin Temple.

**Martyrdom of Cyprian and Justa:** GOODSPEED.

**Martyrs:** RIDDLE.

**Marvick, Elizabeth Wirth,** *joint ed.:* WIRTH, Community Life.

**Marxism: An Autopsy:** PARKES.

**Mary McDowell, Neighbor:** WILSON.

**Mascari, A.** Résumé of Solar Observation Made in 1894 at the Astrophysical Observatory of Catania. 1895. *o.p.*

**Maschke, Heinrich.** Invariants and Covariants of Quadratic Differential Quantics of *n* Variables. Preprint, 1903. *o.p.*

**Mason, Charles Max.** The Electromagnetic Field. By Max Mason and Warren Weaver. 1929. *o.p.*

**Mason, Edward Gay,** *ed.* Early Chicago and Illinois. Edited and Annotated by Edward G. Mason. 1890. *o.p.*
A publication of the Chicago Historical Society.

**Mass Media and Education:** DALE.

**Masserman, Jules.** Behavior and Neurosis. An Experimental Psychoanalytic Approach to Psychobiologic Principles. 1943. BM. *o.p.*

**Masses of the Stars:** RUSSELL.

**Mastaba of Mereruka:** SAKKARAH EXPEDITION.

**Masterman, Ernest William Gurney.** Studies in Galilee. Preface by George Adam Smith. 1909. *o.p.*

**Masters of the Wilderness:** REED.

**Masters of the Wilderness. A Study of the Hudson's Bay Company:** REED.

**Material Logic of John of St. Thomas:** SIMON.

**Material Remains of the Megiddo Cult:** MAY.

**Materials for the Assyrian Dictionary:** *see* ORIENTAL INSTITUTE, PUBLICATIONS OF.

**Materials for Reading:** ROBINSON.

**Materials for the Study of Business** (MSB):
BALABANIS, American Discount Market.
BREWINGTON, Social Concept of Money.
CLARK, Social Control of Business.
COWAN, Sales Analysis from the Management Standpoint.
DOUGLAS, Worker in Modern Economic Society.
GRAHAM, Alternative Laboratory Exercises for Rorem's *Accounting Method.*
GRAHAM, Solutions to *Alternative Laboratory Exercises.*
GRAHAM, Teacher's Manual for *Accounting Method.*
HARDY, Readings in Risk and Risk-bearing.
HITCHCOCK, Forms, Records, and Reports in Personnel Administration.
HODGE, Laboratory Material to Accompany *Principles of Accounting.*
HODGE, Principles of Accounting.
HODGE, Retail Accounting.
JONES, Introduction to Economic Geography.
JONES, Suggestions for Teachers Using *Economic Geography.*
LYON, Education for Business.
MCKINSEY, Managerial Accounting.
MARSHALL, Business Administration.
MARSHALL, Industrial Society.
MARSHALL, Outlines of the Economic Order.
MARSHALL, Quartermaster and Ordnance Supply.
MITCHELL, Production Management.
MOULTON, Financial Organization of Society.
ROREM, Accounting Method.
SPENCER, Law and Business.
SPENCER, Text-Book on Law and Business.

*Special Studies:*
ASSOCIATION OF COLLEGIATE SCHOOLS OF BUSINESS, Social Studies in Secondary Schools.
BAKER, Legal Aspects of Zoning.
CLARK, Adam Smith.
CLARK, Studies in the Economics of Overhead Costs.
DOUGLAS, Wages and the Family.
DUDDY, Cold-Storage Industry in the United States.
FOREMAN, Efficiency and Scarcity Profits.
HOBSON, Some Aspects of Recent British Economics.
INSTITUTE OF AMERICAN MEAT PACKERS, Packing Industry.
KORNHAUSER, How To Study.
KORNHAUSER, Psychological Tests in Business.

LOGAN, History of Trade-Union Organization in Canada.

MAGEE, Trends in Location of the Women's Clothing Industry.

MARSHALL, Business Cases and Problems.

MARSHALL, Collegiate School of Business.

MITCHELL, Uses of Bank Funds.

MONTGOMERY, Industrial Relations in the Chicago Building Trades.

POWELL, History of the United Typothetae.

SCHULTZ, Statistical Laws of Demand and Supply.

VALGREN, Farmers' Mutual Fire Insurance.

VINER, Dumping.

WARNE, Consumers' Co-operative Movement in Illinois.

WEBER, Alfred Weber's Theory of the Location of Industries.

WOLF, Railroad Labor Board.

YNTEMA, Mathematical Reformulation of the General Theory of International Trade.

YOUNG, Advertising Agency Compensation.

*Cases and Problems:*

1. MARSHALL, The Noel Slate and Manufacturing Company.
2. MEECH, The Kansas City Light and Power Company.
3. MCKINSEY, The Walworth Manufacturing Company.
4. MOULTON, The Danner-Kraft Company.
5. BARNES AND LYON, Marketing the Stephens Brake Shoe.
6. MEINE, The Chicago Press Feeders Wage Arbitration Case.
7. MEINE, The Dennison Manufacturing Company.
8. DUDDY, The Chicago Foundry Company.
9. WARNE, The Co-operative Society of America.
10. PALMER, Organization Methods of the Thayer Manufacturing Company.

## Materials for the Study of Elementary Economics: MARSHALL.

## Materials for the Study of Economics (MSE):

CLARK, Readings in the Economics of War.

HAMILTON, Current Economics Problems.

HAMILTON, Exercises in Current Economics.

MARSHALL, Materials for the Study of Elementary Economics.

MARSHALL, Outline of Economics.

MOULTON, Exercises and Questions for Use with *Principles of Money*.

MOULTON, Principles of Banking.

MOULTON, Principles of Money.

NOURSE, Agricultural Economics.

NOURSE, Outlines of Agricultural Economics.

## Maternal Care: ADAIR.

## Maternal Care Complications: ADAIR.

## Maternal Care and Some Complications: ADAIR.

## Mathematical Achievement Tests: BRESLICH.

## Mathematical Biology of Social Behavior: RASHEVSKY.

## Mathematical Biophysics: RASHEVSKY.

## Mathematical Reformulation of the General Theory of International Trade: YNTEMA.

## Mathematical Tools of Economics: TINBERGEN.

## Mathematician Explains: LOGSDON.

## Mathematics Instruction in the University High School: MEMBERS OF THE DEPARTMENT OF MATHEMATICS OF THE UNIVERSITY HIGH SCHOOL OF THE UNIVERSITY OF CHICAGO.

**Matheson, M. Cécile,** *joint author:* CADBURY, Women's Work.

**Mathews, Albert P.:** *see* COWDRY, General Cytology.

**Mathews, Asa A. Lee.** The Lower Triassic Cephalopod Fauna of the Fort Douglas Area, Utah. Published through the Aid of the Kappa Epsilon Pi Fraternity. 1929. *o.p.*

**Mathews, John J.** Talking to the Moon. 1945. *o.p.*

**Mathews, Mitford McLeod.** Beginnings of American English. 1931. ix, 181 p. 21 cm. Paper. P123. $1.50.

**Mathews, Mitford McLeod,** *ed.* A Dictionary of Americanisms on Historical Principles. 1951. xvi, 1,946 p. Illus. 28 cm. 56-2254. $12.50. COBE.

"This is a beautifully legible and eminently readable dictionary of 50,000 terms and meanings that have been coined in the United States or have passed into the English of this country as independent borrowings. . . . It draws on more sources, pays due attention to pronunciation and etymology, and carries its record down to the year 1950. The text has been supplemented by 400 line-drawings of objects now seldom seen. The vocabulary keeps a sensible balance between the historical and the contemporary. . . .

"The result is not only a scholarly dictionary of Americanisms, but an incomparable source book of American life in its most American aspects. It can't be an accident; Mr. Mathews must have planned it that way."—*American Scholar.*

**Mathews, Robert Maurice,** *joint author:* MYERS, Teacher's Manual for First-Year Mathematics.

**Mathews, Robert Maurice:** *see* MYERS, Second-Year Mathematics.

**Mathews, Shailer.** The Message of Jesus to Our Modern Life. 1915. AISL. *o.p.*

**Mathews, Shailer.** The Messianic Hope in the New Testament. 1905. *o.p.*

**Mathews, Shailer.** Scientific Management in the Churches. 1912. *o.p.*

**Mathews, Shailer.** The Social and Ethical Teaching of Jesus. A Series of Direction Sheets for Individual or Class Study of the Social and Ethical Teaching of Jesus as Recorded in the Gospels. New and revised edition. 1907. AISL. *o.p.*

**Mathews, Shailer.** The Student's Gospels. A Harmony of the Synoptics. The Gospel of John. Arranged by Shailer Mathews, Using the *New Testament: An American Translation,* by Edgar J. Goodspeed. 1927. 2d ed. 1934. xii, 252 p. 20 cm. 35-494. CS. $3.50ˢ.

**Mathews, Shailer,** *joint author:* BURTON, Life of Christ.

**Mathews, Shailer,** *joint author:* BURTON, Principles and Ideals for the Sunday School.

**Mathews, Shailer:** *see* BEWER, Religion of the Bible.

**Mathews, Shailer:** *see* BOWER, Church at Work in the Modern World.

**Mathews, Shailer:** *see* GORDON, Truth about the Bible.

**Mathews, Shailer:** *see* SMITH, Guide to the Study of the Christian Religion.

**Mathews, Shailer:** *see* SMITH, Religious Thought in the Last Quarter-Century.

**Matthew Arnold:** BROWN.

**Matthew Arnold:** STANLEY.

**Matthew's Sayings of Jesus:** CASTOR.

**Matthews, R. C. O.** The Business Cycle. 1959. xv, 300 p. 19 cm. 59-10286. Paper. CEH 4. 21 cm. $1.95. USA.

**Mattole, An Athabaskan Language:** LI.

**Maturity in Reading:** GRAY.

**Mauss, Marcel,** *joint author:* DURKHEIM, Primitive Classification.

**Maxey, Mima.** Occupations of the Lower Classes in Roman Society. 1938. *o.p.*

**Maxson, Charles Hartshorn.** The Great Awakening in the Middle Colonies. 1920. *o.p.*

**May, Herbert Gordon.** Material Remains of the Megiddo Cult. By Herbert Gordon May. With a Chapter by Robert M. Engberg. 1935. xiv, 51 p. Illus. 30 cm. 36-3487. OIP, XXVI. $6.00.

**May, Herbert Gordon,** *joint author:* GRAHAM, Culture and Conscience.

**Mayer, Harold M.** The Port of Chicago and the St. Lawrence Seaway. 1957. xi, 335 p. Illus. 23 cm. 57-2850. $5.00ˢ.

**Mayer, Harold M.** Readings in Urban Geography. Edited by Harold M. Mayer and Clyde F. Kohn. 1959. vii, 625 p. Illus. 25 cm. 59-11973. $8.50ᵗ.

**Mayer, Milton.** They Thought They Were Free. The Germans, 1933–45. 1955. Paper. $2.45.

**Mayer, Milton.** What Can a Man Do? Selected Writings. Edited by W. Eric Gustafson with an Introduction by Martin Niemöller. 1964. viii, 310 p. 21 cm. 64-15801. $5.00.

**Mayer, Milton,** *joint author:* ADLER, Revolution in Education.

**Maynard, Leonard A.:** *see* BUCK, Land Utilization in China, Vol. IV.

**Mayow, John.** Medico-physical Works. Being a Translation of *Tractatus quinque medicophysici.* By John Mayow, LL.D., M.D. (1674). 1907. AC. *o.p.*

**Mead, Albert R.** The Giant African Snail. A Problem in Economic Malacology. 1961. xvii, 257 p. Illus. Index. 24 cm. 61-14949. $7.50ˢ.

**Mead, George Herbert.** The Definition of the Psychical. 1903. *o.p.*

**Mead, George Herbert.** George Herbert Mead on Social Psychology. Selected Papers, edited, with an Introduction, by Anselm Strauss. 2d ed. 1964. xxv, 358 p. 21 cm. 64-23419. Cloth. $8.95ˢ. Paper. P170. $2.95.

**Mead, George Herbert.** Mind, Self, and Society. From the Standpoint of a Social Behaviorist. Edited by Charles W. Morris. 1934. xxxviii, 401 p. 24 cm. 35-292. $7.50ˢ.

"It is so full of brilliant insights and on the whole so consistent and systematic, that one is thankful his students have seen fit to give to the wider philosophical community those ideas which proved so stimulating to them."—George E. G. Catlin, in *The Philosophical Review.*

"These posthumous papers represent the ripe fruit of one of America's most original . . . philosophers. . . . Professor Charles Morris is to be congratulated upon a very competent piece of editing. His prefatory essay provides an illuminating introduction to Mead's world of ideas."—Sidney Hook, in *The Nation.*

**Mead, George Herbert.** Movements of Thought in the Nineteenth Century. Edited by Merritt H. Moore. 1936. xi, 510 p. 24 cm. 36-9407. $7.50ˢ.

**Mead, George Herbert.** The Philosophy of the Act. Edited by Charles W. Morris. 1938. lxxiv, 696 p. 24 cm. $10.00ˢ.

**Mead, George Herbert.** A Report on Vocational Training in Chicago and in Other Cities. By a Sub-Committee of the Committee on Public Education, 1910–1911, of the City Club of Chicago. Sub-committee: George H. Mead, Chairman; Ernest A. Wreidt; William J. Bogan. 1912. *o.p.*

**Mead, Margaret,** *ed.* Childhood in Contemporary Cultures. Edited by Margaret Mead and Martha Wolfenstein. 1955. xi, 473 p. 55-10248. Cloth. 25 cm. $7.50ˢ. Paper. P124. 21 cm. $2.95.

**Mead, Margaret,** *ed.* The Study of Culture at a Distance. Edited by Margaret Mead and Rhoda Métraux. 1953. x, 480 p. 25 cm. 53-13135. $7.50ˢ.

**Mead, Sidney E.** Nathaniel William Taylor, 1786–1858. 1942. *o.p.*

**Meade, James E.** Problems of Economic Union. 1953. WFL. *o.p.*

**Meade, Ruth Elizabeth,** *ed.* Sans famille. By Hector Malot. Adapted and edited by Ruth Elizabeth Meade, Grace Cochran, and Helen M. Eddy. HCLS.

**Meadville Theological Seminary.** Theological Study Today. Addresses Delivered at the Seventy-fifth Anniversary of the Meadville Theological School, June 1–3, 1920. 1921. *o.p.*

**Meaning, Communication, and Value:** KECSKEMETI.

**Meaning of Ephesians:** GOODSPEED.

**Meaning of** ἐπὶ τῆς σκηνῆς: FLICKINGER.

**Meaning in History:** LÖWITH.

**Meaning and Necessity:** CARNAP.

**Meaning of Shakespeare:** GODDARD.

**Meaning of Social Science:** SMALL.

**Meaning of Unintelligibility in Modern Art:** ROTHSCHILD.

**Meaning of Work and Retirement:** FRIEDMANN.

**Means, L. L.** The Nocturnal Maximum Occurrence of Thunderstorms in the Midwestern States. 1946. DMMR 16. *o.p.*

**Mears, Eliot Grinnell.** Resident Orientals on the American Pacific Coast. Their Legal and Economic Status. IPR. *o.p.*

**Measure of the Moon:** BALDWIN.

**Measurement of Attitude:** THURSTONE.

**Measurement of Business Activity:** BUTTERBAUGH.

**Measurement of Educational Products:** ASHBAUGH.

**Measurement in Social Work:** MCMILLEN.

**Measurement of Some Standard Wave-Lengths:** LEWIS.

**Measurement of Understanding:** BROWNELL.

**Measurement of Values:** THURSTONE.

**Measurements of Double Stars:** VAN BIESBROECK.

**Measures of Double Stars:** BURNHAM.

**Meat through the Microscope:** MOULTON.

**Mechanisms of Breathing:** JOHNSON.

**Mechanistic Conception of Life:** LOEB.

**Mecklin, John M.** The Passing of the Saint. A Study of a Cultural Type. 1941. *o.p.*

**Medical Administration of Teaching Hospitals:** BAY.

**Medical Care for the American People:** COMMITTEE ON THE COSTS OF MEDICAL CARE.

**Medical Care for 15,000 Workers:** CARPENTER.

**Medical Economics Series** (ME):
BAY, Medical Administration.
BRADBURY, Cost of Adequate Medical Care.
DAVIS, Crisis in Hospital Finance.
DAVIS, Paying Your Sickness Bills.
DAVIS, Public Medical Services.
NEW YORK TUBERCULOSIS AND HEALTH ASSOCIATION. *Committee on Community Dental Service*, Health Dentistry for the Community.
ROREM, Public's Investment in Hospitals.

**Medical Genetics:** LENZ.

**Medical Service of the Homestake Mining Company:** REED.

**Medical Social Case Records.** Submitted in the 1927 Case Competition of the American Association of Hospital Social Workers. Introduction by Sophonisba P. Breckinridge. 1928. SSM. *o.p.*

**Medical World of the Eighteenth Century:** KING.

**Medicine, Science, and Art:** COHN.

**Medicine in Transition:** GALDSTON.

**Medicine and the War:** TALIAFERRO.

**Medico-Physical Works:** MAYOW.

**Medieval and Historiographical Essays in Honor of James Westfall Thompson:** CATE.

**Medieval Islam:** GRUNEBAUM.

**Medieval Latin:** HARRINGTON.

**Medieval Latin Lyrics:** ALLEN.

**Medieval Latin Scientific Writings in the Barberini Collection:** SILVERSTEIN.

**Medieval Library:** THOMPSON.

**Medieval Logic:** BOEHNER.

**Medinet Habu:** EPIGRAPHIC SURVEY.

**Medinet Habu Graffiti:** EDGERTON.

**Medinet Habu, 1924–28:** NELSON.

**Medinet Habu Reports:** NELSON.

**Medinet Habu Studies:** HÖLSCHER.

**Medium-sized Public Library:** CARNOVSKY.

**Meech, Stuart Putnam.** Kansas City Power and Light Company. 1922. MSB. *o.p.*

**Meek, Lois H.** Preschool and Parental Education. Prepared by Lois H. Meek, Chairman of the Society's Committee. 1929. NSSE, 28th Yrbk., Parts I and II. Part I. Organization and Development. Part II. Research and Method. x, 831 p. 24 cm. E29-88. Cloth. $5.00ᵗ. Paper. $3.25ᵗ.

**Meek, Theophile James,** *joint trans.:* SMITH, Old Testament.

**Meek, Theophile James:** *see* BEWER, Religion of the Bible.

**Meek Americans:** BEACH.

**Meeting Individual Differences in Reading:** ROBINSON.

**Megiddo. I:** LAMON.

**Megiddo. II:** LOUD.

**Megiddo Ivories:** LOUD.

**Megiddo Tombs:** GUY.

**Megiddo Water System:** LAMON.

**Meigs, A. James.** Free Reserves and the Money Supply. 1962. xvi, 118 p. 24 cm. 62-17136. ERS. $4.00ˢ.

**Meine, Franklin J.,** *joint ed.:* BLAIR, Half Horse Half Alligator.

**Meine, Franklyn.** The Chicago Press-Feeders Wage Arbitration Case. 1923. MSB. *o.p.*

**Meine, Franklyn.** The Introduction and Development of the Works Committee in the Dennison Manufacturing Company. 1925. MSB. *o.p.*

**Meissner, Bruno.** Beiträge zum assyrischen Wörterbuch. *Vol. I.* 1931. (*o.p.*). *Vol. II.* 1932. vii, 112 p. 2 figures. 25 cm. Paper. AS 4 $1.00.

**Meister (Ponten):** FERNSEMER.

**Melamed, Samuel Max.** Spinoza and Buddha. Visions of a Dead God. 1933. *o.p.*

**Meland, Bernard Eugene.** Higher Education and the Human Spirit. 1953. *o.p.*

**Melville, Herman.** Billy Budd, Sailor. (An Inside Narrative.) Reading Text and Genetic Text Edited from the Manuscript with Introduction and Notes by Harrison Hayford and Merton M. Sealts, Jr. 1962. x, 432 p. Illus. 24 cm. 62-17135. $8.00ˢ.

**Melville, Herman.** Billy Budd, Sailor. (An Inside Narrative.) Reading text only. Edited from the Manuscript with Introduction and Notes by Harrison Hayford and Merton M. Sealts, Jr. 1962. x, 220 p. 21 cm. 62-17135. Paper. P99. $1.50.

**Members of the Department of Mathematics of the University High School of the University of Chicago.** Mathematics Instruction in the University High School. 1940. xiii, 184 p. 25 cm. PLS 8. $3.50ˢ.

**Memories of Eighty Years:** HERRICK.

**Memoirs on Steel and Iron:** RÉAUMUR.

**Men in America:** *see* National Advisory Council on Radio in Education, *Radio Lectures.*

**Men on the Move:** ANDERSON.

**Men and Oil:** WEAVER.

**Men and Planes:** CRAVEN.

**Men of Substance:** JORDAN.

**Mendelson, Wallace.** Justices Black and Frankfurter. Conflict in the Court. 1961. x, 151 p. Index. 21 cm. 61-5781. $5.00ˢ.

**Mental Disorders in Urban Areas:** FARIS.

**Mental Health in Modern Education:** WITTY.

**Mental Retardation:** STEVENS.

**Mental Traits of Sex:** THOMPSON.

**Mentally Disabled and the Law:** LINDMAN.

**Mentally Ill and Public Provision for Their Care:** JAFFARY.

**Mentor Graham:** DUNCAN.

**Merchandising Packinghouse Products:** RHOADES.

**Meriam, Adele Stuart.** The Stepfather in the Family. Edited by Sophonisba P. Breckinridge. 1940. SSM. *o.p.*

**Meriam, Lewis.** Public Service and Special Training. Four Public Lectures Delivered at the University of Chicago, April, 1936. 1936. PA. *o.p.*

**Merriam, Charles Edward.** The Government of the Metropolitan Region of Chicago. By Charles E. Merriam, Spencer D. Parratt, and Albert Lepawsky. 1933. SSCI. *o.p.*

**Merriam, Charles Edward.** The Making of Citizens. A Comparative Study of Methods of Civic Training. 1931. SMC. *o.p.*

**Merriam, Charles Edward.** New Aspects of Politics. 1925. 2d ed. 1931. *o.p.*

**Merriam, Charles Edward.** Non-voting. Causes and Methods of Control. By Charles Edward Merriam and Harold Foote Gosnell. 1924. SSCI. *o.p.*

**Merriam, Charles Edward.** Primary Elections. 1908. Rev. ed. by Charles Edward Merriam and Louise Overacker, 1928. *o.p.*

**Merriam, Charles Edward.** Prologue to Politics. 1939. *o.p.*

**Merriam, Charles Edward.** Report of an Investigation of the Municipal Revenues of Chicago. 1906. CC. *o.p.*

**Merriam, Charles Edward.** Systematic Politics. 1945. xiv, 349 p. 24 cm. $5.00ˢ.

"Here is a masterly attempt to systematize the methods and materials of politics and to relate the whole field to the purposes and hopes of men. The whole course of political evolution is analyzed in order to show how far we have come governmentally and how far we might advance in the light of what we now know."— C. S. Lowry, in *The Mississippi Valley Historical Review.*

**Merriam, Charles Edward.** What Is Democracy? 1941. WFL. *o.p.*

**Merriam, Charles Edward:** *see* SMITH, Chicago.

**Merriam, Charles Edward:** *see* WIRTH, Eleven Twenty-six.

**Merriam, John Campbell:** *see* WHITE, New Social Science.

**Merrifield, Fred,** *joint author:* BURTON, Origin and Teaching of the New Testament Books.

**Merrill, Paul Willard.** Spectra of Long-Period Variable Stars. 1940. AM. *o.p.*

**Merrill, Robert Valentine.** The Platonism of Joachim du Bellay. 1925. *o.p.*

**Merrill, William Dayton.** A Contribution to the Life History of Silphium. 1900. HB. *o.p.*

**Merritt, LeRoy C.** The United States Government as Publisher. 1943. *o.p.*

**Message of Jesus:** MATHEWS.

**Message of the Prophets:** WILLETT.

**Messianic Hope:** MATHEWS.

**Messianic Theme:** WISCHNITZER.

**Mészáros, Julius von.** Die Päkhy-Sprache. 1934. viii, 402 p. Illus. 25 cm. A34-1705. Paper. SAOC 9. $5.00.

Μετανοέω **and** Μεταμέλει **in Greek Literature:** THOMPSON.

**Metal Plutonium:** COFFINBERRY.

**Metaphor and Simile:** CARPENTER.

**Metaphorical Terminology:** VAN HOOK.

**Metaphysics in Modern Times:** GOTSHALK.

**Metaphysics and the New Logic:** WICK.

**Meteorites:** HEIDE.

**Method in Social Anthropology:** RADCLIFFE-BROWN.

**Method and Theory in American Archaeology:** WILLEY.

**Methodists:** SWEET.

**Methods of Ethics:** SIDGWICK.

**Methods for Measuring Teachers' Efficiency:** BOYCE.

**Methods in Plant Histology:** CHAMBERLAIN.

**Methods of Social Science:** RICE.

**Methods of Tissue Culture in Vitro:** BUCHSBAUM.

**Métraux, Rhoda,** *joint ed.:* MEAD, Study of Culture at a Distance.

**Metric Differential Geometry of Curves and Surfaces:** LANE.

**Metropolitan Government:** JONES.

**Metropolitan Library in Action:** JOECKEL.

**Metzger, Bruce M.** The Saturday and Sunday Lessons from Luke in the Greek Gospel Lectionary. 1944. *o.p.*

**Mexican Immigrant:** GAMIO.

**Mexican Immigration to the United States:** GAMIO.

**Mexican War:** SINGLETARY.

**Mexico:** RIPPY.

**Meyer, Charles Ferdinand.** The Diffraction of Light, X-Rays, and Material Particles. An Introductory Treatment. 1934. *o.p.*

**Meyer, Johann Jakab.** Two Twice-told Tales. Preprint, 1903. *o.p.*

**Meyer, Leonard B.** Emotion and Meaning in Music. 1956. With 104 musical examples. xi, 307 p. 56-9130. Cloth. 24 cm. $6.95ˢ. Paper. P56. 21 cm. $1.95.
"Altogether it is a book that should be required reading for any student of music, be he composer, performer, or theorist. It clears the air of many confused notions . . . and lays the groundwork for exhaustive study of the basic problem of music theory and aesthetics, the relationship between pattern and meaning."—David Kraehenbuehl, in *The Journal of Music Theory.*

**Meyer, Leonard B.,** *joint author:* COOPER, Rhythmic Structure of Music.

**Michelson, A. A.** The Echelon Spectroscope. 1898. *o.p.*

**Michelson, Albert Abraham.** Studies in Optics. 1927. Paper. PSS 514. $1.75.
". . . a résumé of his life-long investigations in light . . . even to those readers who have but slight acquaintance with the refined methods of modern experimental physics in the domain where Professor Michelson gained his great renown, the very nature of the contents . . . must convey some kind of thrill."—James P. C. Southall, in *The Nation.*

**Michelson, Albert Abraham.** The Velocity of Light. Preprint, 1902. *o.p.*

**Michelson, Albert Abraham.** Light Waves and Their Uses. 1907. *o.p.*

**Michigan Poor Law:** BRUCE.

**Micrometric Measures of Star Clusters:** BARNARD.

**Micrometrical Observations of Eros:** BARNARD.

**Microscopic Histochemistry:** GOMORI.

**Middle Ages and the Renaissance:** BRÉHIER.

**Middle Ear:** KOBRAK.

**Middle Passage:** COXE.

**Middle West Looks at War:** LAVES.

**Middlehurst, Barbara M.,** *ed.* The Moon, Meteorites, and Comets. (*See* KUIPER: The Solar System.)

**Middlehurst, Barbara M.,** *ed.* see KUIPER, Solar System, Vol. IV. Planets and Satellites.

**Middlehurst, Barbara M.,** *Associate Editor,* KUIPER, Stellar Systems.

**Middlehurst, Barbara M.,** *joint ed.:* KUIPER, Telescopes.

**Midwest at Noon:** HUTTON.

**Midwives, Chiropodists, and Optometrists:** REED.

**Mie prigioni and Francesca da Rimini (Pellico):** McKENZIE.

**Migratory Worker:** HATHWAY.

**Mikesell, Marvin W.,** *joint ed.:* WAGNER, Readings in Cultural Geography.

**Milchrist, Elizabeth Hayward.** State Administration of Child Welfare in Illinois. 1937. SSM. *o.p.*

**Miles, Arnold.** Public Administration and the Library. By Arnold Miles and Lowell Martin. 1941. LS. *o.p.*

**Miles, Arthur Parker.** Federal Aid and Public Assistance in Illinois. 1941. SSM. *o.p.*

**Military Legacy of the Civil War:** LUVAAS.

**Military in the Political Development of New Nations:** JANOWITZ.

**Milk Distribution as a Public Utility:** MORTENSON.

**Mill, John S.** The Spirit of the Age. 1942. *o.p.*

**Mill, John Stuart.** Utilitarianism. Reprinted from the Thirteenth London Edition. 1908. *o.p.*

**Millennial Hope:** CASE.

**Millennium of Hieronymus Bosch:** FRÄNGER.

**Miller, A. C.:** *see* Financial Mobilization for War.

**Miller, David L.,** *joint ed.:* MEAD, The Philosophy of the Act.

**Miller, E. H.** A Proposed Method for the Computation of the 10,000–Foot Tendency Field. By E. H. Miller and W. L. Thompson. 1943. *o.p.*

**Miller, Edward A.** The History of Educational Legislation in Ohio from 1803 to 1850. 1920. SEM 13. *o.p.*

**Miller, Elizabeth Erwin.** The Dramatization of Bible Stories. An Experiment in the Religious Education of Children. 1918. *o.p.*

**Miller, Elizabeth Erwin.** Dramatization in the Church School. A Training Course for Leaders. 1923. *o.p.*

**Miller, Ernest Carl,** *joint author:* REEVES, Trends in University Growth.

**Miller, Frank Justus,** *trans.* The Tragedies of Seneca. Translated into English Verse, to Which Have Been Appended Comparative Analyses of the Corresponding Greek and Roman Plays, and a Mythological Index by Frank Justus Miller. Introduced by an Essay on the Influence of the Tragedies of Seneca upon Early English Drama, by John Matthews Manly. 1907. *o.p.*

**Miller, Frank Justus,** *trans.* Two Dramatizations from Vergil. I. Dido—The Phoenician Queen. II. The Fall of Troy. Arranged and Translated into English Verse by Frank Justus Miller. Stage directions and music for the *Dido* contributed by J. Raleigh Nelson. 1908. *o.p.*

**Miller, G. F.,** *ed.* Le Comte de Monte-Cristo. By Alexandre Dumas. HCLS.

**Miller, Irving Elgar.** The Significance of the Mathematical Element in the Philosophy of Plato. 1904. *o.p.*

**Miller, James E., Jr.** A Critical Guide to *Leaves of Grass.* 1957. xi, 268 p. 24 cm. 57-6982. Cloth. $6.00[s]. Paper. P224. $1.79.

**Miller, Merton Leland.** A Preliminary Study of the Pueblo of Taos, New Mexico. 1898. *o.p.*

**Miller, Raymond Curtis.** James Ford Rhodes, *in* HUTCHINSON, Marcus W. Jernegan Essays.

**Miller, Robert L.,** *joint author:* OLSON, Morphological Integration.

**Miller, Spencer, Jr.,** *ed.* American Labor and the Nation. 1933. *o.p.*

**Millerd, Clara Elizabeth.** On the Interpretation of Empedocles. 1908. *o.p.*

**Millikan, Robert Andrews.** The Electron. Its Isolation and Measurement and the Determination of Some of Its Properties. 1917. Reissued 1963. Edited and with New Introduction by Jesse W. M. DuMond. lxii, 268 p. Illus. 21 cm. 63-20910. Cloth. $6.00ˢ. Paper. PSS523. $2.45.
". . . describes [Millikan's] wonderful researches on the unit of electric charge and the photoelectric effect, for which he received a Nobel prize in 1923. . . . A feature of interest in the present edition is the introduction by . . . DuMond, a close associate of Millikan's during much of his scientific career, who gives a vivid account of his work and personality and of the general picture of research in physics during the first decades of this century."—*Scientific American.*

**Millikan, Robert Andrews.** Electrons (+ and −), Protons, Photons, Neutrons, Mesotrons, and Cosmic Rays. 1935. Rev. ed. 1947. SCI. *o.p.*

**Millikan, Robert Andrews.** New Instruments of Precision from the Ryerson Laboratory. Preprint. 1903. *o.p.*

**Millikan, Robert Andrews.** Radio's Past and Future. [A radio address delivered May 22, 1931. Introduction by Herbert C. Hoover.] 1931. *o.p.*

**Milliken, O. J.** The Chicago Vacation Schools for 1898. By O. J. Milliken. The Vacation School Movement. By Sadie American. 1898. *o.p.*

**Milliman, Jerry,** *joint author:* HIRSHLEIFER, Water Supply.

**Million, John Wilson.** State Aid to Railways in Missouri. 1896. EC. *o.p.*

**Millis, Harry A.** From the Wagner Act to Taft-Hartley. A Study of National Labor Policy and Labor Relations. By Harry A. Millis and Emily Clark Brown. 1950. xi, 724 p. 25 cm. 50-7091. $11.00ˢ.

**Millis, Harry A.** Sickness and Insurance. A Study of the Sickness Problem and Health Insurance. 1937. *o.p.*

**Millott, H. H.:** *see* DARGAN, Studies in Balzac's Realism.

**Mills, Alden Brewster.** The Extent of Illness and of Physical and Mental Defects Prevailing in the United States. A Compilation of Existing Material. 1929. CMC 2. *o.p.*

**Mills, Alden Brewster,** *joint author:* SINAI, Study of Physicians and Dentists.

**Mills, Alden Brewster,** *joint author:* SINAI, Survey of the Medical Facilities of the City of Philadelphia.

**Mills Spectrograph of the Lick Observatory:** CAMPBELL.

**Milton and Others:** WILLIAMSON.

**Milton Papers:** STEVENS.

**Milton's Semitic Studies:** FLETCHER.

**Milyoukov, Paul.** Russia and Its Crisis. Crane Lectures for 1903. 1905. *o.p.*

**Mind of Africa:** ABRAHAM.

**Mind, School, and Civilization:** MACDONALD.

**Mind, Self & Society:** MEAD.

**Miner, Horace.** St. Denis. A French-Canadian Parish. 1939. xx, 300 p. 21 cm. 39-15698. Cloth. $6.50ˢ. Paper. P108. $2.45.

**Miner, W. N.,** *joint ed.:* COFFINBERRY, Metal Plutonium.

**Minimum Essentials in Elementary School Subjects:** WILSON.

**Minister and the Boy:** HOBEN.

**Mints, Lloyd W.** A History of Banking Theory in Great Britain and the United States. 1945. 319 p. 24 cm. A45-4815. $10.00ˢ.

**Mints, Lloyd W.,** *joint author:* MARSHALL, Outlines of the Economic Order.

Mintz, Beatrice, *ed.* Environmental Influences on Prenatal Development. 1958. xiii, 87 p. 24 cm. 58-13251. DBC. $3.00ˢ.

Mir'ât za-Zamân: Yūsuf ibn Ḳis-Ughli.

Mirror for Americans: Tryon.

Mirrors and Windows: Nemerov.

Miscellaneous Studies: Poebel.

Mitchell, Alice Miller. Children and Movies. 1929. *o.p.*

Mitchell, George W.: *see* Leland, State-Local Fiscal Relations.

Mitchell, Hinckley Gilbert Thomas. The Ethics of the Old Testament. 1912. HER. *o.p.*

Mitchell, John W. Growth Regulators for Garden, Field, and Orchard. By John W. Mitchell and Paul C. Marth. 1947. BM. *o.p.*

Mitchell, Kate L., *joint ed.:* Holland, Problems of the Pacific, 1936.

Mitchell, Samuel Alfred: *see* Slocum, Stellar Parallaxes.

Mitchell, Waldo F. The Uses of Bank Funds. 1925. MSB. *o.p.*

Mitchell, Wesley Clair. A History of the Greenbacks, with Special Reference to the Economic Consequences of Their Issue, 1862–65. 1903. Reprint, 1960. v, 577 p. 23 cm. 3-22564. $6.50ˢ.

Mitchell, Wesley Clair: *see* White, New Social Science.

Mitchell, William Norman. Management's Adjustment to the Changing National Economy. 1942. *o.p.*

Mitchell, William Norman. Production Management. 1931. MSB. *o.p.*

Mitchell, William Norman. Trends in Industrial Location in the Chicago Region since 1920. 1933. SBA, IV. *o.p.*

Mitla. Town of the Souls: Parsons.

Mitogenesis: Ducoff.

Mitosis in Pellia: Chamberlain.

Miyakawa, T. Scott. Protestants and Pioneers. Individualism and Conformity on the American Frontier. 1964. 306 p. 23 cm. 64-22247. $7.50ˢ.

Mobile Weather Unit: Ference.

Mobilizing Community Resources for Maladjusted and Delinquent Youth: Bowman.

Modern Algebra for Biologists: Nahikian.

Modern Archives: Schellenberg.

Modern City. Providence, Rhode Island: Kirk.

Modern Constitutions: Dodd.

Modern Discussions of the Dates of Petrarch's Prose Letters: Wilkins.

Modern Elementary Theory of Numbers: Dickson.

Modern Factor Analysis: Harman.

Modern German Grammar. Minimum Essentials Inductively Presented: Hagboldt.

Modern Germany: Kosok.

Modern Higher Algebra: Albert.

Modern Italian Short Stories: Bergin.

Modern Japan and Shinto Nationalism: Holtom.

Modern Philology Monographs of the University of Chicago (MPM):
Cross, Lancelot and Guenevere.
Hazard, Études critiques sur *Manon Lescaut*.
Nitze, Le haut livre du Graal. Perlesvaus.
Northup, Cuento de Tristan de Leonis.
Pietsch, Spanish Grail Fragments.
Plomer, Life and Correspondence of Lodowick Bryskett.
Stevens, Milton Papers.
Wilkins, University of Chicago Manuscript of the Genealogia Deorum Gentilium.

Modern Philosophies and Education: Brubacher.

Modern Political Parties: Neumann.

Modern Spectroscope. XIV: Wadsworth.

Modern Spectroscope. XV: Wadsworth.

Modern Spectroscope. XVII: Newall.

Modern Study of Literature: Moulton.

Modern Tendencies in Sculpture: Taft.

**Modern Trends in Islam:** GIBB.

**Modern Trends in World-Religions:** HAYDON.

**Modern Viola Technique:** DOLĚJŠÍ.

**Modernity of Milton:** LARSON.

**Modernizing a City Government:** CHICAGO HOME RULE COMMISSION.

**Mohr, George Joseph,** *joint author:* HESS, Physical and Mental Growth of Prematurely Born Children.

**Molecular Theory of Matter:** LEMON.

**Monaghan, J.** This Is Illinois. A Pictorial History. 1949. *o.p.*

**Monahan, A. C.** Agricultural Education in Secondary Schools. By A. C. Monahan and others. 1912. NSSE, 11th Yrbk., Part II. *o.p.*

**Monahan, A. C.** The Supervision of Rural Schools. By A. C. Monahan and others. 1913. NSSE, 12th Yrbk., Part II. *o.p.*

**Monasteries of the Fayyūm:** ABBOTT.

**Monetary Chaos and Gold:** PALYI.

**Monetary Stability:** MAHR.

**Money:** ROBERTSON.

**Monograph Supplements to the British Journal of Psychology (BJP):**
- I. 1. WOHLGEMUTH, On the After-effect of Seen Movement.
  2. BALLARD, Obliviscence and Reminiscence.
  3. WEBB, Character and Intelligence.
  4. REANEY, Psychology of the Organized Group Game.
- II. 5. McQUEEN, Distribution of Attention.
  6. WOHLGEMUTH, Pleasure—Unpleasure.
- III. 7. BERNSTEIN, Quickness and Intelligence.
  8. McFARLAND, Study of Practical Ability.
  9. MAGSON, How We Judge Intelligence.
  10. HARGREAVES, "Faculty" of Imagination.
- IV. 11. WELLS, Phenomenology of Acts of Choice.
  12. STEVANOVIC, Experimental Study of the Mental Processes.
  13. FLÜGEL, Practice, Fatigue, and Oscillation.
- V. 14. CATTELL, Subjective Character of Cognition.
  15. LINE, Growth of Visual Perception.
  16. LAWRENCE, Investigation into the Relation between Intelligence and Inheritance.
- VI. 17. PHILPOTT, Fluctuations in Human Output.
  18. RICHARDSON, Growth and Variability of Intelligence.
  19. ALEXANDER, Intelligence, Concrete and Abstract.
- VII. 20. KOUSSY, Investigation into the Factors in Tests Involving the Visual Perception of Space.
  21. PHILP, Experimental Study of Frustration.
  22. DESAI, Surprise.
  23. RICHARDSON, Generalized Foreign Politics.
  24. CLARKE, Predictable Accuracy in Examinations.

**Monroe, Day.** Chicago Families. A Study of Unpublished Census Data. 1932. SSCI. *o.p.*

**Monroe, Marion.** Children Who Cannot Read. The Analysis of Reading Disabilities and the Use of Diagnostic Tests in the Instruction of Retarded Readers. 1932. xvi, 205 p. Illus. 24 cm. 32-12301. $5.00ˢ.

**Monroe, Paul,** *joint author:* CUBBERLEY, Research within the Field of Education.

**Montfort—a Study in Landscape Types in Southwestern Wisconsin:** *see* FINCH, Geographic Surveys.

**Montgomery, John D.** Forced To Be Free. The Artificial Revolutions in Germany and Japan. 1957. (O.I.)

**Montgomery, Louise.** The American Girl in the Stockyards District. 1913. CSC. *o.p.*

**Montgomery, Robert Nathaniel,** ed. The William Rainey Harper Memorial Conference. Held in Connection with the Centennial of Muskingum College, New Concord, Ohio, October 21–22, 1937. 1938. *o.p.*

**Montgomery, Royal Ewert.** Industrial Relations in the Chicago Building Trades. 1927. SE. *o.p.*

**Montgomery, Royal Ewert,** *joint author:* MILLIS, Economics of Labor.

**Monuments of Renaissance Music** (MRM) EDWARD E. LOWINSKY, *General Editor:* SLIM, Musica Nova.

**Monuments of Romanesque Art:** SWARZENSKI.

**Monuments of Sudanese Nubia:** BREASTED.

**Moodie, Roy Lee.** The Antiquity of Disease. 1923. SCI. *o.p.*

**Moodie, Roy Lee,** *ed.:* RUFFER, Studies in the Palaeopathology of Egypt.

**Moon, Parker Thomas,** *joint author:* JONES, United States and the Caribbean.

**Moon:** MARKOV.

**Moon, Meteorites, and Comets:** MIDDLEHURST.

**Mooney, James.** The Ghost-Dance Religion and the Sioux Outbreak of 1890. Abridged with an Introduction by Anthony F. C. Wallace. 1965. xxi, 359 p. 24 cm. 64-24971. CA. Cloth $6.95ˢ. Paper. P176. $2.95.

**Moore, Addison Webster.** Existence, Meaning, and Reality in Locke's Essay on Human Understanding and in Present Epistemology. 1903. *o.p.*

**Moore, Addison Webster.** The Functional versus the Representational Theories of Knowledge in Locke's Essay. 1902. PHI. *o.p.*

**Moore, Addison Webster.** Pragmatism and Its Critics. 1910. *o.p.*

**Moore, Carl Richard,** *joint author:* LILLIE, Laboratory Outline of Embryology.

**Moore, Charlotte Emma,** *joint author:* RUSSELL, Masses of the Stars.

**Moore, Edward Caldwell.** The Spread of Christianity in the Modern World. 1919. HER. *o.p.*

**Moore, Eliakim Hastings.** The Subgroups of the Generalized Finite Modular Group. Preprint. 1903. *o.p.*

**Moore, George Foot,** *joint ed.:* HARPER, Old Testament and Semitic Studies.

**Moore, Jane.** Cityward Migration. Swedish Data. 1938. *o.p.*

**Moore, John Brooks.** The Comic and the Realistic in English Drama. 1925. *o.p.*

**Moore, John Robert.** Daniel Defoe. Citizen of the Modern World. 1958. xv, 409 p. Illus. 25 cm. 58-11950. $7.50ˢ.

**Moore, Maurice E.,** *joint author:* SHAW, Natural History of a Delinquent Career.

**Moore, Merritt Hadden,** *ed.:* MEAD, Movements of Thought in the Nineteenth Century.

**Moore, William Harrison:** *see* HURST, Great Britain and the Dominions.

**Moorman, Lewis Jefferson.** Tuberculosis and Genius. 1940. *o.p.*

**Moral Foundation of Democracy:** HALLOWELL.

**Moral Life:** VIVAS.

**Moral Life of the Hebrews:** SMITH.

**More Contemporary Americans:** BOYNTON.

**More than Lore:** TALBOT.

**More about Psychiatry:** BINGER.

**More Sculpture from the Diyala Region:** FRANKFORT.

**More for Your Money:** BLAIR.

**Morgan, B. Q.** Das Peterle von Nürnberg. HCLS.

**Morgan, B. Q.** *joint author:* HAGBOLDT, Word Book for *Graded German Readers.* HCLS.

**Morgan, Edmund S.** The Birth of the Republic: 1763–89. 1956. ix, 177 p. 21 cm. 56-11003. Cloth. CHAC. $3.50ˢ. Paper. $1.75. ". . . bold and strikingly phrased . . . marked by eminent common sense. . . . It is safe to predict a long and useful life for this urbane book." —Aubrey C. Land, in *The Mississippi Valley Historical Review.*

**Morgan, Lewis H.:** RESEK.

**Morgan, Thomas H.:** *see* COWDRY, General Cytology.

**Morgan, William W.** An Atlas of Stellar Spectra with an Outline of Spectral Classification. By William W. Morgan, P. C. Keenan, and E. Kellman. 1943. AM. *o.p.*

**Morgan, William W.** A Descriptive Study of the Spectra of the A-Type Stars. 1935. YO, VII. *o.p.*

**Morgan, William W.,** *joint author:* LUYTEN, Reobservation of the Orbits of Ten Spectroscopic Binaries.

**Morgenthau, Hans J.** Dilemmas of Politics. 1958. *o.p.*

**Morgenthau, Hans J.** Politics in the 20th Century. 1962. 3 vols. 24 cm. 62-18111. *Vol. I:* The Decline of Democratic Politics. 1962. xii, 432 p. $10.00ˢ. *Vol. II:* The Impasse of American Foreign Policy. 1962. xii, 312 p. $7.50ˢ. *Vol. III:* The Restoration of American Politics. 1962. x, 394 p. $8.95ˢ. *The Set,* $25.00ˢ.

"His monumental trilogy on politics in the 20th century . . . unites Morgenthau's writings of the past quarter century. His attention ranges from nuclear disarmament and the lonely role of the American President to the scholar's obligations to truth and morality."—Robert Colby Nelson, *The Christian Science Monitor.*

**Morgenthau, Hans J.** Scientific Man versus Power Politics. 1946. x, 245 p. 19 cm. A46-23. Cloth. $5.00ˢ. Paper. P189. 21 cm. $1.95.

**Morgenthau, Hans J.,** *ed.* Germany and the Future of Europe. 1951. HFL. (O.I.)

**Morgenthau, Hans J.,** *ed.* Peace, Security, and the United Nations. 1946. *o.p.*

**Morison, Stanley.** The Typographic Book, 1450–1935. By Stanley Morison and Kenneth Day. 1964. 99 p., 377 p. plates. 31 cm. $30.00. OBE.

**Morley, Felix,** *ed.* Aspects of the Depression. 1932. *o.p.*

**Morley, Felix,** *ed.* The Economic World Today. 1933. *o.p.*

**Mormons:** O'DEA.

**Morphet, Edgar L.** Citizen Co-operation for Better Public Schools. Prepared by Edgar L. Morphet, Chairman of the Society's Committee. 1954. xvii, 304, vi p. NSSE, 53d Yrbk., Part I. 24 cm. 54-8085. Cloth. $4.50ᵗ. Paper. $3.75ᵗ.

**Morphological Integration:** OLSON.

**Morphological Study of Certain Asclepiadaceae:** FRYE.

**Morphological Study of the Flower and Embryo of Spiraea:** WEBB.

**Morphological Study of Thuja:** LAND.

**Morphology of Gymnosperms:** COULTER.

**Morris, Adah Vivian.** Anonyms and Pseudonyms. 1933. *o.p.*

**Morris, Charles William.** Foundations of the Theory of Signs. 1938. vii, 59 p. 25 cm. A41-2443. Paper. IEUS, I, 2. $1.50ˢ.

**Morris, Charles William.** Pragmatism and the Crisis of Democracy. 1934. PPP 12. *o.p.*

**Morris, Charles William.** Six Theories of Mind. 1932. (O.I.)

**Morris, Charles William.** Varieties of Human Value. 1956. 232 p. Illus. 24 cm. 56-6641. $5.75ˢ.

**Morris, Charles William,** *ed.:* MEAD, Mind, Self & Society.

**Morris, Charles William,** *ed.:* MEAD, The Philosophy of the Act.

**Morris, Charles William,** *joint ed.:* International Encyclopedia of Unified Science.

**Morris, Charles William:** *see* NEURATH, Encyclopedia and Unified Science.

**Morrison, Henry Clinton.** American Schools. A Critical Study of Our School Systems. 1943. *o.p.*

**Morrison, Henry Clinton.** The Curriculum of the Common School from the Beginning of the Primary School to the End of the Junior College. 1940. *o.p.*

**Morrison, Henry Clinton.** The Management of the School Money. 1932. *o.p.*

**Morrison, Henry Clinton.** The Practice of Teaching in the Secondary School. 1926. Rev. ed. 1931. x, 688 p. 17 figs. 23 cm. 31-9855. $9.00ˢ.

**Morrison, Henry Clinton.** School and Commonwealth. Addresses and Essays. 1937. *o.p.*

**Morrison, Henry Clinton.** School Revenue. 1930. *o.p.*

**Morrison, Henry Clinton.** Some Aspects of High-School Instruction and Administration. By H. C. Morrison and others. 1914. NSSE, 13th Yrbk. Part I. *o.p.*

**Morrison, Henry Clinton.** Studies in Secondary Education. *Vol. I:* University High School, University of Chicago. By Henry C. Morrison and others. 1923. SEM 24. *o.p.*

**Morrison, Jeanette Gertrude.** Children's Preferences for Pictures Commonly Used in Art Appreciation Courses. 1935. *o.p.*

**Morrison, John Alexander,** *joint author:* OSTEN, Discoveries in Anatolia.

**Morrow, Glenn R.,** *joint author:* CLARK, Adam Smith.

**Morse, Jared Kirtland.** Bibliography of Crystal Structure. 1928. *o.p.*

**Morstein Marx, Fritz.** The Administrative State. 1957. x, 202 p. 25 cm. 57-6987. CLCP. $4.00ᵗ.

**Mortenson, William Peter.** Milk Distribution as a Public Utility. 1940. *o.p.*

**Morthland, Rex J.:** *see* LELAND, State-Local Fiscal Relations.

**Morveau, Guyton de:** *see* SCHEELE, Early History of Chlorine.

**Moscow Journal:** SALISBURY.

**Mosher, Arthur T.** Technical Co-operation in Latin-American Agriculture. 1957. NPA. *o.p.*

**Mosher, F. J.,** *joint author:* TAYLOR, Bibliographic History of Anonyma.

**Mossman, Lois Coffey.** The Activity Movement. Prepared by Lois Coffey Mossman, Chairman of the Society's Committee on the Activity Movement. 1934. NSSE, 33d Yrbk., Part II. xi, 320 p. 24 cm. E34-428. Cloth. $2.50ᵗ. Paper. $1.75ᵗ.

**Most Ancient Egypt:** HAYES.

**Motion Pictures in Education:** KOON.

**Moulder, James W.** Biochemistry of Intracellular Parasitism. 1962. xv, 172 p. Illus. 23 cm. 62-12636. SL. BM. $6.00ˢ.

**Moulton, Charles Robert.** Meat through the Microscope. Applications of Chemistry and the Biological Sciences to Some Problems of the Meat Packing Industry. 1929. IMP. *o.p.*

**Moulton, Forest Ray.** An Attempt To Test the Nebular Hypothesis by an Appeal to the Laws of Dynamics. 1900. *o.p.*

**Moulton, Forest Ray.** New Methods in Exterior Ballistics. 1926. *o.p.*

**Moulton, Forest Ray.** On Certain Rigorous Methods of Treating Problems in Celestial Mechanics. Preprint. 1902. *o.p.*

**Moulton, Forest Ray,** *ed.* The World and Man as Science Sees Them. 1937. *o.p.*

**Moulton, Forest Ray:** *see* NEWMAN, Nature of the World and of Man.

**Moulton, Harold Glenn.** The Danner-Kraft Dry Goods Company. 1922. MSB. *o.p.*

**Moulton, Harold Glenn.** Exercises and Questions for Use with *Principles of Money and Banking.* 1916. MSE. *o.p.*

**Moulton, Harold Glenn.** The Financial Organization of Society. 1921. *o.p.*

**Moulton, Harold Glenn.** The War and Industrial Readjustments. 1918. WP. *o.p.*

**Moulton, Harold Glenn,** *ed.* Principles of Banking. A Series of Selected Materials, with Explanatory Introductions. 1917. MSE. *o.p.*
Part ii of *Principles of Money and Banking.*

**Moulton, Harold Glenn,** *ed.* Principles of Money and Banking. A Series of Selected Materials, with Explanatory Introductions. 1916. MSE. *o.p.*

**Moulton, Harold Glenn,** *joint ed.:* CLARK, Readings in the Economics of War.

**Moulton, Harold Glenn:** *see* Financial Mobilization for War.

**Moulton, Harold Glenn:** *see* HUTCHINSON, Democracy and National Unity.

**Moulton, Harold Glenn:** *see* WHITE, New Social Science.

**Moulton, Richard Green.** Book of Illustrations. Ancient Comedy. 1900. *o.p.*

**Moulton, Richard Green.** Book of Illustrations. Ancient Drama. 1894. *o.p.*

**Moulton, Richard Green.** The Modern Study of Literature. An Introduction to Literary Theory and Interpretation. 1915. *o.p.*

**Moulton, William G.** The Sounds of English and German. 1962. xiv, 146 p. 25 cm. 62-20024. Paper. CSS. $2.75ᵗ.

**Mounds in the Plain of Antioch:** BRAIDWOOD.

**Mountain Building:** CRONEIS.

**Mountain Gorilla:** SCHALLER.

**Moussiegt, Henriette,** *ed.* Histoires de bêtes. By Louis Pergaud. Edited by Henriette Moussiegt and Adolphe-Jacques Dickman. HCLS.

**Movement of Money:** DOUGLAS.

**Movements of Thought in the Nineteenth Century:** MEAD.

**Moving Field Radiation Therapy:** WACHSMANN.

**Mowat, Charles Loch.** Britain between the Wars, 1918–40. 1955. lx, 694 p. 23 cm. 55-5139. $8.50ᵗ. USA.

**Mowrer, Ernest Russell.** Domestic Discord. Its Analysis and Treatment. By Ernest R. Mowrer with the Collaboration of Harriet R. Mowrer. 1928. SOC. *o.p.*

**Mowrer, Ernest Russell.** The Family. Its Organization and Disorganization. 1932. SOC. *o.p.*

**Mowrer, Ernest Russell.** Family Disorganization. An Introduction to a Sociological Analysis. 1927. 2d ed. 1939. SOC. *o.p.*

**Mowrer, Harriet Rosenthal:** *see* MOWRER, Domestic Discord.

**Mowry, Lucetta.** The Dead Sea Scrolls and the Early Church. 1962. xii, 260 p. Index. 23 cm. 62-12637. $6.95ˢ.

**Mozart's** *Le Nozze di Figaro:* LEVARIE.

**Mr. Justice:** DUNHAM.

**Muehlberger, Clarence Weinert:** *see* CARLSON, Studies on the Possible Intoxicating Action of 3.2 Per Cent Beer.

**Mueller, John Henry,** *joint trans.:* DURKHEIM, Rules of Sociological Method.

**Muḥammad B. Dāwūd al-Iṣfahānī.** Kitāb al-Zahrah (The Book of the Flower). The First Half. Composed by Abū Bakr Muḥammad ibn Abī Sulaimān Dāwūd al-Iṣfahānī. (A.H. 297/A.D. 909). Edited from the Unique Manuscript at the Egyptian Library by A. R. Nykl in Collaboration with Ibrāhīm Ṭūqān, Nāblus, Palestine. 1932. SAOC 6. *o.p.*

**Muller, George Paul:** *see* FALK, Community Medical Service . . . Roanoke Rapids, N.C.

**Muller, George Paul:** *see* FALK, Organized Medical Service at Fort Benning, Georgia.

**Muller, Herbert J.** Religion and Freedom in the Modern World. 1963. vii, 129 p. 21 cm. 63-20911. WIL. Cloth. $3.95. Paper. P193. $1.50.

**Mullin, Francis Joseph:** *see* KLEITMAN, Sleep Characteristics.

**Multiple-Factor Analysis:** THURSTONE.

**Mumford, Eben.** The Origins of Leadership. 1909. *o.p.*

**Mumford, Lewis,** *joint ed.:* THOMAS, Man's Role in Changing the Face of the Earth.

**Mumford, William Bryant,** *joint author:* EMBREE, Island India Goes to School.

**Municipal Administration:** JAMES.

**Municipal Budget-making:** TAYLOR.

**"Municipal Doctor" System in Rural Saskatchewan:** ROREM.

**Municipal Franchises:** WILCOX.

**Municipal and Institutional Relations within Boston:** LEVI.

**Municipal Revenues:** MERRIAM.

**Municipal Self-insurance of Workmen's Compensation:** BUECHNER.

**Munro, Thomas.** Art in American Life and Education. Prepared by Thomas Munro, Chairman of the Society's Committee. 1941. NSSE, 40th Yrbk. xx, 819, xxxvi p. 24 cm. Cloth. $6.00ᵗ.

**Munro, William B.:** *see* EINSTEIN, Symposium on America and the World Situation.

**Murphy, Walter F.** Congress and the Court. 1962. xi, 308 p. 25 cm. 62-9739. $6.95ˢ. Paper. P196. 21 cm. $2.25.

**Murphy, Walter F.** Elements of Judicial Strategy. 1964. xiii, 249 p. 24 cm. 64-24973. $7.50.

**Murray, Gilbert.** The Literature of Ancient Greece. 1956. *o.p.*

**Music Education:** UHL.

**Musica Nova:** SLIM.

**Muss-Arnolt, William.** Theological and Semitic Literature for the Year 1900. A Supplement to *The American Journal of Theology* and *The American Journal of Semitic Languages and Literatures.* 1901. *o.p.*

**Muss-Arnolt, William.** Theological and Semitic Literature for the Year 1901. A Supplement to *The American Journal of Theology* and *The American Journal of Semitic Languages and Literatures.* 1902. *o.p.*

**Mussey, Robert Daniel.** *see* ADAIR, Maternal Care Complications.

**Mussolini:** FERMI.

**My Life:** BEBEL.

**My Native Land:** TRYON.

**My Sad Captains:** GUNN.

**Myers, Earl Dewey,** *joint author:* FRIED-LANDER, Child Welfare in Germany.

**Myers, George William.** First-Year Mathematics for Secondary Schools. By George William Myers, William R. Wickes, Ernest R. Breslich, Harris F. MacNeish, Ernest A. Wreidt. 1907. *o.p.*

**Myers, George William.** Geometric Exercises for Algebraic Solution. Second-Year Mathematics for Secondary Schools. By George William Myers, William R. Wickes, Ernest A. Wreidt, Ernst R. Breslich. 1907. *o.p.*

**Myers, George William.** Second-Year Mathematics for Secondary Schools. By George William Myers and William R. Wickes, Ernst R. Breslich, Ernest A. Wreidt, Arnold Dresden, assisted by Ernest L. Caldwell and Robert M. Mathews. 1910. UCMS. *o.p.*

**Myers, George William.** Teacher's Manual for First-Year Mathematics. By George William Myers and William R. Wickes, Ernst R. Breslich, Ernest L. Caldwell, Robert M. Mathews, William D. Reeve. 1911. UCMS. *o.p.*

**Myers, Walter Lawrence.** The Later Realism. A Study of Characterization in the British Novel. 1927. *o.p.*

**Mysterious Numbers of the Hebrew Kings:** THIELE.

**Mysticism in Religion:** INGE.

**Myth and Cult among Primitive Peoples:** JENSEN.

**Nagel, Ernest.** Principles of the Theory of Probability. 1939. vii, 80 p. 25 cm. A40-2555. Paper. IEUS, I, 6. $1.50ˢ.

**Nahikian, Howard M.** A Modern Algebra for Biologists. 1964. With a Foreword by N. Rashevsky. x, 236 p. 25 cm. 64-13948. $10.00ᵗ.

**Namba, Maj. R.,** *joint author:* CRESSWELL, A Dictionary of Military Terms.

**Narration:** STEIN.

**Nash, Philleo,** *joint author:* EGGAN, Social Anthropology of North American Tribes.

**Nassau Senior and Classical Economics:** BOWLEY.

**Nasu, Shiroshi:** *see* GINI, Population.

**Natarajan, K.:** *see* HAYDON, Modern Trends in World Religions.

**Nathaniel Fish Moore's Diary:** PARGELLIS.

**Nathaniel William Taylor:** MEAD.

**Nation Takes Shape:** CUNLIFFE.

**National Advisory Council on Radio in Education.** *Committee on Engineering Developments.* Present and Impending Applications to Education of Radio and Allied Arts. Report of the Committee on Engineering Developments. 1934. 2d ed. 1936. NACRE. *o.p.*

*Proceedings of the Assemblies of the National Advisory Council on Radio in Education.* 1931–1935:
Radio and Education. 1931.
Radio and Education. 1932.
Radio and Education. 1933.
Radio and Education. 1934.
Education on the Air . . . and Radio and Education. 1935.

*Information Series.* Bulletins of information:
2. TYSON, What To Read about Radio.
5. *Committee on Engineering Developments,*

Present and Impending Applications to Education of Radio.

7. UNION INTERNATIONALE DE RADIO-DIFFUSION, Broadcasting Abroad.
8. BRITISH INSTITUTE OF ADULT EDUCATION, Group Listening.
10. JANSKY, Problem of the Institutionally Owned Station.
11. WILLIS, Widening Horizons.
12. KOON, Some Public Service Broadcasting.
14. TYSON, Future of Radio.
15. TYSON, Retrospect and Forecast in Radio Education.
16. REED, Four Years of Network Broadcasting.
17. PARKER, School Broadcasting.
18. HYERS, Library and the Radio.
19. GRUENBERG, Use of Radio in Parent Education.

Other titles in the *Information Series* published elsewhere.

*Radio Lectures.* Pamphlets and books publishing broadcasts sponsored by the Council from 1931–1933. *o.p.*:

AMERICAN BAR ASSOCIATION, *Council on Legal Education and Admissions to the Bar*, Lawyer and the Public.
BINGHAM, Psychology Today.
BLAIR, More for Your Money.
FOSTER, Doctors, Dollars, and Disease.
MILLER, American Labor.
MORLEY, Aspects of the Depression.
MORLEY, Economic World Today.
REED, Government in a Depression.
REED, Legislatures.

*Men in America Series:*

DEWEY, American Education.
MILLIKAN, Radio's Past and Future.

*Miscellaneous:*

EINSTEIN, Symposium on America and the World Situation.
FROST, Education's Own Stations.
FROST, Is American Radio Democratic?
LINGEL, Educational Broadcasting. A Bibliography.
TYSON, Debate: Resolved: That the United States Should Adopt the Essential Features of the British System of Radio.

**National Committee on Standard Reports for Institutions of Higher Education.** Financial Reports for Colleges and Universities. Compiled by The National Committee on Standard Reports for Institutions of Higher Education. 1935. *o.p.*

**National Conference of Social Work.**

Proceedings from 1920 to 1938. *o.p.*:

47th Annual Meeting, New Orleans (1920).
48th Annual Meeting, Milwaukee (1921).

49th Annual Meeting, Providence (1922).
50th Annual Meeting, Washington, D.C. (1923).
51st Annual Meeting, Toronto (1924).
52d Annual Meeting, Denver (1925).
53d Annual Meeting, Cleveland (1926).
54th Annual Meeting, Des Moines (1927).
55th Annual Meeting, Memphis (1928).
56th Annual Meeting, San Francisco (1929).
57th Annual Meeting, Boston (1930).
58th Annual Meeting, Minneapolis (1931).
59th Annual Meeting, Philadelphia (1932).
60th Annual Meeting, Detroit (1933).
61st Annual Meeting, Kansas City (1934).
62d Annual Meeting, Montreal (1935).
63d Annual Meeting, Atlantic City (1936).
64th Annual Meeting, Indianapolis (1937).
65th Annual Meeting, Kansas City (1938).

Index to National Conference of Social Work Proceedings. Vols. I to LX.

**National Council of Parent Education:** *see* GRUENBERG, Use of Radio in Parent Education.

**National Country Life Conferences:** *see* American Country Life Association.

**National Labor Relations Act:** SPENCER.

**National Libraries and Foreign Scholarship:** WAPLES.

**National Planning Association** (NPL):

GLICK, Administration of Technical Assistance.
MADDOX, Technical Assistance by Religious Agencies in Latin America.
MOSHER, Technical Co-operation in Latin American Agriculture.

**National Planning and Rural Life:** AMERICAN COUNTRY LIFE ASSOCIATION, Proceedings, No. 17.

**National Policies Affecting Rural Life:** AMERICAN COUNTRY LIFE ASSOCIATION, Proceedings, No. 16.

**National Railroad Adjustment Board:** SPENCER.

**National Self-Determination:** COBBAN.

**National Society of College Teachers of Education.** Publications and Proceedings:

BURNHAM, History of Education.
FARRINGTON, Observation and Practice Teaching.
MACVANNEL, College Course in the Principles of Education.
SPAULDING, Aims, Scope, and Methods of a Uni-

versity Course in Public-School Administration.
Sutton, Organization of the Department of Education.

School Review Monographs:

No. 1. Research within the Field of Education, Its Organization and Encouragement. 1911. *o.p.*

No. 2. Graduate and Undergraduate Courses and Degrees in Education. Normal Schools and University Departments of Education. The Present Status of Education as a Science. 1912. *o.p.*

No. 3. Reports of Investigations by Members of the Society of College Teachers of Education. 1913. *o.p.*

No. 4. List of Approved Colleges and Universities in the North Central Association of Colleges and Secondary Schools for 1913. By Charles H. Judd. 1913. *o.p.*

No. 5. Rating, Placing, and Promotion of Teachers. Educational Surveys. List of Educational Investigations by Members. 1914. *o.p.*

No. 6. Work in Education in Colleges and Universities. Rating, Placing, and Promotion of Teachers. List of Investigations and Other Information of Interest to Members. 1915. *o.p.*

Educational Monographs:

Nos. 7–12. Published elsewhere.

No. 13. Journal of Educational Research, Vol. X, No. 3, October, 1924. College Teachers of Education Number. *o.p.*

No. 14. Studies in Education. 1925.

Studies in Education:

No. 15. Studies in Education. Edited by Stuart Appleton Courtis. 1927. *o.p.*

No. 16. Studies in Education. Edited by Walter S. Monroe. 1928. *o.p.*

No. 17. Current Educational Readjustments in Higher Institutions. Edited by Stuart Appleton Courtis. 1929. *o.p.*

No. 18. Quantitative Measurements in Institutions of Higher Learning. Edited by Stuart Appleton Courtis. 1930. *o.p.*

No. 19. Practices of American Universities in Granting Higher Degrees in Education. A Series of Official Statements Collected and Edited with the Authorization of the Executive Committee of the Society. By Frank N. Freeman. Stuart Appleton Courtis, editor. 1931. *o.p.*

No. 20. The Direct Contribution of Educational Psychology to Teacher Training. Stuart Appleton Courtis, editor. 1932. *o.p.*

No. 21. The Educational Frontier. By William H. Kilpatrick, Boyd H. Bode, John L. Childs, H. Gordon Hullfish, John Dewey, R. B. Raup, V. T. Thayer. Fowler D. Brooks, general editor. 1933. *o.p.*

No. 22. Abstracts of Papers. Fowler D. Brooks, editor. 1934. *o.p.*

No. 23. The Education of Teachers. Fowler D. Brooks, editor. 1935. *o.p.*

No. 24. Abstracts of Papers. Fowler D. Brooks, editor. 1936. *o.p.*

No. 25. The Use of Background in the Interpretation of Educational Issues. Fowler D. Brooks, editor. 1937. *o.p.*

No. 26. Abstracts of Papers. Fowler D. Brooks, editor. 1938. *o.p.*

No. 27. The Study of College Instruction. Fowler D. Brooks, editor. 1939. *o.p.*

No. 28. The Discipline of Practical Judgment in a Democratic Society. 1942. *o.p.*

## National Society for the Study of Education (NSSE) Yearbooks.

The first yearbook was published under the title *Yearbook* of the Herbart Society for the Scientific Study of Teaching. The first and second supplements to the *First Yearbook* and the second to fifth yearbooks were published under the title *Yearbooks* of the National Herbart Society. With the reorganization of the Society in 1901 the title was changed to Yearbooks of the National Society for the Scientific Study of Education. In 1909 the name of the Society was again changed to National Society for the Study of Education.

First to Fifth Yearbooks, 1895–1899. *o.p.*
First Supplement to the First Yearbook. *o.p.*
Second Supplement to the First Yearbook. *o.p.*
Supplement to the Second Yearbook. *o.p.*
Supplement to the Third Yearbook. *o.p.*
Supplement to the Fourth Yearbook. *o.p.*
Supplement to the Fifth Yearbook. *o.p.*

Yearbooks of the NSSE (titles marked with asterisk are out of print):

*First Yearbook, 1902, Part I. Some Principles in the Teaching of History. Lucy M. Salmon.

*First Yearbook, 1902, Part II. The Progress of Geography in the Schools. W. M. Davis and and II. M. Wilson.

*Second Yearbook, 1903, Part I. The Course of Study in History in the Common School. Isabel Lawrence, C. A. McMurry, Frank McMurry, E. C. Page, and E. J. Rice.

*Second Yearbook, 1903, Part II. The Relation of Theory to Practice in Education. M. J. Holmes, J. A. Keith, and Levi Seeley.

*Third Yearbook, 1904, Part I. The Relation of Theory to Practice in the Education of Teachers. John Dewey, Sarah C. Brooks, F. M. McMurry, *et al.*

*Third Yearbook, 1904, Part II. Nature Study. W. S. Jackman.

*Fourth Yearbook, 1905, Part I. The Education

and Training of Secondary Teachers. E. C. Elliott, E. G. Dexter, M. J. Holmes, *et al.*

*Fourth Yearbook, 1905, Part II. The Place of Vocational Subjects in the High-School Curriculum. J. S. Brown, G. B. Morrison, and Ellen Richards.

*Fifth Yearbook, 1906, Part I. On the Teaching of English in Elementary and High Schools. G. P. Brown and Emerson Davis.

Fifth Yearbook, 1906, Part II. The Certification of Teachers. E. P. Cubberley.

*Sixth Yearbook, 1907, Part I. Vocational Studies for College Entrance. C. A. Herrick, H. W. Holmes, T. deLaguna, V. Prettyman, and W. J. S. Bryan.

*Sixth Yearbook, 1907, Part II. The Kindergarten and Its Relation to Elementary Education. Ada Van Stone Harris, E. A. Kirkpatrick, Marie Kraus-Boelté, Patty S. Hill, Harriette M. Mills, and Nina Vandewalker.

*Seventh Yearbook, 1908, Part I. The Relation of Superintendents and Principals to the Training and Professional Improvement of Their Teachers. Charles D. Lowry.

*Seventh Yearbook, 1908, Part II. The Co-ordination of the Kindergarten and the Elementary School. B. J. Gregory, Jennie B. Merrill, Bertha Payne, and Margaret Giddings.

*Eighth Yearbook, 1909, Part I. Education with Reference to Sex. Pathological, Economic, and Social Aspects. C. R. Henderson.

*Eighth Yearbook, 1909, Part II. Education with Reference to Sex. Agencies and Methods. C. R. Henderson and Helen C. Putnam.

*Ninth Yearbook, 1910, Part I. Health and Education. T. D. Wood.

*Ninth Yearbook, 1910, Part II. The Nurse in Education. T. D. Wood *et al.*

*Tenth Yearbook, 1911, Part I. The City School as a Community Center. H. C. Leipziger, Sarah E. Hyre, R. D. Warden, C. Ward Crampton, E. W. Stitt, E. J. Ward, Mrs. E. C. Grice, and C. A. Perry.

*Tenth Yearbook, 1911, Part II. The Rural School as a Community Center. B. H. Crocheron, Jessie Field, F. W. Howe, E. C. Bishop, A. B. Graham, O. J. Kern, M. T. Scudder, and B. M. Davis.

*Eleventh Yearbook, 1912, Part I. Industrial Education. Typical Experiments Described and Interpreted. J. F. Barker, M. Bloomfield, B. W. Johnson, P. Johnson, L. M. Leavitt, G. A. Mirick, M. W. Murray, C. F. Perry, A. L. Safford, and H. B. Wilson.

*Eleventh Yearbook, 1912, Part II. Agricultural Education in Secondary Schools. A. C. Monahan, R. W. Stimson, D. J. Crosby, W. H. French, H. F. Button, F. R. Crane, W. R. Hart, and G. F. Warren.

*Twelfth Yearbook, 1913, Part I. The Supervision of City Schools. Franklin Bobbitt, J. W. Hall, and J. D. Wolcott.

*Twelfth Yearbook, 1913, Part II. The Supervision of Rural Schools. A. C. Monahan, L. J. Hanifan, J. E. Warren, Wallace Lund, U. J. Hoffman, A. S. Cook, E. M. Rapp, Jackson Davis, and J. D. Wolcott.

*Thirteenth Yearbook, 1914, Part I. Some Aspects of High-School Instruction and Administration. H. C. Morrison, E. R. Breslich, W. A. Jessup, and L. D. Coffman.

*Thirteenth Yearbook, 1914, Part II. Plans for Organizing School Surveys, with a Summary of Typical School Surveys. Charles H. Judd and Henry L. Smith.

*Fourteenth Yearbook, 1915, Part I. Minimum Essentials in Elementary School Subjects— Standards and Current Practices. H. B. Wilson, H. W. Holmes, F. E. Thompson, R. G. Jones, S. A. Courtis, W. S. Gray, F. N. Freeman, H. C. Pryor, J. F. Hosic, W. A. Jessup, and W. C. Bagley.

Fourteenth Yearbook, 1915, Part II. Methods for Measuring Teachers' Efficiency. Arthur C. Boyce.

*Fifteenth Yearbook, 1916, Part I. Standards and Tests for the Measurement of the Efficiency of Schools and School Systems. G. D. Strayer, Bird T. Baldwin, B. R. Buckingham, F. W. Ballou, D. C. Bliss, H. G. Childs, S. A. Courtis, E. P. Cubberley, C. H. Judd, George Melcher, E. E. Oberholtzer, J. B. Sears, Daniel Starch, M. R. Trabue, and G. M. Whipple.

*Fifteenth Yearbook, 1916, Part II. The Relationship between Persistence in School and Home Conditions. Charles E. Holley.

*Fifteenth Yearbook, 1916, Part III. The Junior High School. Aubrey A. Douglass.

*Sixteenth Yearbook, 1917, Part I. Second Report of the Committee on Minimum Essentials in Elementary-School Subjects. W. C. Bagley, W. W. Charters, F. N. Freeman, W. S. Gray, Ernest Horn, J. H. Hoskinson, W. S. Monroe, C. F. Munson, H. C. Pryor, L. W. Rapeer, G. M. Wilson, and H. B. Wilson.

*Sixteenth Yearbook, 1917, Part II. The Efficiency of College Students as Conditioned by Age at Entrance and Size of High School. B. F. Pittenger.

*Seventeenth Yearbook, 1918, Part I. Third Report of the Committee on Economy of Time in Education. W. C. Bagley, B. B. Bassett, M. E. Branom, Alice Camerer, J. E. Dealey, C. A. Ellwood, E. B. Greene, A. B. Hart, J. F. Hosic, E. T. Housh, W. H. Mace, L. R. Marston, H. C. McKown, H. E. Mitchell, W. C. Reavis, D. Snedden, and H. B. Wilson.

*Seventeenth Yearbook, 1918, Part II. The Measurement of Educational Products. E. J.

Ashbaugh, W. A. Averill, L. P. Ayers, F. W. Ballou, Edna Bryner, B. R. Buckingham, S. A. Courtis, M. E. Haggerty, C. H. Judd, George Melcher, W. S. Monroe, E. A. Nifenecker, and E. L. Thorndike.

*Eighteenth Yearbook, 1919, Part I. The Professional Preparation of High-School Teachers. G. N. Cade, S. S. Colvin, Charles Fordyce, H. H. Foster, T. S. Gosling, W. S. Gray, L. V. Koos, A. R. Mead, H. L. Miller, W. C. Whitcomb, and Clifford Woody.

Eighteenth Yearbook, 1919, Part II. Fourth Report of Committee on Economy of Time in Education. F. C. Ayer, F. N. Freeman, W. S. Gray, Ernest Horn, W. S. Monroe, and C. E. Seashore.

*Nineteenth Yearbook, 1920, Part I. New Materials of Instruction. Prepared by the Society's Committee on Materials of Instruction.

*Nineteenth Yearbook, 1920, Part II. Classroom Problems in the Education of Gifted Children. T. S. Henry.

*Twentieth Yearbook, 1921, Part I. New Materials of Instruction. Second Report by Society's Committee.

*Twentieth Yearbook, 1921, Part II. Report of the Society's Committee on Silent Reading. M. A. Burgess, S. A. Courtis, C. E. Germane, W. S. Gray, H. A. Greene, Regina R. Heller, J. H. Hoover, J. A. O'Brien, J. L. Packer, Daniel Starch, W. W. Theisen, G. A. Yoakam, and representatives of other school systems.

*Twenty-first Yearbook, 1922, Parts I and II. Intelligence Tests and Their Use. Part I. The Nature, History, and General Principles of Intelligence Testing. E. L. Thorndike. S. S. Colvin, Harold Rugg, G. M. Whipple. Part II. The Administrative Use of Intelligence Tests. H. W. Holmes, W. K. Layton, Helen Davis, Agnes L. Rogers, Rudolf Pintner, M. R. Trabue, W. S. Miller, Bessie L. Gambrill, and others. Two parts are bound together.

*Twenty-second Yearbook, 1923, Part I. English Composition. Its Aims, Methods and Measurements. Earl Hudelson.

*Twenty-second Yearbook, 1923, Part II. The Social Studies in the Elementary and Secondary School. A. S. Barr, J. J. Coss, Henry Harap, R. W. Hatch, H. C. Hill, Ernest Horn, C. H. Judd, L. C. Marshall, F. M. McMurry, Earle Rugg, H. O. Rugg, Emma Schweppe, Mabel Snedaker, and C. W. Washburne.

*Twenty-third Yearbook, 1924, Part I. The Education of Gifted Children. Report of the Society's Committee. Guy M. Whipple, Chairman.

*Twenty-third Yearbook, 1924, Part II. Vocational Guidance and Vocational Education for Industries. A. H. Edgerton and others.

*Twenty-fourth Yearbook, 1925, Part I. Report of the National Committee on Reading. W. S. Gray, Chairman, F. W. Ballou, Rose L. Hardy, Ernest Horn, Francis Jenkins. S. A. Leonard, Estaline Wilson, and Laura Zirbes.

*Twenty-fourth Yearbook, 1925, Part II. Adapting the Schools to Individual Differences. Report of the Society's Committee. Carleton W. Washburn, Chairman.

*Twenty-fifth Yearbook, 1926, Part I. The Present Status of Safety Education. Report of the Society's Committee. Guy M. Whipple, Chairman.

*Twenty-fifth Yearbook, 1926, Part II. Extra-Curricular Activities. Report of the Society's Committee. Leonard V. Koos, Chairman.

*Twenty-sixth Yearbook, 1927, Part I. Curriculum-making, Past and Present. Report of the Society's Committee. Harold O. Rugg, Chairman.

*Twenty-sixth Yearbook, 1927, Part II. The Foundations of Curriculum-making. Prepared by individual members of the Society's Committee. Harold O. Rugg, Chairman.

Twenty-seventh Yearbook. 1928. Part I. Nature and Nurture. Their Influence upon Intelligence. Prepared by the Society's Committee. Lewis M. Terman, Chairman.

*Twenty-seventh Yearbook, 1928, Part II. Nature and Nurture. Their Influence upon Achievement. Prepared by the Society's Committee. Lewis M. Terman, Chairman.

Twenty-eighth Yearbook, 1929, Parts I and II. Preschool and Parental Education. Part I. Organization and Development. Part II. Research and Method. Prepared by the Society's Committee. Lois H. Meek, Chairman. Bound in one volume.

*Twenty-ninth Yearbook, 1930, Parts I and II. Reports of the Society's Committee on Arithmetic. Part I. Some Aspects of Modern Thought on Arithmetic. Part II. Research in Arithmetic. Prepared by the Society's Committee. F. B. Knight, Chairman. Bound in one volume.

Thirtieth Yearbook, 1931, Part I. The Status of Rural Education. First Report of the Society's Committee on Rural Education. Orville G. Brim, Chairman.

Thirtieth Yearbook, 1931, Part II. The Textbook in American Education. Report of the Society's Committee on the Textbook. J. B. Edmonson, Chairman.

Thirty-first Yearbook, 1932, Part I. A Program for Teaching Science. Prepared by the Society's Committee on the Teaching of Science. S. Ralph Powers, Chairman.

Thirty-first Yearbook, 1932, Part II. Changes and Experiments in Liberal-Arts Education. Prepared by Kathryn McHale, with numerous collaborators.

Thirty-second Yearbook, 1933. The Teaching of Geography. Prepared by the Society's Committee on the Teaching of Geography. A. E. Parkins, Chairman.

Thirty-third Yearbook, 1934, Part I. The Planning and Construction of School Buildings. Prepared by the Society's Committee on School Buildings. N. L. Engelhardt, Chairman.

Thirty-third Yearbook, 1934, Part II. The Activity Movement. Prepared by the Society's Committee on the Activity Movement. Lois Coffey Mossman, Chairman.

Thirty-fourth Yearbook, 1935. Educational Diagnosis. Prepared by the Society's Committee on Educational Diagnosis. L. J. Brueckner, Chairman.

*Thirty-fifth Yearbook, 1936, Part I. The Grouping of Pupils. Prepared by the Society's Committee. W. W. Coxe, Chairman.

*Thirty-fifth Yearbook, 1936, Part II. Music Education. Prepared by the Society's Committee. W. L. Uhl, Chairman.

*Thirty-sixth Yearbook, 1937, Part I. The Teaching of Reading. Prepared by the Society's Committee. W. S. Gray, Chairman.

Thirty-sixth Yearbook, 1937, Part II. International Understanding through the Public-School Curriculum. Prepared by the Society's Committee. I. L. Kandel, Chairman.

Thirty-seventh Yearbook, 1938, Part I. Guidance in Educational Institutions. Prepared by the Society's Committee. G. N. Kefauver, Chairman.

Thirty-seventh Yearbook, 1938, Part II. The Scientific Movement in Education. Prepared by the Society's Committee. F. N. Freeman, Chairman.

Thirty-eighth Yearbook, 1939, Part I. Child Development and the Curriculum. Prepared by the Society's Committee. Carleton Washburne, Chairman.

Thirty-eighth Yearbook, 1939, Part II. General Education in the American College. Prepared by the Society's Committee. Alvin Eurich, Chairman.

*Thirty-ninth Yearbook, 1940, Part I. Intelligence: Its Nature and Nurture. Comparative and Critical Exposition. Prepared by the Society's Committee. G. D. Stoddard, Chairman.

Thirty-ninth Yearbook, 1940, Part II. Intelligence: Its Nature and Nurture. Original Studies and Experiments. Prepared by the Society's Committee. G. D. Stoddard, Chairman.

Fortieth Yearbook, 1941. Art in American Life and Education. Prepared by the Society's Committee. Thomas Munro, Chairman.

Forty-first Yearbook, 1942, Part I. Philosophies of Education. Prepared by the Society's Committee. John S. Brubacher, Chairman.

Forty-first Yearbook, 1942, Part II. The Psychology of Learning. Prepared by the Society's Committee. T. R. McConnell, Chairman.

Forty-second Yearbook, 1943, Part I. Vocational Education. Prepared by the Society's Committee. F. J. Keller, Chairman.

Forty-second Yearbook, 1943, Part II. The Library in General Education. Prepared by the Society's Committee. L. R. Wilson, Chairman.

Forty-third Yearbook, 1944, Part I. Adolescence. Prepared by the Society's Committee. Harold E. Jones, Chairman.

Forty-third Yearbook, 1944, Part II. Teaching Language in the Elementary School. Prepared by the Society's Committee. M. R. Traube, Chairman.

Forty-fourth Yearbook, 1945, Part I. American Education in the Postwar Period: Curriculum Reconstruction. Prepared by the Society's Committee. Ralph W. Tyler, Chairman.

Forty-fourth Yearbook, 1945, Part II. American Education in the Postwar Period: Structural Reorganization. Prepared by the Society's Committee. Bess Goodykoontz, Chairman.

Forty-fifth Yearbook, 1946, Part I. The Measurement of Understanding. Prepared by the Society's Committee. William A. Brownell, Chairman.

Forty-fifth Yearbook, 1946, Part II. Changing Conceptions in Educational Administration. Prepared by the Society's Committee. Alonzo G. Grace, Chairman.

Forty-sixth Yearbook, 1947, Part I. Science Education in American Schools. Prepared by the Society's Committee. Victor H. Noll, Chairman.

Forty-sixth Yearbook, 1947, Part II. Early Childhood Education. Prepared by the Society's Committee. N. Searle Light, Chairman.

Forty-seventh Yearbook, 1948, Part I. Juvenile Delinquency and the Schools. Prepared by the Society's Committee. Ruth Strang, Chairman.

Forty-seventh Yearbook, 1948, Part II. Reading in the High School and College. Prepared by the Society's Committee. William S. Gray, Chairman.

Forty-eighth Yearbook, 1949, Part I. Audio-visual Materials of Instruction. Prepared by the Society's Committee. Stephen M. Corey, Chairman.

Forty-eighth Yearbook, 1949, Part II. Reading in the Elementary School. Prepared by the Society's Committee. Arthur I. Gates, Chairman.

Forty-ninth Yearbook, 1950, Part I. Learning and Instruction. Prepared by the Society's Committee. G. Lester Anderson, Chairman.

Forty-ninth Yearbook, 1950, Part II. The Education of Exceptional Children. Prepared by the Society's Committee. Samuel A. Kirk, Chairman.

Fiftieth Yearbook, 1951, Part I. Graduate Study in Education. Prepared by the Society's Board of Directors. Ralph W. Tyler, Chairman.

Fiftieth Yearbook, 1951, Part II. The Teaching of Arithmetic. Prepared by the Society's Committee. G. T. Buswell, Chairman.

Fifty-first Yearbook, 1952, Part I. General Education. Prepared by the Society's Committee. T. R. McConnell, Chairman.

Fifty-first Yearbook, 1952, Part II. Education in Rural Communities. Prepared by the Society's Committee. Ruth Strang, Chairman.

Fifty-second Yearbook, 1953, Part I. Adapting the Secondary-School Program to the Needs of Youth. Prepared by the Society's Committee. William G. Brink, Chairman.

Fifty-second Yearbook, 1953, Part II. The Community School. Prepared by the Society's Committee. Maurice F. Seay, Chairman.

Fifty-third Yearbook, 1954, Part I. Citizen Cooperation for Better Public Schools. Prepared by the Society's Committee. Edgar L. Morphet, Chairman.

Fifty-third Yearbook, 1954, Part II. Mass Media and Education. Prepared by the Society's Committee. Edgar Dale, Chairman.

Fifty-fourth Yearbook, 1955, Part I. Modern Philosophies and Education. Prepared by the Society's Committee. John S. Brubacher, Chairman.

Fifty-fourth Yearbook, 1955, Part II. Mental Health in Modern Education. Prepared by the Society's Committee. Paul A. Witty, Chairman.

Fifty-fifth Yearbook, 1956, Part I. The Public Junior College. Prepared by the Society's Committee. B. Lamar Johnson, Chairman.

Fifty-fifth Yearbook, 1956, Part II. Adult Reading. Prepared by the Society's Committee. David H. Clift, Chairman.

Fifty-sixth Yearbook, 1957, Part I. In-service Education of Teachers, Supervisors, and Administrators. Prepared by the Society's Committee. Stephen N. Corey, Chairman.

Fifty-sixth Yearbook, 1957, Part II. Social Studies in the Elementary School. Prepared by the Society's Committee. Ralph C. Preston, Chairman.

Fifty-seventh Yearbook, 1958, Part I. Basic Concepts in Music Education. Prepared by the Society's Committee. Thurber H. Madison, Chairman.

Fifty-seventh Yearbook, 1958, Part II. Education for the Gifted. Prepared by the Society's Committee. Robert J. Havighurst, Chairman.

Fifty-seventh Yearbook, 1958, Part III. The Integration of Educational Experiences. Prepared by the Society's Committee. Paul L. Dressel, Chairman.

Fifty-eighth Yearbook, 1959, Part I. Community Education. Principles and Practices from World-wide Experience. Prepared by the Society's Committee. C. O. Arndt, Chairman.

Fifty-eighth Yearbook, 1959, Part II. Personnel Services in Education. Prepared by the Society's Committee. Melvene D. Hardee, Chairman.

Fifty-ninth Yearbook, 1960, Part I. Rethinking Science Education. Prepared by the Society's Committee. J. Darrell Barnard, Chairman.

Fifty-ninth Yearbook, 1960, Part II. The Dynamics of Instructional Groups. Prepared by the Society's Committee. Gale E. Jensen, Chairman.

Sixtieth Yearbook, 1961, Part I. Development in and through Reading. Prepared by the Society's Committee. Paul A. Witty, Chairman.

Sixtieth Yearbook, 1961, Part II. Social Forces Influencing American Education. Prepared by the Society's Committee. Ralph W. Tyler, Chairman.

Sixty-first Yearbook, 1962, Part I. Individualizing Instruction. Prepared by the Society's Committee. Fred T. Tyler, Chairman.

Sixty-first Yearbook, 1962, Part II. Education for the Professions. Prepared by the Society's Committee. G. Lester Anderson, Chairman.

Sixty-second Yearbook, 1963, Part I. Child Psychology. Prepared by the Society's Committee. Harold W. Stevenson, Editor.

Sixty-second Yearbook, 1963, Part II. The Impact and Improvement of School Testing Programs. Prepared by the Society's Committee. Warren G. Findley, Editor.

Sixty-third Yearbook, 1964, Part I. Theories of Learning and Instruction. Prepared by the Society's Committee. Ernest R. Hilgard, Editor.

Sixty-third Yearbook, 1964, Part II. Behavioral Science and Educational Administration. Prepared by the Society's Committee. Daniel E. Griffiths, Chairman.

Sixty-fourth Yearbook, 1965. Part I. Vocational Education. Prepared by the Society's Committee. Melvin L. Barlow, Chairman.

Sixty-fourth Yearbook, 1965. Part II. Art Education. Prepared by the Society's Committee. W. Reid Hastie, Chairman.

**Nation's Economic Objectives:** EDWARDS.

**NATO:** OSGOOD.

**Natural History of a Delinquent Career:** SHAW.

**Natural History of Revolution:** EDWARDS.

**Natural Radiation Environment:** ADAMS.

**Natural Right and History:** STRAUSS.

**Naturalist in the Great Lakes Region:** DOWNING.

**Nature and Application of Inductive Logic:** CARNAP.

**Nature of Culture:** KROEBER.

**Nature of Human Society** (NHS). *Edited by* JULIAN PITT-RIVERS *and* ERNEST GELLNER:
ABRAHAM, Mind of Africa.
BAROJA, World of the Witches.
CRICK, In Defence of Politics.
GELLNER, Thought and Change.
MAIR, New Nations.
WORSLEY, Third World.

**Nature and Life:** WHITEHEAD.

**Nature and Nurture:** TERMAN.

**Nature of Psychotherapy:** JASPERS.

**Nature of the Relationship between Ethics and Economics:** AYRES.

**Nature Study:** JACKMAN.

**Nature of the World and of Man:** NEWMAN.

**Navaho Sacrificial Figurines:** HAILE.

**Nazi Conquest of Danzig:** LEONHARDT.

**Near East:** IRELAND.

**Necessary and the Contingent in the Aristotelian System:** HEIDEL.

**Necessary Evil:** KENNEDY, *in his* Plays for Seven Players.

**Needed Readjustments in Higher Education:** GRAY.

**Needed Readjustments in Rural Life:** *see* AMERICAN COUNTRY LIFE ASSOCIATION, Proceedings, No. 8.

**Needham, Rodney.** Structure and Sentiment. 1962. viii, 135 p. 22 cm. 62-9738. $3.50ˢ.

**Neel, James.** Human Heredity. By James V. Neel and William J. Schull. 1954. vii, 361 p. Illus. 22 cm. 54-12698. BM. CLBS. $8.50ᵗ.

**Nef, John.** The Conquest of the Material World. 1964. xii, 408 p. 24 cm. 64-15804. $8.95.

**Nef, John.** The United States and Civilization. 1941. WFL. *o.p.*

**Negatives of the Indo-European Languages:** FOWLER.

**Negro in Chicago:** CHICAGO COMMISSION ON RACE RELATIONS.

**Negro Family in Chicago:** FRAZIER.

**Negro Family in the United States:** FRAZIER.

**Negro Politicians:** GOSNELL.

**Negro Press in the United States:** DETWEILER.

**Negroes in Brazil:** PIERSON.

**Neighborhood:** MCKENZIE.

**Neighborhood Distribution and Consumption of Meat in Pittsburgh:** COVER.

**Nela (Galdós):** CASTILLO.

**Nelson, Harold Hayden.** Key Plans Showing Locations of Theban Temple Decorations. 1941. xi p. 37 double plates. In portfolio. 49 cm. 42-21551. OIP, LVI. $6.00.

**Nelson, Harold Hayden.** Medinet Habu, 1924–28. By Harold H. Nelson and Uvo Hölscher. 1929. xv, 50 p. Illus. 25 cm. 29-13423. Paper. OIC 5. $1.00.

**Nelson, Harold Hayden.** Medinet Habu Reports. 2 parts. *Part I:* The Epigraphic Survey, 1928–31. By Harold H. Nelson. *Part II:* The Architectural Survey, 1929/30. Third Preliminary Report. By Uvo Hölscher. 1931. vii, 69 p. Illus. 25 cm. 29-13423. Paper. OIC 10. $1.00.

**Nelson, Harold Hayden.** Work in Western Thebes, 1931–33. 2 parts. 1934. *Part I:* The Calendar of Feasts and Offerings at Medinet Habu. By Harold H. Nelson. With a Chapter by Siegfried Schott. *Part II:* The Excavations. By Uvo Hölscher. vii, 118 p. Illus. 25 cm. 35-6021. Paper. OIC 18. $1.50.

**Nelson, Harold Hayden:** *see* EPIGRAPHIC SURVEY, Medinet Habu.

**Nelson, Harold Hayden:** *see* EPIGRAPHIC SURVEY, Reliefs and Inscriptions at Karnak.

**Nelson, William H.,** *ed.* Theory and Practice in American Politics. 1964. xv, 149 p. 24 cm. 64-15813. RSS. $5.50ˢ.

**Nemerov, Howard.** Mirrors and Windows. Poems. 1958. *o.p.*

**Nemerov, Howard.** New and Selected Poems. 1960. vi, 116 p. 60-14236. Cloth. 22 cm. $3.95. Paper. 21 cm. $1.95. CUSA.
". . . with the emergence of his *New and Selected Poems* it becomes necessary to class him outside the category of a mere generation; for the book makes it clear that he is one of the best poets writing in English."—Thom Gunn, in *The Yale Review.*

**Nemerov, Howard.** Next Room of the Dream. Poems and Two Plays. 1962. x, 146 p. 62-22328. Cloth. 22 cm. $5.00. Paper. 21 cm. $2.45. CUSA.

**Nerlove, Samuel Henry.** A Decade of Corporate Incomes, 1920 to 1929. 1932. SBA, II. *o.p.*

**Nerlove, Samuel Henry,** *joint author:* MARSHALL, Outlines of the Economic Order.

**Nervous System:** GERARD.

**Ness, Arne,** *joint author:* BRUNSWIK, Theory of Behavior.

**Nethercot, Arthur H.** The First Five Lives of Annie Besant. 1960. xii, 419 p. Illus. 24 cm. 59-11624. $7.50ˢ. COBE AND CONTINENT OF EUROPE.

**Nethercot, Arthur H.** The Last Four Lives of Annie Besant. 1963. 483 p. Illus. 24 cm. $7.50ˢ. COBE AND CONTINENT OF EUROPE.

**Nethercot, Arthur H.** The Road to Tryermaine. A Study of the History, Background, and Purposes of Coleridge's "Christabel." 1939. *o.p.*

**Nethercot, Arthur H.** Sir William D'avenant, Poet Laureate and Playwright-Manager. 1938. *o.p.*

**Nettleship, Richard Lewis.** The Theory of Education in the Republic of Plato. 1906. *o.p.*

**Neuberg, Maurice Joseph.** Right Living. A Discussion Course for Girls and Boys. 1925–1927. CS. *o.p.*

**Neugarten, Bernice L.,** *joint author:* HAVIGHURST, American Indian and White Children.

**Neuman, Margaret W.,** *joint author:* NEUMAN, Chemical Dynamics of Bone Mineral.

**Neuman, William F.** The Chemical Dynamics of Bone Mineral. By William F. Neuman and Margaret W. Neuman. 1958. xi, 209 p. 23 cm. 58-5491. $5.00ˢ.

**Neumann, Sigmund,** *ed.* Modern Political Parties. Approaches to Comparative Politics. 1955. xii, 460 p. 25 cm. 55-10249. $8.50ᵗ.

**Neurath, Otto.** Encyclopedia and Unified Science. By Otto Neurath, Niels Bohr, John Dewey, Bertrand Russell, Rudolf Carnap, Charles W. Morris. 1938. IEUS, I, 1. $1.50ˢ.

**Neurath, Otto.** Foundations of the Social Sciences. 1952. iii, 51 p. 25 cm. A45-483. Paper. IEUS, II, 1. $1.25ˢ.

**Neurath, Otto,** *ed.* International Encyclopedia of Unified Science, Volume I. Edited by Otto Neurath, Rudolf Carnap, and Charles W. Morris. 1955. ix, 700 p. 25 cm. Cloth. $11.00ˢ.

**Neurological Technique:** HARDESTY.

**Neutrality and Collective Security:** WRIGHT.

**New Age of Franklin Roosevelt:** PERKINS.

**New Appreciation of the Bible:** SELLECK.

**New Approach to American History:** BAILEY.

**New Approach to Early European History:** SMITH.

**New Approach to History:** SMITH.

**New Approach to Modern European History:** SMITH.

**New Approach to Poetry:** CHAPIN.

**New Aspects of Politics:** MERRIAM.

**New Deal and Tariff Policy:** FETTER.

**New Definitions of School-Library Service:** FENWICK.

**New Directions in Public Library Development:** ASHEIM.

**New Economic Education:** BROWN.

**New Electoral Law for the Russian Duma:** HARPER.

**New England's Fishing Industry:** ACKERMAN.

**New Essays:** GOLDSMITH.

**New Exposition of Money, Credit, and Prices:** LAUGHLIN.

**New Form of Stellar Photometer:** PICKERING.

**New France:** TANNENBAUM.

**New Frontiers in Collegiate Instruction:** RUSSELL.

**New Inscription of Xerxes:** HERZFELD.

**New Instruments of Precision:** MILLIKAN.

**New Investigations of the Spectrum of β Lyrae:** BÉLOPOLSKY.

**New Latin Primer:** MAXEY.

**New Light from Armageddon:** GUY.

**New or Little-known Vertebrates:** CASE.

**New Materials of Instruction:** COMMITTEE ON MATERIALS (NSSE).

**New Materials of Instruction (Second Report):** COMMITTEE ON MATERIALS (NSSE).

**New Methods in Exterior Ballistics:** MOULTON.

**New Methods for the Study of Literature:** RICKERT.

**New Monetary System of China:** LIN.

**New Nations:** MAIR.

**New Orthodoxy:** AMES.

**New Perspective:** JORDAN.

**New Perspectives on Peace:** HUSZAR.

**New Plan Texts at the University of Chicago** (NPL):
BARTKY, Highlights of Astronomy.
BUCHSBAUM, Animals without Backbones.
CARLSON, Machinery of the Body.
COULTER, Story of the Plant Kingdom.
CRONEIS, Down to Earth.
LEMON, From Galileo to the Nuclear Age.

LOGSDON, Mathematician Explains.
ROMER, Vertebrate Story.
STEPHENSON, Exploring in Physics.

**New Science of Politics:** VOEGELIN.

**New and Selected Poems:** NEMEROV.

**New Social Science:** WHITE.

**New Solutions of New Testament Problems:** GOODSPEED.

**New Star in Gemini.** HALE.

**New Star in Perseus:** HALE.

**New Statecraft:** LISKA.

**New Testament:** GOODSPEED.

**New Testament Life and Literature:** RIDDLE.

**New Testament Literature:** LYONS.

**New Testament Manuscript Studies:** PARVIS.

**New Testament Word Studies:** BURTON.

**New Views of the Nature of Man:** PLATT.

**New York Tuberculosis and Health Association.** *Committee on Community Dental Service.* Health Dentistry for the Community. A Study of Present Needs and General Trends in the Provision of Community-wide Dental Care. 1935. ME. *o.p.*

**New Zealand Becomes a Pacific Power:** GORDON.

**New Zealand in the Making:** CONDLIFFE.

**Newall, Hugh Frank.** The Modern Spectroscope. XVII. Description of a Spectroscope (The Bruce Spectroscope) Recently Constructed for Use in Connection with the 25-Inch Refractor of the Cambridge Observatory. 1896. *o.p.*

**Newberry Gospels:** GOODSPEED.

**Newcomb, Charles Shelton,** *ed.* Census Data of the City of Chicago, 1934. Edited by Charles S. Newcomb and Richard O. Lang. 1934. *o.p.*

**Newcomb, Charles Shelton,** *ed.* Street Address Coding Guide by Census Areas of Chicago, 1930. 1933. *o.p.*

**Newcomb, Charles Shelton,** *joint ed.:* BURGESS, Census Data of the City of Chicago, 1920 . . . 1930.

**Newcomb, Rexford.** Architecture of the Old Northwest Territory. 1950. *o.p.*

**Newcomb Simon.** Aspects of American Astronomy. Address Delivered at the University of Chicago, October 22, 1897, in connection with the Dedication of the Yerkes Observatory. 1897. *o.p.*

**Newell, Edward Theodore:** *see* LAMON, Megiddo. I. Seasons of 1925–34.

**Newell, Edward Theodore:** *see* OSTEN, Alishar Hüyük, Season of 1927, Part II.

**Newell, Edward Theodore:** *see* OSTEN, Alishar Hüyük, Seasons of 1930–32, Part III.

**Newell, Edward Theodore:** *see* OSTEN, Ancient Oriental Seals.

**Newer Knowledge of Bacteriology and Immunology:** JORDAN.

**Newman, Horatio Hackett.** The Biology of Twins (Mammals). 1917. SCI. *o.p.*

**Newman, Horatio Hackett.** Evolution, Genetics, and Eugenics. 1921. 3d ed. 1932. *o.p.*
Originally published under the title *Readings in Evolution, Genetics, and Eugenics.*

**Newman, Horatio Hackett.** The Physiology of Twinning. 1923. SCI. *o.p.*

**Newman, Horatio Hackett.** Twins. A Study of Heredity and Environment. By Horatio H. Newman, Frank N. Freeman, and Karl J. Holzinger. 1937. *o.p.*

**Newman, Horatio Hackett,** *ed.* The Nature of the World and of Man. By W. C. Allee, G. W. Bartelmez, J H. Bretz, A. J. Carlson, R. T. Chamberlin, F.-C. Cole, M. C. Coulter, H. C. Cowles, E. R. Downing, E. O. Jordan, C. H. Judd, H. B. Lemon, F. R. Moulton, H. H. Newman, A. S. Romer, and J. Stieglitz. 1926. 2d ed. 1927. *Educational Edition. o.p.*

**Newman, Horatio Hackett:** *see* MOULTON, World and Man.

**Newman, William Herman.** The Building Industry and Business Cycles. 1935. SBA, V. *o.p.*

**News and the Human Interest Story:** HUGHES.

**Newspaper Chinese by the Inductive Method:** CREEL.

**Newton, Annabel.** Wordsworth in Early American Criticism. 1928. *o.p.*

**Next Room of the Dream:** NEMEROV.

**Nichiporuk, Walter,** *joint ed.:* BROWN, Bibliography on Meteorites.

**Nichiporuk, Walter,** *trans.:* CHERDYNTSEV, Abundance of Chemical Elements.

**Nicholas Biddle:** GOVAN.

**Nicholls, William H.** Labor Productivity Functions in Meat Packing. 1948. *o.p.*

**Nichols, James H.** Romanticism in American Theology. 1961. viii, 328 p. 22 cm. 61-5609. $7.50ˢ.

**Nicholson, Frank C.** Old German Love Songs. Translated from the Minnesingers of the 12th to 14th Centuries. 1907. *o.p.*

**Nicholson, George Albert.** English Words with Native Roots and with Greek, Latin, or Romance Suffixes. 1916. LG. *o.p.*

**Nickols, D. F.,** *joint author:* DUNCAN, Mentor Graham, The Man Who Taught Lincoln.

**Niemer, William T.,** *joint author:* SNIDER, Stereotaxic Atlas of the Cat Brain.

**Nightingale, Augustus Frederick.** Results of the Chicago Experiment in Introducing Latin into the Seventh and Eighth Grades. 1900(?). *o.p.*

**Nikam, N. A.** Edicts of Asoka. Edited and translated by N. A. Nikam and Richard McKeon. 1958. xxvii, 69 p. 19 cm. 59-5748. $2.75ˢ. (Not for sale in South Asia.)

**Nims, Elinor.** The Illinois Adoption Law and Its Administration. 1928. SSM. *o.p.*

**1931 Flood in China:** BUCK.

**Nitobé, Inazo Ota.** Western Influences in Modern Japan. A Series of Papers on Cultural Relations. By Inazo Nitobé and Others. 1931. IPR. *o.p.*

**Nitze, William Albert.** Arthurian Romance and Modern Poetry and Music. 1940. *o.p.*

**Nitze, William Albert.** The French Verb, Its Forms and Tense Uses. By William A. Nitze and Ernest H. Wilkins. 1914. *o.p.*

**Nitze, William Albert,** *ed.* Le Haut Livre du Graal. Perlesvaus. *Vol. I:* Texts, Variants, and Glossary. Edited by William A. Nitze and T. Atkinson Jenkins. 1932. *Vol. II:* Commentary and Notes. Edited by William A. Nitze and collaborators. 1937. MPM. *o.p.*

**Nitze, William Albert,** *joint author:* CROSS, Lancelot and Guenevere.

**No Friendly Voice:** HUTCHINS.

**Noble, Isabel T.,** *joint author:* HALLIDAY, Food Chemistry and Cookery.

**Noble, Isabel T.,** *joint author:* HALLIDAY, How To Buy Beef.

**Noble, Isabel T.,** *joint author:* HALLIDAY, Hows and Whys of Cooking.

**Noble-Gas Compounds:** HYMAN.

**Nocturnal Maximum Occurrence of Thunderstorms:** MEANS.

**Noé, Adolph C.:** *see* STUTZER, Geology of Coal.

**Noel Slate and Manufacturing Company:** MARSHALL.

**Noll, Victor H.** Science Education in American Schools. Prepared by Victor H. Noll, Chairman of the Society's Committee. 1947. NSSE, 46th Yrbk., Part I. xii, 306 p. 24 cm. 48-294. Cloth. $4.50ᵗ. Paper. $3.75ᵗ.

**Nolting, Orin Frederyc,** *joint author:* RIDLEY, City-Manager Profession.

**Nonfrontal Thunderstorms:** BYERS.

**Non-oral Reading:** BUSWELL.

**Non-voting:** MERRIAM.

**Norbeck, Edward,** *joint ed.:* JENNINGS, Prehistoric Man in the New World.

**Normal Schools and University Departments of Education:** NATIONAL SOCIETY OF COLLEGE TEACHERS OF EDUCATION. Proceedings, No. 2.

**Norman, Hilda Laura.** Swindlers and Rogues in French Drama. 1928. *o.p.*

**Norris, Joe L.:** *see* PIERCE, As Others See Chicago.

**Norris, Miriam.** Blindness in Children. By Miriam Norris, Patricia J. Spaulding, and Fern H. Brodie. 1957. xiv, 174 p. 24 cm. 57-6983. $3.00ˢ.

**North, Cecil Clare.** The Sociological Implications of Ricardo's Economics. 1915. *o.p.*

**North American Epicontinental Sea:** LOGAN.

**North of Slavery:** LITWACK.

**Northern Element in English Literature:** CRAIGIE.

**Northmore, Thomas.** Compression of Gases, *in* FARADAY, Liquefaction of Gases.

**Northup, Clark Sutherland.** The Present Bibliographical Status of Modern Philology. By Clark S. Northup. With a Summary of Letters from Representatives of Modern Language Studies by W. N. C. Carlton. Preceded by a Survey of Periodical Bibliography by J. Christian Bay. 1911. *o.p.*

**Northup, George Tyler,** *ed.* El Cuento de Tristan de Leonis. Edited from the unique manuscript, Vatican 6428. 1928. MPM. *o.p.*

**Northup, George Tyler.** An Introduction to Spanish Literature. 1925. 3d enl. ed. 1960. Revised, and with an Introduction by Nicholson B. Adams. 1960. x, 532 p. 21 cm. 60-8127. Cloth. $6.00ˢ. Paper. $3.50ᵗ.

**Norton, Frederick Owen.** A Lexicographical and Historical Study of ΔΙΑΘΗΚΗ from the Earliest Times to the End of the Classical Period. 1908. HLL. *o.p.*

**Norton, Frederick Owen.** The Rise of Christianity. A Historical Study of the Origin of the Christian Religion. 1924. HER. *o.p.*

**Norton, Henry Kittredge:** *see* CASSEL, Foreign Investments.

**Norton, Henry Kittredge:** *see* JONES, United States and the Caribbean.

**Norton, Henry Kittredge:** *see* WOODHEAD, Occidental Interpretations of the Far Eastern Problem.

**Norton, John Foote.** Laboratory Outlines in Bacteriology and Immunology. By John F. Norton and I. S. Falk. 1926. *o.p.*

Notes on the Chalcolithic and Early Bronze Age Pottery of Megiddo: ENGBERG.

Notes on Egyptian Marriage: EDGERTON.

Notes on the Fertilization and Embryogeny of Conifers: COULTER.

Notes on the Megiddo Pottery: SHIPTON.

Notes on Mexican Archaeology: STARR.

Notes on New Testament Grammar: BURTON.

Notes on Quantum Mechanics: FERMI.

Notes on Some Carboniferous Cochliodonts: BRANSON.

Nourse, Edwin Griswold. Outlines of Agricultural Economics. A Class-Book of Questions and Problems. 1917. MSE. *o.p.*

Nourse, Edwin Griswold, *ed.* Agricultural Economics. A Selection of Materials in Which Economic Principles Are Applied to the Practice of Agriculture. 1916. MSE. *o.p.*

Novel and the Modern World: DAICHES.

Novelle (Panzini): DOTY.

Novelle e poesie (Fucini): FURST.

Noy, Dov, *ed.* Folktales of Israel. Translated by Gena Baharav. 1963. xv, 220 p. 22 cm. 63-16721. FW. $4.00. COBE.

Nuclear Physics: FERMI.

Nuclear Studies on Pellia: DAVIS.

Nucleosynthesis in Massive Stars and Supernovae: FOWLER.

Nugent, Walter T. K. The Tolerant Populists. Kansas Populism and Nativism. 1963. xii, 256 p. Index. 22 cm. 63-13069. $6.00ˢ.

Nullification Controversy in South Carolina: BOUCHER.

Number and Arrangement of the Fibers Forming the Spinal Nerves of the Frog: HARDESTY.

Nurse in Education: WOOD.

Nursing Services and Insurance for Medical Care in Brattleboro, Vermont: PEEBLES.

Nutrition Work with Children: *see* MARTIN, Roberts' Nutrition Work with Children.

Nutter, G. Warren. The Extent of Enterprise Monopoly in the United States, 1899–1939. A Quantitative Study of Some Aspects of Monopoly. 1951. *o.p.*

Nuzi Personal Names: GELB.

Nykl, Alois Richard, *ed.:* MUHAMMAD IBN DĀWŪD AL-IṢFAHĀNĪ, Kitāb al-Zahrah.

Oakley, Kenneth P. Man the Tool-maker. 1957. 2d ed. 1959. 128 pages. Illus. 21 cm. 50-13440. Paper. P20 $1.25. COBE.

Oaks, Dallin H., *ed.* The Wall between Church and State. 1963. vii, 179 p. 21 cm. 63-20897. Cloth $6.75ˢ. Paper. P137. $1.95.

Obenhaus, Victor. The Responsible Christian. A Protestant Interpretation. 1957. xi, 219 p. 24 cm. 57-11211. $4.00ˢ.

Oberlé (Bazin): HAYGOOD.

Obliviscence and Reminiscence: BALLARD.

Observation and Practice Teaching: FARRINGTON.

Observations of the Total Solar Eclipse of May 29, 1900: HALE.

Occident and the Orient: CHIROL.

Occidental Interpretations of the Far Eastern Problem: WOODHEAD.

Occupations of the Lower Classes in Roman Society: MAXEY.

Occurrences of Pyramid Texts: ALLEN.

Ocean Analysis: RIEHL.

O'Conner, John Bartholomew. Chapters in the History of Actors and Acting in Ancient Greece Together with a Prosopographia histrionum Graecorum. 1908. *o.p.*

O'Connor, William Van. Sense and Sensibility in Modern Poetry. 1948. *o.p.*

O'Dea, Thomas F. The Mormons. 1957. xii, 288 p. 57-6984. Cloth. 24 cm. $7.50ˢ. Paper. P162. 21 cm. $1.95.

Odes: PINDAR.

Odes and Epodes: HORACE.

**Odishaw, Hugh,** *ed.* The Challenges of Space. 1962. xviii, 379 p. Illus. Index. 23 cm. 62-19627. $6.95s.

**Ogburn, William Fielding.** William F. Ogburn on Culture and Social Change. Selected Papers. Edited and with an Introduction by Otis Dudley Duncan. 1964. xxii, 360 p. 21 cm. 64-23418. HS. Cloth. $7.50s. Paper P171. $2.95.

**Ogburn, William Fielding.** You and Machines. 1935. AP. *o.p.*

**Ogburn, William Fielding,** *ed.* American Society in Wartime. 1943. WFL. *o.p.*

**Ogburn, William Fielding,** *ed.* Recent Social Changes in the United States since the War and Particularly in 1927. 1928. *o.p.*

**Ogburn, William Fielding,** *ed.* Social Change and the New Deal. 1934. *o.p.*

**Ogburn, William Fielding,** *ed.* Social Changes during Depression and Recovery. 1935. *o.p.*

**Ogburn, William Fielding,** *ed.* Social Changes in 1928. 1929. *o.p.*

**Ogburn, William Fielding,** *ed.* Social Changes in 1929. 1930. *o.p.*

**Ogburn, William Fielding,** *ed.* Social Changes in 1930. 1931. *o.p.*

**Ogburn, William Fielding,** *ed.* Social Changes in 1931. 1932. *o.p.*

**Ogburn, William Fielding,** *ed.* Social Changes in 1932. 1933. *o.p.*

**Ogburn, William Fielding,** *ed.* Technology and International Relations. 1949. HFL. *o.p.*

**Ogburn, William Fielding:** *see* WIRTH, Eleven Twenty-six.

**O'Hara, Frank Hurburt.** Today in American Drama. 1939. *o.p.*

**O'Hara, Frank Hurburt.** The University of Chicago. An Official Guide. 1928. 2d ed. 1930. *o.p.*

**O'Hara, Frank Hurburt,** *ed.* University of Chicago Plays, Skits, and Lyrics. With an Introduction to the Plays by Whitford Kane and to the Skits and the Lyrics by Beatrice Lillie. 1936. *o.p.*

**Ohio Poor Law:** KENNEDY.

**O'Keefe, John A.,** *ed.* Tektites. 1963. xii, 228 p. Illus. 25 cm. 63-13070. $10.95s.

**Old Age Assistance:** LINFORD.

**Old Akkadian Writing and Grammar:** GELB.

**Old Chicago Houses:** DRURY.

**Old German Love Songs:** NICHOLSON.

**Old Kaskaskia Records:** ALVORD.

**Old and New Testament Student:** *see* JOURNAL OF RELIGION.

**Old Nobody:** KENNEDY, *in his* Plays for Three Players, Vol. II.

**Old Testament: An American Translation:** SMITH.

**Old Testament and Semitic Studies:** HARPER.

**Old Testament Story:** CORBETT.

**Old Testament Student:** *see* JOURNAL OF RELIGION.

**Oldroyd, Harold.** Insects and Their World. 1960. x, 139 p. 21 cm. Paper. PSS516. $1.95. COBE.

**Oliver, Vincent J.,** *joint author:* ROSSBY, Weather Estimates for Local Aerological Data.

**Olmstead, A. T.** History of Assyria. 1923. Reprint. 1960. xxx, 695, p. 23 cm. 23-17167. $13.50s.

**Olmstead, A. T.** History of the Persian Empire. Achaemenid Period. 1948. xxxii, 568 p. 48-7317. Paper. P36. $2.95.
"Unquestionably . . . a major contribution to the ancient history of western Asia. At last we have an up-to-date and reliable account of the important transitional period dominated by the Achaemenid Persians. . . . Professor Olmstead has reconstructed the whole period, utilizing every scrap of classical and oriental information from an amazing variety of sources."—*The American Historical Review.*

**Olson, Elder.** Collected Poems. 1963. xiii, 194 p. 21 cm. 63-22589. Cloth. $6.50s. Paper. PP.146. $2.45.

**Olson, Elder.** Plays and Poems. 1958. x, 169 p. 24 cm. 58-11951. $4.00s.

**Olson, Elder.** The Poetry of Dylan Thomas. 1954. viii, 120 p. 21 cm. 54-9580. Paper. P72. $1.35.

**Olson, Elder,** *ed.* Aristotle's Poetics and English Literature. A Collection of Critical Essays. Edited with an Introduction by Elder Olson. 1965. xxviii, 236 p. 21 cm. 65-24430. Cloth. $6.50ˢ. Paper. $2.45. PLC. 1.

**Olson, Elder,** *joint author:* CRANE, Critics and Criticism.

**Olson, Everett C.** Morphological Integration. By Everett C. Olson and Robert L. Miller. 1958. viii, 317 p. Illus. 25 cm. 58-5116. $10.00ˢ.

**On Acute and Chronic Diseases:** AURELIANUS.

**On the After-effect of the Seen Movement:** WOHLGEMUTH.

**On Amorphous Sulphur:** SMITH.

**On the "Beckmann Rearrangement":** STIEGLITZ.

**On Cancer and Hormones:** BOYLAND.

**On Certain Rigorous Methods of Treating Problems in Celestial Mechanics:** MOULTON.

**On the Constitution of the Red Spectrum of Argon:** RYDBERG.

**On a Darkling Plain:** WEBSTER.

**On a Difference in the Metabolism of the Sexes:** THOMAS.

**On the Difficulty of Correct Description of Books:** DE MORGAN.

**On Divers Arts:** THEOPHILUS.

**On a Formula for Determining the Weight of the Central Nervous System of the Frog:** DONALDSON.

**On the Genesis of the Aesthetic Categories:** TUFTS.

**On the History and Method of Economics:** KNIGHT.

**On the Interpretation of Empedocles:** MILLERD.

**On the Life-History of Lemna minor:** CALDWELL.

**On the Magnitudes of 919 Fixed Stars:** DOBERCK.

**On the Nature of the Gods:** CICERO.

**On the Nature of Man:** PLATT.

**On the Nature of the Stimulus Causing the Change of Form and Structure in Proserpinaca palustris:** McCALLUM.

**On the Nature of the Stimulus Which Causes the Change in Form in Polymorphic Green Algae:** LIVINGSTON.

**On the Production and Suppression of Muscular Twitchings:** LOEB.

**On the Progress Made in the Last Decade in the Determination of Stellar Motions in the Line of Sight:** VOGEL.

**On Some Photographs of the Great Nebula in Orion:** KEELER.

**On the Spectra of Argon:** KAYSER.

**On the Spectra of Krypton:** RUNGE.

**On the Spectra of Stars of Class IIIb:** DUNÉR.

**On the Structure of the Fore Foot of Dimetrodon:** CASE, *in his* Osteology of the Skull of . . . Dimetrodon.

**On the Teaching of English:** BROWN.

**On the Text of Chaucer's** *Parlement of Foules:* HAMMOND.

**One Hundred Years of Land Values in Chicago:** HOYT.

**One Hundred Years of Public Services:** MA.

**One Year of Sunday School Lessons:** PALMER.

**Oögenesis in Pinus Laricio:** CHAMBERLAIN.

**Oögenesis in Saprolegnia:** DAVIS.

**Opler, Morris Edward.** An Apache Life-Way. The Economic, Social, and Religious Institutions of the Chiricahua Indians. 1941. xiii, 500 p. Illus. 21 cm. AN. $8.50ˢ.

**Opler, Morris Edward,** *joint author:* EGGAN, Social Anthropology of North American Tribes.

**Opler, Morris Edward:** *see* HOIJER, Chiricahua and Mescalero Apache Texts.

**Oppenheim, A. Leo.** Ancient Mesopotamia. Portrait of a Dead Civilization. 1964. 433 p. 14 plates, 4 maps. 24 cm. 64-19847. $8.50.

**Opportunities for Education:** McSwain.

**Opportunities in School and Industry:** Talbert.

**Opportunities for Students at the Yerkes Observatory:** Hale.

**Optical Spectrometric Measurements of High Temperatures:** Dickerman.

**Oral Aspects of Reading:** Robinson.

**Orbit of the Minor Planet (334):** Laves.

**Order of Birth, Parent-Age, and Intelligence:** Thurstone.

**Organization and Administration of the University:** Reeves.

**Organization of the Department of Education:** Sutton.

**Organization and Management of Production:** Mitchell.

**Organization and Methods of the Thayer Manufacturing Company:** Palmer.

**Organization and Methods of the Walworth Manufacturing Company:** McKinsey.

**Organization for Research in the American Sociological Society:** *see* American Sociological Society, Annual Proceedings. Vol. XXVI, No. 2.

**Organization of the Yerkes Observatory:** Hale.

**Organized Labor:** Millis, *in his* Economics of Labor, Vol. III.

**Organized Medical Service at Fort Benning, Georgia:** Falk.

**Organized Scarcity:** Gideonse.

**Oriental Exclusion:** McKenzie.

**Oriental Forerunners of Byzantine Painting:** Breasted.

**Oriental Institute:** Breasted.

**Oriental Institute Discoveries in Iraq, 1933/ 34:** Frankfort.

**Oriental Institute, Publications of:**

**Assyriological Studies (AS):**

Researches based chiefly on cuneiform sources.

1. Meissner, Beiträge zum assyrischen Wörterbuch. I.
2. Poebel, The Sumerian Prefix Forms E- and I- in the Time of the Earlier Princes of Lagaš.
3. Poebel, Das appositionell bestimmte Pronomen der 1. Pers. Sing. in den westsemitischen Inschriften und im Alten Testament.
4. Meissner, Beiträge zum assyrischen Wörterbuch. II.
5. Piepkorn, Historical Prism Inscriptions of Ashurbanipal. I. Editions E, $B_{1-5}$, D, and K.
6. Jacobsen, Philological Notes on Eshnunna and Its Inscriptions.
7. Hallock, The Chicago Syllabary and the Louvre Syllabary AO 7661.
8. Kramer, The Sumerian Prefix Forms Be- and Bi- in the Time of the Earlier Princes of Lagaš.
9. Poebel, Studies in Akkadian Grammar.
10. Kramer, Gilgamesh and the *Huluppu*-Tree. A Reconstructed Sumerian Text.
11. Jacobsen, The Sumerian King List.
12. Kramer, Lamentation over the Destruction of Ur.
13. Heidel, The System of the Quadriliteral Verb in Akkadian.
14. Poebel, Miscellaneous Studies.
15. Poebel, Second Dynasty of Isin.

**Materials for the Assyrian Dictionary (MAD):**

*Edited by* Ignace J. Gelb:

1. Sargonic Texts from the Diyala Region.
2. Old Akkadian Writing and Grammar.
3. Glossary of Old Akkadian.

**Oriental Institute Communications (OIC):**

1. Breasted, The Oriental Institute of the University of Chicago.
2. Osten, Explorations in Hittite Asia Minor. A. Preliminary Report.
3. Sandford, First Report of the Prehistoric Survey Expedition.
4. Fisher, The Excavation of Armageddon.
5. Nelson, Medinet Habu, 1924–28.
6. Osten, Explorations in Hittite Asia Minor, 1927–28.
7. Hölscher, Medinet Habu Studies, 1928/29. I. The Architectural Survey. Wilson, II. The Language of the Historical Texts Commemorating Ramses III.
8. Osten, Explorations in Hittite Asia Minor, 1929.
9. Guy, New Light from Armageddon. Second

Provisional Report (1927–29) on the Excavations at Megiddo in Palestine.

10. I. NELSON, Medinet Habu Reports. The Epigraphic Survey, 1928–31. II. HÖLSCHER, The Architectural Survey, 1929/30.
11. SCHMIDT, Anatolia through the Ages. Discoveries at the Alishar Mound, 1927–29.
12. SPRENGLING, The Alphabet. Its Rise and Development from the Sinai Inscriptions.
13. FRANKFORT, Tell Asmar and Khafaje. The First Season's Work in Eshnunna, 1930/31.
14. OSTEN, Discoveries in Anatolia, 1930–31.
15. HÖLSCHER, Excavations at Ancient Thebes, 1930/31.
16. FRANKFORT, Tell Asmar, Khafaje, and Khorsabad. Second Preliminary Report of the Iraq Expedition.
17. FRANKFORT, Iraq Excavations of the Oriental Institute, 1932/33. Third Preliminary Report of the Iraq Expedition.
18. I. NELSON, Work in Western Thebes, 1931–33. The Calendar of Feasts and Offerings at Medinet Habu. II. HÖLSCHER, The Excavations.
19. FRANKFORT, Oriental Institute Discoveries in Iraq, 1933/34. Fourth Preliminary Report of the Iraq Expedition.
20. FRANKFORT, Progress of the Work of the Oriental Institute in Iraq, 1934/35. Fifth Preliminary Report of the Iraq Expedition.
21. SCHMIDT, The Treasury of Persepolis and Other Discoveries in the Homeland of the Achaemenians.

### Oriental Institute Essays (OIE):

FRANKFORT, Intellectual Adventure of Ancient Man.
FRANKFORT, Kinship and the Gods.
GRUNEBAUM, Medieval Islam.
WILSON, Burden of Egypt.

### Oriental Institute Publications (OIP):

I. BREASTED, Oriental Forerunners of Byzantine Painting.
II. LUCKENBILL, The Annals of Sennacherib.
III–IV. BREASTED, The Edwin Smith Surgical Papyrus.
V. OSTEN, Researches in Anatolia. I. Explorations in Central Anatolia, Season of 1926.
VI–VII. OSTEN, Researches in Anatolia. II–III. The Alishar Hüyük, Season of 1927.
VIII. EPIGRAPHIC SURVEY, Medinet Habu. I. Earlier Historical Records of Ramses III.
IX. EPIGRAPHIC SURVEY, Medinet Habu. II. Later Historical Records of Ramses III.

X. SANDFORD, Prehistoric Survey of Egypt and Western Asia. I. Paleolithic Man and the Nile-Faiyum Divide. A Study of the Region during Pliocene and Pleistocene Times.
XI. CHIERA, Cuneiform Series. I. Sumerian Lexical Texts from the Temple School of Nippur.
XII. WORRELL, The Proverbs of Solomon in Sahidic Coptic According to the Chicago Manuscript.
XIII. GREGORIUS, Barhebraeus' Scholia on the Old Testament. I. Genesis–II Samuel.
XIV. LUCKENBILL, Cuneiform Series. II. Inscriptions from Adab.
XV. CHIERA, Cuneiform Series. III. Sumerian Epics and Myths.
XVI. CHIERA, Cuneiform Series. IV. Sumerian Texts of Varied Contents.
XVII. SANDFORD, Prehistoric Survey of Egypt and Western Asia. II. Paleolithic Man and the Nile Valley in Nubia and Upper Egypt. A Study of the Region during Pliocene and Pleistocene Times.
XVIII. SANDFORD, Prehistoric Survey of Egypt and Western Asia. III. Paleolithic Man and the Nile Valley in Upper and Middle Egypt. A Study of the Region during Pliocene and Pleistocene Times.
XIX–XX. SCHMIDT, Researches in Anatolia. IV–V. The Alishar Hüyük, Seasons of 1928 and 1929.
XXI. HÖLSCHER, The Excavation of Medinet Habu. I. General Plans and Views.
XXII. OSTEN, Ancient Oriental Seals in the Collection of Mr. Edward T. Newell.
XXIII. EPIGRAPHIC SURVEY, Medinet Habu. III. The Calendar, the "Slaughterhouse," and Minor Records of Ramses III.
XXIV. JACOBSEN, Sennacherib's Aqueduct at Jerwan.
XXV. EPIGRAPHIC SURVEY, Reliefs and Inscriptions at Karnak. I. Ramses III's Temple within the Great Inclosure of Amon.
XXVI. MAY, Material Remains of the Megiddo Cult.
XXVII. GELB, Researches in Anatolia. VI. Inscriptions from Alishar and Vicinity.

**Origin and Growth of the Hebrew Religion:** FOWLER.

**Origin and History of Hebrew Law:** SMITH.

**Origin of the Inequality of the Social Classes:** LANDTMAN.

**Origin Legend of the Navaho Flintway:** HAILE.

**Origin of Metamorphic and Metasomatic Rocks:** RAMBERG.

**Origin of Printing in Europe:** BUTLER.

**Origin and Religious Teaching of the Old Testament Books:** *see* CHAMBERLIN, Old Testament Books.

**Origin of Subjectivity:** KITCH.

**Origin and Teaching of the New Testament Books:** BURTON.

**Origins of American Scientists:** KNAPP.

**Origins of Christian Supernaturalism:** CASE.

**Origins and History of Proconsular and Propraetorian Imperium:** JASHEMSKI.

**Origins of Leadership:** MUMFORD.

**Origins of Scientific Thought:** SANTILLANA.

**Origins of Social Liberalism in Germany:** ROHR.

**Origins of Sociology:** SMALL.

**Ornstein, Martha.** The Rôle of Scientific Societies in the Seventeenth Century. Privately printed, 1913. 3d ed. 1938. *o.p.*

**Orton, W. A.** The Economic Role of the State. 1950. WFL. *o.p.*

**Osborn, Loran David.** The Recovery and Restatement of the Gospel. 1903. *o.p.*

**Oscan-Umbrian Verb-System:** BUCK.

**Osgood, Ernest Staples.** The Day of the Cattleman. 1929. ix, 283 p. 21 cm. 29-19222. Paper. P13. $1.95.

**Osgood, Robert Endicott.** Ideals and Self-interest in America's Foreign Relations. The Great Transformation of the Twentieth Century. 1953. xii, 491 p. 24 cm. 53-10532. CSAFP. Cloth. $6.50s. Paper. P160. $2.95.

**Osgood, Robert Endicott.** Limited War. The Challenge to American Strategy. 1957. xi, 315 p. 24 cm. 57-5275. CSAFP. $6.95s.

**Osgood, Robert Endicott.** NATO. The Entangling Alliance. 1962. x, 416 p. 24 cm. 62-8348. $7.50s.

**Osgood, Wilfred Hudson,** *joint author:* FUERTES, Artist and Naturalist.

**Osseous Development in the Hand:** FLORY.

**Osten, Hans Henning von der.** Ancient Oriental Seals in the Collection of Mr. Edward T. Newell. 1934. xiii, 204 p. Illus. 30 cm. 34-15806. OIP, XXII. $6.00.

**Osten, Hans Henning von der.** Ancient Oriental Seals in the Collection of Mrs. Agnes Baldwin Brett. 1936. xi, 76 p. Illus. 30 cm. 36-25523. OIP, XXXVII. $4.00.

**Osten, Hans Henning von der.** Discoveries in Anatolia, 1930–31. By H. H. von der Osten. With the collaboration of R. A. Martin and J. A. Morrison. 1932. xi, 149 p. Illus. 25 cm. 33-13172. Paper. OIC 14, $2.50.

**Osten, Hans Henning von der.** Explorations in Hittite Asia Minor. *Vol. I:* A Preliminary Report. 1927. OIC 2. *o.p. Vol. II:* 1927–28. 1929. vii, 153 p. Illus. 25 cm. Paper. OIC 6. $1.50. *Vol. III:* 1929. 1930. vii, 196 p. Illus. 25 cm. 28-3839. Paper. OIC 8. $2.00.

**Osten, Hans Henning von der.** Researches in Anatolia. *Vol. I:* Explorations in Central Anatolia, Season of 1926. 1929. xix, 167 p. Illus. 30 cm. 29-14658. OIP, V. $5.00. *Vols. II–III:* The Alishar Hüyük, Season of 1927. By H. H. von der Osten and Erich F. Schmidt. 1930–32. *Part I.* 1930. xxii, 284 p. Illus. 30 cm. 30-14678. OIP, VI. $12.00. *Part II.* With a Chapter by Edward T. Newell. 1932. xi, 134 p. Illus. 30 cm. OIP, VII. $6.00. *Vols. VII–IX:* The Alishar Hüyük, Seasons of 1930–32. 1937. *Part I.* xxii, 283 p. Illus. 30 cm. OIP, XXVIII. $20.00. *Part II.* xxii, 481 p. Illus. 30 cm. OIP, XXIX. $35.00. *Part III.* With Contributions by Wilton Marion Krogman and Others. xxiv, 496 p. Illus. 30 cm. OIP, XXX. $25.00.

**Osteology of the Reptiles:** ROMER.

**Osteology of Some American Permian Vertebrates:** WILLISTON.

**Osteology of Some American Permian Vertebrates. II.** WILLISTON.

**Osteology of the Skull of . . . Dimetrodon:** CASE.

**Otterström, Thorvald.** Manual of Harmony. 1941. *o.p.*
Key to Manual of Harmony. 1941. *o.p.*

**Otterström, Thorvald.** A Theory of Modulation. Eine Modulationstheorie. 1935. *o.p.*

**Our Amish Neighbors:** SCHREIBER.

**Our Church:** LOBINGIER.

**Our Generation:** SKELTON.

**Our Living World:** DOWNING.

**Our Physical World:** DOWNING.

**Out of Doors with Youth:** DAVIES.

**Outdoor Labor:** HENDERSON.

**Outline of a Bible-School Curriculum:** PEASE.

**Outline of the Cranial Nerves:** FAVILL.

**Outline of Genetics:** COULTER.

**Outline of New Testament Christology:** GRANBERY.

**Outlines of Agricultural Economics:** NOURSE.

**Outlines of Chinese Art:** FERGUSON.

**Outlines of the Economic Order:** MARSHALL.

**Outlines of Economics:** MARSHALL.

**Outlines of Economics Developed in a Series of Problems:** MARSHALL.

**Outlines of Geologic History:** SALISBURY.

**Outlook for American Prose:** BEACH.

**Outlook for Higher Education:** RUSSELL.

**Outposts of Defense:** HASS.

**Overacker, Louise,** *joint author:* MERRIAM, Primary Elections.

**Overton, James Bertram.** Parthenogenesis in Thalictrum purpurascens. 1902. HB. *o.p.*

**Ovule and Embryo of Potamogeton natans:** HOLFERTY.

**Owen, William Bishop.** Homeric Vocabularies. Greek and English Word-Lists for the Study of Homer. By William Bishop Owen and Edgar Johnson Goodspeed. 1906. 2d ed. 1909. *o.p.*

**Owen Wister Out West:** WISTER.

**Owsley, Frank Lawrence.** King Cotton Diplomacy. Foreign Relations of the Confederate States of America. 1931. 2d ed. revised by Harriet Chappell Owsley. 1959. xxiii, 614 p. 24 cm. 58-11952. $10.00ˢ.
". . . challenges old beliefs and excites new controversies . . . supersedes all other studies of Confederate diplomacy by its thoroughness and its scholarship."—Henry Steele Commager, in *The New Republic.*

**Owsley, Frank Lawrence.** State Rights in the Confederacy. 1925. *o.p.*

**Oxidation and Reduction:** LEMON.

**Pacific: Guadalcanal to Saipan, August 1942 to July 1944:** CRAVEN.

**Pacific: Matterhorn to Nagasaki, June 1944 to August 1945:** CRAVEN.

**Packinghouse Accounting:** GREER.

**Pákhy-Sprache:** MÉSZÁROS.

**Pagan Regeneration:** WILLOUGHBY.

**Pais, Ettore.** Ancient Italy. Historical and Geographical Investigations in Central Italy, Magna Graecia, Sicily, and Sardinia. Translated from the Italian by C. Densmore Curtis. 1908. *o.p.*

**Pain:** BUYTENDIJK.

**Painting and Personality:** ALSCHULER.

**Palacios, Enrique Juan.** The Stone of the Sun and the First Chapter of the History of Mexico. Translated from the Spanish by Frederick Starr. 1921. ANB. *o.p.*

**Paleolithic Man and the Nile Faiyum Divide:** SANDFORD.

**Paleolithic Man and the Nile Valley in Lower Egypt:** SANDFORD.

**Paleolithic Man and the Nile Valley in Nubia and Upper Egypt:** SANDFORD.

**Paleolithic Man and the Nile Valley in Upper and Middle Egypt:** SANDFORD.

**Paleontological Notes:** CASE.

**Palmblad, Harry V. E.,** *ed.* Impressions de voyage. By Alexandre Dumas. HCLS.

**Palmer, Elisabeth,** *trans.:* MARTINET, Elements of General Linguistics.

**Palmer, Florence U.** One Year of Sunday School Lessons for Young Children. A Manual for Teachers and Parents. 1899. 3d ed. 1905. *o.p.*

**Palmer, James Lindley.** Organization and Methods of the Thayer Manufacturing Company. 1925. MSB. *o.p.*

**Palmer, James Lindley,** *joint author:* BJORKLUND, Study of the Prices of Chain and Independent Grocers in Chicago.

**Palmer, Vivien Marie.** Field Studies in Sociology. A Student's Manual. 1928. SSCI. *o.p.*

**Palter, Robert M.** Whitehead's Philosophy of Science. 1960. xv, 250 p. Illus. 24 cm. 60-7211. $7.50s.

**Palyi, Melchior.** The Chicago Credit Market. Organization and Institutional Structure. 1937. SSCI. *o.p.*

**Palyi, Melchior.** Monetary Chaos and Gold. An Address on the European Monetary Problem before the Chicago Council on Foreign Relations. 1934. PPP 11. *o.p.*

**Palyi, Melchior.** Principles of Mortgage Banking Regulation in Europe. 1934. SBA, V. *o.p.*

**Palyi, Melchior,** *joint author:* CLARK, Adam Smith.

**Panchatantra:** RYDER.

**Panhellenism in Aristophanes:** HUGILL.

**Panic of 1837:** McGRANE.

**Papacy and World-Affairs:** ECKHARDT.

**Papers on Etherification:** WILLIAMSON.

**Papers of James Madison:** MADISON.

**Papyri from Karanis:** GOODSPEED.

**Parables of Jesus:** ROBINSON.

**Paradox and Nirvana:** SLATER.

**Parallax of the Andromeda Nebula:** HALE.

**Parallaxes of Eighty Stars:** LEE.

**Parallaxes of Fifty-two Stars:** VAN BIESBROECK.

**Parallel New Testament:** GOODSPEED.

**Parallelism of Mind and Body:** ROGERS.

**Parathyroid Glands:** GAILLARD.

**Pardoning Power:** JENSEN.

**Paré, Ambroise.** The Apologie and Treatise of Ambroise Paré, Containing the Voyages Made into Divers Places, with Many of His Writings upon Surgery. Edited by Geoffrey Keynes. 1952. *o.p.*

**Pargellis, Stanley,** *ed.* Nathaniel Fish Moore's Diary. A Trip from New York to the Falls of St. Anthony in 1845. Edited by Stanley Pargellis and R. L. Butler. 1946. *o.p.*

**Park, Orlando.** A Laboratory Introduction to Animal Ecology and Taxonomy. A Laboratory Guide with Keys Prepared with Particular Reference to Fresh-Water and Terrestrial Habitats of the Deciduous Forest Region in North America. By Orlando Park, W. C. Allee, and V. E. Shelford. 1939. *o.p.*

**Park, Robert Ezra.** The City. By Robert E. Park, Ernest W. Burgess, and Roderick D. McKenzie. With a Bibliography by Louis Wirth. SOC. *o.p.*

**Park, Robert Ezra.** Introduction to the Science of Sociology. By Robert E. Park and Ernest W. Burgess. 1921. 2d ed. 1924. SOC. *o.p.*

**Park, Robert Ezra:** *see* SMITH, Chicago: An Experiment in Social Science Research.

**Parker, Harold Talbot.** The Cult of Antiquity and the French Revolutionaries. A Study in the Development of the Revolutionary Spirit. 1937. *o.p.*

**Parker, Lester Ward.** School Broadcasting in Great Britain. 1937. NACRE. *o.p.*

**Parker, Pierson.** The Gospel before Mark. 1953. *o.p.*

**Parker, Richard A.** Babylonian Chronology, 626 B.C.—A.D. 45. By Richard Parker and W. H. Dubberstein. 1942. SAOC 24. *o.p.*

**Parker, Richard A.** Calendars of Ancient Egypt. 1950. SAOC 26. *o.p.*

**Parkes, Henry Bamford.** Marxism, An Autopsy. 1964. viii, 299 p. 21 cm. Paper. P168. $2.45.

**Parkes, James W.** Judaism and Christianity. 1948. *O.I.*

**Parkhurst, John Adelbert.** Zone +45° of Kapteyn's Selected Areas. Photographic Photometry of 1550 Stars. The preparation for publication was completed after the author's death by Alice Hall Farnsworth. 1927. YO, IV. *o.p.*

**Parkhurst, John Adelbert,** *joint author:* HALE, Spectra of Stars of Secchi's Fourth Type.

**Parkins, A. E.** The Teaching of Geography. Prepared by A. E. Parkins, Chairman of the Society's Committee on the Teaching of Geography. 1933. NSSE, 32d Yrbk. xviii, 571 p. 24 cm. E33-1103. Cloth. $4.50t. Paper. $3.00t.

**Parkins, Maurice Frank.** City Planning in Soviet Russia. 1953. *o.p.*

**Parratt, Spencer Delbert,** *joint author:* MERRIAM, Government of the Metropolitan Region of Chicago.

**Parry, Albert,** *trans.:* LIBERMAN, Building Lenin's Russia.

**Parsons, Elsie Clews.** Mitla. Town of the Souls. And Other Zapoteco-speaking Pueblos of Oaxaca, Mexico, 1936. AN. *o.p.*

**Parsons, Elsie Clews.** Peguche. A Study of Andean Indians. 1945. AN. *o.p.*

**Parsons, Elsie Clews.** Pueblo Indian Religion. 1939. 2 vols. AN. *o.p.*

**Parsons, Ernest William.** A Historical Examination of Some Non-Markan Elements in Luke. 1914. HLL. *o.p.*

**Parsons, Harriet McWilliams.** Astrometric and Photometric Statistics of Certain of Hagen's Fields Photographed with the 24-Inch Reflector. 1928. YO, IV. *o.p.*

**Parthenogenesis in Thalictrum purpurascens:** OVERTON.

**Participle in the Book of Acts:** WILLIAMS.

**Participle in Plautus, Petronius, and Apuleius:** SIDEY.

**Partita a Scacchi (Giacosa):** PHELPS.

**Parts of Body in Later Germanic:** BASKETT.

**Parts of the Body in Older Germanic:** ARNOLDSON.

**Parvis, Merrill M.** New Testament Manuscript Studies. By Merrill M. Parvis and Allen P. Wikgren. 1950. *o.p.*

**Parvis, Merrill M.,** *joint ed.:* LYONS, New Testament Literature.

**Pasch, Alan.** Experience and the Analytic. A Reconsideration of Empiricism. 1958. xvii, 275 p. 24 cm. 58-11953. $6.50s.

**Paschal, George Washington.** A Study of Quintus of Smyrna. 1904. *o.p.*

**Pascua. A Yaqui Village in Arizona:** SPICER.

**Paso a paso:** SPARKMAN.

**Passage Problems for a Stationary Markov Chain:** KEMPERMAN.

**Passarelli, Luigi A.** Les drôles aventures de Renard. By Luigi A. Passarelli and André Pézard. HCLS.

**Passing of the Saint:** MECKLIN.

**Passion for Anonymity:** BROWNLOW.

**Passion for Politics:** BROWNLOW.

**Past and Future:** McNEILL.

**Pasteur, Louis.** Researches on the Molecular Asymmetry of Natural Organic Products (1860). 1902. AC. *o.p.*

**Pathology in General Surgery:** SCHAFER.

**Paton, H. J.** The Categorical Imperative. A Study in Kant's Moral Philosophy. 1948. *O.I.*

**Paton, Lewis Bayles.** Jerusalem in Bible Times. 1908. *o.p.*

**Patterns in the Early Poetry of Israel:** GEVIRTZ.

**Patterns of Literary Criticism** (PLC). *General Editors:* MARSHALL McLUHAN, RICHARD J. SCHOECK, and ERNEST SIRLUCK:

DAVIE, Russian Literature and Modern English Drama.
DOWNER, American Drama and Its Critics.
LEECH, Shakespeare: The Tragedies.
OLSON, Aristotle's Poetics and English Literature.

**Patterns and Problems of Development:** CHILD.

**Patterns of Spanish Pronunciation:** BOWEN.

**Patterson, Robert W.** Early Society in Southern Illinois. 1881. *o.p.*
A publication of the Chicago Historical Society.

**Patterson, W. Bradford,** *ed.* Wound Healing and Tissue Repair. 1958. xi, 83 p. 24 cm. 59-9408. DBC. $2.75ˢ.

**Pauck, Wilhelm:** *see* CASE, Bibliographical Guide to the History of Christianity.

**Paul, John R.** Clinical Epidemiology. 1958. xii, 289 p. Illus. 23 cm. 58-5684. SLBM. $5.00ˢ.

**Paul:** GOODSPEED.

**Paul Becomes a Literary Influence:** BARNETT.

**Paul, Son of Kish:** HENRY.

**Pauvres gens:** BOND.

**Pavlov:** BABKIN.

**Pavlov, D. V.** Leningrad, 1941. The Blockade. Translated by John Clinton Adams. Introduction by Harrison Salisbury. 1965. xxiv, 186 p. 22 cm. 65-24979. $4.50.

**Paying Your Sickness Bills:** DAVIS.

**Payne, Enoch George.** An Experiment in Alien Labor. 1912. *o.p.*

**Payne, Wilson.** Business Behavior, 1919–1922. 1942. SBA. *o.p.*

**Peabody, Emily Clough.** Lives Worth Living. Studies of Women, Biblical and Modern, Especially Adapted for Groups of Young Women in Churches and Clubs. 1915. 2d ed. 1923. CS. *o.p.*

**Peace, Security, and the United Nations:** MORGENTHAU.

**Peaks, Mary Bradford.** The General, Civil and Military Administration of Noricum and Raetia. 1907. *o.p.*

**Pearce, Haywood Jefferson, Jr.** Benjamin H. Hill. Secession and Reconstruction. 1928. *o.p.*

**Peasant Society and Culture:** REDFIELD.

**Pease, George William.** An Outline of a Bible-School Curriculum. 1909. *o.p.*

**Pease, Theodore Calvin.** The Diary of Orville H. Browning. A New Source for Lincoln's Presidency. 1924. *o.p.*
A publication of the Chicago Historical Society.

**Pease, Theodore Calvin.** The Story of Illinois. 3d ed. 1965. Revised by Marguerite Jenison Pease. xvi, 331 p. Illus. 21 cm. 65-17299. $5.95.

**Peattie, Donald Culross.** Vence. Immortal Village. 1945. xxi, 199 p. 21 cm. A45-4042. Paper. P147. $1.75.

**Pechvogel und Glückskind.** Retold and edited after the German of Richard von Volkmann-Leander: HAGBOLDT.

**Peckham, George A.** An Introduction to the Study of Obadiah. 1910. *o.p.*

**Peckham, Howard H.** The Colonial Wars, 1689–1762. 1964. ix, 239 p. 21 cm. 64-12606. CHAC. Cloth. $5.00. Paper. CHAC 21. $1.95.

**Peckham, Howard H.** Pontiac and the Indian Uprising. 1947. xviii, 346 p. Index. 21 cm. 47-11041. Paper. P73. $1.95.

**Peckham, Howard H.** The War for Independence. A Military History. 1958. ix, 226 p. 21 cm. 58-5685. CHAC. Cloth. $4.00ˢ. Paper. $1.95.

**Peddlers and Princes:** GEERTZ.

**Peebles, Allon.** Nursing Services and Insurance for Medical Care in Brattleboro, Vermont. A Study of the Activities of the Thomas Thompson Trust. By Allon Peebles and Valeria D. McDermott. With an Evaluation of the Nursing Program by Violet H. Hodgson and Katharine Tucker. 1932. CMC 17. *o.p.*

**Peebles, Allon.** A Survey of the Medical Facilities of Shelby County, Indiana: 1929. 1930. CMC 6. *o.p.*

**Peebles, Allon.** A Survey of the Medical Facilities of the State of Vermont. 1932. CMC 13. *o.p.*

**Peebles, Allon.** A Survey of Statistical Data on Medical Facilities in the United States. A Compilation of Existing Material. 1929. CMC 3. *o.p.*

**Peguche. A Study of Andean Indians:** PARSONS.

**Peik, Wesley Ernest,** *joint author:* REEVES, Instructional Problems in the University.

**Pelling, Henry.** American Labor. 1960. viii, 247 p. Illus. 21 cm. 60-7247. CHAC. Cloth. $5.00ˢ. Paper. $1.75.

**Pennell, Joseph.** The Graphic Arts. Modern Men and Modern Methods. The Scammon Lectures for 1920. 1921. *o.p.*

**Pennsylvania Germans:** ROSENBERGER.

**Penny Capitalism:** TAX.

**Penrose, E. F.** Food Supply and Raw Materials in Japan. An Index of the Physical Volume of Production of Foodstuffs, Industrial Crops, and Minerals, 1894–1927. 1929. IPR. *o.p.*

**People of Aritama:** REICHEL-DOLMATOFF.

**People and the Land:** *see* AMERICAN COUNTRY LIFE ASSOCIATION, Proceedings, No. 20.

**People of Plenty:** POTTER.

**People and Print:** WAPLES.

**People Shall Judge:** STAFF, SOCIAL SCIENCES 1, THE COLLEGE OF THE UNIVERSITY OF CHICAGO.

**People of the Sierra:** PITT-RIVERS.

**People of the Twilight:** JENNESS.

**People's Architects:** RANSOM.

**Peoples of Siberia:** LEVIN.

**Peoples Speaking to Peoples:** WHITE.

**Percival, M. O.** A Reading of *Moby-Dick*. 1950. *o.p.*

**Peregrinatio aetheriae:** *see* BECHTEL, Sanctae silviae peregrinatio.

**Perfecta casada:** LEÓN.

**Peril and a Hope:** SMITH.

**Perils of Prosperity:** LEUCHTENBURG.

**Period and Elongation Distance of the Fifth Satellite of Jupiter:** HALE.

**Perkins, Anna Louise.** The Comparative Archeology of Early Mesopotamia. 1949. xix, 200 p. Illus. 31 cm. 49-10748. Paper. SAOC 25. $5.00.

**Perkins, Dexter.** The New Age of Franklin Roosevelt, 1932–45. 1957. xi, 194 p. 21 cm. 56-11263. CHAC. Cloth. $4.50ˢ. Paper. $1.95.

**Perlman, Helen Harris.** Social Casework. A Problem-solving Process. 1957. xiii, 268 p. 24 cm. 57-6270. $5.00ᵗ.

"This book has been hailed, and with good reason, as the most significant study of casework since Gordon Hamilton's Theory and Practice. Its author has a rare gift for expressing her ideas in a fresh and arresting way, whether in speech or in writing. This book is no exception. . . . It would be impossible to read this book without stimulus to one's thinking and a deepening of one's understanding of casework."—*Social Work.*

**Perloff, Harvey S.** Puerto Rico's Economic Future. A Study in Planned Development. 1950. *o.p.*

**Perón's Argentine:** BLANKSTEN.

**Perrine (Malot):** SEIBERT.

**Perry, Alfred Morris.** The Sources of Luke's Passion-Narrative. 1920. HLL. *o.p.*

**Perry, Charner M.,** *ed.* The Philosophy of American Democracy. 1943. WFL. *o.p.*

**Persepolis:** SCHMIDT.

**Persepolis Treasury Tablets:** CAMERON.

**Persistent Issues in American Librarianship:** ASHEIM.

**Personal Income Taxation:** SIMONS.

**Personal Knowledge:** POLANYI.

**Personality Development in Children:** CHAVE.

**Personality Schedules:** THURSTONE.

**Personality and the Social Group:** BURGESS.

**Personnel Administration in Libraries:** MARTIN.

**Personnel and Labor Problems:** CARVER.

**Personnel Services in Education:** HARDEE.

**Perspectives in American Indian Culture Change:** SPICER.

**Perspectives in Linguistics:** WATERMAN.

**Perspectives in Medieval History:** DREW.

**Pesek, Boris P.** Gross National Product of Czechoslovakia in Monetary and Real Terms, 1946–58. 1965. xi, 60 p. 24 cm. 65-14429. ERS. $3.00ˢ.

**Peterle von Nürnberg:** MORGAN.

**Peterson, Ruth Camilla.** Attitude toward Capital Punishment. Forms A and B. 1931. TAS 31. *o.p.*

**Peterson, Ruth Camilla.** Attitude toward the Chinese. Forms A and B. 1931. TAS 23. *o.p.*

**Peterson, Ruth Camilla.** Attitude toward the Germans. Forms A and B. 1931. TAS 25. *o.p.*

**Peterson, Ruth Camilla.** Attitude toward War. Forms A and B. 1931. TAS 34. *o.p.*

**Peterson, Walter,** *joint author:* BUCK, Reverse Index of Greek Nouns and Adjectives.

**Peterson, Walter,** *joint ed.:* BUCK, Reverse Index of Greek Nouns and Adjectives.

**Petit chose (Daudet):** LIMPER.

**Petit roi d'Ys (Georges G.-Toudouze):** WEST.

**Petrarch.** Triumphs. Translated by Ernest Hatch Wilkins. 1962. x, 114 p. 7 drawings by Virgil Burnett. 22 cm. 62-19622. $5.00ˢ.

**Petrarch:** *see* WILKINS, Life of Petrarch.

**Petrarch at Vaucluse:** WILKINS.

**Petrarch's Letters to Classical Authors:** COSENZA.

**Pettit, Edison.** The Forms and Motions of the Solar Prominences. 1925. YO, III. *o.p.*

**Pettit, Hannah Bard Steele,** *joint author:* VAN BIESBROECK, Parallaxes of Fifty-two Stars.

**Pézard, André,** *joint author:* PASSARELLI, Les drôles aventures de Renard.

**Pfanner, John Adams, Jr.** A Statistical Study of the Drawing Power of Cities for Retail Trade. 1940. SBA, X. *o.p.*

**Phallicism in Japan:** BUCKLEY.

**Phelan, Eduard J.:** *see* WRIGHT, Unemployment as a World-Problem.

**Phelps, Orme Wheelock.** The Legislative Background of the Fair Labor Standards Act. A Study of the Growth of National Sentiment in Favor of Governmental Regulation of Wages, Hours, and Child Labor. 1939. SBA, IX. *o.p.*

**Phelps, Ruth Shepard.** The Earlier and Later Forms of Petrarch's Canzoniere. 1925. *o.p.*

**Phelps, Ruth Shepard,** *ed.* Una Partita a Scacchi. By Giuseppe Giacosa. HCLS.

**Phenomenology of Acts of Choice:** WELLS.

**Phenomenon of Superconductivity:** BURTON.

**Philbrook, Clarence:** *see* LELAND, State-Local Fiscal Relations.

**Philemon among the Letters of Paul:** KNOX.

**Philippe de Lasalle:** BORLAND.

**Phillips, G. C.,** *ed.* Progress in Fast Neutron Physics. Edited by G. C. Phillips, J. B. Marion, and J. R. Risser. 1963. xiv, 397 p. Illus. Index. 24 cm. 63-18849. RSS. $8.50ˢ.

**Phillips, Grace Darling.** Far Peoples. 1929. PM. *o.p.*

**Phillips, Philip,** *joint author:* WILLEY, Method and Theory in American Archaeology.

**Philological Notes on Eshnunna:** JACOBSEN.

**Philosophers in Hades:** SMITH.

**Philosophers Speak of God:** HARTSHORNE.

**Philosophers Speak for Themselves:** SMITH.

**Philosophic Approach to Communism:** BRAMELD.

**Philosophic Studies** (PS). Issued under the Direction of the Department of Philosophy of the University of Chicago:

1. WRIGHT, Ethical Significance of Feeling.
2. TALBERT, Dualism of Fact and Idea.
3. SUNNE, Some Phases in the Development of the Subjective Point of View.
4. CASTRO, Respective Standpoints of Psychology and Logic.
5. CRAWFORD, Relation of Inference to Fact.
6. TAFT, Woman Movement.
7. KITCH, Origin of Subjectivity.
8. AYRES, Nature of the Relationship between Ethics and Economics.
9. GEIGER, Some Religious Implications.
10. CRANE, Place of the Hypothesis in Logic.

**Philosophic Way of Life:** SMITH.

**Philosophical Greek:** FOBES.

**Philosophical Systems:** HALL.

**Philosophies of Education:** BRUBACHER.

**Philosophy of the Act:** MEAD.

**Philosophy of American Democracy:** PERRY.

**Philosophy of Business:** LODGE.

**Philosophy of Democratic Government:** SIMON.

**Philosophy of Francis Bacon:** ANDERSON.

**Philosophy of the Humanities:** FITZ-HUGH.

**Philosophy of Law in Historical Perspective:** FRIEDRICH.

**Philosophy of Plotinus:** BRÉHIER.

**Philosophy and Policies of Woodrow Wilson:** LATHAM.

**Philosophy and Psychology of Sensation:** HARTSHORNE.

**Philp, Howard Littleton.** An Experimental Study of the Frustration of Will-Acts and Conation. 1936. BJP. *o.p.*

**Philpott, Stanley John Francis.** Fluctuations in Human Output. 1932. BJP. *o.p.*

**"Phiz." Illustrations from the Novels of Charles Dickens:** JOHANNSEN.

**Phoenix Books** (P):

ALEXANDER, Impact of Freudian Psychiatry. (P62.)
ALTICK, English Common Reader. (P140.)
ANDERSON, Hobo. (P71.)

ARTZ, From the Renaissance to Romanticism. (P186.)
BAKER, Short History of Christianity. (P95.)
BASCOM, Continuity and Change in African Cultures. (P85).
BECK, Commentary on Kant's Critique of Practical Reason. (P114.)
BLOCH, Feudal Society. (P156, P157.)
BLUM, Uneasy Case for Progressive Taxation. (P130.)
BOND, Reference Guide to English Studies. (P83.)
BOORSTIN, Genius of American Politics. (P27.)
BOTKIN, Lay My Burden Down. (P24.)
BOVIE, Satires of Horace. (P39.)
BOWEN, Long Encounter. (P132.)
BRAMSTED, Aristocracy and the Middle-Classes in Germany. (P163.)
BRÉHIER, Hellenic Age. (P198.)
BRÉHIER, Hellenistic and Roman Age. (P199.)
BRIDENBAUGH, Colonial Craftsman. (P80.)
BROMBERT, Intellectual Hero. (P158.)
BUCK, Vikings of the Pacific. (P31.)
BURKE, Counterstatement. (P14.)
BUTLER, Introduction to Library Science. (P59.)
CALLAHAN, Education and the Cult of Efficiency. (P149.)
CARNAP, Meaning and Necessity. (P30.)
CASSIRER, Renaissance Philosophy of Man. (P1.)
CECIL, Victorian Novelists. (P26.)
CHIERA, They Wrote on Clay. (P2.)
CLANCY, Odes of Horace. (P47.)
CLARK, History of the Primates. (P21.)
COLWELL, Study of the Bible. (P164.)
COOPER, Learning To Listen. (P79.)
COOPER, Rhythmic Structure of Music. (P118.)
CRANE, Critics and Criticism. (P15.)
CRANE, Shakespeare's Prose. (P127.)
CUNHA, Rebellion in the Backlands. (P22.)
DAICHES, The Novel and the Modern World. (P180.)
DAHL, Preface to Democratic Theory. (P115.)
DANIEL, Poems and A Defence of Ryme. (P200.)
DEAN, Manual of Intergroup Relations. (P129.)
DEWEY, Child and the Curriculum *and* School and Society. (P3.)
DUCKETT, Alfred the Great. (P29.)
DUNHAM, Mr. Justice. (P152.)
EAKIN, Good Books for Children. (P98.)
EISINGER, Fiction of the Forties. (P188.)
EMBRE, Suye Mura. (P173.)
FALLERS, Bantu Bureaucracy. (P197.)
FARIS, Mental Disorders in Urban Areas. (P183.)
FEIDELSON, Symbolism and American Literature. (P37.)
FERMI, Atoms in the Family. (P58.)
FOWLIE, Mallarmé. (P93.)
FREUND, Standards of American Legislation. (P182.)
FRIEDMAN, Capitalism and Freedom. (P111.)

FRIEDRICH, Philosophy of the Law in Historical Perspective. (P135.)

FROMM-REICHMANN, Principles of Intensive Psychotherapy. (P49.)

GELB, Study of Writing. (P109.)

GENNEP, Rites of Passage. (P64.)

GODDARD, Meaning of Shakespeare. (P50, P51.)

GOLDMAN, Ten Commandments. (P141.)

GOODMAN, Structure of Literature. (P91.)

GRAZIA, Political Community. (P116.)

GREENBERG, Essays in Linguistics. (P119.)

GREGG, For Future Doctors. (P126.)

GRENE, Greek Political Theory. (P201.)

GRENE, Greek Tragedies. (P41, P42, P43.)

GRENE, Introduction to Existentialism. (P34.)

GRUNEBAUM, Medieval Islam. (P69.)

HAMILTON, Landmarks in Political Economy. (P100, P101.)

HARRIS, Structural Linguistics. (P52.)

HARTSHORNE, Philosophers Speak of God. (P142.)

HAYEK, Capitalism and the Historians. (P120.)

HAYEK, Road to Serfdom. (P4.)

HEIDEL, Babylonian Genesis. (P133.)

HEIDEL, Gilgamesh Epic and Old Testament Parallels (P136.)

HIMMELFARB, Lord Acton. (P97.)

HOENIGSWALD, Language Change. (P178.)

HOMER, Iliad. (P63.)

HORACE, Odes and Epodes. (P47.)

HORACE, Satires and Epistles. (P39.)

HUGHES, French Canada in Transition. (P139.)

HUTCHINS, University of Utopia. (P151.)

JANOWITZ, Military in the Political Development of New Nations. (P174.)

JASPERS, Future of Mankind. (P143.)

JASPERS, Nature of Psychotherapy. (P187.)

JÁSZI, Dissolution of the Habsburg Monarchy. (P70.)

JENNESS, People of the Twilight. (P32.)

JOUVENEL, Sovereignty. (P121.)

KNAPPER, Tudor Puritanism. (P194.)

KNIGHT, On the History and Method of Economics. (P122.)

KUHN, Structure of Scientific Revolutions. (P159.)

KURLAND, Supreme Court and the Constitution. (P203.)

LA BARRE, Human Animal. (P45.)

LATTIMORE, Greek Lyrics. (P48.)

LATTIMORE, Odes of Pindar. (P33.)

LEVITT, Managerial Psychology. (P96.)

LEFEVRE, Prayers of Kierkegaard. (P131.)

LEHMANN, Thomas Jefferson. (P181.)

LEVI, Introduction to Legal Reasoning. (P84.)

LEWIS, American Adam. (P38.)

LIEBERMAN, Future of Public Education. (P94.)

LINDSEY, Pullman Strike. (P165.)

LITWACK, North of Slavery. (P179.)

LOEWENSTEIN, Political Power and the Governmental Process. (P190.)

LÖWITH, Meaning in History. (P16.)

McDONALD, We the People. (P144.)

McKITRICK, Andrew Johnson and Reconstruction. (P153.)

McNEILL, Past and Future. (P166.)

MAHDI, Ibn Khaldûn's Philosophy of History. (P167.)

MARITAIN, Man and the State. (P5.)

MATHEWS, Beginnings of American English. (P123.)

MEAD, Childhood in Contemporary Cultures. (P124.)

MEAD, George Herbert Mead on Social Psychology. (P170.)

MELVILLE, Billy Budd, Sailor. (P99.)

MEYER, Emotion and Meaning in Music. (P56.)

MINER, St. Denis. (P108.)

MOONEY, Ghost-Dance Religion. (P176.)

MULLER, Religion and Freedom in the Modern World. (P193.)

MURRAY, Literature of Greece. (P12.)

OAKLEY, Man the Tool-maker. (P20.)

OAKS, Wall between Church and State. (P137.)

O'DEA, Mormons. (P162.)

OGBURN, William F. Ogburn on Culture and Social Change. (P171.)

OLMSTEAD, History of the Persian Empire. (P36.)

OLSON, Poetry of Dylan Thomas. (P72.)

OSGOOD, Day of the Cattleman. (P13.)

OSGOOD, Ideals and Self-Interest in America's Foreign Relations. (P160.)

PARKES, Marxism. (P168.)

PEATTIE, Vence. Immortal Village. (P147.)

PECKHAM, Pontiac and the Indian Uprising. (P73.)

PITT-RIVERS, People of the Sierra. (P55.)

POLANYI, Science, Faith and Society. (P155.)

POLANYI, Study of Man. (P128.)

POTTER, People of Plenty. (P28.)

RACINE, Three Plays. (P76.)

REDFIELD, Chan Kom. (P86.)

REDFIELD, Little Community *and* Peasant Society and Culture. (P53.)

REDFIELD, Village That Chose Progress. (P87.)

REICHENBACH, Experience and Prediction. (P81.)

ROSENHEIM, What Happens in Literature. (P77.)

RYDER, Panchatantra. (P169.)

RYDER, The Ten Princes. (P57.)

SANTILLANA, Crime of Galileo. (P40.)

SHOREY, What Plato Said (*abridged*). (P184.)

SIMON, Philosophy of Democratic Government. (P67.)

SIMPSON, Puritanism in Old and New England. (P66.)

SMITH, From Aristotle to Plotinus. (P9.)

SMITH, Berkeley, Hume, and Kant. (P18.)

SMITH, From Descartes to Locke. (P17.)

SMITH, From Thales to Plato. (P8.)

SMITH, T. S. Eliot's Poetry and Plays. (P54.)

STAMPP, And the War Came. (P150.)

**Physical Theory of Neutron Chain Reactors:** WEINBERG.

**Physiographic Ecology of Chicago and Vicinity:** COWLES.

**Physiography of the Region of Chicago:** FRYXELL.

**Physiological Archives.** From Hull Physiological Laboratory of the University of Chicago. Edited by Jacques Loeb. *Vol. I:* Publications of the Year 1895. 1896. *o.p. Vol. II:* 1898. *o.p. Vol. III:* 1900. *o.p.*

**Physiological and Behavioral Aspects of Taste:** KARE.

**Physiology and Biochemistry of the Skin:** ROTHMAN.

**Physiology of Insect Development:** CAMPBELL.

**Physiology and Pharmacology of the Pituitary Body:** VAN DYKE.

**Physiology and Treatment of Peptic Ulcer:** ALLEN.

**Physiology of Twinning:** NEWMAN.

**Picasso, Pablo.** Understanding Picasso. A Study of His Styles and Development. By Helen F. Mackenzie. 1940. *o.p.*

**Pick, Alfred,** *joint author:* KATZ, Interpretation of Electrocardiogram.

**Pick, Alfred,** *joint author:* KATZ, Introduction to the Interpretation of the Electrocardiogram.

**Pickering, Edward Charles.** The Algol Variable +17° 4367. W. Delphini. 1896. *o.p.*

**Pickering, Edward Charles.** The Algol Variable +17° 4367. W. Delphini. 1898. *o.p.*

**Pickering, Edward Charles.** A New Form of Stellar Photometer. 1895. *o.p.*

**Pickersgill, J. W.** The Mackenzie King Record. *Vol. I:* 1939–44. 1960. xiv, 723 p. 24 cm. 60-51004. $12.50ˢ. USA.

**Pickett, Ralph Russell.** Federal Reserve Bank Policy in Iowa. 1931. SBA, II. *o.p.*

**Picó, Rafael:** *see* HAAS, American Empire.

**Piepkorn, Arthur Carl,** *ed. and trans.* Historical Prism Inscriptions of Ashurbanipal. I.

Editions E, B₁₋₅, D, and K. With an Appendix by Joachim Mayr. 1933. xiii, 109 p. 25 cm. 34-127. Paper. AS 5. $1.50.

**Pier, Garrett Chatfield.** Egyptian Antiquities in the Pier Collection. Part I. 1906. *o.p.*

**Pierce, Bessie Louise.** Civic Attitudes in American School Textbooks. 1930. SMC. *o.p.*

**Pierce, Bessie Louise,** *ed.* As Others See Chicago. Impressions of Visitors, 1673–1933. Compiled and Edited by Bessie Louise Pierce with the assistance of Joe L. Norris. 1933. *o.p.*

**Pierce, Paul Revere.** The Origin and Development of the Public School Principalship. 1935. *o.p.*

**Pierce, Paul Revere,** *joint author:* REAVIS, Elementary School.

**Piero di Cosimo:** DOUGLAS.

**Pierre Gringore's Pageants:** BASKERVILL.

**Pierrille (Clarétie):** COCHRAN.

**Pierson, Donald.** Negroes in Brazil. A Study of Race Contact at Bahia. 1942. SOC. *o.p.*

**Pietsch, Karl.** Preliminary Notes on Two Old Spanish Versions of the Disticha Catonis. Preprint, 1902. *o.p.*

**Pietsch, Karl,** *ed.* Spanish Grail Fragments: El Libro de Josep Abarimatia, Le Estoria de Merlin, Lancarote. Edited from the unique manuscript by Karl Pietsch. *Vol. I:* Texts. 1924. *Vol. II:* Commentary. 1925. MPM. *o.p.*

**Pilgrims of Russian-Town:** YOUNG.

**Pillet, Roger A.,** *joint author:* DUNKEL, French in the Elementary School.

**Pindar.** Odes. Translated by Richmond Lattimore. 1947. xii, 170 p. 21 cm. 47-3185. Paper. P33. $1.50.

**Pines, Shlomo,** *trans.:* MAIMONIDES, Guide of the Perplexed.

**Pink Marsh:** ADE.

**Pioneering on Social Frontiers:** TAYLOR.

**Pitt-Rivers, Julian A.,** *joint editor:* Nature of Human Society Series.

**Pitt-Rivers, Julian A.** The People of the Sierra. 1961. Paper. P55. $1.75. USA.

**Pittenger, B. F.** The Efficiency of College Students as Conditioned by Age of Entrance and Size of High School. 1917. NSSE, 16th Yrbk., Part II. *o.p.*

**Place of the Hypothesis in Logic:** CRANE.

**Place of Industries in Elementary Education:** DOPP.

**Place of Vocational Subjects in the High School:** BROWN.

**Planets and Satellites:** *see* KUIPER, Solar System.

**Planning and Construction of School Buildings:** ENGLEHARDT.

**Planning Function in Urban Government:** WALKER.

**Plano-Convex Bricks:** DELOUGAZ.

**Plans and Early Operations, January 1939 to August 1942:** CRAVEN.

**Plans for Organizing School Surveys:** JUDD.

**Plans for World Peace:** HEMLEBEN.

**Plant Genetics:** COULTER.

**Plant Societies:** COWLES.

**Plasma Physics:** CHANDRASEKHAR.

**Plastic Redirections of 20th Century Painting:** SWEENEY.

**Platonism of Joachim du Bellay:** MERRILL.

**Platonism of Philo Judaeus:** BILLINGS.

**Plato's Modern Enemies and the Theory of Natural Law:** WILD.

**Platt, John R.** New Views of the Nature of Man. The Monday Lectures, 1965. By Clifford Geertz, Willard F. Libby, Derek J. de Solla Price, James M. Redfield, Roger W. Sperry, and George Wald. 1965. 152 p. 21 cm. 65-24980. $5.00s.

**Platt, Robert Swanton:** *see* COLBY, Geographic Aspects of International Relations.

**Platt, Robert Swanton:** *see* FINCH, Geographic Surveys.

**Play Behavior and Choice of Play Materials:** VAN ALSTYNE.

**Play Movement in the United States:** RAINWATER.

**Plays and Poems:** OLSON.

**Plays for Seven Players:** KENNEDY.

**Plays for Three Players, Vols. I, II, III:** KENNEDY.

**Pleasure—Unpleasure:** WOHLGEMUTH.

**Plehn, Carl C.:** *see* Financial Mobilization for War.

**Pleistocene Deposits in Warren County, Iowa:** TILTON.

**Plomer, Henry Robert.** The Life and Correspondence of Lodowick Bryskett. By Henry R. Plomer and Tom Peete Cross. 1927. MPM. *o.p.*

**Plotinus:** *see* BRÉHIER, Philosophy of Plotinus.

**Plutarch as a Source of Information on the Greek Theatre:** FLICKINGER.

**Pochard, Henri,** *joint ed.:* DAHL, Le Roi des montagnes.

**Podobed, V. V.** Fundamental Astrometry. Determination of Stellar Co-ordinates. English edition edited by A. N. Vyssotsky. 1965. vii, 236 p. 24 cm. 64-15810. $7.50t.

**Poebel, Arno Max Emil.** Das appositionell bestimmte Pronomen der 1. Pers. sing. in den westsemitischen Inschriften und im Alten Testament. 1932. viii, 86 p. 25 cm. 33-38706. Paper. AS 3. $1.25.

**Poebel, Arno Max Emil.** Miscellaneous Studies. 1947. viii, 122 p. 25 cm. 48-263. Paper. AS 14. $3.50.

**Poebel, Arno Max Emil.** The Second Dynasty of Isin According to a New King-List Tablet. 1955. viii, 41 p. 25 cm. 55-10250. Paper. AS 15. $7.50.

**Poebel, Arno Max Emil.** Studies in Akkadian Grammar. 1939. AS 9. *o.p.*

**Poebel, Arno Max Emil.** The Sumerian Prefix Forms *e-* and *i-* in the Time of the Earlier Princes of Lagaš. 1931. xi, 47 p. 25 cm. 32-4356. Paper. AS 2. $1.00.

**Poems of Anne:** REYNOLDS.

**Poems and A Defence of Ryme:** DANIEL.

**Poet and His Faith:** WOODHOUSE.

**Poetry of Dylan Thomas:** OLSON.

**Poetry and the Modern World:** DAICHES.

**Polak, J. J.** An International Economic System. 1954. *o.p.*

**Polak, J. J.,** *trans.:* TINBERGEN, Dynamics of Business Cycles.

**Polansky, Norman A.** Social Work Research. Method and Methodology. 1960. xii, 306 p. Index. 25 cm. 60-14357. $5.00ᵗ.

**Polanyi, Michael.** The Logic of Liberty. Reflections and Rejoinders. 1951. viii, 206 p. 21 cm. $6.00ˢ. CUSA.

**Polanyi, Michael.** Personal Knowledge. Towards a Post-critical Philosophy. 1958. xiv, 428 p. 25 cm. 58-5162. $7.50ˢ. CUSA.

". . . a passionate and profound attack upon empiricism in its stronghold—the theory of scientific enquiry. . . . It is a vision of the natural history of mankind, brilliantly imagined and expressed in sentences of uninflated eloquence."—Michael Oakeshott, in *Encounter.*

**Polanyi, Michael.** Science, Faith and Society. *Reissue,* 1964. 96 p. 21 cm. Cloth. $3.75. Paper. P155. $1.50.

**Polanyi, Michael.** The Study of Man. 1959. 104 p. 59-4021. Cloth. 19 cm. $2.50ˢ. COBE. Paper. P128. 21 cm. $1.25. CUSA.

**Poley, Irvin C.** Classroom Procedure Test in English Literature for Rating Methods of Teaching in Junior and Senior High Schools. By Irvin C. Poley and Douglas Waples. 1928. *o.p.*

**Police Power:** FREUND.

**Political Community:** GRAZIA.

**Political and Constitutional Study of the Cumberland Road:** YOUNG.

**Political History of Parthia:** DEBEVOISE.

**Political Novels of Joseph Conrad:** HAY.

**Political Philosophy of Hobbes:** STRAUSS.

**Political Power and the Governmental Process:** LOEWENSTEIN.

**Political Realism and Political Idealism:** HERZ.

**Political Thought of Thomas Aquinas:** GILBY.

**Politics and the Constitution in the History of the United States:** CROSSKEY.

**Politics of Discretion:** KRIEGER.

**Politics of Equality:** LIPSON.

**Politics of Modernization:** APTER.

**Politics of Scarcity:** WEINER.

**Politics of the 20th Century:** MORGENTHAU.

**Pollard, Allis Newell,** *ed.* L'Abbé Constantin. By Ludovic Halévy. Adapted and edited by Allis Newell Pollard, Grace Cochran, and Helen M. Eddy. HCLS.

**Polyak, Stephen.** The Retina. The Anatomy and the Histology of the Retina in Man, Ape, and Monkey, Including Physiological Considerations, the History of the Physiological Optics, and the Histological Laboratory Technique. 1941. *o.p.*

**Polyak, Stephen.** The Vertebrate Visual System. Edited by Heinrich Klüver. 1958. xviii, 1,390 p. Illus. 27 cm. $45.00ˢ.

"Sowohl dem *Verfasser,* der dreissig Jahre lang daran gearbeitet hat, wie seinem Freunde *Klüver,* der es unter Opferung von zwei vollen Jahren des eigenen Lebens und Schaffens herausgegeben hat, sind wir dafür zu tiefstem Dank verpflichtet. Für jeden Neuroanatomen, Neurophysiologen, klinischen Neurologen, Neurochirurgen und Opthalmologen, ja für jeden Neurobiologen im umfassenden Sinne dieses Wortes, wird es stets eine unschatzbare Quelle des Studiums, der Anregung, der Belehrung und Begeisterung sein und bleiben."—M. Minkowski, *Swiss Archives for Neurology, Neurosurgery, and Psychiatry Journal.*

"This book of Polyak's will probably serve as a historical landmark. It takes within its compass the speculations of the ancient world, the gross anatomy of the medieval world, and the histology of the modern world, culminating in the beautiful and laborious researches which constituted the author's life work."—*British Journal of Ophthalmology.*

**Pontiac and the Indian Uprising:** PECKHAM.

**Popular Religion:** SCHNEIDER.

Population: GINI.

Population Genetics: LI.

Population in Modern China: TA CHEN.

Population and Peace in the Pacific: THOMPSON.

Population Pressure and Economic Life in Japan: ISHII.

Population and Progress in the Far East: THOMPSON.

Population Statistics and Their Compilation: WOLFENDEN.

Porpoises and Sonar: KELLOGG.

Port of Chicago and the St. Lawrence Seaway: MAYER.

Porter, Charles O., joint author: BLAUSTEIN, The American Lawyer.

Porter, D. F., joint author: HENDRIX, Caballeros y escuderos.

Porter, Kirk Harold. A History of Suffrage in the United States. 1918. o.p.

Portinari, Candido. Portinari. His Life and Art. Introduction by Rockwell Kent. 1940. o.p.

Portrait of Aristotle: GRENE.

Portraits américains: COOK.

Positive Program for Laissez Faire: SIMONS.

Posner, Ernst. American State Archives. 1964. xiv, 397 p. 25 cm. 64-23425. $7.50ᵍ.

Possibility of a Science of Education: SINCLAIR.

Potapov, L. P., joint ed.: LEVIN, Peoples of Siberia.

Poteat, Herbert M., trans.: CICERO, Brutus.

Potter, David. People of Plenty. Economic Abundance and the American Character. 1954. xxvii, 219 p. 21 cm. 54-12797. Cloth. WFL. $4.25ˢ. Paper. P28. $1.35.
". . . this pioneering attempt to unify into a wider social science the historical and the anthropological approaches to human behaviour is stimulating in itself, and full of promise for future developments."—*The Listener*.

Potter, Edith Louise. Fetal and Neonatal Death. A Survey of the Incidence, Etiology, and Anatomic Manifestations of the Conditions Producing Death of the Fetus in Utero and the Infant in the Early Days of Life. By Edith L. Potter, M.D., and Fred L. Adair, M.D. 1940. Rev. ed. 1949. *o.p.*

Potter, Pitman Benjamin. Collective Security and Peaceful Change. The Relations of Order and Progress in International Society. 1937. PPP 24. *o.p.*

Pottery from the Diyala Region: DELOUGAZ.

Powell, John Arthur. How To Write Business Letters. 1925. *o.p.*

Powell, John Arthur, joint author: MANLY, Manual for Writers.

Powell, John Wesley. Exploration of the Colorado River. 1957. viii, 148 p. Illus. 22 cm. 57-6988. $3.75ˢ.

Powell, Leona Margaret. The History of the United Typothetae of America. 1926. SE. *o.p.*

Powell, Thomas Reed: *see* HUTCHINSON, Democracy and National Unity.

Power of Small States: FOX.

Powers, S. Ralph. A Program for Teaching Science. Prepared by S. Ralph Powers, Chairman of the Society's Committee on the Teaching of Science. 1932. NSSE, 31st Yrbk., Part I. xii, 364 p. 24 cm. E33-69. Paper. $1.75ᵗ.

Practical Sociology: HENDERSON.

Practical Theology: SMITH.

Practice of Book Selection: WILSON.

Practice of Dentistry: LEVEN.

Practice, Fatigue, and Oscillation: FLÜGEL.

Practice Teaching for Prospective Secondary Teachers: NATIONAL SOCIETY OF COLLEGE TEACHERS OF EDUCATION, Proceedings, No. 7.

Practice of Teaching in the Secondary School: MORRISON.

**Practices of American Universities in Granting Higher Degrees in Education:** NATIONAL SOCIETY OF COLLEGE TEACHERS OF EDUCATION, Proceedings, No. 19.

**Pragmatic Philosophy of C. S. Peirce:** THOMPSON.

**Pragmatism:** MOORE.

**Pragmatism and the Crisis of Democracy:** MORRIS.

**Pratt, Alice Edwards.** The Use of Color in the Verse of the English Romantic Poets. 1898. *o.p.*

**Pratt, James Bissett:** *see* HAYDON, Modern Trends in World-Religions.

**Pratt, Julius William.** Friends or Enemies? 1935. 2d rev. ed. 1939. AP. *o.p.*

**Pratt, Julius William.** Alfred Thayer Mahan, *in* HUTCHINSON, Marcus W. Jernegan Essays.

**Pratt, Robert A.:** *see* BRYAN, Sources and Analogues of Chaucer's *Canterbury Tales.*

**Prayer Stick Cutting:** HAILE.

**Prayers of Kierkegaard:** LEFEVRE.

**Preaching:** DAVIS.

**Preaching of Peter:** REAGAN.

**Preamble and Boundary Clauses of the Illinois Constitution:** JAMES.

**Preble, Henry,** *trans.:* BERNARD OF CLUNY, Source of "Jerusalem the Golden."

**Predictable Accuracy in Examinations:** CLARKE.

**Preface to an American Philosophy of Art:** McMAHON.

**Preface to Democratic Theory:** DAHL.

**Prehistoric Investigations in Iraqi Kurdistan:** BRAIDWOOD.

**Prehistoric Man in the New World:** JENNINGS.

**Prehistoric Survey of Egypt and Western Asia:** SANDFORD.

**Preliminary Draft of a World Constitution:** BORGESE.

**Preliminary Notes on Two Old Spanish Versions of the Disticha Catonis:** PIETSCH.

**Preliminary Study of the Pueblo of Taos:** MILLER.

**Preliminary Study of the Significance of Partial Tones:** ANGELL.

**Preliminary Table of Solar Spectrum Wave-Lengths:** ROWLAND.

**Première étape:** BOND.

**Premillennialism and Old Testament Prediction:** BERRY.

**Preparation and In-Service Training of College Teachers:** GRAY.

**Pre-Sargonid Temples in the Diyala Region:** DELOUGAZ.

**Preschool and Parental Education:** MEEK.

**Prescott, Henry Washington.** The Development of Virgil's Art. 1927. *o.p.*

**Prescription Notes:** TATUM.

**Present and Impending Applications to Education of Radio:** NATIONAL ADVISORY COUNCIL ON RADIO IN EDUCATION, *Committee on Engineering Developments.*

**Present Bibliographical Status of Modern Philology:** NORTHUP.

**Present Status of Education as a Science:** NATIONAL SOCIETY OF COLLEGE TEACHERS OF EDUCATION, Proceedings, No. 2.

**Present Status of the Inquiry concerning the Genuineness of the Pauline Epistles:** WEISS.

**Present Status of Safety Education:** WHIPPLE.

**Presidency. Crisis and Regeneration:** FINER.

**Press and Politics in Japan:** KAWABÉ.

**Pressure-Height Slide Rule:** BELLAMY.

**Prestige Value of Public Employment in Chicago:** WHITE.

**Preston, Ethel,** *joint author:* WILKINS, First Lessons in Spoken French for Doctors and Nurses.

**Preston, Ethel,** *joint ed.:* SCHOBINGER, Fra le corde d'un contrabasso.

**Preston, Ethel,** *joint ed.:* SCHOBINGER, Scampolo.

**Preston, Ralph C.,** *ed.* Social Studies in the Elementary School. 1957. NSSE, 56th Yrbk., Part II. xl, 320 p. 24 cm. Cloth, $4.50ᵗ. Paper, $3.75ᵗ.

**Pretorian Prefect:** HOWE.

**Preusser, Conrad,** *joint author:* FRANKFORT, Tell Asmar and Khafaje.

**Prévost, Antoine François:** *see* HAZARD, Études critiques sur Manon Lescaut.

**Pribram, Karl:** *see* WRIGHT, Unemployment as a World-Problem.

**Price, Dorothy,** *ed.* Dynamics of Proliferating Tissues. 1958. xv, 96 p. 24 cm. 58-59593. DBC. $3.25ˢ.

**Price, Ira Maurice.** Some Literary Remains of Rim-Sin (Arioch), King of Larsa, about 2285 B.C. 1904. *o.p.*

**Price, Lawrence,** *ed.* Der blinde Geronimo und sein Bruder. By Arthur Schnitzler. HCLS.

**Price Differentials in Wheat Futures:** BALDWIN.

**Price of Power:** AGAR.

**Price and Production Control in British Industry:** LEWIS.

**Priestley, Charles H. B.** Turbulent Transfer in the Lower Atmosphere. 1959. 136 p. Diagrams. 23 cm. 59-10427. $4.50ˢ.

**Priestley, Herbert Ingram:** *see* SAENZ, Some Mexican Problems.

**Priestley, Joseph.** The Discovery of Oxygen. Part 1. Experiments by Joseph Priestley. (1775.) 1902. AC. *o.p.*

**Priestly Element in the Old Testament:** HARPER.

**Primary Elections:** MERRIAM.

**Primary Facts in Religious Thought:** WISHART.

**Primary Mental Abilities:** THURSTONE.

**Primate Thalamus:** WALKER.

**Primeras lecturas españolas:** CASTILLO.

**Primitive Classification:** DURKHEIM.

**Primitive Era of Christianity:** VOTAW.

**Principal Uncial Manuscripts of the New Testament:** HATCH.

**Principles of Accounting:** HODGE.

**Principles of Accrediting Higher Institutions:** ZOOK.

**Principles of Banking:** MOULTON.

**Principles of Christian Living:** SMITH.

**Principles of College Library Administration:** RANDALL.

**Principles of Education as Applied to Art:** CUSHMAN.

**Principles and Ideals for the Sunday School:** BURTON.

**Principles of Intensive Psychotherapy:** FROMM-REICHMANN.

**Principles of Meteorological Analysis:** SAUCIER.

**Principles and Methods of Religious Education (PM):**
ATHEARN, City Institute for Religious Teachers.
BOWER, Survey of Religious Education.
CHAVE, Junior.
DAVIES, Out of Doors with Youth.
EVANS, Sunday-School Building.
GATES, Recreation and the Church.
HEATON, Character Building.
HOBEN, Church School.
HUTCHINS, Graded Social Service.
KRUMBINE, Summer Program for the Church School.
LOBINGIER, Projects in World-Friendship.
LOBINGIER, World-Friendship.
MILLER, Dramatization in the Church School.
MILLER, Dramatization of Bible Stories.
PHILLIPS, Far Peoples.
SHAVER, Church School Projects.
SHAVER, Project Curriculum.
SHAVER, Project Principle in Religious Education.
WARDLE, Handwork in Religious Education.

**Principles of Money and Banking:** MOULTON.

**Principles of Mortgage Banking Regulation in Europe:** PALYI.

**Principles of Preaching:** DAVIS.

**Principles of Stellar Dynamics:** CHANDRASEKHAR.

**Principles of the Theory of Probability:** NAGEL.

Pringle, Henry Fowles: *see* Hutchinson, Democracy and National Unity.

Print, Radio and Film in a Democracy: Waples.

Printing Papers: Wheelwright.

Pritchett, C. Herman. Civil Liberties and the Vinson Court. 1954. *o.p.*

Private Grazing and Public Lands: Calef.

Private Group Clinics: Rorem.

Private Life of Sherlock Holmes: Starrett.

Private and Public Secondary Education: Koos.

Problem of the Angle-Bisectors: Baker.

Problem of Democracy: *see* American Sociological Society, Annual Proceedings, Vol. XIV.

Problem Exercises: Waples.

Problem of Ezekiel: Irwin.

Problem of Induction and Its Solution: Katz.

Problem of the Institutionally Owned Station: Jansky.

Problem-solving Processes of College Students: Bloom.

Problem of Suffering: Smith.

Problems of Boyhood: Johnson.

Problems of Collective Bargaining: Stone.

Problems of Economic Union: Meade.

Problems of Faculty Personnel: Russell.

Problems of Fertilization: Lillie.

Problems in Home Economics Teaching: Bowman.

Problems in Living: Cowles.

Problems of New Testament Translation: Goodspeed.

Problems of the Pacific, 1927: Condliffe.

Problems of the Pacific, 1929: Condliffe.

Problems of the Pacific, 1931: Lasker.

Problems of the Pacific, 1933: Lasker.

Problems of the Pacific, 1936: Holland.

Problems of Preschool Age: Kawin.

Problems of Social Assimilation: American Sociological Association, Annual Proceedings, Vol. VIII.

Problems in Teaching Secondary-School Mathematics: Breslich.

Procedure of Empirical Science: Lenzen.

Procedures Used in Selecting School Books: Whipple.

Proceedings of the Conference Held at the Yerkes Observatory, October 18–31, 1897. 1897. YOB. *o.p.*

Proceedings of the Conference on Problems of Business Administration in Colleges and Universities, 1936: Russell.

Process of Change in the Ottoman Empire: White.

Process of Government: Bentley.

Proconsulate of Julius Agricola: Hendrickson.

Proctor, Addison G. Lincoln and the Convention of 1860. 1918. *o.p.*
A publication of the Chicago Historical Society.

Prodromites: Smith.

Production Management: Mitchell.

Professional Diplomacy in the United States, 1779–1939: Ilchman.

Professional Preparation of High-School Teachers: Cade.

Professional Thief: Sutherland.

Program for Teaching Science: Powers.

Progress in Fast Neutron Physics: Phillips.

Progress of Geography in the Schools: Davis.

Progress of Hellenism in Alexander's Empire: Mahaffy.

Progress of Sociology: American Sociological Society, Annual Proceedings, Vol. XXI.

Progress Tests in French: Eddy.

Progress of Underdeveloped Areas: Hoselitz.

Progress of the Work of the Oriental Institute in Iraq, 1934/35: Frankfort.

Progressive Relaxation: JACOBSON.

Project Curriculum: SHAVER.

Project Principles in Religious Education: SHAVER.

Projective Differential Geometry: LANE.

Projects in Design: SZUKALSKI.

Projects in World-Friendship: LOBINGIER.

Prokosch, Eduard. Elementary Russian Grammar. 1920. *o.p.*

Prolegomena to the Study of the Lectionary Text: COLWELL.

Prologue to Politics: MERRIAM.

Promise of American Politics: SMITH.

Promoting Growth toward Maturity in Interpreting What Is Read: GRAY.

Promoting Maximal Reading Growth: ROBINSON.

Promoting Personal and Social Development through Reading: GRAY.

Pronunciation of Greek and Latin: STURTEVANT.

Pronunciation of the Names of Italian Painters: WILKINS.

Proof of the Sufficiency of Jacobi's Condition: BOLZA.

Proper Wit of Poetry: WILLIAMSON.

Property Taxation in the United States: JENSEN.

Prophetic Element in the Old Testament: HARPER.

Prophets and Israel's Culture: GRAHAM.

Prophets and Their Times: SMITH.

Proposed Genetic Classification of Pleistocene Glacial Formations: CHAMBERLIN.

Proposed Method for the Computation of the 10,000-Foot Tendency Field: MILLER.

Prospects of the Small College: HARPER.

Protection of American Export Trade: SAYRE.

Protestant Era: TILLICH.

Protestants and Pioneers: MIYAKAWA.

Protoplasmic Action and Nervous Action: LILLIE.

Proust Recaptured: JOHNSON.

Proverbs of Solomon: WORRELL.

Provinse, John H., *joint author:* EGGAN, Social Anthropology of North American Tribes.

Provision for the Individual in College Education: GRAY.

Provisional Index to Roman Printing Types: CONDIT.

Psalms: SMITH.

Psalms. Chronologically Treated with a New Translation: BUTTENWIESER.

Pseudo-Ciceronian Consolatio: SAGE.

Psychiatric Social Service in a Children's Hospital: GARTLAND.

Psychological Analysis of the Fundamentals of Arithmetic: JUDD.

Psychological and Ethical Aspects of Mormon Group Life: ERICKSEN.

Psychological Norms: THOMPSON.

Psychological Tests in Business: KORNHAUSER.

Psychologist and the Foreign-Language Teacher: RIVERS.

Psychology of Child Development: KING.

Psychology of Economics: WEISSKOPF.

Psychology of Learning: McCONNELL.

Psychology of the Organized Group Game: REANEY.

Psychology of Prayer: STRONG.

Psychology of Religion: COE.

Psychology and Social Practice: DEWEY.

Psychology Today: BINGHAM.

Psychometric Monographs (PMS):
THURSTONE, Factorial Studies of Intelligence.
THURSTONE, Factorial Studies of Perception.
THURSTONE, Primary Mental Abilities.
WOLFLE, Factor Analysis to 1940.

Psychopathology and Politics: LASSWELL.

Psychotherapeutic Intervention in Schizophrenia: HILL.

Psychotherapy and Personality Change: ROGERS.

Ptolemais: KRAELING.

Public Administration and the Library: MILES.

Public Assistance: ABBOTT.

Public Enterprise: ROBSON.

Public Health Organization in the Chicago Region: STEADMAN.

Public Junior College: JOHNSON.

Public Libraries: BOYD.

Public Medical Services: DAVIS.

Public Opinion and World-Politics: WRIGHT.

Public Policy Pamphlets (PPP).

1. UNIVERSITY OF CHICAGO ROUND TABLE, Balancing the Budget.
2. DIRECTOR, Economics of Technocracy.
3. GILSON, Unemployment Insurance.
4. GIDEONSE, War Debts.
5. TIPPETTS, Autarchy.
6. BRATTER, Should We Turn to Silver?
7. FETTER, New Deal and Tariff Policy.
8. HARDY, Devaluation of the Dollar.
9. MAHR, Monetary Stability.
10. KERWIN, Control of Radio.
11. PALYI, Monetary Chaos and Gold.
12. MORRIS, Pragmatism and the Crisis of Democracy.
13. KALLEN, Education versus Indoctrination in the Schools.
14. HARRIS FOUNDATION COMMITTEE, American Foreign Policy toward International Stability.
15. SIMONS, Positive Program for Laissez Faire.
16. WHITTLESEY, Banking and the New Deal.
17. WRIGHT, United States and Neutrality.
18. STALEY, Foreign Investment and War.
19. GRAY, Land Planning.
20. UNIVERSITY OF CHICAGO ROUND TABLE, Economic Meaning of the Townsend Plan.
21. BOYNTON, Changing Ideas of American Patriotism.
22. DIMOCK, Can Interstate Compacts Succeed?
23. HART, How the National Income Is Divided.
24. POTTER, Collective Security.
25. LEWIS, Price and Production Control in British Industry.
26. GIDEONSE, Commodity Dollar.
27. BUELL, Death by Tariff.
28. SCHMITT, From Versailles to Munich.
29. HAYEK, Freedom and the Economic System.
30. GIDEONSE, Organized Scarcity.
31. HERMENS, Democracy and Proportional Representation.
32. LAVES, The Middle West Looks at War.
33. HART, Economic Policy for Rearmament.
34. KALLEN, The Future of Peace.
35. SULZBACH, "Capitalistic Warmongers."
36. HUTTON, The War as a Factor in Human Progress.
37. HEILPERIN, Economic Policy and Democracy.
38. SCHMITT, What Shall We Do with Germany?
39. PUTTKAMMER, Alien Enemies and Alien Friends in the United States.

*Five pamphlets*

HAAS, Outposts of Defense (A Special Public Policy Pamphlet)

Public Policy and Private Charities: JOHNSON.

Public Schools: CLARK.

Public Service and Special Training: MERIAM.

Public Utility Valuation: GRAHAM.

Public Welfare Administration in Canada: STRONG.

Public Welfare Administration in Louisiana: WISNER.

Public Welfare Administration in the United States: BRECKINRIDGE.

Publications of the Members of the University of Chicago, 1902–16: LAING.

Public's Investment in Hospitals: ROREM.

Pueblo Indian Religion: PARSONS.

Puerto Rico's Economic Future: PERLOFF.

Pullman Strike: LINDSEY.

Punke, Harold H. The Courts and Public-School Property. 1936. *o.p.*

Punke, Harold H. Law and Liability in Pupil Transportation. 1943. *o.p.*

Purchasing Policies and Practices of Chain Drug Companies: WITTE.

Pure Theory of Capital: HAYEK.

Purin, Charles M. Fortunatus. HCLS.

Purin, Charles M. A Standard German Vocabulary of 2,932 Words and 1,500 Idioms. HCLS.

Puritanism and Liberty: WOODHOUSE.

**Puritanism in Old and New England:** SIMPSON.

**Purpose the Variant of Theory:** HOUSE.

**Purves, Pierre M.,** *joint author:* GELB, Nuzi Personal Names.

**Putnam, Helen C.,** *joint author:* HENDERSON, Education with Reference to Sex.

**Putnam, James William.** The Illinois and Michigan Canal. A Study in Economic History. An Illinois Centennial Publication. 1917. *o.p.*
A publication of the Chicago Historical Society.

**Putnam, Samuel,** *trans.:* CUNHA, Rebellion in the Backlands.

**Puttee, Dorothy Frances.** The Illegitimate Child in Illinois. By Dorothy Frances Puttee and Mary Ruth Colby. Edited by Sophonisba P. Breckinridge. 1937. *o.p.*

**Puttkammer, Ernst W.** Administration of Criminal Law. 1953. viii, 249 p. 24 cm. 53-8736. $6.50t.

**Puttkammer, Ernst W.** Alien Enemies and Alien Friends in the United States. 1943. PPP 39. *o.p.*

**Puttkammer, Ernst Wilfred.** A Manual of Criminal Law and Criminal Procedure for Police. Prepared under the auspices of the Citizens' Police Committee, Northwestern University, and the University of Chicago. 1931. *o.p.*

**Puttkammer, Ernst W.,** *ed.* War and the Law. 1944. *o.p.*

**Pyramids:** FAKHRY.

**Quaife, Milo Milton.** Checagou. From Indian Wigwam to Modern City, 1673–1835. 1933. *o.p.*

**Quaife, Milo Milton.** Chicago and the Old Northwest, 1673–1835. A Study of the Evolution of the Northwestern Frontier, together with a History of Fort Dearborn. 1913. *o.p.*

**Quain, Buell.** Fijian Village. 1948. *o.p.*

**Qualitative Nouns in the Pauline Epistles:** SLATEN.

**Quantitative Classification of Igneous Rocks:** CROSS.

**Quantitative Measurement in Institutions of Higher Learning:** NATIONAL SOCIETY OF COLLEGE TEACHERS OF EDUCATION, Proceedings, No. 18.

**Quarter-Centennial Celebration:** ROBERTSON.

**Quarter-Centennial Publications:** *see* UNIVERSITY OF CHICAGO. Quarter-Centennial Publications.

**Quarterly Calendar.** June, 1892–February, 1896. Succeeded by the *University Record.*

**Quartermaster and Ordnance Supply:** MARSHALL.

**Quasi-stellar Sources and Gravitational Collapse:** ROBINSON.

**Queney, Paul.** Theory of Perturbations in Stratified Currents with Applications to Air Flow over Mountain Barriers. 1947. DMMR 23. *o.p.*

**Quest of Seth for the Oil of Life:** QUINN.

**Questions on Shakespeare:** TOLMAN.

**Quickness and Intelligence:** BERNSTEIN.

**Quigley, Harold Scott.** An Introductory Syllabus on Far Eastern Diplomacy. 1931. IPR. *o.p.*

**Quimby, George Irving.** Indian Life in the Upper Great Lakes: 11,000 B.C. to A.D. 1800. 1960. xv, 182 p. Illus. Index. 25 cm. 60-11799. $5.95.

**Quimby, George Irving,** *joint author:* MARTIN, Indians before Columbus.

**Quinn, Esther C.** The Quest of Seth for the Oil of Life. 1962. xii, 196 p. Illus. Index. 22 cm. 62-18120. $5.00s.

**Rabinowitch, Eugene.** The Dawn of a New Age. Essays on Science and Human Affairs. 1963. viii, 352 p. Illus. 24 cm. 63-20898. $6.95.

**Raccontini:** CIOFFARI.

**Rachal, William M. E.,** *joint ed.:* MADISON, Papers of James Madison.

**Racial Contacts and Social Research:** AMERICAN SOCIOLOGICAL SOCIETY, Annual Proceedings. Vol. XXVIII, No. 2.

**Racial Separation:** DVORIN.

**Racial Variations in Immunity to Syphilis:** FRAZIER.

**Racine, Jean Baptiste.** Three Plays. Phaedra, Andromache, Brittanicus. Translated by George Dillon. 1961. xxiii, 183 p. 21 cm. 61-15938. Cloth. $4.00ˢ. Paper. P76. $1.95.

**Racketville, Slumtown, Haulburg:** SPERGEL.

**Radar Meteorology:** BATTAN.

**Radcliffe-Brown, A. R.** Method in Social Anthropology. Edited by M. R. Srinivas. 1958. 216 p. 22 cm. 58-11954. $4.50ˢ.

**Radebaugh, William.** The Boundary Dispute between Illinois and Wisconsin. 1904. *o.p.* A publication of the Chicago Historical Society.

**Radial Velocities of 500 Stars:** FROST.

**Radial Velocities of Twenty Stars:** FROST.

**Radical Surgery:** BRUNSCHWIG.

**Radin, Max.** The Trial of Jesus of Nazareth. 1931. *o.p.*

**Radio and Education, 1931.** Edited by Levering Tyson. Proceedings of the First Assembly of the National Advisory Council on Radio in Education, 1931. 1931. *o.p.*

**Radio and Education, 1932.** Edited by Levering Tyson. Proceedings of the Second Annual Assembly of National Advisory Council on Radio in Education, Inc., 1932. 1932. *o.p.*

**Radio and Education, 1933.** Edited by Levering Tyson. Proceedings of the Third Annual Assembly of National Advisory Council on Radio in Education, Inc., 1933. 1933. *o.p.*

**Radio and Education, 1934.** Edited by Levering Tyson. Proceedings of the Fourth Annual Assembly of the National Advisory Council on Radio in Education, Inc., 1934. 1935. *o.p.*

**Radio and Education, 1935:** *see* EDUCATION ON THE AIR . . . . AND RADIO AND EDUCATION, 1935.

**Radiocarbon Dating:** LIBBY.

**Radio's Past and Future:** MILLIKAN.

**Rae, John B.** The American Automobile. A Brief History. 1965. xiv, 265 p. Illus. 24 cm. 65-24981. CHAC. $5.95.

**Rage for Order:** WARREN.

**Railroad Labor Board:** WOLF.

**Railway Economics:** BUREAU OF RAILWAY ECONOMICS.

**Railway Organiation:** DEWSNUP.

**Railway Terminal Problem:** CITY CLUB OF CHICAGO.

**Rainwater, Clarence Elmer.** The Play Movement in the United States. A Study of Community Recreation. 1922. *o.p.*

**Rall, Harris Franklin:** *see* BEWER, Religion of the Bible.

**Ramazzini, Bernardino.** De morbis artificum, Bernardini Ramazzini, *Diatriba*. Diseases of Workers. The Latin Text of 1713 Revised, with translation and notes, by Wilmer Cave Wright. 1940. *o.p.* In *The History of Medicine Series* issued under the auspices of the Library of the New York Academy of Medicine.

**Ramberg, Hans.** The Origin of Metamorphic and Metasomatic Rocks. A Treatise on Recrystallization and Replacement in the Earth's Crust. 1952. xviii, 317 p. Illus. 26 cm. 53-5810. PS. $12.50ˢ.

**Ranck, Katherine Howland,** *joint author:* CAVAN, Family and the Depression.

**Randall, Clarence B.** A Foreign Economic Policy for the United States. 1954. WFL. *o.p.*

**Randall, William Madison.** The College Library. A Descriptive Study of the Libraries in Four-Year Liberal Arts Colleges in the United States. 1932. *o.p.*

**Randall, William Madison.** Principles of College Library Administration. By William M. Randall and Francis L. D. Goodrich. 1936. Rev. ed. 1941. LS. *o.p.*

**Randall, William Madison,** *ed.* The Acquisition and Cataloging of Books. Papers Presented before the Library Institute at the University of Chicago, July 29 to August 9, 1940. 1940. *o.p.*

**Raney, McKendree Llewellyn.** If Lincoln Had Lived. By M. Llewellyn Raney, Lloyd Lewis, and William E. Dodd. 1935. *o.p.*

**Raney, McKendree Llewellyn.** The University Libraries. 1933. UCS. *o.p.*

**Rank and Title in the Old Kingdom:** BAER.

**Rankama, Kalervo.** Geochemistry. By Kalervo Rankama and Th. G. Sahama. 1950. xvi, 912 p. Illus. 26 cm. 50-7561. PS. $16.50ˢ.

**Rankin, Edwin Moore.** The Rôle of the Μάγειρος in the Life of the Ancient Greeks as Depicted in Greek Literature and Inscriptions. 1907. *o.p.*

**Ransmeier, John C.** Sentence Drill Blanks. Arranged by John C. Ransmeier. HCLS.

**Ransmeier, John C.** Spanish Recognition Grammar. HCLS.

**Ransom, Caroline Louise.** Studies in Ancient Furniture. Couches and Beds of the Greeks, Etruscans, and Romans. 1905. *o.p.*

**Ransom, Harry,** *ed.* The People's Architects. 1964. 120 p. 21 plates. 24 × 24 cm. 64-15812. RSS. $6.95.

**Rappaport, Armin.** Henry L. Stimson and Japan, 1931–33. 1963. ix, 238 p. Illus. Index. 22 cm. 63-18847. $6.00ˢ.

**Rappard, William Emmanuel.** The Crisis of Democracy. 1938. HFL. *o.p.*

**Rashevsky, Nicolas.** Advances and Applications of Mathematical Biology. 1940. SCI. *o.p.*

**Rashevsky, Nicolas.** Mathematical Biology of Social Behavior. 1951. Rev. ed. 1960. xii, 256 p. 25 cm. 51-9381. $6.75ˢ.

**Rashevsky, Nicolas.** Mathematical Biophysics. Physicomathematical Foundations of Biology. 1938. Rev. ed. 1948. *o.p.*

**Rating, Placing, and Promotion of Teachers:** NATIONAL SOCIETY OF COLLEGE TEACHERS OF EDUCATION, Proceedings, Nos. 5, 6.

**Rational Induction:** DUBS.

**Raven, Anton Adolph.** A *Hamlet* Bibliography and Reference Guide, 1877–1935. 1936. *o.p.*

**Ray, David,** *ed.* The Chicago Review Anthology. 1959. xiii, 252 p. 25 cm. 59-11175. $5.00ˢ.

**Ray, Perley Orman.** The Convention That Nominated Lincoln. 1916. *o.p.*
A publication of the Chicago Historical Society.

**Read, Conyers.** England and America. 1918. WP. *o.p.*

**Read, Eaton Van Wert.** An Analysis of the Retail Trading Relationships of Elgin, Illinois: A Satellite City. 1938. SBA, IX. *o.p.*

**Read, Eliphalet Allison.** The Idea of God in Relation to Theology. 1900. *o.p.*

**Reading:** JUDD.

**Reading in the Elementary School:** GATES.

**Reading of George Herbert:** TUVE.

**Reading in the High School and College:** GRAY.

**Reading Instructions in Various Patterns of Grouping:** ROBINSON.

**Reading and the Language Arts:** ROBINSON.

**Reading Method:** BOND.

**Reading of Moby-Dick:** PERCIVAL.

**Reading and Pupil Development:** GRAY.

**Reading in Relation to Experience:** GRAY.

**Readings in Cultural Geography:** WAGNER.

**Readings in Ecology:** BUCHSBAUM.

**Readings in the Economics of War:** CLARK.

**Readings in Evolution, Genetics, and Eugenics:** NEWMAN.

**Readings in General Psychology:** ROBINSON.

**Readings in Industrial Society:** MARSHALL.

**Readings in Managerial Psychology:** LEAVITT.

**Readings in Resource Management and Conservation:** BURTON.

**Readings in Risk and Risk-bearing:** HARDY.

**Readings in Russian Civilization:** RIHA.

**Readings in the Theory and Practice of Medical Social Work:** GOLDSTINE.

**Readings in Urban Geography:** MAYER.

**Reagan, Joseph Nicholas.** The Preaching of Peter. The Beginning of Christian Apologetics. 1923. *o.p.*

**Real Conflict between China and Japan:** MacNAIR.

**Realities of the Christian Religion:** SMITH.

**Reaney, Mabel Jane.** The Psychology of the Organized Group Game with Special Reference to Its Place in the Play System and Its Educational Value. 1916. BJP. *o.p.*

**Réaumur, René Antoine.** Memoirs on Steel and Iron. Translated from the French edition of 1722 by Anneliese Grünhaldt Sisco. With an Introduction and Notes by Cyril Stanley Smith. 1956. xxxiv, 395 p. 27 cm. 56-6637. $6.00ˢ.

**Reavis, William Claude.** Diagnostic Tests in the Fundamental Operation in Arithmetic and Problem Solving. (For Grades VII–XII) 1927, 2d ed. 1935. *o.p.* (For Grades VII, VIII, and IX) 1934. *o.p.* By W. C. Reavis and E. R. Breslich.

**Reavis, William Claude.** The Elementary School. Its Organization and Administration. By William C. Reavis, Paul R. Pierce, and Edward H. Stullken. 1931. Rev. ed. 1938. *o.p.*

**Reavis, William Claude.** Evaluation of Teacher Merit in City School Systems. By William C. Reavis and Dan H. Cooper. 1945. SEM 59. *o.p.*

**Reavis, William Claude.** Studies in Secondary Education. *Vol. II:* University High School, University of Chicago. By William C. Reavis and others. 1925. SEM 26. *o.p.*

**Reavis, William Claude,** ed. Administrative Adjutsments Required by Socio-economic Change. 1941. AOPPS, IV. *o.p.*

**Reavis, William Claude,** ed. Critical Issues in Educational Administration. 1938. AOPPS, I. *o.p.*

**Reavis, William Claude,** ed. Democratic Practices in School Administration. 1939. AOPPS, II. *o.p.*

**Reavis, William Claude,** ed. Educational Administration. A Survey of Progress, Problems, and Needs. 1946. AOPPS, IX. *o.p.*

**Reavis, William Claude,** ed. Evaluating the Work of the School. 1940. AOPPS, III. *o.p.*

**Reavis, William Claude,** ed. Forthcoming Developments in American Education. 1945. AOPPS, VIII. *o.p.*

**Reavis, William Claude,** ed. The School and the Urban Community. 1942. AOPPS, V. *o.p.*

**Reavis, William Claude,** ed. Significant Aspects of American Life and Postwar Education. 1944. AOPPS, VII. *o.p.*

**Reavis, William Claude,** ed. War and Postwar Responsibilities of American Schools. 1943. AOPPS, VI. *o.p.*

**Reavis, William Claude,** *joint author:* WAPLES, Classroom Procedure Test.

**Reavis, William Claude,** *ed.:* CONFERENCE FOR ADMINISTRATIVE OFFICERS OF PUBLIC AND PRIVATE SCHOOLS. Proceedings.

**Reavis, William Claude:** *see* EDWARDS, Education in a Democracy.

**Reavis, William Claude:** *see* WAPLES, Problem Exercises.

**Rebel in Paradise. Biography of Emma Goldman:** DRINNON.

**Rebellion in the Backlands:** CUNHA.

**Recent Developments in Reading:** ROBINSON.

**Recent Mexican Study of the Native Languages of Mexico:** STARR.

**Recent Migration to Chicago:** FREEDMAN.

**Recent Social Changes . . . . in 1927:** OGBURN.

**Recent Theories of Sovereignty:** COHEN.

**Recent Trends in American College Education:** GRAY.

**Recent Trends in Reading:** GRAY.

**Reciprocity with Canada:** WESTERN ECONOMIC SOCIETY.

**Reckless, Walter Cade.** Vice in Chicago. 1933. SOC. *o.p.*

**Recollections of Richard Dewey:** DEWEY.

**Reconstructed Carmelite Missal:** RICKERT.

**Reconstruction after the Civil War:** FRANKLIN.

**Recording America's Past:** VAN TASSEL.

**Recovery and Restatement of the Gospel:** OSBORN.

**Recreation and the Church:** GATES.

**Red Man's America:** UNDERHILL.

**Red Man's Religion:** UNDERHILL.

**Redfield, Charles E.** Communication in Management. A Guide to Administrative Communication. Foreword by John L. Mc-Caffrey. 2d ed. 1958. xiv, 314 p. 22 cm. 58-11955. $6.00ˢ.

**Redfield, Isabel C.,** *joint author:* EDDY, Basic French. Vol. I.

**Redfield, Margaret Park,** *ed.* The Papers of Robert Redfield. *Vol. I:* Human Nature and the Study of Society. 1962. xvi, 508 p. 24 cm. $10.00ˢ. *Vol. II:* The Social Uses of Social Science. 1963. xiii, 287 p. 24 cm. 62-10995. $10.00ˢ.

**Redfield, Margaret Park,** *ed. and trans.:* FEI, China's Gentry.

**Redfield, Robert.** Chan Kom. A Maya Village. By Robert Redfield and Alfonso Villa Rojas. 1934. x, 387 p. Illus. Index. 24 cm. Cloth. $7.50ˢ. Abridged. x, 236 p. 23 cm. 62-2616. Paper. P86. $1.75.

**Redfield, Robert.** The Folk Culture of Yucatan. 1941. xxiii, 416 p. Illus. 24 cm. 41-15380. AN. $7.50ˢ.

**Redfield, Robert.** The Little Community. Viewpoints for the Study of a Human Whole. 1955. 182 p. 24 cm. A55-4511. CSCC. $4.50ˢ.

**Redfield, Robert.** The Little Community *and* Peasant Society and Culture. 1960. 248 p. 21 cm. Paper. P53. $2.25.

**Redfield, Robert.** Peasant Society and Culture. An Anthropological Approach to Civilization. 1956. viii, 164 p. 24 cm. 56-66454. $4.50ˢ.

**Redfield, Robert.** Tepoztlán, a Mexican Village. A Study of Folk Life. 1930. xii, 247 p. Illus. 24 cm. 30-15556. AN. $7.50ˢ.

**Redfield, Robert.** A Village That Chose Progress. Chan Kom Revisited. 1950. xiv, 187 p. 50-5750. Cloth. 24 cm. AN. $5.00ˢ. 1962. Paper. P87. 23 cm. $1.50.

**Redfield, Robert:** *see* WIRTH, Eleven Twenty-six.

**Redfield, Robert, Papers of.** Edited by Margaret Park Redfield.

**Rediscovering Illinois:** COLE.

**Rediscovery of the Frontier:** BOYNTON.

**Redus, Morgan Ward.** The Text of the Major Festivals of the Menologion in the Greek Gospel Lectionary. 1936. LT. *o.p.*

**Reed, Carlos Isaac.** Vitamin D. Chemistry, Physiology, Pharmacology, Pathology. Experimental and Clinical Investigations. By C. I. Reed, Ph.D.; H. C. Struck, Ph.D.; and I. E. Steck, M.D. 1939. CMM. *o.p.*

**Reed, Charles Bert.** The Masters of the Wilderness. 1914. *o.p.*
A publication of the Chicago Historical Society.

**Reed, Charles Bert.** The Masters of the Wilderness. A Study of the Hudson's Bay Company from Its Origin to Modern Times. 1909. *o.p.*
A publication of the Chicago Historical Society.

**Reed, Louis Schultz.** The Ability To Pay for Medical Care. 1933. CMC 25. *o.p.*

**Reed, Louis Schultz.** The Healing Cults. A Study of Sectarian Medical Practice: Its Extent, Causes, and Control. 1932. CMC 16. *o.p.*

**Reed, Louis Schultz.** The Medical Service of the Homestake Mining Company. A Survey of a Community Medical Service Operated under Industrial Auspices. 1932. CMC 18. *o.p.*

**Reed, Louis Schultz.** Midwives, Chiropodists, and Optometrists. Their Place in Medical Care. 1932. CMC 15. *o.p.*

**Reed, Thomas Harrison.** Four Years of Network Broadcasting. A Report by the Committee on Civic Education by Radio of the National Advisory Council on Radio in Education and the American Political Science Association. 1937. *o.p.*

**Reed, Thomas Harrison,** *ed.* Government in a Depression. Constructive Economy in State and Local Government. 1933. *o.p.*

**Reed, Thomas Harrison,** *ed.* Legislatures and Legislative Problems. 1933. *o.p.*

**Re-educating Germany:** RICHTER.

**Reel, A. Frank.** The Case of General Yamashita. 1949. *o.p.*

**Rees, Albert.** The Economics of Trade Unions. 1962. xiv, 208 p. 62-9741. Cloth. 20 cm. $3.50ˢ. Paper. 21 cm. CEH 7. $1.35. OBE.

**Rees, Albert,** *joint ed.:* HAMILTON, Landmarks in Political Economy.

**Rees, Kelley.** The Rule of Three Actors in the Classical Greek Drama. 1908. *o.p.*

**Reese, Herbert Meredith.** An Investigation of the Zeeman Effect. With Reference to Cadmium, Zinc, Magnesium, Iron, Nickel, Titanium, Carbon, Calcium, Aluminum, Silicon, and Mercury. 1900. *o.p.*

**Reese, William L.,** *joint author:* HARTSHORNE, Philosophers Speak of God.

**Reeve, William David.** A Review of High-School Mathematics. By William David Reeve and Raleigh Schorling. 1915. *o.p.*

**Reeve, William David,** *joint author:* MYERS, Teacher's Manual for First-Year Mathematics.

**Reeves, Floyd Wesley.** Admission and Retention of University Students. Prepared under the Direction of a Survey Staff Consisting of Floyd W. Reeves and John Dale Russell. 1933. UCS. *o.p.*

**Reeves, Floyd Wesley.** The Alumni of the Colleges. By Floyd W. Reeves and John Dale Russell. 1933. UCS. *o.p.*

**Reeves, Floyd Wesley.** Class Size and University Costs. By Floyd W. Reeves, Nelson B. Henry, and John Dale Russell. 1933. UCS. *o.p.*

**Reeves, Floyd Wesley.** Instructional Problems in the University. By Floyd W. Reeves, W. E. Peik, and John Dale Russell. 1933. UCS. *o.p.*

**Reeves, Floyd Wesley.** The Liberal Arts College. Based upon Surveys of Thirty-five Colleges Related to the Methodist Episcopal Church. By Floyd W. Reeves, John Dale Russell, H. C. Gregg, A. J. Brumbaugh, and L. E. Blauch. 1932. *o.p.*

**Reeves, Floyd Wesley.** The Organization and Administration of the University. By Floyd W. Reeves, Frederick J. Kelly, John Dale Russell, and George A. Works. 1933. UCS. *o.p.*

**Reeves, Floyd Wesley.** Some University Student Problems. By Floyd W. Reeves and John Dale Russell. 1933. UCS. *o.p.*

**Reeves, Floyd Wesley.** Trends in University Growth. By Floyd W. Reeves, Ernest C. Miller, and John Dale Russell. 1933. UCS. *o.p.*

**Reeves, Floyd Wesley.** University Extension Services. By Floyd W. Reeves, C. O. Thompson, Arthur J. Klein, and John Dale Russell. 1933. UCS. *o.p.*

**Reeves, Floyd Wesley.** The University Faculty. By Floyd W. Reeves, Nelson B. Henry, Frederick J. Kelly, Arthur J. Klein, and John Dale Russell. 1933. UCS. *o.p.*

**Reeves, Floyd Wesley.** University Plant Facilities. By Floyd W. Reeves, Frederick J. Kelly, and John Dale Russell. 1933. UCS. *o.p.*

**Reeves, Floyd Wesley,** *ed.* Education for Rural America. 1945. *o.p.*

**Reeves, Floyd Wesley,** *joint author:* RUSSELL, Administration.

**Reeves, Floyd Wesley,** *joint author:* RUSSELL, Finance.

**Reference Function of the Library:** BUTLER.

**Reference Guide to Edmund Spenser:** CARPENTER.

**Reference Guide to English Studies:** BOND.

**Reference Guide to Milton:** STEVENS.

**Reference Studies in Medieval History:** THOMPSON.

**Regeneration in Vertebrates:** THORNTON.

**Reich, Jerome R.** Leisler's Rebellion. A Study of Democracy in New York, 1664–1720. 1953. *o.p.*

**Reichel, Alicia Dussán de,** *joint author:* REICHEL-DOLMATOFF, People of Aritama.

**Reichel-Dolmatoff, Gerardo.** The People of Aritama. By Gerardo Reichel-Dolmatoff and Alicia Dussán de Reichel. 1962. xviii, 483 p. Illus. Index. 22 cm. 60-14234. $8.50ˢ. COBE.

**Reichenbach, Hans.** Experience and Prediction. An Analysis of the Foundations and the Structure of Knowledge. 1938. x, 408 p. 21 cm. 38-6303. Paper. P81. $1.95.

**Reid, Harvey.** Biographical Sketch of Enoch Long, an Illinois Pioneer. 1884. *o.p.*
A publication of the Chicago Historical Society.

**Reid, Helen Dwight.** International Servitudes in Law and Practice. With a Foreword by Dr. James Brown Scott. 1932. *o.p.*

**Reid, Helen Richmond Young,** *joint author:* YOUNG, Japanese Canadians.

**Reid, Margaret G.** Housing and Income. 1962. xx, 416 p. Index. Illus. 24 cm. 62-19628. $7.50ˢ.

**Reid, William Thomas:** *see* BLISS, Contributions to the Calculus of Variations, 1933–37.

**Reintegrative Process in Psychoanalytic Treatment:** FRENCH.

**Reise durch Deutschland:** LEOPOLD.

**Reiss, Albert J., Jr.,** *ed.:* WIRTH, Louis Wirth on Cities and Social Life.

**Reiss, Albert J., Jr.,** *joint ed.:* WIRTH, Community Life.

**Reiter, Elmar R.** Jet-Stream Meteorology. 1963. xiv, 516 p. Illus. Index. 25 cm. 63-13074. $17.50ˢ.

**Relation of Accelerated, Normal and Retarded Puberty to the Height and Weight of School Children:** RICHEY.

**Relation of the Individual to the Group:** AMERICAN SOCIOLOGICAL SOCIETY, Annual Proceedings, Vol. XXII.

**Relation of Inference to Fact:** CRAWFORD.

**Relation of John Locke to English Deism:** HEFELBOWER.

**Relation of the Medicine-Man to the Origin of the Professional Occupations:** THOMAS.

**Relation between Religion and Science:** WOODBURNE.

**Relation of Superintendents and Principals to the Training and Professional Improvement of Their Teachers:** LOWRY.

**Relation of Theory to Practice in Education:** HOLMES.

**Relation of Theory to Practice in the Education of Teachers:** DEWEY.

**Relations of Structural and Functional Psychology to Philosophy:** ANGELL.

**Relations of the Wisconsin and Kansas Drift Sheets:** BAIN.

**Relationship between Persistence in School and Home Conditions:** HOLLEY.

**Relative Chronologies in Old World Archeology:** EHRICH.

**Relativism, Knowledge, and Faith:** KAUFMAN.

**Relief and Health Problems of a Selected Group of Non-family Men:** JOHNSON.

**Reliefs and Inscriptions at Karnak:** EPIGRAPHIC SURVEY.

**Religion on the American Frontier:** SWEET.

**Religion of the Bible:** BEWER.

**Religion in Country Life:** *see* AMERICAN COUNTRY LIFE ASSOCIATION, Proceedings, No. 7.

**Religion and Freedom in the Modern World:** MULLER.

**Religion in Higher Education:** TOWNER.

**Religion and the Higher Life:** HARPER.

**Religion of Israel:** KAUFMAN.

**Religion in the Kindergarten:** RHODES.

**Religion and the Present Crisis:** KNOX.

**Religion of the Psalms:** SMITH.

**Religion and the Public Order:** GIANNELLA.

**Religions of the World:** BARTON.

Religious Attitude: MACDONALD.

Religious Education: SOARES.

Religious Education in the Family: COPE.

Religious Education in the Public Schools: HALL.

Religious Observances in Tibet: EKVALL.

Religious Thought in the Last Quarter-Century: SMITH.

Remedial Cases in Reading. Their Diagnosis and Treatment: GRAY.

Remedial Reading at the College and Adult Levels: BUSWELL.

Renaissance Philosophy of Man: CASSIRER.

Renaissance of Roman Architecture: JACKSON.

Render unto Caesar: MANWARING.

Renier, Gustaaf Johannes, *trans.*: KAT ANGELINO, Colonial Policy.

Renshaw, Gladys Anne, *joint author:* DELÉRY, France d'Amérique.

Reobservation of the Orbits of Ten Spectroscopic Binaries: LUYTEN.

Repasemos. A Spanish Review Grammar and Elementary Composition Book: SPARKMAN.

Repetition of a Word as a Means of Suspense in the Drama: SCHÜTZE.

Report of the Commission on Length of Elementary Education: BROOKS.

Report of the Educational Commission: HARPER.

Report of an Investigation of the Municipal Revenues of Chicago: MERRIAM.

Report on Reading (National Committee of NSSE): GRAY.

Report of the Society's Committee on Arithmetic: KNIGHT.

Report on Synoptic Conditions in the Mediterranean Area: ROSSBY.

Report on Vocational Training: MEAD.

Reports of Investigations by Members of the Society of College Teachers of Education: NATIONAL SOCIETY OF COLLEGE TEACHERS OF EDUCATION, Proceedings, No. 3.

Reproduction among Mammals: STRANDSKOV.

Requirements for Certification of Teachers: WOELLNER.

Research in Arithmetic (Report of the Society's Committee on Arithmetic, Part II): KNIGHT.

Research within the Field of Education, Its Organization and Encouragement: NATIONAL SOCIETY OF COLLEGE TEACHERS OF EDUCATION, Proceedings, No. 1.

Researches in Anatolia. I, II–III, VII–IX: OSTEN.

Researches in Anatolia. IV–V: SCHMIDT.

Researches in Anatolia. VI: GELB.

Researches on the Arseniates: GRAHAM.

Researches in Assyrian and Babylonian Geography: TOFFTEEN.

Researches into the Early History of Mankind and the Development of Civilization: TYLOR.

Researches on the Molecular Asymmetry of Natural Organic Products: PASTEUR.

Researches on the Spectrum of the Variable Star n Aquilae: BÉLOPOLSKY.

Resek, Carl. Lewis Henry Morgan, American Scholar. 1960. ix, 184 p. Illus. 22 cm. 60-5468. $4.50s.

Resident Orientals on the American Pacific Coast: MEARS.

Resolution into Series of the Third Band of the Carbon Band-Spectrum: THIELE.

Respective Standpoints of Psychology and Logic: CASTRO.

Response to Industrialism: HAYS.

Responsible Christian: OBENHAUS.

Restoration of American Politics: MORGENTHAU.

Restoration and Eighteenth-Century Literature: CAMDEN.

Results of the Chicago Experiment in Introducing Latin into the Seventh and Eighth Grades: NIGHTINGALE.

Résumé of Solar Observation: MASCARI.

Retail Accounting: HODGE.

**Retail Price Behavior:** COVER.

**Rethinking Science Education:** BARNARD.

**Retina:** POLYAK.

**Retrospect and Forecast in Radio Education:** TYSON.

**Reveille for Radicals:** ALINSKY.

**Revelation in Jewish Wisdom Literature:** RYLAARSDAM.

**Revelation of John:** CASE.

**Revelation in Mormonism:** ARBAUGH.

**Reverse Index of Greek Nouns and Adjectives:** BUCK.

**Review of High-School Mathematics:** REEVE.

**Revolution in Education:** ADLER.

**Revzan, David Allen,** *joint author:* DUDDY, Changing Relative Importance of the Central Livestock Market.

**Revzan, David Allen,** *joint author:* DUDDY, Distribution of Livestock from the Chicago Market.

**Revzan, David Allen,** *joint author:* DUDDY, Grain Supply Area of the Chicago Market.

**Revzan, David Allen,** *joint author:* DUDDY, Physical Distribution of Fresh Fruits and Vegetables.

**Revzan, David Allen,** *joint author:* DUDDY, Supply Area of the Chicago Livestock Market.

**Revzan, David Allen,** *joint author:* DUDDY, Use of Transportation Facilities in the Chicago Fruit and Vegetable Market.

**Rey, Jean.** Essays of Jean Rey, Doctor of Medicine. On an Enquiry into the Cause Wherefore Tin and Lead Increase in Weight on Calcination (1630). 1902. AC. *o.p.*

**Reynolds, George Fullmer.** Some Principles of Elizabethan Staging. 1905. *o.p.*

**Reynolds, Myra.** The Treatment of Nature in English Poetry between Pope and Wordsworth. 1896. 2d ed. 1909. ENG. *o.p.*

**Reynolds, Myra,** *ed.* The Poems of Anne, Countess of Winchilsea. From the Original Edition of 1713 and from Unpublished Manuscripts edited with an Introduction and Notes by Myra Reynolds. 1903. *o.p.*

**Rhetoric of Fiction:** BOOTH.

**Rhoades, Elmer Lamont.** Merchandising Packinghouse Products. By E. L. Rhoades, with the Co-operation of Sales Executives of the Packing Industry. 1929. IMP. *o.p.*

**Rhodes, Bertha Marilda.** Religion in the Kindergarten. A Course in Religion for the Beginner's Department in the Sunday School or for Use in the Day School or the Home. 1924–27. CS. *o.p.*

**Rhus dermatitis (Poison Ivy):** McNAIR.

**Rhythmic Structure of Music:** COOPER.

**Rib of Man:** KENNEDY, *in his* Plays for Seven Players.

**Rice, Stuart Arthur,** *ed.* Methods in Social Science. A Case Book, Compiled under the Direction of the Committee on Scientific Method in the Social Sciences of the Social Science Research Council. 1931. *o.p.*

**Rice University Semicentennial Series** (RSS):
ADAMS, Natural Radiation Environment.
CAMDEN, Literary Views.
CAMDEN, Restoration and Eighteenth-Century Literature.
DONNELLY, Earth Sciences.
DREW, Perspectives in Medieval History.
EDWARDS, Nation's Economic Objectives.
ENDERS, Delayed Implantation.
JENNINGS, Prehistoric Man in the New World.
NELSON, Theory and Practice in American Politics.
PHILLIPS, Progress in Fast Neutron Physics.
RANSOM, People's Architects.
VANDIVER, Idea of the South.
WANN, Behaviorism and Phenomenology.

**Rice, William F.,** *ed.* Ariel. By José Enrique Rodó. IICLS.

**Rich, Daniel C.** Seurat and the Evolution of "La Grande Jatte." 1935. MA. *o.p.*

**Rich, Daniel C.,** *ed.* Seurat: Paintings and Drawings. 1958. *o.p.*

**Richards, Ellen Henrietta Swallow.** Food as a Factor in Student Life. A Contribution to the Study of Student Diet. By Ellen H. Richards and Marion Talbot. 1894. *o.p.*

**Richards, I. A.** Speculative Instruments. 1955. xii, 216 p. 22 cm. 56-5037. $4.50s. USA.

**Richardson, Cyril Albert.** The Growth and Variability of Intelligence. 2 parts. 1933. *Part I* by C. A. Richardson and C. W. Stokes. *Part II* by C. A. Richardson. BJP. *o.p.*

**Richardson, E. P.** Washington Allston. A Study of the Romantic Artist in America. 1948. *o.p.*

**Richardson, Emeline.** The Etruscans: Their Art and Civilization. 1964. xvii, 285 p. 48 plates. 64-15817. 24 cm. $7.95.

**Richardson, Lewis Fry.** Generalized Foreign Politics. A Study in Group Psychology. 1939. BJP. *o.p.*

**Richey, Herman Glenn.** The Relation of Acclerated, Normal, and Retarded Puberty to the Height and Weight of School Children. 1937. CD. *o.p.*

**Richter, George Martin.** Andrea dal Castagno. 1943. *o.p.*

**Richter, George Martin.** Giorgio da Castelfranco, Called Giorgione. 1937. *o.p.*

"It combines in a remarkable manner exact scholarship with attractive speculation and both these methods are kept entirely distinct from each other . . . the result is a surprisingly coherent and balanced picture, constructed from hints, disconnected facts, both new and old, and minute indications. The catalogue of Giorgione's works, or possible works, in which all the documents, history, and other facts about each picture are summarized, would by itself make this a necessity, and what is more, a great convenience to every student of the subject."—*The Times Literary Supplement.*

**Richter, Werner.** Re-educating Germany. Translated by Paul Lehman. 1945. *o.p.*

**Rickert, Edith.** New Methods for the Study of Literature. 1927. *o.p.*

**Rickert, Edith,** *joint ed.:* MANLY, Text of *The Canterbury Tales.*

**Rickert, Margaret.** The Reconstructed Carmelite Missal. An English Manuscript of the Late XIV Century in the British Museum. 1952. 151 p. Illus. 28 cm. 52-14782. $10.00s. COBE.

**Rickert, Margaret:** *see* MANLY, Text of *The Canterbury Tales.*

**Ricketts, Howard Taylor.** Contributions to Medical Science by Howard Taylor Ricketts, 1870–1910. Published as a Tribute to His Memory by His Colleagues under the Auspices of the Chicago Pathological Society. 1911. *o.p.*

**Riddle, Donald Wayne.** The Gospels. Their Origin and Growth. 1939. *o.p.*

**Riddle, Donald Wayne.** Jesus and the Pharisees. A Study in Christian Tradition. 1928. *o.p.*

**Riddle, Donald Wayne.** The Martyrs. A Study in Social Control. 1931. *o.p.*

**Riddle, Donald Wayne.** New Testament Life and Literature. By Donald W. Riddle and Harold H. Hutson. 1946. vii, 263 p. 24 cm. A46-2485. $4.00s.

**Riddle, Donald Wayne,** *joint ed.:* COLWELL, Prolegomena to the Study of the Lectionary Text.

**Riddle, Donald Wayne,** *joint ed.:* GOODSPEED, Rockefeller McCormick New Testament.

**Riddle of the Pianist's Finger:** SCHULTZ.

**Ridge, Martin.** Ignatius Donnelly. The Portrait of a Politician. 1962. xii, 428 p. 24 cm. 62-19937. $7.95s.

**Ridgley, Douglas Clay.** The Geography of Illinois. 1921. *o.p.*

**Ridley, Clarence Eugene.** The City-Manager Profession. By Clarence E. Ridley and Orin F. Nolting. With a Foreword by Louis Brownlow. 1934. MM. *o.p.*

**Ridolfi, Roberto.** The Life of Niccolò Machiavelli. Translated from the Italian by Cecil Grayson. 1963. 352 p. Illus. 25 cm. 62-15048. $6.00. COBE.

**Riehl, Herbert.** Ocean Analysis from Coastal Reports. By Herbert Riehl and C. R. Elford. 1943. DMMR 9. *o.p.*

**Riehl, Herbert.** Studies of Upper Air Conditions in Low Latitudes. By Clarence E. Riehl and George P. Cressman. 1948. DMMR 24. *o.p.*

**Riehl, Herbert.** Subtropical Flow Patterns in Summer. 1947. DMMR 22. *o.p.*

**Riehl, Herbert.** Waves in the Easterlies and the Polar Front in the Tropics. DMMR 17. 1945. *o.p.*

**Riese, Hertha.** Heal the Hurt Child. 1962. xxiv, 616 p. Illus. 24 cm. 62-19623. $10.00ˢ.

**Riesman, David:** *see* FALK, Community Medical Service . . . Roanoke Rapids, N.C.

**Riesman, David:** *see* FALK, Organized Medical Service at Fort Benning, Georgia.

**Right Living:** NEUBERG.

**Riha, Thomas,** *ed.* Readings in Russian Civilization. 1964. *Vol. I:* Russia Before Peter the Great, 900–1700. *Vol. II:* Imperial Russia, 1700–1917. *Vol. III:* Soviet Russia, 1917–1963. 1000 p. 23 cm. 64-15814. Cloth, one-vol. ed. $12.50ᵗ. Paper, each vol. $3.75ᵗ.

**Riley, Ralph J.** A Working Manual for Juvenile Court Officers. With an Introductory Note by Sophonisba P. Breckinridge. 1932. SSM. *o.p.*

**Riley, Thomas James.** The Higher Life of Chicago. 1905. *o.p.*

**Ring, Martin, D.,** *joint author:* FALK, Costs of Medical Care.

**Ring Nebula in Lyra:** KEELER.

**Rippy, James Fred.** America and the Strife of Europe. 1938. *o.p.*

**Rippy, James Fred.** Mexico. By J. Fred Rippy, José Vasconcelos, and Guy Stevens. 1928. APA. *o.p.*

**Rippy, James Fred:** *see* LAVES, Foundations of a More Stable World Order.

**Rise of the British Coal Industry:** NEF.

**Rise of Christianity:** NORTON.

**Rise of the North Arabic Script:** ABBOTT.

**Rise of the Skyscraper:** CONDIT.

**Rise of the Transpiration Stream:** COPELAND.

**Rise of the West:** McNEILL.

**Risk and Risk-bearing:** HARDY.

**Risorgimento:** VAN HORNE.

**Risser, J. E.,** *joint ed.:* PHILLIPS, Progress in Fast Neutron Physics.

**Ritchey, George Willis.** Astronomical Photography with the Forty-Inch Refractor and the Two-Foot Reflector of the Yerkes Observatory. Preprint. 1904. *o.p.*

**Rites of Passage:** GENNEP.

**Rivers, Wilga.** The Psychologist and the Foreign-Language Teacher. 1964. viii, 212 p. 22 cm. 64-15809. $4.00ˢ.

**Rivers into Islands:** KNOEPFLE.

**Road to Serfdom:** HAYEK.

**Road to Tryermaine:** NETHERCOT.

**Robbins, Frank Egleston.** The Hexaemeral Literature. A Study of the Greek and Latin Commentaries on Genesis. 1912. *o.p.*

**Robert Burns, His Personality, His Reputation, and His Art:** SNYDER.

**Roberts' Nutrition Work with Children:** MARTIN.

**Robertson, David Allan.** The Quarter-Centennial Celebration of the University of Chicago. June 2 to 6, 1916. A Record by David Allan Robertson. 1918. *o.p.*

**Robertson, David Allan.** The University of Chicago. An Official Guide. 1916. *o.p.*

**Robertson, D. H.** Money. 1959. xvii, 187 p. 21 cm. 59-9825. Paper. CEH 5. $1.75. USA.

**Robinson, Benjamin Willard.** The Life of Paul. 1918. 2d ed. 1928. xvi, 268 p. Illus. 19 cm. 18-19810. HER. $5.00ˢ.

**Robinson, E. A. G.** The Structure of Competitive Industry. 1959. vii, 156 p. 21 cm. 59-6929. Paper. CEH 6. $1.50. USA.

**Robinson, Edward Stevens.** Readings in General Psychology. Edited by Edward Stevens Robinson and Florence Richardson-Robinson. 1923. 2d ed. 1929. *o.p.*

**Robinson, Florence Ella Richardson,** *joint ed.:* ROBINSON, Readings in General Psychology.

**Robinson, Fred N.:** *see* BRYAN, Sources and Analogues of Chaucer's *Canterbury Tales.*

**Robinson, H. Alan.** Meeting Individual Differences in Reading. 1964. ix, 246 p. 25 cm. 64-24978. SEM 94. $4.50$^t$.

**Robinson, H. Alan.** Reading and the Language Arts. 1963. ix, 252 p. 25 cm. 63-23073. SEM 93. $4.50$^t$.

**Robinson, H. Alan.** The Underachiever in Reading. Paper. 1962. x, 198 p. 25 cm. 62-22030. SEM 92. $3.50$^t$.

**Robinson, H. Alan,** *ed.* Recent Developments in Reading. 1965. SEM 95. 240 p. $4.50$^t$.

**Robinson, Helen Mansfield.** Why Pupils Fail in Reading. A Study of Causes and Remedial Treatment. 1946. xiv, 257 p. 24 cm. A46-5912. $5.00$^t$.

**Robinson, Helen Mansfield,** *ed.* Clinical Studies in Reading II. With Emphasis on Vision Problems. 1953. x, 189 p. 25 cm. Paper. SEM 77. $3.75$^t$.

**Robinson, Helen Mansfield,** *ed.* Controversial Issues in Reading and Promising Solutions. 1961. viii, 181 p. 25 cm. 61-18445. Paper. SEM 91. $3.50$^t$.

**Robinson, Helen Mansfield,** *ed.* Corrective Reading in Classroom and Clinic. 1953. viii, 256 p. 25 cm. 54-227. Paper. SEM 79. $4.00$^t$.

**Robinson, Helen Mansfield,** *ed.* Developing Permanent Interest in Reading. 1956. viii, 224 p. 25 cm. 57-6271. Paper. SEM 84. $3.50$^t$.

**Robinson, Helen Mansfield,** *ed.* Evaluation of Reading. 1958. vii, 208 p. 25 cm. 58-59528. Paper. SEM 88. $3.50$^t$.

**Robinson, Helen Mansfield,** *ed.* Materials for Reading. 1957. vii, 231 p. 25 cm. 57-11212. Paper. SEM 86. $3.50$^t$.

**Robinson, Helen Mansfield,** *ed.* Oral Aspects of Reading. 1955. vii, 166 p. 25 cm. 56-5135. Paper. SEM 82, $3.50$^t$.

**Robinson, Helen Mansfield,** *ed.* Promoting Maximal Reading Growth among Able Learners. Proceedings of the Seventeenth Annual Conference on Reading Held at the University of Chicago, 1954. 1954. SEM 81. *o.p.*

**Robinson, Helen Mansfield,** *ed.* Reading Instructions in Various Patterns of Grouping. 1959. viii, 212 p. 25 cm. 60-6681. Paper. SEM 89. $3.50$^t$.

**Robinson, Helen Mansfield,** *ed.* Sequential Development of Reading Abilities. 1960. xv, 251 p. 25 cm. 60-14354. Paper. SEM 90. $3.50$^t$.

**Robinson, Henry Barton.** Syntax of the Participle in the Apostolic Fathers, in the Editio Minor of Gebhardt-Harnack-Zahn. 1913. HLL. *o.p.*

**Robinson, Henry M.:** *see* EINSTEIN, Symposium on America and the World Situation.

**Robinson, Ivor.** Quasi-stellar Sources and Gravitational Collapse. Including the Proceedings of the First Texas Symposium on Relativistic Astrophysics. Edited by Ivor Robinson, Alfred Schild, and E. L. Schucking. 1965. xvii, 475 p. 25 cm. 64-24966. $10.00$^s$.

**Robinson, Willard Haskell.** The Parables of Jesus in Their Relation to His Ministry. 1928. *o.p.*

**Rochedieu, Charles Alfred.** Bibliography of French Translations of English Works, 1700–1800. 1948. *o.p.*

**Rochester and Colgate:** ROSENBERGER.

**Rockefeller, David.** Unused Resources and Economic Waste. 1941. *o.p.*

**Rockefeller McCormick New Testament:** GOODSPEED.

**Roden, Lennart and Kajsa,** *joint trans.:* EHRENSVÄRD, Man on Another World.

**Roehenstart:** SHERBURN.

**Röpke, Wilhelm.** The Social Crisis in Our Time. Translated from the German by Annette and Peter Schiffer Jacobsohn. 1950. *o.p.*

**Rogers, Arthur Kenyon.** The Parallelism of Mind and Body from the Standpoint of Metaphysics. 1899. PHI. *o.p.*

**Rogers, Bernice,** *joint author:* GRAY, Maturity in Reading.

**Rogers, Carl R.,** *ed.* Psychotherapy and Personality Change. Co-ordinated Research Studies in the Client-centered Approach. Edited by Carl R. Rogers and Rosalind F. Dymond. 1954. x, 447 p. 24 cm. 54-11211. $8.50ˢ.

**Rogers, James Edward.** The American Newspaper. 1909. *o.p.*

**Rohr, Donald G.** The Origins of Social Liberalism in Germany. 1963. ix, 179 p. Index. 22 cm. 63-20914. $5.50ˢ.

**Roi des montagnes (About):** DAHL.

**Rojas, Alfonso Villa,** *joint author:* REDFIELD, Chan Kom.

**Roland, Charles P.** The Confederacy. 1960. viii, 218 p. Illus. 21 cm. 60-12573. CHAC. $3.95ˢ. Paper. $1.75.

**Rôle of the Bar in Electing the Bench in Chicago:** MARTIN.

**Role of Diffusion and Osmetic Pressure in Plants:** LIVINGSTONE.

**Role of the Library in Adult Education:** WILSON.

**Rôle of the** Μάγειρος **in the Life of the Ancient Greeks:** RANKIN.

**Role of the Scientific Societies in the Seventeenth Century:** ORNSTEIN.

**Rôles of Men and Women in Eskimo Culture:** GIFFEN.

**Romanticism in American Theology:** NICHOLS.

**Romer, Alfred Sherwood.** Osteology of the Reptiles. 1956. xxi, 772 p. Illus. 25 cm. 55-5143. $20.00ˢ.

**Romer, Alfred Sherwood.** Vertebrate Paleontology. 1933. 2d ed. 1945. ix, 687 p. Illus. 26 cm. A45-4631. BM. $8.50ᵗ.

"Completely up to date. . . . This fine work is recommended without reservation to everyone who has any interest at all in fossil vertebrates."—G. G. SIMPSON, in *The Quarterly Review of Biology.*

"This book, as was true of its predecessor, is indispensable as a reference work in the teaching of vertebrate paleontology."—EVERETT C. OLSON, in *The Journal of Geology.*

**Romer, Alfred Sherwood.** The Vertebrate Story. (Revised edition of *Man and the Vertebrates.*) 1959. vii, 437 p. Illus. 24 cm. 58-11957. $7.00ᵗ.

**Romer, Alfred Sherwood:** *see* MOULTON, World and Man.

**Romer, Alfred Sherwood:** *see* NEWMAN, Nature of the World and of Man.

**Romm, Vladimir:** *see* HARPER, Soviet Union and World-Problems.

**Roofe, Paul G.:** *see* CARPI, Short Introduction to Anatomy.

**Roosevelt and the Caribbean:** HILL.

**Root, Robert K.:** *see* BRYAN, Sources and Analogues of Chaucer's *Canterbury Tales.*

**Root and the Branch:** GORDIS.

**Rorem, Clarence Rufus.** Accounting Method. 1928. 2d ed. 1930. Second edition with Alternative Laboratory Exercises by W. J. Graham. MSB. *o.p.*

**Rorem, Clarence Rufus.** Capital Investment in Hospitals. The Place of "Fixed Charges" in Hospital Financing and Costs. 1930. CMC 7. *o.p.*

**Rorem, Clarence Rufus.** The Costs of Medicines. The Manufacture and Distribution of Drugs and Medicines in the United States and the Services of Pharmacy in Medical Care. By C. Rufus Rorem and Robert P. Fischelis. 1932. CMC 14. *o.p.*

**Rorem, Clarence Rufus.** The "Municipal Doctor" System in Rural Saskatchewan. 1931. CMC 11. *o.p.*

**Rorem, Clarence Rufus.** Private Group Clinics. The Administrative and Economic Aspects of Group Medical Practice, as Represented in the Policies and Procedures of 55 Private Associations of Medical Practitioners. 1931. CMC 8. *o.p.*

**Rorem, Clarence Rufus.** The Public's Investment in Hospitals. 1930. ME. *o.p.*

**Rorem, Clarence Rufus,** *joint author:* DAVIS, Crisis in Hospital Finance.

**Rorem, Clarence Rufus,** *joint author:* FALK, Costs of Medical Care.

**Rorem, Clarence Rufus,** *joint author:* GRAHAM, Teacher's Manual for *Accounting Method.*

**Rosaire, Forrest:** *see* DARGAN, Studies in Balzac's Realism.

**Rosander, Arlyn Custer.** Attitude toward Censorship. Forms A and B. Prepared by A. C. Rosander and L. L. Thurstone. 1931. TAS 28. *o.p.*

**Rosander, Arlyn Custer.** Attitude toward the Constitution of the United States. Forms A and B. Prepared by A. C. Rosander and L. L. Thurstone. 1931. TAS 12. *o.p.*

**Rose, Marc.** Money. By Marc Rose and R. L. Horne. 1935. Rev. ed. 1939. AP. *o.p.*

**Rosen, Alex,** *joint author:* DEAN, Manual of Intergroup Relations.

**Rosén, Haiim B.** A Textbook of Israeli Hebrew. With an Introduction to the Classical Language. 1962. xvi, 398 p. 25 cm. 62-9116. $10.00ᵗ.

**Rosenbaum, Eugene Joseph:** *see* MOULTON, World and Man.

**Rosenberg, Charles E.** The Cholera Years. The United States in 1832, 1849, and 1866. 1962. x, 260 p. 22 cm. 62-18121. $5.95ˢ.

**Rosenberg, S. L. Millard,** *ed.* Horas vividas. Selections from the Verse and Prose of Antonia Heras. Edited by S. L. Millard Rosenberg and Homer Price Earle. HCLS.

**Rosenberger, Jesse Leonard.** In Pennsylvania-German Land, 1928–29. 1929. *o.p.*

**Rosenberger, Jesse Leonard.** The Pennsylvania Germans. A Sketch of Their History and Life, of the Mennonites, and of Side Lights from the Rosenberger Family. 1923. *o.p.*

**Rosenberger, Jesse Leonard.** Rochester and Colgate. Historical Backgrounds of the Two Universites. 1925. *o.p.*

**Rosenberger, Jesse Leonard.** Through Three Centuries. Colver and Rosenberger, Lives and Times, 1620–1922. 1922. *o.p.*

**Rosenfeld, Selma,** *joint ed.:* DIAMOND, Cora. Vier Lausbubengeschichten.

**Rosenheim, Edward W., Jr.** Swift and the Satirist's Art. 1963. xiv, 244 p. Index. 24 cm. 63-11400. $5.95ˢ.

**Rosenheim, Edward W., Jr.** What Happens in Literature. A Student's Guide to Poetry, Drama, and Fiction. 1960. x, 163 p. 21 cm. 60-15458. $3.00ˢ. Paper. P77. $1.25.

**Ross, Frank Elmore.** Atlas of the Northern Milky Way. By Frank E. Ross and Mary R. Calvert. Made from Negatives Secured at the Mount Wilson and Lowell Observatories by Frank E. Ross, with the Assistance of Kenneth Newman at Flagstaff. *Part I.* 1934. *o.p. Part II.* 1936. *o.p.*

**Ross, Helen,** *joint ed.:* ALEXANDER, Dynamic Psychiatry.

**Ross, Helen,** *joint ed.:* ALEXANDER, Impact of Freudian Psychiatry.

**Rossby, Carl G.** Kinematic and Hydrostatic Properties of Certain Long Waves in the Westerlies. 1943. DMMR 5. *o.p.*

**Rossby, Carl G.** A Report on Synoptic Conditions in the Mediterranean Area. 1944. *o.p.*

**Rossby, Carl G.** Weather Estimates from Local Aerological Data: A Preliminary Report. By Carl G. Rossby, Vincent J. Oliver, and Mildred W. Boyden. 1943. DMMR 2. *o.p.*

**Rossby, Carl G.,** *ed.* A Table of Mean Virtual Temperatures for the Air Column between Sea Level and 10,000 feet. 1944. DM. *o.p.*

**Rotary?** UNIVERSITY OF CHICAGO, *Social Science Survey Committee.*

**Rotation Period of the Sun:** FOX.

**Roth, Julius A.,** *joint author:* FRIEDENBERG, Self-perception in the University.

**Roth, Lloyd J.,** *ed.* Isotopes in Experimental Pharmacology. 1965. xiv, 488 p. 24 cm. 65-14430. $12.50ˢ.

**Rothschild, Edward Francis.** The Meaning of Unintelligibility in Modern Art. 1934. MA. *o.p.*

**Rothman, Stephen.** Physiology and Biochemistry of the Skin. 1954. xiii, 741 p. Illus. 24 cm. 54-11218. BM. $19.50ˢ.

". . . a classic. This is not only the best recent book on dermatology, it is probably one of the best medical texts of this generation."—*Bulletin of The Johns Hopkins Hospital.*

". . . the first comprehensive and thorough presentation of physiology and biochemistry of the skin in the English language and should be on the desk or available for reference to any internist as well as to dermatologists and other physicians. . . ."—*Archives of Internal Medicine.*

**Rouse, Irving,** *joint ed.:* TAX, Appraisal of Anthropology.

**Rowland, Durbin,** *ed.* Contes de Maupassant. HCLS.

**Rowland, Henry Augustus.** Arc-Spectrum of Vanadium. Arc-Spectra of Zirconium and Lanthanum. By Henry A. Rowland and Caleb N. Harrison. 1898. *o.p.*

**Rowland, Henry Augustus.** A Preliminary Table of Solar Spectrum Wave-Lengths. 1897. Parts I and II. *o.p.*

**Rowland, Lloyd W.:** *see* WAPLES, Library.

**Rowley, George:** *see* THOMPSON, Civilization of the Renaissance.

**Royce, William Hobart.** A Balzac Bibliography. Writings Relative to the Life and Works of Honoré de Balzac. 1929. SB. *o.p.*

**Royce, William Hobart.** Indexes to A Balzac Bibliography. Containing an Index to Periodicals and a Topical Index to Items in This Bibliography. 1930. SB. *o.p.*

**Rubinow, Isaac Max,** *ed.* The Care of the Aged. Proceedings of the Deutsch Foundation Conference, 1930. 1931. SSM. *o.p.*

**Rudd, Herbert Finley.** Chinese Social Origins. 1928. *o.p.*

**Rudnick, Dorothea,** *ed.* Cytodifferentiation. 1958. xii, 118 p. 24 cm. 58 59709. DBC. $3.75ˢ.

**Rudnick, Dorothea,** *ed.* Embryonic Nutrition. 1958. xi, 114 p. 24 cm. 58-59710. DBC. $3.25ˢ.

**Rudolph, Richard C.,** *joint ed.:* CREEL, Literary Chinese by the Inductive Method.

**Ruffer, Marc Armand.** Studies in the Paleopathology of Egypt. Edited by Roy L. Moodie. 1921. *o.p.*

**Rugg, Harold O.** Curriculum-making: Past and Present. Prepared by Harold O. Rugg, Chairman of the Society's Committee. 1927. NSSE, 26th Yrbk., Part I. *o.p.*

**Rugg, Harold O.** The Foundations of Curriculum-making. Prepared by individual members of the Society's Committee, Harold O. Rugg, Chairman. 1927. NSSE, 26th Yrbk., Part II. *o.p.*

**Rugg, Harold O.** Scientific Method in the Reconstruction of Ninth-Grade Mathematics. A Complete Report of the Investigation of the Illinois Committee on Standardization of Ninth-Grade Mathematics, 1913–1918. By Harold Ordway Rugg and John Roscoe Clark. 1918. SEM 7. *o.p.*

**Rule of Three Actors in the Classical Greek Drama:** REES.

**Rules of Sociological Method:** DURKHEIM.

**Rullkoetter, William.** The Legal Protection of Woman among the Ancient Germans. 1900. *o.p.*

**Rumford Spectroheliograph:** HALE.

**Ruml, Beardsley:** *see* WHITE, New Social Science.

**Ruml, Beardsley:** *see* WIRTH, Eleven Twenty-six.

**Runge, Carl David Tolmé.** On the Spectra of Krypton. 1899. *o.p.*

**Rural America Today:** WORKS.

**Rural Community:** AMERICAN SOCIOLOGICAL SOCIETY, Proceedings, Vol. XXIII.

**Rural Community Organization:** HAYES.

**Rural Government:** AMERICAN COUNTRY LIFE ASSOCIATION, Proceedings, No. 14.

**Rural Health:** AMERICAN COUNTRY LIFE ASSOCIATION, Proceedings, No. 2.

**Rural Home:** AMERICAN COUNTRY LIFE ASSOCIATION, Proceedings, No. 6.

**Rural Mexico:** WHETTEN.

**Rural Mind:** GROVES.

**Rural Organization:** AMERICAN COUNTRY LIFE ASSOCIATION, Proceedings, No. 3, No. 12.

**Rural Public Welfare:** BROWNING.

**Rural School as a Community Center:** CROCHERON.

**Rural Social Conflict:** AMERICAN SOCIOLOGICAL SOCIETY, Proceedings, Vol. XXIV.

**Russell, Bertrand:** *see* NEURATH, Encyclopedia and Unified Science.

**Russell, Henry Norris.** The Masses of the Stars. With a General Catalogue of Dynamical Parallaxes. By Henry Norris Russell and Charlotte E. Moore. 1940. AM. *o.p.*

**Russell, John Dale.** Administration. By John Dale Russell and Floyd W. Reeves. 1937. EHI. *o.p.*

**Russell, John Dale.** Finance. By John Dale Russell and Floyd W. Reeves. 1937. EHI. *o.p.*

**Russell, John Dale.** The Finance of Higher Education. Rev. ed. 1954. xix, 416 p. 24 cm. 54-11212. $8.50ˢ.

**Russell, John Dale,** *ed.* Emergent Responsibilities in Higher Education. Edited by John D. Russell and Donald Mackenzie. 1946. HI. *o.p.*

**Russell, John Dale,** *ed.* Higher Education in the Postwar Period. 1944. HI. *o.p.*

**Russell, John Dale,** *ed.* Higher Education under War Conditions. 1943. HI. *o.p.*

**Russell, John Dale,** *ed.* New Frontiers in Collegiate Instruction. 1941. HI. *o.p.*

**Russell, John Dale,** *ed.* The Outlook for Higher Education. 1939. HI. *o.p.*

**Russell, John Dale,** *ed.* Problems of Faculty Personnel. 1946. HI. *o.p.*

**Russell, John Dale,** *ed.* Proceedings of the Conference on Problems of Business Administration in Colleges and Universities. Held at the University of Chicago, July, 1936. 1936. *o.p.*

**Russell, John Dale,** *ed.* Student Personnel Services in Colleges and Universities. 1941. HI. *o.p.*

**Russell, John Dale,** *ed.* Terminal Education in Higher Institutions. 1942. HI. *o.p.*

**Russell, John Dale,** *joint author:* REEVES, Admission and Retention of University Students.

**Russell, John Dale,** *joint author:* REEVES, Alumni of the Colleges.

**Russell, John Dale,** *joint author:* REEVES, Class Size and University Costs.

**Russell, John Dale,** *joint author:* REEVES, Instructional Problems in the University.

**Russell, John Dale,** *joint author:* REEVES, Liberal Arts College.

**Russell, John Dale,** *joint author:* REEVES, Organization and Administration of the University.

**Russell, John Dale,** *joint author:* REEVES, Some University Student Problems.

**Russell, John Dale,** *joint author:* REEVES, Trends in University Growth.

**Russell, John Dale,** *joint author:* REEVES, University Extension Services.

**Russell, John Dale,** *joint author:* REEVES, University Faculty.

**Russell, John Dale,** *joint author:* REEVES, University Plant Facilities.

**Russell, John Dale:** *see* EDWARDS, Education in a Democracy.

**Russia and Its Crisis:** MILYOUKOV.

**Russia and the Soviet Union:** HORECKY.

**Russian Language Today:** WARD.

**Russian Literature and Modern English Fiction:** DAVIE.

**Russian People. A Reader:** BILL.

**Russian Political Institutions:** KOVALEVSKY.

**Russian Reader:** BOYER.

**Russo, William.** Composing for the Jazz Orchestra. 1961. x, 90 p. 24 cm. 61-8642. $3.50ᵗ.

**Rydberg, Johannes Roberts.** On the Constitution of the Red Spectrum of Argon. 1897. *o.p.*

**Ryder, Arthur W.,** *trans.* The Bhagavadgita. 1929. *o.p.*

**Ryder, Arthur W.,** *trans.* Dandin's Dasha-Kumara-Charita. The Ten Princes. Translated from the Sanskrit by Arthur W. Ryder. 1927. *o.p.*

**Ryder, Arthur W.,** *trans.* Gold's Gloom. Tales from the *Panchatantra.* 1925. *o.p.*

**Ryder, Arthur W.,** *trans.* The Panchatantra. 1925. vi, 470 p. 21 cm. 25-21523. $7.50ˢ. Paper. P169. $2.95.
". . . Ryder is perhaps the most distinguished living translator from the Sanskrit. His . . . Panchatantra, and The Ten Princes, stand among the finest translations in English literature."—Isidor Schneider, in the *New York Evening Sun.*

**Ryder, Arthur W.,** *trans.* The Ten Princes (Dasha-Kumara-Charita). 1927. *o.p.*

**Rylaarsdam, J. Coert.** Revelation in Jewish Wisdom Literature. 1946. *o.p.*

**S. O. Levinson and the Pact of Paris:** STONER.

**Sacher, George A.,** *joint ed.:* BRUES, Aging and Levels of Biological Organization.

**Sacred Fortress:** SIMSON.

**Sacred Oasis:** VINCENT.

**Sacrifice:** HUBERT.

**Saenz, Moises.** Some Mexican Problems. By Moises Saenz and Herbert I. Priestley. 1926. HFL. *o.p.*

**Sage, Evan Taylor.** The Pseudo-Ciceronian consolatio. 1910. *o.p.*

**Sahama, Th. G.,** *joint author:* RANKAMA, Geochemistry.

**St. Denis. A French-Canadian Parish:** MINER.

**St. John, Wallace.** The Contest for Liberty of Conscience in England. 1900. *o.p.*

**Sainte-Beuve's Critical Theory:** MacCLINTOCK.

**Saintonge, Paul Frédéric.** Horace. Three Phases of His Influence. Lectures Given at Mount Holyoke College in Celebration of the Bimillennium Horatianum 1935. By Paul Frédéric Saintonge, Leslie Galc Burgevin, and Helen Griffith. With a Foreword by Cornelia C. Coulter. 1936. *o.p.*

**Saite Demotic Land Leases:** HUGHES.

**Sakkarah Expedition.** The Mastaba of Mereruka. By the Sakkarah Expedition (Prentice Duell, *field director*). 2 vols. *Part I.* 1938. xxv, 18 p. 103 plates (4 in color), 8 plans. OIP, XXXI. $25.00. *Part II.* 1938. xiii p. 116 plates (9 in color), 7 plans. OIP, XXXIX. 30 cm. 38-29617. $25.00. *Set.* $45.00.

**Salaries and Professional Qualifications of Social Workers in Chicago, 1935:** KRUGHOFF.

**Sales Analysis from the Management Standpoint:** COWAN.

**Saleslady:** DONOVAN.

**Salisbury, Harrison.** Moscow Journal. 1961. vii, 450 p. 22 cm. 61-16621. $6.95ˢ.

**Salisbury, Morse,** *joint author:* JANSKY, Problem of the Institutionally Owned Station.

**Salisbury, Rollin D.** Distinct Glacial Epochs and the Criteria for Their Recognition. 1893. *o.p.*

**Salisbury, Rollin D.** The Geography of Chicago and Its Environs. By Rollin D. Salisbury and William C. Alden. 1899. 2d ed. 1920. GSC. *o.p.*
First edition published by Rand McNally; second edition by University of Chicago Press.

**Salisbury, Rollin D.,** *ed.* Outlines of Geologic History with Especial Reference to North America. A Series of Essays Involving a Discussion of Geologic Correlation Presented before Section E of the American Association for the Advancement of Science, in Baltimore, December, 1908. Symposium Organized by Bailey Willis. 1910. *o.p.*

**Salmon, Lucy M.** Some Principles in the Teaching of History. 1902. NSSE, 1st Yrbk., Part I. *o.p.*

**Salutation:** KENNEDY, *in his* Plays for Three Players. Vol. I.

**Šamaš Religious Texts:** GRAY.

**Samuel, Maurice,** *ed.:* GOLDMAN, Ten Commandments.

**Sanctae silviae peregrinatio:** BECHTEL.

**Sandburg, Carl:** *see* RANEY, If Lincoln Had Lived.

**Sanders, Frederick William.** The Standard of Living in Its Relation to Economic Theory and Land Nationalization. An Exposition in Outline of the Relation of Certain Economic Principles to Social Readjustment. 1898. *o.p.*

**Sanders, Jennings Bryan.** John Fiske, *in* HUTCHINSON, Marcus W. Jernegan Essays.

**Sanderson, Ezra Dwight,** *ed.*: AMERICAN COUNTRY LIFE ASSOCIATION. Farm Income and Farm Life.

**Sandford, Kenneth Stuart.** First Report of the Prehistoric Survey Expedition. By K. S. Sandford and W. J. Arkell. 1928. OIC 3. *o.p.*

**Sandford, Kenneth Stuart.** Prehistoric Survey of Egypt and Western Asia. 4 vols. 30 cm. *Vol. I: Paleolithic Man and the Nile-Faiyum Divide.* A Study of the Region during Pliocene and Pleistocene Times. By K. S. Sandford and W. J. Arkell. 1930. xv, 77 p. 25 figures, 11 plates, 1 map. 30-8240. OIP, X. $5.00. *Vol. II: Paleolithic Man and the Nile Valley in Nubia and Upper Egypt.* A Study of the Region during Pliocene and Pleistocene Times. By K. S. Sandford and W. J. Arkell. 1933. OIP, XVII. *o.p. Vol. III: Paleolithic Man and the Nile Valley in Upper and Middle Egypt.* A Study of the Region during Pliocene and Pleistocene Times. 1934. xxi, 131 p. 25 figures, 39 plates, 1 map. 35-2041. OIP, XVIII. $7.00. *Vol. IV: Paleolithic Man and the Nile Valley in Lower Egypt with Some Notes upon a Part of the Red Sea Littoral.* A Study of the Regions during Pliocene and Pleistocene Times. By K. S. Sandford and W. J. Arkell. 1939. OIP, XLVI. *o.p.*

**Sans famille (Malot):** MEADE.

**Santa Eulalia:** LA FARGE.

**Santillana, Giorgio de.** The Crime of Galileo. 1955. xv, 339 p. Illus. 55-7400. Cloth. 24 cm. $6.50ˢ. Paper. P40. 21 cm. $1.95. COBE.

"In the gallery of what might be called the martyrs of thought, the image of Galileo recanting before the Italian Inquisition stirs the minds of educated modern men second only to the picture of Socrates drinking the Hemlock. That image of Galileo is out of focus . . . because it has been distorted by three centuries of rationalist prejudice and clerical polemics. To refocus it clearly,

within the logic of its own time . . . de Santillana has written *The Crime of Galileo*, a masterly intellectual whodunit which traces not the life but the mental footsteps of Galileo on his road to personal tragedy."—*Time.*

**Santillana, Giorgio de.** The Development of Rationalism and Empiricism. By Giorgio de Santillana and Edgar Zilsel. 1941. viii, 94 p. 25 cm. A42-4170. Paper. IEUS, II, 8. $2.50ˢ.

**Santillana, Giorgio de.** The Origins of Scientific Thought. From Alexander to Plotinus, 600 B.C. to A.D. 300. 1961. 320 p. Index. 22 cm. 61-17073. $5.95ˢ. COBE.

**Santillana, Giorgio de,** *ed. and trans.*: GALILEI, Dialogue on the Great World Systems.

**Sargonic Texts from the Diyala Region:** GELB.

**Sarton, George:** *see* THOMPSON, Civilization of the Renaissance.

**Satires and Epistles:** HORACE.

**Saturday and Sunday Lessons from Luke:** METZGER.

**Saucier, Walter J.** Principles of Meteorological Analysis. 1955. xvi, 438 p. Illus. 25 cm. 55-7314. PS. $11.50ᵗ.

**Sauer, Carl O.** The Geography of the Ozark Highland of Missouri. 1920. GSC. *o.p.*

**Sauer, Carl O.** Starved Rock State Park and Its Environs. By Carl O. Sauer, Gilbert H. Cady, and Henry C. Cowles. 1918. GSC. *o.p.*

**Sauer, Carl O.,** *joint ed.*: THOMAS, Man's Role in Changing the Face of the Earth.

**Sauerwein, Jules Auguste:** *see* WRIGHT, Public Opinion and World-Politics.

**Saunders, Kenneth James.** Epochs in Buddhist History. 1924. CR. *o.p.*

**Sayre, Francis Bowes.** The Protection of American Export Trade, 1939. 1940. GFL. *o.p.*

**Scales for the Measurement of Social Attitudes** (TAS). Louis Leon Thurstone, editor.

(NOTE: The irregularity of the numbering below is due to the fact that several contemplated scales were never published.)

  1. THURSTONE, A Scale for Measuring Attitude toward the Church.

2. DROBA, Attitude toward War.
3. HINCKLEY, Attitude toward the Negro.
4. SMITH, Attitude toward Prohibition.
6. THURSTONE, Attitude toward Communism.
9. WANG, Attitude toward the Treatment of Criminals.
11. THIELE, Attitude toward Patriotism.
12. ROSANDER, Attitude toward the Constitution of the United States.
21. WANG, Attitude toward Birth Control.
22. CHAVE, Attitude toward God.
23. PETERSON, Attitude toward the Chinese.
25. PETERSON, Attitude toward the Germans.
26. WANG, Attitude toward Sunday Observance.
27. KATZ, Attitude toward the Law.
28. ROSANDER, Attitude toward Censorship.
29. CHAVE, Attitude toward the Bible.
30. THURSTONE, Attitude toward Evolution.
31. PETERSON, Attitude toward Capital Punishment.
34. PETERSON, Attitude toward War.

**Scammon Lectures at the Art Institute of Chicago** (SL):
BROWN, Lithography for Artists.
CARRINGTON, Engravers and Etchers.
CRAM, Six Lectures on Architecture.
FERGUSON, Outlines of Chinese Art.
PENNELL, The Graphic Arts.
STURGIS, Interdependence of the Arts of Design.
TAFT, Modern Tendencies in Sculpture.

**Scampolo (Niccodemi):** SCHOBINGER.

**Scates, Georgia P.** The Subprimary (Kindergarten) Department: *see* ELEMENTARY SCHOOL RECORD, No. 5.

**Schafer, Paul W.** Pathology in General Surgery. 1950. xv, 581 p. Illus. 28 cm. 50-8667. BM. $20.00ˢ.

**Schaffner, John H.** Contribution to the Life-History of Sagittaria variabilis. 1897. HB. *o.p.*

**Schaffner, John H.** The Development of the Stamens and Carpels of Typha latifolia. 1897. HB. *o.p.*

**Schaffner, John H.,** *joint author:* COULTER, Contribution to the Life-History of Lilium Philadelphicum.

**Schairer, J. F.:** *see* STUDIES IN PETROLOGY.

**Schaller, George B.** The Mountain Gorilla. Ecology and Behavior. 1963. xviii, 432 p. Illus. Index. 24 cm. 63-11401. $10.00.
"In whatever direction further work on primates may proceed, either toward the experimental analysis of behavioral development and physiology or toward the comparative synthesis of information on social systems and their behavioral consequences and ecological significance, the debt to Schaller's pioneering study will be a lasting one. His study sets standards that will be a challenge for future investigators to maintain."—P. Marler, *Science.*

**Schaller, George B.** The Year of the Gorilla. 1964. x, 260 p. Illus. 22 cm. 64-13946. $5.95. COBE.

**Schatzmann, Iman E.** The Country School at Home and Abroad. 1942. *o.p.*

**Schaub, Edward Leroy:** *see* SMITH, Religious Thought in the Last Quarter-Century.

**Scheele, Carl Wilhelm.** The Discovery of Oxygen. Part II. Experiments by Carl Wilhelm Scheele (1777). 1912. AC. *o.p.*

**Scheele, Carl Wilhelm.** The Early History of Chlorine. Papers by Carl Wilhelm Scheele (1774), C. L. Berthollet (1785), Guyton de Morveau (1787), J. L. Gay-Lussac and L. J. Thenard (1809). 1902. AC. *o.p.*

**Scheidemann, Norma Valentine.** Experiments in General Psychology. 1929. Rev. ed. 1939. *o.p.*

**Scheidemann, Norma Valentine.** Lecture Demonstrations for General Psychology. 1939. *o.p.*

**Scheinmann, Daniel:** *see* LELAND, State-Local Fiscal Relations.

**Schellenberg, T. R.** Modern Archives. Principles and Techniques. 1956. xv, 248 p. 23 cm. 56-58525. $6.50ˢ. COBE.

**Schenker, Heinrich.** Harmony. Edited and annotated by Oswald Jonas. Translated by Elisabeth Mann Borgese. 1954. xxxii, 359 p. 24 cm. 54-11213. $8.50ˢ.

**Schevill, Ferdinand.** The Great Elector. 1947. *o.p.*

**Schevill, Ferdinand.** Karl Bitter. A Biography. Issued under the Auspices of The National Sculpture Society. 1917. *o.p.*

**Schevill, Ferdinand.** Six Historians. 1957. xv, 201 p. 22 cm. 56-6635. $5.00ˢ.

**Schevill, Ferdinand:** *see* LAVES, Foundations of a More Stable World Order.

**Schevill, Ferdinand:** *see* THOMPSON, Civilization of the Renaissance.

**Schick, Joseph Schlenter.** The Early Theater in Eastern Iowa. Cultural Beginnings and the Rise of the Theater in Davenport and Eastern Iowa, 1836–63. 1939. *o.p.*

**Schild, Alfred,** *joint ed.*: ROBINSON, Quasistellar Sources and Gravitational Collapse.

**Schindler, Rudolf.** Gastroscopy. The Endoscopic Study of Gastric Pathology. With 89 Text Figures and 96 Color Reproductions of Gastroscopic Observations. With a Preface by Dr. Walter Lincoln Palmer. 1937. Rev. ed. 1950. CMM. *o.p.*

**Schlauch, Margaret:** *see* BRYAN, Sources and Analogues of Chaucer's *Canterbury Tales*.

**Schlenk, Fritz,** *joint author*: SHAPIRO, Transmethylation and Methionine Biosynthesis.

**Schlesinger, Hermann Irving:** *see* MOULTON, World and Man.

**Schmidt, Emanuel.** Solomon's Temple in the Light of Other Oriental Temples. 1902. *o.p.*

**Schmidt, Erich Friedrich.** Anatolia through the Ages. Discoveries at the Alishar Mound, 1927–29. 1931. x, 165 p. Illus. 25 cm. 32-4357. Paper. OIC 11. $2.00.

**Schmidt, Erich Friedrich.** Flights over Ancient Cities of Iran. 1940. *Special Publication of the Oriental Institute of the University of Chicago. o.p.*

**Schmidt, Erich Friedrich.** Persepolis. *Vol. I:* Structures, Reliefs, Inscriptions. 1953. xxix, 297 p. Illus. 42 cm. 53-4329. OIP, LXVII. *O.S.*

"It can be doubted if few more thorough or impressive volumes have ever been published."—Joseph G. Harrison, in *The Christian Science Monitor.*

"This splendid volume . . . imparts to our knowledge of Achaemenian archeology a solidity which was hitherto lacking. . . . The book is . . . a compendium of Achaemenian archeology [dealing] with buildings, sculpture, and inscriptions."—H. Frankfort, in *The Journal of Near Eastern Studies.*

**Schmidt, Erich Friedrich.** Persepolis. *Vol. II:* Contents of the Treasury and Other Discov-

eries. 1956. x, 166 p. Illus. 42 cm. 53-4329. OIP, LXIX. $85.00.

**Schmidt, Erich Friedrich.** Researches in Anatolia. *Vols. IV–V:* The Alishar Hüyük, Seasons of 1928 and 1929. 1932–33. *Part I.* 1932. xxi, 293 p. Illus. 30 cm. OIP, XIX. $16.00. *Part II.* With a Chapter by Wilton Marion Krogman. 1933. xvii, 148 p. Illus. 30 cm. 30-14678. OIP, XX. $8.00.

**Schmidt, Erich Friedrich.** The Treasury of Persepolis and Other Discoveries in the Homeland of the Achaemenians. 1939. OIC 21. *o.p.*

**Schmidt, Erich Friedrich,** *joint author:* OSTEN, Researches in Anatolia. II–III.

**Schmidt, Maarten,** *joint ed.:* BLAAUW, Galactic Structure.

**Schmidt, William Anton.** An Experimental Study in the Psychology of Reading. 1917. SEM 2. *o.p.*

**Schmidt-Wartenberg, Hans Max,** *ed.* Inedita des Heinrich Kaufringer. 1897. GER. *o.p.*

**Schmitt, Bernadotte E.** From Versailles to Munich, 1918–1938. 1939. PPP 28. *o.p.*

**Schmitt, Bernadotte E.** What Shall We Do with Germany? 1943. PPP 38. *o.p.*

**Schmitt, Bernadotte E.,** *ed.* Some Historians of Modern Europe. Essays in Historiography by Former Students of the Department of History. 1942. *o.p.*

**Schneider, David Moses.** The History of Public Welfare in New York State, 1609–1866. 1938. SSM. *o.p.*

**Schneider, David Moses.** The History of Public Welfare in New York State, 1867–1940. By David M. Schneider and Albert Deutsch. 1941. SSM. *o.p.*

**Schneider, Elisabeth.** Coleridge, Opium, and *Kubla Khan.* 1953. *o.p.*

**Schneider, Herbert Wallace.** Making Fascists. By Herbert W. Schneider and Shepard B. Clough. 1929. SMC. *o.p.*

**Schneider, Louis.** Popular Religion. American Inspirational Literature. By Louis Schneider and Sanford M. Dornbusch. 1958. xi, 174 p. 25 cm. 58-11958. $4.50s.

**Schobinger, Elsie,** *ed.* Fra le corde d'un contra-basso. By Salvatore Farina. Edited by Elsie Schobinger and Ethel Preston. HCLS.

**Schobinger, Elsie,** *ed.* Scampolo. By Dario Niccodemi. Edited by Elsie Schobinger and Ethel Preston. HCLS.

**Schoeck, R. J.,** *joint general ed.:* Patterns of Literary Criticism.

**Scholarships for Children of Working Age:** LADEWICK.

**School Broadcasting:** PARKER.

**School and Commonwealth:** MORRISON.

**School Revenue:** MORRISON.

**School Review Monographs:** *see* NATIONAL SOCIETY OF COLLEGE TEACHERS OF EDUCATION. SCHOOL REVIEW.

**School and Society:** DEWEY.

**School and the Urban Community:** REAVIS.

**Schools and City Government:** HENRY.

**Schoonover, Draper Tolman.** A Study of Cn. Domitius Corbulo as Found in the "Annals" of Tacitus. 1909. *o.p.*

**Schorling, Raleigh,** *joint author:* REEVE, A Review of High-School Mathematics.

**Schott, Siegfried.** Wall Scenes from the Mortuary Chapel of the Mayor Paser at Medinet Habu. Translated by Elizabeth B. Hauser. 1957. xi, 21 p. Illus. 25 cm. 57-9891. SAOC 30. $3.50.

**Schott, Siegfried:** *see* NELSON, Work in Western Thebes.

**Schreiber, William I.** Our Amish Neighbors. With drawings by Sybil Gould. 1962. xii, 228 p. 23 cm. 62-17137. $5.95.

**Schucking, E. L.,** *joint ed.:* ROBINSON, Quasi-stellar Sources and Gravitational Collapse.

**Schütze, Martin.** Academic Illusions in the Field of Letters and the Arts. A Survey, a Criticism, a New Approach, and a Comprehensive Plan for Reorganizing the Study of Letters and the Arts. 1933. *o.p.*

**Schütze, Martin.** Repetition of a Word as a Means of Suspense in the Drama under the Influence of Romanticism. An Inquiry into the Structural Foundations of Dramatic Suspense. 1907. *o.p.*

**Schull, William J.,** *joint author:* NEEL, Human Heredity.

**Schultz, Arnold.** The Riddle of the Pianist's Finger and Its Relationship to a Touch-Scheme. 1936. *o.p.*

**Schultz, Henry.** Statistical Laws of Demand and Supply with Special Application to Sugar. 1928. MSB. *o.p.*

**Schultz, Henry.** The Theory and Measurement of Demand. 1938. Reprint. 1957. xxxii, 817 p. Illus. 26 cm. 38-19565. $14.00ˢ.

**Schultz, Theodore W.,** *ed.* Food for the World. 1945. HFL. *o.p.*

**Schuman, Frederick L.** War and Diplomacy in the French Republic. An Inquiry into Political Motivations and the Control of Foreign Policy. 1941. *o.p.*

**Schurman, Donald Mackenzie.** The Education of a Navy. The Development of British Naval Strategic Thought, 1867–1914. 1965. 213 p. 23 cm. 65-24982. $5.50ˢ. COBE.

**Schwabe, Henry Otto.** The Semantic Development of Words for Eating and Drinking in Germanic. 1915. LG. *o.p.*

**Science and Civilization in Islam:** NASR.

**Science Education in American Schools:** NOLL.

**Science, Faith and Society:** POLANYI.

**Science of Finance:** COHN.

**Science française. Readings in General Science:** HADEN.

**Science of Sociology:** HYSLOP.

**Science and the Structure of Ethics:** EDEL.

**Scientific Man versus Power Politics:** MORGENTHAU.

**Scientific Management in the Churches:** MATHEWS.

**Scientific Method in Education:** YOUNG.

**Scientific Method in the Reconstruction of Ninth-Grade Mathematics:** RUGG.

**Scientific Movement in Education:** FREEMAN.

**Scientist's Library. Biology and Medicine** (SL). PETER P. H. DEBRUYN, *General Editor:*
VON BONIN, Evolution of the Human Brain.
CLARK, Fossil Evidence for Human Evolution.
FINNEY, Experimental Design.
MCLEAN, Bone.
MOULDER, Biochemistry of Intracellular Parasitism.
PAUL, Clinical Epidemiology.
SCOTT, Aggression.

**Scofield, Cora Louise.** A Study of the Court of Star Chamber Largely Based on Manuscripts in the British Museum and the Public Record Office. 1900. *o.p.*

**Scott, Arthur Pearson.** Criminal Law in Colonial Virginia. 1930. *o.p.*

**Scott, Arthur Pearson.** George Louis Beer, *in* HUTCHINSON, Marcus W. Jernegan Essays.

**Scott, Arthur Pearson.** An Introduction to the Peace Treaties. 1920. *o.p.*

**Scott, Ernest Findlay:** *see* BEWER, Religion of the Bible.

**Scott, Ernest Findlay:** *see* GORDON, Truth about the Bible.

**Scott, Harold W.,** *ed.:* WALKER, Lectures on Geology.

**Scott, John Adams.** A Comparative Study of Hesiod and Pindar. 1898. *o.p.*

**Scott, John Paul.** Aggression. 1958. xi, 149 p. Illus. 23 cm. 58-11959. SLBM. $4.50ˢ.

**Scott, John Paul.** Animal Behavior. 1958. xi, 281 p. Illus. 22 cm. 57-6989. CLBS. $5.00ˢ.

"Scott has produced a book [which is] at once elementary, comprehensive, and happily, most readable. He gives due attention to experimental psychology, animal ecology, and ethnology. His skillful introduction to the latter science is especially fortunate, since ethnology is making its weight felt increasingly, but seems to be far from adequately understood. . . .

"To anthropologists who realize the importance of the still-to-be-accomplished task of anchoring cultural account to its biological base, this small book will be most welcome.—Earl W. Count, in *The American Anthropologist*."

**Scott, John Paul.** Genetics and the Social Behavior of the Dog. By John Paul Scott

and John L. Fuller. 1965. xviii, 488 p. Illus. 24 cm. 64-23429. $12.50ˢ.

**Scott, William A.:** *see* Financial Mobilization for War.

**Scranton, Robert L.** Aesthetic Aspects of Ancient Art. 1964. xvi, 381 p. 119 plates. 25 cm. 64-24964. $10.00ˢ.

**Scripture and Song in Worship:** SHEPARDSON.

**Sculpture of the Third Millennium B.C. from Tell Asmar and Khafajah:** FRANKFORT.

**Scutage and Knight Service:** BALDWIN.

**Sealts, Merton M., Jr.,** *joint ed.:* MELVILLE, Billy Budd, Sailor.

**Searles, Helen McGaffey.** A Lexicographical Study of the Greek Inscriptions. 1898. Preprint from Volume II, STUDIES IN CLASSICAL PHILOLOGY. *o.p.*

**Sears, Louis Martin.** Woodrow Wilson, *in* HUTCHINSON, Marcus W. Jernegan Essays.

**Seay, Maurice F.** The Community School. Prepared by Maurice F. Seay, Chairman of the Yearbook Committee. 1953. NSSE, 52d Yrbk., Part II. xii, 292, lxxii p. 24 cm. 53-1815. Cloth. $4.50ᵗ. Paper. $3.75ᵗ.

**Secession and Reconstruction:** FERTIG.

**Second Annual Report of the Director of the Yerkes Observatory:** HALE.

**Second Bank of the United States:** CATTERALL.

**Second Dynasty of Isin According to a New King-List Tablet:** POEBEL.

**Second Report of the Committee on Minimum Essentials in Elementary-School Subjects:** BAGLEY.

**Second-Year Mathematics for Secondary Schools:** BRESLICH.

**Second-Year Mathematics for Secondary Schools:** MYERS.

**Sectionalism in Virginia:** AMBLER.

**Seeds of Southern Change:** DYKEMAN.

**Seele, Diederika Millard,** *trans.:* HÖLSCHER, Excavation of Medinet Habu. II–III.

**Seele, Keith Cedric.** The Co-regency of Ramses II with Seti I and the Date of the Great Hypostyle Hall at Karnak. 1940. xiii, 95 p. Illus. 25 cm. A41-1263. Paper. SAOC 19. $2.75.

**Seele, Keith Cedric.** The Tomb of Tjanefer at Thebes. Introduction and 41 plates (without translation). 1960. 24 cm. 40-5781. OIP. LXXXVI. $7.50.

**Seele, Keith Cedric,** *ed.:* HAYES, Most Ancient Egypt.

**Seele, Keith Cedric,** *joint author:* STEINDORFF, When Egypt Ruled the East.

**Seghers, Hercules:** COLLINS.

**Seibert, Louise C.,** *ed.* Perrine. An adaptation of Hector Malot's novel, *En famille.* HCLS.

**Seidman, Joel.** American Labor from Defense to Reconversion. 1953. *o.p.*

**Seidman, Joel.** The Worker Views His Union. By Joel Seidman, Jack London, Bernard Karsh, and Daisy L. Tagliacozzo. 1958. xi, 299 p. 24 cm. 58-5686. $5.75s.

**Seki, Keigo,** *ed.* Folktales of Japan. Translated by Robert J. Adams. 1963. xxii, 222 p. 22 cm. 63-13071. FW. $4.00. COBE.

**Selby, Paul.** Abraham Lincoln. The Evolution of His Emancipation Policy. Published by the Chicago Historical Society in Commemoration of the One Hundredth Anniversary of the Birth of Abraham Lincoln, February 12, 1909. 1909. *o.p.*

**Select Bibliography of British History, 1660–1760:** GROSE.

**Selected References in Education, 1933.** 1934. SEM 41. *o.p.*

**Selected References in Education, 1934.** 1935. SEM 42. *o.p.*

**Selected References In Education, 1935.** 1936. SEM 43. *o.p.*

**Selected References in Education, 1936.** 1937. SEM 44. *o.p.*

**Selected References in Education, 1937.** 1938. SEM 46. *o.p.*

**Selected References in Education, 1938.** 1939. SEM 47. *o.p.*

**Selections from the Lun Yü:** CREEL.

**Selective Character of American Secondary Education:** COUNTS.

**Selective Fertilization:** JONES.

**Self-perception in the University:** FRIEDENBERG.

**Self-Portraits:** GIDE.

**Self-purification of Streams:** JORDAN.

**Seligman, Edwin Robert Anderson:** *see* Financial Mobilization for War.

**Selleck, Willard Chamberlain.** The New Appreciation of the Bible. A Study of the Spiritual Outcome of Biblical Criticism. 1906. *o.p.*

**Sellers, William D.** Physical Climatology. 1965. viii, 272 p. 24 cm. 65-24983. $7.50t.

**Selye, Hans.** Calciphylaxis. 1962. xxxi, 552 p. Illus. Index. 25 cm. 62-13922. $17.50s.

**Semantic Development of Words for Eating and Drinking:** SCHWABE.

**Semantic Development of Words for "Walk, Run" in the Germanic Languages:** IHRIG.

**Semantic Frequency List:** EATON.

**Semeuse:** WOODBRIDGE.

**Semitic Negative:** WALKER.

**Senecan Amble:** WILLIAMSON.

**Senescence and Rejuvenescence:** CHILD.

**Senior High School Curriculum:** COUNTS.

**Senior Mathematics:** BRESLICH.

**Sennacherib's Aqueduct:** JACOBSEN.

**Sense of Movement:** GUNN.

**Sense and Sensibility in Modern Poetry:** O'CONNOR.

**Sensory Order:** HAYEK.

**Sentence Drill Blanks:** RANSMEIER.

**Sentence and Its Parts:** LONG.

**Senturia, Joseph Jacob.** Strikes. With illustrations by Fred G. Cooper. 1935. Rev. ed. 1940. AP. *o.p.*

**Senturia, Joseph Jacob,** *joint author:* CRIGHTON, Business and Government.

**Separation of Church and State in Italian Thought:** HALPERIN.

**Sept-d'un-coup (Dumas):** BOND.

**Sequential Development of Reading Abilities:** ROBINSON.

**Servant in the House:** KENNEDY, *in his* Plays for Seven Players.

**Service, Elman R.** Tobatí. Paraguayan Town. By Elman R. Service and Helen S. Service. 1954. *o.p.*

**Service, Helen S.,** *joint author:* SERVICE, Tobatí.

**Services around the World:** CRAVEN.

**Settlement of Illinois:** BOGGESS.

**Seurat:** RICH.

**Seurat and the Evolution of "La grande jatte":** RICH.

**Seven Questions about the Profession of Librarianship:** ENNIS.

**Seventeenth Century Contexts:** WILLIAMSON.

**Seventeenth-Century Lyrics:** JUDSON.

**Severs, J. Burke:** *see* BRYAN, Sources and Analogues of Chaucer's *Canterbury Tales.*

**Sex Freedom:** MARGOLD.

**Sex and Society:** THOMAS.

**Sforza, Carlo.** The Totalitarian War and After. Recollections and Reflections. 1941. GFL. *o.p.*

**Shadow of the Plantation:** JOHNSON.

**Shaffer, Alice.** The Indiana Poor Law. Its Development and Administration with Special Reference to the Provision of State Care for the Sick Poor. By Alice Shaffer, Mary Wysor Keefer, and Sophonisba P. Breckinridge. 1936. SSM. *o.p.*

**Shakespeare. The Tragedies:** LEECH.

**Shakespeare in Germany, 1590–1700:** BRENNECKE.

**Shakespeare and Jonson:** BENTLEY.

**Shakespeare's Prose:** CRANE.

**Shambaugh, George Elmer.** The Distribution of Blood-Vessels in the Labyrinth of the Ear of Sus Scrofa Domesticus. Preprint. 1903. *o.p.*

**Shanley, J. Lyndon.** The Making of *Walden.* 1957. vi, 218 p. 24 cm. 57-6990. $6.00ˢ.

**Shann, George,** *joint author:* CADBURY, Women's Work.

**Shannon, Edgar F.:** *see* BRYAN, Sources and Analogues of Chaucer's *Canterbury Tales.*

**Shapiro, Maurice,** *trans.:* AUGER, What Are Cosmic Rays?

**Shapiro, Stanley K.,** Transmethylation and Methionine Biosynthesis. Edited by Stanley K. Shapiro and Fritz Schlenk. 1965. vii, 261 p. 24 cm. 64-24975. $12.50ˢ.

**Sharman, Henry Burton.** The Teaching of Jesus about the Future According to the Synoptic Gospels. 1908. *o.p.*

**Sharp, Frank Chapman.** Good Will and Ill Will. A Study of Moral Judgments. 1950. *o.p.*

**Sharp, Malcolm Pitman.** Social Change and Labor Law. By Malcolm Sharp and Charles O. Gregory. 1939. *o.p.*

**Shaver, Erwin Leander.** Church School Projects. A Collection of Seventy-seven Descriptions of Project-teaching Representing All Departments of the Church School. 1924. PM. *o.p.*

**Shaver, Erwin Leander.** A Project Curriculum for Young People. A Method Guide and Source Plan Book for Leaders of Young People's Groups in the Church. 1927. PM. *o.p.*

**Shaver, Edwin Leander.** The Project Principle in Religious Education. A Manual of Theory and Practice for Church-School Leaders. 1924. 2d ed. 1926. PM. *o.p.*

**Shaver, Erwin Leander.** Young People's Projects. Suggested Project Plans for Young People's Groups in Sunday Schools, Churches, Christian Associations, and Week-Day Schools. 1925–1927. CS. *o.p.*

**Shaw, Clifford Robe.** Brothers in Crime. By Clifford R. Shaw with the Assistance of Henry D. McKay and James F. McDonald. With Special Chapters by Harold B. Hanson and Ernest W. Burgess. 1938. BR. *o.p.*

**Shaw, Clifford Robe.** Delinquency Areas. A Study of the Geographic Distribution of School Truants, Juvenile Delinquents, and Adult Offenders in Chicago. By Clifford R. Shaw with the Collaboration of Frederick M. Zorbaugh, Henry D. McKay, and Leonard S. Cottrell. 1929. BR. *o.p.*

**Shaw, Clifford Robe.** The Jack-Roller. A Delinquent Boy's Own Story. 1930. BR. *o.p.*

**Shaw, Clifford Robe.** Juvenile Delinquency and Urban Areas. By Clifford Shaw and Henry McKay. 1942. *o.p.*

**Shaw, Clifford Robe.** The Natural History of a Delinquent Career. By Clifford R. Shaw in Collaboration with Maurice E. Moore. 1931. BR. *o.p.*

**Shaw, Earl B.:** *see* HAAS, American Empire.

**Shelford, Victor Ernest.** Animal Communities in Temperate America as Illustrated in the Chicago Region. A Study in Animal Ecology. 1913. 2d ed. 1937. GSC. *o.p.*

**Shelford, Victor Ernest,** *joint author:* PARK, Laboratory Introduction to Animal Ecology and Taxonomy.

**Shelford, Victor Ernest:** *see* ALLEE, Synoptic Key to the Phyla, Classes, and Orders of Animals.

**Shelley, His Theory of Poetry:** SOLVE.

**Shepardson, Francis Wayland.** Scripture and Song in Worship. A Service Book for the Sunday School. Arranged by Francis Wayland Shepardson and Lester Bartlett Jones. 1909. *o.p.*

**Shepherd, Massey H., Jr.,** *joint author:* BAKER, Short History of Christianity.

**Shera, Jesse H.** Foundations of the Public Library. A Social History of the Public Library Movement in New England from 1629 to 1855. 1949. LS. *o.p.*

**Shera, Jesse H.,** *ed.* Bibliographic Organization. Edited by Jesse H. Shera and Margaret E. Egan. 1951. LS. *o.p.*

**Sherburn, George.** Roehenstart, a Late Stuart Pretender. 1960. vii, 148 p. 22 cm. 60-8402. $5.50ˢ. COBE.

**Sherman, Mandel:** *see* EDWARDS, Education in a Democracy.

**Shields, Harald Gustav.** Junior College Business Education. 1936. SBA, VI. *o.p.*

**Shields, Harald Gustav,** *ed.* Business Education and Money Management. Proceedings of the University of Chicago Conference on Business Education, 1935. 1935. *o.p.*

**Shields, Harald Gustav,** *ed.* Business Education for Everybody. Proceedings of the University of Chicago Conference on Business Education, 1936. 1936. *o.p.*

**Shipton, Geoffrey Morgan.** Notes on the Megiddo Pottery of Strata VI–XX. 1939. xiv, 51 p. Illus. 25 cm. 39-22597. Paper. SAOC 17. $4.00.

**Shipton, Geoffrey Morgan,** *joint author:* ENGBERG, Notes on the Chalcolithic and Early Bronze Age Pottery of Megiddo.

**Shipton, Geoffrey Morgan,** *joint author:* LAMON, Megiddo. I.

**Shorey, Paul.** The Idea of Good in Plato's Republic. A Study in the Logic of Speculative Ethics. 1894. Paper. Preprint from Vol. I, STUDIES IN CLASSICAL PHILOLOGY. *o.p.*

**Shorey, Paul.** The Unity of Plato's Thought. Preprint. 1903. *o.p.*

**Shorey, Paul.** What Plato Said. 1933. vii, 686 p. 24 cm. 33-11964. $11.50ˢ.

". . . [by] the doyen of Platonic studies in the English-speaking world . . . beyond question a great work . . . admirably written."—G. C. Field, in *Classical Review* (England).

". . . we have few examples of contemporary literature of so brilliant a prose style. . . . Shorey puts a large background in Platonic literature into active service and . . . reconquers Plato for . . . all who have the good fortune to read his book."—Horace Gregory, in the *New York Evening Post.*

**Shorey, Paul.** What Plato Said. Abr. ed. 1965. vii, 378 p. 21 cm. 65-14849. Paper. P184. $3.45.

**Shorling, Raleigh,** *joint author:* REEVE, Review of High-School Mathematics.

**Short, James F., Jr.** Group Process and Gang Delinquency. By James F. Short, Jr., and Fred L. Strodtbeck. 1965. xv, 294 p. 23 cm. 65-14434. $7.50ˢ.

**Short, James F., Jr.,** *ed.:* THRASHER, The Gang.

**Short Ballot:** CASSELS.

**Short Bible. The American Translation in Brief:** GOODSPEED.

**Short History of Belgium:** ESSEN.

**Short History of Christianity:** BAKER.

**Short History of Christianity:** GILBERT.

**Short History of Japan:** CLEMENT.

**Short History of Wales:** EDWARDS.

**Short Introduction to Anatomy:** DA CARPI.

**Short Introduction to the Gospels:** BURTON.

**Shorter Lexicon of the Greek New Testament:** GINGRICH.

**Should Papers Dealing with Matters of Scholarship, or Papers on Method, Be the Chief Feature of Teachers' Meeting?** KELSEY.

**Should We Turn to Silver?** BRATTER.

**Si nous écrivions:** HARTSTALL.

**Si nous lisions:** COCHRAN.

**Siam in Transition:** LANDON.

**Siberia and the Exile System:** KENNAN.

**Sibṭ ibn al-Jauzī:** *see* YŪSUF IBN KIS-UGHLI.

**Sick Society:** KRAUS.

**Sickness and Insurance:** MILLIS.

**Sidey, Thomas Kay.** The Participle in Plautus, Petronius, and Apuleius. 1909. *o.p.*

**Sidgwick, Henry.** The Methods of Ethics. 7th ed. revised by E. E. Constance Jones. 1962. xxxvi, 530 p. 22 cm. 62-15049. $5.00ˢ. USA.

**Siegel, Arthur,** *ed.* Chicago's Famous Buildings. A Photographic Guide to the City's Architectural Landmarks and Other Notable Buildings. With descriptive text by Carson Webster. Introductory essays by Hugh Dalziel Duncan and Carl W. Condit. 1965. ix, 230 p. 21 cm. 64-15803. Cloth. $2.95. Paper. $1.50.

**Siemens, Hermann Werner.** General Diagnosis and Treatment of Skin Diseases. Translated by Kurt Wiener. 1957. BM. *o.p.*

**Sigamos leyendo:** CASTILLO.

**Sigerist, Henry E.** Civilization and Disease. 1943. xii, 254 p. 21 cm. Paper. PSS511. $1.95.

**Sigma Chi Accounting System Booklets:** ARNETT.

**Sigma Chi Fraternity Blanks:** ARNETT.

**Sigma Chi Indices:** ARNETT.

**Significance of the Mathematical Element in the Philosophy of Plato:** MILLER.

**Significance of the Problem of Knowledge:** DEWEY.

**Significance of Sociology for Ethics:** SMALL.

**Significant Aspects of American Life and Postwar Education:** REAVIS.

**Signs and Wonders upon Pharaoh:** WILSON.

**Silent Reading:** BURGESS.

**Silent Reading:** JUDD.

**Silent Speech and Silent Reading:** EDFELT.

**Sills, Milton.** Values. A Philosophy of Human Needs. By Milton Sills and Ernest S. Holmes. 1932. *o.p.*

**Silver Age:** MAHAFFY.

**Silverstein, Theodore.** Medieval Latin Scientific Writings in the Barberini Collection. A Provisional Catalogue. 1957. vii, 147 p. 24 cm. 58-5492. $6.00ˢ.

**Silverstein, Theodore,** *ed.:* AUERBACH, Dante, Poet of the Secular World.

**Simon, Margaret Sargent,** *joint author:* EMBREE, Island India Goes to School.

**Simon, Yves R.** Philosophy of Democratic Government. 1951. 324 p. 21 cm. 51-4189. Paper. P67. $2.25.

Simon, Yves R., *trans.* The *Material Logic* of John of St. Thomas. Basic Treatises. Translated by Yves R. Simon, John J. Granville, and G. Donald Hollenhorst. With a Preface by Jacques Maritain. 1955. xxxiv, 638 p. Planographed. 22 cm. 54-11215. CE. $10.00ˢ.

Simons, Algie Martin. The Way of Health Insurance. By A. M. Simons and Nathan Sinai. 1932. ADA. *o.p.*

Simons, Henry C. Economic Policy for a Free Society. 1948. x, 353 p. 22 cm. 47-7075. $6.00ˢ.

Simons, Henry C. Federal Tax Reform. 1950. *o.p.*

Simons, Henry C. Personal Income Taxation. The Definition of Income as a Problem of Fiscal Policy. 1938. xii, 238 p. 21 cm. 38-27193. $6.00ˢ.

Simons, Henry C. A Positive Program for Laissez Faire. Some Proposals for a Liberal Economic Policy. 1934. PPP 15. *o.p.*

Simplified Grammar of the Japanese Language: CHAMBERLAIN.

Simpson, Alan. Puritanism in Old and New England. 1955. vii, 125 p. 21 cm. 55-13637. WFL. Paper. P66. $1.35.

Simpson, Alan. The Wealth of the Gentry, 1540–1650: East Anglian Studies. 1961. vii, 226 p. Index. 23 cm. 61-13873. $5.00ˢ. COBE.

Simson, Otto G. von. Sacred Fortress. Byzantine Art and Statecraft in Ravenna. 1948. xv, 149 p. + 48 plates. 29 cm. $10.00ˢ.

Sinai, Nathan. A Study of Physicians and Dentists in Detroit: 1929. By Nathan Sinai and Alden B. Mills. 1931. CMC 10. *o.p.*

Sinai, Nathan. A Survey of the Medical Facilities of the City of Philadelphia: 1929. (Being in Part a Digest of the "Philadelphia Hospital and Health Survey, 1929.") By Nathan Sinai and Alden B. Mills. 1931. CMC 9. *o.p.*

Sinai, Nathan. A Survey of the Medical Facilities of San Joaquin County, California, 1929. By Nathan Sinai. Statistical Analysis and Presentation by Maurice Leven, Assisted by Elizabeth Sulloway and Kathryn Robertson. 1931. CMC 12. *o.p.*

Sinai, Nathan, *joint author:* FALK, Incidence of Illness.

Sinai, Nathan, *joint author:* SIMONS, Way of Health Insurance.

Sinaiko, Herman. Love, Knowledge, and Discourse in Plato. Dialogue and Dialectic in Phaedrus, Republic, Parmenides. 1965. 312 p. $7.50ˢ.

Sinclair, Elsa M., *trans.:* STRAUSS, Political Philosophy of Hobbes.

Sinclair, Samuel Bower. The Possibility of a Science of Education. 1903. *o.p.*

Singletary, Otis A. The Mexican War. 1960. vii, 181 p. Illus. 21 cm. 60-7248. CHAC. $4.50ˢ. Paper. $1.75.

Sir Arthur Pinero: DUNKEL.

Sir Perceval of Galles: GRIFFITH.

Sir William D'avenant: NETHERCOT.

Sirluck, Ernest, *joint general ed.:* Patterns of Literary Criticism.

Sisco, Anneliese Grünhaldt, *trans.:* RÉAUMUR, Memoirs on Steel and Iron.

Sisco, Anneliese Grünhaldt, *joint trans.:* ECKER, Treatise on Ores.

Sister Arts: HAGSTRUM.

Six Historians: SCHEVILL.

Six Lectures on Architecture: CRAM.

Six Theories of Mind: MORRIS.

Sixteen Causes of War: McLAUGHLIN.

Sixteenth-Century Italian Duel: BRYSON.

Skaggs, Ernest Burton. The Major Forms of Inhibition in Man. 1931. *o.p.*

Skeleton and Satire: HEISERMAN.

Skelton, Oscar Douglas. Our Generation, Its Gains and Losses. Being the Inaugural Course of Lectures Delivered at Westminster College, 1937. 1938. GFL. *o.p.*

Sketch of a Course of Chemical Philosophy: CANNIZZARO.

Sketch of the Linguistic Conditions of Chicago: BUCK.

**Slaten, Arthur Wakefield.** Qualitative Nouns in the Pauline Epistles and Their Translation in the Revised Version. 1918. HLL. *o.p.*

**Slaten, Arthur Wakefield.** What Jesus Taught. For Discussion Groups and Classes. 1922. CS. *o.p.*

**Slater, John Rothwell.** The Sources of Tyndale's Version of the Pentateuch. 1906. *o.p.*

**Slater, Robert Lawson.** Paradox and Nirvana. A Study of Religious Ultimates with Special Reference to Burmese Buddhism. 1951. *o.p.*

**Slater, William.** Man Must Eat. 1964. Foreword by John H. Rust. ix, 112 p. 23 cm. 64-13951. $3.75ˢ.

**Slavery:** ELKINS.

**Slavery in Germanic Society:** WERGELAND.

**Sledd, James H.** Dr. Johnson's *Dictionary.* Essays in the Biography of a Book. By James H. Sledd and Gwin J. Kolb. 1955. *o.p.*

**Sleep Characteristics:** KLEITMAN.

**Sleep and Wakefulness:** KLEITMAN.

**Slide Rule:** BRESLICH.

**Slim, H. Colin.** Musica nova. "Monuments in Renaissance Music." *Vol. I.* Introduction by Edward E. Lowinsky. 1964. xl, 129 p. 36 cm. 64-12258. $15.00ˢ.

**Slocum, Frederick.** Stellar Parallaxes Derived from Photographs Made with the Forty-Inch Refractor. By Frederick Slocum, S. Alfred Mitchell, Oliver J. Lee, Alfred H. Joy, and Georges Van Biesbroeck. With Introductory Note by Edwin B. Frost, Director. 1917. YO, IV. *o.p.*

**Small, Albion Woodbury.** Adam Smith and Modern Sociology. A Study in the Methodology of the Social Sciences. 1907. *o.p.*

**Small, Albion Woodbury.** Americans and the World-Crisis. 1918. WP. *o.p.*

**Small, Albion Woodbury.** The Cameralists. The Pioneers of German Social Polity. 1909. *o.p.*

**Small, Albion Woodbury.** General Sociology. An Exposition of the Main Development in Sociological Theory from Spencer to Ratzenhofer. 1905. *o.p.*

"While the book is principally an outline of the conception on which the study of sociology is based . . . it partakes also of the character of a campaign document. It insists that the sociological argument must be taken into account in the solution of all current social problems and in the interpretation of history."—*Chicago Inter-Ocean.*

**Small, Albion Woodbury.** The Meaning of Social Science. 1910. *o.p.*

**Small, Albion Woodbury.** Origins of Sociology. 1924. *o.p.*

**Small, Albion Woodbury.** The Significance of Sociology for Ethics. 1902. *o.p.*

**Small, Albion Woodbury.** The Sociologists' Point of View. 1897. *o.p.*

**Small Group:** GOLEMBIEWSKI.

**Small-Town Stuff:** BLUMENTHAL.

**Smelser, Neil.** Social Change in the Industrial Revolution. An Application of Theory to the British Cotton Industry. 1959. xii, 440 p. Illus. 22 cm. 59-10743. $6.95ˢ. CUSA.

**Smiddy, Timothy A.:** *see* HURST, Great Britain and the Dominions.

**Smith, A. J. M.,** ed. The Book of Canadian Poetry. A Critical and Historical Anthology. Rev. ed. 1948. *o.p.*

**Smith, Alexander.** On Amorphous Sulphur. By Alexander Smith and Willis B. Holmes. Preprint. 1902. *o.p.*

**Smith, Alexander.** A Laboratory Outline of General Chemistry. 1899. Published by Kent Chemical Laboratory of the University of Chicago. Reprinted 1900 by the University of Chicago Press. 2d ed. 1902. *o.p.*

**Smith, Alexander,** *trans.:* HOFF, Physical Chemistry in the Service of the Sciences.

**Smith, Alice Kimball.** A Peril and a Hope. The Scientists' Movement in America, 1945–47. 1965. xiv, 591 p. 24 cm. 65-17300. $10.00.

**Smith, Arthur Maxson,** *trans.:* LOBSTEIN, Introduction to Protestant Dogmatics.

**Smith, Bruce:** *see* CITIZENS' POLICE COMMITTEE, Chicago Police Problems.

**Smith, Cyril Stanley.** A History of Metallography. 1960. xix, 291 p. Illus. Index. 26 cm. 60-7243. $8.50ˢ.

**Smith, Cyril Stanley,** *joint ed.:* GOMER, Structure and Properties of Solid Surfaces.

**Smith, Cyril Stanley,** *joint trans.:* ECKER, Treatise on Ores.

**Smith, Cyril Stanley,** *joint trans.:* THEOPHILUS: On Divers Arts.

**Smith, Donald P.** Hydrogen in Metals. 1948. PS. *o.p.*

**Smith, Ernest Thomas.** A New Approach to Early European History. Students' Guide Sheets. 1929. *o.p.*

**Smith, Ernest Thomas.** A New Approach to History. Teacher's Manual. To Accompany A New Approach to Early European History, by E. T. Smith; A New Approach to Modern European History, by E. T. Smith; and A New Approach to American History, by D. C. Bailey and E. T. Smith. 1931. *o.p.*

**Smith, Ernest Thomas.** A New Approach to Modern European History. Students' Guide Sheets. 1930. *o.p.*

**Smith, Ernest Thomas:** *see* BAILEY, A New Approach to American History.

**Smith, Gerald Birney.** Current Christian Thinking. 1928. HER. *o.p.*

**Smith, Gerald Birney.** Practical Theology. A Neglected Field in Theological Education. 1903. *o.p.*

**Smith, Gerald Birney.** Principles of Christian Living. A Handbook of Christian Ethics. 1924. *o.p.*

**Smith, Gerald Birney.** The Realities of the Christian Religion. By Gerald B. Smith and Theodore G. Soares. 1918. AISL. *o.p.*

**Smith, Gerald Birney,** *ed.* A Guide to the Study of the Christian Religion. By William Herbert Perry Faunce, Shailer Mathews, J. M. Powis Smith, Ernest DeWitt Burton, Edgar Johnson Goodspeed, Shirley Jackson Case, Francis Albert Christie, George Cross, Errett Gates, Gerald Birney Smith, Theodore Gerald Soares, Charles Richmond Henderson, and George Burman Foster. 1916. *o.p.*

**Smith, Gerald Birney,** *ed.* Religious Thought in the Last Quarter-Century. By J. M. Powis Smith, Shirley Jackson Case, Harold R. Willoughby, John Thomas McNeill, Gerald Birney Smith, Edward L. Schaub, A. Eustace Haydon, Theodore Gerald Soares, Ozora S. Davis, Archibald G. Baker, and Shailer Mathews. 1927. *o.p.*

**Smith, Gerald Birney,** *joint author:* BURTON, Biblical Ideas of Atonement.

**Smith, Gertrude Elisabeth,** *joint author:* BONNER, Administration of Justice from Homer to Aristotle.

**Smith, Grover.** T. S. Eliot's Poetry and Plays. A Study in Sources and Meaning. 1956. xii, 338 p. 56-11001. Cloth. 24 cm. $6.75ˢ. Paper. P54. 21 cm. $2.45.

**Smith, Hattie Nesbit.** Attitude toward Prohibition. Forms A and B. Prepared by Hattie Nesbit Smith and L. L. Thurstone. 1931. TAS 4. *o.p.*

**Smith, Henry L.,** *joint author:* JUDD, Plans for Organizing School Surveys.

**Smith, James Perrin.** Prodromites. A New Ammonite Genus from the Lower Carboniferous. By James Perrin Smith and Stuart Weller. 1901. WM. *o.p.*

**Smith, Joe Patterson.** Francis Parkman, *in* HUTCHINSON, Marcus W. Jernegan Essays.

**Smith, John E.,** *trans.:* KRONER, Kant's Weltanschauung.

**Smith, John Henry.** Tests of Significance: What They Mean and How To Use Them. 1939. SBA, X. *o.p.*

**Smith, John Merlin Powis.** Books for Old Testament Study. An Annotated List for Popular and Professional Use. 1908. *o.p.*

**Smith, John Merlin Powis.** The Day of Yahweh. 1901. *o.p.*

**Smith, John Merlin Powis.** The Moral Life of the Hebrews. 1923. HER. *o.p.*

**Smith, John Merlin Powis.** The Origin and History of Hebrew Law. 1931. Reprint. 1960. 287 p. 21 cm. 31-35707. HER. $4.50ˢ.

**Smith, John Merlin Powis.** The Problem of Suffering in the Old Testament. 1917. AISL. *o.p.*

**Smith, John Merlin Powis.** The Prophets and Their Times. 1925. Rev. ed. by William A. Irwin. 1941. xvii, 342 p. 20 cm. 25-6864. HER. $5.00ˢ.

**Smith, John Merlin Powis.** The Religion of the Psalms. 1922. *o.p.*

**Smith, John Merlin Powis.** The Universal Element in the Psalter. A Series Designed To Promote the Religious Life through the Study of Selected Psalms and Groups of Psalms. Prepared by John Merlin Powis Smith with the Assistance of Georgia Louise Chamberlin. 1908. AISL. *o.p.*

**Smith, John Merlin Powis,** *ed. and trans.* The Bible. An American Translation. The Old Testament Translated by a Group of Scholars under the Editorship of J. M. Powis Smith. The New Testament Translated by Edgar J. Goodspeed. Popular ed. 1935. xx, 1,131 p. 20 cm. 31-28514. Black cloth. $6.00.

**Smith, John Merlin Powis,** *ed. and trans.* The Complete Bible. An American Translation. The Old Testament Translated by J. M. Powis Smith and a Group of Scholars. The Apocrypha and the New Testament Translated by Edgar J. Goodspeed. 1939. xxvi, 1,332 p. 20 cm. 39-28964. Black cloth. $6.75.

"For the first time here is a translation of the whole Bible, including the Apocrypha, in the language of the twentieth century . . . the American Translation is *religious* literature at its very best . . . this translation is more free from prejudice than most."—R. C. Miller, in *The Churchman.*

**Smith, John Merlin Powis,** *ed.* The Old Testament. An American Translation. By Alexander R. Gordon, Theophile J. Meek, J. M. Powis Smith, Leroy Waterman. 1927. *o.p.*

**Smith, John Merlin Powis,** *trans.* The Psalms. An American Translation. 1926. *o.p.*

**Smith, John Merlin Powis,** *joint author:* BURTON. Biblical Ideals of Atonement.

**Smith, John Merlin Powis,** *joint ed.:* GOODSPEED, Short Bible.

**Smith, John Merlin Powis:** *see* GORDON, Truth about the Bible.

**Smith, John Merlin Powis:** *see* SMITH, Guide to the Study of the Christian Religion.

**Smith, John Merlin Powis:** *see* SMITH, Religious Thought in the Last Quarter-Century.

**Smith, Louis.** American Democracy and Military Power. A Study of Civil Control of the Military Power in the United States. 1951. PA. *o.p.*

**Smith, Louis DS.** Introduction to the Pathogenic Anaerobes. 1955. BM. *o.p.*

**Smith, R. Elberton.** Customs Valuation in the United States. A Study in Tariff Administration. 1948. *o.p.*

**Smith, Roy Wilson.** The Acromatic Spindle in the Spore Mother-Cells of Osmunda regalis. 1901. HB. *o.p.*

**Smith, Roy Wilson.** A Contribution to the Life-History of the Pontederiaceæ. 1898. HB. *o.p.*

**Smith, Roy Wilson.** Structure and Development of the Sporophylls and Sporangia of Isoetes. 1900. HB. *o.p.*

**Smith, Thomas Vernor.** The American Philosophy of Equality. 1927. *o.p.*

**Smith, Thomas Vernor.** The Democratic Way of Life. 1926. 2d ed. 1939. *o.p.*

**Smith, Thomas Vernor.** The Legislative Way of Life. 1940. GFL. *o.p.*

**Smith, Thomas Vernor.** Lincoln, Living Legend. 1940. *o.p.*

**Smith, Thomas Vernor.** Philosophers in Hades. 1932. *o.p.*

**Smith, Thomas Vernor.** The Philosophic Way of Life. 1929. *o.p.*

**Smith, Thomas Vernor.** The Promise of American Politics. 1936. 2d ed. 1936. *o.p.*

**Smith, Thomas Vernor,** *ed.* Chicago. An Experiment in Social Science Research. Edited by T. V. Smith and Leonard D. White. 1929. SSCI. *o.p.*

Smith, Thomas Vernor, *ed.* From Descartes to Kant. Readings in the Philosophy of the Renaissance and Enlightenment. By T. V. Smith and Marjorie Grene. 1940. *o.p.*

Smith, Thomas Vernor, *ed.* Philosophers Speak for Themselves. From Thales to Plato. 2d ed. 1956. 412 p. 21 cm. 56-4949. Paper. P8. $1.95.

Smith, Thomas Vernor, *ed.* Philosophers Speak for Themselves. From Aristotle to Plotinus. 2d ed. 1956. 306 p. 21 cm. 56-4949. Paper. P9. $1.50.

Smith, Thomas Vernor, *ed.* Philosophers Speak for Themselves. From Descartes to Locke. Edited by T. V. Smith and Marjorie Grene. 2d ed. 1957. 486 p. 21 cm. 57-7905. Paper. P17. $1.95.

Smith, Thomas Vernor, *ed.* Philosophers Speak for Themselves. Berkeley, Hume, and Kant. Edited by T. V. Smith and Marjorie Grene. 2d ed. 1957. 384 p. 21 cm. 57-7905. Paper. P18. $1.95.

Smith, Thomas Vernor, *ed.* Philosophers Speak for Themselves. Guides and Readings for Greek, Roman, and Early Christian Philosophy. 1934. *o.p.*

Smith, William C. The Stepchild. 1953. *o.p.*

Smith, Wilson, *joint author:* HOFSTADTER, Documentary History of American Education.

Snider, Ray S., A Stereotaxic Atlas of the Cat Brain. By Ray S. Snider and William T. Niemer. 1962. 124 pages of plates and Introduction and Index to Major Structures. Illus. 28 cm. 60-7244. $12.50ˢ.

Snider, Ray S. A Stereotaxic Atlas of the Monkey Brain. By Ray S. Snider and John C. Lee. 1962. Illus. 28 cm. 61-8079. $12.50ˢ.

Snodgrass, M., *joint author:* FERENCE, A Mobile Weather Unit with an Example of a Field Forecast.

Snow, Laetitia M. Some Notes on the Ecology of the Delaware Coast. 1902. HB. *o.p.*

Snyder, Franklyn Bliss. Robert Burns. His Personality, His Reputation and His Art. 1936. *o.p.*

Soares, Theodore Gerald. Heroes of Israel. 1909–1922. CS. *o.p.*

Soares, Theodore Gerald. How To Enjoy the Bible. 1924. AISL. *o.p.*

Soares, Theodore Gerald. Religious Education. 1928. HER. *o.p.*

Soares, Theodore Gerald. The Story of Paul. For Boys and Girls of Junior High School Age. 1930. CS. *o.p.*

Soares, Theodore Gerald. Three Typical Beliefs. 1937. *o.p.*

Soares, Theodore Gerald, *ed.* University of Chicago Sermons by Members of the University Faculties. 1915. *o.p.*

Soares, Theodore Gerald, *joint author:* SMITH, Realities of the Christian Religion.

Soares, Theodore Gerald: *see* GORDON, Truth about the Bible.

Soares, Theodore Gerald: *see* SMITH, Guide to the Study of the Christian Religion.

Soares, Theodore Gerald: *see* SMITH, Religious Thought in the Last Quarter-Century.

Social Anthropology of North American Indian Tribes: EGGAN.

Social Aspects of Farmers' Co-operative Marketing: LANDIS.

Social Base Map of Chicago: UNIVERSITY OF CHICAGO. *Local Community Research Committee.*

Social Behavior and Organization among Vertebrates: ETKIN.

Social Case Records. Family Welfare: DIXON.

Social Case Records from Psychiatric Clinics: TOWLE.

Social Casework: PERLMAN.

Social Change and Labor Law: SHARP.

Social Change in the Industrial Revolution: SMELSER.

Social Change and the New Deal (1933): OGBURN.

Social Changes during Depression and Recovery (1934): OGBURN.

**Social Changes in 1928:** OGBURN.

**Social Changes in 1929:** OGBURN.

**Social Changes in 1930:** OGBURN.

**Social Changes in 1931:** OGBURN.

**Social Changes in 1932:** OGBURN.

**Social Composition of Boards of Education:** COUNTS.

**Social Concept of Money:** BREWINGTON.

**Social Conflicts:** AMERICAN SOCIOLOGICAL SOCIETY, Annual Proceedings. Vol. II, XXV, No. 2.

**Social Control:** AMERICAN SOCIOLOGICAL SOCIETY, Annual Proceedings. Vol. XII.

**Social Control of Business:** CLARK.

**Social Crisis:** RÖPKE.

**Social Currents in Japan:** WILDES.

**Social Duties from the Christian Point of View:** HENDERSON.

**Social and Ethical Teaching of Jesus:** MATHEWS.

**Social Forces Influencing American Education:** TYLER.

**Social Ideals of Alfred Tennyson:** GORDON.

**Social Mind and Education:** VINCENT.

**Social Organization of the Western Apache:** GOODWIN.

**Social Organization of the Western Pueblos:** EGGAN.

**Social Origins of Christianity:** CASE.

**Social Problems and Social Processes:** BOGARDUS.

**Social Process:** AMERICAN SOCIOLOGICAL SOCIETY, Annual Proceedings. Vol. XXVI, No. 3.

**Social Programmes in the West:** HENDERSON.

**Social Relations in the Urban Parish:** FICHTER.

**Social Science Research Council,** *Committee on Scientific Method in the Social Sciences:* see RICE, Methods in Social Science.

**Social Science Studies** (SSCI). Formerly "The University of Chicago Studies in Social Science":

1. MERRIAM, Non-voting.
2. WOODDY, Chicago Primary of 1926.
3. GOODE, Geographic Background of Chicago.
4. GOSNELL, Getting Out the Vote.
5. FRYXELL, Physiography of the Region of Chicago.
6. Chicago Civic Agencies, 1927.
7. JETER, Trends of Population in the Region of Chicago.
8. HOUGHTELING, Income and Standard of Living of Unskilled Laborers in Chicago.
9. WHITE, City Manager.
10. BEYLE, Governmental Reporting in Chicago.
11. JOHNSON, Carter Henry Harrison I.
12. PALMER, Field Studies in Sociology.
13. BECKNER, History of Labor Legislation in Illinois.
14. WHITE, Prestige Value of Public Employment in Chicago.
15. DUDDY, Agriculture in the Chicago Region.
16. STALEY, History of the Illinois State Federation of Labor.
17. SMITH, Chicago, an Experiment in Social Science Research.
18. WHITE, New Social Science.
19. GOSNELL, Why Europe Votes.
20. STEADMAN, Public Health Organization in the Chicago Region.
21. BROWN, Book and Job Printing in Chicago.
22. MONROE, Chicago Families.
23. LEPAWSKY, Judicial System of Metropolitan Chicago.
24. WHITE, Further Contributions to the Prestige Value of Public Employment.
25. WHITE, Whitley Councils in the British Civil Service.
26. MERRIAM, Government of the Metropolitan Region of Chicago.
27. CHRISTENSON, Collective Bargaining in Chicago.
28. EDWARDS, Courts and the Public Schools.
29. KELLOGG, United States Employment Service.
30. WHITE, Water Supply Organization in the Chicago Region.
31. LEPAWSKY, Home Rule for Metropolitan Chicago.
32. GOSNELL, Negro Politicians.
33. PALYI, Chicago Credit Market.
34. GOSNELL, Machine Politics: Chicago Model.
35. CAVAN, Family and the Depression.
36. SCHULTZ, Theory and Measurement of Demand.
37. VIEG, Government of Education.
38. LELAND, State-Local Fiscal Relations.
39. WALKER, Planning Function in Urban Government.

Social Service Exchange in Chicago: HUGHES.

Social Service in Wartime: WRIGHT.

Social Studies in the Elementary School: PRESTON.

Social Studies in the Elementary and Secondary Schools: BARR.

Social Studies in Secondary Schools: ASSOCIATION OF COLLEGIATE SCHOOLS OF BUSINESS.

Social Theory of Georg Simmel: SPYKMAN.

Social Uses of Social Science: REDFIELD.

Social Welfare and Professional Education: ABBOTT.

Social Work and the Courts: BRECKINRIDGE.

Social Work Research: POLANSKY.

Social Work with Travelers and Transients: KIMBLE.

Society and Nature: KELSEN.

Sociological Implications of Ricardo's Economics: NORTH.

Sociological Problems and Methods: AMERICAN SOCIOLOGICAL SOCIETY, Annual Proceedings. Vol. XXVII, No. 2.

Sociological Study of the Bible: WALLIS.

Sociologist's Point of View: SMALL.

Sociology: FICHTER.

Sociology and Education: AMERICAN SOCIOLOGICAL SOCIETY, Annual Proceedings. Vol. XIII.

Sociology of Religion: WACH.

Sociology of Rural Life: AMERICAN SOCIOLOGICAL SOCIETY, Annual Proceedings. Vol. XI.

Sociology of Science: WIRTH.

Sohmen, Egon. Flexible Exchange Rates. Theory and Controversy. 1961. xiv, 172 p. Index. 22 cm. 60-14359. $5.00s.

Solar Eclipse of August 31, 1932: McMATH-HULBERT OBSERVATORY.

Solar Eclipse Problems: HALE.

Solar Phenomena: McMATH-HULBERT OBSERVATORY.

Solar System: KUIPER.

Soldat américain en France: COLEMAN.

Soldiers' Bibles through Three Centuries: WILLOUGHBY.

Solid Geometry: BRESLICH.

Solomon's Temple: SCHMIDT.

Solovay, Sarah A., trans.: DURKHEIM, Rules of Sociological Method.

Solutions to Alternative Laboratory Exercises: GRAHAM.

Solve, Melvin Theodor. Shelley, His Theory of Poetry. 1927. o.p.

Some American Pioneers in Social Welfare: ABBOTT.

Some Aspects of Dynamic Anticyclogenesis: WEXLER.

Some Aspects of High-School Instruction and Administration: MORRISON.

Some Aspects of Modern Thought on Arithmetic (Report of the Society's Committee on Arithmetic, Part I): KNIGHT.

Some Aspects of Recent British Economics: HOBSON.

Some Contemporary Americans: BOYNTON.

Some Historians of Modern Europe: SCHMITT.

Some Indian Landmarks: GROVER.

Some Literary Remains of Rim-Sin: PRICE.

Some Mexican Problems: SAENZ.

Some Newer Problems, National and Social: AMERICAN SOCIOLOGICAL ASSOCIATION, Annual Proceedings. Vol. XV.

Some Notes on the Ecology of the Delaware Coast: SNOW.

Some Paradoxes of the English Romantic Movement: MacCLINTOCK.

Some Phases in the Development of the Subjective Point of View: SUNNE.

Some Principles of Elizabethan Staging: REYNOLDS.

Some Principles of Literary Criticism: BURTON.

**Some Principles in the Teaching of History:** SALMON.

**Some Public Service Broadcasting:** KOON.

**Some Reflections on Culture and Liberty:** MARITAIN.

**Some Religious Implications of Pragmatism:** GEIGER.

**Some 20th Century Historians:** HALPERIN.

**Some Types of Modern Education Theory:** YOUNG.

**Some University Student Problems:** REEVES.

**Sommer in Deutschland:** LEOPOLD.

**Songs for the Latin Club:** FLICKINGER.

**Sons of the Shaking Earth:** WOLF.

**Sophocles:** *see* COMPLETE GREEK TRAGEDIES.

**Soskin, Samuel.** Carbohydrate Metabolism. Correlation of Physiological, Biochemical, and Clinical Aspects. By Samuel Soskin and Rachmiel Levine. 1946. 2d ed. 1952. x, 346 p. Illus. 26 cm. A46-2678. BM. $10.00ˢ.

**Sound Waves and Their Sources:** LEMON.

**Soundings at Tell Fakhariyah:** McEWAN.

**Sounds of English and German:** MOULTON.

**Sounds of English and Italian:** AGARD.

**Sounds of English and Spanish:** STOCKWELL.

**Sounds of French. An Elementary Phonetic Manual:** BOND.

**Source Book of Biological Nature-Study:** DOWNING.

**Source Book for Economic Geography:** COLBY.

**Source Book for Social Origins:** THOMAS.

**Source Book for the Study of the Teaching of Jesus:** BURTON.

**Source of Human Good:** WIEMAN.

**Source of "Jerusalem the Golden":** BERNARD OF CLUNY.

**Sources and Analogues of Chaucer's Canterbury Tales:** BRYAN.

**Sources of Luke's Passion-Narrative:** PERRY.

**Sources of Luke's Perean Section:** WICKES.

**Sources of Tyndale's Version of the Pentateuch:** SLATER.

**South Asia:** TALBOT.

**South Carolina Rice Plantation:** EASTERBY.

**Southeast Asia:** LANDON.

**Southern Parish:** FICHTER.

**Southwestern Archaeology:** McGREGOR.

**Sovereignty:** JOUVENEL.

**Soviet Industrialization, 1928–52:** JASNY.

**Soviet System of Government:** HAZARD.

**Soviet Union and World-Problems:** HARPER.

**Soyeshima, Michimasa.** Oriental Interpretations of the Far Eastern Problem. By Michimasa Soyeshima and P. W. Kuo. 1925. HFL. *o.p.*

**Spain and the Empire:** CHUDOBA.

**Spanish Grail Fragments:** PIETSCH.

**Spanish Recognition Grammar:** RANSMEIER.

**Spanish Wall Charts:** CASTILLO.

**Spanish Workbook To Accompany** *Beginning Spanish:* CASTILLO.

**Spargo, John W.:** *see* BRYAN, Sources and Analogues of Chaucer's *Canterbury Tales.*

**Sparshott, Francis E.** An Enquiry into Goodness. 1958. *o.p.*

**Spaulding, Frank Ellsworth.** The Aims, Scope, and Methods of a University Course in Public-School Administration. By Frank E. Spaulding, William Paxton Burris, and Edward C. Elliott. Published by the National Society of College Teachers of Education. 1910. Transferred to the University of Chicago Press, 1925. *o.p.*

**Spaulding, Patricia J.,** *joint author:* NORRIS, Blindness in Children.

**Spectra of Long-Period Variable Stars:** MERRILL.

**Spectra of Stars of Secchi's Fourth Type:** HALE.

**Spectroscopic Notes:** HUGGINS.

**Spectroscopic Proof of the Meteoric Constitution of Saturn's Rings:** KEELER.

**Spectrum of the High Potential Discharge between Metallic Electrodes in Liquids and Gases at High Pressures:** HALE.

**Speculative Instruments:** RICHARDS.

**Speed in Animals:** HOWELL.

**Spencer, Gladys.** The Chicago Public Library. Origins and Backgrounds. 1943. LS. (O.I.)

**Spencer, William Homer.** Collective Bargaining under Section 7(a) of the National Industrial Recovery Act. 1935. SBA, V. *o.p.*

**Spencer, William Homer.** Law and Business. 3 vols. *o.p.* 1921–22. MSB. *Vol. I:* Introduction. 1921. *Vol. II:* Law and the Market. Law and Finance. 1921. *Vol. III:* Law and Risk-Bearing. Law and Labor. Law and the Form of the Business Unit. 1922.

**Spencer, William Homer.** The National Labor Relations Act. Its Scope, Purposes, and Implications. 1935. SBA, VI. *o.p.*

**Spencer, William Homer.** The National Railroad Adjustment Board. 1938. SBA, VIII. *o.p.*

**Speranskiĭ, Vladimir Nikolaevich,** *joint author:* BOYER, Russian Reader.

**Spergel, Irving.** Racketville, Slumtown, Haulburg. An Exploratory Study of Delinquent Subcultures. 1964. Foreword by Lloyd E. Ohlin. xxiv, 211 p. 22 cm. 64-17165. $5.00ˢ.

**Sphere of Sacrobosco:** THORNDIKE.

**Spicer, Edward H.** Pascua. A Yaqui Village in Arizona. 1940. AN. *o.p.*

**Spicer, Edward H.,** *ed.* Perspectives in American Indian Culture Change. 1961. x, 549 p. 24 cm. 60-14358. $10.00ˢ.

**Spicer, Hazel Inscho,** *joint author:* FALK, Community Medical Service.

**Spicer, Hazel Inscho,** *joint author:* GRISWOLD, University Student Health Services.

**Spicer, Rosamond,** *joint author:* JOSEPH, The Desert People.

**Spier, Leslie.** Yuman Tribes of the Gila River. 1933. AN. *o.p.*

**Spindler, George Washington.** The Life of Karl Follen. A Study in German-American Cultural Relations. 1917. *o.p.*
A Publication of the German-American Historical Society of Illinois. The University of Chicago Press publisher 1917–1938.

**Spinka, Matthew.** John Amos Comenius. That Incomparable Moravian. 1943. *o.p.*

**Spinka, Matthew.** John Hus and Czech Reform. 1941. *o.p.*

**Spinka, Matthew,** *trans.* Chronicle of John Malalas. Books VIII–XVIII. Translated from the Church Slavonic by Matthew Spinka in collaboration with Glanville Downey. 1940. *o.p.*

**Spinka, Matthew,** *joint ed.:* McNEILL, Environmental Factors in Christian History.

**Spinka, Matthew,** *joint author:* BAKER, Short History of Christianity.

**Spinka, Matthew:** *see* CASE, Bibliographical Guide to the History of Christianity.

**Spinoza and Buddha:** MELAMED.

**Spirit of the Age:** MILL.

**Spirit, Soul, and Flesh:** BURTON.

**Spore Mother-Cell of Anthoceros:** DAVIS.

**Sports in American Life:** COZENS.

**Sprague, Arthur Colby,** *ed.:* DANIEL, Poems and A Defence of Ryme.

**Sprague, Rufus Farrington.** The True Nature of Value. 1907. *o.p.*

**Spread of Christianity:** MOORE.

**Sprengling, Martin.** The Alphabet: Its Rise and Development from the Sinai Inscriptions. 1931. OIC 12. *o.p.*

**Sprengling, Martin,** *ed.:* GREGORIUS, Barhebraeus' Scholia on the Old Testament.

**Sprengling, Martin,** *joint author:* GOODSPEED, Descriptive Catalogue of the Manuscripts in the Libraries of the University of Chicago.

**Sprengling, Martin:** *see* HAYDON, Modern Trends in World-Religions.

**Spurrier, Leo.** Common Stocks and Bonds as Long-Term Investments. 1941. SBA, XI. *o.p.*

**Spykman, Nicholas Johannes.** The Social Theory of Georg Simmel. 1925. *o.p.*

**Srinivas, M. R.,** *ed.:* RADCLIFFE-BROWN, Method in Social Anthropology.

**Stabilization of Europe:** DE VISSCHER.

**Stackhouse, Perry James.** Chicago and the Baptists. A Century of Progress. 1933. *o.p.*

**Staff Members of the Institute of Meteorology.** Report on Synoptic Conditions in the Mediterranean Area. 1944. DMMR 14. *o.p.*

**Staff of the Reading Clinics of the University of Chicago.** Clinical Studies in Reading. 1949. xiv, 173 p. 25 cm. 49-6227. Paper. SEM 68. $3.50ᵗ.

**Staff, Social Sciences 1, The College of the University of Chicago.** The People Shall Judge. Readings in the Formation of American Policy. 1949. 2 vols. 25 cm. 49-3028, *Vol. I.* xvi, 797 p. $5.00ᵗ. *Vol. II.* xiv, 931 p. Illus. $5.00ᵗ.

**Staff of the University of Chicago Press.** A Manual of Style. Containing Typographical and Other Rules for Authors, Printers, and Publishers Recommended by the University of Chicago Press, Together with Specimens of Type. 1906. 11th ed. 1949. x, 522 p. 21 cm. 6-40582. $6.00.

**Staley, Alvah Eugene.** Foreign Investment and War. 1935. PPP 18. *o.p.*

**Staley, Alvah Eugene.** History of the Illinois State Federation of Labor. 1930. SSCI. *o.p.*

**Staley, Eugene.** War and the Private Investor. Published elsewhere, 1935. Transferred to the University of Chicago Press, 1941. *o.p.*

**Stampp, Kenneth M.** And the War Came. The North and the Secession Crisis, 1860–61. *Reissue,* 1964. viii, 331 p. Illus. 21 cm. Paper. P150. $2.45.

**Standard German Vocabulary of 2,932 Words and 1,500 Idioms, Illustrated in Typical Phrases and Sentences:** PURIN.

**Standard of Living:** SANDERS.

**Standard of Living in 1860:** MARTIN.

**Standard Usage of English:** UNIVERSITY OF CHICAGO, *University High School.*

**Standardization of American Poetry:** CAVINS.

**Standardization of the Schools:** CLEMENT.

**Standards of American Legislation:** FREUND.

**Standards of Living:** *see* AMERICAN COUNTRY LIFE ASSOCIATION, Proceedings, No. 13.

**Standards and Tests for the Measurement of the Efficiency of Schools and School Systems:** STRAYER.

**Standards of Unemployment Insurance:** DOUGLAS.

**Stanford, Edward B.** Library Extension under the WPA. 1944. *o.p.*

**Stanley, Theodore.** Croquis d'un flâneur. HCLS.

**Stanton, Timothy William.** A Comparative Study of the Lower Cretaceous Formations and Faunas of the United States. 1897. *o.p.*

**Stanton, William.** The Leopard's Spots. Scientific Attitudes toward Race in America, 1815–59. 1960. ix, 245 p. 24 cm. 59-11625. Cloth. $4.00ˢ. Paper. P218. $1.95.

**Staples, William Ewart:** *see* GUY, New Light from Armageddon.

**Stark, Alonzo Rosecrans.** The Christology in the Apostolic Fathers. 1912. *o.p.*

**Stark, Harold.** Art in America from 1600 to 1865. 1934. *o.p.*

**Starr, Frederick.** A Bibliography of Congo Languages. 1908. ANB. *o.p.*

**Starr, Frederick.** The Indians of South Mexico: An Ethnographic Album. 1900. *o.p.*

**Starr, Frederick.** The Little Pottery Objects of Lake Chapala, Mexico. 1897. ANB. *o.p.*

**Starr, Frederick.** The Mapa de Cuauhtlantzinco or Códice Campos. 1898. ANB. *o.p.*

**Starr, Frederick.** Notes on Mexican Archaeology. 1894. ANB. *o.p.*

**Starr, Frederick.** The Physical Characters of the Indians of Southern Mexico. 1902. *o.p.*

**Starr, Frederick.** Recent Mexican Study of the Native Languages of Mexico. 1900. ANB. *o.p.*

**Starr, Frederick,** *trans.:* PALACIOS, Stone of the Sun.

**Starrett, Vincent.** The Private Life of Sherlock Holmes. 1960. viii, 156 p. Illus. 22 cm. 60-7245. $4.75. COBE AND CONTINENT OF EUROPE.

**Stars and Stellar Systems:** KUIPER.

**Stars Upstream:** HALL.

**Starved Rock State Park:** SAUER.

**State Administration of Child Welfare in Illinois:** MILCHRIST.

**State Aid to Railways:** MILLION.

**State Labor Relations Acts:** KILLINGSWORTH.

**State-Local Fiscal Relations in Illinois:** LELAND.

**State Rights in the Confederacy:** OWSLEY.

**State of the Social Sciences:** WHITE.

**Statesmanship and Party Government:** MANSFIELD.

**Statistical Cost Functions of a Hosiery Mill:** DEAN.

**Statistical Determination of Costs:** DEAN.

**Statistical Inference for Markov Processes:** BILLINGSLEY.

**Statistical Laws of Demand and Supply:** SCHULTZ.

**Statistical Methods for Social Workers:** MCMILLEN.

**Statistical Research Monographs** (SRM):

BILLINGSLEY, Statistical Inference for Markov Processes.
KEMPERMAN, Passage Problem for a Stationary Markov Chain.

**Statistical Résumé of the Spearman Two-Factor Theory:** HOLZINGER.

**Statistical Study of Credit Unions in New York State:** WILCOX.

**Statistical Study of the Drawing Power of Cities for Retail Trade:** PFANNER.

**Statistical Tables for Students in Education and Psychology:** HOLZINGER.

**Status of Rural Education:** BRIM.

**Staudt, Calvin Klopp.** The Idea of the Resurrection in the Ante-Nicene Period. 1909. HLL. *o.p.*

**Steadman, Robert Foster.** Public Health Organization in the Chicago Region. 1930. SSCI. *o.p.*

**Stearns, Wallace Nelson,** *ed.* Fragments from Graeco-Jewish Writers. Collected and Edited with Brief Introductions and Notes by Wallace Nelson Stearns. 1908. *o.p.*

**Steck, Irving Elihu,** *joint author:* REED, Vitamin D.

**Stefanski, Elizabeth.** Coptic Ostraca from Medinet Habu. By Elizabeth Stefanski and Miriam Lichtheim. 1952. xi, 51 p. Illus. 31 cm. 52-14490. OIP, LXXI. $12.50.

**Stein, Gertrude.** Narration. Four Lectures by Gertrude Stein. With an Introduction by Thornton Wilder. 1935. *o.p.*
Printed in a limited edition of 120 copies, of which 100, autographed by both Gertrude Stein and Thornton Wilder, were offered for sale.

**Steindorff, George.** Lehrbuch der koptischen Grammatik. 1951. xvi, 250 p. 26 cm. $6.00.

**Steindorff, George.** When Egypt Ruled the East. By George Steindorff and Keith C. Seele. 1942. Rev. ed. 1957. xvi, 284 p. Illus. 57-5276. Cloth. 26 cm. $7.50s. Paper. P125. 21 cm. $2.25.
"When this book first appeared . . . it was recognized at once as one of the best brief histories of Egypt, being based on the soundest scholarship and yet written in a style that can attract the general reader. . . ."—J. W. Swain, in *The Journal of Near Eastern Studies.*

**Steiner, Gary,** *ed.* The Creative Organization. 1965. 267 p. 24 cm. 65-17301. $5.00.

**Steiner, Jesse Frederick.** Education for Social Work. 1921. *o.p.*

**Stellar Atmospheres:** GREENSTEIN.

**Stellar Parallaxes:** SLOCUM.

**Stellar Structure:** ALLER.

**Stepchild:** SMITH.

**Stepfather in the Family:** MERIAM.

**Stephens, G. T.** A Study in Forecasting of Radiation Fog and Status at Omaha. 1943. *o.p.*

**Stephens, G. T.,** *joint ed.:* BICE, Correlations of Isallobaric Patterns.

**Stephenson, Reginald Joseph.** Exploring in Physics. A New Outlook on Problems in Physics. 1935. *o.p.*

**Stephenson, Reginald Joseph,** *ed.* Introductory General Course in the Physical Sciences Syllabus. Edited by Reginald J. Stephenson with the Co-operation of Theodore A. Ashford, Walter Bartky, Gilbert A. Bliss, J Harlen Bretz, Carey Croneis, William C. Krumbein, Harvey B. Lemon, Mayme I. Logsdon, Thornton L. Page, Eugene J. Rosenbaum, Hermann I. Schlesinger, Zens Smith, and Otto Struve. 1931. 11th ed. 1941. *o.p.*

**Stephenson, Reginald Joseph,** *joint author:* FERENCE, Analytical Experimental Physics.

**Stephenson, Reginald Joseph:** *see* MOULTON, World and Man.

**Stephenson, William.** The Study of Behavior. Q-Technique and Its Methodology. 1953. x, 376 p. 24 cm. 53-12540. $8.50ˢ.

**Stereotaxic Atlas of the Cat Brain:** SNIDER.

**Stereotaxic Atlas of the Monkey Brain:** SNIDER.

**Stern, Bernhard Joseph.** Lewis Henry Morgan, Social Evolutionist. 1931. *o.p.*

**Stern-Rubarth, Edgar:** *see* WRIGHT, Public Opinion and World-Politics.

**Steunkel, Francelia,** *joint author:* HUGHES, Social Service Exchange in Chicago.

**Stevanovic, Borislav P.** An Experimental Study of the Mental Processes Involved in Judgment. 1927. BJP. *o.p.*

**Stevens, David Harrison.** Milton Papers. 1927. MPM. *o.p.*

**Stevens, David Harrison.** Reference Guide to Milton from 1800 to the Present Day. 1930. *o.p.*

**Stevens, Frank Lincoln.** The Compound Oösphere of Albugo bliti. 1900. HB. *o.p.*

**Stevens, Frank Lincoln.** The Effect of Aqueous Solutions upon the Germination of Fungus Spores. 1898. HB. *o.p.*

**Stevens, Frank Lincoln.** Gametogenesis and Fertilization in Albugo. 1901. HB. *o.p.*

**Stevens, Guy,** *joint author:* RIPPY, Mexico.

**Stevens, Harvey A.,** *ed.* Mental Retardation. A Review of Research. Edited by Harvey A. Stevens and Rick Heber. 1964. xii, 502 p. 25 cm. 64-15808. $12.50ˢ.

**Stevens, William Harrison Spring.** Unfair Competition. A Study of Certain Practices with Some Reference to the Trust Problem in the United States of America. 1917. *o.p.*

**Stevenson, Arthur Lionel.** Darwin among the Poets. 1932. *o.p.*

**Stevenson, Harold W.,** *ed.* Child Psychology. Prepared by Harold W. Stevenson, Chairman of the Society's Committee. 1963. NSSE, 62d Yrbk., Part I. x, 556 p. 24 cm. $6.50ᵗ.

**Stewart, Irvin,** *ed.* Local Broadcasts to Schools. 1939. *o.p.*

**Stewart, Watt.** George Bancroft, *in* HUTCHINSON, Marcus W. Jernegan Essays.

**Stichometric Scholium to the Medea of Euripides:** FRANK.

**Stickney, J. Clifford,** *joint author:* VAN LIERE, Hypoxia.

**Stigler, George J.** Essays in the History of Economics. 1965. viii, 391 p. 21 cm. 65-14426. $6.95.

**Stieglitz, Julius.** On the "Beckmann Rearrangement." Preprint, 1903. *o.p.*

**Stieglitz, Julius:** *see* NEWMAN, Nature of the World and of Man.

**Stillman, Calvin W.,** *ed.* Africa in the Modern World. Edited by Calvin W. Stillman. With contributions by sixteen political, social, and economic scientists. 1955. x, 342 p. 24 cm. 55-5147. HFL. $7.50ˢ.

**Stipends and Spouses:** DAVIS.

**Stirn, Ernest William.** An Annotated Bibliography of Robert M. La Follette. The Man and His Work. 1937. *o.p.*

**Stivers, Eugene,** *joint author:* Havighurst, Survey of the Education of Gifted Children.

**Stockwell, Robert P.** The Grammatical Structures of English and Spanish. By Robert P. Stockwell, J. Donald Bowen, and John W. Martin. 1965. xi, 315 p. 24 cm. 65-18339. CSS. Paper. $3.75<sup>t</sup>.

**Stockwell, Robert P.** The Sounds of English and Spanish. By Robert P. Stockwell and J. Donald Bowen. 1965. ix, 168 p. 24 cm. 65-17302. CSS. Paper. $2.75<sup>t</sup>.

**Stockwell, Robert P.,** *joint author:* Bowen, Patterns of Spanish Pronunciation. A Drillbook.

**Stoddard, George D.** Intelligence. Its Nature and Nurture. Prepared by George D. Stoddard, Chairman of the Society's Committee. 1940. NSSE, 39th Yrbk., Part II: Original Studies and Experiments. xviii, 409 p. 22 cm. E40-580. Paper. $2.25<sup>t</sup>.

**Stokely, James,** *joint author:* Dykeman, Seeds of Southern Change.

**Stokes, Christopher William,** *joint author:* Richardson, Growth and Variability of Intelligence.

**Stokes, Ella Harrison.** The Conception of a Kingdom of Ends in Augustine, Aquinas, and Leibniz. 1912. *o.p.*

**Stokes Collection of Antarctic Fossils:** Weller.

**Stone, Calvin P:** *see* Lashley, Studies in the Dynamics of Behavior.

**Stone, Charles Arthur,** *joint author:* Breslich, Classroom Procedure Test in Mathematics.

**Stone, Charles Arthur,** *joint author:* Breslich, Slide Rule.

**Stone, Charles Arthur,** *joint author:* Breslich, Trigonometry with Tables.

**Stone, Raleigh Webster.** The Baking Industry under N.R.A. By R. W. Stone and U. B. Stone. 1936. SBA, VI. *o.p.*

**Stone, Raleigh Webster,** *ed.* Problems of Collective Bargaining. Proceedings of the Fourth Midwest Conference on Industrial Relations (Chicago, 1937). 1938. SBA, VIII. *o.p.*

**Stone, Ursula Batchelder,** *joint author:* Stone, Baking Industry under N.R.A.

**Stone of the Sun:** Palacios.

**Stoner, John E.** S. O. Levinson and the Pact of Paris. 1943. *o.p.*

**Stony Island:** Baber.

**Stories of Shepherd Life:** Lobingier.

**Storr, Richard J.** The Beginnings of Graduate Education in America. 1953. x, 195 p. 25 cm. 53-10681. $5.00<sup>s</sup>.

**Story of the Apocrypha:** Goodspeed.

**Story of the Bible:** Goodspeed.

**Story of Eugenia and Philip:** Goodspeed.

**Story of Illinois:** Pease.

**Story of the Maize Plant:** Weatherwax.

**Story of the New Testament:** Goodspeed.

**Story of the Old Testament:** Goodspeed.

**Story of Paul:** Soares.

**Story of Paul of Tarsus:** Atkinson.

**Story of the Plant Kingdom:** Coulter.

**Story of the University of Chicago:** Goodspeed.

**Stourzh, Gerald.** Benjamin Franklin and American Foreign Policy. 1954. CSAFP. *o.p.*

**Stout, John E.** The Development of High-School Curricula in the North Central States from 1860 to 1918. 1921. SEM 15. *o.p.*

**Stover, John F.** American Railroads. 1961. xiv, 302 p. Illus. Index. 21 cm. 61-8081. CHAC. $5.00<sup>s</sup>. Paper. $2.25.

**Strand, K. Aa.,** *ed.* Basic Astronomical Data. ("Stars and Stellar Systems," Vol. III.) 1963. xviii, 496 p. Illus. 25 cm. 63-1402. $12.50<sup>s</sup>.

**Strang, Ruth.** Education in Rural Communities. Prepared by Ruth Strang, Chairman of the Society's Committee. 1952. NSSE, 51st Yrbk., Part II. xiv, 359, lxiv p. 24 cm. 52-7759. Cloth. $4.50<sup>t</sup>. Paper. $3.75<sup>t</sup>.

**Strang, Ruth.** Exploration in Reading Patterns. 1942. *o.p.*

**Strang, Ruth.** Juvenile Delinquency and the Schools. Prepared by Ruth Strang, Chairman of the Society's Committee. 1948. NSSE, 47th Yrbk., Part I. x, 280 p. 24 cm. 48-6850. Cloth. $4.50t.

**Strange New Gospels:** GOODSPEED.

**Strategic Psychological Operations and American Foreign Policy:** HOLT.

**Stratified Cylinder Seals from the Diyala Region:** FRANKFORT.

**Stratton, Alfred William.** Chapters in the History of Greek Noun-Formation. 1899. o.p.

**Stratton, Alfred William.** History of Greek Noun-Formation. I. Suffixes with -μ-. 1899. Preprint from Volume II, STUDIES IN CLASSICAL PHILOLOGY. o.p.

**Stratton, Alfred William:** see STUDIES IN GREEK NOUN-FORMATION.

**Stratton, Samuel Wesley.** A College Course of Laboratory Experiments in General Physics. By Samuel W. Stratton and Robert A. Millikan. 1898. o.p.

**Strauss, Anselm, ed.:** MEAD, George Herbert Mead on Social Psychology.

**Strauss, Anselm, joint author:** BECKER, Boys in White.

**Strauss, Leo.** Natural Right and History. 1953. x, 327 p. 22 cm. 53-12840. WFL. Cloth. $5.00s. Paper. P195. $1.95.
"Is there any foundation in reality for the distinction between right and wrong in ethics and politics? Professor Strauss believes that there is and in presenting his case makes a significant contribution towards an understanding of the intellectual crisis in which we find ourselves. . . . [He] brings to his task an admirable scholarship and a brilliant, incisive mind. His style reflects the lucidity of his thinking and as a consequence his book deserves a wide audience, not only among political theorists, for whom it is indispensable, but among political scientists generally."—JOHN H. HALLOWELL, in *The American Political Science Review*.

**Strauss, Leo.** The Political Philosophy of Hobbes. Its Basis and Its Genesis. Translated from the German MS by Elsa M. Sinclair. 1952. xxii, 172 p. 22 cm. 52-9720. Cloth. $6.00s. Paper. P112. $1.50.

**Strauss, Leo:** see MAIMONIDES, Guide of the Perplexed.

**Strayer, George D.** Standards and Tests for the Measurement of the Efficiency of Schools and School Systems. By G. D. Strayer and others. 1916. NSSE, 15th Yrbk., Part I. o.p.

**Strayer, George D., joint author:** FARRINGTON, Observation and Practice Teaching.

**Street Address Coding Guide:** NEWCOMB.

**Street Corner Society:** WHYTE.

**Streeter, Edward Clark:** see CHOULANT, History and Bibliography of Anatomic Illustration.

**Strevey, Tracy Elmer.** Albert J. Beveridge, in HUTCHINSON, Marcus W. Jernegan Essays.

**Strike:** HILLER.

**Strikes:** SENTURIA.

**Strodtbeck, Fred L., joint author:** SHORT, Group Process and Gang Delinquency.

**Strong, Anna Louise.** The Psychology of Prayer. 1909. o.p.

**Strong, Margaret Kirkpatrick.** Public Welfare Administration in Canada. 1930. SSM. o.p.

**Strophic Structure of Hebrew Poetry:** KRAFT.

**Strout, Ruth French. ed.** Library Catalogs. Changing Dimensions. Twenty-eighth Annual Conference, Graduate Library School. 1964. 127 p. 25 cm. LS. $3.75s.

**Strout, Ruth French, ed.** Toward a Better Cataloging Code. Twenty-first Annual Conference, Graduate Library School. 1957. vi, 116 p. 25 cm. LS. $3.75s.

**Struble, Marguirette M., ed.** Les trois mousquetaires. By Alexandre Dumas. Adapted and edited by Marguirette M. Struble and Helen M. Eddy. HCLS.
*Joint author:*
EDDY, Basic French, Vol. II.
EDDY, Écrivons.

**Struck, Harold Carl, joint author:** REED, Vitamin D.

**Structural Basis of Behavior:** DEUTSCH.

**Structural Linguistics:** HARRIS.

**Structure of Art:** THURSTON.

**Structure of Competitive Industry:** ROBINSON.

**Structure and Development of the Sporophylls and Sporangia of Isoetes:** SMITH.

**Structure of the Glands of Brunner:** BENSLEY.

**Structure of Literature:** GOODMAN.

**Structure and Relationships of Diplocaulus:** DOUTHITT.

**Structure of Scientific Revolutions:** KUHN.

**Structure and Sentiment:** NEEDHAM.

**Structure of the Text of the Book of Amos:** HARPER.

**Structure of the Text of the Book of Hosea:** HARPER.

**Structures, Reliefs, Inscriptions:** SCHMIDT.

**Struggle for Justice:** WALLIS.

**Struggle over Slavery:** WEAVER.

**Struve, Otto,** *joint author:* FROST, Radial Velocities of 500 Stars.

**Struve, Otto,** *joint author:* FROST, Study of the Spectrum of 7ε Aurigae.

**Struve, Otto,** *joint author:* LUYTEN, Reobservation of the Orbits of Ten Spectroscopic Binaries.

**Student Personnel Service:** GARDNER.

**Student Personnel Services in Colleges and Universities:** RUSSELL.

**Student Physician as Psychotherapist:** HEINE.

**Student's Gospels:** MATHEWS.

**Student's Guide for Writing College Papers:** TURABIAN.

**Student's New Testament:** GOODSPEED.

**Studies concerning Adrian IV:** THATCHER.

**Studies in Akkadian Grammar:** POEBEL.

**Studies in Ancient Furniture:** RANSOM.

**Studies in Ancient Oriental Civilization.** *See* ORIENTAL INSTITUTE, PUBLICATIONS OF.

**Studies in Arabic Literary Papyri, I. Historical Texts:** ABBOTT.

**Studies in Balzac's Realism:** DARGAN.

**Studies in Business Administration (SBA):**
I. 1. EDIE, Capital, the Money Market, and Gold.
  2. COX, Appraisal of American Business Forecasts.
  3. DOUGLAS, Movement of Money.
  4. BJORKLUND, Study of the Prices of Chain and Independent Grocers in Chicago.
II. 1. DUDDY, Supply Area of the Chicago Livestock Market.
  2. KEENER, Cutting the Cost of Bank Loans.
  3. PICKETT, Federal Bank Reserve Policy in Iowa.
  4. NERLOVE, Decade of Corporate Incomes.
III. 1. DUDDY, Distribution of Livestock from the Chicago Market.
  2. WITTE, Purchasing Policies and Practices of Chain Drug Companies.
  3. GREER, Customer Turnover Experience.
  4. COVER, Business and Personal Failure and Readjustment in Chicago.
IV. 1. MITCHELL, Trends in Industrial Location in the Chicago Region.
  2. BALDWIN, Price Differentials in Wheat Futures.
  3. GRAHAM, Public Utility Valuation.
  4. DUDDY, Grain Supply Area of the Chicago Market.
V. 1. PALYI, Principles of Mortgage Banking Regulation in Europe.
  2. COVER, Retail Price Behavior.
  3. SPENCER, Collective Bargaining under Section 7(a) of the National Industrial Recovery Act.
  4. NEWMAN, Building Industry and Business Cycles.
VI. 1. SPENCER, National Labor Relations Act.
  2. TOBIN, What Becomes of the Consumer's Meat Dollar?
  3. STONE, Baking Industry under N.R.A.
  4. SHIELDS, Junior College Business Education.
VII. 1. DEAN, Statistical Determination of Costs.
  2. DUDDY, Physical Distribution of Fresh Fruits and Vegetables.
  3. KETCHUM, Fixed Investment Trust.
  4. COVER, Financing the Consumer.
VIII. 1. SWANISH, Trade Disputes Disqualification Clause under the British Unemployment Insurance Acts.
  2. STONE, Problems of Collective Bargaining.
  3. SPENCER, National Railroad Adjustment Board.

4. DUDDY, Changing Relative Importance of the Central Livestock Market.

IX. 1. READ, Analysis of the Retail Trading Relationships of Elgin, Illinois.
2. TANNENBAUM, Costs under the Unfair Practices Acts.
3. PHELPS, Legislative Background of the Fair Labor Standards Act.
4. LEE, Anti-Chain-Store Tax Legislation to 1937.

X. 1. SMITH, Tests of Significance.
2. WILCOX, Statistical Study of Credit Unions in New York State.
3. PFANNER, Statistical Study of the Drawing Power of Cities for Retail Trade.
4. DUDDY, Use of Transportation Facilities.

XI. 1. HART, Anticipations, Uncertainty, and Dynamic Planning.
2. SPURRIER, Common Stocks and Bonds as Long-Term Investments.
3. BARNETT, Business-Cycle Theory in the United States.
4. DEAN, Statistical Cost Functions of a Hosiery Mill.

XII. 1. MITCHELL, Management's Adjustment to the Changing National Economy.
2. BREWINGTON, The Women Graduates of a School of Business.
3. DEAN, The Long-Run Behavior of Costs in a Chain of Shoe Stores.
4–5. PAYNE, Business Behavior, 1919–22.

XIII. 1. WESTON, The Economics of Competitive Bidding.
2. BUTTERBAUGH, The Measurement of Business Activity in the Puget Sound Area.
3. BRODY, Wage Rates and Living Costs in a War Economy.
4. HARTMAN, Hospital Malpractice Insurance.

XIV. 1. REVZAN, The Wholesale Price Structure for Oranges.
2. MORS, Consumer-Credit Theories.
3. HOBBAH, Railroad Transit Privileges.
4. JONES, Secular Trends and Idle Resources.

XV. 1. O'DONNELL, Recent Trends in the Demand for American Cotton.
2. CHACE, Unemployment Compensation Disqualifications.
3. DUFRAIN, The Practicability of Emphasizing Speed before Accuracy in Elementary Typewriting.
4. JONES, Renovated Capitalism.

XVI. 1–2. BROWN, The International Economic Position of New Zealand.
3. FINLAYSON, The Public Utility Holding Company under Federal Regulation.

4. DERRICK, Exemption of Security Interest from Income Taxes in the United States.

XVII. 1. LORIE, Causes of Annual Fluctuations in Production of Livestock.
2. VATTER, The Fund Theory of Accounting and Its Implications for Financial Reports.
3. LEWIS, Studies in Consumer Expenditures.

**Studies in Child Development:** *see* SOCIETY FOR RESEARCH IN CHILD DEVELOPMENT.

**Studies in Chinese Thought:** WRIGHT.

**Studies in Classical Philology** (CP):
*Volume I.* 1895.
BUCK, Oscan-Umbrian Verb-System.
CAPPS, Vitruvius and the Greek Stage.
HALE, Anticipatory Subjunctive.
SHOREY, Idea of Good in Plato's *Republic*.
TARBELL, Direction of Writing on Attic Vases.
*Volume II.* 1899.
SEARLES, Lexicographical Study of the Greek Inscriptions.
STRATTON, History of Greek Noun-Formation.
*Volume III.* 1902.
ABBOTT, Use of Repetition in Latin.
BURGESS, Epideictic Literature.
GOODSPEED, Papyri from Karanis.
*Volume IV.* 1907.
BECHTEL, Sanctae silviae peregrinatio.
PEAKS, General Civil and Military Administration.

**Studies in Dramatic "Preparation" in Roman Comedy:** HARSH.

**Studies in the Dynamics of Behavior:** LASHLEY.

**Studies in the Economics of Overhead Costs:** CLARK.

**Studies in Education:** NATIONAL SOCIETY OF COLLEGE TEACHERS OF EDUCATION.

**Studies of Elementary-School Reading:** GRAY.

**Studies in Fat Necrosis:** WELLS.

**Studies in the First Book of Samuel:** WILLETT.

**Studies in Galilee:** MASTERMAN.

**Studies in General Physiology:** LOEB.

**Studies in the Gospel According to Mark:** BURTON.

**Studies in Greek Noun-Formation** (GN):
BUCK, Dental Terminations.
STURTEVANT, Labial Terminations. I.

STURTEVANT, Labial Terminations. II.

STURTEVANT, Labial Terminations. III and IV.

## Studies in the Lectionary Text of the Greek New Testament (LT):

I. COLWELL, Prolegomena to the Study of the Lectionary Text.

II.   1. BRANTON, Common Text of the Gospel Lectionary.

    2. REDUS, Text of the Major Festivals of the Menologion.

## Studies in Logical Theory: DEWEY.

## Studies in the Making of Citizens (SMC):

BROOKS, Civic Training in Switzerland.

GAUS, Great Britain.

HARPER, Civic Training in Soviet Russia.

HAYES, France: A Nation of Patriots. (Published 1930, by Columbia University Press.)

JÁSZI, Dissolution of the Habsburg Monarchy.

KOSOK, Modern Germany.

MERRIAM, The Making of Citizens.

PIERCE, Civic Attitudes in American School Textbooks.

SCHNEIDER, Making Fascists.

WEBER, Duk-Duks.

## Studies in Mathematical Economics and Econometrics: LANGE.

## Studies of Meaning in Art (MA). 1934–35. Three volumes published for the Renaissance Society of the University of Chicago.

RICH, Seurat and the Evolution of "La grande jatte."

ROTHSCHILD, Meaning of Unintelligibility in Modern Art.

SWEENEY, Plastic Redirections in 20th Century Painting.

## Studies in Minor Folds: DECKER.

## Studies in Municipal Management (MM):

BUECHNER, Municipal Self-Insurance of Workmen's Compensation.

RIDLEY, City-Manager Profession.

## Studies in the New Testament: BOWEN.

## Studies in Optics: MICHELSON.

## Studies in the Palaeopathology of Egypt: RUFFER.

## Studies in Petrology. (Supplementary Number of *The Journal of Geology* in honor of Professor Albert Johannsen.) 1938. *o.p.*

## Studies in Political Science (POL):

I. WALLACE, Constitution of the Argentine Republic and . . . Brazil.

II. FREUND, Legal Nature of Corporations.

III. JAMES, Charters of the City of Chicago.

## Studies in Popular Poetry: ALLEN.

## Studies on the Possible Intoxicating Action of 3.2 Per Cent Beer: CARLSON.

## Studies from the Psychological Laboratory. 1896–1903. *o.p.*

Four STUDIES were published in the University of Chicago Contributions to Philosophy. Of these, three were reprinted from *The Psychological Review:* Vol. I, No. 1, from *The Psychological Review*, May, July, 1896; Vol. II, No. 2, March, November, 1898; Vol. III, No. 2, May, September, 1901, June, 1902, January, May, 1903.

Vol. IV, No. 2. WATSON, Animal Education.

## Studies in Public Administration (PA):

I. DIMOCK, Government-operated Enterprises in the Panama Canal Zone.

II. DIMOCK, British Public Utilities and National Development.

III. WHITE, Government Career Service.

IV. DIMOCK, Developing America's Waterways.

V. MERIAM, Public Service and Special Training.

VI. GAUS, Frontiers of Public Administration.

VII. McDIARMID, Government Corporations.

VIII. HENRY, Schools and City Government.

IX. LIPSON, American Governor.

X. McCAMY, Government Publicity.

XI. BAKER, County Agent.

XII. TRUMAN, Administrative Decentralization. A Study of the Chicago Field Offices of the United States Department of Agriculture.

XIII. LEISERSON, Administrative Regulation.

XIV. CALDWELL, The Administrative Theories of Hamilton and Jefferson.

## Studies in Quantitative and Cultural Sociology: AMERICAN SOCIOLOGICAL SOCIETY, Annual Proceedings. Vol. XXIV, No. 2.

## Studies in the Quantity Theory of Money: FRIEDMAN.

## Studies in Secondary Education: MORRISON.

## Studies in Secondary Education: REAVIS.

## Studies in Stichomythia: HANCOCK.

## Studies in the Theory of Numbers: DICKSON.

## Studies of Upper Air Conditions: RIEHL.

Study of Augustine's Versions of Genesis: McIntosh.

Study of Behavior: Stephenson.

Study of the Bible: Colwell.

Study of the Bible: Willoughby.

Study of Chicago's Stockyard Community: University of Chicago Settlement.

Study of Cn. Domitius Corbulo: Schoonover.

Study of College Instruction: National Society of College Teachers of Education. Proceedings, No. 27.

Study of the Court of Star Chamber: Scofield.

Study of Culture at a Distance: Mead.

Study of Dental Clinics in the United States: Leuck.

Study in Factor Analysis. The Nature of the General, Verbal, and Spatial Bi-factors: Swineford.

Study in Factor Analysis. The Reliability of Bi-factors: Swineford.

Study in Factor Analysis. The Stability of a Bi-factor Solution: Holzinger.

Study in Forecasting of Radiation Fog: Stephens.

Study of the Iliad in Translation: Clark.

Study of Man: Polanyi.

Study Manual of European History: The University of Chicago, *Department of History*.

Study of Physicians and Dentists in Detroit, 1929: Sinai.

Study of Population: Hauser.

Study of Practical Ability: McFarlane.

Study of the Prices of Chain and Independent Grocers in Chicago: Bjorklund.

Study in the Psychology of Ritualism: Henke.

Study of Quintus of Smyrna: Paschal.

Study of the Sepulchral Inscriptions in Buecheler's "Carmina Epigraphica Latina": Tolman.

Study of the Spectrum of 7ε Aurigae: Frost.

Study of the Sporangia and Gametophytes of Selaginella apus and Selaginella rupestris: Lyon.

Study of Stellar Evolution: Hale.

Study of the Technique in Konrad Ferdinand Meyer's Novellen: Taylor.

Study in Theory of Investment: Haavelmo.

Study in Undergraduate Adjustment: Angell.

Study of the Variations between the Original and the Standard Editions of Balzac's *Les Chouans*: Barnes.

Study of War: Wright.

Study of Writing: Gelb.

Studying Children: Bowman.

Stullken, Edward Henry, *joint author:* Reavis, Elementary School.

Stumpf, Florence Scovil, *joint author:* Cozens, Sports in American Life.

Sturgis, Russell. The Interdependence of the Arts of Design. A Series of Six Lectures Delivered at the Art Institute of Chicago. 1905. SL. *o.p.*

Sturtevant, E. H. Labial Terminations I. 1910. GN. *o.p.*

Sturtevant, E. H. Labial Terminations II. Words in -φη or -φᾱ (also -φᾰ)—in -φης or -φᾱς, gen. -φου—and in -φος or -φον, gen. -φου. 1911. GN. *o.p.*

Sturtevant, E. H. Labial Terminations III and IV. Words in -πη or -πᾱ (also -πᾰ)—in -πης or -πᾱς, gen. -που—in -πος and -πον, gen. -που. Words in ψ. Additions and Corrections to Labial Terminations I–IV. 1913. GN. *o.p.*

Sturtevant, E. H. Linguistic Change. An Introduction to the Historical Study of Language. 1917. With a new Introduction by Eric P. Hamp. 1961. 21 cm. 61-1441. Paper. P60. $1.35.

Sturtevant, E. H. The Pronunciation of Greek and Latin. The Sounds and Accents. 1920. *o.p.*

Stutzer, Otto. Geology of Coal. By Otto Stutzer. Translated and Revised by Adolph C. Noé. 1940. *o.p.*

**Subgroups of the Generalized Finite Modular Group:** Moore.

**Subjective Character of Cognition:** Cattell.

**Subjunctive in Tacitus:** Carmody.

**Subtropical Flow Patterns in Summer:** Riehl.

**Such Is Life:** Collins.

**Suicide:** Cavan.

**Sulzbach, Walter.** Capitalistic Warmongers, A Modern Superstition. 1942. PPP 35. *o.p.*

**Sumerian Epics and Myths:** Chiera.

**Sumerian King List:** Jacobsen.

**Sumerian Lexical Texts from the Temple School of Nippur:** Chiera.

**Sumerian Prefix Forms be- and bi-:** Kramer.

**Sumerian Prefix Forms e- and i-:** Poebel.

**Sumerian Texts of Varied Contents:** Chiera.

**Sumerians:** Kramer.

**Summary of Educational Investigations Relating to Arithmetic:** Buswell.

**Summary of Investigations Relating to Grammar, Language, and Composition:** Lyman.

**Summary of Investigations Relating to Reading:** Gray.

**Summer Program for the Church School:** Krumbine.

**Sun:** *see* Kuiper, Solar System.

**Sunday Kindergarten:** Ferris.

**Sunday School Building:** Evans.

**Sunley, Emil.** The Kentucky Poor Law, 1792–1936. 1942. *o.p.*

**Sunne, Dagny Gunhilda.** Some Phases in the Development of the Subjective Point of View during the Post-Aristotelian Period. 1911. PS. *o.p.*

**Superintendents and Principals' Association of Northern Illinois.** Yearbooks. 1906–1913. The University of Chicago Press was agent for yearbooks 1–5 (published by the Association) from December, 1910, to May, 1913, and publisher for yearbooks 6 and 7. All volumes are out of print.

First yearbook. Report of Committee of Seven on Outline of a Course of Study on a Scientific Basis. 1906.

Second yearbook. Report of Committee of Seven on an Outline Course of Study on a Scientific Basis. 1907.

Third yearbook. Report of Committee of Seven on an Outline Course of Study on a Scientific Basis. 1908.

Fourth yearbook. Report of Committee of Seven on an Outline Course of Study on a Scientific Basis. 1909.

Fifth yearbook. Report of Committee of Seven on an Outline Course of Study on a Scientific Basis. Special Subject—Motor Activity in Education. 1910.

Sixth yearbook. Report of Committee of Seven on an Outline Course of Study on a Scientific Basis. Special Subject—Elementary Science. Reprinted from *The Elementary School Teacher*, Vol. XI, No. 8. 1911.

Seventh yearbook. Report of the Committee of Seven. Special Subjects: Third-Grade History Work; Heat as a Topic for the Experimental Science Work of the Eighth Grade: A Study of Corn. Reprinted from *The Elementary School Teacher*, Vol. XII, Nos. 7–8. 1912.

**Superior and Backward Children in Public Schools:** Gossard.

**Supervision of City Schools:** Bobbitt.

**Supervision of Religious Education:** Chave.

**Supervision of Rural Schools:** Monahan.

**Supplemental Drawings for Embryology:** Du Shane.

**Supplementary Educational Monographs (SEM):**

1. Gray, Studies of Elementary-School Reading through Standardized Tests.
2. Schmidt, An Experimental Study in the Psychology of Reading.
3. Koos, The Administration of Secondary-School Units.
4. Counts, Arithmetic Tests and Studies in the Psychology of Arithmetic.
5. Gray, Types of Reading Ability as Exhibited through Tests and Laboratory Experiments.
6. Temple, Survey of Kindergartens of Richmond, Indiana.
7. Rugg, Scientific Method in the Reconstruction of Ninth-Grade Mathematics.
8. Beeley, An Experimental Study in Left-

Handedness, with Practical Suggestions for Schoolroom Tests.

9. FREEMAN, The Handwriting Movement.

10. JUDD, Reading. Its Nature and Development.

11. Hobson, Educational Legislation and Administration in the State of New York.

12. LYON, A Survey of Commercial Education in the Public High Schools of the United States.

13. MILLER, The History of Educational Legislation in Ohio.

14. TRILLING, Home Economics in American Schools.

15. STOUT, The Development of High-School Curricula in the North Central States.

16. WEATHERSBY, A History of Educational Legislation in Mississippi.

17. BUSWELL, An Experimental Study of the Eye-Voice Span in Reading.

18. TERRY, How Numerals Are Read.

19. COUNTS, The Selective Character of American Secondary Education.

20. BOBBITT, Curriculum-making in Los Angeles.

21. BUSWELL, Fundamental Reading Habits. A Study of Their Development.

22. GRAY, Remedial Cases In Reading. Their Diagnosis and Treatment.

23. HUBBARD, Silent Reading. A Study of the Various Forms.

24. MORRISON, Studies in Education I.

25. GLASS, Curiculum Practices in the Junior High School.

26. REAVIS, Studies in Secondary Education II.

27. BUSWELL, Summary of Educational Investigations Relating to Arithmetic.

28. GRAY, Summary of Investigations Relating to Reading.

29. COUNTS, The Senior High School Curriculum.

30. BUSWELL, Diagnostic Studies in Arithmetic.

31. BOBBITT, Curriculum Investigations.

32. JUDD, Psychological Analysis of the Fundamentals of Arithmetic.

33. COUNTS, The Social Composition of Boards of Education.

34. BROOKS, Report of the Commission on Length of Elementary Education.

35. BROWNELL, The Development of Children's Ideas in the Primary Grades.

36. LYMAN, Summary of Investigations Relating to Grammar, Language, and Composition.

37. WOOD, A Graphic Method of Obtaining the Partial-Coefficients.

38. BUSWELL, The Vocabulary of Arithmetic.

39. LYMAN, The Enrichment of the English Curriculum.

40. GRAY, Improving Instruction in Reading.

41. Selected References in Education, 1933.

42. Selected References in Education, 1934.

43. Selected References in Education, 1935.

44. Selected References in Education, 1936.

45. BUSWELL, How Adults Read.

46. Selected References in Education, 1937.

47. Selected References in Education, 1938.

48. HOLZINGER, A Study in Factor Analysis. The Stability of a Bi-factor Solution.

49. GRAY, Recent Trends in Reading. *2d Annual Reading Conference.*

50. BUSWELL, Remedial Reading at the College and Adult Levels.

51. GRAY, Reading and Pupil Development. *3d Annual Reading Conference.*

52. GRAY, Adjusting Reading Programs to Individuals. *4th Annual Reading Conference.*

53. SWINEFORD, A Study in Factor Analysis. The Reliability of Bi-Factors and Their Relation to Other Measures.

54. BURGESS, Environment and Education.

55. McCONNELL, Conceptual Structure of Educational Research.

56. GRAY, Co-operative Effort in Schools to Improve Reading. *5th Annual Reading Conference.*

57. GRAY, Adapting Reading Programs to Wartime Conditions. *6th Annual Reading Conference.*

58. GRAY, Reading in Relation to Experience and Language. *7th Annual Reading Conference.*

59. REAVIS, Evaluation of Teacher Merit in City School Systems.

60. BUSWELL, Non-oral Reading.

61. GRAY, The Appraisal of Current Practices in Reading. *8th Annual Reading Conference.*

62. GRAY, Improving Reading in Content Fields. *9th Annual Reading Conference.*

63. BUSWELL, Arithmetic 1947. *2d Annual Reading Conference on Arithmetic.*

64. GRAY, Promoting Personal and Social Development through Reading. *10th Annual Reading Conference.*

65. GRAY, Basic Instruction in Reading in Elementary and High Schools. *11th Annual Reading Conference.*

66. BUSWELL, Arithmetic 1948. *3d Annual Conference on Arithmetic.*

67. SWINEFORD, A Study in Factor Analysis: The Nature of the General, Verbal, and Spatial Bi-Factors.

68. Staff of the Reading Clinics, Clinical Studies in Reading.

69. GRAY, Classroom Techniques in Improving Reading. 12th *Annual Reading Conference.*

70. BUSWELL, Arithmetic 1949. *4th Annual Conference on Arithmetic.*

71. HERRICK, Toward Improved Curriculum Theory.

72. GRAY, Keeping Reading Programs Abreast of the Times. *13th Annual Reading Conference.*

73. BLOOM, Problem-solving Processes of College Students.

74. GRAY, Promoting Growth toward Maturity in

Interpreting What Is Read. *14th Annual Reading Conference.*

75. HAVIGHURST, Community Youth Development Program.
76. GRAY, Improving Reading in All Curriculum Areas. *15th Annual Reading Conference.*
77. ROBINSON, Clinical Studies in Reading. II.
78. BOWMAN, Studying Children and Training Counselors in a Community Program.
79. ROBINSON, Corrective Reading in Classroom and Clinic. *16th Annual Reading Conference.*
80. FRIEDENBERG, Self-perception in the University.
81. ROBINSON, Promoting Maximal Growth Among Able Learners. *17th Annual Reading Conference.*
82. ROBINSON, Oral Aspects of Reading. *18th Annual Reading Conference.*
83. HAVIGHURST, Survey of the Education of Gifted Children.
84. ROBINSON, Developing Permanent Interest in Reading. *19th Annual Reading Conference.*
85. BOWMAN, Mobilizing Community Resources for Maladjusted and Delinquent Youth.
86. ROBINSON, Materials for Reading. *20th Annual Reading Conference.*
87. GOINS, Visual Perceptual Abilities and Reading Progress.
88. ROBINSON, Evaluation of Reading. *21st Annual Reading Conference.*
89. ROBINSON, Reading Instructions in Various Patterns of Grouping. *22d Annual Reading Conference.*
90. ROBINSON, Sequential Development of Reading Abilities. *23d Annual Reading Conference.*
91. ROBINSON, Controversial Issues in Reading and Promising Solutions. *24th Annual Reading Conference.*
92. ROBINSON, The Underachiever in Reading. *25th Annual Reading Conference.*
93. ROBINSON, Reading and the Language Arts. *26th Annual Reading Conference.*
94. ROBINSON, Meeting Individual Differences in Reading. *27th Annual Reading Conference.*
95. ROBINSON, Recent Developments in Reading. *28th Annual Reading Conference.*

**Supply Area of the Chicago Livestock Market:** DUDDY.

**Supply and Demand:** HENDERSON.

**Supreme Court and the Constitution:** KURLAND.

**Supreme Court Review 1961 . . . 1964:** KURLAND.

**Surprise:** DESAI.

**Survey of Classical Roman Literature:** LOCKWOOD.

**Survey of Commercial Education in the Public High Schools:** LYONS.

**Survey of the Education of Gifted Children:** HAVIGHURST.

**Survey of the Kindergartens of Richmond, Indiana:** TEMPLE.

**Survey of the Medical Facilities of the City of Philadelphia:** SINAI.

**Survey of the Medical Facilities of San Joaquin County, California:** SINAI.

**Survey of the Medical Facilities of Shelby County, Indiana:** PEEBLES.

**Survey of the Medical Facilities of the State of Vermont:** PEEBLES.

**Survey of Religious Education:** BOWER.

**Survey of Statistical Data on Medical Facilities in the United States:** PEEBLES.

**Surveys of the Medical Facilities in Three Representative Southern Counties:** GUILD.

**Sutherland, Edwin Hardin.** The Professional Thief. By a Professional Thief. Annotated and Interpreted by Edwin H. Sutherland. 1937. xiv, 257 p. 20 cm. 37-36112. Cloth. SOC. $5.00ˢ. Paper. P10. $1.70.

**Sutherland, Lucy S.,** *ed.:* BURKE, Correspondence of Edmund Burke, *Vol. II.*

**Sutton, W. S.** The Organization of the Department of Education in Relation to the Other Departments in Colleges and Universities. 1907. *o.p.*

**Sutton, W. S.,** *joint author:* CUBBERLEY, Research within the Field of Education.

**Suye Mura. A Japanese Village:** EMBREE.

**Suzzallo, Henry,** *joint author:* BURNHAM, History of Education.

**Swan, Richard G.** The Theory of Sheaves. 1964. 150 p. 21 cm. 64-24979. CLM. Paper. $2.00ᵗ.

**Swanish, Peter Theodore.** Trade Disputes Disqualification Clause under the British Unemployment Insurance Acts. 1937. SBA, VIII. *o.p.*

**Swanson, Don R.,** *ed.* The Intellectual Foundations of Library Education. Twentyninth Annual Conference, Graduate Library School. 1965. 98 p. 24 cm. LS. $3.75ˢ.

**Swarzenski, Hanns.** Monuments of Romanesque Art. The Art of the Church Treasures in Northwestern Europe. 1955. *o.p.*

**Sweeney, James Johnson.** Plastic Redirections in 20th Century Painting. 1934. MA. *o.p.*

**Sweet, William W.,** *ed.* The Baptists: 1783–1830. A Collection of Source Material. General Introduction by Shirley Jackson Case. 1931. Vol. I, in the series RELIGION ON THE AMERICAN FRONTIER. *o.p.*

**Sweet, William W.,** *ed.* The Congregationalists: 1783–1850. A Collection of Source Materials. 1939. Vol. III, in the series RELIGION ON THE AMERICAN FRONTIER. *o.p.* Vol. II published elsewhere.

**Sweet, William W.,** *ed.* The Methodists, 1783–1840. 1946. Volume IV in the series RELIGION ON THE AMERICAN FRONTIER. *o.p.*

**Sweet, William W.:** *see* BAKER, Short History of Christianity.

**Sweet, William W.:** *see* CASE, Bibliographical Guide to the History of Christianity.

**Swen, Wen-Yuh:** Nutrition Reprints: *see* BUCK, Land Utilization in China, Vol. IV.

**Swift and Anglican Rationalism:** HARTH.

**Swift and the Satirist's Art:** ROSENHEIM.

**Swindlers and Rogues in French Drama:** NORMAN.

**Swineford, Frances.** A Study in Factor Analysis. The Nature of the General, Verbal, and Spatial Bi-factors. 1948. xi, 71 p. Illus. 25 cm. 49-7102. Paper. SEM 67. $2.50ᵗ.

**Swineford, Frances.** A Study in Factor Analysis. The Reliability of Bi-factors and Their Relation to Other Measures. By Frances Swineford and Karl J. Holzinger. 1942. SEM 53. *o.p.*

**Swineford, Frances,** *joint author:* HOLZINGER, A Study in Factor Analysis.

**Swisher, Carl Brent.** The Growth of Constitutional Power in the United States. 1946. x, 261 p. 22 cm. A46-542. Cloth. WFL. $5.00ˢ. Paper. P113. $2.45.

**Syllabus of American Literature:** HASTINGS.

**Symbolism and American Literature:** FEIDELSON.

**Symposium on America and the World Situation:** EINSTEIN.

**Symposium on Molecular Biology:** ZIRKLE.

**Synopsis of the Modal Uses of the Finite Verb:** HALE.

**Synoptic Gospels:** GOODSPEED.

**Synoptic Key to the Phyla, Classes, and Orders of Animals:** ALLEE.

**Syntax of Castilian Prose:** KENISTON.

**Syntax of High-School Latin:** BYRNE.

**Syntax of the Moods and Tenses in New Testament Greek:** BURTON.

**Syntax of the Participle in the Apostolic Fathers:** ROBISON.

**System of the Quadriliteral Verb:** HEIDEL.

**Systematic Method of Calculating the Dimensions of Direct-Current Dynamo-Electric Machines:** KINSLEY.

**Systematic Packing of Spheres:** GRATON.

**Systematic Politics:** MERRIAM.

**Systematic Theology:** TILLICH.

**Szukalski, Stanislaw.** Projects in Design. 1929. Introduction by Roger A. Crane. *o.p.*

**Table of Mean Virtual Temperatures:** ROSSBY.

**Table of Phonetic Changes:** WOOD.

**Tables annuelles de constantes et données numériques de chimie, de physique et de technologie.** Publiées sous le patronage de l'Association internationale des Académies par le Comité international nommé par le VIIᵉ Congrès de Chimie appliquée (Londres, 2 juin 1909). Avec la collaboration de: ... Commission permanente du Comité international: M. Bodenstein; G. Bruni; Ernst Cohen; Ch. Marie; N.-T.-M. Wilsmore. Secrétaire général: Ch. Marie.

(Agency discontinued with Vol. V.)

*Vol. I.* Année 1910. 1912. (*o.p.*)
*Vol. II.* Année 1911. 1913. (*o.p.*)
*Vol. III.* Année 1912. 1914. (*o.p.*)
*Vol. IV.* Années 1913–1914–1915–1916. Première partie. 1921. (*o.p.*)
*Vol. V.* Années 1917–1922. (*o.p.*)

**T. S. Eliot's Poetry and Plays:** SMITH.

**Ta Chen.** Population in Modern China. 1946. *o.p.*

**Taft, Julia Jessie.** The Woman Movement from the Point of View of Social Consciousness. 1916. PS. *o.p.*

**Taft, Lorado.** Modern Tendencies in Sculpture. 1921. SL. *o.p.*

**Tagliacozzo, Daisy L.,** *joint author:* SEIDMAN, Worker Views His Union.

**Takeuchi, Tatsuji.** War and Diplomacy in the Japanese Empire. 1941. *o.p.*

**Taki, Seiichi:** *see* Manyōshū.

**Talbert, Ernest Lynn.** The Dualism of Fact and Idea in Its Social Implications. 1910. *o.p.*

**Talbert, Ernest Lynn.** Opportunities in School and Industry for Children of the Stockyards District. 1912. CSC. *o.p.*

**Talbot, Marion.** The Education of Women. 1910. *o.p.*

**Talbot, Marion.** More than Lore. Reminiscences of Marion Talbot, Dean of Women, The University of Chicago, 1892–1925. 1936. *o.p.*

**Talbot, Marion,** *joint author:* RICHARDS, Food.

**Talbot, Phillips,** *ed.* South Asia in the World Today. 1950. HFL. *o.p.*

**Tales of Ancient India:** VAN BUITENEN.

**Taliaferro, William H.,** *ed.* Medicine and the War. 1944. BM. WFL. *o.p.*

**Taliaferro, William H.:** *see* MOULTON, World and Man.

**Talking to the Moon:** MATHEWS.

**Tall-i-Bakun A, Season of 1932:** LANGSDORFF.

**Tallmadge, Thomas Eddy.** Architecture in Old Chicago. 1941. *o.p.*

**Talmage, Roy V.,** *joint ed.:* GAILLARD, The Parathyroid Glands.

**Tannenbaum, Edward.** The New France. 1961. viii, 252 p. Illus. 24 cm. 61-8076. $5.00s.

**Tannenbaum, Robert.** Cost under the Unfair Practices Acts. 1939. SBA, IX. *o.p.*

**Tanner, Amy Eliza.** Association of Ideas. A Preliminary Study. 1900. PHI. *o.p.*

**Tarahumara. An Indian Tribe of Northern Mexico.** BENNETT.

**Tarbell, Frank Bigelow.** A Cantharus from the Factory of Brygos in the Boston Museum of Fine Arts.
Bound with TARBELL, Greek Hand-Mirror (see below).

**Tarbell, Frank Bigelow.** The Direction of Writing on Attic Vases. 1894. Preprint from Volume I, STUDIES IN CLASSICAL PHILOLOGY. *o.p.*

**Tarbell, Frank Bigelow.** A Greek Hand-Mirror in the Art Institute of Chicago. A Cantharus from the Factory of Brygos in the Boston Museum of Fine Arts. Preprint. 1902. *o.p.*

**Tashiro, Shiro.** A Chemical Sign of Life. 1917. SCI. *o.p.*

**Tatlock, J. S. P.:** *see* BRYAN, Sources and Analogues of Chaucer's *Canterbury Tales*.

**Tatum, Arthur Lawrie.** Prescription Notes. 1925. *o.p.*

**Tauber, Maurice F.,** *joint ed.:* WILSON, The University Library.

**Tave, Stuart M.** The Amiable Humorist. A Study in the Comic Theory and Criticism of the Eighteenth and Early Nineteenth Centuries. 1960. xi, 304 p. 22 cm. 59-11627. $5.00s.

"This is one of the best studies of the eighteenth-century outlook that has appeared for some years."—D. W. Jefferson, in *The Modern Language Review.*

". . . careful and witty . . . remarkably successful in making the significant connections between his material and its wide-ranging associations."—W. R. Irwin, in *The Philological Quarterly.*

**Tax, Sol.** Penny Capitalism. 1953. Reprint. 1963. x, 230 p. Map. Index. 27 cm. 63-9730. $5.75ˢ.

**Tax, Sol.** *ed.* Acculturation in the Americas. 1952. *o.p.*

**Tax, Sol.** *ed.* Anthropology Today. Selections. 1962. viii, 481 p. 24 cm. 62-17960. Paper. P105. $2.95. *See also* KROEBER, Anthropology Today.

**Tax, Sol.** *ed.* An Appraisal of Anthropology Today. Edited by Sol Tax, Loren C. Eiseley, Irving Rouse, and Carl F. Voegelin. 1952. *o.p.*

**Tax, Sol,** *ed.* The Civilizations of Ancient America. 1951. *o.p.*

**Tax, Sol.** *ed.* Evolution after Darwin. *The University of Chicago Centennial.* 1960.
*Vol. I:* The Evolution of Life. Its Origin, History, and Future. vi, 628 p. Index. 24 cm. 60-10575. $10.00ˢ.
*Vol. II:* The Evolution of Man. Mind, Culture, and Society. vi, 473 p. Index. 24 cm. 60-10575. $10.00ˢ.
*Vol. III:* Issues in Evolution. The University of Chicago Centennial Discussions. Edited by Sol Tax and Charles Callender. viii, 310 p. Index. 24 cm. 60-10575. $7.50ˢ.
*Set of three volumes.* $25.00ˢ.

**Tax, Sol,** *ed.* Indian Tribes of Aboriginal America. 1952. *o.p.*

**Tax, Sol,** *joint author:* EGGAN, Social Anthropology of North American Tribes.

**Taxi-Dance Hall:** CRESSEY.

**Taylor, Alva Wilmot:** *see* HAYDON, Modern Trends in World-Religions.

**Taylor, Archer.** A Bibliographical History of Anonyma and Pseudonyma. By Archer Taylor and F. J. Mosher. 1951. *o.p.*

**Taylor, Archer.** "Edward" and "Sven i Rosengård." A Study in the Dissemination of a Ballad. 1931. *o.p.*

**Taylor, Archer:** *see* BRYAN, Sources and Analogues of Chaucer's *Canterbury Tales.*

**Taylor, Earl A.** Controlled Reading. A Correlation of Diagnostic, Teaching, and Corrective Techniques. 1937. *o.p.*

**Taylor, Graham.** Pioneering on Social Frontiers. 1930. *o.p.*

**Taylor, Hasseltine Byrd.** Law of Guardian and Ward. 1935. SSM. *o.p.*

**Taylor, Joshua C.** Learning To Look. A Handbook for the Visual Arts. 1957. vii, 152 p. Illus. 25 cm. 57-11213. Cloth. $3.75ˢ. Paper. P78. $1.95.

**Taylor, Joshua C.** William Page, the American Titian. 1957. *o.p.*

**Taylor, Marion Lee.** A Study of the Technique in Konrad Ferdinand Meyer's Novellen. 1909. *o.p.*

**Taylor, Mary E.,** *joint author:* FIELD, Atlas of Cat Anatomy.

**Taylor, Robert Emmett.** Municipal Budget-making. 1925. *o.p.*

**Teacher's Manual.** To Accompany the Chicago Spanish Series: SPARKMAN.

**Teacher's Manual for Accounting Method:** GRAHAM.

**Teacher's Manual for First-Year Mathematics:** MYERS.

**Teacher's Rating Scales for Pupil Adjustment:** FREEMAN.

**Teaching of Arithmetic:** BUSWELL.

**Teaching in the Army:** LEWIS.

**Teaching of General Science:** EICKENBERRY.

**Teaching of Geography:** PARKINS.

**Teaching of German:** HAGBOLDT.

**Teaching High-School Latin:** GAME.

**Teaching of Jesus about the Future:** SHARMAN.

**Teaching Language in the Elementary School:** TRABUE.

**Teaching of Reading:** GRAY.

**Teaching Science:** DOWNING.

**Tear, Daniel Ambrose.** The Logical Basis of Educational Theory from the Standpoint of "Instrumental" Logic. 1908. *o.p.*

**Technical Assistance by Religious Agencies:** MADDOX.

**Technical Co-operation in Latin-American Agriculture:** MOSHER.

**Technique of Teaching Secondary-School Mathematics:** BRESLICH.

**Technique of Theory Construction:** WOODGER.

**Technique of Thomas Hardy:** BEACH.

**Technology and International Relations:** OGBURN.

**Tektites:** O'KEEFE.

**Telescopes:** KUIPER.

**Tell Asmar and Khafaje:** FRANKFORT.

**Tell Asmar, Khafaje, and Khorsabad:** FRANKFORT.

**Temple, Alice.** Survey of the Kindergartens of Richmond, Indiana. 1917. SEM 60. *o.p.*

**Temple of King Sethos I:** CALVERLEY.

**Temple Oval at Khafājah:** DELOUGAZ.

**Temples of Lower Nubia:** BREASTED.

**Templeton, Frederic E.** X-Ray Examination of the Stomach. A Description of the Roentgenologic Anatomy, Physiology, and Pathology of the Esophagus, Stomach, and Duodenum. 2d ed. 1964. xviii, 598 p. Illus. 24 cm. $15.00ˢ.

**Ten Commandments:** GOLDMAN.

**Ten Princes:** RYDER.

**Tenements of Chicago:** ABBOTT.

**Têng Ssŭ-yü.** Advanced Conversational Chinese. 1965. xv, 293 p. 29 cm. 65 12042. $5.50ᵗ.

**Têng Ssŭ-yü.** Chang Hsi and the Treaty of Nanking, 1842. 1944. *o.p.*

**Têng Ssŭ-yü.** Conversational Chinese. With Grammatical Notes. 1947. x, 441 p. 26 cm. 47-30857. $7.00ᵗ. (NOTE.—All lessons available on records. Inquiry should be addressed to S. Y. Têng, Department of History, Indiana University, Bloomington. Indiana.) SOUTH ASIA.

**Têng Ssŭ-yü,** *joint ed.:* CREEL, Newspaper Chinese by the Inductive Method.

**Têng Ssŭ-yü,** *joint ed.:* CREEL, Translations of Text Selections and Exercises in Newspaper Chinese.

**Tentative Chronological List of Petrarch's Prose Letters:** WILKINS.

**Tenth-Century Document of Arabic Literary Theory:** GRUNEBAUM.

**Tepoztlán:** REDFIELD.

**Teratology:** WILSON.

**Terman, Lewis M.** Nature and Nurture. Prepared by L. M. Terman, Chairman of the Society's Committee. 1928. NSSE, 27th Yrbk., Part II. *o.p.*

**Terminal Education in Higher Institutions:** RUSSELL.

**Terminology of Operations:** JENKINS.

**Ternary Orthogonal Group:** DICKSON.

**Terre de France: Premières lectures:** BOND.

**Terrible Meek:** KENNEDY, *in his* Plays for Seven Players.

**Terry, Paul W.** How Numerals Are Read. An Experimental Study of the Reading of Isolated Numerals in Arithmetic Problems. 1922. SEM 18. *o.p.*

**Tests and Measurements in Higher Education:** GRAY.

**Tests of Significance. What They Mean and How To Use Them:** SMITH.

**Tests To Accompany** *A Brief Course in German:* HAGBOLDT.

**Teter, Lucius:** *see* Financial Mobilization for War.

**Texas Navy:** HILL.

**Text of the** *Canterbury Tales:* MANLY.

**Text of the Major Festivals of the Menologion:** REDUS.

**Textbook in American Education:** EDMONSON.

**Textbook of Israeli Hebrew:** ROSÉN.

**Textbook on Law and Business:** SPENCER.

**Thatcher, Oliver Joseph.** Studies concerning Adrian IV. 1903. *o.p.*

**The Russia I Believe In:** HARPER.

**Theatre on the Frontier:** CARSON.

**Their Majesties the Mob:** CAUGHEY.

**Thelen, Herbert A.** Dynamics of Groups at Work. Principles and Practices. 1954. ix, 379 p. 54-11600. Cloth. 24 cm. $6.75ˢ. Paper. P117. 21 cm. $2.45.

**Thenard, Louis Jacques:** *see* SCHEELE, Early History of Chlorine.

**Theological and Semitic Literature for the Year 1900:** MUSS-ARNOLT.

**Theological and Semitic Literature for the Year 1901:** MUSS-ARNOLT.

**Theological Study Today:** MEADVILLE THEOLOGICAL SEMINARY.

**Theology of Schleiermacher:** CROSS.

**Theophilus.** On Divers Arts. Translated from the medieval Latin with Introduction and Notes by John G. Hawthorne and Cyril Stanley Smith. 1963. xxxv, 216 p. 25 cm. 63-11397. $8.50ˢ.

**Theoretical Considerations Respecting the Dependence of Wave-Length on Pressure:** WILSING.

**Theories of Learning:** HILGARD.

**Theory of Behavior:** BRUNSWIK.

**Theory of Education in the Republic of Plato:** NETTLESHIP.

**Theory of Ground-Water Motion:** HUBBERT.

**Theory of Legislation:** JORDAN.

**Theory and Measurement of Demand:** SCHULTZ.

**Theory of Modulation:** OTTERSTRÖM.

**Theory of Perturbations:** QUENEY.

**Theory and Practice in American Politics:** NELSON.

**Theory of Sheaves:** SWAN.

**Theory of Valuation:** DEWEY.

**They Found the Buried Cities:** WAUCHOPE.

**They Thought They Were Free:** MAYER.

**They Wrote on Clay:** CHIERA.

**Thief of Love:** DIMOCK.

**Thiele, Edwin R.** The Mysterious Numbers of the Hebrew Kings. A Reconstruction of the Chronology of the Kingdoms of Israel and Judah. 1951. *o.p.*

**Thiele, Marie Barbara.** Patriotism. Forms A and B. Prepared by Marie B. Thiele and L. L. Thurstone. 1931. TAS 11. *o.p.*

**Thiele, Thorwald Nicolai.** Resolution into Series of the Third Band of the Carbon Band-Spectrum. 1898. *o.p.*

**Things Seen and Heard:** GOODSPEED.

**Thinking Machine:** HERRICK.

**Third and Fourth Generation:** DOWNING.

**Third World:** WORSLEY.

**Third-Year Mathematics for Secondary Schools:** BRESLICH.

**This Is Illinois:** MONAGHAN.

**Thomas Jefferson:** LEHMANN.

**Thomas, Joseph,** *trans.:* BRÉHIER, Hellenic Age. History of Philosophy.

**Thomas, Joseph,** *trans.:* BRÉHIER, Philosophy of Plotinus.

**Thomas, Milton Halsey.** John Dewey. A Centennial Bibliography. Rev. ed. 1962. xiv, 370 p. Index. 22 cm. 62-12638. $6.50ˢ.

**Thomas, Russell Brown,** *joint author:* CHAPIN, New Approach to Poetry.

**Thomas, William Isaac.** On a Difference in the Metabolism of the Sexes. 1897. *o.p.*

**Thomas, William Isaac.** The Polish Peasant in Europe and America: Monograph of an Immigrant Group. By William I. Thomas and Florian Znaniecki. 1918. *Vol. I:* Primary-Group Organization. *o.p. Vol. II:* Primary-Group Organization. *o.p. Vol. III:* Primary-Group Organization. *o.p.*

**Thomas, William Isaac.** The Relation of the Medicine-Man to the Origin of the Professional Occupations. 1903. *o.p.*

**Thomas, William Isaac.** Sex and Society. Studies in the Social Psychology of Sex. 1907. *o.p.*

Thomas, William Isaac, ed. Source Book for Social Origins. Ethnological Materials, Psychological Standpoint, Classified and Annotated Bibliographies for the Interpretation of Savage Society. 1909. *o.p.*

Thomas, William L., Jr., ed. Current Anthropology. A Supplement to Anthropology Today. 1956. *o.p.*

Thomas, William L., Jr., ed. Man's Role in Changing the Face of the Earth. Edited by William L. Thomas, Jr., in collaboration with Carl O. Sauer, Marston Bates, and Lewis Mumford. 1956. xxxviii, 1,193 p. Illus. 25 cm. 56-5865. $15.00ˢ.

Thomas Wakefield Goodspeed: GOODSPEED.

Thomism and Aristotelianism: JAFFA.

Thompson, Clem Oren. The Extension Program of the University of Chicago. 1933. *o.p.*

Thompson, Clem Oren: *see* REEVES, University Extension Services.

Thompson, Craig R., *trans.:* ERASMUS, Colloquies of Erasmus.

Thompson, Effie Freeman. Μετανοέω and Μεταμέλει in Greek Literature until 100 A.D. Including Discussion of Their Cognates and of Their Hebrew Equivalents. 1908. HLL. *o.p.*

Thompson, Era Bell. American Daughter. 1946. *o.p.*

Thompson, Helen Bradford. The Mental Traits of Sex. An Experimental Investigation of the Normal Mind in Men and Women. 1903. *o.p.*

Thompson, Helen Bradford. Psychological Norms in Men and Women. 1903. PHI. *o.p.*

Thompson, Helen Bradford, *joint author:* TUFTS, Individual and His Relation to Society.

Thompson, James Westfall. The Civilization of the Renaissance. By James Westfall Thompson, George Rowley, Ferdinand Schevill, and George Sarton. 1929. *o.p.*

Thompson, James Westfall. The Decline of Missi Dominici in Frankish Gaul. 1903. *o.p.*

Thompson, James Westfall. The Development of the French Monarchy under Louis VI, le Gros, 1108–1137. 1895. *o.p.*

Thompson, James Westfall. Feudal Germany. 1928. *o.p.*

Thompson, James Westfall. The Medieval Library. 1939. *o.p.*

Thompson, James Westfall. Reference Studies in Medieval History. Revised and enlarged edition, 1923. (First two editions privately printed, 1907 and 1914.) *Part I:* The Dark Ages, 180–814. *o.p. Part II:* The Feudal Age, 814–1291. *o.p. Part III:* The End of the Middle Ages, 1291–1498. *o.p.*

Thompson, James Westfall. The Wars of Religion in France, 1559–76. The Huguenots, Catherine de Medici and Philip II. 1909. *o.p.*

Thompson, Laura. The Hopi Way. By Laura Thompson and Alice Joseph. 1945. *o.p.*

Thompson, Manley. The Pragmatic Philosophy of C. S. Peirce. 1953. xvii, 317 p. 21 cm. A45-4598. Paper. P110. $1.95.

Thompson, Silvanus, *trans.:* HUYGENS, Treatise on Light.

Thompson, Stith: *see* BRYAN, Sources and Analogues of Chaucer's *Canterbury Tales.*

Thompson, W. L., *joint author:* MILLER, A Proposed Method for the Computation of the 10,000-Foot Tendency Field.

Thompson, Warren S. Population and Peace in the Pacific. 1946. *o.p.*

Thompson, Warren S. Population and Progress in the Far East. 1959. ix, 443 p. Illus. 24 cm. 59-10428. $7.50ˢ.

Thomson, Thomas.: *see* DALTON, Foundations of the Atomic Theory.

Thorndike, Lynn. Latin Treatises on Comets. Between A.D. 1238 and 1368. 1950. *o.p.*

Thorndike, Lynn. The Sphere of Sacrobosco and Its Commentators. 1949. *o.p.*

Thorndike, Lynn, ed. The Herbal of Rufinus. Edited by Lynn Thorndike, L. T. and F. S. Benjamin. 1946. *o.p.*

**Thorndyke, Edward L.** Intelligence Tests and Their Use. By E. L. Thorndyke and others. 1922. NSSE, 21st Yrbk., Part I. Bound with Part II, The Administrative Use of Intelligence Tests. *o.p.*

**Thorndyke, Edward L.,** *joint author:* CUBBERLEY, Research within the Field of Education.

**Thorne, Kip S.,** *joint author:* HARRISON, Gravitation Theory and Gravitational Collapse.

**Thornton, Charles S.,** *ed.* Regeneration in Vertebrates. 1958. ix, 108 p. 24 cm. 59-8869. DBC. $3.25ˢ.

**Thornton, Harrison John.** The History of the Quaker Oats Company. 1933. *o.p.*

**Thornton, Harrison John.** Theodore Roosevelt, *in* HUTCHINSON, Marcus W. Jernegan Essays.

**Thorpe, Clarence DeWitt,** *ed.* Fred Newton Scott Anniversary Papers.

**Thought, Action, and Passion:** MCKEON.

**Thought and Change:** GELLNER.

**Thraldom in Ancient Iceland:** WILLIAMS.

**Thrasher, Frederic Milton.** Chicago's Gangland. A Social Base Map. 1927. (Included in THRASHER, Gang.) SOC. *o.p.*

**Thrasher, Frederic Milton.** The Gang. A Study of 1,313 Gangs in Chicago. 1927. Abridged and with new Introduction by James F. Short, Jr. 1963. lviii, 388 p. 22 cm. 63-20899. Cloth. SOC. $7.50ˢ. Paper. P138. $2.95.
"No one conversant in the social sciences would challenge the designation of Thrasher's work as a 'modern classic.' It is so for a variety of reasons. It stands, first of all, after more than three and a half decades as the most comprehensive study of the phenomenon of adolescent gangs ever undertaken. So complete was it that, at least in part because of this fact, no other great survey of its type has been undertaken."—James F. Short, Jr., in the Introduction to the 1963 edition.

**Threat of German World-Politics:** JUDSON.

**Three Centuries of Poor Law Administration . . . Rhode Island:** CREECH.

**Three Greek Tragedies:** GRENE.

**Three Plays:** RACINE.

**Three Typical Beliefs:** SOARES.

**Through Routes for Chicago's Steam Railroads:** HOOKER.

**Through Three Centuries. Colver and Rosenberger . . . 1620–1922.** ROSENBERGER.

**Thrupp, Sylvia.** The Merchant Class of Medieval London, 1300–1500. 1948. (O.I.)

**Thunderstorm Electricity:** BYERS.

**Thurston, Carl.** The Structure of Art. 1940. *o.p.*

**Thurstone, Louis Leon.** A Factorial Study of Perception. By L. L. and T. G. Thurstone. 1944. PMS 4. *o.p.*

**Thurstone, Louis Leon.** The Measurement of Attitude. A Psychophysical Method and Some Experiments with a Scale for Measuring Attitude toward the Church. By L. L. Thurstone and E. J. Chave. 1929. xii, 97 p. Illus. 21 cm. 30-4383. Paper. $2.50ˢ.

**Thurstone, Louis Leon.** The Measurement of Values. 1959. viii, 322 p. 24 cm. 58-11960. $7.50ˢ.

**Thurstone, Louis Leon.** Multiple-Factor Analysis. A Development and Expansion of *The Vectors of Mind.* 1947. xx, 535 p. Illus. 24 cm. 47-2981. BM. $8.50ˢ.
". . . no book by an American psychologist has been so frequently studied and quoted in this country as Thurstone's *Vectors of Mind;* and I venture to predict that his new volume on factorial methods will arouse an even wider interest. . . . It is much more than a revised edition . . . a large amount of new material, much of which has hitherto been accessible only in isolated articles, has now been brought together for the first time. . . . The book thus presents a complete and systematic statement of Thurstone's views on factor-analysis up to date, and will be indispensable to every advanced student."—Cyril Burt, in *The British Journal of Educational Psychology.*

**Thurstone, Louis Leon.** Order of Birth, Parent-Age, and Intelligence. By L. L. Thurstone and Richard L. Jenkins. 1931. BR. *o.p.*

**Thurstone, Louis Leon.** Personality Schedule. Arranged by L. L. Thurstone and Thelma Gwinn Thurstone. 1929. 4 p. Package of 25, $2.00ˢ. Specimen set, including 1 Schedule, Instructions, and Scoring Sheet, postpaid, $0.25. Instruction Sheet, $0.05.

**Thurstone, Louis Leon.** Primary Mental Abilities. 1938. Rev. ed. 1957. PMS. *o.p.*

**Thurstone, Louis Leon.** A Scale for Measuring Attitude toward the Church. By L. L. Thurstone and E. J. Chave. 1929. TAS 1. *o.p.*

**Thurstone, Louis Leon.** A Scale for Measuring Attitude toward Communism. Forms A and B. 1929. TAS 6. *o.p.*

**Thurstone, Louis Leon.** The Vectors of Mind. Multiple-Factor Analysis for the Isolation of Primary Traits. 1935. SCI. *o.p.*

**Thurstone, Louis Leon,** *ed.* Factorial Studies of Intelligence. Edited by L. L. Thurstone and Thelma Gwinn Thurstone. 1941. PMS. *o.p.*

**Thurstone, Louis Leon,** *Editor:* SCALES FOR THE MEASUREMENT OF SOCIAL ATTITUDES.

**Thurstone, Louis Leon:** *see* WIRTH, Eleven Twenty-six.

**Thurstone, Thelma Gwinn.** Attitude toward Evolution. Forms A and B. 1931. TAS 30. *o.p.*

**Thurstone, Thelma Gwinn,** *joint editor:* THURSTONE, Factorial Studies of Intelligence.

**Thurstone, Thelma Gwinn,** *joint author:* THURSTONE, Factorial Studies of Perception.

**Thurstone, Thelma Gwinn,** *joint author:* THURSTONE, Personality Schedules.

**Thutmosid Succession:** EDGERTON.

**Tibbitts, Clark.** Handbook of Social Gerontology. Societal Aspects of Aging. 1960. xviii, 776 p. Illus. Index. 25 cm. 60-5469. HSG. $10.00ᵗ.

**Tiffany, Lewis H.** The Algae of Illinois. By Lewis H. Tiffany and M. E. Britton. 1952. BM. (O.I.)

**Tillich, Paul.** Biblical Religion and the Search for Ultimate Reality. 1955. x, 85 p. 21 cm. 55-5149. Cloth. $2.50ˢ. Paper. P154. $1.00. COBE.

**Tillich, Paul.** The Protestant Era. Translated by James Luther Adams. 1957. Abridged. xxvii, 242 p. 21 cm. Paper. P19. $1.50. COBE.

**Tillich, Paul.** Systematic Theology, *Vol. I.* 1951. xii, 300 p. 24 cm. 51-2235. $5.50. *Vol. II.* 1957. xii, 199 p. 24 cm. 51-2235. $4.50. *Vol. III.* 1963. xiv, 434 p. 24 cm. 51-2235. $6.95. COBE.

"The whole is a work of such breadth and penetration that one marvels at the power and comprehensiveness of Tillich's thought. . . . The question which concerns me most . . . has to do with that element in his philosophical structure, adopted from the neo-Platonic mystical tradition, which holds that the split between subjectivity and objectivity is the source of the ambiguities of existence and is therefore the primary sign of man's separation from God. Paul Tillich brings high intellectuality, aesthetic sensitivity and courageous participation in history to his interpretation of the Christian faith that God in his grace overcomes human estrangement. His theology will serve countless seekers and believers who crave a faith which permits and requires involvement in the human struggle for truth."—D. D. Williams in *The Christian Century.*

**Tilton, John Littlefield.** The Pleistocene Deposits in Warren County, Iowa. 1911. *o.p.*

**Time, Space, and Man:** BRAIDWOOD.

**Time's Arrow in Society:** WOODS.

**Tinbergen, Jan.** The Dynamics of Business Cycles. Translated and adapted by J. J. Polak. 1950. *o.p.*

**Tippetts, Charles Sanford.** Autarchy: National Self-sufficiency. 1933. PPP 5. *o.p.*

**Titelbaum, Sydney:** *see* KLEITMAN, Sleep Characteristics.

**Tobatí:** SERVICE.

**Tobias Smollett:** KAHRL.

**Tobin, Bernard Freeman.** What Becomes of the Consumer's Meat Dollar? Introduction and Summary by Howard C. Greer. 1936. SBA, VI. *o.p.*

**Toda, Kenji.** Japanese Scroll Painting. 1935. *o.p.*

**Toda, Kenji,** *joint author:* DRISCOLL, Chinese Calligraphy.

**Today in American Drama:** O'HARA.

**Todd, Arthur Jones,** *joint editor:* FARIS, Intelligent Philanthropy.

**Todd, Jessie Mabel.** Enjoyment and Use of Art in the Elementary School. By Jessie Todd and Ann Van Nice Gale. 1933. *o.p.*

**Todd, Jessie Mabel.** Learning To Draw. Sets I, II, and III. Forty-eight individual practice sheets per set for use in the elementary grades. 1931. *o.p.*

**Toeplitz, Otto.** The Calculus. A Genetic Approach. Edited by Gottfried Köthe. Translated by Luise Lange. 1963. xiv, 192 p. Index. 24 cm. 63-9731. Cloth. $6.50ˢ. Paper. PSS520. $1.95.

**Toffteen, Olaf Alfred.** Ancient Chronology, 1907. [Vol. I, Researches in Biblical Archaeology.] Published for the Oriental Society of the Western Theological Seminary. *o.p.*

**Toffteen, Olaf Alfred.** The Historic Exodus. 1909. [Vol. II, Researches in Biblical Archaeology.] Published for the Oriental Society of the Western Theological Seminary. *o.p.*

**Toffteen, Olaf Alfred.** Researches in Assyrian and Babylonian Geography. 1908. *o.p.*

**Toledo Manuscript of the Germania of Tacitus:** ABBOTT.

**Tolerant Populists:** NUGENT.

**Tolman, Albert Harris.** Questions on Shakespeare. 1910–1912. *o.p.*

Part I. Introductory. 1910.

Part II. The First Histories, Poems, Comedies. 1910.

Questions on the following plays were issued in pamphlet form. *o.p.*

*As You Like It.* 1912. *I Henry IV.* 1912. *The Merchant of Venice.* 1912. *A Midsummer-Night's Dream.* 1912. *Much Ado about Nothing.* 1912. *II Henry IV.* 1912. *The Tempest.* 1912. *Twelfth Night.* 1912.

**Tolman, Albert Harris.** What Has Become of Shakespeare's Play, "Love's Labour's Won"? Preprint. 1902. *o.p.*

**Tolman, Judson Allen.** A Study of the Sepulchral Inscriptions in Buecheler's "Carmina epigraphica Latina." 1910. *o.p.*

**Tomb of Tjanefer at Thebes:** SEELE.

**Tomorrow's Chicago:** HILLMAN.

**Tongue, Ruth L.,** *joint ed.:* BRIGGS, Folktales of England.

**Topping, Coral Wesley.** Canadian Penal Institutions. 1930. SSM. *o.p.*

**Torchiana, Henry Albert Willem van Coenen.** Tropical Holland. Java and Other Islands. An Essay on the Birth, Growth and Development of Popular Government in an Oriental Possession. 1921. 2d ed. 1923. *o.p.*

**Toronto Gospels:** GOODSPEED.

**Torrey, Charles Cutler.** Ezra Studies. 1910. *o.p.*

**Totalitarian War—and After:** SFORZA.

**Toussaint, Auguste.** History of the Indian Ocean. Translated by June Guicharnaud. 1965. 292 p. $6.00ˢ. COBE.

**Toward a Better Cataloging Code:** STROUT.

**Toward Improved Curriculum Theory:** HERRICK.

**Toward the New Spain:** BRANDT.

**Toward Understanding Germany:** LOWIE.

**Tower, William Lawrence.** The Development of the Colors and Color Patterns of Coleoptera, with Observations upon the Development of Color in Other Orders of Insects. Preprint. 1903. *o.p.*

**Tower, William Lawrence:** *see* CASTLE, Heredity and Eugenics.

**Towle, Charlotte.** The Learner in Education for the Professions. As Seen in Education for Social Work. 1954. xxv, 432 p. 24 cm. 54-11216. $8.50ᵗ.

**Towle, Charlotte.** Social Case Records from Psychiatric Clinics. With Discussion Notes. 1941. *o.p.*

**Town and Country Relations:** AMERICAN COUNTRY LIFE ASSOCIATION, Proceedings No. 4.

**Towner, Milton Carsley,** *ed.* Religion in Higher Education. Containing the Principal Papers Read at the Conference of Church Workers, Chicago, Illinois, December 31, 1930—January 2, 1931, with Other Contributions to the Permanent Literature of Higher Education. With introductions by Shailer Mathews and Frederick J. Kelly. 1931. *o.p.*

**Trabue, M. R.** Teaching Language in the Elementary School. Prepared by M. R. Trabue, Chairman of the Society's Committee. 1944. NSSE, 43d Yrbk., Part II. ix, 257 p. 24 cm. Cloth. E44-72. $2.75ᵗ. Paper. $2.00ᵗ.

**Trade Disputes Disqualification Clause under the British Unemployment Insurance Acts:** SWANISH.

**Trade and Politics in Ancient Greece:** HASEBROEK.

**Tradition and Enlightenment in Tuscan Academies:** COCHRANE.

**Tragedies of Seneca:** MILLER.

**Training of College Teachers:** GRAY.

**Training for Recreation under the W.P.A.:** CLINE.

**Transactions of the Illinois Society for Child-Study, 1894–1901.** Quarterly. Vols. III–IV. 1898–99.

**Transition to an Objective Standard of Social Control:** BERNARD.

**Translations of Text Selections and Exercises in Newspaper Chinese:** CREEL.

**Translators to the Reader: Preface to the King James Version of 1611:** GOODSPEED.

**Transmethylation and Methionine Biosynthesis:** SCHLENK.

**Treasury of Persepolis:** SCHMIDT.

**Treatise on Light:** HUYGENS.

**Treatise on Ores and Assaying:** ERCKER.

**Treatise on Projective Differential Geometry:** LANE.

**Treatise on Weights and Measures:** EPIPHANIUS.

**Treatment of Clay Tablets in the Field:** DELOUGAZ.

**Treatment of the Misdemeanant in Indiana:** WILSON.

**Treatment of Nature in English Poetry:** REYNOLDS.

**Treatment of Nature in German Literature:** BATT.

**Treatment of Nature in the Works of Nikolaus Lenau:** KLENZE.

**Treatment of the Problem of Capital and Labor:** BLACHLY.

**Tree-Ring Analysis and Dating in the Mississippi Drainage:** HAWLEY.

**Trehan, S. K.:** *see* CHANDRASEKHAR, Plasma Physics.

**Trend in Higher Education:** HARPER.

**Trend of Our Civilization:** AMERICAN SOCIOLOGICAL SOCIETY, Vol. XIX.

**Trend of Population:** AMERICAN SOCIOLOGICAL SOCIETY, Vol. XVIII.

**Trends in Consumer Credit Legislation:** CURRAN.

**Trends in Industrial Location in the Chicago Region:** MITCHELL.

**Trends in Location of the Women's Clothing Industry:** MAGEE.

**Trends of Population in the Region of Chicago:** JETER.

**Trends in University Growth:** REEVES.

**Trever, Albert Augustus.** A History of Greek Economic Thought. 1916. Paper. *o.p.*

**Trexler, Harrison Anthony.** The Confederate Ironclad "Virginia" ("Merrimac"). 1938.

**Trial of Jesus:** RADIN.

**Triggs, Oscar Lovell,** *ed.:* LYDGATE, Assembly of Gods.

**Trigonometry with Tables:** BRESLICH.

**Trilling, Mabel B.** Home Economics in American Schools. By Mabel B. Trilling and others. 1920. SEM 14. *o.p.*

**Tristi amori (Giacosa):** ALTROCCHI.

**Triumphs:** PETRARCH.

**Trois mousquetaires (Dumas):** STRUBLE.

**Tropical Holland:** TORCHIANA.

**Trotter, R. C.,** *joint ed.:* HADEN, Science française. Readings in General Science.

**Troyanovsky, Alexander Antonovīch:** *see* HARPER, Soviet Union and World-Problems.

**Truancy and Non-attendance:** ABBOTT.

**True Nature of Value:** SPRAGUE.

**Truman, David Bicknell.** Administrative Decentralization. A Study of the Chicago Field Offices of the United States Department of Agriculture. 1940. *o.p.*

**Trump, J. Lloyd.** High-School Extracurricular Activities: Their Management in the Public High Schools of the North Central Association. 1944. *o.p.*

**Truth about the Bible:** GORDON.

**Truth and Denotation:** MARTIN.

**Tryon, Rolla Milton.** Household Manufactures in the United States, 1640–1860. A Study in Industrial History. 1917. *o.p.*

**Tryon, Warren S.,** *ed.* A Mirror for Americans. Life and Manners in the United States, 1790–1870, as Recorded by American Travelers. 3 vols. *Vol. I:* Life in the East. *Vol. II:* The Cotton Kingdom. *Vol. III:* The Frontier Moves West. 1952. *o.p.*

**Tryon, Warren S.** *ed.* My Native Land. Life in America, 1790–1870. A shortened version of *A Mirror for Americans.* 1961. 21 cm. Paper. P61. $1.95.

**Ts'ai T'ing-kan,** *trans.* Chinese Poems in English Rhyme. 1932. IPR. *o.p.*

**Tsien, T. H.** Written on Bamboo and Silk. The Beginnings of Chinese Books and Inscriptions. 1962. xiv, 234 p. Illus. 25 cm. 61-11897. LS. $7.50ˢ.

**Tsou, Tang.** America's Failure in China, 1941–50. 1963. xviii, 614 p. 24 cm. 63-13072. $12.50.

**Tsu, Yu Yue:** *see* HAYDON, Modern Trends in World-Religions.

**Tsurumi, Yusuke:** *see* WRIGHT, Interpretations of American Foreign Policy.

**Tuberculosis and Genius:** MOORMAN.

**Tuber-like Rootlets of Cycas revoluta:** LIFE.

**Tudor Puritanism:** KNAPPEN.

**Tufts, James Hayden.** The Individual and His Relation to Society as Reflected in British Ethics. PHI.

*Part I:* The Individual in Relation to Law and Institutions. By James H. Tufts and Helen B. Thompson. 1898. *o.p.*
*Part II:* The Individual in Social and Economic Relations. 1904. *o.p.*

**Tufts, James Hayden.** On the Genesis of the Aesthetic Categories. 1902. *o.p.*

**Tugwell, Rexford Guy.** A Chronicle of Jeopardy, 1945–55. 1955. *o.p.*

**Tulchin, Simon H.** Intelligence and Crime. A Study of Penitentiary and Reformatory Offenders. 1939. BR. *o.p.*

**Tunison, Joseph Salathiel.** Dramatic Traditions of the Dark Ages. 1907. *o.p.*

**Tupper, Frederick:** *see* BRYAN, Sources and Analogues of Chaucer's *Canterbury Tales.*

**Tūqān, Ibrāhīm,** *joint ed.:* MUḤAMMAD IBN DĀWŪD AL-IṢFAHĀNĪ, Kitāb al-Zahrah.

**Turabian, Kate L.** A Manual for the Writers of Term Papers, Theses, and Dissertations. 1937. Rev. ed. 1955. viii, 110 p. 21 cm. 55-5151. Cloth. $2.50ˢ. Paper. P146. $1.00.

**Turabian, Kate L.** Student's Guide for Writing College Papers. 1963. vii, 172 p. 21 cm. 63-19753. Cloth. $3.75ˢ. Paper. P134. $1.25.

**Turbulent Transfer in the Lower Atmosphere:** PRIESTLEY.

**Turkish Transformation:** ALLEN.

**Turner, Albert Morton.** The Making of *The Cloister and the Hearth.* 1938. *o.p.*

**Turner, Dorothea.** Handbook of Diet Therapy. 1946. 4th ed. rev. 1965. xv, 260 p. Illus. 24 cm. 65-24984. BM. $5.50ᵗ.

**Turner, Lorenzo Dow.** Africanisms in the Gullah Dialect. 1949. *o.p.*

**Tuve, Rosemond.** Elizabethan and Metaphysical Imagery. Renaissance Poetic and Twentieth-Century Critics. 1947. xiv, 442 p. 47-4244. Cloth. 24 cm. $7.50ˢ. Paper. P68. 21 cm. $2.25.

"It is not often that one encounters a work of the depth and scope of . . . *Elizabethan and Metaphysical Imagery.* The author has performed an enormous labor of scholarship, and to this she has added some critical insights which must be taken into account from now on by those who judge modern poetry."—Richard M. Weaver, in *Poetry.*

**Tuve, Rosemond.** A Reading of George Herbert. 1952. 215 p. 22 cm. $6.00. COBE.

**TVA:** CLAPP.

**Twins. A Study of Heredity and Environment:** NEWMAN.

**Two Dramatizations from Vergil:** MILLER.

**Two Queens of Baghdad:** ABBOTT.

**Two Solar Families:** CHAMBERLIN.

**Two Twice-told Tales:** MEYER.

**Tyler, Fred T.** Individualizing Instruction. Prepared by Fred T. Tyler, Chairman of the Society's Committee. 1962. NSSE, 61st Yrbk., Part I. xiv, 338, xi p. 24 cm. 62-2192. $4.50ᵗ.

**Tyler, Ralph W.** American Education in the Postwar Period. Curriculum Reconstruction. Prepared by Ralph W. Tyler, Chairman of the Society's Committee. 1945. NSSE, 44th Yrbk., Part I. x, 292 p. 24 cm. E46-52. Cloth. $3.00ᵗ. Paper. $2.25ᵗ.

**Tyler, Ralph W.** Graduate Study in Education. Prepared by Ralph W. Tyler, Chairman of the Society's Board of Directors. 1951. NSSE, 50th Yrbk., Part I. xix, 369 p. 24 cm. 51-6258. Cloth. $4.50ᵗ. Paper. $3.75.ᵗ

**Tyler, Ralph W.** Social Forces Influencing American Education. Prepared by Ralph W. Tyler, Chairman of the Society's Committee. 1961. NSSE, 60th Yrbk., Part II. x, 252, xcvi p. 24 cm. 61-1759. Cloth. $4.50ᵗ.

**Tyler, Ralph W.,** *joint author:* EELLS, Intelligence and Cultural Differences.

**Tyler, Ralph W.,** *joint author:* WAPLES, What People Want To Read About.

**Tyler, Ralph W.,** *joint ed.:* HERRICK, Toward Improved Curriculum Theory.

**Tyler, Ralph W.:** *see* EDWARDS, Education in a Democracy.

**Tylor, Edward B.** Researches into the Early History of Mankind and the Development of Civilization. Abridged and with an Introduction by Paul Bohannan. 1964. xvii, 295 p. 21 cm. 64-23416. CA. Cloth. $6.95ˢ. Paper. P175. $2.95.

**Types of Aesthetic Judgment:** BARTLETT.

**Types of Reading Ability:** TRUMAN.

**Types of Religious Experience:** WACH.

**Typographic Book 1450–1935:** MORISON.

**Tyrant's War:** HERMENS.

**Tyson, Levering.** Debate. Resolved: That the United States Should Adopt the Essential Features of the British System of Radio Control and Operation. Affirmative: E. C. Buehler, C. C. Cunningham, H. L. Ewband. Negative: Harry W. Chase, C. H. Judd, T. V. Smith. Chairman, Levering Tyson. 1933. NACRE. *o.p.*

**Tyson, Levering.** The Future of Radio and Educational Broadcasting. By Levering Tyson and Judith Waller. 1934. NACRE. *o.p.*

**Tyson, Levering.** Retrospect and Forecast in Radio Education. By Levering Tyson and William J. Donovan. 1936. NACRE. *o.p.*

**Tyson, Levering.** What To Read about Radio. 1933. NACRE. *o.p.*

**Tyson, Levering,** *ed.* EDUCATION ON THE AIR. . . . AND RADIO AND EDUCATION, 1935.

**Tyson, Levering,** *ed.* RADIO AND EDUCATION.


**Udden, Johan August.** Erosion, Transportation, and Sedimentation Performed by the Atmosphere. 1894. *o.p.*

**Übersichtstabellen zur Lautentsprechungen:** WOOD.

**Ugo Benzi:** LOCKWOOD.

**Uhl, W. L.** Music Education. Prepared by W. L. Uhl, Chairman of the Society's Committee. 1936. NSSE, 35th Yrbk., Part II. *o.p.*

**Ukrainians in the United States:** HALICH.

**Ultraviolet Light and Vitamin D in Nutrition:** BLUNT.

**Underhill, Ruth Murray.** Red Man's America. A History of Indians in the United States. Illustrations by Marianne Stoller. 1953. x, 400 p. Illus. 26 cm. 53-10535. $7.50ᵗ.

"Underhill's excellent compendium may not yet be the epitomized treatment of the whole broad subject of Indian life which has been so greatly needed, but it comes nearer to that accomplishment than any single volume yet published. . . . a massive job of condensation. The book should serve the purposes of general reference for years to come."—D'Arcy McNickle in the *American Anthropologist.*

**Underhill, Ruth Murray.** Red Man's Religion. Beliefs and Practices of the Indians North of Mexico. 1965. x, 301 p. 25 cm. 65-24985. Illus. $7.95.

**Understanding Picasso:** PICASSO.

**Uneasy Case for Progressive Taxation:** BLUM.

**Unemployment as a World-Problem:** WRIGHT.

**Unemployment Insurance:** GILSON.

**Unfair Competition:** STEVENS.

**Unfolding of Personality:** MARK.

**Union Internationale de Radio-Diffusion.** Broadcasting Abroad. Compiled by the Union Internationale de Radio-Diffusion, Geneva, Switzerland, A. R. Burrows, Secretary General. With a Supplemental Memorandum on Radio Broadcasting in the Far East and Southern Pacific, by the American Council, Institute of Pacific Relations. 1932. 2d ed. 1934. NACRE. *o.p.*

**Unionism and Relative Wages in the United States:** LEWIS.

**United States and the Caribbean:** JONES.

**United States and Civilization:** NEF.

**United States Employment Service:** KELLOGG.

**United States Government as Publisher:** MERRITT.

**United States and Great Britain:** FISH.

**United States and Neutrality:** WRIGHT.

**Unity of Plato's Thought:** SHOREY.

**Unity and Variety in Muslim Civilization:** GRUNEBAUM.

**Universal Element in the Psalter:** SMITH.

**University Chapel:** GOODSPEED.

**University of Chicago.** Abstracts of Theses. Humanistic Series, 9 volumes. Science Series, 9 volumes. *o.p.*

As the abstract plan has been discontinued, Volume IX is the last volume in each series.

**University of Chicago.** *Alumni Council.* Alumni Directory, 1861–1910. 1910. *o.p.* 1861–1913. 1913. *o.p.* 1919. 1920. *o.p.*

**University of Chicago.** *Committee on Development.* Great University Memorials. With a Reference to the Plans for the Development of the University of Chicago. 1925. *o.p.*

**University of Chicago.** *Department of Anthropology.* Bulletins. (ANB.) 1894–1921. *o.p.* Bulletin: I. STARR, Notes on Mexican Archaeology. II. STARR, Little Pottery Objects. III. STARR, Mapa de Cuauhtlantzinco. IV. STARR, Recent Mexican Study of the Native Languages of Mexico. V. STARR, Bibliography of Congo Languages. VI. PALACIOS, Stone of the Sun.

**University of Chicago.** *Department of English.* The Manly Anniversary Studies in Language and Literature. 1923. *o.p.*

**University of Chicago.** *Department of History.* Study Manual for European History. 1920. *o.p.*

**University of Chicago.** *Department of Political Economy.* Bibliography of Economics for 1909. A Cumulation of Bibliography Appearing in the *Journal of Political Economy* from February, 1909, to January, 1910, inclusive. 1910. *o.p.*

**University of Chicago:** FLINT.

**University of Chicago.** *Local Community Research Committee.* Social Base Map of Chicago Showing Industrial Areas, Parks, Transportation, and Language Groups. 1926. SOC. *o.p.*

**University of Chicago.** *Local Community Research Committee: see* FRYXELL, Physiography of the Chicago Region.

**University of Chicago.** An Official Guide: O'HARA.

**University of Chicago.** An Official Guide: ROBERTSON.

**University of Chicago.** Oriental Institute: *see* ORIENTAL INSTITUTE.

**University of Chicago.** *School of Commerce and Administration: see* Institute of American Meat Packers.

**University of Chicago.** *The Social Science Survey Committee.* Rotary? A University Group Looks at the Rotary Club of Chicago. 1934. *o.p.*

**University of Chicago.** *University High School; Department of English.* Standard Usage in English. Standards of Capitalization, Punctuation, Handwriting, Spelling, and Sentence Structure, required of all classes in the University High School. 1921. 3d ed. 1941. Original edition edited by Rollo Lyman; 3d ed. by Harold Anderson. *o.p.*

**University of Chicago Biographical Sketches:** GOODSPEED.

**University of Chicago Chapel:** GOODSPEED.

**University of Chicago Conference on Business Education.** Proceedings of the University of Chicago Conference on Business Education.

SHIELDS, Business Education and Money Management, 1935.

SHIELDS, Business Education for Everybody, 1936.

BREWINGTON, Business as a Social Institution, 1938.

DUDDY, Business Education in School Situations, 1939.

KORNHAUSER, Business Education for What? 1940.

**University of Chicago Contributions to Philosophy (PHI).**

Succeeded by PHILOSOPHIC STUDIES.

VOL.

I. No. 1. Studies from the Psychological Laboratory.

No. 2. HEIDEL, The Necessary and Contingent in the Aristotelian System.

No. 3. DEWEY, Significance of the Problem of Knowledge.

No. 4. MacLENNAN, Impersonal Judgment.

No. 5. TUFTS, Individual and His Relation to Society, Part I.

No. 6. TUFTS, Individual and His Relation to Society, Part II.

II. No. 1. ROGERS, Parallelism of Mind and Body.

No. 2. Studies from the Psychological Laboratory.

No. 3. TANNER, Association of Ideas.

No. 4. GORE, Imagination in Spinoza and Hume.

III. No. 1. MOORE, Functional versus the Representational Theories of Knowledge.

No. 2. Studies from the Psychological Laboratory.

IV. No. 1. THOMPSON, Psychological Norms.

No. 2. Studies from the Psychological Laboratory: WATSON, Animal Education.

**University of Chicago Historical and Linguistic Studies in Literature Related to the New Testament (HLL).**

*First Series: Texts:*

Vol. I. Ethiopic Martyrdoms. By Edgar J. Goodspeed. 1931.

The Texts here assembled were first published in the *American Journal of Semitic Languages and Literatures,* Vols. XVII, XIX–XXI, 1901–1904.

The following Parts were also published separately:

Part 1. GOODSPEED, Book of Thekla.

2. GOODSPEED, Martyrdom of Cyprian and Justa.

3. GOODSPEED, Epistle of Pelagia.

4. GOODSPEED, Story of Eugenia and Philip.

Vol. II. Greek Gospel Texts in America. By Edgar J. Goodspeed. 1931.

The following Parts were also published separately:

Part 1. GOODSPEED, The Newberry Gospels.

2. GOODSPEED, Toronto Gospels.

3. GOODSPEED, Freer Gospels.

4. GOODSPEED, Bixby Gospels.

5. GOODSPEED, Haskell Gospels.

6. GOODSPEED, Harvard Gospels.

*Second Series: Linguistic and Exegetical Studies:*

Vol. I. 1909. Parts also published separately:

Part 1. HOBEN, Virgin Birth.

2. HERRICK, Kingdom of God.

3. HOBSON, Diatessaron of Tatian.

4. ALLEN, Infinitive in Polybius.

5. THOMPSON, Μετανοέω and Μεταμέλει in Greek Literature.

6. NORTON, Lexicographical and Historical study of Διαθήκη.

7. LEWIS, Irenaeus Testimony.

8. STAUDT, Idea of the Resurrection.

Vol. II. 1909. Parts also published separately:

Part 1. GRANBERY, Outline of New Testament Christology.

2. WICKES, Sources of Luke's Perean Section.

3. FERGUSON, Legal Terms Common to the Macedonian Inscriptions.

4. MacNEILL, Christology of the Epistle to the Hebrews.

5. ROBINSON, Syntax of the Participle in the Apostolic Fathers.

6. PARSONS, Historical Examination of Some Non-Markan Elements in Luke.

Vol. III. BURTON, Spirit, Soul, and Flesh,

Vol. IV. Published only in parts.

Part 1. SLATEN, Qualitative Nouns in the Pauline Epistles.

2. PERRY, Sources of Luke's Passion-Narrative.

Vol. V. BURTON, New Testament Word Studies.

**University of Chicago Home Economics Series (HE):**

BLUNT, Ultraviolet Light and Vitamin D in Nutrition.

BOWMAN, Problems in Home Economics Teaching.

CLARK, Art in Home Economics.

HALBERT, Better Homes Manual.

HALLIDAY, How To Buy Beef.

HALLIDAY, Hows and Whys of Cooking.

ROBERTS, Nutrition Work with Children.

**University of Chicago Manuscript of the Genealogia deorum gentilium:** WILKINS.

**University of Chicago Mathematical Series (UCMS):**

BRESLICH, Correlated Mathematics.

BRESLICH, First Year Mathematics.

BRESLICH, Logarithmic and Trigonometric Tables and Mathematical Formulas.

BRESLICH, Mathematical Achievement Tests.

BRESLICH, Second Year Mathematics.

BRESLICH, Senior Mathematics. Book I.

BRESLICH, Senior Mathematics. Book II.

BRESLICH, Senior Mathematics. Book III.

BRESLICH, Slide Rule.

BRESLICH, Solid Geometry.

BRESLICH, Third Year Mathematics.

BRESLICH, Trigonometry.

MYERS, Second-Year Mathematics.

MYERS, Teacher's Manual for First-Year Mathematics.

**University of Chicago Monographs in Medicine (CMM).**

Name of editorial committee changed in 1941 to *Committee on Publications in Biology and Medicine*. The designation BM was assigned to all volumes issued after 1941.

BAILEY, Intracranial Tumors.

HOLCK, Diet.

HORRALL, Bile.

JACOBSON, Progressive Relaxation.

KLEITMAN, Sleep and Wakefulness.

LEE, Childbirth.

REED, Vitamin D.

SCHINDLER, Gastroscopy.

VAN DYKE, Physiology and Pharmacology of the Pituitary Body.

WALKER, The Primate Thalamus.

**University of Chicago Nature-Study Series (NS):**

DOWNING, A Field and Laboratory Guide in Biological Nature-Study.

DOWNING, A Field and Laboratory Guide in Physical Nature-Study.

DOWNING, A Naturalist in the Great Lakes Region.

DOWNING. Our Living World.

DOWNING, Our Physical World.

**University of Chicago Plays, Skits, and Lyrics:** O'HARA.

**University of Chicago Poems:** LEWIS.

**University of Chicago Press.** A Manual of Style. Containing Typographical and Other Rules for Authors, Printers, and Publishers Recommended by the University of Chicago Press, Together with Specimens of Type. 1906. 11th ed. 1949. x, 522 p. 21 cm. 6-40582. $6.00.

"Differences of opinion concerning capitalization, punctuation, italics, footnotes, indexing, and scores of other points have been settled for 30 years by the authority of this work. . . ."— *Printing Industry*.

". . . beautifully illustrates the principles and practices upon which it places its authoritative stamp of approval . . . a fine example of modern bookmaking. . . . The world of scholarship is under great obligations to the staff . . . and to the Press itself for making available so useful and authoritative a book. . . ."—Henry Grattan Doyle, in *Modern Language Journal*.

**University of Chicago Publications in Anthropology (AN):**

BARTON, Kalingas.

BENNETT, Archaeological Explorations in Jo Daviess County, Illinois.

BENNETT, Tarahumara.

BOWERS, Mandan Social and Ceremonial Organization.

COLE, Kincaid.

COLE, Rediscovering Illinois.

EGGAN, Social Anthropology of North American Tribes.

EGGAN, Social Organization of the Western Pueblos.

EKVALL, Cultural Relations on the Kansu-Tibetan Border.

EMBREE, Suye Mura: A Japanese Village.

GIFFEN, Roles of Men and Women in Eskimo Culture.

GOODWIN, The Social Organization of the Western Apache.

HAILE, Origin Legend of the Navaho Flintway.

HAWLEY, Tree-Ring Analysis.

HOIJER, Chiricahua and Mascalero Apache Texts.

KROGMAN, Bibliography of Human Morphology.

LA FARGE, Santa Eulalia.

LI, Mattole, An Athabaskan language.

MINER, St. Denis.

OPLER, An Apache Life-Way.
PARSONS, Mitla.
PARSONS, Peguche.
PARSONS, Pueblo Indian Religion.
REDFIELD, Folk Culture of Yucatan.
REDFIELD, Tepoztlán.
REDFIELD, Village That Chose Progress.
SPICER, Pascua, A Yaqui Village in Arizona.
SPIER, Yuman Tribes of the Gila River.
WISDOM, Chorti Indians of Guatemala.

## University of Chicago Publications in Religious Education.

CONSTRUCTIVE STUDIES (CS).
HANDBOOKS IN ETHICS AND RELIGION (HER).
PRINCIPLES AND METHODS OF RELIGIOUS EDUCATION (PM).

## University of Chicago Round Table. Balancing the Budget. Federal Fiscal Policy during Depression. 1933. PPP 1. *o.p.*

## University of Chicago Round Table. The Economic Meaning of the Townsend Plan. 1936. PPP 20. *o.p.*

## University of Chicago Science Series (SCI):

ALBERT, Modern Higher Algebra.
BLICHFELDT, Finite Collineation Groups.
CHAMBERLAIN, Living Cycads.
CHAMBERLIN, Origin of the Earth.
CHAMBERLIN, Two Solar Families.
CHILD, Individuality in Organisms.
CHILD, Origin and Development of the Nervous System.
COULTER, Evolution of Sex in Plants.
DICKSON, Algebras and Their Arithmetics.
DICKSON, Studies in the Theory of Numbers.
HEISENBERG, Physical Principles of the Quantum Theory.
JONES, Selective Fertilization.
JORDAN, Food Poisoning and Food-borne Infection.
LANE, Projective Differential Geometry.
LILLIE, Problems of Fertilization.
LILLIE, Protoplasmic Action.
MICHELSON, Studies in Optics.
MILLIKAN, Electrons (+ and —).
MOODIE, Antiquity of Disease.
NEWMAN, Biology of Twins.
NEWMAN, Physiology of Twinning.
RASHEVSKY, Advances and Applications of Mathematical Biology.
TASHIBO, A Chemical Sign of Life.
THURSTONE, Vectors of Mind.
WEATHERWAX, Story of the Maize Plant.

## University of Chicago Sermons: SOARES.

## University of Chicago Settlement. A Study of Chicago's Stockyard Community. An Investigation Carried On under the Direction of the Board of the University of Chicago Settlement. 1912–1914. (CSC). *o.p.* I. TALBERT, Opportunities in School and Industry. II. MONTGOMERY, American Girl. III. KENNEDY, Wages and Family Budgets.

## University of Chicago Social Service Monographs (SSM). Published in Conjunction with the *Social Service Review*.

ABBOTT, Tenements of Chicago.
ADDITION, City Planning for Girls.
BEELEY, Bail System in Chicago.
BOAN, History of Poor Relief Legislation and Administration in Missouri.
BRADWAY, Law and Social Work.
BRECKINRIDGE, Illinois Poor Law.
BRECKINRIDGE, Marriage and the Civic Rights of Women.
BRISTOL, Handbook for Field Work Students.
BRISTOL, Handbook on Social Case Recording.
BROWN, A History of Public Assistance in Chicago.
BROWNING, Development of Poor Relief Legislation in Kansas.
BRUCE, Michigan Poor Law.
CREECH, Three Centuries of Poor Law Administration . . . Rhode Island.
DOUGLAS, Standards of Unemployment Insurance.
FRASER, Licensing of Boarding Homes.
FRIEDLANDER, Child Welfare in Germany.
GARDINER, Convalescent Care in Great Britain.
GARTLAND, Psychiatric Social Service in a Children's Hospital.
GLICK, Illinois Emergency Relief Commission.
HATHWAY, Migratory Worker.
HATHWAY, Young Cripple and His Job.
HUGHES, Social Service Exchange in Chicago.
JAFFARY, The Mentally Ill in Illinois.
JANSON, Background of Swedish Immigration.
JERNEGAN, Laboring and Dependent Classes in Colonial America.
JOHNSON, Public Policy and Private Charities.
JOHNSON, Relief and Health Problems of a Selected Group of Non-family Men.
KENNEDY, Ohio Poor Law.
KIMBLE, Social Work with Travelers.
KLEIN, Work Accidents to Minors.
KRUGHOFF, Salaries and Professional Qualifications of Social Workers in Chicago, 1935.
LADEWICK, Scholarships for Children of Working Age.
MA, One Hundred Years of Public Services for Children.
MACDONALD, Federal Grants for Vocational Rehabilitation.

McKELVEY, American Prisons.
McMILLEN, Measurement in Social Work.
Medical Social Case Records.
MERIAM, Stepfather in the Family.
MILCHRIST, State Administration of Child Welfare in Illinois.
MILES, Federal Aid and Public Assistance in Illinois.
NIMS, Illinois Adoption Law.
PUTTEE, Illegitimate Child in Illinois.
RILEY, Working Manual for Juvenile Court Officers.
RUBINOW, Care of the Aged.
SCHNEIDER, History of Public Welfare in New York State. Vols. I–II.
SHAFFER, Indiana Poor Law.
STRONG, Public Welfare Administration in Canada.
SUNLEY, Kentucky Poor Law.
TAYLOR, Law of Guardian and Ward.
TOPPING, Canadian Penal Institutions.
VEEDER, Development of the Montana Poor Law.
WARNER, Juvenile Detention in the United States.
WEBB, History of Contagious Disease Care in Chicago.
WHITE, Administering Unemployment Compensation.
WILSON, Treatment of the Misdemeanant in Indiana.
WISNER, Public Welfare Administration in Louisiana.

## University of Chicago Social Service Series (SSS):

ABBOTT, Child and the State. Two volumes.
ABBOTT, Historical Aspects of the Immigration Problem.
ABBOTT, Immigration.
ABBOTT, Public Assistance.
ABBOTT, Some American Pioneers in Social Welfare.
BRECKINRIDGE, Family and the State.
BRECKINRIDGE, Family Welfare Work in a Metropolitan Community.
BRECKINRIDGE, Public Welfare Administration in the United States.
BRECKINRIDGE, Social Work and the Courts.
BROWNING, Rural Public Welfare.
DIXON, Social Case Records.
TOWLE, Social Case Records from Psychiatric Clinics.
WALKER, Child Welfare Case Records.

## University of Chicago Sociological Series (SOC):

ANDERSON, Hobo.
ANDERSON, Men on the Move.
BLUMENTHAL, Small-Town Stuff.
BURGESS, Personality and the Social Group.

BURGESS, Urban Community.
CAVAN, Suicide.
CRESSEY, Taxi-Dance Hall.
DONOVAN, Saleslady.
DURKHEIM, Rules of Sociological Method.
EDWARDS, Natural History of Revolution.
FARIS, Mental Disorders in Urban Areas.
FRAZIER, Negro Family in Chicago.
FRAZIER, Negro Family in the United States.
HILLER, Strike.
HUGHES, News and the Human Interest Story.
KAWABÉ, Press and Politics in Japan.
MARGOLD, Sex Freedom and Social Control.
MOWRER, Domestic Discord.
MOWRER, Family.
MOWRER, Family Disorganization.
PARK, The City.
PARK, Introduction to the Science of Sociology.
RECKLESS, Vice in Chicago.
SUTHERLAND, Professional Thief.
THRASHER, The Gang.
THRASHER, Map of Chicago's Gangland.
UNIVERSITY OF CHICAGO, THE. *Local Community Research Committee*. Social Base Map of Chicago.
WIRTH, Ghetto.
WILDES, Social Currents in Japan.
YOUNG, Pilgrims of Russian-Town.
ZORBAUGH, Gold Coast and the Slum.

## University of Chicago Songs. 1900(?). *o.p.*

## University of Chicago Spanish Dictionary: CASTILLO.

## University of Chicago Studies in Balzac (SB):

DARGAN, Studies in Balzac's Realism.
ROYCE, Balzac Bibliography.
ROYCE, Indexes to *A Balzac Bibliography*.

## University of Chicago Studies in Economics (SE):

CLARK, Adam Smith.
CLARK, Studies in the Economics of Overhead Costs.
FIELD, Essays on Population.
JENSEN, Property Taxation in the United States.
LOGAN, History of Trade-Union Organization in Canada.
MAGEE, Trends in Location of the Women's Clothing Industry.
MONTGOMERY, Industrial Relations in the Chicago Building Trades.
POWELL, History of the United Typothetae.
SCHULTZ, Statistical Laws of Demand and Supply.
VINER, Dumping.
WARNE, Consumers' Co-operative Movement in Illinois.
WOLF, Railroad Labor Board.

**University of Chicago Studies in Library Science** (LS):

ASHEIM, New Directions in Public Library Development.

ASHEIM, Persistent Issues in American Librarianship.

BUTLER, Introduction to Library Science.

BUTLER, Librarians, Scholars, and Booksellers.

BUTLER, Origin of Printing in Europe.

CARNOVSKY, International Aspects of Librarianship.

CARNOVSKY, Medium-sized Public Library.

CONDIT, Pamphlet about Pamphlets.

ENNIS, Seven Questions about the Profession of Librarianship.

FENWICK, New Definitions of School-Library Service.

FUSSLER, Photographic Reproduction for Libraries.

GLEASON, The Southern Negro and the Public Library.

GRAY, What Makes a Book Readable.

HANSON, Comparative Study of Catalogue Rules.

HAYGOOD, Who Uses the Public Library?

JOECKEL, Government of the American Public Library.

JOECKEL, Metropolitan Library in Action.

MERRITT, The United States Government as Publisher.

MILES, Public Administration and the Library.

POSNER, American State Archives.

RANDALL, Principles of College Library Administration.

SCHNELLENBERG, Modern Archives.

SHERA, Bibliographic Organization.

SHERA, Foundations of the Public Library.

SPENCER, Chicago Public Library.

STANFORD, Library Extension Under the WPA.

STROUT, Library Catalogs.

THOMPSON, Medieval Libraries.

TSIEN, Written on Bamboo and Silk.

WAPLES, Investigating Library Problems.

WAPLES, Libraries and Readers.

WAPLES, National Libraries and Foreign Scholarship.

WAPLES, People and Print.

WAPLES, What Reading Does to People.

WILSON, County Library Service.

WILSON, Geography of Reading.

WILSON, Library in General Education.

WINGER, Iron Curtains and Scholarship.

*Proceedings of the Library Institutes at the University of Chicago.*

1936. WILSON, Library Trends.

1937. WILSON, Role of the Library in Adult Education.

1938. JOECKEL, Current Issues in Library Administration.

1939. WILSON, Practice of Book Selection.

1940. RANDALL, The Acquisition and Cataloging of Books.

1941. WAPLES, Print, Radio, and Film in a Democracy.

1942. BUTLER, The Reference Function of the Library.

1943. CARNOVSKY, The Library in the Community.

1944. JOECKEL, Library Extension.

1945. MARTIN, Personnel Administration in Libraries.

**University of Chicago Survey** (UCS).

Published in twelve volumes the major results of an intensive critical investigation of the University of Chicago, directed by Floyd W. Reeves, extending from October 1, 1929, to April, 1933, and embracing forty to fifty separate projects.

   I. REEVES, Trends in University Growth.

  II. REEVES, Organization and Administration of the University.

 III. REEVES, University Faculty.

 IV. REEVES, Instructional Problems in the University.

  V. REEVES, Admission and Retention of University Students.

 VI. REEVES, Alumni of the College.

 VII. RANEY, University Libraries.

VIII. REEVES, University Extension Services.

 IX. REEVES, University Plant Facilities.

  X. REEVES, Some University Student Problems.

 XI. REEVES, Class Size and University Costs.

 XII. BREASTED, Oriental Institute.

**University of Chicago War Papers** (WP):

1. JUDSON, Threat of German World-Politics.
2. SMALL, Americans and the World-Crisis.
3. BRAMHALL, Democracy.
4. McLAUGHLIN, Sixteen Causes of War.
5. MOULTON, War and Industrial Readjustments.
6. READ, England and America.
7. JUDD, Democracy and American Schools.
8. ABBOTT, Democracy and Social Progress.

**University Extension Services:** REEVES.

**University Extension World.** 1893–1895. First three volumes were monthly journals, the last volume issued as a quarterly journal. *o.p.*

**University Faculty:** REEVES.

**University Libraries:** RANEY.

**University Library:** WILSON.

**University Plant Facilities:** REEVES.

**University Record.** 1896–1902 (weekly); 1902–1905 (monthly); 1905–8 (quarterly). Incorporated into The University of Chicago Magazine in 1908. Resumed independent publication as the *University Record* in 1915, discontinued 1933.

**University Student Health Services:** GRISWOLD.

**University of Utopia:** HUTCHINS.

**Unpopular Government:** KALES.

**Unused Resources and Economic Waste:** ROCKEFELLER.

**Upper-Air Trajectories and Weather Forecasting:** FULTZ.

**Urban Community:** BURGESS.

**Urban Frontier:** WADE.

**Urban Redevelopment:** WOODBURY.

**Urist, Marshall R.,** *joint author:* McLEAN, Bone.

**Use of Background in the Interpretation of Educational Issues:** NATIONAL SOCIETY OF COLLEGE TEACHERS OF EDUCATION, Proceedings, No. 25.

**Use of Color in Verse:** PRATT.

**Use of Loan Credit:** VEBLEN.

**Use of Φύσις in Fifth-Century Greek Literature:** BEARDSLEE.

**Use of Radio in Parent Education:** GRUENBERG.

**Use of Repetition in Latin To Secure Emphasis, Intensity, and Distinctness of Impression:** ABBOTT.

**Use of Transportation Facilities in the Chicago Fruit and Vegetable Market:** DUDDY.

**Uses of Bank Funds:** MITCHELL.

**Utilitarianism:** MILL.

**Utilization of Radiosonde Flights:** WULF.

**Utopian Vision of D. H. Lawrence:** GOODHEART.

**Utter, William Thomas.** Vernon Louis Parrington, *in* HUTCHINSON, Marcus W. Jernegan Essays.

**Utterances of Amos:** HARPER.

**Vaillant, Paule,** *joint author:* VAILLANT, Introduction to French Pronunciation.

**Vaillant, René:** Introduction to French Pronunciation and Diction. A manual for the Erpi. . . . Records. *See* MODERN LANGUAGE RECORDS. FRENCH.

**Vaillant, René:** *see* MODERN LANGUAGE RECORDS. FRENCH.

**Valéry, Paul:** *see* GIDE, Self-Portraits.

**Valgren, Victor Nelson.** Farmers' Mutual Fire Insurance in the United States. 1924. MSB. *o.p.*

**Value and Distribution:** DAVENPORT.

**Values:** SILLS.

**Van Alstyne, Dorothy Mabel.** Play Behavior and Choice of Play Materials of Pre-school Children. The Behavior Research Fund Co-operating with the Garden Apartments Nursery Schools and the Winnetka and Franklin Public School Nurseries. 1932. BR. *o.p.*

**Van Biesbroeck, George.** Definitive Orbit of Comet Delavan. 1913 f=1914 V. 1927. YO, V. *o.p.*

**Van Biesbroeck, George.** The Definitive Orbit of Comet Geddes (1932 VI). 1937. YO, VIII. *o.p.*

**Van Biesbroeck, George.** The Definitive Orbit of Comet Morehouse, 1908 III. 1943. YO, VIII. *o.p.*

**Van Biesbroeck, George.** The Definitive Orbits of Comets Van Biesbroeck, 1935 d, and of Barnard-Brooks, 1889 I. 1940. YO, VIII. *o.p.*

**Van Biesbroeck, George.** Measurements of Double Stars. 1927. YO, V. *o.p.*

**Van Biesbroeck, George.** Measurements of Double Stars. 1936. YO, VIII. *o.p.*

**Van Biesbroeck, George.** Measurements of Double Stars. 1954. PS. *o.p.*

**Van Biesbroeck, George.** Parallaxes of Fifty-two Stars. By George Van Biesbroeck and Mrs. Hannah Steele Pettit. 1920. YO, IV. *o.p.*

**Van Biesbroeck, George,** *joint ed.:* BARNARD, Micrometric Measures of Star Clusters.

**Van Biesbroeck, George:** *see* SLOCUM, Stellar Parallaxes.

**Van Buitenen, J. A. B.,** *trans.* Tales of Ancient India. 1959. xi, 260 p. 23 cm. 59-10430. $5.50s.

**Vandiver, Frank E.,** *ed.* The Idea of the South. Pursuit of a Central Theme. With Contributions by Richard B. Harwell, Hugh B. Patterson, Jr., Louis D. Rubin, Jr., George B. Tindall, Frank E. Vandiver, Walter Prescott Webb, and T. Harry Williams. 1964. ix, 82 p. 23 cm. 64-15818. RSS. $3.95.

**Van Dyke, Harry Benjamin.** The Physiology and Pharmacology of the Pituitary Body. *Vol. I.* 1936. *Vol. II.* 1939. CMM. *o.p.*

"It is to be hoped that those who feel tempted to discuss the role of the pituitary in the etiology of diseases and disorders in terms of plausible analogies to our experimental knowledge of the gland will take the trouble to discover from these two volumes what that knowledge really amounts to."—*The Journal of the American Medical Association.*

**Van Hook, Larue.** The Metaphorical Terminology of Greek Rhetoric and Literary Criticism. 1905. *o.p.*

**Van Horne, John.** Il Risorgimento. HCLS.

**Van Liere, Edward J.** Anoxia. Its Effect on the Body. 1942. BM. *o.p.*

**Van Liere, Edward J.** Hypoxia. By Edward J. van Liere, M.D. and J. Clifford Stickney. 1963. x, 381 p. Illus. Index. 25 cm. 63-16722. $8.75s.

**Van Tassel, David D.** Recording America's Past. An Interpretation of the Development of Historical Studies in America, 1607–1884. 1960. xii, 224 p. Index. 24 cm. 60-14404. $6.00s.

**Variable Star Observations:** HALE.

**Varieties of Human Value:** MORRIS.

**Vasconcelos, José.** Aspects of Mexican Civilization. By José Vasconcelos and Manuel Gamio. 1926. HFL. *o.p.*

**Vasconcelos, José:** *see* RIPPY, Mexico.

**Vascular Responses:** ABRAMSON.

**Vatter, William J.** The Fund Theory of Accounting and Its Implications for Financial Reports. 1947. vi, 141 p. 25 cm. A48-8794. Paper. $2.75s.

**Veblen, Thorstein Bunde.** The Use of Loan Credit in Modern Business. 1903. *o.p.*

**Veblen, Thorstein Bunde:** *see* COHN, Science of Finance.

**Vecchio della montagna (Deledda):** FUCILLA.

**Vectors of Mind:** THURSTONE.

**Veeder, Frederic R.** The Development of the Montana Poor Law. With Editor's Preface by Sophonisba P. Breckinridge. 1938. SSM. *o.p.*

**Vegetation of the Chicago Region:** FULLER.

**Veith, Ilza.** Hysteria. The History of a Disease. 1965. xvi, 301 p. Illus. 24 cm. 65-24429. $7.95.

**Velde, Robert W. van de,** *joint author:* HOLT, Strategic Operations and American Foreign Policy.

**Velocity of Chemical Reactions:** LEMON.

**Velocity of Light:** MICHELSON.

**Vence. Immortal Village:** PEATTIE.

**Vermeule, Emily.** Greece in the Bronze Age. 1964. xix, 406 p. 25 cm. 48 plates. 64-23427. $10.00.

**Verner's Law in Gothic:** WOOD.

**Vertebrate Paleontology:** ROMER.

**Vertebrate Story:** ROMER.

**Vertebrate Visual System:** POLYAK.

**Vertebrates from the Permian Bone Bed of Vermilian County, Illinois:** CASE.

**Very, Frank Washington.** Heliographic Positions. 1938. *o.p.*

**Veysey, Laurence R.** The Emergence of the American University. 1965. xiv, 505 p. 24 cm. 65-24427. $10.00s.

**Vice in Chicago:** RECKLESS.

**Victor Lawson:** DENNIS.

**Victorian Novelists:** CECIL.

**Victorian People:** BRIGGS.

**Vieg, John Albert.** The Government of Education in Metropolitan Chicago. 1939. SSCI. *o.p.*

**Vigneron, Pierre Robert.** *Explication de textes* and Its Adaptation to the Teaching of Modern Languages. 1928. *o.p.*

**Vikings of the Pacific:** BUCK.

**Villa Rojas, Alfonso,** *joint author:* REDFIELD, Chan Kom.

**Village India:** MARRIOTT.

**Village Japan:** BEARDSLEY.

**Village That Chose Progress:** REDFIELD.

**Vincent, George Edgar.** The Social Mind and Education. 1897. *o.p.*

**Vincent, Irene Vongehr.** The Sacred Oasis. Caves of the Thousand Buddhas: Tun Huang. Preface by Pearl Buck. 1953. *o.p.*

**Vincent, John B.,** *joint author:* GRAY, Buddhist Cave Paintings at Tun-huang.

**Viner, Jacob.** Dumping. A Problem in International Trade. 1923. MSB. *o.p.*

**Viner, Jacob,** *joint author:* CLARK, Adam Smith.

**Viner, Jacob:** *see* LAVES, Foundations of a More Stable World Order.

**Viner, Jacob:** *see* WRIGHT, Gold and Monetary Stabilization.

**Virgil.** Virgil's Georgics. Translated by Smith Palmer Bovie. 1956. xxx, 111 p. Illus. 20 cm. 56-11264. $3.75ˢ.

**Virgin Birth:** HOBEN.

**Virginia and the French and Indian War:** BAKER-CROTHERS.

**Visual Education:** FREEMAN.

**Visual Perception of Space:** E. L. KOUSSY.

**Visual Perceptual Abilities and Reading Progress:** GOINS.

**Vitamin D:** REED.

**Vitruvius and the Greek Stage:** CAPPS.

**Vivas, Eliseo.** The Moral Life and the Ethical Life. 1950. *o.p.*

**Vizedom, Monika B.,** *joint trans.:* GENNEP, Rites of Passage.

**Vocabulary of Arithmetic:** BUSWELL.

**Vocabulary Drill Book for Graded French Readers (Books 1–5):** BOND.

**Vocational Education:** BARLOW.

**Vocational Education:** KELLER.

**Vocational Guidance and Vocational Education:** EDGERTON.

**Vocational Studies for College Entrance:** HERRICK.

**Voegelin, Carl F.,** *joint ed.:* TAX, Appraisal of Anthropology.

**Voegelin, Eric.** The New Science of Politics. An Introduction. 1952. xiv, 193 p. 23 cm. 52-13531. WFL. $4.50ˢ.

**Vogel, Hermann Carl.** On the Progress Made in the Last Decade in the Determination of Stellar Motions in the Line of Sight *and* Description of the Spectrographs for the Great Refractor at Potsdam. 1900. *o.p.*

**Vogt, Evon Z.** Water Witching U.S.A. By Evon Z. Zogt and Roy Hyman. 1959. xi, 298 p. Illus. 23 cm. 58-11961. $4.95ˢ.

**Voices from Unoccupied Japan:** MACNAIR.

**Volcanoes in Action:** CRONEIS.

**von Bonin, Gerhardt.** The Evolution of the Human Brain. 1963. xiv, 92 p. Index. 23 cm. 63-13062. SLBM. $5.00ˢ.

**Von deutscher Sprache und Dichtung:** HAGBOLDT.

**Votaw, Clyde Weber.** Books Recommended for New Testament Study. Prepared by Clyde W. Votaw and Charles F. Bradley. 1901. 3d ed. 1911. *o.p.*

**Votaw, Clyde Weber.** The Primitive Era of Christianity. As Recorded in the Acts of the Apostles, 30–63 A.D. A Series of Inductive Studies in the English Bible. 1898. *o.p.*

**Voting:** BERELSON.

**Vuelo a México. Lecturas:** CASTILLO.

**Vyssotsky, A. N.,** *see:* PODOBED, Fundamental Astrometry.

**Wach, Joachim.** Sociology of Religion. 1944. ix, 418 p. 21 cm. Paper. P92. $2.45.

"Joachim Wach has done the first major sociology of religion in English. Everyone working in this field will have great appreciation for this outstanding contribution."—SAMUEL C. KINCHELOE, in *The Christian Century*.

**Wach, Joachim.** Types of Religious Experience. Christian and Non-Christian. 1951. xvi, 275 p. 22 cm. A51-9885. $4.50ˢ. COBE.

**Wachsmann, F.** Moving-Field Radiation Therapy. By F. Wachsmann and G. Barth. From *Die Bewegnungsbestrahlung*. Adapted by L. H. Lanzl and J. W. J. Carpender. Translated by Elisabeth Lanzl. 1962. xviii, 268 p. Illus. Index. 25 cm. 62-10994. $10.95ˢ.

**Wade, Louise.** Graham Taylor. Pioneer for Social Justice, 1851–1938. 1964. 268 p. 24 cm. Illus. 64-24976. $7.50ˢ.

**Wade, Richard C.** The Urban Frontier. Pioneer Life in Early Pittsburgh, Cincinnati, Lexington, Louisville, and St. Louis. *Reissue,* 1964. 360 p. 21 cm. 59-9285. Paper. P161. $2.45.

**Wadsworth, Frank Lawton Olcott.** The Modern Spectroscope. XIV. Fixed Arm Concave Grating Spectroscopes. 1895. *o.p.*

**Wadsworth, Frank Lawton Olcott.** The Modern Spectroscope. XV. On the Use and Mounting of the Concave Grating as an Analyzing or Direct Comparison Spectroscope. 1896. *o.p.*

**Wage Rates and Living Costs:** BRODY.

**Wager, Lewis.** The Life and Repentaunce of Marie Magdalene. By Lewis Wager, *fl.* 1566. A Morality Play Reprinted from the Original Edition of 1566. Edited with Introduction, Notes, and Glossarial Index, by Frederic Ives Carpenter. 1904. *o.p.*

**Wages and the Family:** DOUGLAS.

**Wages and Family Budgets:** KENNEDY.

**Wagner, Philip L.,** *ed.* Readings in Cultural Geography. Edited by Philip L. Wagner and Marvin W. Mikesell. 1962. xii, 598 p. 25 cm. 62-9740. $8.50ᵗ.

**Wakano, Masami,** *joint author:* HARRISON, Gravitation Theory and Gravitational Collapse.

**Walgreen Foundation Lectures** (WFL):
ARENDT, Human Condition.
BIDDLE, World's Best Hope.
BOORSTIN, Genius of American Politics.
BUTLER, Books and Libraries in Wartime.
CLAPP, TVA.
CRAVEN, Democracy in American Life.
DAHL, Preface to Democratic Theory.
DOUGLAS, Economy in the National Government.
EDWARDS, Education in a Democracy.
ELLIS, American Catholicism.
GLAZER, American Judaism.
HALLOWELL, Moral Foundation of Democracy.
HUTCHINS, University of Utopia.
HUTCHINSON, Democracy and National Unity.
HUSZAR, New Perspectives on Peace.
KENNAN, American Diplomacy.
KERWIN, Civil-Military Relationships.
KNOX, Religion and the Present Crisis.
LOEWENSTEIN, Political Power and the Governmental Process.
MARITAIN, Man and the State.
MEAD, Problems of Economic Union.
MERRIAM, What is Democracy?
NEF, The United States and Civilization.
OGBURN, American Society in Wartime.
ORTON, Economic Role of the State.
PERRY, Philosophy of American Democracy.
POTTER, People of Plenty.
PUTTKAMMER, War and the Law.
RANDALL, Foreign Economic Policy for the United States.
SIMON, Philosophy of Democratic Government.
SIMPSON, Puritanism in Old and New England.
STRAUSS, Natural Right and History.
SWISHER, Growth of Constitutional Power in the United States.
TALIAFERRO, Medicine and the War.
VOEGELIN, New Science of Politics.
WHITE, Civil Service in Wartime.
WRIGHT, Social Service in Wartime.

**Walker, Arthur Earl.** The Primate Thalamus. 1938. xxiv, 321 p. Illus. 24 cm. $8.50. CMM.

**Walker, Daniel P.** The Decline of Hell. Discussions of Eternal Torment in the 17th Century. 1964. 288 p. Illus. 64-19849. $5.95ˢ. OBE.

**Walker, Dean Augustus.** The Semitic Negative with Special Reference to the Negative Hebrew. 1896. *o.p.*

**Walker, E. Ronald.** From Economic Theory to Policy. 1943. *o.p.*

**Walker, John.** Lectures on Geology. Edited by Harold W. Scott. 1966. 376 p. 65-24986. $8.50.

**Walker, Robert A.** The Planning Function in Urban Government. 1941. Rev. ed. 1950. SSCI. *o.p.*

**Walker, Wilma,** *ed.* Child Welfare Case Records. 1937. *o.p.*

**Walker, Williston.** Great Men of the Christian Church. 1908. CS. *o.p.*

**Wall between Church and State:** OAKS.

**Wall Scenes from the Mortuary Chapel of the Mayor Paser at Medinet Habu:** SCHOTT.

**Wallace, Anthony F. C.,** *ed.:* MOONEY, Ghost-Dance Religion and the Sioux Outbreak of 1890.

**Wallace, Elizabeth.** The Constitution of the Argentine Republic. The Constitution of the United States of Brazil. With Historical Introduction and Notes. 1894. POL. *o.p.*

**Wallace, Elizabeth:** *see* LEÓN, La perfecta casada.

**Wallace, Sarah Agnes,** *ed.,* The Journal of Benjamin Moran. 1857–65. Edited by Sarah A. Wallace and Frances Elma Gillespie. 2 vols. 1949. *o.p.*

**Waller, Judith,** *joint author:* TYSON, Future of Radio.

**Wallis, Louis.** Egoism. A Study in the Social Premises of Religion. 1905. *o.p.*

**Wallis, Louis.** God and the Social Process. A Study in Hebrew History. 1935. *o.p.*

**Wallis, Louis.** Sociological Study of the Bible. 1912. *o.p.*

**Wallis, Louis.** The Struggle for Justice. 1916. *o.p.*

**Walpole, Hugh.** Foundations of English for Foreign Students. 1946. 2d ed. 1950. vii, 59 p. 25 cm. 51-3299. Paper. $1.25ᵗ.

**Walther, Arnold:** *see* SMITH, Origin and History of Hebrew Law.

**Wang, Charles Kilord Athen.** Attitude toward Birth Control. Forms A and B. Prepared by Charles K. A. Wang and L. L. Thurstone. 1930. TAS 21. *o.p.*

**Wang, Charles Kilord Athen.** Attitude toward Sunday Observance. Forms A and B. Prepared by Charles K. A. Wang and L. L. Thurstone. 1931. TAS 26. *o.p.*

**Wang, Charles Kilord Athen.** Attitude toward the Treatment of Criminals. Forms A and B. Prepared by Charles K. A. Wang and L. L. Thurstone. 1931. TAS 9. *o.p.*

**Wann, T. W.,** *ed.* Behaviorism and Phenomenology. Contrasting Bases for Modern Psychology. With Contributions by Sigmund Koch, R. B. Macleod, B. F. Skinner, Carl R. Rogers, Norman Malcolm, and Michael Scriven. 1964. ix, 190 p. 23 cm. 64-12257. RSS. $5.00ˢ.

**Wanted: Intelligent Local Self-government:** FAIRWEATHER.

**Waples, Douglas.** Classroom Procedure Test for Rating Methods of Teaching in Junior and Senior High Schools. By Douglas Waples and W. C. Reavis. 1926. *o.p.*

**Waples, Douglas.** Investigating Library Problems. 1939. LS. *o.p.*

**Waples, Douglas.** Libraries and Readers in the State of New York. The State's Administration of Public and School Libraries with Reference to the Educational Values of Library Services. By Douglas Waples and Leon Carnovsky. 1939. xiv, 160 p. 22 cm. 39-27568. LS. $3.00ˢ.

**Waples, Douglas.** The Library. By Douglas Waples in Collaboration with Leon Carnovsky, E. W. McDiarmid, Jr., Lloyd W. Rowland, Edward A. Wight. 1936. EHI. *o.p.*

**Waples, Douglas.** National Libraries and Foreign Scholarship. (Notes on Recent Selections in Social Science.) By Douglas Waples and Harold D. Lasswell. 1936. LS. *o.p.*

**Waples, Douglas.** People and Print. Social Aspects of Reading in the Depression. 1937. LS. *o.p.*

**Waples, Douglas.** Problem Exercises for High-School Teachers. A Series of Classroom Problems in English, Social Studies, Mathematics, Science, and General Method. By Douglas Waples, in Collaboration with W. C. Reavis and Others. 1928. *o.p.*

**Waples, Douglas.** What People Want To Read About. A Study of Group Interests and a Survey of Problems in Adult Reading. By Douglas Waples and Ralph W. Tyler. 1931. *o.p.*

**Waples, Douglas.** What Reading Does to People. A Summary of Evidence on the Social Effects of Reading and a Statement of Problems for Research. By Douglas Waples, Bernard Berelson, Franklyn R. Bradshaw. 1940. LS. *o.p.*

**Waples, Douglas,** *ed.* Print, Radio, and Film in a Democracy. Papers presented before the Sixth Library Institute at the University of Chicago, August, 1941. 1942. *o.p.*

**Waples, Douglas,** *joint author:* ANDERSON, Classroom Procedure Test in English Composition.

**Waples, Douglas,** *joint author:* CHARTERS, Check-List of Teachers' Activities.

**Waples, Douglas,** *joint author:* CHARTERS, Commonwealth Teacher-training Study.

**Waples, Douglas,** *joint author:* CUNNINGHAM, Classroom Procedure Test in Natural Science.

**Waples, Douglas,** *joint author:* POLEY, Classroom Procedure Test in English Literature.

**Waples, Douglas,** *joint author:* WILSON, Classroom Procedure Test in History.

**War Debts:** GIDEONSE.

**War and Diplomacy in the French Republic:** SCHUMAN.

**War and Diplomacy in the Japanese Empire:** TAKEUCHI.

**War of 1812:** COLES.

**War as a Factor in Human Progress:** HUTTON.

**War for Independence:** PECKHAM.

**War and Industrial Readjustments:** MOULTON.

**War and the Law:** PUTTKAMMER.

**War and Militarism in Their Sociological Aspects:** AMERICAN SOCIOLOGICAL SOCIETY, Vol. X.

**War and Postwar Responsibilities of American Schools:** REAVIS.

**War and the Private Investor:** STALEY.

**Ward, Dennis.** The Russian Language Today. System and Anomaly. 1965. 297 p. 21 cm. 65-25439. Paper. P191. $2.25. CUSA.

**Ward, F. C.,** *ed.* The Idea and Practice of General Education. An Account of the College of the University of Chicago by present and former Members of the College. 1950. *o.p.*

**Ward, Robert E.,** *joint author:* BEARDSLEY, Village Japan.

**Ward, Robert S.** Asia for the Asiatics? The Technique of Japanese Occupation. 1945. *o.p.*

**Wardle, Addie Grace.** Handwork in Religious Education. 1916. PM. *o.p.*

**Waring, Henry F.** Christianity and Its Bible. A Textbook and for Private Reading. 1907. CS. *o.p.*

**Warkany, Josef,** *joint ed.:* WILSON, Teratology.

**Warne, Colston Estey.** The Consumers' Cooperative Movement in Illinois. 1926. SE. *o.p.*

**Warne, Colston Estey.** The Co-operative Society of America. 1924. MSB. *o.p.*

**Warner, Florence Mary.** Juvenile Detention in the United States. Report of a Field Survey of the National Probation Association. With a Foreword by Charles L. Chute. 1933. SSM. *o.p.*

**Warner, W. Lloyd.** American Life. Dream and Reality. Rev. ed. 1962. xi, 292 p. Index. 21 cm. $6.50s. Paper. P82. $1.95.

**Warner, W. Lloyd:** *see* DAVIS, Deep South.

**Warren, Austin.** Rage for Order. Essays in Criticism. 1948. *o.p.*

**Warren, Charles:** *see* WRIGHT, Neutrality and Collective Security.

**Warriors without Weapons:** MACGREGOR.

**Wars of Religion in France, 1559–1576:** THOMPSON.

**Wartburg, Walther von.** Evolution et structure de la langue française. Par W. v. Wartburg. 1934. [B. G. Teubner, Leipzig.] Deuxième édition. (Published in the United States, 1937.) *o.p.*

**Washburne, Carleton W.** Adapting the Schools to Individual Differences. Prepared by Carleton W. Washburne, Chairman of the Society's Committee. 1925. NSSE, 24th Yrbk., Part II. *o.p.*

**Washburne, Carleton W.** Child Development and the Curriculum. Prepared by the Society's Committee on Maturity. Carleton W. Washburne, Chairman. 1939. NSSE, 38th Yrbk., Part I. x, 442 p. 22 cm. E39-268. Cloth. $3.25$^t$. Paper. $2.50$^t$.

**Washburne, Elihu Benjamin,** *ed.* The Edwards Papers; Being a Portion of the Collection of the Letters, Papers, and Manuscripts of Ninian Edwards. Presented to the Chicago Historical Society, October 16th, 1883, by His Son, Ninian Wirt Edwards. Edited by E. B. Washburne. 1884. *o.p.*
A publication of the Chicago Historical Society.

**Washburne, Elihu Benjamin:** *see* FLOWER, History of the English Settlement in Edwards County, Illinois.

**Washington Allston:** RICHARDSON.

**Washington's Map of Mount Vernon.** Reproduced in Facsimile from the Original in the Huntington Library. With an Introduction by Lawrence Martin. 1937. *o.p.*

**Water Reptiles of the Past and Present:** WILLISTON.

**Water Supply:** HIRSHLEIFER.

**Water Supply Organization in the Chicago Region:** WHITE.

**Water Witching U.S.A.:** VOGT.

**Waterman, John T.** Perspectives in Linguistics. 1963. ix, 105 p. 21 cm. 63-9732. Cloth. $4.00$^s$. Paper. P106. $1.95.

**Waterman, Leroy,** *joint trans.:* SMITH, Old Testament.

**Watson, John B.** Animal Education. 1903. PHI. *o.p.*

**Watson, John B.** Behaviorism. 1924. Rev. ed. 1930. x, 308 p. 21 cm. 58-14680. Cloth. $5.00$^s$. Paper. P23. $1.75.

**Watterson, Ray L.,** *ed.* Endocrines in Development. 1959. xiii, 142 p. 24 cm. 59-8868. DBC. $4.00$^s$.

**Watts, Alan W.** The Legacy of Asia and Western Man. A Study of the Middle Way. 1938. *o.p.*

**Wauchope, Robert.** Lost Tribes and Sunken Continents. Myth and Method in the Study of American Indians. 1962. x, 156 p. Illus. 21 cm. 62-18112. $3.95$^s$.

**Wauchope, Robert.** They Found the Buried Cities. Exploration and Excavation in the American Tropics. 1965. viii, 382 p. Illus. 24 cm. 65-24433. $7.50.

**Waves in the Easterlies:** RIEHL.

**Way of Health Insurance:** SIMONS.

**Wax and Gold:** LEVINE.

**We the People:** MCDONALD.

**Wealth of the Gentry:** SIMPSON.

**Weapon of Silence:** KOOP.

**Wearing, Thomas.** The World-View of the Fourth Gospel. A Genetic Study. 1918. *o.p.*

**Weather and Climate of Chicago:** COX.

**Weather Estimates from Local Aerological Data:** ROSSBY.

**Weather-Map Construction and Forecasting:** JONES.

**Weathersby, William H.** A History of Educational Legislation in Mississippi from 1798 to 1860. 1921. SEM 16. *o.p.*

**Weatherwax, Paul.** The Story of the Maize Plant. 1923. SCI. *o.p.*

**Weaver, Richard M.** Ideas Have Consequences. 1948. vii, 190 p. Paper. P44. $1.50.

**Weaver, Robert Bartow.** Amusements and Sports in American Life. 1939. *o.p.*

**Weaver, Robert Bartow.** Men and Oil. 1938. *o.p.*

**Weaver, Robert Bartow.** The Struggle over Slavery. 1938. *o.p.*

**Weaver, Warren,** *joint author:* MASON, Electromagnetic Field.

**Webb, Constance Bell.** A History of Contagious Disease Care in Chicago before the Great Fire. 1940. SSM. *o.p.*

**Webb, Edward.** Character and Intelligence. An Attempt at an Exact Study of Character. 1915. BJP. *o.p.*

**Webb, Jonathan E.** A Morphological Study of the Flower and Embryo of Spiræa. 1902. HB. *o.p.*

**Weber, Elizabeth Anne.** The Duk-Duks. Primitive and Historic Types of Citizenship. 1929. SMC. *o.p.*

**Weber's Theory of Location of Industries:** FRIEDRICH.

**Webster, Harvey Curtis.** On a Darkling Plain. The Art and Thought of Thomas Hardy. 1947. *o.p.*

**Webster, Ralph Waldo.** A Contribution to the Physical Analysis of the Phenomena of Absorption of Liquids by Animal Tissues. Preprint. 1902. *o.p.*

**Webster, Ralph Waldo.** A Laboratory Manual of Physiological Chemistry. By Ralph W. Webster and Waldemar Koch. 1903. *o.p.*

**Wedel, Mildred Mott:** *see* HAWLEY, Tree-Ring Analysis and Dating.

**Weed Seedlings:** KUMMER.

**Weedon, Vivian,** *joint author:* HEATON, Failing Student.

**Weidenreich, Franz.** Apes, Giants, and Man. 1946. viii, 122 p. 90 figures. 24 cm. A46-3798. BM. $3.75ˢ.

**Weil Institute Lectures (WIL):**
HOWE, Garden and the Wilderness.
MULLER, Religion and Freedom in the Modern World.
WOODHOUSE, Poet and His Faith.

**Weinberg, Alvin M.** The Physical Theory of Neutron Chain Reactors. By Alvin M. Weinberg and Eugene P. Wigner. 1958. xii, 801 p. Illus. 24 cm. 58-8507. $15.00ᵗ.

"The features which most distinguish this work from earlier ones are its thoroughness, its careful consideration of fundamental concepts, and the modern character of the treatment."—HERBERT KOUTS, in *Science.*

"The publication of this book is a milestone in the history of Nuclear Engineering. There is finally available a deep, broad, definitive treatment of the basic physics of nuclear reactors. . . . I am certain that [the] book will be, for many years, the primary reference work. . . ."—IRVING KAPLAN, in *Review of Scientific Instruments.*

"Ce livre d'une grande clarté et d'une grande clarté et d'une grande précision comprend l'ensemble des connaissances de physique requises pour un ingénieur nucléaire. C'est un ouvrage théorique de premier ordre, écrit dans le langage mathématique habituel et accessible à tout étudiant scientifique."—*Journal de Physique et Le Radium.*

"Das Buch von Weinberg und Wigner ist *das* Buch über Reaktortheorie für den Physiker."—H. MAIER-LEIBNITZ, in *Nukleonik.*

"Eine reichliche Ausstattung mit Literaturhinweisen und Tabellen macht das Buch zugleich zu einem Nachschlagewerk."—T. SPRINGER, in *Zeitschrift für Angewandte Physik.*

**Weinberg, Bernard.** The Art of Jean Racine. 1963. xv. 355 p. 22 cm. 63-20900. $7.50ˢ.

**Weinberg, Bernard.** History of Literary Criticism in the Italian Renaissance. 1961. 2 vols. 1,184 p. Index. 24 cm. 60-5470. $20.00ˢ.

". . . will be invaluable to the literary historian, and provide a mine of information for the student of the literary and artistic theory of the Cinquecento. These two massive volumes will doubtless remain, for a long time to come, the fundamental work on the subject."—*Times Literary Supplement.*

"On considérera donc ce grand ouvrage comme le livre de déférence qui nous éclairera à la fois sur les doctrines particulières et sur les mouvements d'ensemble d'une période essentielle pour la théorie littéraire."—R. POUILLIART, in *Les Lettres Romanes.*

**Weinberg, Bernard,** *joint author:* CRANE, Critics and Criticism.

**Weinberg, Bernard,** *joint ed.:* DARGAN, The Evolution of Balzac's *Comédie humaine.*

**Weiner, Myron.** The Politics of Scarcity. Public Pressure and Political Response in India. 1962. xx, 252 p. 24 cm. 62-15047. $5.00ˢ. (Not for sale in South Asia.)

**Weisberger, Bernard A.** The American News-paperman. 1961. xii, 226 p. Illus. 21 cm. 61-8647. CHAC. $4.50ˢ.

**Weiss, Karl Philipp Bernhard.** The Present Status of the Inquiry concerning the Genuineness of the Pauline Epistles. 1897. *o.p.*

**Weiss, Paul.** Genetic Neurology. Problems of the Development, Growth, and Regeneration of the Nervous System and of Its Function. 1950. BM. *o.p.*

**Weiss, Paul,** *co-ordinator:* DEVELOPMENTAL BIOLOGY CONFERENCE (1956) SERIES.

**Weisskopf, Walter A.** The Psychology of Economics. 1955. *o.p.*

**Weissleder, Wolfgang,** *joint trans.:* JENSEN, Myth and Cult.

**Weitz, Morris.** Hamlet and the Philosophy of Literary Criticism. 1964. xvi, 335 p. 24 cm. 64-22245. $6.75ˢ. COBE.

**Weizsäcker, C. F. von.** The History of Nature. Translated by Fred D. Wieck. 1949. vi, 192 p. 21 cm. 49-10907. Paper. P35. $1.25. COBE.

"A short review must fail to do more than hint at the depth and richness of this remarkable book. After all, it ranges over geological aeons, and spaces unimaginable. . . . The scope is nothing less than Nature, past, present and to come."
—ALAN DEVOE, in *The Commonweal.*

**Weizsäcker, C. F. von.** The World View of Physics. Translated by Marjorie Grene. 1952. *o.p.*

**Weller, Stuart.** (1) Atactocrinus, a New Crinoid Genus from the Richmond of Illinois. (2) Description of a Ste Genevieve Limestone Fauna from Monroe County, Illinois. 1916. WM. *o.p.*

**Weller, Stuart.** Francesco di Giorgio, 1439–1501. 1943. *o.p.*

**Weller, Stuart.** The Stokes Collection of Antarctic Fossils. 1903. WM. *o.p.*

**Weller, Stuart,** *joint author:* SMITH, Pro-dromites.

**Wells, Harry Gideon.** Studies in Fat Necrosis. Preprint, 1903. *o.p.*

**Wells, Honoria Marian.** The Phenomenology of Acts of Choice. An Analysis of Volitional Consciousness. 1927. BJP. *o.p.*

**Wells, James M.,** *ed.:* The Scholar Printers. 1964. 64 p. 22 cm. $3.50ˢ.

**Wenger, M. A.,** *joint author:* FREEMAN, The Chicago Mental Health Battery.

**Wergeland, Agnes Mathilde.** History of the Working Classes in France. A Review of Levasseur's *Histoire des classes ouvrières et de l'industrie en France avant 1789.* 1916. *o.p.*

**Wergeland, Agnes Mathilde.** Slavery in Germanic Society during the Middle Ages. 1916. *o.p.*

**Wertime, T. A.** The Coming of the Age of Steel. 1962. xvi, 330 p. 25 cm. Illus. 60-14362. *Not UK or Europe.* $6.95ˢ.

**Wessel, Bessie Bloom.** An Ethnic Survey of Woonsocket, Rhode Island. 1931. *o.p.*

**West, Edith Maddock,** *joint author:* BAPTIST CONGRESS, Annual Sessions. Author, Title, and Subject Index.

**West, Michael.** A Grouped-Frequency French Word List. Based on the *French Word Book* of Vander Beke. By Michael West and Otto F. Bond. 1939. *o.p.*

**West, Michael.** Le petit roi d'Ys. By Georges G.-Toudouze. Adapted and edited by Michael West. HCLS.

**Western Economic Society.** Reciprocity with Canada. The Topic of the First Meeting of the Society Held in Chicago, June 3, 1911. Publications of the Western Economic Society: Proceedings, Vol. I, Part 1. 1911. *o.p.*

**Western Economic Society:** *see* Financial Mobilization for War.

**Western Influences in Modern Japan:** NITOBÉ.

**Weston, John F.** The Economics of Competitive Bidding in the Sale of Securities. 1943. *o.p.*

**Wexler, Harry.** Some Aspects of Dynamic Anticyclogenesis. 1943. DMMR. *o.p.*

**What Are Cosmic Rays?:** AUGER.

**What Becomes of the Consumer's Meat Dollar?** TOBIN.

**What Can a Man Do?:** MAYER.

**What Happens in Literature:** ROSENHEIM.

**What Has Become of Shakespeare's Play "Love's Labour's Won"?:** TOLMAN.

**What Is the Best New Testament?:** COLWELL.

**What Is Christianity?:** CROSS.

**What Is Democracy?:** MERRIAM.

**What Jesus Taught:** SLATEN.

**What Makes a Book Readable:** GRAY.

**What People Want To Read About:** WAPLES.

**What Plato Said:** SHOREY.

**What Reading Does to People:** WAPLES.

**What Shall We Do with Germany?:** SCHMITT.

**What To Read about Radio:** TYSON.

**What's Ahead for Rural America:** *see* AMERICAN COUNTRY LIFE ASSOCIATION, Proceedings. No. 22.

**Wheat Economy:** BRITNELL.

**Wheeler, John Archibald,** *joint author:* HARRISON, Gravitation Theory and Gravitational Collapse.

**Wheelwright, William Bond.** Printing Papers. Foreword by Otto G. Kress. 1936. *o.p.*

**When Democracy Builds:** WRIGHT.

**When Egypt Ruled the East:** STEINDORFF.

**Whetten, Nathan L.** Rural Mexico. Foreword by Manuel Gamio. 1948. xxvi, 671 p. Illus. 26 cm. 48-8023. $12.50ˢ.

**Whipple, Gertrude.** Procedures Used in Selecting School Books. 1936. *o.p.*

**Whipple, Gertrude,** *joint author:* GRAY, Improving Instruction in Reading.

**Whipple, Guy M.** The Education of Gifted Children. Prepared by Guy M. Whipple, Chairman of the Society's Committee. 1924. NSSE, 23d Yrbk., Part I. *o.p.*

**Whipple, Guy M.** The Present Status of Safety Education. Prepared by Guy M. Whipple, Chairman of the Society's Committee. 1926. NSSE, 25th Yrbk., Part I. *o.p.*

**Whipple, Guy M.,** *joint author:* CUBBERLEY, Research within the Field of Education.

**Whirligig of Politics:** HOLLINGSWORTH.

**White, Henry Kirke.** History of the Union Pacific Railway. 1895. EC. *o.p.*

**White, Horace.** The Lincoln and Douglas Debates. 1914. *o.p.*
A publication of the Chicago Historical Society.

**White, Leonard Dupee.** The City Manager. 1927. SSCI. *o.p.*

**White, Leonard Dupee.** Further Contributions to the Prestige Value of Public Employment. 1932. SSCI. *o.p.*

**White, Leonard Dupee.** Government Career Service. 1935. PA. *o.p.*

**White, Leonard Dupee.** The Prestige Value of Public Employment in Chicago. An Experimental Study. 1929. SSCI. *o.p.*

**White, Leonard Dupee.** Whitley Councils in the British Civil Service. A Study in Conciliation and Arbitration. 1933. SSCI. *o.p.*

**White, Leonard Dupee,** ed. The Civil Service in the Modern State. A Collection of Documents Published under the Auspices of the International Congress of the Administrative Sciences. 1930. *o.p.*

**White, Leonard Dupee,** ed. The Civil Service in Wartime. 1945. WFL. *o.p.*

**White, Leonard Dupee,** ed. The Future of Government in the United States. Essays in Honor of Charles E. Merriam. 1942. *o.p.*

**White, Leonard Dupee,** ed. The New Social Science. 1930. SSCI. *o.p.*

**White, Leonard Dupee,** ed. The State of the Social Sciences. 1956. xiv, 504 p. 24 cm. 56-9131. $8.00ˢ.

**White, Leonard Dupee,** *joint author:* GAUS, Frontiers of Public Administration.

**White, Leonard Dupee,** *joint ed.:* SMITH, Chicago: An Experiment in Social Science Research.

**White, Llewellyn.** The American Radio. 1947. *o.p.*

**White, Llewellyn.** Peoples Speaking to Peoples. A Report on International Mass Communications from the Commission on Freedom of the Press. By Llewellyn White and Robert D. Leigh. 1946. *o.p.*

**White, Max Richard.** Water Supply Organization in the Chicago Region. 1934. SSCI. *o.p.*

**White, Reuel Clyde.** Administering Unemployment Compensation. A Comparison and a Critique. 1939. SSM. *o.p.*

**White, Wilbur Wallace.** The Process of Change in the Ottoman Empire. 1937. *o.p.*

**Whitehead, Alfred North.** Nature and Life. 1934. *o.p.*

**Whitehead's Philosophy of Science:** PALTER.

**Whitford, Harry Nichols.** The Genetic Development of the Forests of Northern Michigan. A Study in Physiographic Ecology. 1901. HB. *o.p.*

**Whiting, Bartlett J.:** *see* BRYAN, Sources and Analogues of Chaucer's *Canterbury Tales*.

**Whitley Councils in the British Civil Service:** WHITE.

**Whitman's Manuscripts:** BOWERS.

**Whitmore, Charles Edward,** *joint ed.:* Fred Newton Scott Anniversary Papers.

**Whittlesey, Charles Raymond.** Banking and the New Deal. 1935. PPP 16. *o.p.*

**Whittlesey, Derwent Stainthorpe,** *joint author:* JONES, Introduction to Economic Geography.

**Whittlesey, Derwent Stainthorpe,** *joint author:* Jones and Whittlesey Economic Geography Maps.

**Whittlesey, Derwent Stainthorpe:** *see* COLBY, Geographic Aspects of International Relations.

**Who Uses the Public Library:** HAYGOOD.

**Why Europe Votes:** GOSNELL.

**Why Pupils Fail in Reading:** ROBINSON.

**Whyte, William Foote.** Street Corner Society. The Social Structure of an Italian Slum. Rev. ed. 1955. xxii, 366 p. Illus. 22 cm. 55-5152. Cloth. $6.00ˢ. Paper. $3.75ᵗ.
". . . his analysis has a warmth and interest, in no way detracting from its scientific value, which will appeal to the lay reader as well as to the social scientist. . . . But what gives his study authority and conviction is that he has successfully avoided reducing his data to dreary statistics or to monotonous case histories."—WILLIAM S. LYNCH, in *The Saturday Review*.

**Wick, Warner.** Metaphysics and the New Logic. 1942. *o.p.*

**Wickes, Dean Rockwell.** The Sources of Luke's Perean Section. 1912. HLL. *o.p.*

**Wickes, William Rockwell,** *joint author:* MYERS, First-Year Mathematics.

**Wickes, William Rockwell,** *joint author:* MYERS, Geometric Exercises for Algebraic Solution.

**Wickes, William Rockwell,** *joint author:* MYERS, Second-Year Mathematics.

**Wickes, William Rockwell,** *joint author:* MYERS, Teachers' Manual for First-Year Mathematics.

**Widening Horizons:** WILLIS.

**Wieck, Fred D.,** *trans.:* WEIZSÄCKER, History of Nature.

**Wieman, Henry N.** The Source of Human Good. 1946. *o.p.*

**Wiener, Kurt,** *trans.:* WIENER, General Diagnosis and Treatment of Skin Diseases.

**Wiese, Mildred Janovsky.** Let's Talk It Over. By Mildred J. Wiese, Lyman Bryson, and Wilbur C. Hallenbeck. 1936. AP. *o.p.*

**Wight, Edward Allen:** *see* WAPLES, Library.

**Wight, Edward Allen,** *joint author:* WILSON, County Library Service.

**Wight, William Ward.** Eleazer Williams. Not the Dauphin of France. 1903. *o.p.*
A publication of the Chicago Historical Society.

**Wigner, Eugene P.,** *joint author:* WEINBERG, Physical Theory of Neutron Chain Reactors.

**Wikgren, Allen P.** Hellenistic Greek Texts. By Allen Wikgren. With the collaboration of Ernest Cadman Colwell and Ralph Marcus. 1947. xxvi, 277 p. 24 cm. 47-4029. $5.00ᵗ.

**Wikgren, Allen P.,** *joint author:* PARVIS, New Testament Manuscript Studies.

**Wilcox, Delos Franklin.** Analysis of the Electric Railway Problem. Published by the Author, 1921, New York City. Republished by the University of Chicago Press, 1930. *o.p.*

**Wilcox, Delos Franklin.** Municipal Franchises. A Description of the Terms and Conditions upon Which Private Corporations Enjoy Special Privileges in the Streets of American Cities. 2 vols. 1930.
*Vol. I:* Introductory. Pipe and Wire Franchises. *o.p.*
*Vol. II:* Transportation Franchises. Taxation and Control of Public Utilities. *o.p.*

**Wilcox, Francis E.** A Statistical Study of Credit Unions in New York. 1940. Vol. X. SBA. *o.p.*

**Wilcox, Francis O.,** *joint author:* LAVES, Middle West Looks at War.

**Wild, John.** Plato's Modern Enemies and the Theory of Natural Law. 1953. xii, 259 p. 25 cm. 53-2434. $6.75ˢ.

**Wildes, Harry Emerson.** Social Currents in Japan with Special Reference to the Press. 1927. SOC. *o.p.*

**Wilkins, Eithne,** *joint trans.:* FRÄNGER, Millennium of Hieronymus Bosch.

**Wilkins, Eliza Gregory.** The Delphic Maxims in Literature. 1929. *o.p.*

**Wilkins, Ernest Hatch.** Above Pompeii. 1930. *o.p.*

**Wilkins, Ernest Hatch.** Army French. An Introduction to Spoken French for Men in Military Service. By Ernest H. Wilkins and Algernon Coleman. 1918. 2d ed. 1918. *o.p.*

**Wilkins, Ernest Hatch.** The Changing College. 1927. *o.p.*

**Wilkins, Ernest Hatch.** Dante. Poet and Apostle. 1921. *o.p.*

**Wilkins, Ernest Hatch.** First Italian Book. 1920. HCLS.

**Wilkins, Ernest Hatch.** First Lessons in Spoken French for Doctors and Nurses. By Ernest H. Wilkins, Algernon Coleman, and Ethel Preston. 1917. *o.p.*

**Wilkins, Ernest Hatch.** First Lessons in Spoken French for Men in Military Service. By Ernest H. Wilkins, Algernon Coleman, and Howard R. Huse. 1917. *o.p.*

**Wilkins, Ernest Hatch.** French Verb Blank. 1914. *o.p.*

**Wilkins, Ernest Hatch.** L'Italia. By Ernest Hatch Wilkins and Antonio Marinoni. 1921. HCLS.

**Wilkins, Ernest Hatch.** Life of Petrarch. 1961. vii, 276 p. 61-15939. Cloth. $6.50ˢ. Paper. P148. 21 cm. $1.95.

**Wilkins, Ernest Hatch.** Modern Discussions of the Dates of Petrarch's Prose Letters. 1929. *o.p.*

**Wilkins, Ernest Hatch.** The Pronunciation of the Names of Italian Painters. 1920. *o.p.*

**Wilkins, Ernest Hatch.** A Tentative Chronological List of Petrarch's Prose Letters. 1929. *o.p.*

**Wilkins, Ernest Hatch.** The University of Chicago Manuscript of the *Genealogia deorum gentilium* of Boccaccio. 1927. *o.p.*

**Wilkins, Ernest Hatch,** *ed. and trans.* Petrarch at Vaucluse. 1958. xi, 215 p. 26 cm. 58-5658. $7.50ˢ.

**Wilkins, Ernest Hatch,** *trans.:* PETRARCH, Triumphs.

**Wilkins, Ernest Hatch,** *joint author:* NITZE, French Verb.

**Willett, Herbert Lockwood.** The Message of the Prophets of Israel to the Twentieth Century. 1916. AISL. *o.p.*

**Willett, Herbert Lockwood.** Studies in the First Book of Samuel. For the Use of Classes in Secondary Schools and in the Secondary Division of the Sunday School. 1909. CS. *o.p.*

**Willey, Gordon R.** Method and Theory in American Archaeology. By Gordon R. Willey and Philip Phillips. 1957. ix, 270 p. 21 cm. 57-11215. Paper. P88. $1.50.

"As an organized picture of New World prehistory, this is an impressive accomplishment, which few scholars could have undertaken. As a discussion of present archeological theory, it is a significant half-way house . . . [the authors'] broad approach to developmental interpretation is a firm step toward a modern evolutionary approach."—*American Scientist.*

**William Blake, Poet and Painter:** HAGSTRUM.

**William F. Ogburn on Culture and Social Change:** OGBURN.

**William James and Henri Bergson:** KALLEN.

**William Page:** TAYLOR.

**William Rainey Harper:** GOODSPEED.

**William Rainey Harper Memorial Conference:** MONTGOMERY.

**Williams, Carl O.** Thraldom in Ancient Iceland. 1937. *o.p.*

**Williams, Charles Bray.** The Participle in the Book of Acts. 1909. *o.p.*

**Williams, Florence B.,** *ed.* Madame Thérèse. By Erckmann-Chatrian. Adapted and edited by Florence B. Williams, Grace Cochran, and Helen M. Eddy. HCLS.

**Williams, Florence B.,** *joint author:* EDDY, Basic French. Vol. II.

**Williams, Henry Shaler.** Elements of the Geological Time-Scale. 1893. *o.p.*

**Williams, John Henry:** *see* WRIGHT, Gold and Monetary Stabilization.

**Williams, Philip Francis:** *see* ADAIR, Maternal Care Complications.

**Williamson, Alexander William.** Papers on Etherification and on the Constitution of Salts. By Alexander W. Williamson (1850–1856). 1902. AC. *o.p.*

**Williamson, Edward John.** Grillparzer's Attitude toward Romanticism. 1910. *o.p.*

**Williamson, George.** Milton and Others. 1965. 227 p. 22 cm. 65-26302. $5.50. USA.

**Williamson, George.** The Proper Wit of Poetry. 1962. 136 p. 22 cm. 61-16729. $4.00ˢ. USA.

"Together with [his *Senecan Amble*] it comprises our most sophisticated inquiry into seventeenth-century style."—VICTOR HARRIS, in *Philological Quarterly.*

". . . Mr. Williamson shows again the extent to which he possesses those special gifts so rarely united in the single person of historian, theorist, and perceptive reader of poetry. In a series of six chapters, he follows more or less chronologically the discussion of poetic wit throughout the seventeenth century. . . ."—BERNARD N. SCHILLING, *Criticism.*

**Williamson, George.** The Senecan Amble. A Study in Prose Form from Bacon to Collier. 1951. (O.I.)

**Williamson, George.** Seventeenth Century Contexts. 1961. 291 p. 24 cm. 61-1450. $6.00ˢ. USA.

**Willis, Frederic Arthur.** Widening Horizons. 1934. *o.p.*

**Willis, Henry Parker.** A History of the Latin Monetary Union. A Study of International Monetary Action. 1901. *o.p.*

**Willis, Henry Parker:** *see* WRIGHT, Gold and Monetary Stabilization.

**Williston, Samuel Wendell.** American Permian Vertebrates. 1911. *o.p.*

**Williston, Samuel Wendell.** (1) The Evolution of Vertebrae. (2) The Osteology of Some American Permian Vertebrates. III. 1918. WM. *o.p.*

**Williston, Samuel Wendell.** Labidosaurus Cope, a Lower Permian Cotylosaur Reptile from Texas. 1917. WM. *o.p.*

**Williston, Samuel Wendell.** The Osteology of Some American Permian Vertebrates. 1914. WM. *o.p.*

**Williston, Samuel Wendell.** The Osteology of Some American Permian Vertebrates. II. Synopsis of the American Permocarboniferous Tetrapoda. 1916. WM. *o.p.*

**Williston, Samuel Wendell.** The Phylogeny and Classification of Reptiles. 1917. WM. *o.p.*

**Williston, Samuel Wendell.** Water Reptiles of the Past and Present. 1914. *o.p.*

**Willoughby, Harold Rideout.** The First Authorized English Bible and the Granmer Preface. 1942. *o.p.*

**Willoughby, Harold Rideout.** Pagan Regeneration. A Study of Mystery Initiations in the Graeco-Roman World. 1929. Reprint. 1960. xi, 307 p. 21 cm. 29-22404. $4.50ˢ.

**Willoughby, Harold Rideout.** Soldiers' Bibles Through Three Centuries. 1944. *o.p.*

**Willoughby, Harold Rideout,** *ed.:* BURTON, Christianity in the Modern World.

**Willoughby, Harold Rideout,** *ed.:* BURTON, Education in a Democratic World.

**Willoughby, Harold Rideout,** *ed.* The Elizabeth Day McCormick Apocalypse. Edited by Harold Rideout Willoughby and Ernest Cadman Colwell. 2 vols. 1940. *Vol. I: A* Greek Corpus of Revelation Iconography. By Harold R. Willoughby. With an Introduction by Mlle Juliette Renaud. *o.p. Vol. II:* History and Text. By Ernest Cadman Colwell. With English Version of Prefaces of Three Early Greek Translators by J. Merle Rife. *o.p.*

**Willoughby, Harold Rideout,** *ed.* The Study of the Bible Today and Tomorrow. 1947. *o.p.*

**Willoughby, Harold Rideout,** *joint ed.:* COLWELL, Four Gospels of Karahissar.

**Willoughby, Harold Rideout,** *joint ed.:* McNEILL, Environmental Factors in Christian History.

**Willoughby, Harold Rideout:** *see* BURTON, Short Introduction to the Gospels.

**Willoughby, Harold Rideout:** *see* GOODSPEED, Rockefeller McCormick New Testament.

**Willoughby, Harold Rideout:** *see* SMITH, Religious Thought in the Last Quarter-Century.

**Wilsing, Johannes.** Theoretical Considerations Respecting the Dependence of Wave-Length on Pressure Which Messrs. Humphreys and Mohler Have Observed in the Arc-Spectra of Certain Elements. 1898. *o.p.*

**Wilson, Charles Ray.** Hermann Eduard von Holst, *in* HUTCHINSON, Marcus W. Jernegan Essays.

**Wilson, Edmund B.:** *see* COWDRY, General Cytology.

**Wilson, Edwin Bidwell:** *see* WHITE, New Social Science.

**Wilson, H. B.** Minimum Essentials in Elementary School Subjects—Standards and Current Practices. By H. B. Wilson and others. 1915. NSSE, 14th Yrbk., Part I. *o.p.*

**Wilson, H. M.,** *joint author:* DAVIS, The Progress of Geography in the Schools.

**Wilson, Helen.** The Treatment of the Misdemeanant in Indiana, 1816–1936. 1938. SSM. *o.p.*

**Wilson, Howard Eugene.** Classroom Procedure Test in History and Other Social Studies for Rating Methods of Teaching in Junior and Senior High Schools. By Howard E. Wilson and Douglas Waples. 1928. *o.p.*

**Wilson, Howard Eugene.** Mary McDowell, Neighbor. 1928. *o.p.*

**Wilson, James G.** Teratology. Principles and Techniques. Edited by James G. Wilson and Josef Warkany. 1965. viii, 279 p. 25 cm. 64-14432. $5.50ˢ.

**Wilson, James Q.** The Amateur Democrat. Club Politics in Three Cities. 1962. xv, 378 p. Illus. Index. 23 cm. 62-13564. $6.95ˢ.

**Wilson, John Albert.** The Burden of Egypt. An Interpretation of Ancient Egyptian Culture. 1951. xx, 332 p. Illus. 25 cm. 51-9735. OIE. $6.00ˢ.
". . . undoubtedly the most significant, stimulating, and provocative contribution on Egyptian history and culture to see the light in recent years."—SAMUEL N. KRAMER, in *The Saturday Review.*

**Wilson, John Albert.** The Culture of Ancient Egypt. 1956. (Originally published as *The Burden of Egypt.*) 344 p. 21 cm. 56-4923. Paper. P11. $1.95.

**Wilson, John Albert.** Signs and Wonders upon Pharaoh. A History of American Egyptology. 1964. xxv, 243 p. Illus. 24 cm. 64-23535. $5.95.

**Wilson, John Albert,** *joint trans.:* EDGERTON, Historical Records of Ramses III.

**Wilson, John Albert,** *joint author:* FRANKFORT. Intellectual Adventure of Ancient Man.

**Wilson, John Albert,** *joint author:* HÖLSCHER, Medinet Habu Studies. *Part II.*

**Wilson, John Harold.** All the King's Ladies. Actresses of the Restoration. 1958. *o.p.*

**Wilson, Louis Round.** County Library Service in the South. A Study of the Rosenwald County Library Demonstration. By Louis R. Wilson and Edward A. Wight. 1935. LS. *o.p.*

**Wilson, Louis Round.** The Geography of Reading. A Study of the Distribution and Status of Libraries in the United States. 1938. LS. *o.p.*

A joint publication with the American Library Association.

**Wilson, Louis Round.** The Library in General Education. 1943. Prepared by Louis R. Wilson, Chairman of the Society's Committee. NSSE, 42d Yrbk., Part II. xiv, 383, xlii p. 24 cm. Cloth. $3.00t. Paper $2.25t.

**Wilson, Louis Round,** *ed.* Library Trends. Papers Presented before the First Library Institute at the University of Chicago, 1936. Edited with an Introduction by Louis R. Wilson. 1937. *o.p.*

**Wilson, Louis Round,** *ed.* The Practice of Book Selection. Papers Presented before the [Fourth] Library Institute at the University of Chicago, 1939. Edited with an Introduction by Louis R. Wilson. 1940. LS. *o.p.*

**Wilson, Louis Round,** *ed.* The Role of the Library in Adult Education. Papers Presented before the [Second] Library Institute at the University of Chicago, 1937. Edited with an Introduction by Louis R. Wilson. 1937. LS. *o.p.*

**Wilson, Louis Round,** *ed.* The University Library. Its Organization, Administration, and Functions. Edited by Louis R. Wilson and Maurice F. Tauber. 1945. LS. *o.p.*

**Wilson, Woodrow, Philosophy and Policies of:** LATHAM.

**Wimberly, Lowry Charles.** Folklore in the English and Scottish Ballads. 1928. *o.p.*

**Windy McPherson's Son:** ANDERSON.

**Winger, Howard W.,** *ed.* Iron Curtains and Scholarship. Twenty-third Annual Conference, Graduate Library School. 1958. v, 132 p. 24 cm. 59-1497. LS. $3.75s.

**Winger, Howard W.,** *joint ed.:* CARNOVSKY, The Medium-sized Public Library.

**Winger, Howard W.,** *joint ed.:* ENNIS, Seven Questions about the Profession of Librarianship.

**Winter Characters of Certain Sporangia:** CHAMBERLAIN.

**Winterfeast:** KENNEDY, *in his* Plays for Seven Players.

**Winternitz, Milton Charles:** *see* WHITE, New Social Science.

**Wirth, Louis.** Community Life and Social Policy. Selected Papers by Louis Wirth. Edited by Elizabeth Wirth Marvick and Albert J. Reiss, Jr. 1956. (O.I.)

**Wirth, Louis.** The Ghetto. Woodcut illustrations by Todros Geller. 1928. 306 p. 21 cm. 56-14116. Paper. P7, $1.65.

". . . a first-rate study . . . packed with information . . . made from the point of view of the Jewish ghetto, but his conclusions, which touch many problems of cultural history, are applicable to many other types of the sectarian community."—*The Times Literary Supplement.*

**Wirth, Louis,** *ed.* Local Community Fact Book of Chicago. Edited by Louis Wirth and Eleanor H. Bernert. 1949. xii, 156 p. Illus. Paper. $5.50s.

**Wirth, Louis.** Louis Wirth on Cities and Social Life. Selected Papers, edited with an Introduction by Albert J. Reiss, Jr. 1964. xxx, 350 p. 21 cm. 64-24970. Cloth. $7.50s. Paper. P172. $2.95.

**Wirth, Louis,** *ed.* Contemporary Social Problems. A Tentative Formulation for Teachers of Social Studies. 1940. *o.p.*

**Wirth, Louis,** *ed.* Eleven Twenty-six. A Decade of Social Science Research. Contributors: Robert Maynard Hutchins, Henry Bruère, Beardsley Ruml, Charles E. Merriam, Robert Redfield, Louis Wirth, W. F. Ogburn, L. L. Thurstone. 1940. *o.p.*

**Wischnitzer, Rachel.** The Messianic Theme in the Paintings of the Dura Synagogue. 1948. *o.p.*

**Wisdom, Charles.** The Chorti Indians of Guatemala. 1940. AN. *o.p.*

**Wise Choice of Toys:** KAWIN.

**Wishart, Alfred Wesley.** Primary Facts in Religious Thought. Seven Essays Dealing in a Simple and Practical Manner with the Nature, Expressions, and Relations of Religion. 1905. *o.p.*

**Wisner, Elizabeth.** Public Welfare Administration in Louisiana. 1930. SSM. *o.p.*

**Wister, Fanny Kemble,** *ed.* Owen Wister Out West. His Journal and Letters. 1958. xix, 269 p. Illus. 23 cm. 58-9609. $6.50ˢ. COBE.

**With the Procession:** FULLER.

**Witte, Ernest Frederic.** Purchasing Policies and Practices of Chain Drug Companies. 1933. SBA, III. *o.p.*

**Wittick, Eugene C.** The Development of Power. 1939. *o.p.*

**Wittke, Carl.** Against the Current. The Life of Karl Heinzen. 1945. *o.p.*

**Witty, Paul A.** Development in and through Reading. Prepared by Paul A. Witty, Chairman of the Society's Committee. 1961. NSSE, 60th Yrbk., Part I. xviii, 406, vi p. 24 cm. 61-1837. Cloth. $5.00ᵗ. Paper. $4.25ᵗ.

**Witty, Paul A.** Mental Health in Modern Education. Prepared by Paul A. Witty, Chairman of the Society's Committee. 1955. NSSE, 54th Yrbk., Part II. xi, 397 p. 24 cm. 55-14176. Cloth. $4.50ᵗ. Paper. $3.75ᵗ.

**Wobbly:** CHAPLIN.

**Woellner, Elizabeth H.** Requirements for Certification of Teachers, Counselors, Librarians, Administrators for Elementary Schools, Secondary Schools, Junior Colleges. By Elizabeth H. Woellner and M. Aurilla Wood. 30th ed., 1965. Map. 28 cm. Paper. $3.75ˢ.

**Wohlgemuth, Adolf.** On the After-effect of Seen Movement. 1911. BJP. *o.p.*

**Wohlgemuth, Adolf.** Pleasure—Unpleasure. An Experimental Investigation on the Feeling-Elements. 1919. BJP. *o.p.*

**Wolcott, J. D.,** *joint author:* BOBBITT, Supervision of City Schools.

**Wolf, Eric.** Sons of the Shaking Earth. 1959. viii, 303 p. Illus. 21 cm. 59-12290. Cloth. $5.00ˢ. Paper. P90. $1.50.

**Wolf, Harry DeMerle.** The Railroad Labor Board. 1927. SE. *o.p.*

**Wolf, Hazel C.,** *joint author:* HESSELTINE, Blue and the Gray on the Nile.

**Wolfenden, Hugh H.** Population Statistics and Their Compilation. 1954. xxiii, 228 p. 24 cm. 54-10735. $7.50ˢ.

**Wolfenstein, Martha,** *joint ed.:* MEAD, Childhood in Contemporary Cultures.

**Wolfle, Dael L.** Factor Analysis to 1940. PMS. 1940. *o.p.*

**Woll, Matthew:** *see* HUTCHINSON, Democracy and National Unity.

**Wollaston, William Hyde:** *see* DOLTON, Foundations of the Atomic Theory.

**Woman Movement from the Point of View of Social Consciousness:** TAFT.

**Women Graduates of a Collegiate School of Business:** BREWINGTON.

**Women and Wealth:** BRANCH.

**Women's Work:** CADBURY.

**Wood, Ernest R.** A Graphic Method of Obtaining the Partial-Correlation Coefficients and the Partial-Regression Coefficients of Three or More Variables. 1931. SEM 37. *o.p.*

**Wood, Francis Asbury.** Tables of Phonetic Changes. 1906. *o.p.*

**Wood, Francis Asbury.** Übersichtstabellen zu Lautentsprechungen und zur Casusbildung des Nomens und Adjektivs im Germanischen. Zusammengestellt von Francis A. Wood. 1911. *o.p.*

**Wood, Francis Asbury.** I. Verner's Law in Gothic. II. The Reduplicating Verbs in Germanic. 1895. GER. *o.p.*

**Wood, Francis Asbury,** *trans.* The Hilde-brandslied. Translated from the Old High German into English Alliterative Verse, by Francis A. Wood. 1914. *o.p.*

**Wood, Leland Foster:** *see* SMITH, Principles of Christian Living.

**Wood, M. Aurilla,** *joint author:* WOELLNER, Requirements for Certification.

**Wood, Mary Adele,** *joint author:* McAULEY, Economies in Food.

**Wood, T. D.** Health and Education. 1910. NSSE, 9th Yrbk., Part I. *o.p.*

**Wood, T. D.** The Nurse in Education. By T. D. Wood and others. 1910. NSSE, 9th Yrbk., Part II. *o.p.*

**Woodbridge, Benjamin M.** La Semeuse. HCLS.

**Woodbridge, Benjamin M.,** *joint ed.:* ALTROC-CHI, Tristi amori.

**Woodburne, Angus Stewart.** The Relation between Religion and Science. A Biological Approach. 1920. *o.p.*

**Woodbury, Coleman,** *ed.* The Future of Cities and Urban Redevelopment. Edited by Coleman Woodbury. With Contributions by Catherine Bauer, Henry S. Church-ill, Frank Cliffe, Vernon de Mars, Richard Dewey, Arthur Gallion, Victor Jones, G. Holmes Perkins, William Slayton, Robert C. Weinberg, and Coleman Woodbury. 1953. xx, 764 p. 26 cm. 53-7679. $11.50s.

**Woodbury, Coleman,** *ed.* Urban Redevelopment. Problems and Practices. Edited by Coleman Woodbury. With Contributions by Charles S. Ascher, William H. Ludlow, Jack Meltzer, Sheilah Orloff, Ira S. Rob-bins, William Slayton, Allan A. Twichell, and Marian Perry Yankauer. 1953. xvi, 525 p. Illus. 26 cm. 53-7678. $9.00s.

**Wooddy, Carroll Hill.** The Case of Frank L. Smith. A Study in Representative Government. 1931. *o.p.*

**Wooddy, Carroll Hill.** The Chicago Primary of 1926. A Study in Election Methods. 1926. SSCI. *o.p.*

**Woodger, J. H.** The Technique of Theory Construction. 1939. vii, 81 p. 25 cm. A42-5469. Paper. IEUS, II, 5. $1.75s.

**Woodhead, Henry George Wandesforde.** Occidental Interpretations of the Far Eastern Problem. By H. G. W. Woodhead, Julean Arnold, and Henry Kittredge Norton. 1926. HFL. *o.p.*

**Woodhouse, A. S. P.** The Poet and his Faith. Religion and Poetry in England from Spenser to Eliot and Auden. 1965. xii, 304 p. 21 cm. 65-24428. WIL. $6.95s.

**Woodhouse, A. S. P.,** *ed.* Puritanism and Liberty. Being the Army Debates (1647–49) from the Clarke Manuscripts with Sup-plementary Documents. With a Foreword by A. D. Lindsay. 1951. 506 p. 24 cm. $7.50s.

**Woods, Anderson.** Time's Arrow in Society. A Philosophy of Progress. 1935. *o.p.*

**Woods, J. A.,** *ed.* Correspondence of Edmund Burke (*Vol. IV*).

**Woods Hole Marine Biological Laboratory:** LILLIE.

**Word Book for Graded German Readers, Books 1–10 (with B. Q. Morgan).** HCLS.

**Wordsworth in Early American Criticism:** NEWTON.

**Work, James A.:** *see* BRYAN, Sources and Analogues of Chaucer's *Canterbury Tales.*

**Work Accidents to Minors:** KLEIN.

**Work of the Atmosphere:** CRONEIS.

**Work in Education in Colleges and Universi-ties:** NATIONAL SOCIETY OF COLLEGE TEACH-ERS OF EDUCATION, Proceedings, No. 6.

**Work of the Kidneys:** CARLSON.

**Work of the Old Testament Priests:** HARPER.

**Work of the Old Testament Sages:** HARPER.

**Work of Rivers:** CRONEIS.

**Work in Western Thebes:** NELSON.

**Workbook To Accompany The Sentence and Its Parts:** LONG.

**Worker in Modern Economic Society:** DOUG-LAS.

**Worker Views His Union:** SEIDMAN.

**Working Manual for Juvenile Court Officers:** RILEY.

**Workman, E. J.:** see HAWLEY, Tree-Ring Analysis and Dating.

**Works, George A.** Rural America Today. Its Schools and Community Life. By George Works and Simon Lesser. 1942. *o.p.*

**Works, George A.:** see EDWARDS, Education in a Democracy.

**Works, George A.:** see REEVES, Organization and Administration of the University.

**Works of the Mind:** HEYWOOD.

**Works of Sir Thomas Browne:** BROWNE.

**World Community:** WRIGHT.

**World of the First Australians:** BERNDT.

**World-Friendship:** LOBINGIER.

**World and Man:** MOULTON.

**World Politics and Personal Insecurity:** LASSWELL.

**World-View of the Fourth Gospel:** WEARING.

**World View of Physics:** WEIZSÄCKER.

**World of the Witches:** BAROJA.

**World's Best Hope:** BIDDLE.

**Worrell, William Hoyt,** *ed.* The Proverbs of Solomon in Sahidic Coptic According to the Chicago Manuscript. 1931. xxx, 107 p. 30 cm. OIP, XII. $5.00.

**Worsley, Peter.** The Third World. 1965. x, 317 p. 23 cm. NHS. $5.50ˢ. OBE.

**Wound Healing and Tissue Repair:** PATTERSON.

**Wreidt, Ernest August,** *joint author:* MYERS, First-Year Mathematics.

**Wreidt, Ernest August,** *joint author:* Myers, Geometric Exercises for Algebraic Solution.

**Wreidt, Ernest August,** *joint author:* MYERS, Second-Year Mathematics.

**Wright, Arthur F.,** *ed.* Studies in Chinese Thought. Edited by Arthur F. Wright. With Contributions by Derk Bodde, Schuyler Cammann, W. Theodore de Bary, Achilles Fang, Arnold Isenberg, J. R. Levenson, David Nivison, and I. A. Rich-

ards. 1953. xiv, 317 p. Illus. 26 cm. 53-13533. CSCC. $4.50ˢ.

**Wright, Austin McGiffert.** The American Short Story in the Twenties. 1961. xi, 425 p. Index. 24 cm. 61-14536. $7.50ˢ.

**Wright, Austin McGiffert.** Joseph Spence. A Critical Biography. 1950. *o.p.*

**Wright, Chester,** *ed.* Economic Problems of War and its Aftermath. 1942. WFL. *o.p.*

**Wright, Chester W.,** *joint ed.:* MARSHALL, Materials for the Study of Elementary Economics.

**Wright, Elizabeth Quincy Sewall,** *joint author:* WRIGHT, Elizur Wright.

**Wright, Frank Lloyd.** When Democracy Builds. 1945. *o.p.*

**Wright, G. Ernest.** The Challenge of Israel's Faith. 1944. x, 108 p. 21 cm. A44-1354. $2.50ˢ.

**Wright, Helen R.,** *ed.* Social Service in Wartime. 1944. WFL. *o.p.*

**Wright, Philip Green.** The American Tariff and Oriental Trade. 1931. IPR. *o.p.*

**Wright, Philip Green.** Elizur Wright. The Father of Life Insurance. By Philip Green Wright and Elizabeth Q. Wright. 1937. *o.p.*

**Wright, Quincy.** Mandates under the League of Nations. 1930. *o.p.*

**Wright, Quincy.** A Study of War. 1942. 2d ed. 1965. xii, 1,637 p. 24 cm. 65-5396. $20.00ˢ.

"Professor Quincy Wright has unquestionably won for himself the position of the foremost living student of war as an institution."—H. E. BARNES, in *The Harvard Law Review.*

"As a work of reference to which to go to discover whence wars have come and how they have been fought and to what ends, I know nothing in its class. . . ."—PAUL HUTCHINSON, in *The Christian Century.*

**Wright, Quincy.** A Study of War. Abridged by Louise Leonard Wright. 1964. xiv, 451 p. 24 cm. Cloth. $7.50. Paper. P185. $2.95.

**Wright, Quincy.** The United States and Neutrality. 1935. PPP 17. *o.p.*

**Wright, Quincy.** The World Community. 1948. HFL. *o.p.*

**Wright, Quincy.** *ed.* A Foreign Policy for the United States. 1947. HFL. *o.p.*

**Wright, Quincy,** *ed.* Gold and Monetary Stabilization. By Jacob Viner, Gottfried Haberler, H. Parker Willis, Lionel D. Edie, and John H. Williams. 1932. HFL. *o.p.*

**Wright, Quincy,** *ed.* Interpretations of American Foreign Policy. By George H. Blakeslee, Percy Ellwood Corbett, George Young, Victor Andres Belaunde, and Yusuke Tsurumi. 1930. HFL. *o.p.*

**Wright, Quincy,** *ed.* Neutrality and Collective Security. By Alfred Zimmern, William Edward Dodd, Charles Warren, and Edwin DeWitt Dickinson. 1936. HFL. *o.p.*

**Wright, Quincy,** *ed.* Public Opinion and World-Politics. By John W. Dafoe, Jules Auguste Sauerwein, Edgar Stern-Rubarth, Ralph Haswell Lutz, and Harold Dwight Lasswell. 1933. HFL. *o.p.*

**Wright, Quincy,** *ed.* Unemployment as a World-Problem. By John Maynard Keynes, Karl Pribram, and E. J. Phelan. 1931. HFL. *o.p.*

**Wright, Quincy:** *see* LAVES, The Foundations of a More Stable World Order.

**Wright, William Kelly.** The Ethical Significance of Feeling, Pleasure, and Happiness in Modern Non-hedonistic Systems. 1907. PS. *o.p.*

**Wright, Wilmer Cave,** *trans.:* RAMAZZINI, De morbis artificum.

**Written on Bamboo and Silk:** TSIEN.

**Wulf, Oliver R.** The Utilization of the Entire Course of Radiosonde Flights in Weather Diagnosis. 1944. *o.p.*

**Wulf, Oliver R.** The Meteorological Conditions in the Upper Reaches of the Radiosonde. Flights over the United States, Parts I and II. 1946. *o.p.*

**Wyant, Andrew Robert Elmer,** *ed.:* HULBERT, English Reformation.

**Wyckoff, Charles Truman.** Feudal Relations between the Kings of England and Scotland under the Early Plantagenets. 1897. *o.p.*

**X-Ray Examination of the Stomach:** TEMPLETON.

**Yamanouchi, Shigeo.** The Life-History of Polysiphonia. 1907. *o.p.*

**Yamey, Basil,** *joint author:* BAUER, Economics of Under-developed Countries.

**Yates, Frances A.** Giordano Bruno and the Hermetic Tradition. 1964. xiv, 466 p. 22 cm. 64-10094. $7.50s. OBE.

**Year of the Gorilla:** SCHALLER.

**Yeomans, Alfred Beaver,** *ed.* City Residential Land Development. Studies in Planning. Competitive Plans for Subdividing a Typical Quarter-Section of Land in the Outskirts of Chicago. 1916. CC. *o.p.*

**Yerkes Observatory of the University of Chicago Bulletins** (YOB).

Announcements of results, brief descriptions of new buildings and instruments, and notes on the work of the Observatory.

1. HALE, Organization of the Yerkes Observatory.
2. HALE, Completion of the Yerkes Telescope.
3. HALE, Dedication of the Yerkes Observatory.
4. Addresses Delivered in Connection with the Dedication of the Yerkes Observatory.
5. Proceedings of the Conferences Held at the Yerkes Observatory.
6. HALE, Parallax of the Andromeda Nebula.
7. HALE, Spectra of Stars of Secchi's Fourth Type.
8. HALE, Opportunities for Students.
9. HALE, Comparison of Stellar Spectra.
10. HALE, Period and Elongation Distance of the Fifth Satellite of Jupiter.
11. HALE, Heat Radiation of the Stars.
12. HALE, Carbon in the Chromosphere.
13. HALE, Variable Star Observations.
14. HALE, Observations of the Total Solar Eclipse of May 28, 1900.
15. HALE, Photographs of Star Clusters.
16. HALE, New Star in Perseus.
17. HALE, Changes in the Spectrum of Nova Persei.

18. Hale, Latitude and Longitude of the Yerkes Observatory.
19. Hale, New Star in Gemini.

## Yerkes Observatory of the University of Chicago: Publications (YO):

VOLUME

| | | |
|---|---|---|
| I. | | Burnham, General Catalogue of 1290 Double Stars. |
| II. | | Decennial Papers on Astronomy and Astrophysics |
| III. | Part I. | Hale, Rumford Spectroheliograph. |
| | Part II. | Hale, Spectrum of the High Potential Discharge between Metallic Electrodes. |
| | Part III. | Fox, Rotation Period of the Sun. |
| | Part IV. | Pettit. Forms and Motions of the Solar Prominences. |
| IV. | Part I. | Slocum, Stellar Parallaxes. |
| | Part II. | Hubble, Photographic Investigations of Faint Nebulae. |
| | Part III. | Van Biesbroeck, Parallaxes of Fifty-two Stars. |
| | Part IV. | Lee, Zone +45° of Kapteyn's Selected Areas. |
| | Part V. | Farnsworth, Comparison of the Photometric Fields of the 6-Inch Doublet, 24-Inch Reflector, and 40-Inch Refractor of the Yerkes Observatory. |
| | Part VI. | Parkhurst, Zone +45° of Kapteyn's Selected Areas. |
| | Part VII. | Parsons, Astrometric and Photometric Statistics of Certain of Hagen's Fields. |
| V. | Part I. | Van Biesbroeck, Measurements of Double Stars. [I.] |
| | Part II. | Van Biesbroeck, Definitive Orbit of Comet Delavan. |
| VI. | Part I. | Barnard, Micrometric Measures of Star Clusters. |
| VII. | Part I. | Frost, Radial Velocities of 500 Stars. |
| | Part II. | Frost, Study of the Spectrum of 7 ε Aurigae. |
| | Part III. | Morgan, Descriptive Study of the Spectra of the A-Type Stars. |
| | Part IV. | Luyten, Reobservation of the Orbits of Ten Spectroscopic Binaries. |
| VIII. | Part I. | Lee, Parallaxes of Eighty Stars. |
| | Part II. | Van Biesbroeck, Measurements of Double Stars. [II.] |
| | Part III. | Van Biesbroeck, Definitive Orbit of Comet Geddes. |
| | Part IV. | Van Biesbroeck, Definitive Orbits of Comets Van Biesbroeck, 1935 d, and of Barnard-Brooks, 1889 I. By George Van Biesbroeck. 1940. |
| | Part V. | Van Biesbroeck, The Definitive Orbit of the Comet Morehouse, 1908 III. |

**Yntema, Theodore Otte.** A Mathematical Reformulation of the General Theory of International Trade. 1932. MSB. *o.p.*

**Yntema, Theodore Otte,** *joint ed.:* Lange, Studies in Mathematical Economics and Econometrics.

**You and Machines:** Ogburn.

**You Must Relax:** Jacobson.

**Young, Carl Walter.** The International Relations of Manchuria. A Digest and Analysis of Treaties, Agreements, and Negotiations concerning the Three Eastern Provinces of China. Prepared for the 1929 Conference of the Institute of Pacific Relations in Kyoto, Japan. 1929. IPR. *o.p.*

**Young, Ella Flagg.** Ethics in the School. 1902. CE. *o.p.*

**Young, Ella Flagg.** Isolation in the School. 1901. CE. *o.p.*

**Young, Ella Flagg.** Scientific Method in Education. Preprint. 1903. *o.p.*

**Young, Ella Flagg.** Some Types of Modern Educational Theory. 1902. CE. *o.p.*

**Young, George:** *see* Wright, Interpretations of American Foreign Policy.

**Young, James Webb.** Advertising Agency Compensation in Relation to the Total Cost of Advertising. 1933. MSB. *o.p.*

**Young, Jeremiah Simeon.** A Political and Constitutional Study of the Cumberland Road. 1904. *o.p.*

**Young, Karl:** *see* Bryan, Sources and Analogues of Chaucer's *Canterbury Tales.*

**Young, Pauline Vislick.** The Pilgrims of Russian-Town. Introduction by Robert E. Park. 1932. SOC. *o.p.*

**Young Cripple and His Job:** Hathway.

**Young People's Projects:** Shaver.

**Younger American Scholar:** Knapp.

**Your Business and Postwar Readjustment:** LYON.

**Youth of André Gide:** DELAY.

**Youth in the Depression:** DAVIS.

**Youth Development Series** (YDS):
1. HAVIGHURST, Community Youth Development Program.
2. BOWMAN, Studying Children and Training Counselors.
3. BOWMAN, Mobilizing Community Resources for Maladjusted and Delinquent Youth.

**Yuman Tribes of the Gila River:** SPIER.

**Yūsuf ibn Ḳis-Ughli.** Mirʾât za-Zamân (A.H. 495–654). By Šams ad-Dîn Abū 'l-Muzaffar Yûsuf ben Qizughlū ben ʿAbdallāh, Commonly Known by the Surname of Sibṭ ibn al-Jauzī. A Facsimile Reproduction of Manuscript No. 136 of the Landberg Collection of Arabic Manuscripts Belonging to Yale University. Edited with Introduction by James Richard Jewett. 1907. *o.p.*

**Zeisler, Ernest Bloomfield,** *joint author:* LEVINSON, Law of Gravitation.

**Zener, Clarence.** Elasticity and Anelasticity of Metals. 1948. x, 170 p. Illus. 24 cm. 48-3902. PS. $5.75ˢ.

**Zesbaugh, Helen Ann.** Children's Drawings of the Human Figure. 1934. *o.p.*

**Zilsel, Edgar,** *joint author:* SANTILLANA, The Development of Rationalism and Empiricism.

**Zimmern, Alfred Eckhard:** *see* WRIGHT, Neutrality and Collective Security.

**Zingg, Robert Mowry,** *joint author:* BENNETT, Tarahumara.

**Zirkle, Raymond E.,** *ed.* A Symposium on Molecular Biology. 1959. viii, 348 p. Illus. 25 cm. 58-13032. $7.50ˢ.

**Znaniecki, Florian.** Cultural Reality. 1919. *o.p.*

**Znaniecki, Florian,** *joint author:* THOMAS, Polish Peasant.

**Zone +45° of Kapteyn's Selected Areas:** LEE.

**Zone +45° of Kapteyn's Selected Areas:** PARKHURST.

**Zook, George Frederick.** Principles of Accrediting Higher Institutions. By George F. Zook and M. E. Haggerty. 1936. EHI. *o.p.*

**Zorbaugh, Frederick McClure,** *joint author:* SHAW, Delinquency Areas.

**Zorbaugh, Harvey Warren.** The Gold Coast and the Slum. A Sociological Study of Chicago's Near North Side. 1929. xvi, 287 p. 15 maps. 20 cm. 29-12607. SOC. $6.00ˢ.

**Zueblin, Charles.** A Decade of Civic Development. 1905. *o.p.*

**Zumbrunnen, Albert Clay.** The Community Church. A Probable Method of Approach to and Bases for Denominational Unity. 1922. *o.p.*

**Zweifel, Frances W.** A Handbook of Biological Illustration. 1961. xi, 131 p. 21 cm. 61-19734. Paper. PSS510. $1.95.

# Subject Listings

## AGRICULTURE:

ACKERMAN, Family Farm Policy.
BAKER, County Agent.
BALDWIN, Price Differentials in Wheat Futures.
BUCK, Chinese Farm Economy.
BUCK, Land Utilization in China.
BUTTERFIELD, Chapters in Rural Progress.
DILLER, Farm Ownership.
DUDDY, Agriculture in the Chicago Region.
DUDDY, Conference on Economic Policy.
EASTERBROOK, Farm Credit in Canada.
GRAY, Land Planning.
HARDIN, Freedom in Agricultural Education.
HORNE, Farm Business.
HUGHES, Saite Demotic Land Leases.
INSTITUTE OF PACIFIC RELATIONS, *Research Staff of the Secretariat.* Agrarian China.
JOHNSON, Forward Prices for Agriculture.
JOHNSON, Grain Yields and the American Food Supply.
KNAPP, Hard Winter Wheat Pools.
LEE, Land Utilization and Rural Economy in Korea.
LIND, Island Community.
*See also* AMERICAN COUNTRY LIFE ASSOCIATION.

## ANTHROPOLOGY:

BAROJA, World of the Witches.
BARTON, Kalingas.
BASCOM, Continuity and Change in African Cultures.
BEARDSLEY, Village Japan.
BECKWITH, The Kumulipo. A Hawaiian Creation Chant.
BERNDT, Excess and Restraint.
BERNDT, From Black to White in South Australia.
BERNDT, World of the First Australians.

BOWERS, Mandan Social and Ceremonial Organization.
BRAIDWOOD, Time, Space, and Man.
BRANDT, Hopi Ethics.
BUCK, Vikings of the Pacific.
CLARK, Fossil Evidence for Human Evolution.
CLARK, History of the Primates.
COLLIER, Awakening Valley.
DRIVER, Indians of North America.
DURKHEIM, Primitive Classification.
EGGAN, Social Anthropology of North American Tribes.
EGGAN, Social Organization of the Western Pueblos.
EKVALL, Religious Observances in Tibet.
FALLERS, Bantu Bureaucracy.
EMBREE, Suye Mura.
FOREMAN, Last Trek of the Indians.
GEERTZ, Peddlers and Princes.
GENNEP, Rites of Passage.
GRUNEBAUM, Unity and Variety in Muslim Civilization.
HAILE, Navaho Sacrificial Figurines.
HAILE, Origin Legend of the Navaho Flintway.
HAILE, Prayer Stick Cutting.
HAVIGHURST, American Indian and White Children.
HUBERT, Sacrifice.
JACOBS, Content and Style of an Oral Literature.
JENNESS, People of the Twilight.
JENNINGS, Prehistoric Man in the New World.
JENSEN, Myth and Cult among Primitive Peoples.
KROEBER, Anthropology Today.
KROEBER, Nature of Culture.
LA BARRE, Human Animal.
LEVIN, Peoples of Siberia.

LOWIE, Toward Understanding Germany.
MACGREGOR, Warriors without Weapons.
MACY, Chemical Anthropology.
MAIR, New Nations.
MARRIOTT, Village India.
MARTIN, Indians before Columbus.
MEAD, Childhood in Contemporary Cultures.
MEAD, Study of Culture at a Distance.
MINER, St. Denis, French-Canadian Parish.
MOONEY, Ghost-Dance Religion.
MORRIS, Varieties of Human Value.
NEEDHAM, Structure and Sentiment.
OAKLEY, Man the Tool-maker.
OPLER, Apache Life-Way.
PITT-RIVERS, People of the Sierra.
QUAIN, Fijian Village.
QUIMBY, Indian Life in the Upper Great Lakes.
RADCLIFFE-BROWN, Method in Social Anthropology.
REDFIELD, Chan Kom.
REDFIELD, Folk Culture of Yucatan.
REDFIELD, Human Nature and the Study of Society.
REDFIELD, Little Community.
REDFIELD, Papers of Robert Redfield.
REDFIELD, Peasant Society and Culture.
REDFIELD, Tepoztlán.
REDFIELD, Village That Chose Progress.
REICHEL-DOLMATOFF, People of Aritama.
RESEK, Lewis Henry Morgan.
SCHALLER, Mountain Gorilla.
SERVICE, Tobatí.
SPICER, Perspectives in American Indian Culture Change.
STANTON, Leopard's Spots.
TAX, Acculturation in the Americas.
TAX, Anthropology Today: Selections.
TAX, Civilizations of Ancient America.
TAX, Evolution after Darwin.
TAX, Indian Tribes of Aboriginal America.
TAX, Penny Capitalism.
THOMAS, Man's Role in Changing the Face of the Earth.
THOMAS, Current Anthropology.
THOMPSON, The Hopi Way.
TURNER, Africanisms in the Gullah Dialect.
TYLOR, Early History of Mankind.
UNDERHILL, Red Man's America.
UNDERHILL, Red Man's Religion.
WAGNER, Readings in Cultural Geography.
WAUCHOPE, Lost Tribes and Sunken Continents.

WAUCHOPE, They Found the Buried Cities.
WEIDENREICH, Apes, Giants, and Man.
WESSELL, Ethnic Survey of Woonsocket, Rhode Island.
WILLEY, Method and Theory in American Archaeology.
WOLF, Sons of the Shaking Earth.
WRIGHT, World Community.

## ARCHEOLOGY:

ADAMS, Land behind Baghdad.
ALLEN, Handbook of the Egyptian Collection.
BAER, Rank and Title in the Old Kingdom.
BENNETT, Archaeological Explorations in Jo Daviess County, Illinois.
CHIERA, They Wrote on Clay.
COLE, Kincaid.
COLE, Rediscovering Illinois.
DELOUGAZ, Pottery from the Diyala Region.
DELOUGAZ, Pre-Sargonid Temples in the Diyala Region.
EHRICH, Chronologies in Old World Archaeology.
EHRICH, Relative Chronologies in Old World Archeology.
FAKHRY, Pyramids.
FRANKFORT, Arrest and Movement.
FRANKFORT, Gimilsin Temple.
FRANKFORT, Intellectual Adventure of Ancient Man.
FRANKFORT, Kingship and the Gods.
FRANKFORT, More Sculpture from the Diyala Region.
FRANKFORT, Stratified Cylinder Seals from the Diyala Region.
GELB, Study of Writing.
GRAHAM, Culture and Conscience.
GRIFFIN, Archeology of Eastern United States.
HAYES, Most Ancient Egypt.
JENNINGS, Prehistoric Man in the New World.
KEES, Ancient Egypt.
KRAMER, Sumerians.
LIBBY, Radiocarbon Dating.
MARTIN, Indians before Columbus.
OAKLEY, Man the Tool-maker.
OPPENHEIM, Ancient Mesopotamia.
PERKINS, Comparative Archeology of Early Mesopotamia.
POEBEL, Second Dynasty of Isn.
QUIMBY, Indian Life in the Upper Great Lakes.

RANSOM, Studies in Ancient Furniture.
RICHARDSON, Etruscans.
SANDFORD, First Report of the Prehistoric Survey Expedition.
SANDFORD, Paleolithic Man and the Nile-Faiyum Divide.
SANDFORD, Paleolithic Man and the Nile Valley in Nubia and Upper Egypt.
SANDFORD, Paleolithic Man and the Nile Valley in Upper and Middle Egypt.
SANDFORD, Prehistoric Survey of Egypt and Western Asia.
SCRANTON, Aesthetic Aspects of Ancient Art.
STARR, Notes on Mexican Archaeology.
STEINDORFF, When Egypt Ruled the East.
TOFFTEEN, Ancient Chronology.
TOFFTEEN, Historic Exodus.
VERMEULE, Greece in the Bronze Age.
WILLEY, Method and Theory in American Archaeology.
WILSON, Burden of Egypt.
WILSON, Culture of Ancient Egypt.
WILSON, Signs and Wonders upon Pharaoh.
WOLF, Sons of the Shaking Earth.
See also ORIENTAL INSTITUTE, PUBLICATIONS OF

## ARCHITECTURE:

CONDIT, Chicago School of Architecture.
CONDIT, Rise of the Skyscraper.
CRAM, Six Lectures on Architecture.
DELOUGAZ, Plano-Convex Bricks and the Methods of Their Employment.
DELOUGAZ, Pre-Sargonid Temples.
DELOUGAZ, Temple Oval at Khafājah.
DRURY, Old Chicago Houses.
FRANKFORT, Gimilsin Temple.
GOODMAN, Communitas.
HALBERT, Better Homes Manual.
HILL, Islamic Architecture and Its Decoration.
HÖLSCHER, Excavation of Medinet Habu.
JACKSON, Byzantine and Romanesque Architecture.
JACKSON, Gothic Architecture.
JACOBSEN, Sennacherib's Aqueduct.
LOUD, Khorsabad.
NEWCOMB, Architecture of the Old Northwest Territory.
RANSOM, People's Architects.
SCHMIDT, Persepolis I.
SCHMIDT, Persepolis II.
SIEGEL, Chicago's Famous Buildings.

STURGIS, Interdependence of the Arts of Design.
SZUKALSKI, Projects in Design.
WRIGHT, When Democracy Builds.

## ART:

ALLEN, Handbook of the Egyptian Collection.
ALSCHULER, Painting and Personality.
ARTZ, From the Renaissance to Romanticism.
BREASTED, Oriental Forerunners of Byzantine Painting.
BUSWELL, How People Look at Pictures.
CALVERLEY, Temple of King Sethos.
CARPENTER, Greek Sculpture.
CHRIST-JANER, Boardman Robinson.
COLLEGE OF THE UNIVERSITY OF CHICAGO, Humanities I Handbook.
COLLINS, Hercules Seghers.
COHN, Medicine, Science, and Art.
DAVIES, Ancient Egyptian Paintings.
DOUGLAS, Leonardo da Vinci.
DOUGLAS, Piero di Cosimo.
DRISCOLL, Chinese Calligraphy.
EATON, Landscape Artist in America.
EITNER, Géricault.
ELKIN, Art in Arnhem Land.
FERGUSON, Chinese Painting.
FERGUSON, Outlines of Chinese Art.
FRÄNGER, Millennium of Hieronymus Bosch.
FRANKFORT, Arrest and Movement.
GALE, Children's Preferences for Colors.
GOTSHALK, Art and the Social Order.
GRAY, Buddhist Cave Paintings.
HAGSTRUM, Sister Arts.
HAGSTRUM, William Blake: Poet and Painter.
JOHANNSEN, "Phiz." Illustrations from the Novels of Charles Dickens.
KERNODLE, From Art to Theatre.
McDERMOTT, Lost Panoramas of the Mississippi.
McMAHON, Preface to an American Philosophy of Art.
MARCH, China and Japan in Our Museums.
MORRISON, Children's Preferences for Pictures.
MUNRO, Art in American Life and Education.
PICASSO, Understanding Picasso.
PORTINARI, Portinari, His Life and Work.
RICHARDSON, Washington Allston.
RICH, Seurat.
RICHTER, Andrea dal Castagno.

RICHTER, Giorgio da Castelfranco.
RICKERT, Reconstructed Carmelite Missal.
SAKKARAH EXPEDITION, Mastaba of Mereruka.
SCRANTON, Aesthetic Aspects of Ancient Art.
SIMSON, Sacred Fortress.
SWARZENSKI, Monuments of Romanesque Art.
TARBELL, Cantharus from the Factory of Brygos.
TARBELL, Greek Hand-Mirror.
TAYLOR, Learning To Look.
TAYLOR, William Page.
THURSTON, Structure of Art.
TODA, Japanese Scroll Painting.
TODD, Enjoyment and Use of Art in the Elementary School.
TODD, Learning To Draw.
VINCENT, Sacred Oasis.
WELLER, Francesco di Giorgio, 1439–1501.
WISCHNITZER, Messianic Theme in the Paintings of the Dura Synagogue.
ZESBAUGH, Children's Drawings of the Human Figure.

## ASTRONOMY:

ALLER, Stellar Structure.
ĀRYABHAṬA, Āryabhaṭiya of Āryabhaṭa.
BALDWIN, Face of the Moon.
BALDWIN, Measure of the Moon.
BARNARD, Micrometrical Observations of Eros.
BARRETT, Geography of the Heavens.
BARTKY, Highlights of Astronomy.
BLAAUW, Galactic Structure.
BROWN, Bibliography on Meteorites.
BURNHAM, Measures of Double Stars.
CHAMBERLIN, Origin of the Earth.
CHAMBERLIN, Two Solar Families.
FINLAY-FREUNDLICH, Cosmology.
FOWLER, Nucleosynthesis in Massive Stars and Supernovae.
FROST, Radial Velocities of 500 Stars.
GALILEI, Dialogue on the Great World Systems.
GREENSTEIN, Stellar Atmospheres.
HALE, Spectra of Stars of Secchi's Fourth Type.
HALE, Study of Stellar Evolution.
HARRISON, Gravitation Theory and Gravitational Collapse.
HEIDE, Meteorites.
HILTNER, Astronomical Techniques.
KUIPER, Atmospheres of the Earth and Planets.

KUIPER, Photographic Lunar Atlas.
KUIPER, Solar System. (Series.)
KUIPER, Telescopes.
LAVES, Orbit of the Minor Planet (334).
MARKOV, Moon.
MIDDLEHURST, Moon, Meteorites, and Comets.
MOULTON, On Certain Rigorous Methods of Treating Problems in Celestial Mechanics.
ODISHAW, Challenges of Space.
O'KEEFE, Tektites.
PODOBED, Fundamental Astrometry.
RITCHEY, Astronomical Photography.
ROBINSON, Quasi-stellar Sources and Gravitational Collapse.
ROSS, Atlas of the Northern Milky Way.
SANTILLANA, Crime of Galileo.
STRAND, Basic Astronomical Data.
THORNDIKE, Latin Treatises on Comets.
THORNDIKE, Sphere of Sacrobosco and Its Commentators.
*See also* ASTROPHYSICAL JOURNAL REPRINTS; ASTROPHYSICAL MONOGRAPHS; YERKES OBSERVATORY BULLETINS; YERKES OBSERVATORY PUBLICATIONS.

## BACTERIOLOGY:

DACK, Food Poisoning.
FROST, Frost's Culture Charts.
HEINEMANN, Laboratory Guide in Bacteriology.
JORDAN, Food-Poisoning and Food-borne Infection.
JORDAN, Newer Knowledge of Bacteriology and Immunology.
JORDAN, Self-purification of Streams.
NORTON, Laboratory Outlines in Bacteriology and Immunology.
SMITH, Introduction to Pathogenic Anaerobes.

## BIBLE:

CHAMBERLIN, Books of the Holy Bible.
CHAMBERLIN, Introduction to the Bible.
COLWELL, Study of the Bible.
DAICHES, King James Version of the English Bible.
GOODSPEED, Short Bible.
GOODSPEED, Story of the Apocrypha.
GOODSPEED, Story of the Bible.
GOODSPEED, Translators to the Reader.
GORDON, Truth about the Bible.
LEWIS, How the Bible Grew.
MILLER, Dramatization of Bible Stories.

REDUS, Text of the Major Festivals of the Menologion in the Greek Gospel Lectionary.

SELLECK, New Appreciation of the Bible.

SMITH, Bible. An American Translation.

SMITH, Complete Bible.

SOARES, How To Enjoy the Bible.

THIELE, Mysterious Numbers of the Hebrew Kings.

WALLIS, Sociological Study of the Bible.

WIKGREN, Hellenistic Greek Religious Texts.

WILLOUGHBY, First Authorized English Bible.

WILLOUGHBY, Study of the Bible Today and Tomorrow.

## BIBLE. NEW TESTAMENT:

ARNDT, Greek-English Lexicon of the New Testament and Other Early Christian Literature.

BOWEN, Studies in the New Testament.

BRANTON, Common Text of the Gospel Lectionary.

BRAY, Weekday Lessons from Luke in the Greek Gospel Lectionary.

BUCK, Johannine Lessons in the Greek Gospel Lectionary.

BURTON, Harmony of the Synoptic Gospels.

BURTON, Origin and Teaching of the New Testament Books.

BURTON, Short Introduction to the Gospels.

BURTON, Some Principles of Literary Criticism and Their Application to the Synoptic Problem.

BURTON, Studies in the Gospel According to Mark.

BURTON, Syntax of the Moods and Tenses in New Testament Greek.

CASE, Book of Revelation.

CASE, Historicity of Jesus.

CASE, Jesus, A New Biography.

CASE, Jesus through the Centuries.

CASTOR, Matthew's Sayings of Jesus.

CLARK, Descriptive Catalogue of Greek New Testaments.

CLARK, Eight American Paraxapostoloi.

COLWELL, Four Gospels of Karahissar.

COLWELL, Greek of the Fourth Gospel.

COLWELL, Prolegomena to the Study of the Lectionary Text.

COLWELL, What Is The Best New Testament?

FUNK, Greek Grammar of the New Testament.

GINGRICH, Shorter Lexicon of the Greek New Testament.

GOODSPEED, Ethiopic Martyrdoms.

GOODSPEED, Formation of the New Testament.

GOODSPEED, Goodspeed Parallel New Testament.

GOODSPEED, History of Early Christian Literature.

GOODSPEED, Introduction to the New Testament.

GOODSPEED, Key to Ephesians.

GOODSPEED, Making of the English New Testament.

GOODSPEED, Meaning of Ephesians.

GOODSPEED, New Solutions of New Testament Problems.

GOODSPEED, New Testament.

GOODSPEED, Rockefeller-McCormick New Testament.

GOODSPEED, Story of the New Testament.

GOODSPEED, Strange New Gospels.

GOODSPEED, Student's New Testament.

GOODSPEED, Synoptic Gospels.

HATCH, Principal Uncial Manuscripts.

HENRY, Paul, Son of Kish.

HOBEN, Virgin Birth.

HOBSON, Diatessaron of Tatian.

KNOX, Philemon.

LEWIS, Irenaeus Testimony.

LYONS, New Testament Literature.

MATHEWS, Message of Jesus.

MATHEWS, Messianic Hope.

MATHEWS, Student's Gospels.

METZGER, Saturday and Sunday Lessons from Luke.

OSBORN, Recovery and Restatement of the Gospel.

PARSONS, Historical Examination of Some Non-Markan Elements in Luke.

PARVIS, New Testament Manuscript Studies.

PERRY, Sources of Luke's Passion Narrative.

RADIN, Trial of Jesus.

REDUS, Text of the Major Festivals of Menologion.

RIDDLE, Gospels.

RIDDLE, Jesus and the Pharisees.

RIDDLE, New Testament Life and Literature.

ROBINSON, Life of Paul.

ROBINSON, Parables of Jesus.

SEIDEL, In the Time of Jesus.

SHARMAN, Teaching of Jesus.

VOTAW, Books Recommended for New Testament Study.

VOTAW, Primitive Era of Christianty.

WEARING, World-View of the Fourth Gospel.

WEISS, Present Status of the Inquiry concerning the Genuineness of the Pauline Epistles.

WICKES, Sources of Luke's Perean Section.

WILLOUGHBY, Elizabeth Day McCormick Apocalypse.

*See also* HISTORICAL AND LINGUISTIC STUDIES IN LITERATURE RELATED TO THE NEW TESTAMENT; AMERICAN INSTITUTE OF SACRED LITERATURE.

## BIBLE. OLD TESTAMENT:

ASADA, Hebrew Text of Zechariah.

BERRY, Premillennialism and Old Testament Prediction.

BUTTENWIESER, Psalms.

CHAMBERLIN, Making the Bible Live.

CORBETT, Old Testament Story.

FOWLER, Origin and Growth of the Hebrew Religion.

GEVIRTZ, Patterns in the Early Poetry of Israel.

GOLDMAN, Ten Commandments.

GOODSPEED, Apocrypha.

GOODSPEED, Story of the Apocrypha.

GOODSPEED, Story of the Old Testament.

GRAHAM, Culture and Conscience.

GRAHAM, Prophets and Israel's Culture.

GREGORIUS, Barhebraeus' Scholia on the Old Testament.

HARPER, Book of Job.

HARPER, Old Testament and Semitic Studies.

HARPER, Priestly Element in the Old Testament.

HARPER, Prophetic Element in the Old Testament.

HARPER, Structure of the Text of the Book of Hosea.

HARPER, Utterances of Amos.

HARPER, Work of the Old Testament Priests.

HARPER, Work of the Old Testament Sages.

HEIDEL, Babylonian Genesis.

HEIDEL, Gilgamesh Epic and Old Testament Parallels.

HIRSCHY, Artaxerxes III.

HOUGHTON, Hebrew Life.

IRWIN, Problems of Ezekiel.

KAUFMANN, Religion of Israel.

KRAFT, Strophic Structure of Hebrew Poetry.

McINTOSH, Study of Augustine's Versions of Genesis.

MAIMONIDES, Guide to the Perplexed.

MITCHELL, Ethics of the Old Testament.

PECKHAM, Introduction to the Study of Obadiah.

POEBEL, Appositionell bestimmte Pronomen.

QUINN, Quest of Seth for the Oil of Life.

ROBBINS, Hexaemeral Literature.

SLATER, Sources of Tyndale's Version of the Pentateuch.

SMITH, Books for Old Testament Study.

SMITH, Day of Yahweh.

SMITH, Old Testament.

SMITH, Origin and History of Hebrew Law.

SMITH, Problem of Suffering.

SMITH, Prophets and Their Times.

SMITH, Psalms.

SMITH, Religion of the Psalms.

SMITH, Universal Element in the Psalter.

TORREY, Ezra Studies.

WALLIS, Sociological Study of the Bible.

WORRELL, Proverbs of Solomon.

WRIGHT, Challenge of Israel's Faith.

## BIBLIOGRAPHY:

BLOOMFIELD, Bibliography of Internal Medicine.

BOND, Reference Guide to English Studies.

BREWINGTON, Social Concept of Money.

COLE, Index to Bibliographical Papers.

COLEMAN, Analytical Bibliography of Modern Language Teaching, 1927–1932.

COLEMAN, Analytical Bibliography of Modern Language Teaching, 1932–1937.

COOPER, Bibliography on Educational Broadcasting.

CROSS, Bibliographical Guide to English Studies.

DE MORGAN, On the Difficulty of Correct Description of Books.

DOE, Bibliography of the Works of Ambroise Paré.

FEIPEL, Elements of Bibliography.

GROSE, Select Bibliography of British History, 1660–1760.

HORECKY, Basic Russian Publications.

HORECKY, Russia and the Soviet Union.

JOSEPHSON, Bibliographies of Bibliographies.

KRAMER, History of Stone & Kimball and Herbert S. Stone & Co.

KROGMAN, Bibliography of Human Morphology.

LYONS, New Testament Literature. An Annotated Bibliography.

RAVEN, *Hamlet* Bibliography.

ROCHEDIEU, Bibliography of French Translations of English Works.

SCHELLENBERG, Modern Archives.

SHERA, Bibliographic Organization.

SILVERSTEIN, Medieval Latin Scientific Writings.

TAYLOR, Bibliographical History of Anonyma and Pseudonyma.

THOMAS, John Dewey.

## BIOCHEMISTRY:

COWDRY, General Cytology.

DAVENPORT, ABC of Acid-Base Chemistry.

EVANS, Biochemical Studies of Bacterial Viruses.

GERARD, Food for Life.

GOMORI, Microscopic Histochemistry.

MACY, Chemical Anthropology.

MOULDER, Biochemistry of Intercellular Parasitism.

NEUMAN, Chemical Dynamics of Bone Material.

RASHEVSKY, Mathematical Biophysics.

ROTHMAN, Physiology and Biochemistry of the Skin.

SCHLENK, Transmethylation and Methionine Biosynthesis.

SELYE, Calciphylaxis.

SOSKIN, Carbohydrate Metabolism.

TASHIRO, Chemical Sign of Life.

WATTERSON, Endocrines in Development.

WEBSTER, Laboratory Manual of Physiological Chemistry.

WEISS, Genetic Neurology.

ZIRKLE, Symposium on Molecular Biology.

## BIOLOGY:

ANDREWARTHA, Distribution and Abundance of Animals.

ANDREWARTHA, Introduction to the Study of Animal Populations.

BAYER, Growth Diagnosis.

BIRREN, Handbook of Aging and the Individual.

BUCHSBAUM, Animals without Backbones.

BUCHSBAUM, Readings in Ecology.

CAMPBELL, Physiology of Insect Development.

CARLSON, Machinery of the Body.

CHILD, Individuality in Organisms.

CHILD, Origin and Development of the Nervous System.

CHILD, Patterns and Problems of Development.

CLARK, Fossil Evidence for Human Evolution.

CLARK, History of the Primates.

COULTER, Story of the Plant Kingdom.

COWDRY, General Cytology.

DACK, Food Poisoning.

DOWNING, Our Living World.

DOWNING, Field and Laboratory Guide in Biological Nature-Study.

DUCOFF, Mitogenesis.

DuSHANE, Supplemental Drawings for Embryology.

EDDS, Immunology and Development.

EHRENSVÄRD, Life.

EHRENSVÄRD, Man on Another World.

ENDERS, Delayed Implantation.

ETKIN, Social Behavior and Organization among Vertebrates.

EVANS, Biochemical Studies of Bacterial Viruses.

FIELD, Atlas of Cat Anatomy.

FINNEY, Experimental Design.

GALTON, Haematology and Blood Groups.

GREENBLATT, Cat Musculature.

HAMBURGER, Manual of Experimental Embryology.

HAYEK, Sensory Order.

HESS, The Biology of Mind.

HYMAN, Comparative Vertebrate Anatomy.

JONES, Selective Fertilization.

KARE, Physiological and Behavioral Aspects of Taste.

KELLOGG, Porpoises and Sonar.

KLEITMAN, Sleep and Wakefulness.

KLÜVER, Behavior Mechanisms in Monkeys.

KUMMER, Weed Seedlings.

LENZ, Medical Genetics,

LEWIS, Biology of the Negro.

LI, Population Genetics.

LIBBY, Comparative Vertebrate Anatomy.

LILLIE, General Biology and Philosophy of Organism.

LILLIE, Laboratory Outline of Embryology.

LILLIE, Problems of Fertilization.

LILLIE, Woods Hole Marine Biological Laboratory.

LOEB, Artificial Production of Spores of Monas.

LOEB, Mechanistic Conception of Life.

LOUTIT, Irradiation of Mice and Men.

LURIE, Louis Agassiz.

McLEAN, Bone.

MAINX, Foundations of Biology.

MARTIN, Roberts' Nutrition Work with Children.

MEAD, Giant African Snail.

MINTZ, Environmental Influences on Prenatal Development.
MITCHELL, Growth Regulators.
NAHIKIAN, Modern Algebra for Biologists.
NEEL, Human Heredity.
NEUMAN, Chemical Dynamics of Bone Material.
NEWMAN, Evolution, Genetics, and Eugenics.
NEWMAN, Twins.
OLSON, Morphological Integration.
PATTERSON, Wound Healing and Tissue Repair.
PAUL, Clinical Epidemiology.
POLYAK, Vertebrate Visual System.
PRICE, Dynamics of Proliferating Tissues.
RASHEVSKY, Advances and Applications of Mathematical Biology.
RASHEVSKY, Mathematical Biology of Social Behavior.
RASHEVSKY, Mathematical Biophysics.
ROMER, Osteology of the Reptiles.
ROMER, Vertebrate Story.
RUDNICK, Cytodifferentiation.
RUDNICK, Embryonic Nutrition.
SCHALLER, Mountain Gorilla.
SCOTT, Animal Behavior.
SCOTT, Genetics and the Social Behavior of the Dog.
SHAPIRO, Transmethylation and Methionine Biosynthesis.
SMITH, Introduction to Pathogenic Anaerobes.
SNIDER, Stereotaxic Atlas of the Cat Brain.
SNIDER, Stereotaxic Atlas of the Monkey Brain.
TAX, Evolution after Darwin.
THORNTON, Regeneration in Vertebrates.
VON BONIN, Evolution of the Human Brain.
WATTERSON, Endocrines in Development.
WEIDENREICH, Apes, Giants and Man.
ZIRKLE, Symposium on Molecular Biology.
ZWEIFEL, Handbook of Biological Illustration.

## BOTANY:

BARROWS, Ethno-Botany of the Coahuilla Indians.
BRAY, Ecological Relations of the Vegetation of Western Texas.
CHAMBERLAIN, Gymnosperms.
CHAMBERLAIN, Living Cycads.
CHAMBERLAIN, Methods in Plant Histology.
CHAMBERLAIN, Mitosis in Pellia.
CHAMBERLAIN, Oögenesis in Pinus laricio.

COULTER, Evolution of Sex in Plants.
COULTER, Morphology of Gymnosperms.
COULTER, Outline of Genetics.
COULTER, Phylogeny of Angiosperms.
COULTER, Plant Genetics.
COULTER, Story of the Plant Kingdom.
COWLES, Ecological Relations of the Vegetation of the Sand Dunes.
COWLES, Plant Societies.
DAVIS, Oögenesis in Saprolegnia.
FULLER, Vegetation of the Chicago Region.
JEFFREY, Anatomy of Woody Plants.
KUMMER, Weed Seedlings.
LIVINGSTON, Rôle of Diffusion and Osmotic Pressure in Plants.
McNAIR, Rhus Dermatitis.
MITCHELL, Growth Regulators for Garden, Field, and Orchard.
OVERTON, Parthenogenesis in Thalictrum purpurascens.
SAUER, Starved Rock State Park.
SHELFORD, Bio-ecology.
SMITH, Structure and Development of the Sporophylls and Sporangia of Isoetes.
TAX, Evolution after Darwin.
THORNDIKE, Herbal of Rufinus.
TIFFANY, Algae of Illinois.
WEATHERWAX, Story of the Maize Plant.
YAMANOUCHI, Life-History of Polysiphonia.

## BUSINESS:

ARNETT, Blank Accounting Blanks.
ARNETT, Sigma Chi Accounting System Booklets.
ARNETT, Sigma Chi Fraternity Blanks.
ARNETT, Sigma Chi Indices.
BAKER, Legal Aspects of Zoning.
BARNES, Marketing the Stephens Brake Shoe.
BREWINGTON, Social Concept of Money.
CALHOUN, Business Life in Ancient Athens.
COVER, Business and Personal Failure and Readjustment in Chicago.
COWAN, Sales Analysis.
DUDDY, Grain Supply Area of the Chicago Market.
DUDDY, Use of Transportation Facilities in the Chicago Fruit and Vegetable Market.
DUDDY, Physical Distribution of Fresh Fruits and Vegetables.
EMMET, Catalogues and Counters.
FRIEDMAN, Studies in the Quantity Theory of Money.
FRIEDRICH, Alfred Weber's Theory of the Location of Industries.

GRAHAM, Alternative Laboratory Exercises for Rorem's *Accounting Method.*

GRAHAM, Solutions to *Alternative Laboratory Exercises.*

GRAHAM, Teacher's Manual for *Accounting Method.*

GREER, Packinghouse Accounting.

HAAVELMO, Study in Theory of Investment.

HARBERGER, Demand for Durable Goods.

HODGE, Laboratory Material.

HODGE, Principles of Accounting.

HODGE, Retail Accounting.

HOYT, One Hundred Years of Land Values in Chicago.

JAMES, Education of Business Men.

JUDSON, Higher Education as a Training for Business.

KEMP, Canadian Marketing Problems.

KNOWLTON, Air Transportation in the United States.

LEAVITT, Managerial Psychology.

LEAVITT, Readings in Managerial Psychology.

LODGE, Philosophy of Business.

LYON, Education for Business.

McKINSEY, Managerial Accounting.

MARSHALL, Collegiate School of Business.

MATTHEWS, Business Cycle.

MEAD, Report on Vocational Training.

MINTS, History of Banking Theory.

MORTENSON, Milk Distribution.

NEWMAN, Building Industry and Business Cycles.

NICHOLLS, Labor Productivity Functions in Meat Packing.

NUTTER, Extent of Enterprise Monopoly in the United States, 1899–1939.

RANDALL, Foreign Economic Policy for the United States.

REDFIELD, Communication in Management.

RHODES, Merchandising Packinghouse Products.

ROBERTSON, Money.

ROBINSON, Structure of Competitive Industry.

ROREM, Accounting Method.

RUSSELL, Proceedings of the Conference on Problems of Business Administration in Colleges and Universities, 1936.

SCHULTZ, Statistical Laws of Demand and Supply.

SCHULTZ, Theory and Measurement of Demand.

SHIELDS, Junior College Business Education.

VATTER, Fund Theory of Accounting.

YNTEMA, Mathematical Reformulation of the General Theory of International Trade.

YOUNG, Advertising Agency Compensation.

*See also* MATERIALS FOR THE STUDY OF BUSINESS; STUDIES IN BUSINESS ADMINISTRATION; UNIVERSITY OF CHICAGO CONFERENCE ON BUSINESS EDUCATION.

## CHEMISTRY:

CHERDYNTSEV, Abundance of Chemical Elements.

DAVENPORT, ABC of Acid-Base Chemistry.

EITEL, Physical Chemistry of the Silicates.

GARNER, Condensations with Benzoin.

GERARD, Food for Life.

HALLIDAY, Food Chemistry and Cookery.

HOFF, Physical Chemistry.

HYMAN, Noble-Gas Compounds.

KOCH, Lecithans.

LADENBURG, Lectures on the History of the Development of Chemistry.

McCOY, Equilibrium.

MACY, Chemical Anthropology.

RANKAMA, Geochemistry.

ROTHMAN, Physiology and Biochemistry of the Skin.

RYDBERG, On the Constitution of the Red Spectrum of Argon.

SMITH, Hydrogen in Metals.

SMITH, Laboratory Outline of General Chemistry.

SMITH, On Amorphous Sulphur.

STIEGLITZ, On the "Beckmann Rearrangement."

TABLES ANNUELLES DE CONSTANTES.

WEBSTER, Contribution to the Physical Analysis of the Phenomena of Absorption.

WEBSTER, Laboratory Manual of Physiological Chemistry.

## CHICAGO:

ABBOTT, Tenements of Chicago.

ABBOTT, Truancy and Non-attendance.

ANDERSON, Hobo.

BEELEY, Bail System.

BEYLE, Governmental Reporting in Chicago.

BJORKLUND, Study of Prices of Chain and Independent Grocers.

BLOUNT, Excursion through the Rivers and Harbors of Chicago.

BRECKINRIDGE, Family Welfare Work in a Metropolitan Community.

BRISTOL, Handbook for Field Work Students.

BROWN, Book and Job Printing.

Buck, Sketch of the Linguistic Conditions of Chicago.

Burgess, Census Data of the City of Chicago, 1920.

Burgess, Census Data of the City of Chicago, 1930.

Cavan, Family and the Depression.

Chicago Commission on Race Relations, Negro in Chicago.

Christenson, Collective Bargaining.

City Club of Chicago, Railway Terminal Problem.

Clark, Public Schools.

Condit, Chicago School of Architecture.

Cover, Business and Personal Failure.

Cox, Weather and Climate of Chicago.

Cressey, Taxi-Dance Hall.

Drury, Old Chicago Houses.

Duddy, Agriculture in the Chicago Region.

Duddy, Changing Relative Importance of Central Livestock Market.

Duddy, Chicago Foundry Company.

Duddy, Distribution of Livestock.

Duddy, Grain Supply Area of the Chicago Market.

Duddy, Supply Area of Chicago Livestock Market.

Duddy, Use of Transportation Facilities.

Duncan, Negro Population of Chicago.

Fairweather, Wanted. Intelligent Local Self-Government.

Faris, Mental Disorders in Urban Areas.

Frazier, Negro Family in Chicago.

Freedman, Recent Migration to Chicago.

Fryxell, Physiography of the Region of Chicago.

Fuller, Vegetation in the Chicago Region.

Goode, Geographic Background of Chicago.

Gosnell, Machine Politics.

Gosnell, Negro Politicians.

Harper, Report of the Educational Commission.

Hillman, Tomorrow's Chicago.

Hooker, Through Routes for Chicago's Steam Railroads.

Houghteling, Income and Standard of Living.

Hoyt, One Hundred Years of Land Values in Chicago.

Hughes, Social Service Exchange in Chicago.

James, Charters of the City of Chicago.

Jeter, Trends of Population in the Region of Chicago.

Koeckel, Metropolitan Library in Action.

Johnson, Relief and Health Problems of a Selected Group of Non-Family Men.

Kennedy, Wages and Family Budgets.

Krughoff, Salaries and Professional Qualifications of Social Workers in Chicago, 1935.

Lepawsky, Home Rule for Metropolitan Chicago.

Lepawsky, Judicial System of Metropolitan Chicago.

Local Community Research Committee, *The University of Chicago.* Social Base Map of Chicago.

Lyon, Governmental Problems in the Chicago Metropolitan Area.

Lyon, Modernizing a City Government.

Martin, Role of the Bar in Electing the Bench.

Mayer, Port of Chicago and the St. Lawrence Seaway.

Merriam, Government of the Metropolitan Region of Chicago.

Mitchell, Trends in Industrial Location in the Chicago Region.

Monroe, Chicago Families.

Montgomery, American Girl.

Montgomery, Industrial Relations.

Newcomb, Census Data of the City of Chicago, 1934.

Newcomb, Street Address Coding Guide.

Palyi, Chicago Credit Market.

Pierce, As Others See Chicago.

Quaife, Chicago and the Old Northwest.

Reckless, Vice in Chicago.

Riley, Higher Life.

Salisbury, Geography of Chicago.

Shaw, Delinquency Areas.

Short, Group Process and Gang Delinquency.

Siegel, Chicago's Famous Buildings.

Smith, Chicago, An Experiment in Social Science Research.

Steadman, Public Health Organization.

Talbert, Opportunities in School and Industry.

Tallmadge, Architecture in Old Chicago.

Taylor, Pioneering on Social Frontiers.

Thrasher, Gang.

University of Chicago, *The Social Science Survey Committee,* Rotary?

Vieg, Government of Education.

Webb, Contagious Disease Care.

White, Prestige Value of Public Employment in Chicago.

WHITE, Water Supply Organization.
WIRTH, Local Community Fact Book of Chicago.
ZORBAUGH, Gold Coast and the Slum.
*See also* CHICAGO HISTORICAL SOCIETY.

## CHILD STUDY:

ABBOTT, Child and the State.
ABBOTT, From Relief to Social Security.
ACKERSON, Children's Behavior Problems.
ALSCHULER, Painting and Personality.
BAYER, Growth Diagnosis.
BOWMAN, Studying Children and Training Counselors.
BOWMAN, Mobilizing Community Resources.
CHAVE, Junior.
CHAVE, Personality Development in Children.
DAWSON, Child and His Religion.
DeHAAN, Educating Gifted Children.
DEWEY, Child and the Curiculum.
DEWEY, Child and the Curiculum *and* The School and Society.
FRASER, Licensing of Boarding Homes.
GALE, Children's Preferences for Colors.
GARTLAND, Psychiatric Social Service in a Children's Hospital.
GOSSARD, Superior and Backward Children.
GRAY, Growth in Private School Children.
HARDY, Healthy Growth.
HAVIGHURST, Community Youth Development Program.
HAVIGHURST, Education for the Gifted in School and College.
HAVIGHURST, Survey of the Education of Gifted Children.
HESS, Physical and Mental Growth of Prematurely Born Children.
JONES, Adolescence.
KAWIN, Children of Preschool Age.
KAWIN, Comparative Study of a Nursery-School versus a Non-Nursery-School Group.
KAWIN, Problems of Preschool Age.
KAWIN, Wise Choice of Toys.
KING, Psychology of Child Development.
KIRK, Education of Exceptional Children.
LADEWICK, Scholarships.
LIGHT, Early Childhood Education.
MARTIN, Roberts' Nutrition Work with Children.
MEAD, Childhood in Contemporary Cultures.
MILCHRIST, State Administration of Child Welfare in Illinois.

MONROE, Children Who Cannot Read.
MORRISON, Children's Preferences for Pictures.
NIMS, Illinois Adoption Law.
NORRIS, Blindness in Children.
PUTTEE, Illegitimate Child in Illinois.
RIESE, Heal the Hurt Child.
RILEY, Working Manual for Juvenile Court Officers.
SMITH, Stepchild.
STEVENSON, Child Psychology.
STRANG, Juvenile Delinquency and the Schools.
TAYLOR, Law of Guardian and Ward.
THURSTONE, Order of Birth, Parent Age, and Intelligence.
VAN ALSTYNE, Play Behavior and Choice of Play Materials.
WASHBURNE, Child Development and the Curriculum.
WHIPPLE, Report of the Society's Committee on the Education of Gifted Children.
WHYTE, Street-Corner Society.
ZESBAUGH, Children's Drawings of the Human Figure.
*See also* CHICAGO ASSOCIATION FOR CHILD STUDY; TRANSACTIONS OF THE ILLINOIS SOCIETY FOR CHILD STUDY.

## CRIMINOLOGY:

ABBOTT, Child and the State.
ADDITON, City Planning for Girls.
BEELEY, Bail System in Chicago.
CHICAGO, *Citizens' Police Committee*, Chicago Police Problems.
LARSON, Lying and Its Detection.
McKELVEY, American Prisons.
RILEY, Working Manual for Juvenile Court Officers.
SHAW, Brothers in Crime.
SHAW, Delinquency Areas.
SHAW, Jack-Roller.
SHAW, Natural History of a Delinquent Career.
SUTHERLAND, Professional Thief.
THRASHER, The Gang.
TOPPING, Canadian Penal Institutions.
TULCHIN, Intelligence and Crime.
WARNER, Juvenile Detention in the United States.
WILSON, Treatment of the Misdemeanant in Indiana.

## DRAMA:

BASKERVILL, Elizabethan Jig.
BENTLEY, Shakespeare and Jonson.
CAPPS, Introduction of Comedy.
CAPPS, Vitruvius and the Greek Stage.
CARSON, Theatre on the Frontier.
DIGNAN, Idle Actor in Aeschylus.
DOWNER, Modern American Drama and Its Critics.
DUNKEL, Sir Arthur Pinero.
FLICKINGER, Greek Theatre.
FLICKINGER, Meaning of ἐπὶ τῆς σκηνῆς in Writers of the Fourth Century.
FLICKINGER, Plutarch as a Source of Information on the Greek Theatre.
GODDARD, Meaning of Shakespeare.
HANCOCK, Studies in Stichomythia.
JOHNSON, Six Proust Reconstructions.
KENNEDY, Plays for Seven Players.
KENNEDY, Plays for Three Players.
KERNODLE, From Art to Theatre.
KUEFFNER, Development of the Historic Drama.
LEECH, Shakespeare. The Tragedies.
MILLER, Two Dramatizations from Vergil.
MOORE, Comic and the Realistic in English Drama.
MOULTON, Book of Illustrations.
NETHERCOT, Sir William D'avenant.
O'CONNER, Chapters in the History of Actors and Acting.
O'HARA, Today in American Drama.
O'HARA, University of Chicago Plays, Skits, and Lyrics.
OLSON, Plays and Poems.
RAVEN, *Hamlet* Bibliography and Reference Guide.
REES, Rule of Three Actors.
REYNOLDS, Some Principles of Elizabethan Staging.
SCHICK, Early Theatre in Eastern Iowa.
SMITH, T. S. Eliot's Poetry and Plays.
TUNISON, Dramatic Traditions.
WILSON, All the King's Ladies.
*See also* COMPLETE GREEK TRAGEDIES.

## ECONOMICS:

ACKERMAN, Family Farm Policy.
ACKERMAN, Japan's Natural Resources and Their Relation to Japan's Economic Future.
ACKERMAN, New England's Fishing Industry.
AYRES, Nature of the Relationship between Ethics and Economics.
BALABANIS, American Discount Market.
BAUER, Economics of Under-developed Countries.
BECKER, Economics of Discrimination.
BJORKLUND, Study of the Prices of Chain and Independent Grocers.
BLAIR, More for Your Money.
BLOCH, Economics of Military Occupation.
BLOOMFIELD, Capital Imports and the American Balance of Payments.
BLUM, Uneasy Cases for Progressive Taxation.
BRANCH, Women and Wealth.
BRATTER, Should We Turn to Silver?
BRECKINRIDGE, Legal Tender.
BREWINGTON, Social Conception of Money.
BRITNELL, Wheat Economy.
BUELL, Death by Tariff.
CARVER, Personnel and Labor Problems.
CATTERALL, Second Bank of the United States.
CASSEL, Foreign Investments.
CHAPLIN, Wobbly. The Rough-and-Tumble Story of an American Radical.
CLAPP, TVA.
CLARK, Studies in the Economics of Overhead Costs.
COHN, Science of Finance.
CONDLIFFE, New Zealand in the Making.
COVER, Financing the Consumer.
COVER, Retail Price Behavior.
DAVENPORT, Exercises in Value Theory.
DAVENPORT, Value and Distribution.
DEAN, Statistical Determination of Costs.
DIRECTOR, Defense, Controls, and Inflation.
DIRECTOR, Economics of Technocracy.
DOUGLAS, Economy in the National Government.
DOUGLAS, Movement of Money.
EASTERBY, South Carolina Rice Plantation.
EDIE, Capital, the Money Market, and Gold.
EDWARDS, Nation's Economic Objectives.
ELLSTAETTER, Indian Silver Currency.
EUCKEN, Foundations of Economics.
FETTER, New Deal and Tariff Policy.
Financial Mobilization for War.
FRIEDMAN, Capitalism and Freedom.
FRIEDMAN, Essays in Positive Economics.
FRIEDMAN, Studies in the Quantity Theory of Money.
FRIEDRICH, Alfred Weber's Theory of the Location of Industries.
GIDEONSE, Commodity Dollar.

GINSBURG, Atlas of Economic Development.
GLICK, Administration of Technical Assistance.
GRODINSKY, Iowa Pool.
HAAVELMO, Study in the Theory of Investment.
HAMILTON, Current Economic Problems.
HAMILTON, Exercises in Current Economics.
HAMILTON, Landmarks of Political Economy.
HARBERGER, Demand for Durable Goods.
HARDY, Devaluation of the Dollar.
HARROD, International Economics.
HART, Anticipations, Uncertainty, and Dynamic Planning.
HART, How the National Income Is Divided.
HATFIELD, Lectures on Commerce.
HAYEK, Capitalism and the Historians.
HAYEK, Constitution of Liberty.
HAYEK, Freedom and the Economic System.
HAYEK, Individualism and the Economic Order.
HAYEK, Pure Theory of Capitalism.
HAYEK, Road to Serfdom.
HENDERSON, Supply and Demand.
HIRSHLEIFER, Water Supply.
HOSELITZ, Progress of Underdeveloped Areas.
INNIS, Essays in Political Economy.
JASNY, Soviet Industrialization, 1928–52.
JENSEN, Property Taxation in the United States.
JOHNSON, Forward Prices for Agriculture.
JOHNSON, Grain Yields and the American Food Supply.
KEENER, Cutting the Cost of Bank Loans.
KNIGHT, On the History and Method of Economics.
KYRK, Family in the American Economy.
LANGE, Studies in Mathematical Economics.
LAUGHLIN, Gold and Prices since 1873.
LAUGHLIN, New Exposition of Money, Credit, and Prices.
LEE, Anti Chain-Store Tax Legislation.
LELAND, State-Local Fiscal Relations in Illinois.
LEWIS, Unionism and Relative Wages in the United States.
LIPSON, Politics of Equality.
LINDSEY, Pullman Strike.
MADDOX, Technical Assistance by Religious Agencies in Latin America.
MAHR, Monetary Stability.
MARSHALL, Industrial Society.
MARSHALL, Materials for the Study of Elementary Economics.

MARSHALL, Outline of Economics.
MARSHALL, Outlines of the Economic Order.
MARTIN, Standard of Living in 1860.
MATTHEWS, Business Cycle.
MEADE, Problems of Economic Union.
MEIGS, Free Reserves and the Money Supply.
MERRIAM, Government and the Economic Order.
MILLIS, From Wagner Act to Taft-Hartley.
MINTS, History of Banking Theory.
MITCHELL, History of the Greenbacks.
MITCHELL, Uses of Bank Funds.
MORLEY, Economic World Today.
MOSHER, Technical Co-operation in Latin American Agriculture.
MOULTON, Danner-Kraft Dry Goods Company.
MOULTON, Exercises and Questions for Use with *Principles of Money.*
MOULTON, Principles of Banking.
MOULTON, Principles of Money and Banking.
NICHOLLS, Labor Productivity Functions in Meat Packing.
NORTH, Sociological Implications of Ricardo's Economics.
NUTTER, Extent of Enterprise Monopoly in the United States.
ORTON, Economic Role of the State.
PALYI, Chicago Credit Market.
PALYI, Monetary Chaos and Gold.
PALYI, Principles of Mortgage Banking Regulation in Europe.
PELLING, American Labor.
PERLOFF, Puerto Rico's Economic Future.
PESEK, Gross National Product of Czechoslovakia.
PICKETT, Federal Reserve Bank Policy in Iowa.
POLAK, International Economic System.
POTTER, People of Plenty.
RANDALL, Foreign Economic Policy for the United States.
REES, Economics of Trade Unions.
REID, Housing and Income.
ROBERTSON, Money.
ROBINSON, Structure of Competitive Industry.
ROCKEFELLER, Unused Resources and Economic Waste.
RÖPKE, Social Crisis in Our Time.
ROSE, Money.
SANDERS, Standard of Living.

SAYER, Protection of American Export Trade.

SCHULTZ, Statistical Laws of Demand and Supply.

SCHULTZ, Theory and Measurement of Demand.

SEIDMAN, Worker Views His Union.

SIMONS, Economic Policy for a Free Society.

SIMONS, Federal Tax Reform.

SIMONS, Personal Income Taxation.

SIMONS, Positive Program for Laissez Faire.

SMALL, Adam Smith and Modern Sociology.

SMITH, Customs Valuation in the United States.

SOHMEN, Flexible Exchange Rates.

SPRAGUE, True Nature of Value.

SPURRIER, Common Stocks and Bonds as Long-Term Investments.

STALEY, War and the Private Investor.

TIPPETTS, Autarchy.

THORNTON, History of the Quaker Oats Company.

TINBERGEN, Dynamics of Business Cycles.

TOBIN, What Becomes of the Consumer's Meat Dollar?

UNIVERSITY OF CHICAGO, *Department of Political Economy*, Bibliography of Economics.

VEBLEN, Use of Loan Credit.

VINER, Dumping.

WALKER, From Economic Theory to Policy.

WEISSKOPF, Psychology of Economics.

WHITE, State of the Social Sciences.

WILCOX, Credit Unions in New York State.

WILCOX, Statistical Study of Credit Unions.

WRIGHT, American Tariff and Oriental Trade.

WRIGHT, Economic Problems of War.

WRIGHT, Gold and Monetary Stabilization.

WRIGHT, World Community.

YNTEMA, Mathematical Reformulation of the General Theory of International Trade.

*See also* ECONOMIC STUDIES OF THE UNIVERSITY OF CHICAGO; MATERIALS FOR THE STUDY OF ECONOMICS.

## EDUCATION:

ABBOTT, Truancy and Non-attendance.

ADLER, Revolution in Education.

ALSCHULER, Painting and Personality.

ANDERSON, Learning and Instruction.

ARNDT, Community Education.

ASHBAUGH, Measurement of Educational Products.

AYER, Fourth Report of the Committee on Economy of Time in Education.

BAGLEY, Third Report of the Committee on Economy of Time in Education.

BARKER, Industrial Education.

BARNARD, Rethinking Science Education.

BOWER, Church and State in Education.

BOYCE, Methods for Measuring Teacher's Efficiency.

BRESLICH, Problems in Teaching Secondary-School Mathematics.

BRIM, Status of Rural Education.

BRUBACHER, Modern Philosophies and Education.

BRUBACHER, Philosophies of Education.

BUSWELL, Summary of Educational Investigations Relating to Arithmetic.

BUSWELL, Teaching Arithmetic.

CADE, Professional Preparation of High-School Teachers.

CALLAHAN, Education and the Cult of Efficiency.

CHARTERS, Check List of Teacher's Activities.

CHARTERS, Commonwealth Teacher-training Study.

CLEMENT, Standardization of the Schools.

CLIFT, Adult Reading.

COE, Law and Freedom.

COMENIUS, Analytical Didactic of Comenius.

COMMITTEE ON NEW MATERIALS OF INSTRUCTION, New Materials of Instruction.

COMMITTEE ON NEW MATERIALS OF INSTRUCTION, Second Report.

COOPER, Administrative Planning for School Programs and Plants.

COOPER, Bibliography on Educational Broadcasting.

COREY, Audio-Visual Materials of Instruction.

COREY, In-Service Education for Teachers, Supervisors, and Administrators.

COXE, Grouping of Pupils.

COULTER, Introductory General Course in the Biological Sciences, Syllabus.

CROCHERON, Rural School as a Community Center.

CUBBERLEY, Certification of Teachers.

CUNNINGHAM, Classroom Procedure Test in Natural Science.

DALE, Mass Media and Education.

DeHAAN, Educating Gifted Children.

DEPARTMENT OF PHYSICAL EDUCATION AND HEALTH, Physical Education and Health of School Children.

DEWEY, American Education, Past and Present.

DEWEY, Child and the Curriculum.

DEWEY, Educational Situation.

DEWEY, Ethical Principles.

DEWEY, Relation of Theory to Practice in the Education of Teachers.

DEWEY, School and Society.

DOWNING, Introduction to the Teaching of Science.

DOWNING, Teaching Science.

DRESSEL, Integration of Educational Experiences.

EAKIN, Good Books for Children.

EDGERTON, Vocational Guidance and Vocational Education for Industries.

EDMONSON, Textbook in American Education.

EDWARDS, Courts and the Public Schools.

EDWARDS, Education in a Democracy.

EICKENBERRY, Teaching of General Science.

ELLIOTT, Education and Training of Teachers.

EMBREE, Island India Goes to School.

ENGLEHARDT, Planning and Construction of School Buildings.

EURICH, General Education in the American College.

FARRINGTON, Observation and Practice Teaching.

FINDLEY, Impact and Improvement of School Testing Programs.

FREEMAN, Scientific Movement in Education.

GILLAND, Origin and Development of the Power and Duties of the City-School Superintendent.

GOODYKOONTZ, American Education in the Postwar Period.

GOSSARD, Superior and Backward Children.

GRACE, Changing Conceptions in Educational Administration.

GRACE, Leadership in American Education.

GRAY, Promoting Growth toward Maturity in Interpreting What Is Read.

HARDEE, Personnel Services in Education.

HARDIN, Freedom in Agricultural Education.

HARDY, Healthy Growth.

HATHWAY, Young Cripple and His Job.

HAVIGHURST, Developmental Tasks and Education.

HAVIGHURST, Education for the Gifted in School and College.

HAVIGHURST, Survey of the Education of Gifted Children.

HEATON, Character Emphasis in Education.

HEATON, College Curriculum Based on Functional Needs of Students.

HEATON, Professional Education for Experienced Students.

HENDERSON, Education with Reference to Sex.

HENDERSON, Introduction to Philosophy of Education.

HENRY, Classroom Problems in the Education of Gifted Children.

HENRY, Schools and City Government.

HERRICK, Toward Improved Curriculum Theory.

HERRICK, Vocational Studies for College Entrance.

HOBSON, Educational Legislation and Administration in the State of New York.

HOLLEY, Relationship between Persistence in School and Home Conditions.

HOLZINGER, Statistical Tables for Students in Education and Psychology.

HUTCHINS, No Friendly Voice.

JACKMAN, Nature Study.

JENSEN, Dynamics of Instructional Groups.

JONES, Character and Citizenship Training.

JUDD, Democracy and American Schools.

JUDD, Plans for Organizing School Surveys.

KALLEN, Education versus Indoctrination in the Schools.

KANDEL, International Understanding through the Public-School Curriculum.

KAWIN, Wise Choice of Toys.

KEFAUVER, Guidance in Educational Institutions.

KELLER, Vocational Education.

KELSEY, Should Papers Dealing with Matters of Scholarship, or Papers on Method Be the Chief Feature of Teacher Meetings?

KIRK, Education of Exceptional Children.

KNAPP, Origins of American Scientists.

KOOS, Extra-curricular Activities.

KOOS, Private and Public Secondary Education.

KORNHAUSER, How To Study.

LAWLER, Educational Administration in an Era of Transition.

LAWRENCE, Course of Study in History in the Common School.

LAWSON, Curriculum Development in City-School Systems.

LEIPZIGER, City School as a Community Center.

LIEBERMAN, Future of Public Education.

LOWRY, Relation of Superintendents and Principals to the Training and Professional Improvement of Their Teachers.

MCCONNELL, General Education.

MACDONALD, Mind, School, and Civilization.

MCSWAIN, Opportunities for Education in the Next Decade.

MACVANNEL, College Course in the Principles of Education.

MADISON, Basic Concepts of Music Education.

MEAD, Report on Vocational Training.

MEEK, Preschool and Parental Education.

MILLER, History of Educational Legislation in Ohio.

MONAHAN, Supervision of Rural Schools.

MONROE, Children Who Cannot Read.

MORRISON, American Schools.

MORRISON, Curriculum of the Common School.

MORRISON, Management of the School Money.

MORRISON, School Revenue.

MOSSMAN, Activity Movement.

NATIONAL COMMITTEE ON STANDARD REPORTS FOR INSTITUTIONS OF HIGHER EDUCATION, Financial Reports for Colleges and Universities.

NETTLESHIP, Theory of Education.

NOLL, Science Education in American Schools.

NORRIS, Blindness in Children.

PARKINS, Teaching of Geography.

PIERCE, Origin and Development of the Public-School Principalship.

POWERS, Program for Teaching Science.

PUNKE, Courts and Public-School Property.

PUNKE, Law and Liability in Pupil Transportation.

RANDALL, College Library.

REAVIS, Administrative Adjustments Required by Socioeconomic Change.

REAVIS, Critical Issues in Educational Administration.

REAVIS, Democratic Practices in School Administration.

REAVIS, Educational Administration.

REAVIS, Evaluation of Teacher Merit in City School Systems.

REAVIS, Significant Aspects of American Life and Postwar Education.

REAVIS, War and Postwar Responsibilities of American Schools.

REEVES, Education for Rural America.

RICHTER, Re-educating Germany.

ROBINSON, Why Pupils Fail in Reading.

RUGG, Foundations and Technique of Curriculum Construction.

SALMON, Some Principles in the Teaching of History.

SCHATZMANN, Country School.

SEAY, Community School.

SINCLAIR, Possibility of a Science Education.

SPAULDING, Aims, Scope, and Methods of a University Course in Public-School Administration.

STEPHENSON, Introductory General Course in the Physical Sciences, Syllabus.

STEVENSON, Child Psychology.

STEWART, Local Broadcasts to Schools.

STODDARD, Intelligence. Its Nature and Nurture. Comparative and Critical Exposition.

STODDARD, Intelligence. Its Nature and Nurture. Original Studies and Experiments.

STRANG, Education in Rural Communities.

STRANG, Exploration in Reading Patterns.

STRANG, Juvenile Delinquency and the Schools.

STRAYER, Standards and Tests for the Measurement of Efficiency of Schools and School Systems.

SUTTON, Organization of the Department of Education.

TEAR, Logical Basis of Educational Theory.

TERMAN, Nature and Nurture.

TRUMP, High-School Extracurricular Activities.

TYLER, American Education in the Postwar Period.

TYLER, Basic Principles of Curriculum and Instruction.

TYLER, Individualizing Instruction.

TYLER, Social Forces Influencing American Education.

UHL, Music Education.

VIEG, Government of Education in Chicago.

VIEG, Government of Education in Metropolitan Chicago.

VINCENT, Social Mind and Education.

WAPLES, Classroom Procedure Test.

WAPLES, Problem Exercises.

WAPLES, What Reading Does to People.

WASHBURNE, Adapting the Schools to Individual Differences.

WASHBURNE, Child Development and Curriculum.

WHIPPLE, Present Status of Safety Education.

WHIPPLE, Procedures Used in Selecting School Books.

TOWLE, Learner in Education for the Professions.

TOWNER, Religion in Higher Education.

TYLER, Graduate Study in Education.

VEYSEY, Emergence of the American University.

WARD, Idea and Practice of General Education.

WILKINS, Changing College.

## EDUCATION. SECONDARY:

ASSOCIATION, OF COLLEGIATE SCHOOLS OF BUSINESS, Social Studies in Secondary Schools.

BRESLICH, Administration of Mathematics in Secondary Schools.

BRINK, Adapting the Secondary-School Program to the Needs of Youth.

BROWN, Place of Vocational Subjects in the High-School Curriculum.

BUTLER, Improvement of Teaching in Secondary Schools.

CHASE, High School in a New Era.

COUNTS, Senior High School Curriculum.

DEWEY, Child and the Curriculum.

DOUGLASS, Junior High School.

EDUCATIONAL CONFERENCE OF THE ACADEMIES AND HIGH SCHOOLS AFFILIATING OR CO-OPERATING WITH THE UNIVERSITY OF CHICAGO.

GLASS, Curriculum Practices in the Junior High School.

GRAY, Academic and Professional Preparation of Secondary-School Teachers.

KIRK, Education of Exceptional Children.

KOOS, Administration of Secondary-School Units.

KOOS, Private and Public Secondary Education.

LOCKE, Bibliography of Secondary Education.

MONAHAN, Agricultural Education in Secondary Schools.

MORRISON, Practice of Teaching in the Secondary School.

MORRISON, Some Aspects of High-School Instruction and Administration.

MORRISON, Studies in Secondary Education, Vol. I.

REAVIS, Studies in Secondary Education, Vol. II.

*See also* CONFERENCE FOR ADMINISTRATIVE OFFICERS OF PUBLIC AND PRIVATE SCHOOLS; CONTRIBUTIONS TO EDUCATION; CURRICULUM ENRICHMENT MATERIALS; EVALUATION OF HIGHER INSTITUTIONS; INSTITUTE FOR AD-MINISTRATIVE OFFICERS OF HIGHER INSTITUTIONS; NATIONAL SOCIETY FOR THE STUDY OF EDUCATION; NATIONAL SOCIETY OF COLLEGE TEACHERS OF EDUCATION; SUPPLEMENTARY EDUCATIONAL MONOGRAPHS.

## FOLKLORE:

BLAIR, Half Horse Half Alligator.

BOTKIN, Lay My Burden Down.

BRIGGS, Folktales of England.

BROWNLOW, Anatomy of the Anecdote.

CHRISTIANSEN, Folktales of Norway.

COWPER, Italian Folk Tales and Folk Songs.

DÉGH, Folktales of Hungary.

DIMOCK, Thief of Love.

DORSON, American Folklore.

DORSON, Buying the Wind.

EBERHARD, Folktales of China.

NOY, Folktales of Israel.

SEKI, Folktales of Japan.

## GEOGRAPHY:

BURTON, Readings in Resource Management and Conservation.

CALEF, Private Grazing and Public Lands.

COLBY, Geographic Aspects of International Relations.

COLBY, Source Book for Economic Geography.

COULTER, Fiji.

DAVIS, Physical Geography.

FRYXELL, Physiography of Chicago.

GINSBURG, Atlas of Economic Development.

GOODE, Geographic Background of Chicago.

GREENHOOD, Mapping.

HASS, American Empire.

HASS, Outposts of Defense.

HUZAR, New Perspectives on Peace.

JONES, Introduction to Economic Geography.

MAYER, Readings in Urban Geography.

PARKINS, Teaching of Geography.

RIDGLEY, Geography of Illinois.

TAYLOR, Environment and Nation.

TAYLOR, Environment, Race, and Migration.

THOMAS, Man's Role in Changing the Face of the Earth.

WAGNER, Readings in Cultural Geography.

WHITE, State of the Social Sciences.

*See also* GEOGRAPHIC SOCIETY OF CHICAGO.

## GEOLOGY:

BABER, Stony Island.

BACKLUND, Studies in Petrology.

BAIN, Relations of the Wisconsin and Kansas Drift Sheets.

BURWASH, Geology of Vancouver.

CHAMBERLIN, Attempt To Frame a Working Hypothesis of the Cause of Glacial Periods.

CHAMBERLIN, Classification of American Glacial Deposits.

CHAMBERLIN, Contribution to the Theory of Glacial Motion.

CHAMBERLIN, Proposed Genetic Classification of Pleistocene Glacial Formations.

CRESSEY, Indiana Sand Dunes.

CRONEIS, Down to Earth.

CROSS, Quantitative Classification of Igneous Rocks.

DECKER, Studies in Minor Folds.

DONNELLY, Earth Sciences.

DOWNING, Naturalist in the Great Lakes Region.

EITEL, Physical Chemistry of the Silicates.

FENNER, Bore-Hole Investigations.

FRASER, Experimental Study of the Porosity and Permeability of Clastic Sediments.

GEIKIE, Classification of European Glacial Deposits.

GRATON, Systematic Packing of Spheres.

HATCH, Introduction to the Study of Ore Deposits.

HUBBERT, Theory of Ground-Water Motion.

JOHANNSEN, Descriptive Petrography of the Igneous Rocks.

JOHANNSEN, Essentials for the Microscopic Determination of Rock-forming Minerals.

LOGAN, North American Epicontinental Sea.

RAMBERG, Origin of Metamorphic and Metasomatic Rocks.

RANKAMA, Geochemistry.

ROMER, Vertebrate Paleontology.

SALISBURY, Distinct Glacial Epochs.

SALISBURY, Outlines of Geologic History.

SANDFORD, First Report of the Prehistoric Survey Expedition.

SANDFORD, Prehistoric Survey of Egypt and Western Asia.

SAUER, Starved Rock State Park.

STUTZER, Geology of Coal.

THOMAS, Man's Role in Changing the Face of the Earth.

TILTON, Pleistocene Deposits in Warren County, Iowa.

UDDEN, Erosion, Transportation, and Sedimentation.

WILLIAMS, Elements of the Geological Time-Scale.

WILLISTON, American Permian Vertebrates.

WILLISTON, Water Reptiles of the Past and Present.

## HISTORY. GENERAL:

ABBOTT, Two Queens of Baghdad.

ALLEN, Turkish Transformation.

ANDERSON, First Moroccan Crisis.

ARTZ, From the Renaissance to Romanticism.

BALDWIN, Scutage and Knight Service.

BAROJA, World of the Witches.

BENEŠ, International Security.

BENÍTEZ, Century after Cortés.

BLOCH, Feudal Society.

BONDURANT, Decimus Junius Brutus Albinus.

BRAMSTED, Aristocracy and the Middle-Classes in Germany.

BRANDT, Toward the New Spain.

BRIGGS, Victorian People.

BRYSON, Sixteenth-Century Italian Duel.

CASPARI, Humanism and the Social Order in Tudor England.

CHIERA, They Wrote on Clay.

CHUDOBA, Spain and the Empire.

CLIFFORD, Knight of Great Renown.

COCHRANE, Tradition and Enlightment in the Tuscan Academies.

CREEL, Chinese Thought from Confucius to Mao Tsê-tung.

CROZIER, Bureaucratic Phenomenon.

CUNHA, Rebellion in the Backlands.

DEBEVOISE, Political History of Parthia.

DE JONG, German Fifth Column in the Second World War.

DE VISSCHER, Stabilization of Europe.

DOWNS, Essays in Honor of Conyers Read.

DREW, Perspectives in Medieval History.

DUCKETT, Alfred the Great.

ECKHARDT, Papacy and World-Affairs.

ENNIS, French Policy and Developments in Indochina.

ESSEN, Short History of Belgium.

FERMI, Mussolini.

FISH, United States and Great Britain.

FRANKFORT, Intellectual Adventure of Ancient Man.

GIFFEN, Fashoda.

GOLAY, Founding of the Federal Republic of Germany.

GOTTSCHALK, Generalization in the Writing of History.

GROSE, Select Bibliography of British History, 1660–1760.

GRUNEBAUM, Medieval Islam.

HALPERIN, Diplomat under Stress.

HALPERIN, Italy and the Vatican at War.

HALPERIN, Separation of Church and State in Italian Thought from Cavour to Mussolini.

HALPERIN, Some 20th Century Historians.

HARPER, The Russia I Believe In.

HARRIS, All Coherence Gone.

HARRIS, Britain and the Bulgarian Horrors of 1876.

HAYEK, Capitalism and the Historians.

HEMLEBEN, Plans for World Peace through Six Centuries.

HIMMELFARB, Lord Acton.

HOWE, Pretorian Prefect.

HULBERT, English Reformation.

JASHEMSKI, Origins and History of the Proconsular and Propraetorian Imperium.

JÁSZI, Dissolution of the Habsburg Empire.

JUDSON, Threat of German World-Politics.

KENNAN, Siberia and the Exile System.

KING, Medical World of the Eighteenth Century.

KNAPPEN, Tudor Puritanism.

KRIEGER, Politics of Discretion.

LACH, Asia in the Making of Europe.

LANGLOIS, Historic Role of France.

LIBERMAN, Building Lenin's Russia.

LOCKWOOD, Ugo Benzi.

LÖWITH, Meaning in History.

LUVAAS, Education of an Army.

LYNN, College Professor of the Renaissance.

McFAYDEN, History of the Title *Imperator.*

McNEILL, Europe's Steppe Frontier.

McNEILL, History Handbook of Western Civilization.

McNEILL, Past and Future.

McNEILL, Rise of the West.

MAHDI, Ibn Khaldûn's Philosophy of History.

MANSFIELD, Statesmanship and Party Government.

MAXEY, Occupations of the Lower Classes.

MOWAT, Britain between the Wars.

NEF, Conquest of the Material World.

NEF, United States and Civilization.

NETHERCOT, First Five Lives of Annie Besant.

NETHERCOT, Last Four Lives of Annie Besant.

OLMSTEAD, History of Assyria.

OLMSTEAD, History of the Persian Empire.

ORNSTEIN, Role of the Scientific Societies in the Seventeenth Century.

PARKER, Cult of Antiquity and the French Revolution.

PAVLOV, Leningrad, 1941.

PEAKS, General, Civil and Military Administration.

PEATTIE, Immortal Village.

PICKERSGILL, Mackenzie King Record.

READ, England and America.

REED, Masters of the Wilderness. A Study of the Hudson's Bay Company.

REEL, Case of General Yamashita.

RIDOLFI, Life of Niccolò Machiavelli.

RIHA, Readings in Russian Civilization.

ROHR, Origins of Social Liberalism in Germany.

SALISBURY, Moscow Journal.

SANTILLANA, Crime of Galileo.

SCHEVILL, Great Elector.

SCHEVILL, Six Historians.

SCHMITT, From Versailles to Munich.

SCHMITT, Some Historians of Modern Europe.

SCHURMAN, Education of a Navy.

SFORZA, Totalitarian War.

SHERBURN, Roehenstart, a Late Stuart Pretender.

SIMPSON, Wealth of the Gentry.

SIMSON, Sacred Fortress.

SMITH, New Approach to Early European History.

SMITH, New Approach to Modern History.

SMITH, New Approach to History.

STEINDORFF, When Egypt Ruled the East.

STONER, S. O. Levinson and the Pact of Paris.

STRAUSS, Natural Right and History.

TANNENBAUM, New France.

TÊNG, Chang Hsi and the Treaty of Nanking, 1842.

THATCHER, Studies concerning Adrian IV.

THOMPSON, Decline of the Missi Dominici in Frankish Gaul.

THOMPSON, Development of the French Monarchy.

THOMPSON, Medieval Library.

THOMPSON, Reference Studies in Medieval History.

THRUPP, Merchant Class in Medieval London.

TOUSSAINT, History of the Indian Ocean.

TREXLER, Confederate Ironclad "Virginia" ("Merrimac").

UNIVERSITY OF CHICAGO, *Department of History,* Study Manual of European History.

WEIZSÄCKER, History of Nature.

WHITE, Process of Change in the Ottoman Empire.

WILLIAMS, Thraldom in Ancient Iceland.

WILSON, Classroom Procedure Test in History.

WITTKE, Against the Current. The Life of Karl Heinzen.

WRIGHT, Study of War.

WYCOFF, Feudal Relations between the Kings of England and Scotland.

YATES, Giordano Bruno and the Hermetic Tradition.

## HISTORY. AMERICAN:

AGAR, Price of Power.

ANGLE, Created Equal?

BAILEY, New Approach to American History.

BAKER-CROTHERS, Virginia and the French and Indian War.

BLAIR, Half Horse Half Alligator.

BOGUE, From Prairie to Corn Belt.

BOTKIN, Lay My Burden Down.

BREMNER, American Philanthropy.

BRIDENBAUGH, Colonial Craftsman.

BROWNLOW, Passion for Anonymity.

BROWNLOW, Passion for Politics.

CALDWELL, Administrative Theories of Hamilton and Jefferson.

CATTERALL, Second Bank of the United States.

CAUGHEY, In Clear and Present Danger.

CAUGHEY, Their Majesties the Mob.

CAWELTI, Apostles of the Self-made Man.

CHAPLIN, Wobbly, The Rough-and-Tumble Story of an American Radical.

COLES, War of 1812.

CRAVEN, Army Air Forces in World War II.

CRAVEN, Essays in Honor of William E. Dodd.

CRAVEN, Historian and the Civil War.

CUNLIFFE, Nation Takes Shape.

DORSON, American Folklore.

DRINNON, Rebel in Paradise. Biography of Emma Goldman.

DUNCAN, Mentor Graham, The Man Who Taught Lincoln.

DYKEMAN, Seeds of Southern Change.

EARHART, Frances Willard.

EASUM, Americanization of Carl Schurz.

ELAZAR, American Partnership.

ELKINS, Slavery.

ELLIS, American Catholicism.

FINER, Presidency. Crisis and Regeneration.

FOREMAN, Last Trek of the Indians.

FRANKLIN, Reconstruction after the Civil War.

GLAZER, American Judaism.

GOTTSCHALK, Lafayette and the Close of the American Revolution.

GOTTSCHALK, Lafayette between the American and the French Revolution.

GOTTSCHALK, Lafayette Comes to America.

GOTTSCHALK, Lafayette Joins the American Army.

GOVAN, Nicholas Biddle.

GRAEBNER, Troubled Union.

HAAS, American Empire.

HABER, Efficiency and Uplift.

HAGAN, American Indians.

HALICH, Ukrainians in the United States.

HARASZTI, Bay Psalm Book.

HASTINGS, Life and Works of Francis Hopkinson.

HAYEK, Road to Serfdom.

HAYS, Response to Industrialism.

HENDERSON, Civil War.

HESSELTINE, Blue and Gray on the Nile.

HILL, Roosevelt and the Caribbean.

HODGES, Life and Times of Emil Grubbe.

HOFSTADTER, Documentary History of American Higher Education.

HOLLINGSWORTH, Whirligig of Politics. Democracy of Cleveland and Bryan.

HUDSON, American Protestantism.

HUDSON, John Ponet.

HUTCHINSON, Lowden of Illinois.

HUTCHINSON, Marcus W. Jernegan Essays in American Historiography.

HUTTON, Midwest at Noon.

ILCHMAN, Professional Diplomacy in the United States, 1779–1939.

JAMES, Life of George Rogers Clark.

JOHNSON, Battle against Isolation.

JOHNSON, Fulbright Program.

JONES, American Immigration.

JORDAN, Men of Substance.

KENNAN, American Diplomacy.

KIRK, Randolph of Roanoke.

KLEMENT, Copperheads in the Middle West.

LEHMANN, Thomas Jefferson.

LEUCHTENBURG, Perils of Prosperity.

LINDSEY, Pullman Strike.

LITWACK, North of Slavery.

LUVAAS, Military Legacy of the Civil War.

McCLOSKEY, American Supreme Court.

McDONALD, Insull.

McDONALD, We the People.

McGRANE, Panic of 1837.

McKITRICK, Andrew Johnson and Reconstruction.

MADISON, Papers of James Madison.

MANWARING, Render unto Caesar.

MITCHELL, History of the Greenbacks.

MIYAKAWA, Protestants and Pioneers.
MONAGHAN, This Is Illinois.
MORGAN, Birth of the Republic.
MULLER, Religion and Freedom in the Modern World.
NUGENT, Tolerant Populists.
O'DEA, Mormons.
OSGOOD, Day of the Cattleman.
OWSLEY, King Cotton Diplomacy.
OWSLEY, State Rights in the Confederacy.
PARGELLIS, Nathaniel Fish Moore's Diary.
PEARCE, Benjamin H. Hill.
PEASE, The Story of Illinois.
PECKHAM, Colonial Wars.
PECKHAM, Pontiac and the Indian Uprising.
PECKHAM, War for Independence.
PELLING, American Labor.
PERKINS, New Age of Franklin Roosevelt.
POTTER, People of Plenty.
POWELL, Exploration of the Colorado River.
RAE, American Automobile.
RAPPAPORT, Henry L. Stimson and Japan.
REICH, Leisler's Rebellion.
RIDGE, Ignatius Donnelly.
ROLAND, Confederacy.
SCHREIBER, Our Amish Neighbors.
SIMPSON, Puritanism in Old and New England.
SINGLETARY, Mexican War.
SMITH, Peril and a Hope.
STANTON, Leopard's Spots.
STOURZH, Benjamin Franklin and American Foreign Policy.
STOVER, American Railroads.
THOMAS, John Dewey.
TRYON, Mirror for Americans.
TRYON, My Native Land.
TSOU, America's Failure in China.
VANDIVER, Idea of the South.
VAN TASSEL, Recording America's Past.
WADE, Graham Taylor.
WADE, Urban Frontier.
WALLACE, Journal of Benjamin Moran, 1857–65.
WEISBERGER, American Newspaperman.
WISTER, Owen Wister Out West.

## HISTORY OF SCIENCE:

APOSTLE, Aristotle's Philosophy of Mathematics.
AURELIANUS, On Acute Diseases and Chronic Diseases.
BABKIN, Pavlov.

BREASTED, Edwin Smith Surgical Papyrus.
CARPI, Short Introduction to Anatomy.
DALTON, Foundations of the Atomic Theory.
DALTON, Foundations of the Molecular Theory.
FERMI, Collected Papers.
FRANK, Foundations of Physics.
GALILEI, Dialogue on the Great World Systems.
HUYGENS, Treatise on Light.
KING, Growth of Medical Thought.
KING, Medical World of the Eighteenth Century.
LOCKWOOD, Ugo Benzi.
MAYOW, Medico-physical Works.
ORNSTEIN, Role of the Scientific Societies in the 17th Century.
RAMAZZINI, De morbis artificum.
RÉAUMUR, Memoirs on Steel and Iron.
ROSENBERG, Cholera Years.
SANTILLANA, Crime of Galileo.
SANTILLANA, Origins of Scientific Thought.
SIGERIST, Civilization and Disease.
SILVERSTEIN, Medieval Latin Scientific Writings.
SMITH, History of Metallography.
SMITH, Peril and a Hope.
THEOPHILUS, On Divers Arts.
WERTIME, Coming of the Age of Steel.

## ILLINOIS:

ALVORD, Old Kaskaskia Records.
BECKNER, History of Labor Legislation in Illinois.
BLATCHFORD, Biographical Sketch of Hon. Joseph Duncan.
BLOUNT, Excursion on the Rock River of Illinois.
BOGGESS, Settlement of Illinois.
BRECKINRIDGE, Illinois Poor Law.
BROWN, Biographical Sketch of Hon. John Peter Altgeld.
COLE, Rediscovering Illinois.
DODD, Government in Illinois.
FLOWER, History of the English Settlement in Edwards County, Illinois.
GROVER, Some Indian Land Marks.
HUTCHINSON, Lowden of Illinois.
INGRAHAM, Elmer E. Ellsworth.
JAMES, Preamble and Boundary Clauses of the Illinois Constitution.
MILCHRIST, State Administration of Child Welfare in Illinois.
MONAGHAN, This Is Illinois.

NIMS, Illinois Adoption Law.
PATTERSON, Early Society in Southern Illinois.
PEASE, Story of Illinois.
PUTNAM, Illinois and Michigan Canal.
PUTTEE, Illegitimate Child in Illinois.
RADEBAUGH, Boundary Dispute.
RIDGLEY, Geography of Illinois.
TIFFANY, Algae of Illinois.
WASHBURNE, Edwards Papers.
WOODDY, Case of Frank L. Smith.

## INDIANS OF NORTH AMERICA AND MEXICO:

BARROWS, Ethno-Botany of the Coahuilla Indians.
BENNETT, Tarahumara.
BRANDT, Hopi Ethics.
COLE, Rediscovering Illinois.
COX, Indian as a Diplomatic Factor.
DRIVER, Indians of North America.
EGGAN, Social Anthropology.
EGGAN, Social Organization of the Western Pueblos.
FOREMAN, Last Trek of the Indians.
GOODWIN, Social Organization of the Western Apache.
GRIFFIN, Archeology of Eastern United States.
GROVER, Some Indian Land Marks.
HAGAN, American Indians.
HAILE, Navaho Sacrificial Figurines.
HAILE, Origin Legend of the Navaho Flintway.
HAILE, Prayer Stick Cutting.
HOIJER, Chiricahua and Mescalero Apache Texts.
JACOBS, Content and Style of an Oral Literature.
JENNESS, People of the Twilight.
JENNINGS, Prehistoric Man in the New World.
JOSEPH, Desert People.
LI, Mattole.
MACGREGOR, Warriors without Weapons.
MARTIN, Indians before Columbus.
MILLER, Preliminary Study of the Pueblo of Taos.
OPLER, Apache Life-Way.
PARSONS, Mitla.
PARSONS, Pueblo Indian Religion.
PECKHAM, Pontiac and the Indian Uprising.
QUIMBY, Indian Life in the Upper Great Lakes.
REDFIELD, Folk Culture of Yucatan.

REDFIELD, Tepoztlán.
SPICER, Pascua, A Yaqui Village in Arizona.
SPICER, Perspectives in American Indian Culture Change.
SPIER, Yuman Tribes of the Gila River.
STARR, Indians of South Mexico.
STARR, Little Pottery Objects.
STARR, Physical Characters of the Indians.
STARR, Recent Mexican Study of the Native Languages of Mexico.
TAX, Indian Tribes of Aboriginal America.
THOMPSON, Hopi Way.
UNDERHILL, Red Man's America.
UNDERHILL, Red Man's Religion.
WAUCHOPE, Lost Tribes and Sunken Continents.
WISDOM, Chorti Indians of Guatemala.
WOLF, Sons of the Shaking Earth.

## LABOR:

ANDERSON, Men on the Move.
BECKNER, History of Labor Legislation in Illinois.
BLACHLY, Treatment of the Problem of Capital and Labor.
CADBURY, Women's Work.
CALKINS, CIO and the Democratic Party.
CARVER, Personnel and Labor Problems.
CHRISTENSON, Collective Bargaining in Chicago.
DAVIS, Youth in the Depression.
DENOOD, Jobs or the Dole?
DOUGLAS, Standards of Unemployment Insurance.
DOUGLAS, Wages and the Family.
DOUGLAS, Worker in the Modern Economic Society.
DRINNON, Rebel in Paradise. Biography of Emma Goldman.
GILSON, Unemployment Insurance.
GLICK, Illinois Emergency Relief Commission.
HATHWAY, Migratory Worker.
HILLER, Strike.
HOUGHTELING, Income and Standard of Living.
JERNEGAN, Laboring and Dependent Classes.
JOHNSON, Relief and Health Problems of a Selected Group of Non-family Men.
KENNEDY, Wages and Family Budgets.
KILLINGSWORTH, State Labor Relations Acts.
LEWIS, Unionism and Relative Wages in the United States.
LINDSEY, Pullman Strike.

LOGAN, History of Trade-Union Organization in Canada.

McCARTHY, Labor Looks at Unemployment Insurance.

MAXEY, Occupations of the Lower Classes.

MILLER, American Labor.

MILLIS, From the Wagner Act to Taft-Hartley.

MONTGOMERY, Industrial Relations in the Chicago Building Trades.

OGBURN, You and Machines.

PAYNE, Experiment in Alien Labor.

PELLING, American Labor.

PHELPS, Legislative Background of the Fair Labor Standards Act.

REES, Economics of Trade Unions.

SEIDMAN, American Labor from Defense to Reconstruction.

SEIDMAN, Worker Views His Union.

SENTURIA, Strikes.

SHARP, Social Change and Labor Law.

SPENCER, Collective Bargaining.

SPENCER, National Labor Relations Act.

STALEY, History of the Illinois State Federation of Labor.

STONE, Problems of Collective Bargaining.

SWANISH, Trade Disputes Disqualification Clause under the British Unemployment Insurance Acts.

WERGELAND, History of the Working Class.

WHITE, Administering Unemployment Compensation.

## LANGUAGE AND LINGUISTICS:

### ENGLISH LANGUAGE

AGARD, Grammatical Structures of English and Italian.

AGARD, Sounds of English and Italian.

ANDERSON, Classroom Procedure Test in English Composition.

ANDERSON, Standard Usage in English.

Annual Bibliography of English Language and Literature.

CARPENTER, Metaphor and Simile.

COX, Arte or Crafte of Rhethoryke.

CRESSWELL, Dictionary of Military Terms.

CRAIGIE, Dictionary of American English.

CRAIGIE, Dictionary of the Older Scottish Tongue.

HOSIC, Elementary Course in English.

HUDELSON, English Composition.

HULBERT, Effective English.

LONG, Sentence and Its Parts.

LONG, Workbook for *The Sentence and Its Parts*.

LEWIS, History of the English Paragraph.

MATHEWS, Beginnings of American English.

MATHEWS, Dictionary of American English.

MATHEWS, Dictionary of Americanisms.

NICHOLSON, English Words with Native Roots.

SLEDD, Dr. Johnson's *Dictionary*.

STOCKWELL, Grammatical Structures of English and Spanish.

STOCKWELL, Sounds of English and Spanish.

UNIVERSITY OF CHICAGO, UNIVERSITY HIGH SCHOOL, DEPARTMENT OF ENGLISH, Standard Usage in English.

UNIVERSITY OF CHICAGO, DEPARTMENT OF ENGLISH, Manly Anniversary Studies.

WALPOLE, Foundations of English for Foreign Students.

### FRENCH LANGUAGE

BOND, Reading Method.

COLEMAN, Soldat américain en France.

DUNKEL, French in the Elementary School.

INGRES, Cours complet de langue française.

NITZE, French Verb.

VIGNERON, Explication de textes.

WARTBURG, Evolution et structure de la langue française.

WEST, Grouped-Frequency French Word List.

WILKINS, Army French.

WILKINS, First Lessons in Spoken French for Doctors and Nurses.

WILKINS, First Lessons in Spoken French for Men in Military Service.

WILKINS, French Verb Blanks.

### GERMAN LANGUAGE

ARNOLDSON, Parts of the Body in Older Germanic.

BASKETT, Parts of the Body in Later Germanic.

CUTTING, Concerning the Modern German Relatives, "Das" and "Was."

CUTTING, Conjunktiv bei Hartmann von Aue.

IHRIG, Semantic Development of Words for "Walk," "Run."

KUFNER, Grammatical Structures of English and German.

MOULTON, Sounds of English and German.

SCHÜTZE, Repetition of a Word.

SCHWABE, Semantic Development of Words for Eating and Drinking.

STEINDORFF, Lehrbuch der Koptischen Grammatik.

WOOD, Table of Phonetic Changes.

WOOD, Übersichtstabellen zu Lautentsprechungen.

WOOD, Vernor's Law in Gothic.

## GREEK LANGUAGE

ALLEN, Infinitive in Polybius.

ARNDT, Greek-English Lexicon of the New Testament.

BEARDSLEE, Use of Φύσις.

BUCK, Comparative Grammar of Greek and Latin.

BUCK, Greek Dialects.

BUCK, Reverse Index of Greek Nouns and Adjectives.

BURTON, Notes on New Testament Grammar.

BURTON, Spirit, Soul, and Flesh.

BURTON, Syntax of the Moods and Tenses in New Testament Greek.

COLWELL, Greek of the Fourth Gospel.

COLWELL, Hellenistic Greek Reader.

FERGUSON, Legal Terms Common to the Macedonian Inscriptions.

FLICKINGER, Meaning of ἐπὶ τῆς σκηνῆς.

FOBES, Philosophical Greek.

FUNK, Greek Grammar of the New Testament.

GOODSPEED, Greek Papyri from the Cairo Museum.

GOODSPEED, Greek Papyrus Reader.

GUNNERSON, History of U-Stems.

HALE, Anticipatory Subjunctive.

HOFFMAN, Everyday Greek.

NORTON, Lexicographical and Historical Study of Διαθήκη.

OWEN, Homeric Vocabularies.

ROBINSON, Syntax of the Participle in the Apostolic Fathers.

SEARLES, Lexicographical Study of the Greek Inscriptions.

SLATEN, Qualitative Nouns in the Pauline Epistles.

STRATTON, History of Greek Noun-Formation.

Studies in Greek Noun Formation.

STURTEVANT, Pronunciation of Greek and Latin.

THOMPSON, Μετανοέω and Μεταμέλει in Greek Literature.

VAN HOOK, Metaphorical Terminology.

WIKGREN, Hellenistic Greek Texts.

WILLIAMS, Participle in the Book of Acts.

## LATIN LANGUAGE

ABBOTT, Use of Repetition in Latin.

BUCK, Comparative Grammar of Greek and Latin.

BUCK, Oscan-Umbrian Verb-System.

BYRNE, Syntax of High-School Latin.

CARMODY, Subjunctive in Tacitus.

GAME, Teaching High-School Latin.

HALE, Anticipatory Subjunctive.

HALE, Synopsis of the Modal Uses of the Finite Verb.

HARRINGTON, Medieval Latin.

LAING, Genitive of Value.

LEVY, Latin Reader for Colleges.

LINSCOTT, Latin Third Declension.

LOCKWOOD, Survey of Classical Roman Literature.

MORE, Latin Epigrams of Thomas More.

NIGHTINGALE, Results of the Chicago Experiment in Latin.

SIDEY, Participle in Plautus, Petronius, and Apuleius.

STURTEVANT, Pronunciation of Greek and Latin.

## RUSSIAN LANGUAGE

BILL, Russian People. A Reader.

BOYER, Russian Reader.

PROKOSCH, Elementary Russian Grammar.

WARD, Russian Language Today.

## SPANISH LANGUAGE

BOWEN, Patterns of Spanish Pronunciation.

CASTILLO, University of Chicago Spanish Dictionary.

EATON, Semantic Frequency List.

KANY, American-Spanish Syntax.

KENISTON, Basic List of Spanish Words.

KENISTON, Syntax of Castilian Prose.

PIETSCH, Preliminary Notes on Two Old Spanish Versions of the Disticha Catonis.

## OTHER

ALTROCCHI, Deceptive Cognates.

BLOOMFIELD, Linguistic Aspects of Science.

BUCK, Dictionary of Selected Synonyms in the Principal Indo-European Languages.

COLEMAN, Analytical Bibliography of Modern Language Teaching, 1927–32.

COLEMAN, Analytical Bibliography of Modern Language Teaching, 1932–37.

COLEMAN, Experiments and Studies in Modern Language Teaching.

CREEL, Literary Chinese by the Inductive Method.

CREEL, Newspaper Chinese by the Inductive Method.

DUNCAN, Language and Literature in Society.

EATON, Semantic Frequency List.

GELB, Nuzi Personal Names.

GREENBERG, Essays in Linguistics.

HAGBOLDT, How To Study Modern Languages.

HAGBOLDT, How To Study Modern Languages in College.

HAGBOLDT, How To Study Modern Languages in High School.

HAGBOLDT, Language Learning.

HARPER, Elements of Hebrew by an Inductive Method.

HARPER, Introductory Hebrew.

HARRIS, Structural Linguistics.

HOENIGSWALD, Language Change and Linguistic Reconstruction.

HOIJER, Language in Culture.

LADEFOGED, Elements of Acoustic Phonetics.

LYMAN, Summary of Investigations Relating to Grammar, Language, and Composition.

McILROY, Chamberlain's Japanese Grammar.

MARTIN, Truth and Denotation.

MARTINET, Elements of General Linguistics.

MÉSZÁROS, Päkhy-Sprache.

MUSS-ARNOLT, Theological and Semitic Literature.

POEBEL, Das appositionell bestimmte Pronomen.

RIVERS, Psychologist and the Foreign-Language Teacher.

ROSÉN, Textbook of Israeli Hebrew.

STARR, Bibliography of Congo Languages.

STARR, Recent Mexican Study of the Native Languages of Mexico.

STURTEVANT, Linguistic Change.

TAYLOR, Bibliographical History of Anonyma and Pseudonyma.

TÊNG, Conversational Chinese.

TÊNG, Advanced Conversational Chinese.

TURNER, Africanisms in the Gullah Dialect.

WALKER, Semitic Negative.

WATERMAN, Perspectives in Linguistics.

## LAW

ABBOTT, Child and the State.

ALLEN, Borderland of Criminal Justice.

BAKER, Legal Aspects of Zoning.

BECKNER, History of Labor Legislation in Illinois.

BEELEY, Bail System in Chicago.

BLAUSTEIN, American Lawyer.

BLUM, Uneasy Case for Progressive Taxation.

BONNER, Administration of Justice from Homer to Aristotle.

BONNER, Evidence in Athenian Courts.

BONNER, Lawyers and Litigants in Ancient Athens.

BRADWAY, Law and Social Work.

CHAFEE, Government and Mass Communications.

COUNTRYMAN, Discrimination and the Law.

CREECH, Three Centuries of Poor Law Administration.

CROSSKEY, Politics and the Constitution in the History of the United States.

CURRAN, Trends in Consumer Credit Legislation.

DIRECTOR, Defense, Controls, and Inflation.

DUNHAM, Mr. Justice.

DUYVENDAK, Book of Lord Shang.

EDWARDS, Courts and the Public Schools.

ELLIOT, Conflicting Penal Theories in Statutory Criminal Law.

FELLMAN, Constitutional Right of Association.

FITZGIBBON, Constitutions of the Americas.

FREUND, Administrative Powers over Persons and Property.

FREUND, Legal Nature of Corporations.

FREUND, Police Power.

FREUND, Standards of American Legislation.

FRIEDRICH, Philosophy of Law in Historical Perspective.

GETTYS, Law of Citizenship in the United States.

GIANNELLA, Religion and the Public Order.

GREGORY, Legislative Loss Distribution.

ḤAMMURABI, Code.

HOWE, Garden and the Wilderness.

JENSEN, Property Taxation in the United States.

KATZ, An Introduction to Accounting for Students of Law.

KILLINGSWORTH, State Labor Relations Acts.

KISH, Jews in Medieval Germany.

KURLAND, Supreme Court and the Constitution.

KURLAND, Supreme Court Review.

LEPAWSKY, Judicial System of Metropolitan Chicago.

LEVI, Introduction to Legal Reasoning.

LINDMAN, Mentally Disabled and the Law.

LLEWELLYN, Jurisprudence.

McCLOSKEY, American Supreme Court.
McDONALD, We the People.
MANWARING, Render unto Caesar.
MENDELSON, Justices Black and Frankfurter.
MURPHY, Congress and the Court.
MURPHY, Elements of Judicial Strategy.
OAKS, Wall between Church and State.
PRITCHETT, Civil Liberties and the Vinson Court.
PUNKE, Courts and Public School Property.
PUNKE, Law and Liability in Pupil Transportation.
PUTTKAMMER, Administration of Criminal Law.
PUTTKAMMER, Alien Enemies and Alien Friends.
PUTTKAMMER, Manual of Criminal Law.
PUTTKAMMER, War and the Law.
REEL, Case of General Yamashita.
REID, International Servitudes in Law.
RILEY, Working Manual for Juvenile Court Officers.
SCOTT, Criminal Law in Colonial Virginia.
SHARP, Social Change and Labor Law.
SMITH, Origin and History of Hebrew Law.
SPENCER, Collective Bargaining.
SPENCER, National Labor Relations Act.
SPENCER, National Railroad Adjustment Board.
SPENCER, Law and Business.

**LIBRARY SCIENCE:**

ASHEIM, Future of the Book.
ASHEIM, New Directions in Public Library Development.
ASHEIM, Persistent Issues in American Librarianship.
BOYD, Public Libraries and Literary Culture in Ancient Rome.
BUTLER, Books and Libraries in Wartime.
BUTLER, Introduction to Library Science.
BUTLER, Librarians, Scholars, and Booksellers at Mid-century.
BUTLER, Reference Function of the Library.
CARNOVSKY, International Aspects of Librarianship.
ENNIS, Seven Questions about the Profession of Librarianship.
FENWICK, New Definitions of School-Library Service.
GLEASON, Southern Negro and the Public Library.
HANSON, Comparative Study of Cataloging Rules.

HAYGOOD, Who Uses the Public Library.
HYERS, Library and the Radio.
POSNER, American State Archives.
RANDALL, Acquisition and Cataloging of Books.
RANDALL, College Library.
RANEY, University Libraries.
SCHELLENBERG, Modern Archives.
SHERA, Bibliographic Organization.
SHERA, Foundations of the Public Library.
SPENCER, Chicago Public Library.
STROUT, Library Catalogs.
STROUT, Toward a Better Cataloging Code.
SWANSON, Intellectual Foundations of Library Education.
TSIEN, Written on Bamboo and Silk.
WAPLES, Libraries and Readers in the State of New York.
WAPLES, National Libraries and Foreign Scholarship.
WAPLES, Library.
WAPLES, What People Want To Read About.
WILSON, Library in General Education.
WILSON, University Library.
WINGER, Iron Curtains and Scholarship.
*See also* UNIVERSITY OF CHICAGO STUDIES IN LIBRARY SCIENCE.

**LITERATURE AND LITERARY CRITICISM:**

## AMERICAN LITERATURE

ADE, Artie *and* Pink Marsh.
ANDERSON, Windy McPherson's Son.
ATKINS, Edna St. Vincent Millay.
BEACH, Outlook for American Prose.
BLAIR, Half Horse Half Alligator.
BLAIR, Horse Sense in American Humor.
BOOTH, Rhetoric of Fiction.
BOTKIN, Lay My Burden Down.
BOWEN, Long Encounter.
BOWERS, Whitman's Manuscripts.
BOYNTON, America in Contemporary Fiction.
BOYNTON, More Contemporary Americans.
BOYNTON, Rediscovery of the Frontier.
BOYNTON, Some Contemporary Americans.
BRONSON, American Poems.
BRONSON, American Prose.
BROWNLOW, Anatomy of the Anecdote.
CAMDEN, Literary Views.
CARSON, Theatre on the Frontier.
CAVINS, Standardization of American Poetry.
CHAPIN, New Approach to Poetry.
CRANE, Critics and Criticism.
CUNHA, Rebellion in the Backlands.

DENNEY, Astonished Muse.
DENNIS, Victor Lawson.
DOWNER, Modern American Drama and its Critics.
DUNBAR, A House in Chicago.
EAKIN, Good Books for Children.
EISINGER, Fiction of the Forties.
FEIDELSON, Symbolism and American Literature.
FULLER, With the Procession.
GOODMAN, Structure of Literature.
GOODSPEED, Buying Happiness.
GOODSPEED, Things Seen and Heard.
GRABO, Creative Critic.
HARASZTI, Bay Psalm Book.
HARRIS, Bomb.
HASTINGS, Life and Works of Francis Hopkinson.
HASTINGS, Syllabus of American Literature.
HECHT, Erik Dorn.
HOWARD, Connecticut Wits.
JACOBS, Content and Style of An Oral Literature.
LARDNER, Gullible's Travels.
LEWIS, American Adam.
LOCHER, German Histories of American Literature.
MARBLE, Heralds of American Literature.
MELVILLE, Billy Budd, Sailor.
MILLER, Critical Guide to *Leaves of Grass*.
O'CONNOR, Sense and Sensibility in Modern Poetry.
PERCIVAL, A Reading of *Moby-Dick*.
RAY, Chicago Review Anthology.
RICHARDS, Speculative Instruments.
ROSENHEIM, What Happens in Literature.
SCHNEIDER, Popular Religion.
SHANLEY, Making of *Walden*.
SMITH, Book of Canadian Poetry.
STEIN, Narration.
WISTER, Owen Wister Out West.
WRIGHT, American Short Story in the Twenties.
*See also* POETRY.

## ENGLISH LITERATURE

ALTICK, English Common Reader.
AMES, Aesthetics of the Novel.
ARTZ, From the Renaissance to Romanticism.
BASKERVILL, Elizabethan Jig.
BEACH, Technique of Thomas Hardy.
BENNETT, Evolution of the *Faerie Queene*.
BENTLEY, Shakespeare and Jonson.
BOYNTON, London in English Literature.

BRADNER, Edmund Spenser and the *Faerie Queene*.
BRENNECKE, Shakespeare in Germany. 1590–1700.
BROWN, Matthew Arnold.
BROWNE, Works of Sir Thomas Browne.
BRYAN, Sources and Analogues of Chaucer's *Canterbury Tales*.
BUCKLEY, Atheism in the English Renaissance.
BURKE, Counter-Statement.
CAMDEN, Restoration and Eighteenth-Century Literature.
CARPENTER, Reference Guide to Edmund Spenser.
CASPARI, Humanism and the Social Order in Tudor England.
CECIL, Victorian Novelists.
CHAPIN, New Approach to Poetry.
COLLINS, Such Is Life.
CRAIGIE, Northern Element in English Literature.
CRANE, Shakespeare's Prose.
CROSS, Bibliographical Guide to English Studies.
DAICHES, Novel and the Modern World.
DAICHES, Poetry and the Modern World.
DANIEL, Poems and A Defence of Ryme.
DAVIE, Russian Literature and Modern English Fiction.
DILLON, Early Irish Literature.
DUNKEL, Sir Arthur Pinero.
FLETCHER, Milton's Semitic Studies.
FRIEDMAN, Ballad Revival.
GARDNER, Gawain-Poet.
GARNER, Henry Vaughan.
GODDARD, Meaning of Shakespeare.
GOLDSMITH, New Essays.
GOODHEART, Utopian Vision of D. H. Lawrence.
GORDON, Social Ideals of Alfred Tennyson.
GRIFFITH, Sir Perceval of Galles.
HAGSTRUM, Sister Arts.
HAGSTRUM, William Blake, Poet and Painter.
HANGEN, Concordance to the Complete Poetical Works of Sir Thomas Wyatt.
HARTH, Swift and Anglican Rationalism.
HAY, Political Novels of Joseph Conrad.
HEISERMAN, Skelton and Satire.
JOHANNSEN, "Phiz." Illustrations from the Novels of Charles Dickens.
JONSON, Case Is Altered.
JUDSON, Seventeenth-Century Lyrics.
KAHRL, Tobias Smollett.

KAIN, Fabulous Voyages.
KOGAN, The Great EB.
LARSON, Modernity of Milton.
LEECH, Shakespeare. The Tragedies.
LEFEVRE, Prayers of Kierkegaard.
LYDGATE, Assembly of Gods.
MACCLINTOCK, Some Paradoxes of the English Romantic Movement.
MAGOUN, Chaucer Gazetteer.
MANLY, Text of *The Canterbury Tales*.
MARSH, Four Dialectical Theories of Poetry.
MOORE, Comic and the Realistic in English Drama.
MOORE, Daniel Defoe.
MORRIS, Anonyms and Pseudonyms.
MYERS, Later Realism.
NETHERCOT, Road to Tryermaine.
NETHERCOT, Sir. William D'avenant.
NEWTON, Wordsworth.
NEWTON, Wordsworth in Early American Criticism.
NITZE, Arthurian Romance and Modern Poetry and Music.
OLSON, Aristotle's Poetics and English Literature.
OLSON, Poetry of Dylan Thomas.
PRATT, Use of Color in Verse.
RAVEN, *Hamlet* Bibliography.
REYNOLDS, Poems of Anne.
REYNOLDS, Treatment of Nature in English Poetry.
RICHARDS, Speculative Instruments.
ROSENHEIM, Swift and the Art of Satire.
SCHNEIDER, Coleridge, Opium, and *Kubla Khan*.
SLEDD, Dr. Johnson's *Dictionary*.
SMITH, T. S. Eliot's Poetry and Plays.
SOLVE, Shelley, His Theory of Poetry.
STARRETT, Private Life of Sherlock Holmes.
STEVENS, Milton Papers.
STEVENS, Reference Guide to Milton.
STEVENSON, Darwin among the Poets.
TAVE, Amiable Humorist.
TAYLOR, "Edward" and "Sven I Rosengård."
TOLMAN, Questions on Shakespeare.
TOLMAN, What Has Become of Shakespeare's Play, *Love's Labour's Won?*
TURNER, Making of *The Cloister and the Hearth*.
TUVE, Elizabethan and Metaphysical Imagery.
TUVE, Reading of George Herbert.
UNIVERSITY OF CHICAGO, *Department of English*, Manly Anniversary Studies.

WAGER, Life and Repentaunce of Marie Magdalene.
WARREN, Rage for Order.
WEBSTER, On a Darkling Plain.
WEITZ, *Hamlet* and the Philosophy of Literary Criticism.
WILLIAMSON, Milton and Others.
WILLIAMSON, Proper Wit of Poetry.
WILLIAMSON, Senecan Amble.
WILLIAMSON, Seventeenth Century Contexts.
WIMBERLY, Folklore in the English and Scottish Ballads.
WOODHOUSE, The Poet and His Faith.
*See also* POETRY.

## FRENCH LITERATURE

BARNES, Study of the Variations between the Original and the Standard Editions of Balzac's *Les Chouans*.
BASKERVILL, Pierre Gringore's Pageants.
CROSS, Lancelot and Guenevere.
DARGAN, Honoré de Balzac.
DARGAN, Studies in Balzac's Realism.
DELAY, Youth of André Gide.
FOWLIE, Mallarmé.
GIDE, Self-Portraits.
HAZARD, Études critiques sur *Manon Lescaut*.
JENKINS, Espurgatoire Saint Patriz.
JOHNSON, Proust Recaptured.
MACCLINTOCK, Sainte-Beuve's Critical Theory.
MERRILL, Platonism of Joachim du Bellay.
NITZE, Le haut livre du Graal. Perlesvaus.
NORMAN, Swindlers and Rogues in French Drama.
RACINE, Three Plays.
ROCHEDIEU, Bibliography of French Translations of English Works.
ROYCE, Balzac Bibliography.
ROYCE, Indexes to *A Balzac Bibliography*.
WEINBERG, Art of Jean Racine.

## GERMAN LITERATURE

ALLEN, Studies in Popular Poetry.
BATT, Treatment of Nature in German Literature.
BERGSTRÄSSER, Deutsche Beiträge zur geistigen Überlieferung.
FAIRLEY, Goethe as Revealed in His Poetry.
KLENZE, Interpretation of Italy.
KLENZE, Treatment of Nature in the Works of Nikolaus Lenau.
NICHOLSON, Old German Love Songs.

Schmidt-Wartenberg, Inedita des Heinrich Kaufringer.

Taylor, Study of the Technique in Konrad Ferdinand Meyer's Novellen.

Williamson, Grillparzer's Attitude toward Romanticism.

Wood, Hildebrandslied.

## GREEK LITERATURE

Burgess, Epideictic Literature.

Capps, Introduction of Comedy into the City Dionysia.

Clark, Study of the *Iliad*.

College of the University of Chicago, Humanities I Handbook.

Flickinger, Greek Theatre and Its Drama.

Frank, Stichometric Scholium to the *Medea* of Euripides.

Grene, Complete Greek Tragedies.

Grene, Greek Tragedies (Phoenix).

Grene, Three Greek Tragedies in Translation.

Homer, Iliad.

Hugill, Panhellenism in Aristophanes.

Hull, Aesop's Fables.

Lattimore, Greek Lyrics.

Murray, Literature of Ancient Greece.

Paschal, Study of Quintus of Smyrna.

Pindar, Odes.

Rankin, Role of the Μάγειρος in the Life of the Ancient Greeks.

Scott, Comparative Study of Hesiod and Pindar.

Shorey, Idea of Good in Plato's Republic.

Shorey, What Plato Said.

Stearns, Fragments from Graeco-Jewish Writers.

Wilkins, Delphic Maxims.

## ITALIAN AND LATIN LITERATURE

Abbott, Toledo Manuscript of the *Germania* of Tacitus.

Allen, Medieval Latin Lyrics.

Auerbach, Dante, Poet of the Secular World.

Axtell, Deification of Abstract Ideas in Roman Literature.

Bechtel, Sanctae silviae peregrinatio.

Cicero, Brutus, *On the Nature of the Gods, On Divination, On Duties.*

Gordis, Estimates of Moral Values.

Harsh, Studies in Dramatic "Preparation."

Henderson, Commentariolum petitionis.

Hendrickson, Proconsulate of Julius Agricola.

Horace, Odes and Epodes.

Horace, Satires and Epistles.

Jones, Boccaccio and His Imitators.

Miller, Tragedies of Seneca.

Miller, Two Dramatizations from Vergil.

Petrarch, Triumphs.

Phelps, Earlier and Later Forms of Petrarch's Canzoniere.

Pietsch, Preliminary Notes on Two Old Spanish Versions of the *Disticha Catonis*.

Prescott, Development of Virgil's Art.

Sage, Pseudo-Ciceronian Consolatio.

Saintonge, Horace. Three Phases of His Influence.

Schoonover, Study of Cn. Domitius Corbulo.

Virgil, Georgics.

Weinberg, History of Literary Criticism in the Italian Renaissance.

Wilkins, Dante: Poet and Apostle.

Wilkins, Life of Petrarch.

Wilkins: Modern Discussions of the Dates of Petrarch's Prose Letters.

Wilkins, Petrarch at Vaucluse.

Wilkins, Tentative Chronological List of Petrarch's Prose Letters.

Wilkins, University of Chicago Manuscript of the Genealogia Deorum Gentilium.

## SPANISH LITERATURE

Castillo, Antología de la literatura mexicana.

Hayton, Flor de las ystorias de Orient.

León, La perfecta casada.

Northup, Cuento de Tristan de Leonis.

Northup, Introduction to Spanish Literature.

Pietsch, Spanish Grail Fragments.

## OTHER

Clark, Āryabhaṭiya of Āryabhaṭa.

Grunebaum, Tenth-Century Document of Arabic Literary Theory and Criticism.

Kerner, Foundations of Slavic Bibliography.

Liu, Art of Chinese Poetry.

Meyer, Two Twice-told Tales.

Moulton, Modern Study of Literature.

Nikam, Edicts of Asoka.

Northup, Introduction to Spanish Literature.

Poley, Classroom Procedure Test in English Literature.

Rickert, New Method for the Study of Literature.

RYDER, Bhagavad-gita.
RYDER, Gold's Gloom.
RYDER, Panchatantra.
RYDER, The Ten Princes.
SCHÜTZE, Academic Illusions.
THORPE, Fred Newton Scott Anniversary Papers.
VAN BUITENEN, Tales of Ancient India.
WRIGHT, Joseph Spence.

## MATHEMATICS:

ALBERT, College Algebra.
ALBERT, Fundamental Concepts of Higher Algebra.
ALBERT, Introduction to Algebraic Theories.
ALBERT, Modern Higher Algebra.
APOSTLE, Aristotle's Philosophy of Mathematics.
ĀRYABHAṬA, Āryabhaṭiya.
BAKER, Problem of the Angle-Bisectors.
BILLINGSLEY, Statistical Inference for Markov Process.
BLICHFELDT, Finite Collineation Groups.
BLISS, Contributions to the Calculus of Variations, 1930 . . . 1931–32 . . . 1933–37 . . . 1938–41.
BLISS, Lectures on the Calculus of Variations.
BOLZA, Concerning Geodesic Curvature.
BOLZA, Lectures on the Calculus of Variations.
BRESLICH, Administration of Mathematics in Secondary Schools.
BRESLICH, Classroom Procedure Tests in Mathematics.
BRESLICH, Correlated Mathematics.
BRESLICH, Problems in Teaching Secondary-School Mathematics.
BRESLICH, Slide Rule.
BRESLICH, Technique of Teaching Secondary-School Mathematics.
BUSWELL, Arithmetic, 1947.
BUSWELL, Arithmetic, 1949.
BUSWELL, Summary of Educational Investigations Relating to Arithmetic.
BUSWELL, Teaching of Arithmetic.
CARNAP, Foundations of Logic and Mathematics.
CARNAP, Logical Foundations of Probability.
COUNTS, Arithmetic Tests.
DICKSON, Algebras and Their Arithmetics.
DICKSON, Groups Defined for a General Field.
DICKSON, Introduction to the Theory of Numbers.

DICKSON, Modern Elementary Theory of Numbers.
DICKSON, Studies in the Theory of Numbers.
DICKSON, Ternary Orthogonal Group.
HARMAN, Modern Factor Analysis.
HOLZINGER, Factor Analysis.
KEMPERMAN, Passage Problem for a Stationary Markov Chain.
KHINCHIN, Continued Fractions.
KNIGHT, Report of the Society's Committee on Arithmetic.
LANE, Metric Differential Geometry of Curves and Surfaces.
LANE, Projective Differential Geometry.
LANE, Treatise on Projective Differential Geometry.
LEVINSON, Law of Gravitation in Relativity.
LOGSDON, Mathematician Explains.
MACNEISH, Linear Polars of the $k$-Hedron in $n$-Space.
MASCHKE, Invariants and Covariants of Quadratic Differential Quantics of $n$-Variables.
MEMBERS OF THE DEPARTMENT OF MATHEMATICS OF THE UNIVERSITY HIGH SCHOOL OF THE UNIVERSITY OF CHICAGO, Mathematics Instruction in the University High School.
MILLER, Significance of the Mathematical Element in the Philosophy of Plato.
MOORE, Subgroups of the Generalized Finite Modular Group.
MYERS, First-Year Mathematics for Secondary Schools.
MYERS, Geometric Exercises.
MYERS, Second-Year Mathematics for Secondary Schools.
MYERS, Teacher's Manual for First-Year Mathematics.
NAGEL, Principles of the Theory of Probability.
NAHIKIAN, Modern Algebra for Biologists.
RASHEVSKY, Mathematical Biology of Social Behavior.
RASHEVSKY, Mathematical Biophysics.
REEVE, Review of High-School Mathematics.
RUGG, Scientific Method in the Reconstruction of Ninth-Grade Mathematics.
SWAN, Theory of Sheaves.
TOEPLITZ, Calculus.
*See also* STATISTICS; UNIVERSITY OF CHICAGO MATHEMATICAL SERIES.

## MEDICAL SCIENCES:

ADAIR, Maternal Care.

ADAIR, Maternal Care and Some Complications.

ADAIR, Maternal Care Complications.

ALLEN, Physiology and Treatment of Peptic Ulcer.

AURELIANUS, On Acute Diseases and Chronic Diseases.

BABKIN, Pavlov.

BAILEY, Intracranial Tumors.

BARKER, Description of the Brains and Spinal Cords of Two Brothers.

BAY, Medical Administration.

BECKER, Boys in White.

BIRREN, Handbook of Aging and the Individual.

BLOOMFIELD, Bibliography of Internal Medicine.

BOYLAND, On Cancer and Hormones.

BREASTED, Edwin Smith Surgical Papyrus.

BURGESS, Aging in Western Societies.

CARPI, Short Introduction to Anatomy.

DACK, Food Poisoning.

DAVENPORT, ABC of Acid-Base Chemistry.

DAVIS, Crisis in Hospital Finance.

DOE, Bibliography of the Works of Ambroise Paré.

FAVILL, Outline of the Cranial Nerves.

FOSTER, Doctors, Dollars, and Disease.

FRAZIER, Racial Variations in Immunity to Syphilis.

FROMM-REICHMANN, Principles of Intensive Psychotherapy.

GAILLARD, Parathyroid Glands.

GALTON, Haematology and Blood Groups.

GARDINER, Convalescent Care.

GREGG, For Future Doctors.

HANKE, Diet and Dental Health.

HARDESTY, Neurological Technique.

HEINE, Student Physician as Psychotherapist.

HERRICK, Memories of Eighty Years.

HESS, Physical and Mental Growth of Prematurely Born Children.

HILL, Psychotherapeutic Intervention in Schizophrenia.

HODGES, An Epiphyseal Chart.

HODGES, Life and Times of Emil H. Grubbe.

HORRALL, Bile.

HUFF, Manual of Medical Parasitology.

INGLE, Dozen Doctors.

JACOBSON, Progressive Relaxation.

JENKINS, Terminology of Operations.

JONES, Evolution of the Atherosclerotic Plaque.

KATZ, Elements of Electrocardiographic Interpretation.

KATZ, Introduction to the Interpretation of the Electrocardiogram.

KING, Growth of Medical Thought.

KING, Medical World of the Eighteenth Century.

KLIGLER, Epidemiology and Control of Malaria in Palestine.

KOBRAK, Middle Ear.

LEE, Childbirth.

LENZ, Medical Genetics.

LEVEN, Incomes of Physicians.

LOCKWOOD, Ugo Benzi: Medieval Philosopher and Physician.

LOUTIT, Irradiation of Mice and Men.

McINTYRE, Curare.

McLEAN, Bone.

MILLIS, Sickness and Insurance.

MOORMAN, Tuberculosis and Genius.

NEW YORK TUBERCULOSIS AND HEALTH ASSOCIATION, *Committee on Community Dental Service,* Health Dentistry for the Community.

ORNSTEIN, Role of Scientific Societies.

PAUL, Clinical Epidemiology.

POTTER, Fetal and Neonatal Death.

RAMAZZINI, De morbis artificum.

REED, Vitamin D.

RICKETTS, Contribution to Medical Science.

ROREM, Capital Investment in Hospitals.

ROREM, Public's Investment in Hospitals.

ROSENBERG, Cholera Years.

ROTH, Isotopes in Experimental Pharmacology.

ROTHMAN, Physiology and Biochemistry of the Skin.

SCHAFER, Pathology in General Surgery.

SCHINDLER, Gastroscopy.

SELYE, Calciphylaxis.

SIGERIST, Civilization and Disease.

SINAI, Study of Physicians and Dentists.

SNIDER, Stereotaxic Atlas of the Cat Brain.

SNIDER, Stereotaxic Atlas of the Monkey Brain.

STEVENS, Mental Retardation.

TALIAFERRO, Medicine and the War.

TEMPLETON, X-Ray Examination of the Stomach.

VAN LIERE, Anoxia.

VAN LIERE, Hypoxia.

VEITH, Hysteria.

WACHSMANN, Moving-Field Radiation Therapy.
WILSON, Teratology.
WOOD, Health and Education.
*See also* PSYCHIATRY; PSYCHOLOGY.

## METEOROLOGY:

BATTAN, Radar Meteorology.
BROWN, Bibliography of Meteorites.
BYERS, Elements of Cloud Physics.
BYERS, Thunderstorm Electricity.
COX, Weather and Climate of Chicago.
DEPARTMENT OF METEOROLOGY, Tephigram Chart.
FULTZ, Upper-Air Trajectories and Weather Forecasting.
PRIESTLEY, Turbulent Transfer in the Lower Atmosphere.
REITER, Jet-Stream Meteorology.
SAUCIER, Principles of Meteorological Analysis.
SELLERS, Physical Climatology.
*See also* PUBLICATIONS OF THE UNIVERSITY OF CHICAGO DEPARTMENT OF METEOROLOGY.

## MUSIC:

ARTZ, From the Renaissance to Romanticism.
COOPER, Learning to Listen.
COOPER, Rhythmic Structure in Music.
DOLĚJŠÍ, Modern Viola Technique.
DUSHKIN, Fun with Flutes.
HARASZTI, Bay Psalm Book.
LEONARD, Jazz and the White Americans.
LEVARIE, Mozart's *Le Nozze di Figaro*.
MADISON, Basic Concepts of Music Education.
MEYER, Emotion and Meaning in Music.
OTTERSTRÖM, Key to Manual of Harmony.
OTTERSTRÖM, Manual of Harmony.
OTTERSTRÖM, Theory of Modulation.
RUSSO, Composing for Jazz Orchestra.
SCHENKER, Harmony.
SCHULTZ, Riddle of the Pianist's Finger.
SLIM, Musica nova.

## NUTRITION:

BOGERT, Good Nutrition for Everybody.
BORLAND, Philippe de Lasalle.
CUMMINGS, American and His Food.
DACK, Food Poisoning.
GERARD, Food for Life.
HALLIDAY, Food Chemistry and Cookery.
HALLIDAY, Hows and Whys of Cooking.
HANKE, Diet and Dental Health.

HOLCK, Diet and Efficiency.
KYRK, Family in the American Economy.
MCAULEY, Economies in Food.
MARTIN, Robert's Nutrition Work with Children.
RICHARDS, Food.
SCHULTZ, Food for the World.
SLATER, Man Must Eat.
TURNER, Handbook of Diet Therapy.

## PALEONTOLOGY:

CLARK, Fossil Evidence for Human Evolution.
CLARK, History of the Primates.
HILZHEIMER, Animal Remains from Tell Asmar.
MATHEWS, Lower Triassic Cephalopod Fauna.
ROMER, Osteology of the Reptiles.
ROMER, Vertebrate Paleontology.
STANTON, Comparative Study of the Lower Cretaceous Formations.
WEIDENREICH, Apes, Giants, and Man.
WILLISTON, American Permian Vertebrates.
WILLISTON, Phylogeny and Classification of Reptiles.
WILLISTON, Water Reptiles.
*See also* CONTRIBUTIONS FROM WALKER MUSEUM.

## PHILOSOPHY:

ANDERSON, Philosophy of Francis Bacon.
APOSTLE, Aristotle's Philosophy of Mathematics.
ARENDT, Human Condition.
AYRES, Nature of the Relationship between Ethics and Economics.
BECK, Commentary on Kant's *Critique of Practical Reason*.
BILLINGS, Platonism of Philo Judaeus.
BRAMELD, Philosophic Approach to Communism.
BRANDT, Hopi Ethics.
BRÉHIER, Hellenic Age.
BRÉHIER, Middle Ages and the Renaissance.
BRÉHIER, Philosophy of Plotinus.
CARNAP, Logical Foundations of Probability.
CARNAP, Meaning and Necessity.
CASE, Christian Philosophy of History.
CASSIRER, Renaissance Philosophy of Man.
CICERO, Brutus, On the Nature of the Gods, On Divination, On Duties.
CREEL, Chinese Thought from Confucius to Mao Tsê-tung.
DEWEY, Theory of Valuation.
DEWEY, Essay in Experimental Logic.

DEWEY, Logical Conditions of a Scientific Treatment of Morality.

DEWEY, Significance of the Problem of Knowledge.

DEWEY, Studies in Logical Theory.

DEWEY, Ethical Principles.

DUBS, Rational Induction.

EDEL, Science and the Structure of Ethics.

EWING, Short Commentary on Kant's *Critique of Pure Reason*.

FAIRBANK, Chinese Thought and Institutions.

FOBES, Philosophical Greek.

FRANK, Foundations of Science.

FRANKFORT, Intellectual Adventure of Ancient Man.

FRIEDMAN, Martin Buber.

FRIEDRICH, Philosophy of Law in Historical Perspective.

GALILEI, Dialogue on the Great World Systems.

GORE, Imagination in Spinoza and Hume.

GOTSHALK, Art and the Social Order.

GOTSHALK, Metaphysics in Modern Times.

GRENE, Greek Political Theory.

GRENE, Introduction to Existentialism.

GRENE, Man in His Pride.

GRENE, Portrait of Aristotle.

HALL, Philosophical Systems.

HALLOWELL, Moral Foundation of Democracy.

HARRIS, All Coherence Gone.

HARTSHORNE, Philosophers Speak of God.

HARTSHORNE, Philosophy and Psychology of Sensation.

HAYEK, Constitution of Liberty.

HEATH, Concept of Time.

HEFELBOWER, Relation of John Locke to English Deism.

HEIDEL, Necessary and the Contingent in the Aristotelian System.

HEMPEL, Foundations of Concept Formation in Empirical Science.

HEMPEL, Fundamentals of Concept Formation.

HENDERSON, Introduction to Philosophy of Education.

HERTZ, Chance and Symbol.

HERZ, Political Realism and Political Idealism.

HEYWOOD, Works of the Mind.

HUSZAR, New Perspectives on Peace.

JAFFA, Thomism and Aristotelianism.

JOAD, Critique of Logical Positivism.

JASPERS, Future of Mankind.

JOERGENSEN, Development of Logical Empiricism.

JORDAN, Essays in Criticism.

JORDAN, Good Life.

JORDAN, New Perspective.

JORDAN, Theory of Legislation.

JOUVENEL, Sovereignty.

KALLEN, William James and Henri Bergson.

KANT, *Critique of Practical Reason* and Other Writings in Moral Philosophy.

KANT, Foundations of the Metaphysics of Morals.

KATZ, Problem of Induction and Its Solution.

KAUFMAN, Relativism, Knowledge, and Faith.

KECSKEMETI, Meaning, Communication, and Value.

KRIEGER, Politics of Discretion.

KROEBER, Nature of Culture.

KRONER, Kant's Weltanschauung.

KUHN, Structure of Scientific Revolutions.

LEE, Existence and Inquiry.

LEFEVRE, Prayers of Kierkegaard.

LEIBNIZ, Philosophical Papers and Letters.

LENZEN, Procedures of Empirical Science.

LEPRINCE-RINGUET, Atoms and Men.

LILLIE, General Biology and Philosophy of Organism.

LÖWITH, Meaning in History.

McKEON, Thought, Action, and Passion.

MAHDI, Ibn Khaldûn's Philosophy of History.

MAIMONIDES, Guide of the Perplexed.

MARITAIN, Man and the State.

MARTIN, Truth and Denotation.

MEAD, George Herbert Mead on Social Psychology.

MEAD, Mind, Self, and Society.

MEAD, Movements of Thought in the Nineteenth Century.

MEAD, Philosophy of the Act.

MELAND, Higher Education and the Human Spirit.

MELAMED, Spinoza and Buddha.

MEYER, Emotion and Meaning in Music.

MILL, Spirit of the Age.

MILL, Utilitarianism.

MILLER, Significance of the Mathematical Element in the Philosophy of Plato.

MILLERD, On the Interpretation of Empedocles.

MISES, Kleines Lehrbuch des Positivismus.

MOORE, Existence, Meaning, and Reality.

MORRIS, Foundations of the Theory of Signs.

MOORE, Functional versus the Representational Theories of Knowledge.

MOORE, Pragmatism.
MORRIS, Six Theories of Mind.
NEURATH, Encyclopedia of Unified Science.
NIKAM, Edicts of Asoka.
PALTER, Whitehead's Philosophy of Science.
PASCH, Experience and the Analytic.
PATON, Categorical Imperative.
PERRY, Philosophy of American Democracy.
PLATT, New Views of the Nature of Man.
POLANYI, Logic of Liberty.
POLANYI, Personal Knowledge.
POLANYI, Science, Faith, and Society.
POLANYI, Study of Man.
REICHENBACH, Experience and Prediction.
RÖPKE, Social Crisis in Our Time.
ROGERS, Parallelism of Mind and Body.
SANTILLANA, Development of Rationalism and Empiricism.
SHARP, Good Will and Ill Will.
SHOREY, Idea of Good in Plato's Republic.
SHOREY, Unity of Plato's Thought.
SHOREY, What Plato Said.
SIDGWICK, Methods of Ethics.
SILLS, *Values*.
SIMON, *Material Logic* of John of St. Thomas.
SIMON, Philosophy of Democratic Government.
SINAIKO, Love, Knowledge, and Discourse in Plato.
SMITH, American Philosophy of Equality.
SMITH, From Descartes to Kant.
SMITH, Moral Life of the Hebrews.
SMITH, Philosophers Speak for Themselves.
SMITH, Philosophic Way of Life.
SPARSHOTT, Enquiry into Goodness.
STRAUSS, Natural Right and History.
STRAUSS, Political Philosophy of Hobbes.
STRAUSS, Social Psychology of George Herbert Mead.
THOMPSON, Pragmatic Philosophy of C. S. Peirce.
TUFTS, Individual and His Relation to Society.
TUFTS, On the Genesis of the Aesthetic Categories.
VIVAS, Moral and Ethical Life.
WALKER, Decline of Hell.
WATTS, Legacy of Asia.
WEAVER, Ideas Have Consequences.
WEIZSÄCKER, History of Nature.
WEIZSÄCKER, World View of Physics.
WHITEHEAD, Nature and Life.
WIEMAN, Source of Human Good.
WICK, Metaphysics and the New Logic.

WILD, Plato's Modern Enemies and the Theory of Natural Law.
WOOD, Time's Arrow in Society.
WOODGER, Technique of Theory Construction.
WRIGHT, Studies in Chinese Thought.

**PHYSICS:**

ADAMS, Natural Radiation Environment.
BATTAN, Radar Meteorology.
BYERS, Thunderstorm Electricity.
CALDER, Living with the Atom.
CHANDRASEKHAR, Plasma Physics.
CHERDYNTSEV, Abundance of Chemical Elements.
COFFINBERRY, Metal Plutonism.
DALTON, Foundations of Atomic Theory.
DALTON, Foundations of the Molecular Theory.
DICKERMAN, Optical Spectrometric Measurements of High Temperatures.
FERENCE, Analytical Experimental Physics.
FERMI, Atoms in the Family.
FERMI, Atoms for the World.
FERMI, Collected Papers.
FERMI, Notes on Quantum Mechanics.
FERMI, Nuclear Physics.
FISHER, Statistical Theory of Liquids.
FRANK, Foundations of Physics.
GOMER, Structure and Properties of Solid Surfaces.
HEISENBERG, Physical Principles of the Quantum Theory.
HUYGENS, Treatise on Light.
HYMAN, Noble-Gas Compounds.
LEMON, Analytical Experimental Physics.
LEMON, Demonstration Laboratory of Physics.
LEMON, From Galileo to the Nuclear Age.
LEPRINCE-RINGUET, Atoms and Men.
LEVINSON, Law of Gravitation in Relativity.
LEVI SETTI, Elementary Particles.
LIBBY, Radiocarbon Dating.
MASON, Electromagnetic Field.
MEYER, Diffraction of Light.
MICHELSON, Light Waves.
MICHELSON, Studies in Optics.
MICHELSON, Velocity of Light.
MILLIKAN, Electron.
MILLIKAN, Electrons (+ and −).
MOULTON, New Method on Exterior Ballistics.
PHILLIPS, Progress in Fast Neutron Physics.
PRIESTLEY, Turbulent Transfer in the Lower Atmosphere.

REITER, Jet Stream Meteorology.
SAUCIER, Principles of Meteorological Analysis.
SMITH, Hydrogen in Metals.
STEPHENSON, Exploring in Physics.
STRATTON, College Course of Laboratory Experiments.
WEINBERG, Physical Theory of Neutron Chain Reactors.
WEIZSÄCKER, World View of Physics.
ZENER, Elasticity and Anelasticity of Metals.

## PHYSIOLOGY:

ABRAMSON, Vascular Responses in the Extremities of Man.
BENSLEY, Handbook of Histological and Cytological Technique.
BENSLEY, Structure of the Glands of Brunner.
BUYTENDIJK, Pain.
CAMPBELL, Physiology of Insect Development.
CARLSON, Control of Hunger.
CARLSON, Machinery of the Body.
CARLSON, Studies on the Possible Intoxicating Action of 3.2 Per Cent Beer.
CHILD, Senescence and Rejuvenescence.
D'AMOUR, Basic Physiology.
D'AMOUR, Manual for Laboratory Work in Mammalian Physiology.
ENDERS, Delayed Implantation.
FIELD, Atlas of Cat Anatomy.
GAILLARD, Parathyroid Glands.
GERARD, Food for Life.
GREENBLATT, Cat Musculature.
HALSTEAD, Brain and Intelligence.
HAYEK, Sensory Order.
HERRICK, Brain of the Tiger Salamander.
HERRICK, Thinking Machine.
HESS, Biology of Mind.
HODGES, Epiphyseal Chart.
HYMAN, Comparative Vertebrate Anatomy.
HYMAN, Laboratory Manual for Comparative Vertebrate Anatomy.
JACOBSON, Progressive Relaxation.
KARE, Physiological and Behavioral Aspects of Taste.
KLEITMAN, Sleep and Wakefulness.
KLEITMAN, Sleep Characteristics.
LEWIS, Biology of the Negro.
LILLIE, Protoplasmic Action.
LOEB, On the Production and Suppression of Muscular Twitchings.
LOEB, Studies in General Physiology.
LYON, Contribution to the Comparative Physiology of Compensatory Motions.

McLEAN, Bone.
MITCHELL, Growth Regulators.
NEWMAN, Physiology of Twinning.
NEUMAN, Chemical Dynamics of Bone Mineral.
PATTERSON, Wound Healing and Tissue Repair.
POLYAK, Retina.
POLYAK, Vertebrate Visual System.
PRICE, Dynamics of Proliferating Tissues.
REED, Vitamin D.
ROTHMAN, Physiology and Biochemistry of the Skin.
SHAMBAUGH, Distribution of Blood Vessels.
SOSKIN, Carbohydrate Metabolism.
THOMAS, On a Difference in the Metabolism of the Sexes.
THORNTON, Regeneration in Vertebrates.
VAN DYKE, Physiology and Pharmacology of the Pituitary Body.
VAN LIERE, Anoxia.
VAN LIERE, Hypoxia.
WEBSTER, Laboratory Manual of Physiological Chemistry.
WEISS, Genetic Neurology.

## POETRY:

BELITT, Enemy Joy.
BOWERS, Whitman's Manuscripts. Leaves of Grass.
CLANCY, Odes and Epodes of Horace.
COXE, Middle Passage.
DENNEY, In Praise of Adam.
GARDNER, Looking Glass.
GUNN, My Sad Captains.
GUNN, Sense of Movement.
HOMER, Iliad.
HULL, Aesop's Fables.
KNOEPFLE, Rivers into Islands.
LATTIMORE, Greek Lyrics.
LOGAN, Ghosts of the Heart.
NEMEROV, Mirrors and Windows.
NEMEROV, New and Selected Poems.
NEMEROV, Next Room of the Dream.
OLSON, Collected Poems.
OLSON, Plays and Poems.
PETRARCH, Triumphs.
PINDAR, Odes.
VIRGIL, Georgics.

## POLITICAL SCIENCE:

APTER, Politics of Modernization.
BARR, Let's Join the Human Race.

BENTLEY, Process of Government.
BEYLE, Identification and Analysis of Attribute-Cluster-Blocs.
BERELSON, Voting.
BLAU, Dynamics of Bureaucracy.
BORGESE, Foundations of the World Republic.
BRAMELD, Philosophical Approach to Communism.
BRANDT, Toward the New Spain.
BROWNLOW, Passion for Politics.
BUCK, Amateurs and Professionals in British Politics, 1918–59.
BURKE, Correspondence of Edmund Burke.
BURTON, Assembly of the League of Nations.
CALEF, Private Grazing and Public Lands.
CASSELS, Short Ballot.
CAUGHEY, In Clear and Present Danger.
CAUGHEY, Their Majesties the Mob.
CHRISTOPH, Capital Punishment and British Politics.
COBBAN, National Self-determination.
COHEN, Communism of Mao Tse-tung.
COHEN, Recent Theories of Sovereignty.
CRAVEN, Democracy in American Life.
CRICK, In Defense of Politics.
CROSSKEY, Politics and the Constitution in the History of the United States.
CURRIE, Federalism in the New Nations.
DAHL, Preface to Democratic Theory.
DE GRAZIA, Political Community.
DE JONG, German Fifth Column in the Second World War.
DIVINE, Illusion of Neutrality.
DUVERGER, French Political System.
DUYVENDAK, Book of Lord Shang.
ELAZAR, American Partnership.
ENNIS, French Policy and Developments in Indochina.
EPSTEIN, Britain—Uneasy Ally.
FELLMAN, Constitutional Right of Association.
FERMI, Mussolini.
FINER, Presidency.
FITZGIBBONS, Constitutions of the Americas.
FOX, Power of Small States.
FREUND, Empire and Sovereignty.
FREUND, Standards of American Legislation.
GETTYS, Law of Citizenship in the United States.
GIFFEN, Fashoda.
GILBY, Political Thought of Thomas Aquinas.
GLICK, Administration of Technical Assistance.
GORDON, New Zealand Becomes a Pacific Power.

GOSNELL, Boss Platt and His New York Machine.
GOSNELL, Getting Out the Vote.
GOSNELL, Machine Politics, Chicago Model.
GOSNELL, Negro Politicians.
GOSNELL, Why Europe Votes.
GRODZINS, Americans Betrayed.
GRODZINS, Loyal and the Disloyal.
HALLOWELL, Moral Foundation of Democracy.
HARDIN, Freedom in Agricultural Education.
HASS, American Empire.
HAYEK, Constitution of Liberty.
HAYEK, Road to Serfdom.
HAZARD, Soviet System of Government.
HEMLEBEN, Plans for World Peace through Six Centuries.
HERMENS, Tyrants' War and the Peoples' Peace.
HERZ, Political Realism and Political Idealism.
HOCKING, Freedom of the Press.
HOLT, Strategic Psychological Operations.
HOLTOM, Modern Japan and Shinto Nationalism.
HOWE, Garden and the Wilderness.
HUDSON, John Ponet.
HUTCHINSON, Democracy and National Unity.
ILCHMAN, Professional Diplomacy in the United States.
INGLIS, Freedom of the Movies
JANOWITZ, Military in the Political Development of New Nations.
JASNY, Soviet Industrialization.
JASPERS, Future of Mankind.
JORDAN, Theory of Legislation.
JOUVENEL, Sovereignty.
KAWAI, Japan's American Interlude.
KENNAN, American Diplomacy, 1900–1950.
KILLINGSWORTH, State Labor Relations Acts.
KIRK, Randolph of Roanoke.
KLEMENT, Copperheads in the Middle West.
KNAPPEN, And Call It Peace.
KURLAND, Supreme Court Review.
LASSWELL, Psychopathology and Politics.
LATHAM, Philosophy and Policies of Woodrow Wilson.
LEIGH, Free and Responsible Press.
LEONHARDT, Nazi Conquest of Danzig.
LIPSON, Politics of Equality: New Zealand's Adventure in Democracy.
LOEWENSTEIN, Political Power and the Governmental Process.
LYON, Governmental Problems in the Chicago Metropolitan Area.

McCLOSKEY, American Supreme Court.
McDONALD, We the People.
McGOVNEY, American Suffrage Medley.
McKEON, Democracy in a World of Tensions.
MacNAIR, China in Revolution.
MacNAIR, Real Conflict between China and Japan.
MADISON, Papers of James Madison.
MANSFIELD, Statesmanship and Party Government.
MANWARING, Render unto Caesar.
MERRIAM, New Aspects of Politics.
MERRIAM, New Aspects of Voting.
MERRIAM, Non-voting.
MERRIAM, Primary Elections.
MERRIAM, Prologue to Politics.
MERRIAM, Systematic Politics.
MERRIAM, What Is Democracy?
MORGENTHAU, Decline of Democratic Politics.
MORGENTHAU, Germany and the Future of Europe.
MORGENTHAU, Impasse of American Foreign Policy.
MORGENTHAU, Politics in the 20th Century.
MORGENTHAU, Restoration of American Politics.
MORGENTHAU, Scientific Man versus Power Politics.
MONTGOMERY, Forced To Be Free.
MORSTEIN MARX, Administrative State.
MURPHY, Congress and the Court.
MURPHY, Elements of Judicial Strategy.
NEF, United States and Civilization.
NELSON, Theory and Practice of American Politics.
NEUMANN, Modern Political Parties.
OAKS, Wall between Church and State.
OSGOOD, Ideals and Self-Interest in America's Foreign Relations.
OSGOOD, Limited War.
OSGOOD, NATO.
PARKES, Marxism. An Autopsy.
PERLOFF, Puerto Rico's Economic Future.
PERRY, Philosophy of American Democracy.
POLANYI, Logic of Liberty.
PORTER, History of Suffrage.
PRITCHETT, Civil Liberties and the Vinson Court.
RABINOWITCH, Dawn of a New Age.
REED, Legislatures.
REICH, Leisler's Rebellion.
REID, International Servitudes in Law and Peace.
RICHTER, Re-educating Germany.

RIDGE, Ignatius Donnelly.
RIDLEY, City-Manager Profession.
RIDOLFI, Life of Niccolò Machiavelli.
RIPPY, America and the Strife of Europe.
RÖPKE, Social Crisis in Our Time.
SAYRE, Protection of American Export Trade.
SCHNEIDER, Making Fascists.
SCHUMAN, War and Diplomacy in the French Republic.
SFORZA, Totalitarian War.
SIMON, Philosophy of Democratic Government.
SIMONS, Federal Tax Reform.
SMITH, American Democracy and Military Power.
SMITH, Legislative Way of Life.
SMITH, Promise of American Politics.
SPENCER, Collective Bargaining.
STAFF, SOCIAL SCIENCES 1, THE COLLEGE OF THE UNIVERSITY OF CHICAGO, People Shall Judge.
STALEY, War and the Private Investor.
STILLMAN, Africa in the Modern World.
STONER, S. O. Levinson and the Pact of Paris.
STOURZH, Benjamin Franklin and American Foreign Policy.
STRAUSS, Natural Right and History.
STRAUSS, Political Philosophy of Hobbes.
SWISHER, Growth of Constitutional Power in the United States.
TALBOT, South Asia in the World Today.
TÊNG, Chang Hsi and the Treaty of Nanking.
THOMPSON, Future of the Pacific World.
THOMPSON, Population and Peace in the Pacific.
VOEGELIN, New Science of Politics.
WALKER, Planning Function in Urban Government.
WARD, Asia for the Asiatics?
WEINER, Politics of Scarcity.
WHITE, Civil Service in the Modern State.
WHITE, Future of Government in the United States.
WHITE, Whitley Councils in the British Civil Service.
WHITE, State of the Social Sciences.
WILSON, Amateur Democrat.
WOODHOUSE, Puritanism and Liberty.
WOODDY, Case of Frank L. Smith.
WOODDY, Chicago Primary of 1926.
WRIGHT, Mandates under the League of Nations.
WRIGHT, Study of War.
WRIGHT, World Community.

Rogers, Psychotherapy and Personality Change.

Scheidemann, Experiments in General Psychology.

Scheidemann, Lecture Demonstrations for General Psychology.

Scott, Aggression.

Scott, Animal Behavior.

Scott, Genetics and the Social Behavior of Dogs.

Skaggs, Major Forms of Inhibition.

Stephenson, Study of Behavior.

Stevenson, Child Psychology.

Strauss, Social Psychology of George Herbert Mead.

Swineford, Study in Factor Analysis.

Tanner, Association of Ideas.

Thelen, Dynamics of Groups at Work.

Thompson, Mental Traits of Sex.

Thompson, Psychological Norms.

Thurstone, Factorial Study of Perception.

Thurstone, Measurement of Attitude.

Thurstone, Measurement of Values.

Thurstone, Multiple-Factor Analysis.

Thurstone, Personality Schedules.

Thurstone, Primary Mental Abilities.

Thurstone, Vectors of Mind.

Tibbitts, Handbook of Social Gerontology.

Wann, Behaviorism and Phenomenology.

Watson, Animal Education.

Watson, Behaviorism.

White, State of the Social Sciences.

*See also* Behavior Research Fund Monographs; Monograph Supplements to the British Journal of Psychology; Psychometric Monographs; Scales for the Measurement of Socal Attitudes; Studies from the Psychological Laboratory.

## READING:

Burgess, Report of the Society's Committee on Silent Reading.

Buswell, Experimental Study of the Eye-Voice Span in Reading.

Buswell, Non-oral Reading.

Clift, Adult Reading.

Colburn, Books and Library Reading for Pupils of the Intermediate Grades.

Edfelt, Silent Speech and Silent Reading.

Gates, Reading in the Elementary School.

Goins, Visual Perceptual Abilities and Reading Progress.

Gray, Adapting Reading Programs to Wartime Needs.

Gray, Basic Instruction in Reading in the Elementary and High Schools.

Gray, Improving Reading in All Curriculum Areas.

Gray, Keeping Reading Programs Abreast of the Times.

Gray, Maturity in Reading.

Gray, Promoting Growth toward Maturity in Interpreting What Is Read.

Gray, Reading in the High School and College.

Gray, Report of the National Committee on Reading.

Gray, Studies of Elementary-School Reading.

Gray, Teaching of Reading.

Gray, What Makes a Book Readable.

Haygood, Who Uses the Public Library.

Judd, Reading.

Monroe, Children Who Cannot Read.

Robinson, Clinical Studies in Reading II.

Robinson, Controversial Issues in Reading and Promising Solutions.

Robinson, Corrective Reading in Classroom and Clinic.

Robinson, Developing Permanent Interest in Reading.

Robinson, Evaluation of Reading.

Robinson, Materials for Reading.

Robinson, Meeting Individual Differences in Reading.

Robinson, Oral Aspects of Reading.

Robinson, Promoting Maximal Reading Growth among Able Learners.

Robinson, Reading Instructions in Various Patterns of Grouping.

Robinson, Reading and the Language Arts.

Robinson, Recent Developments in Reading.

Robinson, Sequential Development of Reading Abilities.

Robinson, Underachiever in Reading.

Robinson, Why Pupils Fail in Reading.

Schmidt, Experimental Study in the Psychology of Reading.

Staff of the Reading Clinic, Clinical Studies in Reading I.

Strang, Exploration in Reading Patterns.

Taylor, Controlled Reading.

Truman, Types of Reading Ability.

Waples, Libraries and Readers.

Waples, People and Print.

Waples, What People Want To Read About.

WAPLES, What Reading Does to People.
WILSON, Role of the Library in Adult Education.
WITTY, Development in and through Reading.

## REFERENCE BOOKS:

BOND, Reference Guide to English Studies.
CASTILLO, University of Chicago Spanish Dictionary.
CRAIGIE, Dictionary of American English on Historical Principles.
CRAIGIE, Dictionary of the Older Scottish Tongue.
MATHEWS, Dictionary of Americanisms.
TURABIAN, Manual for the Writers of Term Papers, Theses, and Dissertations.
TURABIAN, Student's Guide for Writing College Papers.
UNIVERSITY OF CHICAGO PRESS, Manual of Style.

## RELIGION AND THEOLOGY:

AMES, Beyond Theology.
AMES, New Orthodoxy.
ARBAUGH, Revelation in Mormonism.
ARPEE, Armenian Awakening.
ATHEARN, City Institute for Religious Teachers.
BAKER, Short History of Christianity.
BARTON, Religions of the World.
BEWER, Religion of the Bible.
BOWER, Church and State in Education.
BOWER, Survey of Religious Education.
BRAY, Weekday Lessons from Luke in the Greek Gospel Lectionary.
BUCK, Johannine Lessons in the Greek Gospel Lectionary.
BURGESS, Life of Christ.
BURTON, Biblical Ideas of Atonement.
BURTON, Christianity in the Modern World.
BURTON, Jesus of Nazareth.
BURTON, Founding of the Christian Church.
BURTON, Life of Christ.
BURTON, Origin and Teaching of the New Testament Books.
BURTON, Principles and Ideals for the Sunday School.
BURTON, Source Book for the Study of the Teaching of Jesus.
CASE, Bibliographical Guide to the History of Christianity.

CASE, Christian Philosophy of History.
CASE, Evolution of Early Christianity.
CASE, Historicity of Jesus
CASE, Incarnation and Modern Thought.
CASE, Jesus.
CASE, Jesus through the Centuries.
CASE, Millennial Hope.
CASE, Origins of Christian Supernaturalism.
CASE, Social Origins of Christianity.
CHAVE, Functional Approach to Religious Education.
CHAVE, The Junior.
CHAVE, Personality Development in Children.
CHAVE, Supervision of Religious Education.
CLEVELAND, Great Revival in the West.
CROSS, Christian Salvation.
CROSS, Hebrew Family.
CROSS, Horace Bushnell.
CROSS, What Is Christianity?
DAWSON, Child and His Religion.
EBY, God in You.
ECKHARDT, Papacy and World-Affairs.
EKVALL, Religious Observations in Tibet.
ELIADE, History of Religions.
ELLIS, American Catholicism.
ERICKSEN, Psychological and Ethical Aspects of Mormon Group Life.
Essays concerning Jesus.
EVANS, Sunday-School Building.
FICHTER, Social Relations in the Urban Parish.
FICHTER, Southern Parish.
FOSTER, Finality of the Christian Religion.
FOSTER, Function of Religion.
FOWLER, Origin and Growth of the Hebrew Religion.
FRANKFORT, Kingship and the Gods.
FRIEDMAN, Martin Buber.
GATES, Life of Jesus.
GIANELLA, Religion and the Public Order.
GIBB, Modern Trends in Islam.
GILBY, Political Thought of Thomas Aquinas.
GILKEY, Jesus and Our Generation.
GLAZER, American Judaism.
GOLDIN, Living Talmud.
GOLDMAN, Ten Commandments.
GOODSPEED, History of Early Christian Literature.
GOODSPEED, Key to Ephesians.
GORDIS, Root and Branch.
GRAHAM, Culture and Conscience.
GRAHAM, Prophets and Israel's Culture.
GRANBERY, Outline of New Testament Christology.

GRAY, Šamaš Religious Texts.

GRUNEBAUM, Unity and Variety in Muslim Civilization.

GURNEY, Evolution, the Bible, and Religion.

HALL, Christ and the Eastern Soul.

HALL, Christian Belief.

HALL, Religious Education in the Public Schools.

HALPERIN, Italy and the Vatican at War.

HALPERIN, Separation of Church and State.

HAMILTON, Buddhism.

HARPER, Foreshadowings of the Christ.

HARPER, Religion and the Higher Life.

HARTH, Swift and Anglican Rationalism.

HARTSHORNE, Philosophers Speak of God.

HAYDON, Modern Trends in World-Religions.

HEGEL, Early Theological Writings.

HEIDEL, Gilgamesh Epic.

HERRICK, Kingdom of God.

HOBEN, Church School.

HOBEN, Minister and the Boy.

HOBEN, Virgin Birth.

HOLTOM, Modern Japan and Shinto Nationalism.

HOOKER, Of the Laws of Ecclesiastical Polity.

HOWE, Garden and the Wilderness.

HUDSON, American Protestantism.

HUDSON, John Ponet.

HUTCHINS, Graded Social Service.

INGE, Mysticism in Religion.

JENSEN, Myth and Cult.

JOHNSON, Have We the Likeness of Christ?

KAUFMAN, Relativism, Knowledge, and Faith.

KAUFMANN, Religion of Israel.

KNOX, Religion and the Present Crisis.

KOENKER, Liturgical Renaissance in the Roman Catholic Church.

KRONER, Culture and Faith.

KRUMBINE, Summer Program for the Church School.

LANDON, Southeast Asia.

LEFEVRE, Prayers of Kierkegaard.

LOBINGIER, Hebrew Home Life.

LOBINGIER, Projects in World-Friendship.

LOBINGIER, World-Friendship.

LÖWITH, Meaning in History.

McCONNELL, Christian Ideal.

McNEILL, Environmental Factors in Christian History.

MAIMONIDES, Guide of the Perplexed.

MATHEWS, Message of Jesus.

MATHEWS, Social and Ethical Teaching of Jesus.

MAXSON, Great Awakening.

MAY, Material Remains of the Megiddo Cult.

MEAD, Nathaniel William Taylor.

MEADVILLE THEOLOGICAL SEMINARY, Theological Study Today.

MELAMED, Spinoza and Buddha.

MILLER, Dramatization in the Church School.

MILLER, Dramatization of Bible Stories.

MOORE, Spread of Christianity.

MOWRY, Dead Sea Scrolls.

MULLER, Religion and Freedom in the Modern World.

MUSS-ARNOLT, Theological and Semitic Literature for the Year 1900.

MUSS-ARNOLT, Theological and Semitic Literature for the Year 1901.

NICHOLS, Romanticism and American Theology.

NORTON, Rise of Christianity.

OBENHAUS, Responsible Christian.

O'DEA, Mormons.

PALMER, One Year of Sunday-School Lessons.

PARKER, Gospel before Mark.

PARKES, Judaism and Christianity.

PEASE, Outline of a Bible-School Curriculum.

QUINN, Quest of Seth for the Oil of Life.

RADIN, Trial of Jesus.

READ, Idea of God.

REAGAN, Preaching of Peter.

RIDDLE, Jesus and the Pharisees.

RIDDLE, Martyrs.

ROBINSON, Life of Paul.

ROBINSON, Parables of Jesus.

RYLAARSDAM, Revelation in Jewish Wisdom Literature.

ST. JOHN, Contest for Liberty of Conscience.

SAUNDERS, Epochs in Buddhist History.

SCHNEIDER, Popular Religion.

SHARMAN, Teaching of Jesus about the Future.

SHAVER, Church School Projects.

SHAVER, Project Curriculum.

SHAVER, Project Principle in Religious Education.

SLATEN, What Jesus Taught.

SLATER, Paradox and Nirvana.

SMITH, Current Christian Thinking.

SMITH, Guide to the Study of the Christian Religion.

SMITH, Origin and History of Hebrew Law.

SMITH, Practical Theology.

SMITH, Principle of Christian Living.

SMITH, Prophets and Their Times.

SMITH, Realities of the Christian Religion.

SMITH, Religious Thought in the Last Quarter-Century.
SOARES, How To Enjoy the Bible.
SOARES, Three Typical Beliefs.
SPINKA, Chronicle of John Malalas.
STACKHOUSE, Chicago and the Baptists.
STARK, Christology.
STAUDT, Idea of the Resurrection.
SWEET, Baptists.
SWEET, Congregationalists.
SWEET, Methodists.
TILLICH, Biblical Religion and the Search for Ultimate Reality.
TILLICH, Protestant Era.
TILLICH, Systematic Theology.
THATCHER, Studies concerning Adrian IV.
THIELE, Mysterious Numbers of the Hebrew Kings.
TOWNER, Religion in Higher Education.
VOTAW, Primitive Era of Christianity.
WACH, Sociology of Religion.
WACH, Types of Religious Experience.
WALLIS, Egoism.
WALLIS, God and the Social Process.
WALLIS, Sociological Study of the Bible.
WARDLE, Handwork in Religious Education.
WATTS, Legacy of Asia.
WIEMAN, Source of Human Good.
WILLETT, Message of the Prophets.
WILLOUGHBY, Pagan Regeneration.
WIRTH, Ghetto.
WISCHNITZER, Messianic Theme in the Paintings of the Dura Synagogue.
WISHART, Primary Facts in Religious Thought.
WOODBURNE, Relation between Religion and Science.

## SCIENCE, GENERAL:

AUGER, What Are Cosmic Rays?
CALDER, Living with the Atom.
COHN, Medicine, Science, and Art.
DOWNING, Our Living World.
EHRENSVÄRD, Life.
EHRENSVÄRD, Man on Another World.
FERMI, Atoms in the Family.
FERMI, Atoms for the World.
FOSTER, Doctors, Dollars, and Disease.
GREGG, For Future Doctors.
HERRICK, Memories of Eighty Years.
KUHN, Structure of Scientific Revolutions.
LEPRINCE-RINGUET, Atoms and Men.
MOULTON, World and Man.
NEURATH, Encyclopedia of Unified Science.

ODISHAW, Challenges of Space.
SCHALLER, Year of the Gorilla.
SIGERIST, Civilization and Disease.
TALIAFERRO, Medicine and the War.
TAX, Evolution after Darwin.
WEIZSÄCKER, History of Nature.

## SOCIAL SERVICE:

ABBOTT, From Relief to Social Security.
ABBOTT, Immigration.
ABBOTT, Public Assistance.
ABBOTT, Social Welfare and Professional Education.
ABBOTT, Tenements of Chicago.
ABBOTT, Truancy and Non-attendance in the Chicago Schools.
BOAN, History of Poor Relief Legislation and Administration in Missouri.
BRECKINRIDGE, Illinois Poor Law.
BRECKINRIDGE, Madeline McDowell Breckinridge.
BROWNING, Development of Poor Relief in Kansas.
BROWNING, Rural Public Welfare.
BRUCE, Michigan Poor Law.
BURKE, Administration of Private Social Service Agencies.
COMMITTEE ON COMMUNITY DENTAL SERVICE, Health Dentistry for the Community.
CREECH, Three Centuries of Poor Law Administration.
DAVIS, Stipends and Spouses.
FARIS, Intelligent Philanthropy.
GOLDSTINE, Expanding Horizons in Medical Social Work.
GOLDSTINE, Readings in the Theory and Practice of Medical Social Work.
GRODZINS, Loyal and the Disloyal.
HALICH, Ukrainians in the United States.
HATHWAY, Young Cripple and His Job.
JOHNSON, Public Policy and Private Charities.
JUNKER, Field Work.
KENNEDY, Ohio Poor Law.
LINFORD, Old Age Assistance in Massachusetts.
MA, One Hundred Years of Public Services for Children in Minnesota.
MACDONALD, Federal Grants for Vocational Rehabilitation.
McMILLEN, Community Organization for Social Welfare.
McMILLEN, Statistical Methods for Social Workers.
PERLMAN, Social Casework.

POLANSKY, Social Work Research.

RADCLIFFE-BROWN, Method of Social Anthropology.

RIESE, Heal the Hurt Child.

SCHNEIDER, History of Public Welfare in New York State.

SHAFFER, Indiana Poor Law.

SMITH, Stepchild.

SPERGEL, Racketville, Slumtown, Haulburg.

STEINER, Education for Social Work.

STRONG, Public Welfare Administration in Canada.

TAYLOR, Pioneering on Social Frontiers.

TOWLE, Learner in Education for the Professions.

TOWLE, Social Case Records.

VEEDER, Development of the Montana Poor Law.

WADE, Graham Taylor.

WHITE, State of the Social Sciences.

WILSON, Mary McDowell: Neighbor.

WISNER, Public Welfare Administration in Louisiana.

WRIGHT, Social Service in Wartime.

*See also* UNIVERSITY OF CHICAGO SOCIAL SERVICE SERIES; UNIVERSITY OF CHICAGO SOCIAL SERVICE MONOGRAPHS.

## SOCIOLOGY:

ACKOFF, Design of Social Research.

ANDERSON, Desert Saints.

ANDERSON, Hobo.

BARNES, Introduction to the History of Sociology.

BECKER, Boys in White.

BECKER, Economics of Discrimination.

BERELSON, Voting.

BERNARD, Transition to an Objective Standard of Social Control.

BLAU, Dynamics of Bureaucracy.

BLAUNER, Alienation and Freedom.

BOGARDUS, Social Problems and Social Processes.

BREESE, Daytime Population of the Central Business District of Downtown Chicago.

BRISTOL, Handbook for Field Work Students.

BURGESS, Contributions to Urban Sociology.

BURGESS, Function of Socialization.

BURGESS, Personality and the Social Group.

BUTTERFIELD, Chapters in Rural Progress.

BUTTERFIELD, Country Church.

CAVAN, Family and the Depression.

CHICAGO COMMISSION ON RACE RELATIONS, Negro in Chicago.

CONDLIFFE, New Zealand in the Making.

CROCHERON, Rural School as a Community Center.

CROSS, Hebrew Family.

CROZIER, Bureaucratic Phenomenon.

DAVIS, Deep South.

DAVIS, Stipends and Spouses.

DEAN, Manual of Intergroup Relations.

DIXON, Social Case Records.

DOUGLAS, Wages and the Family.

DOYLE, Etiquette of Race Relations.

DUNCAN, Language and Literature in Society.

DUNN, Analysis of the Social Structure of a Western Town.

EELLS, Intelligence and Cultural Differences.

ELKINS, Slavery.

ELLIOTT, Conflicting Penal Theories in Statutory Criminal Law.

ESSIEN-UDOM, Black Nationalism.

FARIS, Intelligent Philanthropy.

FARIS, Mental Disorders in Urban Areas.

FEI, China's Gentry.

FEI, Earthbound China.

FICHTER, Social Relations in the Urban Parish.

FICHTER, Sociology.

FICHTER, Southern Parish.

FOOTE, Identity and Interpersonal Competence.

FOSTER, Education and Social Change in Ghana.

FRAZIER, Negro Family in Chicago

FRAZIER, Negro Family in the United States.

FREEDMAN, Recent Migration to Chicago.

FRIEDMANN, Meaning of Work and Retirement.

GAMIO, Mexican Immigration to the United States.

GAMIO, Mexican Immigrant.

GENNEP, Rites of Passage.

GILLETTE, Culture Agencies of a Typical Manufacturing Group.

GLEASON, Southern Negro and the Public Library.

GOLEMBIEWSKI, Small Group.

GOSNELL, Negro Politicians.

GOTSHALK, Art and the Social Order.

GROVES, Rural Mind.

HASTINGS, Bibliography of Sociology.

HAYES, Rural Community Organization.

HESS, Family Worlds.

HENDERSON, Practical Sociology.

HENDERSON, Social Programmes in the West.
HOWARD, History of Matrimonial Institutions.
HUGHES, French Canada in Transition.
HYMAN, Interviewing in Social Research.
HYSLOP, Science of Sociology.
JOHNSON, Shadow of the Plantation.
JUNKER, Field Work.
KELSEN, Society and Nature.
KISCH, Jews in Medieval Germany.
KNAPP, Origins of American Scientists.
KRAUS, Sick Society.
KYRK, Family in the American Economy.
LA BARRE, Human Animal.
LANDTMAN, Origin of the Inequality of the Social Classes.
LEVI, Municipal and Institutional Relations within Boston.
LIND, Island Community.
MEAD, George Herbert Mead and Social Psychology.
MEAD, Mind, Self, and Society.
MECKLIN, Passing of the Saint.
MERIAM, Stepfather in the Family.
MIYAKAWA, Protestants and Pioneers.
MONROE, Chicago Families.
MOWRER, Domestic Discord.
MOWRER, Family.
MOWRER, Family Disorganization.
MUMFORD, Origins of Leadership.
NEURATH, Foundations of the Social Sciences.
O'DEA, Mormons.
OGBURN, American Society in Wartime.
OGBURN, Recent Social Changes in the United States.
OGBURN, Social Changes in 1928 . . . 1929 . . . 1930 . . . 1931 . . . 1932.
OGBURN, Social Change and the New Deal.
OGBURN, Social Changes during the Depression and Recovery.
OGBURN, Technology and International Relations.
OGBURN, William F. Ogburn on Culture and Social Change.
PALMER, Field Studies in Sociology.
PARK, The City.
RASHEVSKY, Mathematical Biology of Social Behavior.
REDFIELD, Village That Chose Progress.
RICE, Methods in Social Science.
SANDERS, Standard of Living.
SCHREIBER, Our Amish Neighbors.
SCHULTZ, Food for the World.
SIGERIST, Civilization and Disease.

SKELTON, Our Generation.
SMALL, Cameralists.
SMALL, General Sociology.
SMALL, Meaning of Social Science.
SMALL, Origins of Sociology.
SMALL, Significance of Sociology for Ethics.
SMALL, Sociologist's Point of View.
SMELSER, Social Change in the Industrial Revolution.
SPERGEL, Racketville, Slumtown, Haulburg.
SPYKMAN, Social Theory of Georg Simmel.
STANTON, Leopard's Spots.
STRANG, Juvenile Delinquency and the Schools.
SUTHERLAND, Professional Thief.
THELEN, Dynamics of Groups at Work.
THOMAS, Source Book for Social Origins.
THRASHER, Gang.
THRUPP, Merchant Class in Medieval London.
WACH, Sociology of Religion.
WACH, Types of Religious Experience.
WALKER, Planning Function in Urban Government.
WALLIS, Struggle for Justice.
WARNER, American Life.
WESSEL, Ethnic Survey of Woonsocket, Rhode Island.
WHETTEN, Rural Mexico.
WHITE, State of the Social Sciences.
WHYTE, Street Corner Society.
WIRTH, Community Life and Social Policy.
WIRTH, Contemporary Social Problems.
WIRTH, Ghetto.
WIRTH, Local Community Fact Book of Chicago.
WIRTH, Louis Wirth on Cities and Social Life.
WORSLEY, Third World.
WRIGHT, World Community.
ZNANIECKI, Cultural Reality.
ZNANIECKI, Laws of Social Psychology.
ZORBAUGH, Gold Coast and the Slum.
See also AMERICAN COUNTRY LIFE ASSOCIATION; AMERICAN SOCIOLOGICAL SOCIETY; BEHAVIOR RESEARCH FUND PUBLICATIONS; UNIVERSITY OF CHICAGO SOCIOLOGICAL SERIES.

### STATISTICS:

BILLINGSLEY, Statistical Inference for Markov Processes.
FINNEY, Experimental Design and Its Statistical Basis.

FINNEY, Introduction to the Theory of Experimental Design.

HARMAN, Modern Factor Analysis.

HOLZINGER, Factor Analysis.

HOLZINGER, Statistical Résumé of the Spearman Two-Factor Theory.

HOLZINGER, Statistical Tables for Students in Education and Psychology.

KEMPERMAN, Passage Problem for a Stationary Markov Chain.

McMILLEN, Measurement in Social Work.

SMITH, Tests of Significance.

STEPHENSON, Study of Behavior.

THURSTONE, Multiple-Factor Analysis.

WOLFENDEN, Population Statistics and Their Compilation.

WOOD, Graphic Method.

## UNIVERSITY OF CHICAGO:

BOUCHER, Chicago College Plan.

FLINT, University of Chicago: A Sketch.

GOODSPEED, History of the University of Chicago.

GOODSPEED, Story of the University of Chicago.

LAING, Publications of the Members of the University of Chicago, 1902–1916.

O'HARA, University of Chicago. An Official Guide.

ROBERTSON, Quarter-Centennial Celebration.

ROBERTSON, University of Chicago. An Official Guide.

TALBOT, More than Lore.

THOMPSON, Extension Program of the University of Chicago.

## URBAN PLANNING:

ARNDT, Community Education.

BAUER, Economics of Under-developed Countries.

BEYLE, Governmental Reporting in Chicago.

BOYD, Chinese Architecture and Town Planning.

BUECHNER, Municipal Self-insurance of Workman's Compensation.

BURGESS, Contributions to Urban Sociology.

CHICAGO HOME RULE COMMISSION, Modernizing City Government.

FAIRWEATHER, Wanted: Intelligent Local Self-government.

GLICK, Administration of Technical Assistance.

GOSNELL, Boss Platt.

GOSNELL, Machine Politics.

HENRY, Schools and City Government.

HOSELITZ, Progress of Underdeveloped Areas.

JAMES, Municipal Administration in Germany.

KRAELING, City Invincible.

LEVI, Municipal and Institutional Relations within Boston.

LEPAWSKY, Home Rule for Metropolitan Chicago.

LEPAWSKY, Judicial System of Metropolitan Chicago.

LYON, Governmental Problems in the Chicago Metropolitan Area.

MAYER, Readings in Urban Geography.

MERRIAM, Government of the Metropolitan Region of Chicago.

MERRIAM, Municipal Revenues.

PARKINS, City Planning in Soviet Russia.

RIDLEY, City-Manager Profession.

TAYLOR, Municipal Budget-making.

THOMAS, Man's Role in Changing the Face of the Earth.

VIEG, Government of Education.

WALKER, The Planning Function in Urban Government.

WHITE, City Manager.

WHITE, Further Contributions to the Prestige Value of Public Employment.

WHITE, Prestige Value of Public Employment in Chicago.

WIRTH, Community Life and Social Policy.

WOODBURY, Future of Cities and Urban Redevelopment.

WOODBURY, Urban Redevelopment.

## ZOÖLOGY:

ANDREWARTHA, Distribution and Abundance of Animals.

ANDREWARTHA, Introduction to the Study of Animal Populations.

ALLEE, Animal Aggregations.

ALLEE, Synoptic Key to the Phyla, Classes, and Orders of Animals.

BLAKE, Birds of Mexico.

BUCHSBAUM, Animals without Backbones.

BUCHSBAUM, Readings in Ecology.

CLARK, Fossil Evidence for Human Evolution.

CRANDALL, Management of Wild Mammals in Captivity.

DAVENPORT, Animal Ecology in the Cold Spring Sand Spit.

ENDERS, Delayed Implantation.

ETKIN, Social Behavior and Organization among Vertebrates.

EYCLESHYMER, Early Development of Lepidosteus osseus.

FIELD, Atlas of Cat Anatomy.

GREENBLATT, Cat Musculature.

GUYER, Animal Micrology.

HERRICK, Brain of the Tiger Salamander.

HOWELL, Speed in Animals.

HYMAN, Comparative Vertebrate Anatomy.

HYMAN, Laboratory Manual for Elementary Zoölogy.

KELLOGG, Porpoises and Sonar.

LILLIE, Woods Hole Marine Biological Laboratory.

MEAD, Giant African Snail.

NEWMAN, Evolution, Genetics, and Eugenics.

NEWMAN, Twins.

OLDROYD, Insects and Their World.

PARK, Laboratory Introduction to Animal Ecology and Taxonomy.

ROMER, Osteology of the Reptiles.

ROMER, Vertebrate Paleontology.

ROMER, Vertebrate Story.

SCHALLER, Mountain Gorilla.

SCHALLER, Year of the Gorilla.

SCOTT, Animal Behavior.

SCOTT, Genetics and the Social Behavior of Dogs.

SHELFORD, Animal Communities.

SHELFORD, Bio-ecology.

TAX, Evolution after Darwin.

THORNTON, Regeneration in Vertebrates.

TOWER, Development of the Colors and the Color Patterns of Coleoptera.

WEIDENREICH, Apes, Giants, and Man.

WILLISTON, Water Reptiles.

# The Journals

## ACTA CYTOLOGICA

Publication discontinued.

## AMERICAN JOURNAL OF SEMITIC LANGUAGES AND LITERATURE

*See* Journal of Near Eastern Studies

## THE AMERICAN JOURNAL OF SOCIOLOGY

The growing complexity of man's relationship to men in society produced an increasing need for a co-ordinated social philosophy in the last century. In the 1830's, the word *sociologie* was originated by Auguste Comte. By the 1890's fragmentary popular opinion and the lack of systematized thinking regarding these problems pointed up the necessity for a more precise, scientific study of past and present human associations to form a theoretical basis for the new social science as well as for social reform. To fill this need THE AMERICAN JOURNAL OF SOCIOLOGY was founded in 1895 by Albion W. Small with the support of President William Rainey Harper. Small discussed the purpose of the JOURNAL in his opening editorial: "The Journal will thus be primarily technical. It will be devoted to the organization of knowledge pertaining to the relations of men in society into a sociology that shall represent the best American scholarship."

Today THE AMERICAN JOURNAL OF SOCIOLOGY, the oldest journal in the world devoted to sociology, maintains the same scholarship criteria. It is a professional journal of fundamental sociological analysis, research, and theory.

In addition to a careful selection of papers on social research and theory, articles are published in neighboring areas such as cultural anthropology and political science. Regular features include research notes, commentary and debates, book reviews, and a list of current publications. From time to time special issues devoted to a single topic of particular interest, as well as annotated bibliographies, are published.

The following selection of articles are classics which have been published in the past in THE AMERICAN JOURNAL OF SOCIOLOGY:

*The Number of Members as Determining the Sociological Form of the Group,* by Georg Simmel (1902)
*The Roots of Social Knowledge,* by Charles Horton Cooley (1926)
*Human Migration and the Marginal Man,* by Robert E. Park (1928)
*The Primary Group: Essence and Accident,* by Ellsworth Faris (1932)
*Institutional Office and the Person,* by Everett C. Hughes (1937)
*Social Behavior as Exchange,* by George C. Homans (1958)
*Some Aspects of Women's Ambition,* by Ralph H. Turner (1964)
*Mathematical Methods for the Study of Systems of Groups,* by Leo A. Goodman (1964)
*The Professionalization of Everyone?* by Harold L. Wilensky (1964)

SUPPLEMENTARY MONOGRAPHS:

*The Moral Integration of American Cities,* by Robert Cooley Angell (1951)
*Misunderstandings in Human Relations,* by Gustav Ichheiser (1949)

SPECIAL ISSUES:

Special semicentennial issue:
*Sociological Developments in the Last Fifty Years* (1945)
*Public Opinion and Propaganda* (1950)
*Sociology of Religion* (1955)
*The Interview in Social Research* (1956)
*Studies in Political Sociology* (1958)
*Formal Organizations* (1962)

After the founding of THE AMERICAN JOURNAL OF SOCIOLOGY, Small edited the publication for over thirty years. During his editorship the JOURNAL became the official organ of the American Sociological Society (now the American Sociological Association), remaining its official publication until 1936.

Small was followed by a succession of eminent scholars who continued his editorial policies. Ellsworth Faris, Ernest W. Burgess, Herbert Blumer, and Everett C. Hughes consecutively edited the publication. In 1960 Peter M. Blau became editor of THE AMERICAN JOURNAL OF SOCIOLOGY. He was succeeded by the present editor, C. Arnold Anderson, in 1966.

THE AMERICAN JOURNAL OF SOCIOLOGY is published bimonthly in July, September, November, January, March, and May. The size of the journal is six and three-quarters inches by nine and one-half inches, and each issue contains approximately one hundred and forty pages.

| SUBSCRIPTIONS: | ONE YEAR | TWO YEARS | THREE YEARS |
|---|---|---|---|
| United States and possessions . . . . | $8.00 | $15.00 | $21.50 |
| Canada and Pan American Postal Union . . . . . . . | 8.50 | 16.00 | 23.00 |
| All other countries . . . . . . . | 9.00 | 17.00 | 24.50 |

SINGLE COPY, $2.00

## AMERICAN JOURNAL OF THEOLOGY

*See* The Journal of Religion

## ASTRONOMY AND ASTROPHYSICS

*See* The Astrophysical Journal

## THE ASTROPHYSICAL JOURNAL

Almost as old as the University of Chicago itself, THE ASTROPHYSICAL JOURNAL was first edited by George E. Hale and James E. Keeler in 1895. The publication was a continuation of the original SIDEREAL MESSENGER which was retitled ASTRONOMY AND ASTROPHYSICS. As the foremost professional astronomical publication in the world, THE ASTROPHYSICAL JOURNAL has a long and distinguished record of having published in its pages most of the great astronomical discoveries of our times.

The JOURNAL published Hale's announcement of his fundamental discovery of the presence of magnetic fields in sunspots in 1907. The paper by Milton L. Humason and Edwin P. Hubble published in 1931 established the phenomenon of the expanding universe. The papers of Henry Norris Russell published in 1934 established the modern astrophysical methods for determining the abundances of the elements in the cosmos. W. Baade's recognition of the occurrence of different kinds of stellar populations (fundamental to so much current astronomical thinking) was described in papers published in 1944. And more recently the papers by Allan Sandage, Maarten Schmidt, and Martin Ryle on the quasi-stellar objects have been published in the JOURNAL.

Articles on current investigation and discovery, improved observation methods, and the application of modern physical theories to astronomy in the fields of spectroscopy and astronomical physics are features of THE ASTROPHYSICAL JOURNAL. The following papers manifest the scope of the JOURNAL:

*The Quasi-stellar Radio Sources 3C 48 and 3C 273,* by Jesse L. Greenstein and Maarten Schmidt
*Gravitational Collapse to a Small Volume,* by G. C. McVittie
*Infrared Spectra of Red-Giant Stars,* by N. J. Woolf, M. Schwarzschild, and W. K. Rose

*Composition of the Clouds of Venus* by Murk Bottema, William Plummer, John Strong, and Rodolphe Zander

*The Optical Spectrum of 3C 273,* by J. B. Oke

*Explorer XI Experiment on Cosmic Gamma Rays,* by W. Kraushaar, G. W. Clark, G. Garmire, H. Helmken, P. Higbie, and M. Agogino

*Stellar Evolution. I. The Approach to the Main Sequence,* by Icko Iben, Jr.

*Large Redshifts of Five Quasi-stellar Sources,* by Maarten Schmidt

*Spectral and Photometric Measurements of Solar X-Ray Emission below 60 Å,* by R. L. Blake, T. A. Chubb, H. Friedman, and A. E. Unzicker

*Observations of Extremely Cool Stars,* by G. Neugebauer, D. E. Martz, and R. B. Leighton

*Cosmic Black-Body Radiation,* by R. H. Dicke, P. J. E. Peebles, P. G. Roll, and D. T. Wilkinson

*The Optical Identification of Three New Radio Objects of the 3C 48 Class,* by M. Ryle and A. Sandage

*The Synthesis and Destruction of Elements in Peculiar Stars of Types A and B,* by William A. Fowler, E. Margaret Burbidge, G. R. Burbidge, and Fred Hoyle

THE ASTROPHYSICAL JOURNAL SUPPLEMENT SERIES has been published since 1953 at irregular intervals in conjunction with THE ASTROPHYSICAL JOURNAL. This *Series* provides a medium for the publication of extensive investigations and original memoirs on such matters as wavelength lists of stars, photometric data, results of numerical integrations pertaining to stellar interiors, and stellar atmospheres. Each SUPPLEMENT usually consists of a single paper, although some issues include several related papers. Typical examples of the SERIES are:

*Neutrino Processes and Pair Formation in Massive Stars and Supernovae,* by William A. Fowler and F. Hoyle

*General Catalogue of Discrete Radio Sources,* by William E. Howard III and Stephen P. Maran, and *A Uniform Flux-Density System for Observations of Discrete Radio Sources,* by William E. Howard III, Tom R. Dennis, Stephen P. Maran, and Hugh D. Aller

Distinguished previous managing editors of THE ASTROPHYSICAL JOURNAL include Hale and Keeler, E. B. Frost, H. G. Gale, O. Struve, and W. W. Morgan. Since 1952 the JOURNAL has enjoyed the excellent editorial craftsmanship of S. Chandrasekhar, Morton D. Hull Distinguished Service Professor. Dr. Chandrasekhar is a theoretical astrophysicist whose eminent works have placed him foremost in his profession. He has received numerous awards, and his publications include: *An Introduction to the Study of Stellar Structure, Principles of Stellar Dynamics, Radiative Transfer,* and *Hydrodynamic and Hydromagnetic Stability*. Working with Dr. Chandrasekhar on the editorial staff and board are scholars of great ability and repute.

THE ASTROPHYSICAL JOURNAL is sponsored by the American Astronomical Society and is published monthly. The size of the JOURNAL is six and three-quarters inches by nine and one-half inches. Each issue contains approximately three hundred and sixty pages.

| PRICE LIST: | SINGLE COPY | ONE-YEAR SUBSCRIPTION |
|---|---|---|
| United States and possessions. . . . . . . . | $6.00 | $35.00 |
| Canada and Pan American | | |
| Postal Union . . . . . . . . . . | 6.20 | 37.50 |
| All other countries . . . . . . . . . | 7.50 | 40.00 |

Members of the American Astronomical Society must send their subscriptions and remittances to the treasurer of the Society; and members of various national astronomical societies must in the first instance write to the managing editor for reduced rates.

THE ASTROPHYSICAL JOURNAL SUPPLEMENT SERIES is published irregularly. Issues are collected into volumes of about five hundred pages.

| PRICE LIST: | SINGLE VOLUME |
|---|---|
| United States and possessions . . . . . . . . . | $12.00 |
| Canada and Pan American Postal Union . . . . . . | 12.75 |
| All other countries . . . . . . . . . . | 13.50 |

The price of single copies varies and is announced as each SUPPLEMENT is issued.

## BIBLICAL WORLD

*See* The Journal of Religion

## BOTANICAL GAZETTE

From modest, unpretentious beginnings in 1875, the BOTANICAL GAZETTE matured into a potent force in the molding of botanical thought under the guidance of Dr. John M. Coulter, who founded the journal and edited it for the following fifty years. The GAZETTE grew from a pamphlet devoted to the naturalistic phase of the field (then almost the whole of botany) into a full-fledged journal covering a greatly expanded science, including morphology, physiology, and ecology.

Dr. Coulter brought the journal to the University of Chicago in 1896, five years after the founding of the University. Published by The University Press since that time, and edited by a succession of outstanding botanists after

Dr. Coulter's retirement, the GAZETTE has gained an international reputation as a highly important organ reporting the botanical research of investigators in the United States and in many other countries.

With the exception of a few review articles, the BOTANICAL GAZETTE is devoted to reporting original research. As the science has grown, the journal has broadened its scope, thus maintaining its policy of publishing theoretical articles in many fields of botany rather than specializing in one segment of the science.

The following selection of outstanding articles published in the BOTANI-CAL GAZETTE during the past twenty-five years reflects the range of subject matter covered by the journal:

> *Sexual Hormones in Achlya. VII. The Hormonal Mechanism in Homothallic Species,* by John R. Raper (1950)
> *Rates of Succession in Soil Changes on Southern Lake Michigan Sand Dunes,* by Jerry S. Olson (1958) (Mercer Award)
> *Photocontrol of Plant Development by Simultaneous Excitation of Two Interconvertible Pigments. III. Control of Seed Germination and Axis Elongation,* by S. B. Hendricks, E. H. Toole, V. K. Toole, and H. A. Borthwick (1959)
> *Development of Sieve-Plate Pores,* by Katherine Esau, V. I. Cheadle, and E. B. Risley (1962)
> *Action Spectra Studies of Phycocyanin Formation in a Mutant of* Cyanidium caldarium, by Kenneth E. Nichols and Lawrence Bogorad (1962)
> *Natural Introgression between* Bothriochloa ischaemum *and B. intermedia in West Pakistan,* by Jack R. Harlan (1963)
> *Genetics of Phytopathogenic Fungi. XII. Detection of Esterases and Phosphatases in Culture Filtrates of* Fusarium oxysporum *and F. xylarioides, by Starch-Gel Zone Electrophoresis,* by J. A. Meyer, E. D. Garber, and Susan G. Shaeffer (1964)
> *Effects of Peroxyacetyl Nitrate on Ultrastructure of Chloroplasts,* by William D. Thomson, W. M. Dugger, Jr., and R. L. Palmer (1965)
> *Meiosis and Sporogenesis in Excised Fern Leaves Grown in Sterile Culture,* by Mary E. Clutter and Ian M. Sussex (1965)

Coulter was an outstanding taxonomist and morphologist. His breadth of view, soundness of judgment, and plasticity of mind and ideas marked the GAZETTE from the beginning with flexibility and vision. Henry C. Cowles, a well-known ecologist and outstanding teacher, succeeded Dr. Coulter in 1928. Following Dr. Cowles in 1933 was Ezra J. Kraus, a man of exceptional ability and influence, who was an inspiration to students at the University and to collaborators in the United States Department of Agriculture. He was a renowned plant physiologist, anatomist, and horticulturist.

Succeeding Dr. Kraus in 1946, Charles E. Olmsted, a well-known ecologist, served as editor until 1959. Dr. Barbara F. Palser, a specialist in anatomy and morphology, was editor of the BOTANICAL GAZETTE from 1959 until 1965, when Dr. Olmsted resumed the editorship. The major fields of botany are represented by the editors of the journal, members of the Department of Botany at the University of Chicago.

BOTANICAL GAZETTE is published quarterly in March, June, September, and December. The size of the journal is seven and three-quarter inches by ten and one-half inches, and it averages eighty pages per issue.

| SUBSCRIPTIONS: | ONE YEAR | TWO YEARS | THREE YEARS |
|---|---|---|---|
| United States and possessions . . . . | $10.00 | $19.00 | $27.50 |
| Canada and Pan American | | | |
| Postal Union . . . . . . . . | 10.50 | 20.00 | 29.00 |
| All other countries . . . . . . . | 11.00 | 21.00 | 30.50 |

SINGLE COPY, $3.00

## BULLETIN OF THE ATOMIC SCIENTISTS

No longer published by The University of Chicago Press; address inquiries to 935 East Sixtieth Street, Chicago, Illinois 60637.

## BULLETIN OF THE BIBLIOGRAPHIC SOCIETY OF AMERICA

*See* Bibliographical Society of America in catalogue of books

## BULLETIN OF THE CENTER FOR CHILDREN'S BOOKS

The Center for Children's Books was originated in 1945 at the University of Chicago by the Education Library. A collection of trade books for children was set up by the Center for purposes of analysis in terms of uses and appeals, and evaluations in terms of quality. Within the department a memorandum began to circulate which contained information about new trade books for children. By 1947 the memorandum grew into the BULLETIN OF THE CENTER FOR CHILDREN'S BOOKS, now sponsored by the Graduate Library School.

The BULLETIN OF THE CENTER FOR CHILDREN'S BOOKS provides a service of extreme value: (1) to librarians, by saving time and money and eliminating mediocre material; (2) to teachers, for supplementary curricular use of trade books; (3) to students of children's literature, by giving them training in judging books; (4) and to parents, as a guide to good books at appropriate reading levels. The criteria for evaluating each book are literary quality—form and organization—quality of content, suitability of style, and quality of format.

Current trade books for children together with some adult books suitable for young people are critically evaluated and reviewed in terms of reading level, literary merit, and appropriateness of concepts. Curricular use and developmental values are suggested; strengths and weaknesses are pointed out; the importance of the book relative to others on the same subject is noted. Reading levels of books are determined by the appropriateness of the subject matter, the concepts involved, and the reading-level difficulty.

Former distinguished staff members of the BULLETIN OF THE CENTER FOR CHILDREN'S BOOKS include Miss Mary K. Eakin and Miss Frances Henne. Miss Eakin is the author of *Good Books for Children* and coauthor of *Subject Index to Books for Primary Grades*. Miss Henne is the author of *School Library Standards*.

Mrs. Zena Sutherland, the present editor, is on the Newberry-Caldecott and Notable Books committees of the American Library Association. The acting supervising editor of the journal is Miss Sara Fenwick, who is president of the American Association of School Librarians.

The BULLETIN OF THE CENTER FOR CHILDREN'S BOOKS is published monthly except August. It is six and three-quarter inches by nine and one-half inches and contains approximately seventy to eighty book reviews in each issue.

| SUBSCRIPTIONS: | ONE YEAR | TWO YEARS | THREE YEARS |
|---|---|---|---|
| No foreign postage . . . . . . . | $4.50 | $9.00 | $13.50 |

SINGLE COPY, $0.75

## THE BULLETIN OF MATHEMATICAL BIOPHYSICS

No longer published by The University of Chicago Press; address inquiries to Dr. N. Rashevsky, Editor, University of Michigan, Ann Arbor, Michigan 48106.

## CANCER RESEARCH

No longer published by The University of Chicago Press; address inquiries to Williams and Wilkins Company, 428 East Preston Street, Baltimore, Maryland 21202.

## CHICAGO ALUMNI MAGAZINE

*See* University of Chicago Magazine

# CHILD DEVELOPMENT PUBLICATIONS

The child-development movement in the United States began to flower in the early 1920's, but its roots had developed much earlier. The nineteenth century had witnessed a curious mixture, on the one hand, of exploitation of children in industry and, on the other, of an enhanced interest in the welfare and education of children. Movements related to child study were active during the late nineteenth and early twentieth centuries. The U.S. Children's Bureau was established during this period.

In the midst of such activities the Laura Spelman Rockefeller Memorial instituted a program dedicated to the welfare of women and children. Beardsley Ruml, director, and Laurence K. Frank conceived the idea of bringing together scientists from different disciplines to integrate research on the development of the child.

The scientific status of this movement received formal recognition in 1922–23 through the appointment of a subcommittee on Child Development under the Division of Anthropology and Psychology of the National Research Council. This became the Committee on Child Development in 1925. The purpose of the Committee was to integrate and stimulate research activities in this area. In 1927 the committee published a *Directory of Research in Child Development;* the same year the first volume of CHILD DEVELOPMENT ABSTRACTS AND BIBLIOGRAPHY was published. The Committee on Child Development was disbanded in 1933 and the Society for Research in Child Development was formed.

The Society is a professional organization concerned with the study of the behavior and development of children. Members represent the fields of anthropology, anatomy, physiology, nutrition, public health, psychiatry, psychology, sociology, and medicine. Its purpose is to provide opportunity for people from different disciplines to extend their horizons, to become cognizant of the techniques and tools of research in allied fields, and to evaluate critically their own approaches to the study of children in the light of knowledge in related areas.

Published by The University of Chicago Press for the Society are the following journals:

CHILD DEVELOPMENT is a quarterly containing original articles on current research and theory concerning human development from the fetal period through adolescence. It was established in 1930 and came to The University of Chicago Press in 1965. The editor is Alberta Engvall Siegel, research associate in psychiatry and lecturer in psychology, School of Medicine, Stanford University.

The following list of articles published by CHILD DEVELOPMENT suggests the scope of the journal:

*American Longitudinal Research on Psychological Development,* by Jerome Kagan

*Individual Variation in the Rate of Skeletal Maturation between Five and Eighteen Years,* by Francis E. Johnston

*Patterns of Imitative Behavior in Adolescents,* by Willard W. Hartup

CHILD DEVELOPMENT ABSTRACTS AND BIBLIOGRAPHY, published triannually, includes abstracts of research studies and notices of books concerning child development. The books selected for brief, factual summaries are generally of a technical or professional nature, though selected non-technical materials prepared by professionals are included. The journal was established in 1927. The editor is Dale B. Harris, professor, Department of Psychology, The Pennsylvania State University.

MONOGRAPHS OF THE SOCIETY FOR RESEARCH IN CHILD DEVELOPMENT, published irregularly, contributes more extensive research studies in child development. The editor is Mildred C. Templin, professor, Institute of Child Development, The University of Minnesota. Recent issues include:

*Basic Cognitive Processes in Children,* edited by John C. Wright and Jerome Kagan

*The Acquisition of Language,* edited by Ursula Bellugi and Roger Brown

*Improving the Physical Fitness of Youth,* by Thomas K. Cureton and Alan J. Barry

*Mathematical Learning,* edited by Lloyd N. Morrisett and John Vinsonhaler

*European Research in Cognitive Development,* edited by Paul H. Mussen

CHILD DEVELOPMENT is published quarterly in March, June, September, and December. Each issue contains approximately two hundred and sixty pages.

CHILD DEVELOPMENT ABSTRACTS AND BIBLIOGRAPHY is published triannually with two numbers appearing in each issue; February–April, June–August, and October–December. Each issue contains approximately eighty pages.

MONOGRAPHS FOR THE SOCIETY FOR RESEARCH IN CHILD DEVELOPMENT are published irregularly. The number of pages in each monograph varies depending on the nature of the subject treated.

Each of the three publications is six inches by nine inches.

| SUBSCRIPTIONS (ONE YEAR): | CHILD DEVELPM. | ABSTRACTS | MONOGR. | CLUB (ALL THREE) |
|---|---|---|---|---|
| United States and possessions | $15.00 | $8.00 | $12.00 | $25.00 |
| Canada and Pan American Postal Union | 15.50 | 8.50 | 12.50 | 26.00 |
| All other countries | 16.00 | 9.00 | 13.00 | 27.00 |
| SINGLE COPY | 4.00 | 3.00 | 3.00 | .... |

## CLASSICAL JOURNAL

No longer published by The University of Chicago Press; address inquiries to the Department of Classics, Indiana University, Bloomington, Indiana 47401.

## CLASSICAL PHILOLOGY

E. T. Merrill, one of the founders of CLASSICAL PHILOLOGY, in an article appearing in the second volume of the journal (1907), wrote: "Intimate knowledge of the personality of ancient peoples is nearly confined to that of two races only, the Hellenic and the Italic, or, as we commonly call them, the Greek and the Roman." He goes on to declare that nothing can interfere with "the permanence of our vast mental and spiritual inheritance from the Greeks and Romans." It has been the purpose of CLASSICAL PHILOLOGY from its first issue to the present to increase our knowledge and understanding of this inheritance.

President William R. Harper was instrumental in establishing CLASSICAL PHILOLOGY. For six decades it has exerted an increasing influence upon classical scholarship throughout the world. Its policy has been and remains to publish only material that embodies the results of original research and which significantly contributes to our knowledge of antiquity.

In addition to major articles, each issue contains a number of shorter articles in a section entitled "Notes and Discussions." Each issue also contains numerous reviews of current publications of interest to classical scholars.

The following articles are typical of the contents of the journal:

*Bacon and Tacitus,* by E. B. Benjamin
*The Virtues of Admetus,* by A. P. Burnett
*Vida and Virgil: Review Article,* by R. T. Bruère
*The Lesbia Love Lyrics,* by W. M. A. Grimaldi, S.J.
*One Word Less,* by P. B. Corbett
*Early Christianity and Greek Comic Poetry,* by R. M. Grant
*The Revolt of Heraclian,* by S. I. Oost
*Silius and Suillius,* by T. A. Dorey
*Livia as Artemis Boulaia at Athens,* by J. H. Oliver
*Statius and the Late Latin Epithalamia,* by Z. Pavlovskis

For almost thirty years CLASSICAL PHILOLOGY was edited by the eminent Platonist Paul Shorey. Thereafter it was successively edited by Charles H. Beeson, well known for his paleographical studies, and J. A. O. Larsen, historian and authority on representative government in Greece and Rome. Since 1951 the editor has been R. T. Bruère, Professor of Latin and chairman of the Department of Classical Languages and Literatures, University of Chicago.

CLASSICAL PHILOLOGY is published quarterly in January, April, July, and October. The size of the journal is six and three-quarters inches by nine and one-half inches, and each issue contains approximately eighty pages.

| SUBSCRIPTIONS: | ONE YEAR | TWO YEARS | THREE YEARS |
|---|---|---|---|
| United States and possessions . . . . | $8.00 | $15.00 | $21.50 |
| Canada and Pan American | | | |
| Postal Union . . . . . . . | 8.50 | 16.00 | 23.00 |
| All other countries . . . . . . | 9.00 | 17.00 | 24.50 |

SINGLE COPY, $2.75

## COLLEGE ENGLISH

No longer published by The University of Chicago Press; address inquiries to the editor, James E. Miller, Jr., 508 South Sixth Street, Champaign, Illinois 61822.

## COMMERCE AND ADMINISTRATION

*See* The Journal of Business

## COMMON CAUSE

Publication discontinued.

## DENTAL PROGRESS

Publication discontinued.

## DIOGENES

No longer published by The University of Chicago Press; address inquiries to 1519 Pine Avenue West, Montreal 25, Canada.

## ECONOMIC DEVELOPMENT AND CULTURAL CHANGE

The Research Center in Economic Development and Cultural Change published the first issue of this journal in 1952. It was sent free to interested researchers in the social sciences as a medium for discussion of pressing current problems. The response was immediate and overwhelming. From the large number of manuscripts received it became apparent that a quarterly journal was needed. The absence of a theoretical framework for this field of study, the complexity of the problems involved, and the wide area of research to be covered indicated the need for theoretical research in many fields and the discussion and dissemination of these findings.

The interdisciplinary contents of ECONOMIC DEVELOPMENT AND CULTURAL CHANGE are divided among papers with mainly theoretical orientation and others which present significant new data. Of value to the teacher, the research worker, and the student, the journal publishes articles in the fields of economics, anthropology, sociology, history, geography, political science, and ancillary areas of study. It is designed for exploratory discussion of the problems of economic development and cultural change.

In addition to the articles on current research, ECONOMIC DEVELOPMENT AND CULTURAL CHANGE publishes a section of significant analytical book reviews. Each issue also contains a listing of books pertinent to this field of study that have been received from publishers. At least once a year a special supplementary issue is published and distributed free of charge to subscribers. These have been reports of conferences or parts of a larger work by Simon Kuznets, *Quantitative Aspects of the Economic Growth of Nations.*

From time to time special issues are published which deal with different aspects of one particular problem. Typical examples appear below:

> *The Contribution of Land Reform to Agricultural Development: An Analytical Framework,* by Philip M. Raup
> *The Sudan's Three Towns,* by Peter F. M. McLaughlin (published in three parts)
> *Breakdowns of Modernization,* by S. N. Eisenstadt
> *On Staging,* by George G. S. Murphy
> *Formalizing the Shimomura Growth Model,* by Martin Bronfenbrenner

SPECIAL SUPPLEMENTS:

> *State Income of Delhi State, 1951–52 and 1955–56,* by Mahinder D. Chaudhry and Bert F. Hoselitz (April, 1963)
> *Regional Inequality and the Process of National Development: A Description of the Patterns,* by Jeffrey G. Williamson (July, 1965)

ECONOMIC DEVELOPMENT AND CULTURAL CHANGE is edited at the Research Center for Economic Development and Cultural Change at the University of Chicago. For the first two years after its founding, the journal was edited by R. Richard Wohl, a specialist in American economic history and urban sociology.

Bert F. Hoselitz, director of the Research Center, succeeded Wohl and served as editor for seven years. Mr. Hoselitz is a specialist in economic growth, economic history, and the history of economic thought. He was succeeded by Manning Nash, who was followed by Robert Dernberger. In 1965 Mr. Hoselitz resumed his position as editor of the journal.

ECONOMIC DEVELOPMENT AND CULTURAL CHANGE is published quarterly in October, January, April, and July. The size of the journal is six and three-quarters inches by nine and one-half inches. Each issue contains approximately one hundred and twelve pages. At least one supplement a year is published containing approximately one hundred and twenty pages.

| SUBSCRIPTIONS: | ONE YEAR | TWO YEARS | THREE YEARS |
|---|---|---|---|
| United States and possessions . . . . | $6.00 | $11.50 | $16.50 |
| Canada and Pan American | | | |
| Postal Union . . . . . . . | 6.50 | 12.50 | 18.00 |
| All other countries . . . . . . | 7.00 | 13.50 | 19.50 |

SINGLE COPY, $2.00

## THE ELEMENTARY SCHOOL JOURNAL

In 1900 Colonel Francis W. Parker established a journal which was entitled COURSE OF STUDY, a record of the experimental work conducted by the Chicago Institute for parents and teachers interested in the new education. It contained many practical suggestions for the application of fundamental principles to daily schoolroom work. In 1901 the journal was renamed THE ELEMENTARY SCHOOL TEACHER and functioned as an organ of the Elementary School of the University of Chicago. The publication assumed its present name, THE ELEMENTARY SCHOOL JOURNAL, in 1914 as an indication of its adoption of a more general range of subjects, including administrative discussions. Since 1918 it has been published by The University of Chicago Press in conjunction with the Department of Education.

THE ELEMENTARY SCHOOL JOURNAL, more than any other publication in its field, has devoted its articles and editorials to the treatment of elementary-school problems from a scientific point of view. The objective of the publication is to keep the reader up to date on current developments in elementary education, particularly on research in the field. It is a medium for professional discussion of the problems of education at the elementary-school level, for promoting scholarship, and for improvement of education.

The publication includes: *reports* of scientific investigations which throw light on classroom procedure, evaluation of teaching, supervision, school administration, the place of the school in a changing society, child development, the curriculum, preparation of teachers, and other topics of current interest to administrators, teachers, and students of education; *descriptions* of useful and innovating educational practices; *expositions* of educational theories and philosophies; and *guides* to new and helpful instructional materials, especially in monthly lists of new books and pamphlets, and occasional book reviews carefully prepared by authorities in the field of the book under review.

Among the articles published during the past few years are:

*The Elementary School of 1980: A Suburban Superintendent Makes a Prediction,* by Lester B. Ball
*An Anniversary,* by Kenneth J. Rehage
*Individualized Reading,* by Helen M. Robinson
*What Shall We Do about Poetry in the Schools?* by Lindley J. Stiles
*Are "Toughs" Teachable?* by Gladys Natchez
*Who Are the Deprived Children?* by Charles A. Glatt
*Kindergarten—Education or Babysitting?* by Marilyn Church
*When Your Child Stutters,* by Ruth FitzSimons
*The Guv'ners: Venture in Group Guidance,* by Arthur A. Attwell and Robert R. Odom
*A Day in an Eskimo School,* by Dorothy H. Johnson

In the first issue of the JOURNAL, Francis W. Parker said, "Education . . . implies a recognition of the pupil's right to the privilege of initiative." This philosophy of education was furthered by John Dewey as director of the School of Education. With a concept of education involving fulfilment of character and all aspects of community living, the field of education became more extensive and complex. In 1951 Kenneth J. Rehage began editing THE ELEMENTARY SCHOOL JOURNAL, continuing the policy of publishing worthy manuscripts from a wide variety of sources, providing a broad base for professional discussion of current problems. Mr. Rehage is professor of education and director of the University of Chicago–Pakistan Education Project.

THE ELEMENTARY SCHOOL JOURNAL is published monthly, October through May. The size of the JOURNAL is six and three-quarters inches by nine and one-half inches. Each issue contains approximately sixty pages exclusive of advertising.

| SUBSCRIPTIONS: | ONE YEAR | TWO YEARS | THREE YEARS |
|---|---|---|---|
| United States and possessions . . . . | $6.00 | $11.00 | $15.50 |
| Canada and Pan American | | | |
| Postal Union . . . . . . . | 6.50 | 12.00 | 17.00 |
| All other countries . . . . . . . | 7.00 | 13.00 | 18.50 |

SINGLE COPY, $1.25

## ELEMENTARY SCHOOL TEACHER

*See* The Elementary School Journal

## ELEMENTARY SCHOOL TEACHER AND COURSE OF STUDY

*See* The Elementary School Journal

## THE ENGLISH JOURNAL

No longer published by The University of Chicago Press; address inquiries to the editor, Dwight L. Burton, 508 South Sixth Street, Champaign, Illinois 61822.

## ETHICS: An International Journal of Social, Political, and Legal Philosophy

The International Journal of Ethics was established in 1890 as an outgrowth of The Ethical Record, published by the Ethical Societies. For thirty-three years the journal operated as a private, non-profit publication controlled by a managing editor and an international editorial committee of famous scholars. Responsibility for publication was assumed by The University of Chicago Press in 1923, and in 1938 the title was shortened to Ethics.

The purpose of Ethics is to develop and clarify ideas and principles relevant to practical problems—individual, social, political, and international. Such principles arise from the generalization and rationalization of procedures used in handling specific problems and from interpretation and synthesis of the results of specialized research. Ethics thus provides communication of ideas uniquely spanning the fields of philosophy and social science. Articles are published in ethical theory, social science, and jurisprudence, contributing to an understanding of the basic structure of civilization and society.

In one publication, Ethics presents a significant sample of the advanced thinking of philosophers, economists, lawyers, political scientists, and sociologists from various countries on topics of practical relevance and general interest.

Each issue of Ethics presents essays, discussions, book reviews (significant critical analyses), shorter notices, and notes on new books. The kind and variety of articles published in the journal are indicated by the following list:

> *The Limits of Effective Legal Action,* by Roscoe Pound (1917)
> *Putting Politics in Its Place,* by Charles E. Merriam (1936)
> *The Twilight of International Morality,* by Hans Morgenthau (1948)
> *Managing Complexity,* by Paul H. Appleby (1954)
> *Intelligence and Social Policy,* by Frank H. Knight (1957)
> *Freedom, Reason, and Tradition,* by Friedrich A. Hayek (1958)
> *The Ideological Component of Indian Development,* by José Arsenio Torres (1962)
> *Urbanism and American Democracy,* by Francis E. Rourke (1964)
> *Economic Growth versus Existential Balance,* by Walter A. Weisskopf (1965)
> *Limits to the Moral Claim in Civil Disobedience,* by Harry Prosch (1965)
> *The Paradox of American Legal Realism,* by Wilfrid E. Rumble (1965)

Since Ethics was first established in 1890, four men of note have occupied the editorial chair. The first was S. Burns Weston, director of the Philadelphia Society for Ethical Culture. James H. Tufts, professor of philosophy and vice-president of the University of Chicago, was the second editor. He was succeeded by T. V. Smith, professor of philosophy, Illinois senator, and congressman-at-large. Since 1933 Charner Marquis Perry has edited Ethics, working as coeditor with Smith until 1948. Mr. Perry is professor of philosophy. His fields of special inquiry include social philosophy, theory and logic of social sciences, political philosophy, ethics, economics, and political theory.

Ethics is published quarterly in October, January, April, and July. The size of the journal is six and three-quarters inches by nine and one-half inches. Each issue contains approximately eighty pages.

| Subscriptions: | One Year | Two Years | Three Years |
|---|---|---|---|
| United States and possessions . . . . | $8.00 | $15.00 | $21.50 |
| Canada and Pan American | | | |
| Postal Union . . . . . . . . | 8.50 | 16.00 | 23.00 |
| All other countries . . . . . . . | 9.00 | 17.00 | 24.50 |

Single copy, $2.75

Supplementary Monographs ($2.25 each):

*The Normative Impact of the Behavioral Sciences,* by Harold D. Lasswell (1957)

*Political Decisions in Modern Society,* by Kurt Riezler (1954)

*Aggression: A Study of Values and Law,* by Malcolm Sharp (1947)

# HEBRAICA

*See* Journal of Near Eastern Studies

# HEBREW STUDENT

*See* The Journal of Religion

# HISTORY OF RELIGIONS: An International Journal for Comparative Historical Studies

Concern for the study and teaching of the history of religions has been growing steadily in American universities. The methods and principles of this discipline, however, are taught in only a few American universities. Scholars of the science in Europe and America recognize the University of Chicago as the leading center for this study in America. It has the longest tradition of teaching history of religions and over the past two decades has attracted two of the most famous scholars in the field, Joachim Wach (1945–54) and Mircea Eliade (1956——).

Professor Wach and Professor Eliade were concerned to introduce the history of religions as a definite area of study in America. With the growing demand for teachers in this field, the University of Chicago has become the center for training.

Until the appearance of HISTORY OF RELIGIONS in 1961, no journal in America had devoted itself exclusively to the history of religions. The new journal has filled a vacuum among American periodicals. One of the primary aims of HISTORY OF RELIGIONS is the integration of results of the several disciplines of the science of religion. The journal is also intended as an organ of communication between scholars in this field in America, Europe, and Asia.

The journal promotes studies and discussions on the central themes of the history of religions, such as the meaning and function of myth and ritual, the structure of religious symbolism, the problem of the high god, of mana, of totemism, and others. It also encourages methodological studies and critical surveys and reviews of recent works on specific subjects, such as prehistoric religions and shamanism. The articles often have a synthetical character in order to acquaint the reader with the progress being made in the general area of the history of religions and to co-ordinate results of related disciplines, particularly ethnology, sociology, anthropology, and specialized area studies. The journal is international in scope, as to both contributors and subscribers. Although the journal is published in English, the editors accept and translate articles written in other languages by European and Asian scholars.

Some of the manuscripts by internationally known scholars which have appeared in recent issues are:

> *Mazdak and Porphyrios,* by Franz Altheim
> *The Large Ātman,* by J. A. B. van Buitenen
> *The Last Giants,* by Marie Delcourt
> *Crisis and Renewal in History of Religions,* by Mircea Eliade
> *Of Change and Adaptation in Judaism,* by Judah Goldin
> *Gods and Drinking Serpents,* by Carl Hentze
> *Islam and Image,* by Marshall G. S. Hodgson
> *The Buddhist Transformation in Japan,* by Joseph M. Kitagawa
> *The Triple Structure of Creation in the Ṛg Veda,* by Stella Kramrisch
> *Approaches to the Religion of Early Paleolithic Man,* by Karl J. Narr
> *The Decline of the Almohads: Reflections on the Viability of*
>    *Religious Movements,* by W. Montgomery Watt
> *Buddhist Self-immolation in Medieval China,* by Jan Yün-Hua

Mircea Eliade, Joseph M. Kitagawa, and Charles H. Long have edited HISTORY OF RELIGIONS since it was established. The already classic works of Professor Eliade on shamanism, yoga, initiation, mythology, and religious symbolism, as well as his synthetic work, *Patterns in Comparative Religion,* establish him as one of the great historians of religion. Professor Kitagawa is an expert in Mahayana Buddhism, religions of Japan, and the relation of Christianity to other religions. Professor Long's interests lie in primitive religions and in methodological problems.

History of Religions is published quarterly in August, November, February, and May. The size of the journal is six inches by nine inches, and each issue contains approximately one hundred pages.

| SUBSCRIPTIONS: | ONE YEAR | TWO YEARS | THREE YEARS |
|---|---|---|---|
| No foreign postage . . . . . . | $8.00 | $15.50 | $22.50 |

SINGLE COPY:
  Prior to August, 1966, $3.75
  Current, $2.50

## INTERNATIONAL JOURNAL OF ETHICS

*See* Ethics

## JOURNAL OF THE ASSOCIATION OF COLLEGIATE ALUMNAE

No longer published by The University of Chicago Press; now the Journal of the American Association of University Women; address inquiries to 2401 Virginia Avenue, N.W., Washington, D.C. 20207.

## THE JOURNAL OF BUSINESS

In order to achieve its present form and sustain its present editorial policy, The Journal of Business was first subjected to the maelstrom of organization and reorganization, of flux and change of editorial policy, finally emerging to take its place among the scholarly journals in this field of study. The publication, initially called Commerce and Administration, became The University Journal of Business and was published in co operation with several other universities. Reorganized in 1928, it became The Journal of Business, and in 1930 the University of Chicago became sole publisher.

Intended for the academic reader, the advanced student, and the business executive or staff person with an interest in the study of a wide range of business problems at an advanced level, The Journal of Business maintains a quantitative or analytic rather than a descriptive approach to the current research which it publishes.

The Journal of Business publishes papers which deal with both the theoretical and the applied aspects of studies of the world of business. While

the JOURNAL emphasizes articles contributing to the theory of business behavior and advanced economic or mathematical analysis by academicians,
papers by businessmen, consultants, and government executives provide a
balance with studies devoted to particular phases of current business problems.

In addition to the major articles, the JOURNAL publishes in each issue a
selection of reviews of recent books and a listing of personnel changes, grants
received, and dissertations awarded by members of the American Association
of Collegiate Schools of Business.

In the last decade, the JOURNAL has become an important medium of
publication for research work in the area of capital management and finance.
Recent contributions in this field have been:

> *Public Regulation of the Securities Markets,* by G. S. Stigler
> *Dividend Policy, Growth, and the Valuation of Shares,* by
>   M. H. Miller and Franco Modigliani
> *Psychological and Objective Factors in the Prediction of Brand
>   Choice: Ford vs. Chevrolet,* by F. Evans
> *Oil Prices in the Long Run,* by M. A. Adelman
> *Rates of Return on Investments in Common Stocks,* by L. Fisher
> *The Future of Business Education,* by R. M. Cyert and W. R. Dill
> *Marketing Research Expenditures: A Decision Model,* by F. M. Boss

From 1920 until 1930 THE JOURNAL OF BUSINESS was published by students of the School of Commerce and Administration of the University of
Chicago in co-operation with students of business of the University of Illinois, Indiana University, the University of Minnesota, the University of
Nebraska, Ohio State University, and the University of Wisconsin. In 1930
Edward A. Duddy became the first editor of the JOURNAL after the University
of Chicago took over publication. He was professor of marketing and a specialist in general marketing and the marketing of agricultural products. An
eminent member of his profession, he was instrumental in setting policy and
in broadening the JOURNAL.

Duddy was succeeded in 1948 by Eli Shapiro, professor of finance. Mr.
Shapiro is a consultant and an author of books on finance and banking. He
includes monetary economics, financial administration, and capital markets
in his fields of particular research. Royal S. Van de Woestyne, professor of
business administration and a specialist in state control of local finance,
edited the JOURNAL during 1953. From 1954 to 1957 Ezra Solomon, professor
of finance, functioned as editor. A consultant and author, Mr. Solomon has
specialized in monetary economics, regional economics, and business forecasting.

In 1957 Irving Schweiger, professor in the Graduate School of Business,
succeeded Ezra Solomon as editor. Mr. Schweiger is a consultant and author

of numerous articles on consumer market behavior, business forecasting, business finance, and banking.

THE JOURNAL OF BUSINESS is published quarterly in January, April, July, and October. The size of the journal is six and three-quarters inches by nine and one-half inches. Each issue contains approximately one hundred and ten pages.

| SUBSCRIPTIONS: | ONE YEAR | TWO YEARS | THREE YEARS |
|---|---|---|---|
| United States and possessions . . . . | $8.00 | $15.00 | $21.50 |
| Canada and Pan American | | | |
| Postal Union . . . . . . . . | 8.50 | 16.00 | 23.00 |
| All other countries . . . . . . . | 9.00 | 17.00 | 24.50 |

SINGLE COPY, $2.75

## JOURNAL OF CONFLICT RESOLUTION

Publication discontinued.

## JOURNAL OF DENTAL RESEARCH

No longer published by The University of Chicago Press; address inquiries to the American Dental Association, 211 East Chicago Avenue, Chicago, Illinois 60611.

## JOURNAL OF GENERAL EDUCATION

No longer published by The University of Chicago Press; address inquiries to the Pennsylvania State University Press, University Park, Pennsylvania 16802.

## THE JOURNAL OF GEOLOGY

The second journal to be published by The University of Chicago Press was THE JOURNAL OF GEOLOGY, which was founded in 1893 by Thomas C. Chamberlin, author of the planetesimal hypothesis. It was the founder's belief that since the job of the universities should be not only to educate young geologists but to develop science for science's sake, the co-ordinate function of a university journal of geology should be to promote the growth of systematic philosophical and fundamental geology and to educate professional geologists. The opening of new fields of research and the rapid progress of several new and important departments of the science served to emphasize the already prevalent need for a periodical to invite discussion of fundamental and theoretical themes and of investigations of international and intercontinental relations.

The objectives of THE JOURNAL OF GEOLOGY have not changed. It is a publication devoted to the entire field of geology, avoiding narrow specialization. New ideas and concepts presented in the JOURNAL keep the geologist aware of recent developments in the broad field of geology as well as in his own field of specialization.

The current studies published in THE JOURNAL OF GEOLOGY are of indispensable value to geologists in both the academic and the applied aspects of the science. The full range of the field is covered, from highly physical studies in geochemistry and geophysics to the biological areas such as paleontology and paleoecology. The JOURNAL includes major, original contributions; shorter contributions and comments under "Geological Notes"; some book reviews; and "Communications and Announcements" in each issue.

Recently published articles reflecting the scope of THE JOURNAL OF GEOLOGY include:

> *Classification and Environmental Significance of Algal Stromatolites,* by B. W. Logan, R. Rezak, and R. N. Ginsburg
>
> *Ages of Zircon and Feldspar Concentrates from North American Beach and River Sands,* by D. Ledent, C. Patterson, and G. R. Tilton
>
> *Mineralogy of Amphibolite Interlayers in the Gneiss Complex, Northwest Adirondack Mountains, New York,* by A. E. J. Engel, Celeste C. Engel, and R. G. Havens
>
> *Pleistocene Vegetational Studies in the Whitewater Basin, Southeastern Indiana,* by Ronald O. Kapp and Ansel M. Gooding
>
> *The Petrography and Isotopic-Mineral Age Relations of a Contact Zone in the Front Range, Colorado,* by S. R. Hart
>
> *Turbidities and Topography of North End of San Diego Trough, California,* by Bryce M. Hand and K. O. Emery
>
> *Experimental Evidence of Basal Slip in Quartz,* by J. M. Christie, D. T. Griggs, and N. L. Carter
>
> *Stability Fields of Iron Minerals in Anaerobic Marine Sediments,* by Robert A. Berner
>
> *Wrench Faulting in Cyprus,* by Paul Stanley Bagnall
>
> *Paleographic Reconstructions by Absolute Age Determinations of Sand Particles,* by Andrew B. Vistelius

In addition to prominent members of the University of Chicago faculty, outstanding geologists have been chosen over the past seventy years to serve on the editorial staff: Sir Archibald Geikie, England; G. K. Gilbert, U.S. Geological Survey; George M. Dennison, Canada; H. Rosenbush, Germany; William B. Clark, Johns Hopkins University; C. D. Walcott, U.S. Geological Survey; Charles Leith, University of Wisconsin; Bailey Willis, Stanford University; and Richard Penrose, Jr., Philadelphia.

Everett C. Olson, professor, Department of Geophysical Sciences, and a specialist in vertebrate paleontology, became editor of THE JOURNAL OF GEOLOGY in 1962. Mr. Olson and the associate editors form a distinguished editorial group and reflect the international aspect of the journal.

THE JOURNAL OF GEOLOGY is published bimonthly in January, March, May, July, September, and November. The size of the journal is six and three-quarters inches by nine and one-half inches. Each issue contains approximately one hundred and twenty-eight pages.

| SUBSCRIPTIONS: | ONE YEAR | TWO YEARS | THREE YEARS |
|---|---|---|---|
| United States and possessions . . . | $14.00 | $27.50 | $40.50 |
| Canada and Pan American | | | |
| Postal Union . . . . . . . | 14.50 | 28.50 | 42.00 |
| All other countries . . . . . . | 15.00 | 29.50 | 43.50 |

SINGLE COPY, $3.25

SUPPLEMENTS AND SPECIAL ISSUES ($3.25 EACH):
*The Theory of Ground-Water Motion,* by M. King Hubbert
*Glaciological Issue*
*Penrose Memorial Issue*

## THE JOURNAL OF INFECTIOUS DISEASES

In 1904 THE JOURNAL OF INFECTIOUS DISEASES was established in connection with the John Rockefeller McCormick Memorial Institute for Infectious Diseases. This was made possible through the generosity of the late Mrs. Edith Rockefeller McCormick and the late Harold F. McCormick. Ludwig Hektoen and Edwin O. Jordan were instrumental in the founding of the publication, serving as coeditors for many years.

In 1941 the John Rockefeller McCormick Memorial Fund was set up, utilizing assets of the old McCormick Institute. Income from the present fund has been used by the Department of Microbiology of the University of Chicago to support studies of representatives of all the larger groups of organisms producing disease in man and animals and to assist in publishing THE JOURNAL OF INFECTIOUS DISEASES. Although the publication has served the University of Chicago as an outlet for such research, 80 per cent of its space is devoted to research from other institutions both here and abroad.

THE JOURNAL OF INFECTIOUS DISEASES is devoted to the publication of original investigations dealing with the general phenomena, causation, and prevention of infectious diseases. The biology and chemistry of the various pathogenic organisms, the physiology and anatomy of the morbid processes they initiate, and the hygienic and sanitary problems to which they give rise are considered to be especially within the scope of the JOURNAL.

The following articles published in recent issues of THE JOURNAL OF INFECTIOUS DISEASES reflect the purposes of the publication:

> *Nontransmissible Lysis of Mouse Leukemia Cells by Myxoviruses,* by Malcolm Slifkin and Peter Isacson
>
> *Passive Immunity in Experimental Cholera,* by M. V. Panse, H. I. Jhala, and N. K. Dutta
>
> *Attenuation of the Myxoma Virus and Use of the Living Attenuated Virus as an Immunizing Agent for Myxomatosis,* by J. K. Saito, D. G. McKercher, and G. Castrucci
>
> *Species Identity and Epidemiology of* Brucella *Strains from Alaskan Eskimos,* by Margaret E. Meyer
>
> *The Relationship between Antibody Formation and the Appearance of Plasma Cells in Newborn Hamsters,* by R. L. Young, H. Ward, D. Hartshorn, and M. Block
>
> *Reduced Activity of Histaminase in Rats and Guinea Pigs Sensitized with Culture Supernatants of* Bordetella pertussis, by Makato Niwa, Yutaka Yamadeya, and Yoshio Kuwajima
>
> *Studies on the Nutrition and Metabolism of Animal Cells in Serum-free Media,* by Henry R. Tribble, Jr., and Kiyoshi Higuchi
>
> *Inactivation of Two Arboviruses and Their Associated Nucleic Acids,* by Leonard A. Mika, Julius E. Officer, and Arthur Brown
>
> *Immunological Injury of Mast Cells in Mice Actively and Passively Sensitized to Antigens from* Trichinella spiralis, by N. Theodore Briggs

Distinguished scientists who have played prominent roles in the development of microbiology at the University of Chicago and in the United States as a whole have edited THE JOURNAL OF INFECTIOUS DISEASES since it was founded in 1904. Hektoen was professor and head of the Department of Pathology at the University of Chicago and the recipient of many high honors in the fields of pathology and bacteriology. Jordan was professor and head of the Department of Hygiene and Bacteriology (now Microbiology) and was an outstanding figure in the early history of bacteriology in the United States.

William H. Taliaferro, still serving as an advisory editor for the JOURNAL, is the Eliakim H. Moore Distinguished Service Professor Emeritus of Microbiology. His eminence in the fields of microbiology and immunology is reflected in the many medals and honors which he has received during a lifetime of scholarly endeavor.

The present editor of THE JOURNAL OF INFECTIOUS DISEASES is James W. Moulder, chairman of the Department of Microbiology. His research interests cover intermediary metabolism, biochemistry and immunology of malarial parasites and trypanosomes, biochemistry of the psittacosis-lymphogranuloma group of viruses, and the mechanism of action of chemotherapeutic agents.

THE JOURNAL OF INFECTIOUS DISEASES is published five times a year, in February, April, June, October, and December. The size of the journal is six and three-quarters inches by ten inches. Each issue is approximately one hundred and twelve pages in length.

| SUBSCRIPTIONS: | ONE YEAR | TWO YEARS | THREE YEARS |
|---|---|---|---|
| United States and possessions . . . | $14.00 | $27.00 | $40.00 |
| Canada and Pan American | | | |
| Postal Union . . . . . . | 14.50 | 28.00 | 41.50 |
| All other countries . . . . . | 15.00 | 29.00 | 43.00 |

SINGLE COPY, $3.50

## JOURNAL OF MEDICAL EDUCATION

No longer published by The University of Chicago Press; address inquiries to Service Printers, Inc., 120 North Green Street, Chicago, Illinois 60607.

## THE JOURNAL OF MODERN HISTORY

The first issue of THE JOURNAL OF MODERN HISTORY was published in 1929 under the direction of two eminent scholars, Bernadotte E. Schmitt and Louis Gottschalk. The JOURNAL was founded by the Modern History Section of the American Historical Association and The University of Chicago Press. The response from students and teachers of modern history in the United States was immediate and encouraging; in addition to subscriptions, they manifested a willingness to contribute articles, prepare reviews of books, and otherwise assist with the publication of the JOURNAL. Since that time the JOURNAL has steadily grown and expanded, with present readers and contributors from all parts of the world reflecting the global character of the clientele as well as the broad coverage of the published material.

THE JOURNAL OF MODERN HISTORY publishes articles that provide either new information or new interpretations of known phenomena. Of value to both the student and the teacher, the JOURNAL is concerned with the history of the arts and sciences as well as with the political, diplomatic, military, religious, social, and economic aspects of history.

THE JOURNAL OF MODERN HISTORY publishes historical, bibliographical, and historiographical articles, documents, and reviews of books. The book review section presents critical analyses of current publications and is a significant part of the JOURNAL. The JOURNAL deals with world history from the Renaissance to the present with the exception of the domestic history of the American Republics. During the past thirty-odd years of publication, papers by many distinguished scholars and authors have appeared in the JOURNAL. The following typical articles were published between 1955 and 1965:

> *Machiavelli, 1940–1960,* by Eric Cochrane
> *Benito Mussolini: A Guide to the Biographical Literature,* by Charles F. Delzell
> *Education and Militarism in Modern China,* by Donald Gillin
> *Arms and the British Diplomats in the French Revolutionary Era,* by Richard Glover
> *How Success Spoiled the Risorgimento,* by Raymond Grew
> *Arkad'evich Stolpin: A Political Appraisal,* by Alfred Levin
> *The Historical Work of Pieter Geyle,* by Herbert H. Rowen
> *1914 and 1939,* by Bernadotte E. Schmitt
> *The Constructive Opposition to Emigration [in Sweden],* by Franklin D. Scott
> *The Historian's Dilemma,* by William B. Willcox

Schmitt and Gottschalk, both of the University of Chicago, edited THE JOURNAL OF MODERN HISTORY from 1929 until 1946. Under their expert guidance the JOURNAL grew in concept and importance. Schmitt, author of note, recipient of the G. L. Beer Prize and the Pulitzer Prize, is the MacLeish Distinguished Service Professor Emeritus. Gottschalk is the Gustavus F. and Ann M. Swift Distinguished Service Professor. He has received the James Hazen Hyde Prize and the American Council of Learned Societies' Prize for Distinguished Scholarship in the Humanities.

S. William Halperin, professor of modern history and an expert in the fields of recent French, German, and Italian history, was succeeded by Hanna H. and Charles M. Gray, the present editors.

THE JOURNAL OF MODERN HISTORY is published quarterly in March, June, September, and December. The size of the JOURNAL is six and three-quarters inches by nine and one-half inches. Each issue contains approximately one hundred and twenty-six pages.

| SUBSCRIPTIONS: | ONE YEAR | TWO YEARS | THREE YEARS |
|---|---|---|---|
| United States and possessions . . . | $8.00 | $15.00 | $21.50 |
| Canada and Pan American | | | |
| Postal Union . . . . . . . | 8.50 | 16.00 | 23.00 |
| All other countries . . . . . . | 9.00 | 17.00 | 24.50 |

SINGLE COPY, $2.75

# JOURNAL OF NEAR EASTERN STUDIES

HEBRAICA, founded by William Rainey Harper in 1884, has been retitled twice, each change reflecting a growth and broadening of the fields of interest covered by the publication. In 1895 it became the AMERICAN JOURNAL OF SEMITIC LANGUAGES AND LITERATURES and was given its present designation, JOURNAL OF NEAR EASTERN STUDIES, in 1942. From the narrow, purely biblical emphasis on Old Testament studies, NEAR EASTERN STUDIES has gradually broadened its scope until it now offers a forum for the scholarly treatment of any Near Eastern problem of antiquity.

THE JOURNAL OF NEAR EASTERN STUDIES is of particular value to (1) specialists in the history and culture of the countries of the ancient Near East (including Islam, which is not, strictly speaking, "ancient"), (2) to clergymen who will find the JOURNAL helpful in their preaching and religious leadership and study of the Bible, and (3) to college and university teachers who may not be professional Orientalists but who will profit from the researches of the specialists.

The JOURNAL OF NEAR EASTERN STUDIES offers findings on the political, social, and religious life of cultures now extinct, including results of recent archeological discovery. Interpretation of Old Testament books, chronology, and literature of the ancient Orient, including translations and commentaries, are frequently published.

Book reviews direct attention to the most important publications in the fields covered by the articles in the JOURNAL. From time to time, the JOURNAL OF NEAR EASTERN STUDIES publishes "Oriental Institute Museum Notes" by Helene J. Kantor and other scholars. This is an eminent series of articles devoted to objects in the Oriental Institute Museum.

The following selections of recent articles reflect the specialized fields covered by the JOURNAL in the last twenty-four years:

*The Assyrian King List from Khorsabad,* by Arno Poebel
*A Ninth-Century Fragment of the "Thousand Nights,"* by Nabia Abbott
*Jahreszeiten im Sumerisch-Akkadischen,* by Benno Landsberger
*Egyptian Art in the Collection of Albert Gallatin,* by John D. Cooney
*Achaemenid Jewelry in the Oriental Institute,* by Helene J. Kantor
*The Earliest History of the Constellations in the Near East and the Motif of the Lion-Bull Combat,* by Willy Hartner
*The Topography of the Jews of Medieval Egypt,* by Norman Golb
*Un motif "scythe" en Iran et en Grèce,* by P. Amandry

William Rainey Harper edited the JOURNAL OF NEAR EASTERN STUDIES for twenty-two years after he founded it. Other illustrious names connected with the JOURNAL through its years of growth are to be found among the cooperating editors: James Henry Breasted, founder of the Oriental Institute of the University of Chicago and noted Egyptologist; Albert T. Olmstead, Assyriologist; William A. Irwin, eminent Old Testament scholar and translator; and Arno Poebel, famous Sumerologist.

Keith C. Seele, well-known Egyptologist and educator, has edited the JOURNAL OF NEAR EASTERN STUDIES since 1948. He is an Oriental Institute professor emeritus and director of the Oriental Institute Nubian Expedition. Mr. Seele is an expert in the field of Egyptian culture, history, and philology and the author of a number of publications, including *The Coregency of Ramses II with Seti I and the Date of the Great Hypostyle Hall at Karnak, When Egypt Ruled the East,* and *The Tomb of Tjanefer at Thebes.*

JOURNAL OF NEAR EASTERN STUDIES is published quarterly in January, April, July, and October. The size of the journal is six and three-quarters inches by nine and one-half inches. Each issue contains approximately seventy-two pages.

| SUBSCRIPTIONS: | ONE YEAR | TWO YEARS | THREE YEARS |
|---|---|---|---|
| United States and possessions . . . . | $8.00 | $15.00 | $21.50 |
| Canada and Pan American | | | |
| Postal Union . . . . . . . | 8.50 | 16.00 | 23.00 |
| All other countries . . . . . . | 9.00 | 17.00 | 24.50 |

SINGLE COPY, $2.75

## THE JOURNAL OF POLITICAL ECONOMY

THE JOURNAL OF POLITICAL ECONOMY was one of the first scholarly journals established by the University of Chicago; it began publication during the new university's first academic year. J. Laurence Laughlin founded it in the belief that communication of the scope, method, and principles of scientific work in political economy would facilitate public understanding of practical economic problems. "Political economy," he wrote, "is a means of analyzing the play of economic motives, of measuring their force, of discovering and explaining the relations between concrete truths, and of ascertaining their causes and effects." The JOURNAL welcomed the discussion of economic theory but emphasized the study of practical problems of economics, finance, and statistics.

The general editorial purposes of the publication remain the same today, although the type of material published has changed with the professionalization of economics and the growth of other media for commentary on public affairs.

The JOURNAL imposes few restrictions on subject matter and has published articles in such diverse fields as economic history, history of economic thought, economic development, the theory of economic planning, the theory of political choice, and the economics of education, in addition to articles in economic theory, labor economics, agricultural economics, money, industrial organization, and international trade.

Short notes and comments, book reviews, and occasional review articles on books of outstanding importance are also published in the JOURNAL.

The following list of articles illustrates the scope and quality of THE JOURNAL OF POLITICAL ECONOMY:

*A Difficulty in the Concept of Social Welfare,* by K. J. Arrow

*A Dynamic Aggregative Model,* by James Tobin

*An Economic Theory of Political Action in a Democracy,* by Anthony Downs

*The Sources of Measured Productivity Growth: United States Agriculture, 1940–66,* by Zvi Griliches

*Industrial Research and Development Expenditures: Determinants, Prospects, and Relation to Size of Firm and Inventive Output,* by Edwin Mansfield

*Investment in Human Capital: A Theoretical Analysis,* by Gary S. Becker

*Wealth, Saving, and the Rate of Interest,* by L. A. Metzler

*Advertising and Competition,* by Lester G. Telser

*The Theory of Underemployment in Backward Economies,* by Harvey Leibenstein

*The Demand for Money: Some Theoretical and Empirical Results,* by Milton Friedman

J. Laurence Laughlin, first professor of political economy at the University of Chicago, edited THE JOURNAL OF POLITICAL ECONOMY during its early years of publication. Succeeding editors, men of international reputation in the profession of economics, include Thorstein B. Veblen, J. M. Clark, Frank H. Knight, Jacob Viner, William H. Nicholls, Earl J. Hamilton, and Albert Rees.

Harry G. Johnson, professor in the Department of Economics, is the present editor of the JOURNAL. He has also served in an editorial capacity on several other journals. His academic background and high standing in his profession have brought him many honors. His publications include *Canadian Quandary: Economic Problems and Policies; Money, Trade, and Economic Growth;* and *International Trade and Economic Growth.*

THE JOURNAL OF POLITICAL ECONOMY is published bimonthly in February, April, June, August, October, and December. The JOURNAL is six and three-quarters inches by nine and one-half inches in size. It contains approximately one hundred and ten pages in each issue.

| SUBSCRIPTIONS: | ONE YEAR | TWO YEARS | THREE YEARS |
|---|---|---|---|
| United States and possessions . . . . | $10.00 | $19.00 | $27.50 |
| Canada and Pan American | | | |
| Postal Union . . . . . . . | 10.50 | 20.00 | 29.00 |
| All other countries . . . . . . | 11.00 | 21.00 | 30.50 |

SINGLE COPY, $2.50

## THE JOURNAL OF RELIGION

The history of the JOURNAL reaches back into the last century. Founded by William Rainey Harper in 1882, it passed through several changes of name and policy, ever broadening its scope and field of study. THE JOURNAL OF RELIGION first appeared under its present name in 1921, replacing THE BIBLICAL WORLD and the AMERICAN JOURNAL OF THEOLOGY. THE BIBLICAL WORLD was a continuation of THE HEBREW STUDENT, founded by Harper, which was retitled THE OLD TESTAMENT STUDENT and, later, THE OLD AND NEW TESTAMENT STUDENT. At this time, the aim of the JOURNAL, in keeping with the emphasis of theological study at the Divinity School at the University of Chicago, was to advance the scientific interpretation of religion with a special emphasis upon sociological and psychological studies in religion.

During the early forties a shift in emphasis occurred, veering toward a more theological and philosophical discussion of religious problems, reflecting the existential concern in theological study itself as it developed during this period.

The purpose of the JOURNAL at present is to make available authoritative and provocative articles on religious subjects. It offers both historical and contemporary studies, but its aim is to throw light upon religious problems that are currently relevant and insistent, including in its offerings articles dealing with topics that concern the wider intellectual community. Although some technical studies in theology and philosophy of religion are published, THE JOURNAL OF RELIGION is devoted primarily to scholarly articles of general interest. It provides definitive analyses rather than topical or survey-type discussion.

Significant studies in the following fields of interest have been published in the JOURNAL: biblical study, history of Christianity, theology, philosophy of religion and philosophical theology, history and sociology of religion, ethics and society, religion and art, religion and personality.

A selected list of articles published in THE JOURNAL OF RELIGION reflects the timeliness and the scope of the publication:

> *The Concept of Providence in Contemporary Theology,* by Langdon B. Gilkey
>
> *A Word in Defense of Schleiermacher's Theological Method,* by Van A. Harvey
>
> *The Shekhina,* by Raphael Patai
>
> *Dostoevski and Satanism,* by George A. Panichas
>
> *Karl Jaspers' Christology,* by Harold A. Durfee
>
> *The Necessity of Myth: An Answer to Rudolph Bultmann,* by Richard F. Grabau
>
> *What Sense Does It Make To Say, "God Acts in History"?* by Schubert M. Ogden

*Is Tragedy Essential to Knowing? Critique to Dr. Tillich's Aesthetic,* by John Dixon, Jr.

*Futuristic and Realized Eschatology in the Earliest Stages of Christianity,* by Werner Georg Kummel

*I-Thou and I-It: An Attempted Clarification of Their Relationship,* by W. Taylor Stevenson

Well-known scholars and authors have served as editors for THE JOURNAL OF RELIGION since 1921. Successive editors were Gerald Birney Smith, Shirley Jackson Case, John Knox, John McNeill, Amos Wilder, James H. Nichols, and James Luther Adams.

J. Coert Rylaarsdam and Nathan A. Scott, Jr., are the present coeditors of the publication. Rylaarsdam is chairman of the Biblical Field in the Divinity School, specializing in Old Testament theology. Scott is a professor in the Divinity School and in the Department of Theology and Imaginative Literature. Both editors have published important contributions in their fields.

THE JOURNAL OF RELIGION is issued by the Divinity School of the University of Chicago and is published quarterly in January, April, July, and October. The size of the JOURNAL is six and three-quarters inches by nine inches, and each issue contains approximately ninety-six pages.

| SUBSCRIPTIONS: | ONE YEAR | TWO YEARS | THREE YEARS |
|---|---|---|---|
| United States and possessions . . . . | $8.00 | $15.00 | $21.50 |
| Canada and Pan American | | | |
| Postal Union . . . . . . . . | 8.50 | 16.00 | 23.00 |
| All other countries . . . . . . . | 9.00 | 17.00 | 24.50 |

SINGLE COPY, $2.75

## THE LIBRARY QUARTERLY

THE LIBRARY QUARTERLY is the research journal of librarianship. It was established in 1931 by the Graduate Library School of the University of Chicago with the assistance of a grant from the Carnegie Corporation and with the co-operation of the American Library Association and the Bibliographical Society of America. From the beginning it has published research articles submitted by contributors from all over the world. In addition, it publishes comprehensive and logical expositions of issues basic to librarianship and related fields. Its extensive reviewing section presents critical reviews of the serious works on librarianship appearing in all the countries and languages of the world.

As Karl J. Weintraub, in a LIBRARY QUARTERLY article, wrote, "Ortega y Gasset envisages the future librarian as a sensitive filter standing between the flood of print and man. This image ought to haunt the profession." This expressive image has in fact haunted the QUARTERLY from its beginning. It is interested in mass communications, in reading audiences, and, generally, in the people on the other side of the filter. A major focus is the filter—the technical operations of libraries and the role of the librarian.

A yearly feature of THE LIBRARY QUARTERLY is one issue devoted to the proceedings of the annual conference of the Graduate Library School. These conferences feature a series of papers on a central topic of current interest. From each of them come seven to ten articles written by specialists in librarianship and by eminent scholars in other fields. The conference issues of THE LIBRARY QUARTERLY are important additions to the unified body of library literature. Recent conference topics have been "Seven Questions about the Profession of Librarianship," "The Intellectual Foundations of Library Education," "New Definitions of School Library Service," and "Library Catalogs: Changing Dimensions."

Another important feature of the journal is the publication of the lists of graduate theses accepted by library schools in the United States.

Selected articles which have been published during the past few years are typical of the journal:

> The Librarian: From Occupation to Profession? by William H. Goode
> Main Entries and Citations: One Test of the Revised Cataloging Code, by Elizabeth L. Tate
> The Evidence Underlying the Cranfield Results, by Don R. Swanson
> Regulations Relating to the Book Trade in London from 1357 to 1586, by Howard W. Winger
> The Library Consumer: Patterns and Trends, by Philip H. Ennis
> Postwar Publishing Trends in Japan, by Natsuko Y. Furuya
> Far Eastern Resources in American Libraries, by G. Raymond Nunn and Tsuen-hsuin Tsien
> The Adolescent in School, by Robert D. Hess
> Soviet Library Literature: A Survey of Selected Manuals of Methodology, by Elizabeth Beyerly
> The Historical Background of Departmental and Collegiate Libraries, by Lawrence Thompson
> The National Library of Medicine, by Dorothy M. Schullian and Frank B. Rogers

William M. Randall was managing editor of THE LIBRARY QUARTERLY from the time of its founding in 1931 until 1942. He set the tone of the publication as a journal of research and guided it through its first years of growth. He was succeeded by Leon Carnovsky, internationally known as a library scholar, who maintained and expanded the reputation of THE LIBRARY QUARTERLY from 1943 until 1961, when he resigned to devote more time to other scholarly projects, although continuing to serve the journal as an associate editor.

Since 1961 Howard W. Winger, an associate professor in the Graduate Library School, has been the managing editor of the journal. He is an expert in library science, historical bibliography, and history of the public diffusion of knowledge. The members of the Board of Editors are on the faculty of the Graduate Library School at the University of Chicago.

THE LIBRARY QUARTERLY is published quarterly in January, April, July, and October. The size of the journal is six and three-quarters inches by nine and one-half inches, and each issue contains approximately ninety-six pages.

| SUBSCRIPTIONS: | ONE YEAR | TWO YEARS | THREE YEARS |
|---|---|---|---|
| United States and possessions . . . | $8.00 | $15.00 | $21.50 |
| Canada and Pan American | | | |
| Postal Union . . . . . . . | 8.50 | 16.00 | 23.00 |
| All other countries . . . . . . | 9.00 | 17.00 | 24.50 |

SINGLE COPY, $2.75

## MANUAL TRAINING MAGAZINE

Publication transferred in 1903.

## MECHANICAL TRANSLATION AND COMPUTATIONAL LINGUISTICS

W. N. Locke and Victor H. Yngve founded MECHANICAL TRANSLATION at the Massachusetts Institute of Technology in 1955 with a grant from the Rockefeller Foundation. The new journal was published on an irregular basis producing eight volumes in eleven years. Testimony to the need and success of the journal is evident in the growing number of subscribers in a narrowly specialized field.

Several years ago a professional society was formed, called the Association for Machine Translation and Computational Linguistics. In 1964, the association voted to accept MECHANICAL TRANSLATION as its official organ. In 1966, the journal was added to the Chicago list. Beginning with Volume IX, the first to be published by The University of Chicago Press, MECHANICAL TRANSLATION became a quarterly.

The following articles were published in Volume VIII, Numbers 3 and 4:

*Machine Methods for Proving Logical Arguments Expressed in English,* by Jared L. Darlington
*Automatic Paraphrasing in Essay Format,* by Sheldon Klein
*The Nature of Affixing Written English,* by H. L. Resnikoff and J. L. Dolby

*Experiments in Semantic Classification,* by K. Sparck Jones
*An Applied Radical Semantics,* by M. Zarechnak
*Applications of the Theory of Clumps,* by R. M. Needham

After several years W. N. Locke resigned as coeditor of Mechanical Translation. Victor H. Yngve continued to edit the journal with the help of an editorial advisory board consisting of leading people in the field of mechanical translation from England, France, Germany, Italy, Japan, Mexico, the U.S.S.R., and the United States.

Yngve holds a joint appointment in the Graduate Library School, the Department of Linguistics, and the Committee for Information Sciences as professor of information science. He was the first president of the Association for Machine Translation and Computational Linguistics and has actively participated in the efforts made by the American Standards Association to standardize computer programming languages. He has published many papers in the fields of mechanical translation, linguistics, and programming languages and is the author of two books: *Introduction to Comit Programming* and *Comit Programmers' Reference Manual.*

Mechanical Translation and Computational Linguistics is published quarterly in March, June, September, and December. The journal is seven and five-eighths inches by ten and one-half inches. It contains approximately sixty-four pages in each issue.

| Subscriptions: | ONE YEAR | TWO YEARS | THREE YEARS |
|---|---|---|---|
| No foreign postage . . . . . . . | $10.00 | $20.00 | $30.00 |

Single copy, $3.00

## MIDWAY

A new venture in ideas emerged with the publication of the first issue of Midway by The University of Chicago Press in January, 1960. Midway was designed to acquaint both the scholar and the educated general reader with the results of current investigations in the sciences and the humanities, the illumination of analytic and speculative thought, and the interests and concerns of the scholarly world. For the scholar Midway offers research in fields of interest other than his own, and for the intelligent layman access to material which is found only in specialized journals and books. The new magazine filled a particular need, bridging the gap between the specialist and the interested and intelligent reader—midway between scholar and scholar, scholar and layman.

With a wealth of material at hand in the publications of the Press, subject matter is unlimited. Midway covers all aspects of the arts and sciences, providing an imaginative and intriguing balance of articles in each issue.

Well-known authors from all fields of scholarly study have contributed to MIDWAY, including Julian Huxley, Paul Tillich, David Daiches, Frieda Fromm-Reichmann, Harrison E. Salisbury, Reuel Denney, Thom Gunn, Howard Nemerov, Joshua C. Taylor, Gerardo Reichel-Dolmatoff, Isabella Gardner, A. Leo Oppenheim, Percival Bailey, Moses Hadas, Vincent Starrett, Denison B. Hull, Daniel J. Boorstin, Pamela Hansford Johnson, Winthrop N. Kellogg, and Karl Jaspers.

Indicative of the scope of MIDWAY are the following selections which have been published in the journal:

> *Consistent Theology,* by Paul Tillich
> *The Dimensions of Economic Freedom,* by Kenneth E. Boulding
> *The Mysteries of Galaxy M87,* by W. A. Hiltner
> *Black Nationalism: A Search for an Identity,* by E. U. Essien-Udom
> *The Action of the Nervous System,* by Charles Darwin
> *The Poetic Method of Aristotle,* by Elder Olson
> *The Test of the Accepted Past,* by George Herbert Mead
> *Secrecy and the Army,* by Alice Kimball Smith
> *Some Modern Interpretations of Witchcraft,* by Julio Caro Baroja
> *Advanced Consciousness,* by Gösta Ehrensvärd

John H. Kendrick is the editor of MIDWAY. The editorial board is composed of the editors of The University of Chicago Press.

MIDWAY is published quarterly in January, April, July, and October. The size of the journal is five and one-half inches by eight inches. Each issue contains one hundred and twenty-eight pages.

| SUBSCRIPTIONS: | ONE YEAR | TWO YEARS | THREE YEARS |
|---|---|---|---|
| United States and possessions . . . . | $4.50 | $8.50 | $12.00 |
| Canada and Pan American | | | |
| Postal Union . . . . . . . . | 5.50 | 10.00 | 14.00 |
| All other countries . . . . . . | 6.00 | 11.00 | 15.50 |

SINGLE COPY, $1.50

# MODERN PHILOLOGY

Founded in 1903 by a group of humanists invited to the University of Chicago by William Rainey Harper, MODERN PHILOLOGY is one of the oldest American journals devoted to the publication of substantial articles in all areas of medieval and modern literature. In the early part of the century John Matthews Manly, with the collaboration of such scholars as

C. R. Baskervill, William A. Nitze, and Tom Peete Cross, brought the journal to a position of high international repute.

The next editor, Ronald S. Crane, introduced several innovations in response to the changing currents of literary study during the 1930's. Articles of a purely linguistic character were dropped, and critical reviewing was given more prominence, especially through the review article. MODERN PHILOLOGY was one of the first American scholarly journals to open its pages to papers on the history of criticism and on problems in critical theory and method. The succeeding editor, George Williamson, who directed the journal until 1960, broadened this emphasis to comprehend a wider range of critical interests. A diversity of articles and reviews reflected his special concern for poetic interpretation disciplined by learning.

Under the present editor, Donald F. Bond, MODERN PHILOLOGY continues to publish papers of both scholarly and critical interest. Articles range from edited texts and documents to extended pieces on literary history, interpretation, and theory. In addition to the review articles, book reviews of current works appear that are generally critical and analytical rather than descriptive.

The following list of articles, selected from recent and current numbers, illustrates MODERN PHILOLOGY's present scope:

> Christian Elements and the Genesis of Beowulf, by Robert D. Stevick
> Don Quixote: Story or History? by Bruce W. Wardropper
> Baroque in England, by Mario Praz
> Une Traduction française du "Sublime" de Longin vers 1645, by Bernard Weinberg
> Fielding and "Conservation of Character," by John S. Coolidge
> Dryden, Corneille, and the Heroic Play, by Arthur C. Kirsch
> Gide et Vielé-Griffin: Documents inédits, by Beatrice W. Jasinski
> Die Sprache des "Spiels" und des "Antispiels" in den frühen Dramen Schillers, by Matthijs Jolles
> Joyce's Sermon on Hell: Its Source and Its Backgrounds, by James R. Thrane
> Gerard Manley Hopkins and His Public, 1889–1918, by Edgar W. Mellown

The editors of MODERN PHILOLOGY have been distinguished members of the University of Chicago faculty. Philip S. Allen, the first editor, was a medievalist of note, with interests in the Latin and vernacular lyric. J. M. Manly was the well-known editor of Chaucer and student of the earlier English poetry and drama. Crane has worked in a number of areas, but chiefly in the eighteenth century and in criticism as a leading figure among a group of theorists who have been called the Chicago School. George Williamson's books on Donne and the seventeenth century and on T. S. Eliot and contemporary poetry have long been influential. The present editor, Donald F.

Bond, a professor emeritus of the Department of English, is an accomplished eighteenth-century bibliographer and literary historian, whose critical edition of the *Spectator* appeared in 1965.

MODERN PHILOLOGY is published quarterly in August, November, February, and May. The size of the journal is six and three-quarters inches by nine and one-half inches. Each issue contains ninety-six pages.

| SUBSCRIPTIONS: | ONE YEAR | TWO YEARS | THREE YEARS |
|---|---|---|---|
| United States and possessions . . . . | $8.00 | $15.00 | $21.50 |
| Canada and Pan American Postal Union . . . . . . . | 8.50 | 16.00 | 23.00 |
| All other countries . . . . . . . | 9.00 | 17.00 | 24.50 |

SINGLE COPY, $2.75

# THE OLD AND NEW TESTAMENT STUDENT

*See* The Journal of Religion

# PERSPECTIVES IN BIOLOGY AND MEDICINE

Dwight J. Ingle founded PERSPECTIVES IN BIOLOGY AND MEDICINE in 1957 for the communication of ideas in biology and medicine. Most of the great ideas about life and disease have concerned some basic process of life. Nevertheless, there is no well-developed body of theory in biology and medicine, such as in the physical sciences. Theory and experiment remain parts of the same tool. There is no theory without at least observational data and no experiment which is not motivated by an idea.

PERSPECTIVES is published for all those engaged in creative scientific effort in laboratories, clinics, and classrooms. Papers which enlarge biological horizons and bring specific medical problems into perspective with investigative work on life processes are published. The journal is oriented toward man and his illnesses, but with appreciation of the fact that the roots of medical theory reach into all fields of biology.

PERSPECTIVES also publishes autobiographical sketches of leaders in biology and medicine (by invitation), book reviews, and letters to the editor.

A few of the significant articles published in PERSPECTIVES over the past few years are:

> *Evolution of Photosynthetic Mechanisms,* by Melvin Calvin
> *History of Cancer Quackery,* by Morris Fishbein
> *A Defense of Beanbag Genetics,* by J. B. S. Haldane
> *The Cybernetics of Competition: A Biologist's View of Society,* by Garrett Hardin

*A Scientific Career,* by George von Hevesy
*Claude Bernard on Experimental Medicine: Some Unpublished Notes,* by
  Hebbel E. Hoff, Roger Guillemin, and Edouard Sakiz
*The Emergence of Darwinism,* by Sir Julian Huxley
*The Guidance of Human Evolution,* by Hermann J. Muller
*A Guide to the Theory of Arterial Hypertension,* by Irvine H. Page, J. W.
  McCubbin, and A. C. Corcoran
*On Scientific Creativity,* by Albert Szent-Györgyi

Dr. Ingle has edited PERSPECTIVES IN BIOLOGY AND MEDICINE since 1957 with the sponsorship of the Division of the Biological Sciences at the University of Chicago. He is chairman of the Department of Physiology at the University of Chicago and has been honored with the Upjohn Prize and the Roche-Organon Award of the Laurentian Hormone Conference. Dr. Ingle is the author of many scientific papers and the book *Principles of Research in Biology and Medicine.* He has edited a book of selected essays from PERSPECTIVES entitled *New Outlooks in Medicine.* Dr. S. O. Waife, of the medical division of Eli Lilly and Company Research Laboratories, is coeditor of the journal. He is co-author of the book *Clinical Investigation of New Drugs.*

PERSPECTIVES IN BIOLOGY AND MEDICINE is published quarterly in the Autumn, Winter, Spring, and Summer. The journal is six and three-quarters inches by nine and one-half inches, and each issue contains approximately one hundred and twenty-eight pages.

| SUBSCRIPTIONS (INDIVIDUAL): | ONE YEAR | TWO YEARS | THREE YEARS |
|---|---|---|---|
| United States and possessions . . . . | $10.00 | $19.00 | $28.00 |
| Canada and Pan American | | | |
| Postal Union . . . . . . . | 10.50 | 20.00 | 29.50 |
| All other countries . . . . . . | 11.00 | 21.00 | 31.00 |
| SUBSCRIPTIONS (INSTITUTIONAL) . . . . . | 15.00 | 29.00 | 43.00 |

SINGLE COPY, $3.00

## PHYSIOLOGICAL ZOÖLOGY

PHYSIOLOGICAL ZOÖLOGY was founded in 1928 by C. M. Child and W. C. Allee, who felt that there was the need for another research publication devoted to general experimental zoölogy. Physiological zoölogy is so fundamental and broad that a journal to record current researches in the field was considered by them to be imperative.

Published in PHYSIOLOGICAL ZOÖLOGY are those manuscripts which are essentially experimental and/or analytical in character, and which are original contributions to knowledge within the areas of zoölogy as described by the following statement: For the purposes of this journal "physiological zoölogy" is interpreted as including the physiological aspects of all fields of zoölogy, some of which—cytology, genetics, and ecology, for example—cannot be included in their entirety.

More specifically stated, physiological zoölogy is regarded as comprising: physiology of the cell and of protoplasm; physiology of the nervous system and behavior in the stricter sense; physiology of populations; hormones and other features of chemical correlation that are of general biological interest; sex in its physiological aspects; and the physiological phases of genetics.

The range of PHYSIOLOGICAL ZOÖLOGY is evident from the following articles published in 1964 and 1965:

*The Role of the Sun's Altitude in Sun Orientation of Fish,* by Horst O. Schwassmann and Arthur D. Hasler

*Body Temperature, Oxygen Consumption, and Heart Rate in Three Species of Australian Flying Foxes,* by George A. Bartholomew, Philip Leitner, and John E. Nelson

*The Generality of Temperature Effects on Developmental Rate and on Oxygen Consumption in Insect Eggs,* by A. Glenn Richards

*Genetic Strains and Competition in Populations of* Tribolium, by Thomas Park, P. H. Leslie, and David B. Mertz

*Water Balance in a Carnivorous Desert Rodent, the Grasshopper Mouse,* by K. Schmidt-Nielsen and H. B. Haines

*Population Dynamics of Brown Trout in Different Environments,* by James T. McFadden and Edwin L. Cooper

*Acclimation to Temperature in Terrestrial Isopods. I. Lethal Temperatures,* by E. B. Edney

*Acclimation to Temperature in Terrestrial Isopods. II. Heart Rate and Standard Metabolic Rate,* by E. B. Edney

*Temperature Effects on Responses in the Auditory System of the Little Brown Bat* Myotis l. lucifugus, by Jean Burch Harrison

*Water Relation and Internal Body Temperature of Isopods from Mesic and Xeric Habitats,* by Michael R. Warburg

Child was the first of the three editors who have been responsible for the publication of PHYSIOLOGICAL ZOÖLOGY. He was followed by Allee, who had also been instrumental in starting the journal. Thomas Park, the present editor, is professor of zoölogy and is a former editor of ECOLOGY.

PHYSIOLOGICAL ZOÖLOGY is published quarterly in January, April, July, and October. The size of the journal is six and three-quarters inches by nine and one-half inches, and each issue is approximately eighty-eight pages in length.

| SUBSCRIPTIONS: | ONE YEAR | TWO YEARS | THREE YEARS |
|---|---|---|---|
| United States and possessions . . . . | $12.00 | $23.00 | $33.50 |
| Canada and Pan American | | | |
| Postal Union . . . . . . . . | 12.50 | 24.00 | 35.00 |
| All other countries . . . . . . | 13.00 | 25.00 | 36.50 |

SINGLE COPY, $3.50

## POETRY

No longer published by The University of Chicago Press; address inquiries to the editor, 1018 North State Street, Chicago, Illinois 60610.

## PROCEEDINGS OF THE NATIONAL ACADEMY OF SCIENCES

No longer published by The University of Chicago Press; address inquiries to 2101 Constitution Avenue, Washington, D.C. 20225.

## QUARTERLY CALENDAR

Published June, 1892–February, 1896; succeeded by the University Record.

## QUARTERLY JOURNAL OF PUBLIC SPEAKING

No longer published by The University of Chicago Press; now the QUARTERLY JOURNAL OF SPEECH; address inquiries to the editor, R. M. R. Jeffrey, Department of Speech, Indiana University, Bloomington, Indiana 47401.

## THE SCHOOL REVIEW

The first issue of THE SCHOOL REVIEW appeared in 1893, a product of the wisdom and imagination of Jacob G. Schurman, president of Cornell University. The journal was established for the high school and academy, and Mr. Schurman delineated its objectives in his introductory editorial: "The problems of secondary education are so numerous and difficult, and they are so different from the problems of primary education, that they demand an organ for separate treatment . . . a meeting place of the philosophy and the practice of education . . . catholic and impartial in tone and spirit."

Until very recently THE SCHOOL REVIEW continued to emphasize secondary education, but it no longer seemed fruitful to restrict discussion of theory, of philosophy, and of policy and practice to one sector and level of the educational system.

Thus the outlook of the REVIEW now is to all parts of the educational enterprise. The purpose of THE SCHOOL REVIEW is to encourage reflection and discussion by all persons who are interested in or concerned about education. The REVIEW centers its attention on specific questions of educational policy and practice and on fundamental philosophical and theoretical issues.

Over the years THE SCHOOL REVIEW has published important papers by many distinguished figures in American education, including Charles W. Eliot, G. Stanley Hall, John Dewey, George S. Counts, Henry C. Morrison, Edward L. Thorndike, Charles Hubbard Judd, Ella Flagg Young, H. O. Rugg, and Frank N. Freeman.

Articles of continuing importance in educational research and policy were published in recent special issues of the REVIEW:

*Effects of Current Curriculum Projects on Educational Policy and Practice*
*Dewey Centennial Issue*
*Social Climates in School and College*
*The Nature and Effects of Non-public Schooling*
*Teaching: A Profession and a Process*
*The Arts in American Education*

After founding THE SCHOOL REVIEW Schurman remained the editor for several years. The journal was then taken over by Charles H. Thurber, president of Colgate Academy, and brought to the University of Chicago in 1896. Published by The University Press with the Department of Education of the University, the editorial function has been executed by various members of the department, including Judd, Leonard V. Koos, Nelson B. Henry, Maurice L. Hartung, Roald F. Campbell, and Francis S. Chase, prominent educators and authors. The chairman of the present editorial board is Charles E. Bidwell, associate professor of education. He is author of numerous papers on school in the social order.

THE SCHOOL REVIEW is published quarterly in March, June, September, and December. The size of the journal is six and three-quarters inches by nine and one-half inches, and each issue contains one hundred and twenty-eight pages.

| SUBSCRIPTIONS: | ONE YEAR | TWO YEARS | THREE YEARS |
|---|---|---|---|
| United States and possessions . . . | $8.00 | $15.00 | $21.50 |
| Canada and Pan American | | | |
| Postal Union . . . . . . | 8.50 | 16.00 | 23.00 |
| All other countries . . . . . | 9.00 | 17.00 | 24.50 |

SINGLE COPY, $2.75

## THE SIDEREAL MESSENGER

*See* The Astrophysical Journal

## THE SOCIAL SERVICE REVIEW

THE SOCIAL SERVICE REVIEW began publication in 1927. Edith Abbott and Sophonisba P. Breckinridge founded the journal as "a quarterly devoted to the scientific and professional interests of social work." Under their gifted leadership, the REVIEW quickly took its place as one of the genuinely significant professional journals in the world. In 1927 social work, as a relatively new profession, was struggling to develop its identity. Both students and practicing social workers needed a means of keeping up with new developments. The journal sought to provide case materials for students, to stimulate research in social welfare and related fields, and to encourage scholarly analysis of current issues in social work.

Through the depression, World War II, and the ensuing uneasy peace, the publication has provided a continuing record and analysis of the important social issues. THE SOCIAL SERVICE REVIEW emphasizes original research while maintaining a balance of highly specialized articles and those that deal broadly with social issues or problems. Because of the dynamic quality of the social work profession, the journal has retained flexibility to meet the changes in range and focus of the work in this field.

The scope of THE SOCIAL SERVICE REVIEW is wide. It deals with problems from economics to sociology, political science to law, and psychology to psychiatry. These articles report the results of research, throw new light on history, or deal with issues and problems in social work education.

In addition to the analytical articles, a section of "Notes and Comments" is included. The extensive reviews of books and government documents are also of great value to both the theoretician and the practitioner.

Selected papers from recent issues of THE SOCIAL SERVICE REVIEW are typical of the journal:

> *Toward a Psychoanalytic Definition of Social Casework,* by Justin Simon, M.D.
> *The Philosophy of Social Work,* by Paul Tillich
> *Power and Politics: A Road to Social Reform,* by Peter H. Rossi
> *The State of Crisis: Some Theoretical Considerations,* by Lydia Rapoport
> *The Welfare State: Images and Realities,* by Richard M. Titmuss
> *Identity Problems, Role, and Casework Treatment,* by Helen Harris Perlman
> *The Place of Help in Supervision,* by Charlotte Towle

Any list of social welfare pioneers in the United States would include the names of three persons who were intimately involved in the development of THE SOCIAL SERVICE REVIEW. The three—Sophonisba P. Breckinridge and Edith and Grace Abbott—were members of that remarkable group of people who gathered at Hull-House to share in some of the most creative developments of the early twentieth century. Sophonisba Breckinridge, a legal scholar and social worker, was a long-time member of the University of Chicago faculty. Edith Abbott, a noted authority on public welfare, served for many years as dean of the School of Social Service Administration and as editor of the REVIEW. Her sister, Grace Abbott, served as chief of the U.S. Children's Bureau. Upon her resignation in 1934 she became a member of the Chicago faculty and served as managing editor of the REVIEW until her death in 1939. Other members of the REVIEW board have been Wayne McMillen, a recognized authority on community organization, and Helen Russell Wright, research teacher and second dean of the School of Social Service Administration. All of these people have been recognized for their selfless dedication to social betterment. The present editor, Rachel B. Marks, is professor and associate dean of the School of Social Service Administration.

THE SOCIAL SERVICE REVIEW is published quarterly in March, June, September, and December. The size of the journal is six and three-quarters inches by nine and one-half inches, and each issue contains approximately one hundred and twenty pages.

| SUBSCRIPTIONS: | ONE YEAR | TWO YEARS | THREE YEARS |
|---|---|---|---|
| United States and possessions . . . | $8.00 | $15.00 | $21.50 |
| Canada and Pan American | | | |
| Postal Union . . . . | 8.50 | 16.00 | 23.00 |
| All other countries . . . . | 9.00 | 17.00 | 24.50 |

SINGLE COPY, $2.75

# STUDIES IN PUBLIC COMMUNICATION

Publication discontinued.

# TECHNOLOGY AND CULTURE

The Society for the History of Technology was formed in 1958 to encourage the study of the development of technology and its relations with society and culture. In 1960 Technology and Culture was founded as the official quarterly journal for the Society. Publication was begun in response to a growing, imperative need for a systematic and scholarly study of the development of technology. The tremendous interest in this field was not limited to engineering educators and historians, but academicians in all disciplines were becoming increasingly aware of the impact of technology upon their own special fields, just as technologists were becoming cognizant of the interaction of society with their work. Sociologists, economists, and political scientists as well as scholars working in the humanities and fine arts recognized the significance of technology and its role in the development of civilization. The "underdeveloped" areas of the world, with their explosive and far-reaching reactions to other, more advanced cultures are also a concern of Technology and Culture.

Articles of general interest in the field of technology and culture, along with material concerned with the history of technical devices and processes, are contributed by scholars from many nations.

A bibliography is published annually in the journal and each issue contains significant, analytical book reviews.

Representative of the coverage Technology and Culture affords its readers are the following articles:

> *Tools and the Man,* by Lewis Mumford
> *Ideas, History, Technology,* by Howard Mumford Jones
> *The Legend of Eli Whitney and Interchangeable Parts,* by Robert S. Woodbury
> *Future Exploration and Utilization of Outer Space,* by Hugh L. Dryden
> *The Interaction of Science and Practice in the History of Metallurgy,* by Cyril S. Smith
> *The Redstone, Jupiter, and Juno,* by Wernher von Braun
> *Technology in the Modern World,* by Sir Robert Watson-Watt
> *Technology and Man: A Christian Vision,* by W. Morris Clarke, S.J.
> *The Changing Technical Act,* by A. Rupert Hall
> *Modern Technology and Ancient Jobs,* by Peter Drucker

Editor-in-chief of the journal since its inception, Melvin Kranzberg is professor of history and director of the Graduate Program in Science and Technology in Society at Case Institute of Technology. He is the author of numerous papers and books and member of both professional and scientific societies. Editors of Technology and Culture are Carl W. Condit, Northwestern University, and Eugene S. Ferguson, Iowa State University.

Technology and Culture is published quarterly in January, April,

July, and October. The size of the journal is six inches by nine inches, and each issue contains approximately one hundred and sixty pages.

SUBSCRIPTIONS:    ONE YEAR    TWO YEARS    THREE YEARS

No foreign postage . . . . . . . $10.00    $19.50    $28.50

SINGLE COPY, $3.00

## TERRESTRIAL MAGNETISM

Publication transferred to Johns Hopkins University in September, 1899.

## TRANSACTIONS OF THE ILLINOIS SOCIETY FOR CHILD STUDY

Publication discontinued in 1901.

## THE UNIVERSITY OF CHICAGO LAW REVIEW

No longer published by The University of Chicago Press; address inquiries to the Law School, The University of Chicago, Chicago, Illinois 60637.

## UNIVERSITY OF CHICAGO MAGAZINE

Continuing the CHICAGO ALUMNI MAGAZINE, published March, 1907— October, 1908; since 1915 published by The University of Chicago Alumni Association, 5733 University Avenue, Chicago, Illinois 60637.

## UNIVERSITY EXTENSION WORLD

Publication discontinued in 1895.

## UNIVERSITY JOURNAL OF BUSINESS

*See* The Journal of Business

## UNIVERSITY RECORD

Incorporated into the UNIVERSITY OF CHICAGO MAGAZINE in 1908; resumed independent publication as the UNIVERSITY RECORD in 1915; discontinued 1933.

## WEEKLY CALENDAR

Formerly called THE WEEKLY OFFICIAL BULLETIN OF THE UNIVERSITY OF CHICAGO, established in 1893; calendar (one sheet, 11⅛ × 18½) of public lectures and other events at the University. Subscription, $3.00 a year.

## ZYGON: JOURNAL OF RELIGION AND SCIENCE

ZYGON was founded in 1966 as a medium through which modern religions can seek and promote human values with full cognizance and acceptance of the scientific pictures of reality. ZYGON is a bridge, a sorely needed communicative path over which ideas travel back and forth between scientists who have in the past struggled to avoid problems of values and theologians who have spoken of "true myths" without serious concern for scientific images of reality.

Past cultures possessed ways of describing the realities with which men must deal, and their religions and values were integrated with their reality images. Today, however, science has emerged as the most effective way of refining reality images. Modern man, in trying to assimilate the expanding knowledge at a rapid rate, faces a continuing crisis of his own making. ZYGON brings together the growing number of presently isolated scholars working on these concerns—the scientists, the theologians, the humanists—and through mutual exploration and criticism aids in the evolution of a common wisdom.

The following articles and commentaries were presented at the 1965 Meadville Conference and were subsequently published in Volume I, Number 1 of ZYGON:

THEOLOGICAL RESOURCES FROM THE PHYSICAL SCIENCES:
    *Can Physics Contribute to Theology?* by Sanborn C. Brown
    Commentaries by Filmer S. C. Northrop, Ian G. Barbour, John F. Hayward, and John R. Platt
THEOLOGICAL RESOURCES FROM THE BIOLOGICAL SCIENCES:
    *The Search for Common Ground,* by George Wald
    Commentaries by H. J. Muller, Robert B. Tapp, Alfred E. Emerson, and Bernard M. Loomer
THEOLOGICAL RESOURCES FROM THE SOCIAL SCIENCES:
    *Rituals: Sacred and Profane,* by Anthony F. C. Wallace
    Commentaries by Henry N. Wieman, Lawrence K. Frank, Ralph Wendell Burhoe, and Melford Spiro
*Science and the Search for a Rational Religious Faith,* by Donald S. Harrington
*The Sciences and Theological Education,* by Malcolm R. Sutherland, Jr.

ZYGON was founded by Ralph Wendell Burhoe and Robert B. Tapp as editor and managing editor, respectively, representing the Joint Publication

Board of the Institute on Religion in an Age of Science and the Meadville Theological School of Lombard College. Burhoe and Tapp are both professors at the Meadville Theological School. In addition to the Joint Publication Board, ZYGON has an editorial advisory board that includes scholars of high repute in the fields of theology and the sciences.

ZYGON: JOURNAL OF RELIGION AND SCIENCE is published quarterly in March, June, September, and December. The JOURNAL is six inches by nine inches in size. Each issue contains approximately ninety-six pages.

| SUBSCRIPTIONS: | ONE YEAR | TWO YEARS | THREE YEARS |
|---|---|---|---|
| United States and possessions . . . . | $8.00 | $15.50 | $22.50 |
| Canada and Pan American | | | |
| Postal Union . . . . . . . | 8.50 | 16.50 | 24.00 |
| All other countries . . . . . . | 9.00 | 17.50 | 25.50 |

SINGLE COPY, $2.50